rock 'n' roll sweepstakes

ian hunter

the authorised biography
campbell devine

volume two:
hunter by proxy

T0333304

OMNIBUS PRESS

London / New York / Paris / Sydney / Copenhagen / Berlin / Madrid / Tokyo

Ian Hunter

All of The Good Ones Are Taken

Ian Hunter's
Dirty Laundry

rock 'n' roll sweepstakes

For Mick Ronson (1946–1993) and Richie Anderson (1948–2017)

All-American Alien Boy

Well I packed my bags, in the land of rags
'Cos I don't believe, in them dimmo drags
Don't want to vote for the left wing, don't want to vote for the right
I gotta have both, to make me fly

Just a whitey from Blighty, heading out west
I got my little green card, 'n' my bulletproof vest
I'm going to old tube city, where the buzz is the best
On down the line, down the line

Well I was born, and I was raised
I was schooled, and I was fazed
And I was used, and I was dazed
I just had to split, 'cos I was crazed

And I remember all the good times, me 'n' Miller enjoyed
Up and down the M1, in some luminous yo-yo toy
But the future had to change, and to change I've got to destroy
Oh, look out Lennon here I come, land ahoy-hoy-hoy

All-American Alien Boy

Ian Hunter (1975)

Contents

Preface

Rock 'n' Roll Sweepstakes is Ian Hunter's story – the life, the art and the heart – the purpose, the passion and the perception – in his own words and through the tales of colleagues and collaborators.

"Long, long time ago", in November 1992, I was invited to compile a new fanzine feature on the late-lamented Mott the Hoople. Eventually, I surrendered and interviewed Verden Allen, and a wonderful trip to Hereford became the launchpad for a book.

Over a six-year period my original biography project was underpinned with input and support from Ian Hunter, the original members of Mott the Hoople and many associates of the band. Of note, the most active participant in that book was Mott drummer Dale Griffin. After six years of work, *All the Young Dudes: The Official Biography of Mott the Hoople and Ian Hunter* was released by Cherry Red Books as a companion to *All the Young Dudes: The Anthology*, a box set that I instigated with Sony Music and their superb team of Phil Savill, Chris Black and the late Hugh Attwooll.

The "journey" preparing the *Dudes* biography was interesting to say the least, confirming that the outside world largely sees one aspect of the music business – the positive side. Fans and the record-buying public are mostly sheltered from the niggling and negative elements, and so, whilst I tried to document stories told and untold in that 1992–98 period, I also embraced loyalty and humour. Crucially, I respected "the code of the road" and I have continued to adopt the same tone.

This biography, fully authorised by Ian Hunter, is based on acres of new work and fresh collaborations. After *All the Young Dudes*, a wider field opened up and over 200 people have assisted directly on this project through interviews, discussions and emails.

Ian Hunter's life story spans fifty years of accomplishment and musical magic, so Omnibus Press decided that Ian's unique journey should be travelled via two volumes.

Rock 'n' Roll Sweepstakes: Volume One covered Ian's youth and formative rock 'n' roll days alongside the likes of Freddie 'Fingers' Lee and Miller Anderson, Mott the Hoople's formation, David Bowie's intervention as a fan of the band, Mott's rise to international stardom and their tortured break-up.

Volume Two reflects on Hunter's partnership with guitarist Mick Ronson, his collaborations with the likes of Jaco Pastorius, The E Street Band and Ringo Starr, and his colossal solo achievements across an astonishing artistic landscape.

Collectively, the two volumes look in depth at Mott the Hoople's classic albums – *Brain Capers*, *All the Young Dudes* and *Mott* – as well as Hunter's eclectic solo recordings – from the commercially successful *Ian Hunter* and *You're Never Alone with a Schizophrenic*, through the left-field *All-American Alien Boy* and *Short Back n' Sides*, to the astonishing *Shrunken Heads* and *Fingers Crossed*.

Devoid of borrowed information and recycled press clippings, *Rock 'n' Roll Sweepstakes* contains inside stories, controversial quotes and previously unpublished views. I have collaborated with Ian Hunter, who provides revealing anecdotes, and there are contributions from all the members of Mott the Hoople, Hunter Ronson and The Rant Band, Queen's Brian May, Mick Jones of The Clash, Def Leppard's Joe Elliott and many other important sources.

With this personal input from key players, *Rock 'n' Roll Sweepstakes* traces strife and stardom with honesty and humour. Peppered with untold tales, this is a story of determination, adversity and triumph. It is a unique and exciting musical journey that will be welcomed by committed and casual rock readers and by all Dudes – young, post-young and now quite old.

Twenty years after publication of *All the Young Dudes*, the time had arrived to update Ian Hunter's remarkable story – not just because his decade as the driving force behind *Brain Capers*, *Mott*, *The Hoople*, *Ian Hunter*, *All-American Alien Boy* and *You're Never Alone with a Schizophrenic* assured him legendary status, but because he remains one of the most interesting figures in popular music thanks to a stunning quintet of albums, starting with *Rant* in 2001 and extending to the recent *Fingers Crossed*; because these remarkable, riveting and resonant recordings have been widely acclaimed; and because Ian consistently delivers emotional performances that put many younger artists to shame.

Hunter's influence on fellow musicians has been significant. In 2005, *Classic Rock* presented Ian with the magazine's first Classic Songwriter Award, and, in 2016, his career was celebrated with the thirty-disc box set *Stranded in Reality*. The book from that project included a section titled "Go Tell the Superstar" and I received dozens of quotations from luminaries and legends who were all eager to pay homage to Ian. Longer passages were written by some of the collaborators, and so, adopting a Hunter-style "Do what you want to do" mantra, four wonderful essays are presented in the two volumes of *Rock 'n' Roll Sweepstakes*.

It has been a privilege to share such close and unprecedented observations of Ian's work and life. He has defied the recognised arc of commercialism by being his own man – delivering some of his best music over the last twenty years.

It was once expounded that anything is classic if it endures.

Ian Hunter has.

Campbell Devine
September 2019

Foreword

A MATTER OF TIME

It's 1973 and I'm in Mott the Hoople. We're riding high with our album *Mott*, after the success of our previous release, *All the Young Dudes*, saved us from the brink of breaking up. There are huge adoring crowds, chatty DJs and reporters who want to know everything about us, travel to exotic places like Cleveland and Los Angeles – in other words, all the rewards and shackles of fame. The high point of each day for me is playing 'All the Way from Memphis' and 'I Wish I Was Your Mother'. The low point is, the rest of the band doesn't know who I am, the neighbours are constantly complaining about the noise, and I'm thirteen years old and every morning I must drag myself to school instead of sleep in late in some posh hotel suite. Life is bittersweet.

Had my time machine not been broken, I would have been able to not feel so down over the next twenty-five years, because I would have known then that I would someday meet Ian Hunter and play in his band again, only this time with a real guitar instead of one made of air. The years we spent apart did us both some good. For Ian, the foreboding black shades lightened a bit. And though this may have made his appearance seem softer, his already astute songwriting skills sharpened to katana sword-like ferocity. His ability to cut to the chase of a situation, to describe a feeling or setting, and to sheath it in a musical scabbard that very few are worthy to wear always catches me by surprise – the type of cut that at first appears like nothing, but then you notice you're suddenly bleeding all over the floor, wondering how it happened.

What that same stretch of time did for me before my Escher-like musical staircase climb to meeting Ian was prepare me for the unexpected. What seems good is not good enough. What seems finished isn't quite done. What appears honest needs more light. You should zig when everyone tells you to zag. This is how Ian operates, and I've accepted it as a good way to be. It's all you really need to know to get you through the day, month, or the next twenty-five years.

James Mastro
The Rant Band

Acknowledgements

I would like to thank the following for their support and contributions:

Ian Hunter, Trudi Hunter, Verden Allen, Robbie Alter, Miller Anderson, Richie Anderson, Geoff Appleby, Peter Arnesen, Dick Asher, Dan Atkinson, Alan Baguste, Dan Baird, Roy Thomas Baker, Mick Barakan, Dave Bargeron, Darrell Bath, Ariel Bender, Leee Black Childers, Colin Blunstone, Trevor Bolder, Mark Bosch, Angela Bowie, Michael Bradley, Tony Brainsby, Martin Briley, Harvey Brooks, Mick Brown, Andy Burton, Ricky Byrd, John Cambridge, Vivian Campbell, Chris Carter, David Cassidy, Martin Chambers, Bobby Chen, Tim Clark, Marc Coker, Martin Colley, Bobby Colomby, George Cowan, Billy Cross, Paul Cuddeford, Kal David, Dennis DiBrizzi, Johnnie Dee, Sandy Dillon, Billy Duffy, Rusty Egan, Shawn Eisenberg, Roy Eldridge, Dennis Elliott, Joe Elliott, Alejandro Escovedo, Morgan Fisher, Ellen Foley, Shane Fontayne, Paul Francis, David Fricke, Mike Garson, Bobby Gillespie, Dana Gillespie, Gus Goad, Imogen Gordon Clark, Kris Gray, Dale Griffin, Guy Griffin, Alex Gross, Luther Grosvenor, Paul Guerin, Ian Hampton, Steve Harley, Bob Harris, Laurie Heath, Fred Heller, Howard Helm, Robert Hirschman, John Holbrook, Steve Holley, The Horse, Tracie Hunter, Luke Hyams, Steve Hyams, Paul Hyde, Barry Imhoff, John Jansen, David Johansen, Phil John, Mick Jones, Pat Kilbride, Marty Kristian, Corky

Laing, Frankie La Rocka, John Leckie, Per Lindvall, Dan Loggins, Carmela Long, Graham Maby, Russell Mael, Ray Major, Tommy Mandel, Willard Manus, Benny Mardones, Phil Martini, James Mastro, Glen Matlock, Brian May, Robin Mayhew, Roger McGuinn, Wilson McLean, George Meyer, Sham Morris, Tommy Morrongiello, Bjørn Nessjø, Bob Neuwirth, Steve New, Les Nicol, Peter Oxendale, David Oxtoby, Rich Pagano, Paul Page, Eric Parker, Graham Parker, Jesse Patterson, Annette Peacock, Marco Pirroni, Simon Phillips, Honest John Plain, Mac Poole, Steve Popovich, Graham Preskett, David Quantick, Philip Rambow, Mick Ralphs, Genya Ravan, Rob Rawlinson, Bob Rock, Mick Rock, Jim Rodford, Dave Roe, Mats Ronander, Mick Ronson, Suzi Ronson, Lisa Ronson, Maggi Ronson, David Ronson, Rick Rose, Mick Rossi, Tom Semioli, Earl Slick, Gene Simmons, Curly Smith, Amy Speace, Casino Steel, Diane Stevens, James Stevenson, John Justin 'J.J.' Stewart, Sting, Roslaw Szaybo, John Taylor, Roger Taylor, Rick Tedesco, Ian Thomas, Stan Tippins, Martin Turner, Cherry Vanilla, Tony Visconti, Kosmo Vinyl, Johan Wahlstrom, Ricky Warwick, Norman Watt-Roy, Pete Watts, Blue Weaver, Richard Weaver, Max Weinberg, Ginger Wildheart, Peter Wolf, Woody Woodmansey, Trevor Wyatt, Sami Yaffa, Andy York, Roy Young and Robin Zander.

I also acknowledge Robert Christgau, Chrysalis Records, Ian Crockett, Steve Davis, Ben Duke, Ben Edmonds, EMI Records, Hugh Gilmour, Sven Gusevik, Bill Henderson, David Hepworth, Drew Hill, Nicky Horne, JJM Music, Anthony Keates, Dave Ling, Charles Shaar Murray, New West Records, Proper Music, Michael O'Connell, Alan Price, Justin Purington, Nigel Reeve, Scott Rowley, Carlton Sandercock, Phil Savill, Sony Music, Johnnie Walker and Ray Zell.

My special appreciation is extended to:
Iain McNay and Cherry Red Books who supported and published my first biography, *All the Young Dudes*, when there were few "True Believers" left standing who remained actively interested in Mott the Hoople and Ian Hunter. Iain came to the party then and has blessed this new project; I will always be grateful to him…

David Barraclough of Omnibus Press, who has been a tremendous supporter. David gave this biography project huge commitment from the outset; without him you might not be reading this…

Debra and Hunter for enduring all the music mania…

Billy Henry [Fingles Cave Management] for empathy and encouragement…

'Lieutenant' James Mastro and 'Wing Commander' Joe Elliott for their wonderful reflections…

Ian Hunter Patterson for his involvement and the *Hunter by Proxy* and *Rock 'n' Roll Sweepstakes* titles, the latter his preferred branding for *Diary of a Rock 'n' Roll Star*, until commerciality came calling. As Ian says, "If you wait long enough…"

I send special appreciation to the incredible Trudi Hunter…

And thank you once again to four gems: the gentle Steve Hyams, the charming Hugh Attwooll, the wonderful Richie Anderson and the incredible Mick Ronson – four of the finest, fun people I ever met. Boy do we miss them!

Now it's recreational skull diving time, so… plunge in, think and enjoy!

Campbell Devine
September 2019

Hunter Turns Killer

Marc Bolan gravely said, "I must admit Ian,
I've always underestimated you."

The loner, the alien boy, the outsider – distinctive, articulate, truthful.

Ian Hunter's story is that of a gifted songwriter; a profound influence on many musicians and fans; a peerless journeyman who has spent decades writing and delivering some of rock's most intelligent songs.

Always concerned with creating his next record rather than trading on the past, Ian Hunter has been a source of inspiration through his observations, his attitude and his lyrics. He was honoured with *Classic Rock*'s first ever Roll of Honour – Classic Songwriter Award. His musical admirers include Cheap Trick, The Clash and Def Leppard. *The New Yorker* remarked of Hunter that "the main draw" is his voice. But dig-deep and you will find that Ian has written a wealth of amazing and varied songs: eclectic melodies and literate lyricism; odysseys of lived words rather than imagined situations; commentaries about hopes and history; tales of relationships, frustrations and events.

In the early Seventies Ian Hunter was the face, the voice and the soul of Mott the Hoople – a stylish, rambunctious rock band, adored by a cult following. Ian had experienced life before he joined Island Record's most ramshackle group, and, fired by rejection, a fear of returning to the factory floor and sheer determination, he craved musical recognition and fame. These arrived through a combination of his emblematic songs ('Hymn for the Dudes', 'All the Way from Memphis', 'Roll Away the Stone'), classic albums (*Brain Capers*, *All the Young Dudes*, *Mott*) and sensational concerts – "banned" from the Royal Albert Hall, famed for "The Battle of Hammersmith" and acknowledged as the first rock act to appear on Broadway.

Born in Oswestry, England on 3rd June 1939, Ian Hunter Patterson spent his childhood in Hamilton, Scotland before moving back to Shropshire. His musical passion was ignited by the lightning bolt of late Fifties rock 'n' roll, and especially by Little Richard and Jerry Lee Lewis. Abandoning an early career in journalism, Hunter alternated between manual, factory and engineering-based jobs but he also started to dip his toes into the revolutionary musical scene that turned post-war Britain from monochrome to glorious colour.

Ian played guitar in early skiffle and rock 'n' roll groups, including The Apex and Hurricane Henry and the Shriekers, then switched to bass with Freddie Lee, The Scenery, At Last the 1958 Rock and Roll Show and Charlie Woolfe. He also became a staff songwriter in Denmark Street, at the musical heart of London, where one of his early compositions was recorded by Dave Berry. Hunter never thought he would make it as a professional musician, but Sixties sojourns to Germany with Freddie Lee proved to be amongst the most exhilarating times of his life and he started to believe that he might carve out a life in music.

In 1969 Ian backed Sixties pop idol Billy Fury on bass, joined a short-lived version of The New Yardbirds and then auditioned for Island Records, Guy Stevens and a band named Silence, whose line-up included guitarist Mick Ralphs, organist Verden Allen, bassist Peter Overend Watts and drummer Dale 'Buffin' Griffin. Silence had evolved via several Herefordshire groups including The Soulents,

17

The Buddies, The Shakedown Sound and The Doc Thomas Group. Wearing black Zimmerman-style shades and a bland suit, Ian sat at a piano in a dingy Denmark Street basement and stumbled through renditions of Bob Dylan's 'Like a Rolling Stone' and Sonny Bono's 'Laugh at Me'. None of Silence realised that Hunter would become their most valuable asset, but, somewhat reluctantly, Guy invited him to join the band. Here was *the* opportunity that Ian Hunter Patterson had been waiting for.

The re-vamped Silence signed to Island Records, Britain's most eclectic label whose impressive roster already included Traffic, Free and King Crimson. Silence was swiftly re-named Savage Rose and Fixable by Stevens, then Mott the Hoople, the title of a novel by American author Willard Manus featuring the escapades of Norman Mott, an eccentric and rebellious misfit. Guy thought the band's name would look good written down, but it confused some people: "Mott the Who?" "What the Hoople?" "Mouser Hoop…" – "Oh, Mott the Hoople."

Guy Stevens was central to Mott's conception and he was on a mission, thirsting for a band that could place the rock 'n' roll energy of The Rolling Stones alongside the poetic balladry of Bob Dylan, with a touch of Procol Harum keyboards thrown in for good measure. Razor-thin and maniacal, Guy ran on high octane. In a recording studio he was the sworn enemy of moveable furniture, but he was a passionate instigator and energiser who became Mott's mentor. He was also a magpie with an instinct for procuring distinctive names and titles, including Procol Harum, *Sticky Fingers*, 'Death May Be Your Santa Claus' and 'The Wheel of the Quivering Meat Conception', many of them lifted from strange or disturbing sources.

Crucially, though, the man at the Hoople helm was Ian Hunter: the tousle-haired, raspy-voiced, sometimes controversial rocker with the impenetrable black shades; a journalist's delight; an intelligent figure who would arm Mott the Hoople with a stockpile of stunning songs. The band recorded four albums at Island Records between 1969 and 1971: their Dylan-flavoured debut,

Mott the Hoople, with its M.C. Escher sleeve, featured their first epic, 'Half Moon Bay'; *Mad Shadows* was a darker offering, containing Hunter's buoyant 'Walking with a Mountain', captured in the presence of Mick Jagger; *Wildlife* had a gentler atmosphere, exemplified by 'Waterlow', one of Ian's finest compositions; while *Brain Capers* became Mott's Island swansong, the dejected group going down blazing, recording an astonishing album in only five days. The cornerstone of *Brain Capers* was 'The Moon Upstairs', a song that bled frustration and gave credence to the "godfather of punk" description subsequently claimed for Ian.

Hunter had rapidly become a distinctive facet of Mott the Hoople, writing several startling songs including 'Backsliding Fearlessly', 'I Can Feel', 'Angel of Eighth Avenue' and 'The Journey'. Whilst the group's schizophrenic recordings did not storm the charts, Mott had become a significant live draw and a dynamic and powerful unit, admired by the likes of Slade, Status Quo and King Crimson's Robert Fripp. The group pounded the UK motorways, gigging extensively, and their explosive shows often caused mayhem, culminating in a ban from London's Royal Albert Hall. Guitarist Mick Ralphs considered that Mott was always wild and magic in concert; a pre-punk punk band that went against convention, was ahead of its time and was never accepted for what it was. Mott the Hoople was a force of rock 'n' roll, but their failure to gain mass acceptance led to growing frustration. Following two snarling shows in Switzerland, band tensions were high once more and Mott the Hoople decided to split on 26th March 1972. Strangely, M.C. Escher, whose artwork had adorned their debut album, died the following day.

Mott notified Island Records of their demise, but were "heavily heavied" to honour a British concert tour, 'Mott the Hoople's Rock and Roll Circus'. In the shadows, however, soon-to-be-superstar David Bowie, a fan of *Brain Capers* and an admirer of Hunter's onstage persona, learned of the band's demise and charged to the rescue. Bowie offered a pre-*Ziggy Stardust* tape of 'Suffragette City' for the group to record, but when Hunter turned it down, David gifted

'All the Young Dudes'. Recognising a hit, Mott reunited, switched to CBS Records and 'Dudes' swaggered to No.3 in Britain, propelling the band towards a mainstream audience. In the studio, Mott the Hoople learned from David and his sidekick Mick Ronson, but they also bolstered Bowie's song with individuality and conviction. Ian defines 'All the Young Dudes' as "a classic", comparable with 'Layla', and whilst lyrically 'Dudes' was David's conception, it was Mott's instrumental assault and Hunter's vocals that created a genuine anthem. The Bowie-produced *All the Young Dudes* album hit No.21 in Britain and featured Ian's 'Sea Diver', showcasing one of Ronson's stunning orchestral arrangements. Subsequently, 'All the Young Dudes' was voted No.33 in *Mojo*'s 'All-Time Top 100 Singles' and No.1 in *Uncut*'s 2018 'Greatest Glam Singles Chart', while *All the Young Dudes* ranks at No.491 on *Rolling Stone*'s '500 Greatest Albums' listing.

Through Bowie's intervention, Mott was reborn and Hunter felt rejuvenated as the group was finally armed with a huge hit, but organist Verden Allen opted to quit. Temporarily reduced to a quartet, the band considered engaging John Lennon, Glitter maestro Mike Leander or Roy Wood of Move–ELO–Wizzard fame to produce their next LP but, encouraged by Roxy Music, who were recording *For Your Pleasure* in an adjacent room at AIR Studios, Mott the Hoople took the reins and delivered their masterpiece. Chronicling the trials and tribulations of rock 'n' roll, *Mott* is still regarded as a classic Seventies album; 'Ballad of Mott the Hoople (26th March 1972, Zurich)', 'Hymn for the Dudes' and 'I Wish I Was Your Mother' were some of Hunter's finest songs and the proto-punk 'Violence' successfully retained the anger of the group's earlier work. The *Mott* album got to No.7 in the UK charts and, in 2003, was ranked at No.366 in *Rolling Stone*'s '500 Greatest Albums'.

Sell-out tours were wrapped around *Mott*, punctuated with a string of successful UK hit singles penned by Ian – 'Honaloochie Boogie' (No.12), 'All the Way from Memphis' (No.10), 'Roll Away the Stone' (No.8) and 'The Golden Age of Rock 'n' Roll' (No.16)

– while Hunter blazed across the front pages of the world's music press and the band's popularity soared. However, following unease during the *Mott* sessions and unhappy with the band's post-Bowie direction, Mick Ralphs left to form Bad Company with Free vocalist Paul Rodgers. Ralphs' replacement was former Spooky Tooth guitarist Luther Grosvenor, who joined as Ariel Bender, while Verden Allen's role was filled by ex-Love Affair keyboard player Morgan Fisher.

In late 1973 Mott the Hoople played a sold-out British tour, culminating in a performance at London's Hammersmith Odeon that created more sensational headlines when roadies and fans fought with stewards at the climax of Mott's swashbuckling show. Crowds swarmed the stage and rock 'n' roll madness ran rampant – a dramatic illustration of the band's power at their zenith.

Ian Hunter was now Mott's focal point and their principal songwriter but he rose to the challenge and composed some amazing material for their final studio album. *The Hoople* (UK No.11, US No.28) contained an eclectic mix of songs and marked a solid progression in Hunter's writing. The highly charged 'Crash Street Kidds' related the tale of a socially disillusioned gang that wanted to take over Britain, while the equally dramatic 'Marionette' was Ian's "five-minute opera", driven by his feelings towards the stresses of and demands imposed by the music industry. Hunter modestly described 'Marionette' as a nervous breakdown on record, but it was surely an influence on Queen's 'Bohemian Rhapsody' and its sentiments were echoed in the David Essex movie *Stardust*. As Mott drummer Dale Griffin later remarked, Ian possessed astonishing flashes of perception, brilliantly foretelling the mood of the punk era and early Eighties civil unrest.

During the spring of 1974, Mott the Hoople became the first rock band to sell out a week of Broadway concerts at The Uris Theatre in New York. On their opening night, however, Led Zeppelin arrived backstage, antagonised the band and brawled when drummer John Bonham was refused permission to play on 'All the Young Dudes'. Zeppelin's manager, Peter Grant, apologised to Hunter and the fracas was noted by one journalist who felt strongly that "Zep should have known better". In contrast, Mott guitarist Luther Grosvenor was philosophical, reflecting that "Led Zeppelin had simply come to Broadway to see THE greatest rock 'n' roll band in the world at that time – MOTT THE HOOPLE!"

The opening act for Mott's back-to-back British and American tours was Queen, who wrote of their inspirational experiences alongside Hunter and the band, referencing "the Hoople" in their hit single 'Now I'm Here'. Queen guitarist Brian May described his first impressions of Mott the Hoople as "an agglomeration of bright colours, scarves, leather, sunglasses, velvet, huge boots, strange felt hats, blending seamlessly into the masses of hair, beer bottles, fags, battered guitar cases covered with stickers and SWAGGER. They looked lived-in; they exuded Attitude and easy humour and the utter confidence born of 'Knowing you are Good.' They were!"

Diary of a Rock 'n' Roll Star, written by Ian Hunter on Mott's 1972 US tour, was published in 1974. Filled with wise observations about the highs, lows and emptiness of stardom, it was subsequently cherished as a "bible" by several upcoming musicians and was ultimately acclaimed by Q magazine as "the greatest music book ever written".

Mott the Hoople had become chart fixtures during this peak period for Hunter and the group; however, the pressure was building. Now at loggerheads over the choice and style of their music, *The Hoople* had been something of a compromise, accommodating new personnel and an expanded use of keyboards. In truth, after Allen and Ralphs departed, Mott had started to dissolve. Hunter's 'Foxy, Foxy' was released as a British single but it only reached No.33 in the charts and the band lost momentum. Then, despite the whirlwind energy and renewed spirit that he had injected into the group, Luther Grosvenor left.

With a final throw of the dice, Ian engaged Mick Ronson as Grosvenor's replacement. Bowie's former guitarist and musical arranger joined Mott the Hoople firing on all cylinders, fresh from recording two excellent solo albums. Mick contributed to Hunter's self-referential and valedictory single 'Saturday Gigs'; this was deemed a huge potential hit, but it stalled inexplicably, this time at No.41 on the UK chart. Ronson spoke excitedly of recording the next Mott studio album but, whilst a series of European concerts in October 1974 were publicly praised, increasing tensions behind the scenes started to fracture the group. CBS released *Mott the Hoople Live*, but Ian was subsequently hospitalised with exhaustion in New York, leading to the cancellation of a sold-out British tour.

Hunter realised that glam rock was waning and that Mott the Hoople had run its course. The new commercial expectations surrounding the band had started to affect Ian and his writing; he had discovered the shallowness of fame and the pressures attached to it. Frustrations and arguments within the group had also caused him increasing upset. In the end, 'Saturday Gigs' turned out to be Mott's epitaph and a classic way to close the book on the band's history, for, in spite of persuasion from their original guiding light, Guy Stevens, Hunter quit the group. By December 1974, Mott the Hoople had ceased to exist. For Ian Hunter, it was time for a different artistic environment.

Ian Hunter: "Mott the Hoople was crazy and they were great times, but the band was over. We'd hit a brick wall, creatively. When Mick Ronson joined, I saw things through his eyes. We had to come up with something new to continue in Mott, but I wasn't getting much cooperation. People always relied on me in the band which made them lazy, but Ronson and I were changing. Ends are never easy and the split was not entirely amicable. Looking back, Mott went awry when Verden quit and very wrong when Ralphs left. After Bowie, Ralpher thought I got caught up in the 'writing-three-minute-singles' syndrome, but they were good songs and they got Mott the Hoople out of the shit. There had been an alternative; I should have left when Mick did after the *Mott* album. After Ralphs we recruited Luther Grosvenor, who was an excellent chap, but we made no great strides. We'd done *Mott* and *The Hoople*, and that said *Mott the Hoople*, so I guess there was nowhere to go.

"Then Ronson arrived gung-ho for Mott the Hoople and for showing Bowie that he could do it somewhere else; however, the band was exhausted by this point. Mick came in afresh, and observed and said what was wrong with Mott, but the others didn't want advice. Ralphs had been good for me because he would argue in the studio and that's why I got Ronson in; I knew he'd argue too. I felt I was pulling Mott along and Ronson started pulling with me. I really respected him, but some of the others resented him for that. I guess I re-joined the band with Mick and didn't like what I saw – not just the others – me as well. It got to the stage where I couldn't work with them. Dale and I did not get on and I couldn't bear to look at him by the end. I realised that my days with the band were over. There had been so much pressure; we'd had lawyers, not managers, in Mott, so I would spend time trying to manage and that's tough. We'd really become a business and I hadn't been smiling for a long time.

"I flew over to the States between Mott's European and British tours and flaked out. They did a battery of tests on me in a New Jersey hospital and a doctor there said that if I didn't get away from the pressures and re-think my life, I'd be on my way to an early grave. He wrote me medical paperwork and I left Mott. We were due to play Madison Square Garden on my birthday, 3rd June 1975, which I would loved to have done, but I went into complete depression. Mott the Hoople had been a big part of my life, but rock 'n' roll's not much good to you when you're lying on your back in a hospital. Really, you get things in proportion.

"I didn't enjoy Mott the Hoople anymore and there was no way back. When we split, I remember Guy Stevens talking to me for hours, saying, 'You are Mott the Hoople. You are Mott the Hoople. You must stay Mott the Hoople.' The Mott pressure was gone but then, suddenly, there was other

> pressure placed on me from Guy. I realised in one way that I was Mott the Hoople and Guy wanted me to be that, but to be honest, I was sick of Mott the Hoople. I just wanted to be Ian Hunter."

Mott's manager Fred Heller had also been unable to convince Hunter to stay in the band. "I had been saying to Ian before the split, 'Hang in there. 'You're about to do 20,000 seaters. Suck it up. You'll be a millionaire,' but Hunter wanted out," says Fred. "There had been a tremendous amount of pressure on him during Mott's European tour. The whole show was on Ian and he felt the band's reputation trapped him into doing hard rockers, while his great slow numbers were overshadowed. Ian decided to record and tour under his own name."

Fred Heller retained his artist management role for Watts, Griffin and Fisher in a revamped Mott, and he would represent Hunter too. Heller was also the manager of Blood Sweat & Tears and was close to the group's drummer Bobby Colomby, so, following initial recuperation, Ian spent time resting at Bobby's residence in Rockland, New York. There was talk of Hunter working with former Spirit and Jo Jo Gunne figure Jay Ferguson, who loved Mott the Hoople; Jay described Hunter as a genius, but he opted for a solo career. Parallel speculation included the whisper of Ronson's candidacy to replace Mick Taylor, who had quit The Rolling Stones; 'HULL STAR TIPPED TO GO ROCKING WITH THE STONES' revealed the *Hull Daily Mail* in January 1975, but the rumour evaporated. Hunter later declared that he had heard Ronson was on the Stones' shortlist, but that Mick was never asked. Instead, Ronson joined Hunter at Colomby's home and Mick sensed an opportunity; he was conscious of Ian's position, but he was also aware that emotional situations were a rarity and that the pair could achieve something special amidst the upset and chaos.

IH: "Bobby Colomby offered me his house while he was on tour and Ronson came over and stayed with me in America.

Mick and I sat and wondered what to do, then he said, 'Get in the studio and do an album *now*, while you're feeling the way you're feeling, because there are a lot of emotions flying about.' Ronson was really intuitive; he knew I was emotionally charged and said, 'We have to make a record *right now*. This is when you make 'em! This is when you make 'em!' So, I said, 'We haven't got a band,' but Mick said, 'I'll go back and get one.' So Ronno went back to England and put a band together, while I started writing songs as fast as I could. I remember I wrote 'Boy' at Bobby's house. I hadn't planned on doing an album until the summer, but Mick was right and he made everything sound so easy. I had got in such a state that I had to do something. I'd figured I was going to be alright because I could write songs, so I realised that Mick and me would be fine. We had a lot to live up to, but Ronson had a name, and I had a name and now we were both as free as birds."

Having opted to record a solo album with Ronson and divorced from the treadmill that Mott the Hoople had become, Ian composed with a new sense of space. He had sometimes written to the demands and image of Mott, but his new songs would be different. Heller negotiated a solo contract with Columbia Records, Hunter asking for a four-album option, and Mott the Hoople's mammoth 1975 tour was re-planned as a shorter solo outing, to follow Ian's recording sessions. Some of the material and song ideas that Hunter would take into the studio had been partly written in Mott, but whilst everyone anticipated a degree of Hoople echo, Ian's record would showcase a new direction.

The engagement of "a band" for Hunter's sessions became straightforward when Mick introduced bassist Geoff Appleby, who had played alongside Ronson in Hull. "I'd known Mick since our teenage years in the Sixties when we were in The Rats together," recalled Geoff. "We had a great time – young, single and skint – so skint that I remember Mick forging his dad's signature to get hire purchase to buy musical equipment for The Rats' legendary trip to France. He was in big, big bother when we got back – and homeless for quite a while."

Ronson also knew Simon Phillips through MainMan Management and Dana Gillespie, and the drummer was wanted for Hunter's album. "I had just signed to Jet Records and Don Arden Management with a band called Chopyn and couldn't join Ian Hunter, but I remember a session with him," says Simon. "I'd been to New York with Dana and Mick was flying with us, so I visited Hunter at AIR Studios. I have a recollection of being in the control room with Mick and Ian, but I think it was purely social." Instead of Phillips, Hunter engaged drummer Dennis Elliott, who had plied his trade with The Ferris Wheel and Island Records band If.

> **IH:** "Simon Phillips had drummed with Mick and me one day, by chance, at the very end of Mott – we jammed on 'All the Way from Memphis' and we got on well. Simon was only seventeen at the time and went on to be one of Britain's greatest drummers; his father, Sid, had led a big band. Simon was great and made my songs come to life so Ronson and I asked him to join us, but he couldn't come to the US and that was part of the deal at the time. When I got back to London after Mott, I met Dennis Elliott and his wife Iona. Dennis was a swing drummer and I've always liked swing drummers, so he came down and we agreed he would play. Dennis is great. He'd been in If, a jazz-rock band, and jazz-based drummers are always great in rock bands."

After Christmas, Ian and Mick entered Tony Pike Studio in South-west London to rehearse the songs that Hunter had prepared in America. 'Tepee' was an independent demo facility in Putney, where early recordings had been made by Genesis and John Martyn, and Hunter Ronson put the new band through their paces there and checked the recording potential of several songs. Then, on 13th January 1975, the ensemble moved into AIR (London) Studio No.2 at Oxford Circus to record, using the studio time previously booked for Mott the Hoople. Ronson would act as arranger and co-produce the album with Hunter, assisted by Bill Price, AIR's amazing recording engineer who had been central to *Mott* and *The Hoople*.

For Ian's sessions, Mick also introduced Hans-Peter Arnesen, a student of piano from Salzburg and Seattle universities who had played keyboards with If, The Dana Gillespie Band and successful pop act The Rubettes. Arnesen recorded several tracks "from basics" with Hunter and the band, but also overdubbed on some earlier takes. "I quit The Rubettes after three hit singles and joined Hunter Ronson through Mick, the connection being MainMan," says Peter. "I knew Simon Phillips as we were in Dana's band, but it was Mick who phoned me about Ian. I met Dennis Elliott and Geoff Appleby for the first time at AIR Studios and we recorded tracks together over two or three sessions; I did a lot of overdubs too. I recall Rod Stewart being in the adjoining studio."

In time-honoured fashion, Ian's solo debut would be eponymously titled, and the *Ian Hunter* sessions progressed well. Having been constricted by commercial considerations and a situation where so many agendas had to be satisfied within Mott, Hunter was unleashed and liberated. There was a charged and introspective lyrical content, the music was direct and uncluttered, and Mick added great strength with intelligent arrangements and exciting guitar work that complemented Ian's writing and vocals.

Ian Hunter would feature nine sparkling tracks: 'Once Bitten Twice Shy', 'Who Do You Love', 'Lounge Lizard', 'Boy', '3,000 Miles from Here', 'The Truth, the Whole Truth, Nuthin' But the Truth', It Ain't Easy When You Fall', 'Shades Off' and 'I Get So Excited'. Hunter had entered AIR Studios with a handful of songs rehearsed, but during recording new material emerged and the album evolved with elements of accident and chance, which Ian found exciting. Hunter knew that he had written lyrics to fill *The Hoople* to a certain extent, so he started discarding songs at AIR that reminded him of any recent heritage. *Ian Hunter* changed in mid-flight and, having anticipated a transitional record, Ian was delighted that the album captured an identity of its own. As *Rolling Stone* proclaimed, this was "Hunter Ronson: Not the Hoople".

Five of the songs first slated for *Ian Hunter* had been partially hatched in Mott the Hoople. 'Colwater High', 'One Fine Day' and 'Lounge Lizard' were considered for Mott singles but shelved; the band had also rehearsed other Hunter fragments – 'Did You See Them Run', which would be extended and developed as 'Boy', and 'Shades Off', a poem that Ian had written in 1973, travelling in Scotland during a short Hoople tour. At the *Ian Hunter* sessions, 'Lounge Lizard' was re-recorded, while 'Colwater High' and 'One Fine Day' were commenced but not completed.

> **IH:** "We kept kicking songs out as we went along during the sessions because I found that I was writing as we recorded. Half the album was written in the studio and it was great because Ronson had pounced on the crisis of the moment. Something different came out and we were lucky. Geoff, Dennis and Pete were great to work with and Mick was positively brilliant, both in the booth and in the studio. Ronson and I made a quicker transition from Mott into that band than we could ever have hoped for. The songs had swing and differed from Mott the Hoople mainly in the speeds and funkiness of it all. When we started, we had 'Boy', 'Lounge Lizard', 'One Fine Day' and 'Colwater High', and although we changed things, we still did the album in six weeks. Doing my first solo album so quickly proved to be a catharsis."

When *Ian Hunter* hit British record stores on 28th March 1975, the LP was unveiled as a remarkable release and a significant departure from Mott. Gone were the saxophones, cellos and over-ornate, multi-layered production of *The Hoople*; the new album's essence was much more direct. Ronson's guitar playing excelled, the musical backing and dynamics were powerful and sympathetic, and the structural layout of the record was clever.

With the vinyl branded 'Part One' and 'Part Two', rather than the customary 'Side One' and 'Side Two', Hunter's first three songs combined to offer a terrific rock 'n' roll triptych, including riffs and rhythms that refracted influential echoes of Chuck Berry and The Rolling Stones.

The album's opening track, 'Once Bitten Twice Shy', was Hunter's favourite song from the LP. Carrying an intimate lyrical message and praised for having beat, build and restraint, Ian had crafted a clever rock song that struck swiftly and stuck in the memory. Completed during the latter stages of the AIR sessions, it was written in open G tuning and started with a basic 'Little Queenie' rhythm guitar vamp and spoken introductory *"'Allo"* from Hunter, a direct counterpoint to the repeated *"Goodbye"* that concluded Mott's swansong single, 'Saturday Gigs'. 'Once Bitten Twice Shy' climbed in intensity for two minutes, verse after verse, until a laid-back flurry of drums and simple chords created some breathing space before the band slammed into overdrive; then, in mid-flight, Ronson's expressive guitar solo sparkled, culminating in a magical fifteen-second, single-note vibrato held over the bridge, before Ian's frenzied home run, hinged around a classic chorus. Released as the first 45 to promote *Ian Hunter*, this was glorious rock 'n' roll for the singles chart and the song would thrive in Hunter's live repertoire throughout his career.

> **IH:** "I remember I originally got the verse for 'Once Bitten' at a Mott rehearsal, piddling about at the end of a session one day. I was stuck but I found the middle later, then I finished it off one day at Ronson's flat behind the Albert Hall, with Suzi coming in and bringing me coffee as I was writing. Mick had a little drum machine and me and the drum machine got along just fine. I had the verse and the bridge for 'Once Bitten' but I didn't get the hook until sometime later. One night I was sitting with a drummer in the Speakeasy talking about the song and he tapped something out while we were both sitting there drunk. A bell went off in my head and I

rushed home. I was saying something on 'Once Bitten' but covered it up by using a girl. It's partly about Mott's break-up, but it's also about the rock business in broader terms. I wrote about the industry quite a bit back then. That was the best track on the album, and it has been a great song for me. The great song is the one that comes altogether, at once – words and music – and whilst I had some of it in advance, really 'Once Bitten Twice Shy' took ten hours. We recorded it 'backwards' at AIR Studios in that the guitar went on with a click-track, then the drums went on last. That was quite daring at the time. When we did the real drums I just sat and listened, and Dennis had it on the second take! The 'hello' intro just came out of my mouth and was unplanned. It was a soulful song and subconsciously it was just me moving out of one situation into another: a beginning."

Variously described as pop's cosmic dancer, a flowerchild and an ambitious figure, Marc Bolan of T. Rex appeared at AIR Studios during the *Ian Hunter* sessions. Bolan had been championed by DJ John Peel in the early days of Tyrannosaurus Rex, until the pair fell out, and publicist B.P. Fallon later opined that it was easy to underestimate Marc because he overestimated himself. Bolan asked to hear some of Hunter's new work at AIR, and Ian observed Marc with interest.

IH: "Marc Bolan was popping in and out during our time at AIR Studios. He wanted Mick to listen to the entire album that he was doing, and Ronson was rolling his eyes but went to the mixing room to please Marc in the end. I think Bolan was also doing a solo for ELO in AIR No.1 while we were in AIR No.2, which was the studio I preferred. I remember Marc coming in like King Rocker when Mick and I were doing 'Once Bitten'. Never short of regal confidence, he asked us to play something. So, we played him something and it turned out to be 'Once Bitten Twice Shy'. Marc Bolan listened, then turned to me and gravely said, 'I must admit, Ian, I've always underestimated you.' Better late than never! That was the only time we spoke. Bolan had some extremely good singles, but I never listened to his albums. He was a great self-promoter, always telling the British press how huge he was in the US when he wasn't. He was cheeky, engaging and rather pompous regarding his standing in British rock but he still has vociferous supporters. I don't think there was ever really much weight with Marc. He never said anything other than, 'Buy my records, I want to be a fucking star.' T. Rex was a great singles band though. My mate Miller Anderson was with Bolan for a few years later on and Miller thought Marc was great."

'Who Do You Love', a road-weary freeway tale referencing Detroit City was an infectious toe-tapper with funky harmonica and boogie piano. Whereas American audiences took to 'Once Bitten Twice Shy', British listeners seemed to embrace 'Who Do You Love', so it became CBS's second single from the LP. The track would later be covered by The Pointer Sisters, Def Leppard and Joe Elliott's Down 'n' Outz, but Hunter says he struggles to remember the origins of the song.

> **IH:** "I can't remember who 'Who Do You Love' was written about. I don't think it was a disc jockey in Detroit as some people thought. I think it was put together as we liked the groove. Lyrically, it was fabricated with atomised elements of truth."

'Lounge Lizard' completed Ian's trio of tracks exhibiting Sixties influences and was another "rock 'n' roll women" song, but stronger and more sure-footed than Mott the Hoople's earlier interpretation. With 'Honky Tonk Women' cowbell, another attention-grabbing Ronson guitar motif and a stalwart appearance from Roxy Music bassist John Gustafson, the re-born 'Lizard' moved with slinky

32

rhythm, sassy swing and sardonic lyrics, as Hunter sang of a real "speakeasy sleazer" encounter.

> **IH:** "It was a year before I met Trudi after I split from my first wife and I was pulling women out of the Speakeasy in the middle of the night. That was the subject matter for 'Lounge Lizard'. Originally, I recorded the track with Mott for the B-side of 'Saturday Gigs', but ditched it. There was no imagination in Mott's 'Lizard' – they were just bashing it out. Mick and I re-did it in a different style at AIR, with Johnny Gustafson on bass. Like 'Who Do You Love', 'Lounge Lizard' was a song that spoke of a girl, but as a cover-up for something else I was trying to say."

After three up-tempo rock songs, Hunter deftly moderated the mood with 'Boy', an atmospheric, nine-minute story of reprimand and reassurance that concluded 'Part One' of *Ian Hunter* with class and conviction. Ian completed 'Boy' with arrangement assistance from Ronson and there would be some speculation about the song's content. Hunter's mention of genocide and coke undoubtedly referenced *Diamond Dogs* and Bowie, and Ronson later stated that 'Boy' was partly about David. In fact, the stylish song was a composite tale, including a cautionary message for Joe Cocker and admonishment to Hunter himself. 'Boy' was also the album's intended centrepiece.

The intensely impassioned Cocker had flown high with his early albums, a live appearance at Woodstock and the 'Mad Dogs and Englishmen' tour alongside Leon Russell. Having dropped off the music map, in 1974 Joe's booze-laden comeback gig at the Roxy in Los Angeles damaged his career in front of invited record industry personnel. Cocker was unique and had become known for erratic behaviour, but he would fight his way back after being written off as another casualty of Seventies' rock 'n' roll excess. Because Ronson had contributed greatly to the arrangement of Hunter's song and to the entire album, Ian co-credited Mick on 'Boy' so that he gained some publishing benefit.

IH: "'Boy' was probably the first song I 'wrote' with Ronson although he never actually composed anything with me. Mick wasn't interested in writing. His focus was the song and his guitar solos were songs within songs, but he always had ideas and made great contributions that I would never think of. We did deals on these and with 'Boy' we are both credited, but I wrote the song. Originally it was even longer than the finished article and went into another area which Mick didn't like, so I dropped that section. The co-write was just that he'd edited it and done such a beautiful job on the arrangement and other tracks too, so I thought he should be paid more and felt obligated to share the song with him. That's the way it went down.

"'Boy' was a lyrical compendium of people in my life. It was a bunch of bits and pieces that all sounded good, so I threw a lot of different things together. It wasn't about one particular person. It was two or three people I was intrigued by around that time, and a bit of myself is in there too. Everyone thought it was about Bowie, but I wouldn't give away eight minutes to David. The song was never specifically about Bowie, although his manager might have got a couple of references. Predominantly 'Boy' was about Joe Cocker, because I'd known him a little during the Mott days at Island. I loved Leon Russell who got a bad rap about taking over Cocker's 'Mad Dogs' tour; I just felt that somebody had to take the reins and I always rated Leon very highly, so 'Boy' was intended as a bit of encouragement towards Joe. 'Boy' was an amalgamation of images and, like Joe Cocker, David Bowie did play a role in that movie."

'Part Two' of *Ian Hunter* began with '3,000 Miles from Here', a tranquil, sub-three-minute, fleeting vignette about a lady of the road. Comprising lightly treated acoustic guitar and Hunter's vocal, the lyrics were so devastating in their simplicity and the song so understated that it almost had the aura of a demo. It was certainly a concise and charmingly effective track, and a contrasting way to mark the halfway stage of the record.

> **IH:** "'3,000 Miles from Here' was a song that was partly left over from Mott the Hoople and I remember I finished it quickly at the end of the sessions. It's nice and sparse and was part-written in the studio because we were two songs short for the record. It's a sad little song, but I thought it had to be said. Some very sad and romantic things happen on the road, and some of '3,000 Miles from Here' was about the early days. That's how it was then."

Hunter's song remains vastly underrated and, in 2014, manager Fred Heller reflected that Ian was delivering something very special on his first solo album. "Hunter was often in a dark place and hurt himself by not socialising enough with other musicians in my view," said Fred. "But, in the studio, in 1975, with acoustic guitar in hand, Ian Hunter was the British Bob Dylan."

Siting 'The Truth, the Whole Truth, Nuthin' But the Truth' as a direct contrast to '3,000 Miles from Here', Hunter's album got stronger and stronger with each succeeding track. The stark, ominous riff and Ian's vocal on 'The Truth' were marvellous, but the piece also provided a platform for Mick's inspirational guitar style. Ronson's light touches and aggressive playing laced Ian's song with passion, centred around an ascending, almost apocalyptic solo that remains one of Mick's most extraordinary offerings. British reviewer Ray Fox-Cumming described the track as epic and the best thing Hunter had ever written, adding: "It exemplifies why Ian and Ronno are so good for each other. A bunch of songs looking for a sound meets a head full of sounds looking for some songs." *Phonograph Record* in the US opined that the track would become "a classic – enshrined in anyone's hard-rock hall of fame".

35

Across the *Ian Hunter* album, Mick's creative presence seemed to encourage Ian to reach vocal performances surpassing any of Mott the Hoople's work, and 'The Truth' was an example of Hunter's writing inspiring Ronson's musicianship too. Def Leppard guitarist Vivian Campbell, who was blown away when Joe Elliott first played him Ian's track on a tour bus, recently enthused: "'The Truth, the Whole Truth, Nuthin' But the Truth' featured one of rock's greatest-ever guitar solos – from one of rock's greatest-ever guitarists."

> **IH:** "I found the main riff for that song by going up and down the fretboard in E position. It was an ambiguous lyric, but I wrote it musically with Mick in mind and as a vehicle for his incredible playing, especially the whole middle section where the scream occurs. The minute Mick heard it he was taken. That was Ronson's speed; he liked slow groove songs and the slower the better. It was very simple and I knew Mick would play the shit out of it. I remember just before the session in AIR, he got a review for his solo album, *Play Don't Worry*, which was vicious and personal. So Mick read this scathing review and went bright red and we were doing the track and went out to do the solo. We got it in five minutes flat. If he hadn't read that review it would have taken us about three days. Mick was extremely picky and a purist with his solos. He'd do a lot of them and he'd constantly chop and change. He wasn't too keen on the heavy-handed approach and he wasn't a fan of running up and down the fretboard just to show off. His whole thing was melody. Concert trained, perfect ear, I just let him get on with it. Whatever he finished up with was fine by me, and 'The Truth' was something special. Mick was fabulous on that track."

A refreshing aspect of the *Ian Hunter* album was the expression and eclecticism of Ian's writing. 'It Ain't Easy When You Fall' reflected on the fragility of fame and success, but Ian held a trump card.

After tender verses, intelligent piano interludes and captivating, harmony-laden choruses, with a creative brushstroke Hunter placed 'Shades Off' as a moving spoken section over the song's extended outro. Cushioned by a beautiful repeat chorus as a backdrop, the poetic verses conveyed the observations of a travelling musician with an element of rock star confusion and awareness. With 'Shades Off' appended to 'It Ain't Easy When You Fall', Ian had created a monolithic classic. Arguably the cornerstone of the record, 'It Ain't Easy' could have been Hunter's song to himself, at the peak of his recent breakdown, but he later confessed that the lyrical inspiration was Mott guitarist Mick Ralphs.

> **IH:** "'It Ain't Easy When You Fall' wasn't anything to do with me. It was written about Mick Ralphs. Maybe I was telling Mick how I felt and how I was. He really did talk about boats and planes; he'd talk about anything other than getting down to business. I had written 'Shades Off' on a short tour of Scotland with Mott the Hoople in early 1973. My father was born in Scotland, so I'm half Scottish, and parts of the country are quite amazing. I was on the tour bus, gazing out of the window and those words just started coming into my head. So, I started writing and it didn't take long to do; maybe ten minutes. We'd had the D.H. Lawrence poem on *Mott* and Baudelaire on *Mad Shadows*, and I'd written 'Shades Off' which was intended for the *Ian Hunter* album cover and that was all. Then we had this long tail on 'It Ain't Easy When You Fall', because we were a bit short of material and sometimes you do long endings, 'just in case'. I was supposed to do some scat singing over the fade out, but it didn't sound too good. Then I remembered I had this handy book of poems and we thought we'd drop 'Shades Off' in, to make the side a bit longer. I felt embarrassed about doing it, but I read the poem and we overdubbed it and killed two birds with one stone. It was a personal statement and I did feel self-conscious, but I figured I should do what

I want. The *'uncontrollable light'* line in 'Shades Off' refers to that extremely rare occasion when you nail it, dead on, in songwriting. You're lucky if you get that once in a lifetime. I've felt it maybe half a dozen times."

Bookending *Ian Hunter* with another exuberant rock song, Ian concluded proceedings with the energetic power-pop of 'I Get So Excited'. Formulated with vibrant verses, a simple chorus and gleeful lyrics, Ronson's rampant guitarwork and Dennis Elliott's drumming shine throughout – but the song's finale was also stirring, the frantic instrumental section suddenly halted with a scissored end, leaving band and listener breathless. Hunter always envisaged 'Once Bitten Twice Shy' as *the* album cut for single release – and he won – but 'I Get So Excited' was the commercial choice of CBS Records. It may not have been Ian's most complex song and it didn't carry the lyrical prowess of 'Boy', but the sheer joy of hell-for-leather rock 'n' roll is simply expressed and exemplified in 'I Get So Excited.'

> **IH:** "I remember we put that song together after we dropped several numbers during the sessions at AIR. We'd started running out of material, so 'I Get So Excited' was done over the last few days. We had a hell of a job with it. Ronno fished the track back from the outtake pond and it was the hardest song to do on the whole album. We needed two songs actually, so '3,000 Miles from Here' and 'I Get So Excited' were done quickly as we were up against the clock. I wasn't singing 'I Get So Excited' that well, so we added every echo in the book."

Ian Hunter far exceeded post-Hoople expectations – the album proved that the combination of 'Mott and Mick' could have been sensational, Ronson's sparkling guitar adding a gorgeous gloss to some of Ian's finest compositions. Hunter was appreciative that CBS had granted him freedom on his first solo project and felt that the new band possessed erratic magic. The musicians were happy, the experience was full of high spirits and Dennis Elliott had turned out to be an ace in the pack, as Ian admitted at the time.

> **IH:** "The drummer has been the surprise. That's why the album is much more rhythmic. I swore I'd get a swing drummer if I left Mott. I love this album. It's the best thing I've been involved in, in terms of the sound, clarity and songs."

Musically, the *Ian Hunter* recordings were imaginative and colourful, and so was the album artwork. Featuring M.C. Escher's surrealistic 1956 image, 'Bond of Union', the cover presented a parallel to Escher's 'Reptiles' that had adorned Mott the Hoople's debut LP, but *Ian Hunter* incorporated only half of the Dutch artist's monochrome lithograph. Based on a self-portrait of Maurits and his wife Jetta, the original 'Bond of Union' portrays the expressionless faces of two people in peaceful double unity. Composed from merged spiral ribbons that gave the appearance of fruit peel, the interlinked heads are constructed simply, transcending the environment and floating spheres around them, in another mysterious, futuristic world of Escher shapes and symmetry. Symbolically, the peeled face on Hunter's cover was connected to the concept of shedding outdated situations, so in the light of Ian's disconnection from Mott the Hoople, the artistic representation was appropriate.

CBS Art Director Roslaw Szaybo recalled that the label sought permission to use part of 'Bond of Union' for *Ian Hunter*, but reflected that the black-and-white art and 'Shades Off' poem on the inner record liner should have been employed inside a gatefold sleeve. The original Escher lithograph was adapted by illustrator Martin Springett, who designed covers and inner sleeves for other Columbia artists, including Argent. Springett utilised the left-hand head from Escher's work and expanded the illustration with eagles, planets, multicoloured flashes and Hunter's signature shades.

"Roslaw had seen my work when the group I was in delivered a tape to the record company," says Martin. "They didn't care for the music but Roslaw was taken with my art on a poster that I'd created for our band, so I was hired to do the cover for *Ian Hunter*. I met Ian briefly when I worked on his sleeve. I was living in a freezing cold flat in Finchley and that's where the artwork was done. I think I decided on the female half of 'Bond of Union' simply because it faced the right way; there was no deep reason. Roslaw was keen on using Ian's dark glasses and I was left alone to add whatever I wanted, so all the surrounding images were mine. I was keen on birds of prey at the time! As usual, these sorts of intriguing artistic moments have many sides. I was not really into Ian's stuff – I was more Yes and Genesis – so, my creative instincts sent me off on tangents that are perhaps not entirely related to Ian's music on the album, but that's okay. As for any connection between the imagery and the music, I leave that to the listener. Some folks consider *Ian Hunter* a classic album cover and I was contacted once by a German music magazine to unlock some of the visual mysteries on the cover. 'Why the baby in the cabbage?' Who knows? For me, it was just having fun with the image."

> **IH:** "Guy Stevens had turned me on to Escher when he picked 'Reptiles' for the *Mott the Hoople* cover in 1969. I like any challenge to normalcy and I had loved the artwork for the first Mott album, so I asked Roslaw as Art Director at CBS to experiment with another Escher. I really liked what he came up with and that was that. Much of M.C. Escher's work dealt with infinity and cycles, and he certainly makes you think. His spirals led me to the beautiful 'Bond of Union'. The uniqueness of his art was such that it made him a loner. He had a wife and children and was tortured by the fact that he needed to be selfish with his time. Why is it that people are called self-obsessed or selfish when all they are trying to do is something special?"

Hunter had delivered an amazing album against all the odds and the LP cover included an important personal dedication: "*I would like to thank my manager Fred Heller, Trudi, Suzi Baby and Guy Stevens for making this album a happy memory. Organized Under Stress by Richie Anderson.*"

The British music press commended *Ian Hunter*, noting that the record was a solid reflection on one of rock's most exciting combinations. *NME* enthused: "'The Truth, the Whole Truth, Nuthin' But the Truth' is just great. Play it loud. That's L-O-U-D. It's Killersville!" *DISC* considered that Ronson had played no better on record since Bowie's *Aladdin Sane* and remarked: "*Ian Hunter* is a blend of very tasty, heavy r'n'r countered by simpler 'own-up' tracks – what a pleasant surprise this is going to be for the mourners of Mott the Hoople." *Melody Maker*'s 'Heartful Hunter' review conceded: "*Ian Hunter* is a surprising leap forward. There is a thread that runs through *Hunter* giving it a cohesion and direction." Under the headline 'Hunter Turns Killer', Bill Henderson raved in *Sounds*, describing Ronson's sweet and corrosive guitar as "sharper than a serpent's tooth", Hunter as "someone who has always been our best rock chronicler" and the album's three opening cuts as "a rock 'n' roll masterpiece".

America was also excited about Ian's new album; *Hit Parader* termed Hunter one of the most recognizable rock 'n' roll stars of the decade and *Circus* praised *Ian Hunter* as one of the most impressive debut LPs ever released. *Phonograph Record* wrote: "It's a superb album, with strong initial impact but a much more profound effect after repeated exposure. There's a new exploitation of build-up and tension – a mastery of intonation that makes Bob Dylan sound ludicrously overblown – plus lyrical injections of intellectual substance." In their lead 'Records' review, under the headline 'Ian Hunter Professes Faith: Rock Saves', *Rolling Stone* opined, "'Once Bitten', 'Boy', 'It Ain't Easy' and 'So Excited' are near masterpieces. The singer's salvation through rock & roll is apparently complete." Columbia Records' press ads, headed 'Night of the Hunter', proclaimed: "The man who made Mott so hot is out on his own.

Ian Hunter, last of the great English rock crazies and soul of Mott the Hoople, unleashes himself on a solo career. Teaming up with Mick Ronson, guitar powerhouse and one-time Bowie honcho, for a mammoth American tour and a debut album that's already a British smash."

CBS released *Ian Hunter* in late March, so British concert-goers heard some of Ian's new material in advance during a thirteen-date UK tour. Engaging Mott the Hoople stalwarts Richie Anderson and Phil John as road crew, Hunter Ronson made their first live appearance playing a warm-up show at Exeter University on 15th March, a gig that Ian described as amazing.

"When planning the UK leg of the Hunter Ronson tour in 1975, the promoter Harvey Goldsmith asked my thoughts on which venues we should play," recalled Richie. "I suggested a second London show, over at East Ham Granada. It later turned out to be a pretty bad choice. I remember some years earlier, during an Island recording session, Guy Stevens asked what I thought of a Mott playback. I tentatively said it sounded thin and they should add some 'oomph'. Guy agreed and had the engineer do whatever was needed to fatten it up. Both times I was left slightly confused by having experts ask my opinion of things that I really didn't know much about, and then act on what I said. Harvey and Guy were both brilliant in their own ways and to be asked my opinion was quite flattering, but I looked at people and events around Mott the Hoople and Ian, and their careers, and I think they were dogged by some really poor advice and weak representation. They needed a tough, committed and capable manager. I don't believe that person didn't exist somewhere, but sadly the connection was never made."

Hunter's British tour started in earnest at Aylesbury Assembly Hall and the itinerary included Glasgow Apollo, Newcastle City Hall and Hammersmith Odeon. Billed as 'Ian Hunter and Mick Ronson', the shows comprised songs from *Ian Hunter*, Ronson's *Slaughter on 10th Avenue* and *Play Don't Worry* albums and a climactic flurry of Mott the Hoople hits. Hunter Ronson was supported by Jet, a new CBS band featuring Peter Oxendale, Martin Gordon and

Davy O'List, a trio with Sparks and Roxy Music connections. RCA Records had deferred the release of *Play Don't Worry* to coincide with Hunter Ronson's concerts, its glossy black gatefold cover featuring Mick in four dramatic poses, brandishing his iconic maple Les Paul. The tour was re-scheduled to conclude at East Ham on 2nd April, as Ian planned to move to America and needed to exit Britain by the end of the tax year.

Echoing ambitious strategies adopted by Genesis and The Who for *The Lamb Lies Down on Broadway* and *Quadrophenia*, CBS let Hunter embark on live dates with his solo LP ready but not yet released. Ian was still delighted with the shows and audience responses given that they played a live set with several songs from an unreleased album. Ronson seemed more confident and re-charged sharing the stage with Hunter, and 'The Truth, the Whole Truth, Nuthin' But the Truth' became Mick's blistering guitar showcase each night.

> **IH:** "At the Glasgow Apollo, Mick played this great enormous solo on 'The Truth' which went on for about twenty minutes. We just rode along with it and I forgot half the words because I was listening."

Hunter Ronson's live line-up included Geoff Appleby and Dennis Elliott from the album sessions, but Peter Arnesen was hospitalised before the start of the British tour, so former Mott the Hoople organist Blue Weaver stepped in on keyboards. Blue had been recording with The Bee Gees in America when he received Ian's call, flying in to rehearse briefly, before Hunter Ronson played their opening show at Exeter.

"It was great to join Ian again and play piano and organ with Hunter Ronson," says Blue. "I had two days of rehearsal and had only played organ on the Mott the Hoople material, so I spent time with chord sheets in front of me. It was good for me because piano is more physical and good fun. It was an excellent tour and there was no noticeable difference between the earlier concerts with

Mott. There was still Mott the Hoople fans and Mick's fans and the Bowie overflow, and Hunter Ronson was a really good band. 'Slaughter on 10th Avenue' made me a bit nervous though; I'd originally heard Mike Garson playing that and he was incredible. Ian Hunter is a true star in every sense of the word. The fans love him, other musicians and singers love him, and everyone that ever played with him loves him."

Def Leppard's Joe Elliott, a die-hard Hoople, Hunter and Ronson fan, first experienced Mott's music in 1971 via 'Original Mixed-Up Kid' on an Island Records sampler, *El Pea*, and the band's third single, 'Downtown', played on Radio Luxembourg. Elliott never saw the original Mott the Hoople play, but witnessed Hunter Ronson at Sheffield City Hall in 1975. It was the beginning of a lifelong passion for Ian's music.

Former Mott the Hoople benefactor Dan Loggins recalls: "*Ian Hunter* was very well received by critics and public, the 'Once Bitten Twice Shy' single was a hit and the album cover art made a classy statement. Hunter Ronson's appearance at Hammersmith Odeon was also a sensation, with energy and visual impact – stage left was Ian, resplendent all in white, and on the right Ronno still shone, dressed all in black. The image was perfect – 'yin and yang' – the performance rocked, and the audience was with them from beginning to end. It was a triumph and one of the highlights of that year, or any year. It was also a logical step and notable progression in Ian and Mick's musical evolution. Hunter Ronson should have been one of the biggest and most successful touring acts to hit the UK and the US in 1975, but the business side soon got in the way."

On 29th March, Ian and Mick were featured on the front page of *DISC*. Under the headline 'Hunter Ronson Walking on Guilded Odds', the article spoke of the duo's dual management and label situation: "The spectacular concept of Ian Hunter and Mick Ronson fronting their own supergroup officially began in Sheffield last Thursday at the start of an extensive British tour. Two major artists on two different labels, attempting to beat the business odds with the sheer weight of their need to combine forces, Hunter on CBS,

Ronson on RCA – meaning their music will possibly never exist under the proper dual album. It will be a series of solo albums in disguise."

During their infancy at Island Records, Mott the Hoople's output had meandered across four diverse albums, but CBS expected Hunter Ronson to make an instant impact. *Ian Hunter* entered the British charts on 12th April, peaking at No.21 while, in America, the album reached No.50 on *Billboard*. The LP stayed on both charts for fifteen weeks and was certified for a Silver Disc.

An edited version of 'Once Bitten Twice Shy', backed with '3,000 Miles from Here', was released as a single on 4th April, hitting the British chart on 3rd May where it spent ten weeks, climbing to No.14. *Record Mirror* described the disc as "an insidious toe-tapper with a strong hook", while John Peel, writing in *Sounds*, termed the "rowdy guitaring" single "a most seductive three minutes, fifty seconds". A colourful in-performance promo video was filmed by CBS and Hunter's driving rock brightened the British charts. 'Once Bitten Twice Shy' was later covered by Shaun Cassidy, Status Quo and Great White, who scored an American Top Five single in 1989. It paid royalties, but Hunter was bewildered when Great White's lead singer was nominated for a Grammy.

> **IH:** "'Once Bitten Twice Shy' was really Seventies Chuck Berry and I think it was a great song: subtle and simple, but with a twist. I was sure it was going to be a hit because it really gave me a buzz like 'Dudes' had done in Mott. I only had that feeling on those two occasions. 'Once Bitten' made the UK Top Twenty when Mick and I did it, and the US Top Five when it was covered by Great White. Originally, the song was 'wanted' by Guns N' Roses, which would have meant gold dust for me. Axl Rose told me at The Palace in Hollywood in 1989 that he 'found' 'Once Bitten Twice Shy' and played it to Alan Niven who was managing Guns N' Roses and Great White. Axl wanted to record it, but Niven wanted it for Great White and 'gave' it to them.

Great White's cover was alright. It gave them a career. The Great White album, *Twice Shy*, that had 'Once Bitten' on it sold 2 million copies. The Guns N' Roses album that 'Once Bitten' would have been on went on to sell 7 million copies. I lost out there, but the royalty cheques were still amazing. I believe Great White's version went double platinum. They gave me the first platinum disc but wanted to charge me 75 dollars for the second one. Welcome to the music biz!

"I remember when 'Once Bitten Twice Shy' went into the Top Twenty in England, Ronson and I got on a plane to fly back to perform on *Top of the Pops*, which would have taken it into the Top Ten. I knew the show was heavy union, but we got off the flight at Heathrow Airport and then Mick asked, 'Are you in the Musicians' Union?' I said, 'Of course; you can't go on TV if you're not in the Union!' Ronno says, 'Ah!' I said, 'Mick, we've flown first class, we're going to do *Top of the Pops* and you tell me you're not in the Union, right?' 'I might not be,' says Ronson. 'I'm not sure.' That was it. Cancelled! I didn't know what to do, but this was Mick; I could have killed him at least once a week."

Before Hunter went back to America, he appeared on BBC Radio One's *My Top Twelve* with legendary British DJ, Brian Matthew. Ian's inspired song selection of favourite tracks included 'Whole Lotta Shakin' Goin' On' by Jerry Lee Lewis, Little Richard's 'Good Golly Miss Molly', The Righteous Brothers' 'You've Lost That Loving Feeling', Lorraine Ellison's 'Stay with Me Baby', 'I Got You Babe' by Sonny and Cher, Mountain's 'Mississippi Queen', The Rolling Stones' 'Brown Sugar', 'Sail Away' by Randy Newman, Free's 'Catch a Train', Leon Russell's 'Delta Lady', 'Life On Mars?' by David Bowie and, inevitably, Bob Dylan's 'Like a Rolling Stone'.

IH: "'Brown Sugar' is the greatest, most amazing rock riff ever and Lorraine Ellison's 'Stay with Me Baby' is probably my all-time favourite song. She only did two albums and this was on the first one. The story is that Frank Sinatra walked out of a studio session one day and they arranged and recorded this on the spot, with Frank's forty-eight-piece orchestra. Lorraine just went in and did it, and it's incredible; the only orgasm on record that I've ever heard. I auditioned for Mott with 'Like a Rolling Stone' so it will always be big in my memory. Dylan grabbed me; the look of him, the voice, everything about him."

On *My Top Twelve*, Hunter confessed to Matthew that he was still not ready to talk about what really happened with the demise of Mott. Ian was discreet about the reasons for leaving at the time, saying he didn't want to cause upset as he felt Mott the Hoople was cherished by many people. When asked how strong his desire for musical success really was, Hunter explained that he couldn't compromise with what he writes.

> **IH:** "It's just a question of timing and zeroing in on that point where everybody thinks the same way you do, and then you become huge. If they don't, then you never become huge. If you're asking me if I'd like to be huge, I'd say yes, obviously, but on my writing, not on a compromise trip – then it'll be me."

After Hunter Ronson's UK tour, Mick appeared on BBC TV's *The Old Grey Whistle Test* backed by Dana Gillespie guitarist John Turnbull, Geoff Appleby, Blue Weaver and Colin Blunstone drummer Jim Toomey. The slot had been booked for Hunter Ronson promotion but, with Ian back in America, Mick played 'Angel No.9' and the title track from *Play Don't Worry*. Programme host Bob Harris considered Ronson's LP a model of thoughtful production and arrangement, citing 'Angel No.9' as his favourite track. Def Leppard's Joe Elliott was a further admirer of Mick's solo records.

"Ronson didn't write much of the material for *Play Don't Worry* but it features some phenomenal work," says Joe. "Mick did several covers and it was almost a desperate attempt to make a record. He pulled out 'White Light/White Heat' that he'd done with Bowie, but there are some songs that are to die for. 'The Empty Bed', a beautiful acoustic string ballad, and 'This Is for You' are stunning. 'Billy Porter', which Mick wrote, is almost a French chanteuse kind of thing. 'Angel No. 9', written by Craig Fuller from Pure Prairie League is amazing, but Mick's version is killer, just for the guitar playing alone. *Play Don't Worry* wasn't a big seller, and I'm probably in a club with about 25 people who give a shit, but it's a truly fantastic album."

The Hunter Ronson band hit the US in April and was scheduled to play over two dozen dates. America had always appealed to Ian in so many ways and, as it was also an inspirational source for writing, he finally opted to quit London for New York.

IH: "I decided to leave the UK and move to the States when I was standing on Charing Cross Road one day and a van was passing by. Its back door slid open and two housepainters threw a bucket of paint water all over me. They thought this was funny; they had such a laugh; but I thought, 'Why am I paying ninety per cent of my money back to a country that has people like this?' I know it sounds odd, but that really was the last straw. I'd never had a penny in my life as I'd been a semi-skilled worker. Then I joined Mott and wrote a couple of songs that were hits, and I remember when I suddenly got a thirty-grand royalty cheque in the mail. I didn't know what to do with it as I'd never seen more than two hundred quid. I soon found out that the £30,000 cheque wasn't really worth that, as I had to give £27,000 of it back to the British Government in tax. I had very little confidence in myself and thought this might be the only real money I'd get, so I was off like a shot to America and I wasn't the only musician that left. I didn't choose to leave Britain. I was kicked out, at least that's the way I looked at it. Mott's former tour manager Stan Tippins is the most patriotic Englishman there is and, forty years later, Stan admitted he wished he'd done what I did."

Hunter had chosen America as his base for a year, declaring that it was natural for him to gravitate towards New York City because it was extreme, colourful and inspiring. He found New York a fast environment, London medium-paced and Los Angeles slow, so his metabolism drew him to the Eastern seaboard. Hunter had explained to Brian Matthew that the move was also necessary for artistic reasons.

> **IH:** "I think that every person, if they're fortunate enough to have amassed a few quid, should live somewhere other than England. If you're seventy-five, and you look back on your life, and you didn't spend a year somewhere else, then I think you might be a bit narrow-minded. I'm drawn to America, possibly for the same reason Lennon was. I live on nervous energy, so therefore I find it a little bit slow in England. I really worked hard on the lyrics for the *Ian Hunter* album, but I was getting a little bit more into fiction and I want to live the lyric. New York has always got me. I can go there for a week and get two lyrics, because I'm always better as an observer in a different situation. If you try to write songs over any length of time, which I've done, you run out of topics. You don't want to keep on approaching the same things, so you've got to move to places that will keep you going, otherwise it can dry up. I like New York for lots of reasons. I think it's an incredible place."

Ready to take up American residency, Hunter stayed at Fred Heller's home in Pleasantville, Westchester County, before he and Trudi moved into a rambling redwood house on Kipp Street in Chappaqua, a neighbouring town located forty miles north of New York.

IH: "My manager Fred Heller lived north of New York City so I got a house in Chappaqua, now Bill Clinton territory. Later we moved to Katonah and points north because every ten miles you got an extra bedroom for your money. Then I visited Dennis Elliott one day who had moved to Connecticut. I loved it there; it's so different to New York State. Trudi and I moved to Connecticut and rented a place, then we bought a house and stayed for life. I've lived in Connecticut since 1991. Initially, I went to America because of Harold Wilson and Ted Heath, but there's also more room in America and it's cheaper. Movies, and then music, made it a natural progression for me too, but the English tax situation did play a big part because they didn't seem to be doing much with the tax we paid. It made more sense in the US to me and when my youngest kid went to school there, I just stayed. There was no long-term plan. I fully intended to come back when I left England in 1975, but I became settled."

Opening in Wisconsin, Hunter Ronson toured the USA from 17th April to 23rd May. The gigs were predominantly founded on the new *Ian Hunter* album, but the itinerary was detailed on MainMan Management documentation. Peter Arnesen returned on keyboards and Hunter Ronson played in several regions where Mott the Hoople had never toured. At Grand Rapids, Michigan and a packed Philadelphia Spectrum, audiences were ecstatic, while a review of their raucous Felt Forum show in New York City was headed 'The Lid Blows Off'. But *Melody Maker* journalist Chris Charlesworth threw down the gauntlet when Hunter Ronson abandoned some US dates; Ian admitted in 1975 that a few venues did not sell out and some shows were scratched after horrendous PA problems, while Chris casually reflected in 2015 that "the tour was cancelled because no one bought any tickets".

IH: "We toured with the *Ian Hunter* album barely released, billed as 'Ian Hunter and Mick Ronson', but we played to great crowds. One show in Toledo was pulled by the promoter and we had some sound problems, so we found out how many gigs we had to do without being sued and played them with a different sound company each night. The tour was portrayed as a disaster by Chris Charlesworth, but I remember it differently. I wrote to *Melody Maker* telling them to get off my back. I even sent slips to prove the attendance figures and eventually they stopped. Mick and I played The Spectrum and sold the place out, so I thought it was a great tour. I remember Ronson's camp saying on the way to one gig that nobody was turning up, but I also remember getting there and it was mobbed. Press and management – all that stuff didn't help my career at all."

Phil John: "I think it was in Milwaukee, April 1975, during last-minute rehearsals for the US leg of the Hunter Ronson tour, that I was sitting on a flight case with Ian as he dictated the running order for the set list. I imagine he's just bummed a fag off me and feels like a chat. As I write down the song list, Hunter says, 'You know the secret for a good gig Phil – light and shade. Between every couple of rock songs, slip in a slow number and bring the pace down – this gives the audience time to get their breath back – follow with a slow build and start the process over again – until you reach the last fifteen or so minutes – then you hit them with all you've got and leave them yelling for more.' I pondered. A bit like shagging really."

Alongside *Melody Maker*'s Hunter Ronson tickets discourse, *New Musical Express* writer Nick Kent jousted with Ian too.

IH: "The journalist Nick Kent called me a 'cross-eyed old rocker' in 1975. Nick was a big deal at the time, but he also had two problems: one was ego; the other was he could pass out anywhere. I think he'd been flattered by association. Because he was good at his job, he'd been on

51

a few 'big' tours and the resulting disadvantages had sadly occurred. Nick also desperately wanted to embrace punk rock, the next new thing. I got a lot of flak around that time, but it was amusing to see the about-turn a couple of years later."

On 21st June, *The Old Grey Whistle Test* broadcast the CBS promo film of "Ronson and Hunter" playing 'Once Bitten Twice Shy' and the label released 'Who Do You Love' as a UK single on 25th July, backed with a fragmented four-minute edit of 'Boy'. The single received virtually no airplay and, with promotional activity completed, the touring band was put on ice pending future recording. Ian and Mick wanted to write and produce a second album as a Hunter Ronson release, but they ran into resistance. Signed to CBS and RCA Records, and having separate management agreements with Heller and Defries, Ian and Mick were prevented from working jointly. Contractually, the next project was meant to be "a Mick Ronson album", the intention being the re-engagement of Elliott, Appleby and Arnesen on future sessions.

> IH: "We came off the road in 1975, split up and then we were offered gigs in Japan and Australia, but it was too late. I couldn't keep the band together. Mick's management was supposed to be paying half the band and I was supposed to pay the other half. Then, Dennis Elliott came to me one day saying he hadn't been paid for a few weeks. It was a great pity, because that was the nearest Ronson and I got to touring Japan."

During the summer, Ian and Mick set to work writing material in the rehearsal and taping room in Hunter's Chappaqua basement. Ian drafted songs for Mick, but the pair still fought for a Hunter Ronson record as they wanted their joint name to become established. Ian didn't wish to tour performing parts of *Slaughter on 10th Avenue* and *The Hoople*; he aimed to play new songs starting with his solo debut, which he considered to be a Hunter Ronson album anyway. Hunter intended to take time preparing material, and although he became increasingly frustrated with managerial and record label entanglements, the collaboration continued, Ronson admiring Hunter's writing and Ian respecting Mick as a formidable musician and arranger. In the end, whilst RCA contemplated some single releases from Mick, having declined a follow-up to *Play Don't Worry*, no new Ronson tracks were recorded. The push for a Hunter Ronson record proved pointless and Ian felt he could no longer work with Mick while he was represented by Tony Defries. The Hunter Ronson relationship was a friendship and an artistic alliance, but the managerial and label impasse split a special musical partnership.

> **IH:** "The original plan was for us to start work on a new Ronson solo record, then we had to shelve that idea; apparently RCA didn't want another album as the first two had lost money – at least that's how I understood the situation. By this time, I'd already got four songs that I was really pleased with, written specifically for Mick, and we were going to go in and cut them. After all the drama of H&H and MainMan with Mott, it remained difficult when we were Hunter Ronson because Defries was still Mick's manager. CBS Records and Heller wanted me to be a solo artist, not linked with Ronson, so I offered Mick half my bread. I said that the album would have to go out as Ian Hunter, but that Ronson would make the same money as me. Mick wasn't keen on that idea and wanted us to form a group. We couldn't think of a name for a band, but we really didn't try to.
>
> "The outcome of it all was that to do a second album, Ronson's management wanted more for him than I was going to get and I told Mick I couldn't put up with that. He would agree with me but then he'd see Tony, who was a very hypnotic character, and he'd come back with a different mindset. Defries and I were not getting along at all. We couldn't get

agreement on anything and the Hunter Ronson group folded because of political infighting. It was a great band, the first album was great, Ronson was in top form and we had a hit, but with all the managerial games, Mick and I drifted apart. He moved into Dana Gillespie's vacant apartment in Manhattan and, in the end, I said to Ronson, 'I can't work with you any more as long as you're with MainMan.' I never forgave Fred or Tony because, in the end, we lost three years when Mick and I could have been working."

Following Hunter Ronson, Dennis Elliott joined Foreigner, a band that would shine as one of rock music's greatest AoR successes. Peter Arnesen collaborated with Leo Sayer, The Hollies and Sheena Easton, and became a music lecturer at Mozarteum University in Salzburg. Geoff Appleby released some solo singles and played with Buzz, U-Boat and The Screen Idols, but his music career came to a tragic and premature end when he suffered two brain haemorrhages. Geoff described the Hunter Ronson experience as great fun and noted a magical communication, respect and friendship between Ian and Mick.

IH: "Dennis went on to fame and fortune with Foreigner after working with Mick and me, and later lived in Florida with his wife Iona, creating sculptures and fine art out of turned wood. Great drummer! Unfortunately, Geoff our bass player had a few mishaps and became confined to a wheelchair. This happened when he was young but he was fortunate that he had a loyal girlfriend, Moi, who basically sacrificed her life to look after Geoff. We would see Geoff now and again, over the years, usually in Leeds. He was a great lad who had rotten luck."

Geoff Appleby: "To tour and record in Hunter Ronson was a memorable experience. For all his success and fame, Mick never let it go to his head. He was always the same down-to-earth guy he

CHAPTER ONE: HUNTER TURNS KILLER

was when we first met, complete with Hull accent, which he never lost. He was a good friend and a real gentleman."

Dennis Elliott: "I was twenty-four when I got my break with Ian and Mick. Although I had been touring with different bands since I was sixteen, this was my first look at the big time. I really felt that I was working with two legends; well that's what Ian Hunter used to tell me. It was a privilege working on Ian's first solo project as I think he could have had any drummer he wanted. Everyone was so professional, except when Ian had a disagreement with the studio's pinball machine one night and put his fist through it; at least we got some work done while he was getting stitched-up. If it wasn't for Ian's friendship I would never have met up with Mick Jones and landed the gig with Foreigner. Mick Ronson always had a smile, always had a can-do attitude and was always willing to try something new to make a song better. Artist – perfectionist – Mick was always the one with ideas and they invariably worked."

Peter Arnesen: "Playing on and touring the *Ian Hunter* album was one of the high points of my career. I admired 'Boy' – the sheer craft of the record and the atmosphere of creativity. Hunter and Ronson were a great combination and the live dates were rock at its very best. I remember our Felt Forum show in New York and it was magical. I lost track of Ian and Mick but one day, about three years after the tour, I was driving round Marble Arch in London and suddenly Mick Ronson pulled up beside me. He leapt out of his car and stood and spoke with me, holding up all the traffic. He was a great person. Sadly, I never saw Mick again after that."

Following the US Hunter Ronson tour, Phil John and Richie Anderson re-joined Mott for some British live dates until Queen drummer Roger Taylor called. Richie joined the band's road crew while Phil aided Luther Grosvenor in Widowmaker before entering "The Court of Queen". Phil left within a year for pastures new and, while Richie stayed on for seven years, he always considered that his time with Queen never matched the sheer magic of Mott. "Queen might have been a better business," said Anderson, "but it wasn't Ian Hunter and Mott the Hoople."

In 2005, Sony BMG released a 30th Anniversary Edition of *Ian Hunter* with adapted Escher artwork. The expanded CD included six extra tracks including the CBS single edits of 'Once Bitten Twice Shy', 'Who Do You Love' and 'Boy' – plus 'One Fine Day' and 'Colwater High' featuring newly written lyrics and vocals that Hunter had overdubbed at London's Riverside Studios in April 1999. *Classic Rock*'s 9/10 review described Ian's debut as a monumental album that has stood the test of time fantastically well; *Ian Hunter* was placed at No.2 in their 2005 Top Fifty 'Best Reissue' poll.

> **IH:** "Although Dennis Elliott thought it was a sure-fire hit at the time, 'One Fine Day' sounded terrible to me when we did it at AIR, so that song was shelved, along with 'Colwater High'. They were epic, dramatic things and, all of a sudden, tracks were coming through like 'Who Do You Love' and 'The Truth', and we started axing songs. I'd struggled with the lyrics for 'One Fine Day' and 'Colwater High' for weeks; I couldn't get them right at the time, so 'Once Bitten Twice Shy' and 'Who Do You Love' went on *Ian Hunter* and we just left the backing tracks of the other two on tape. Fast forward twenty-five years and I was prevailed upon by a friend to finish off 'Colwater High' and 'One Fine Day' for a Sony compilation. To my surprise I sat down and wrote both lyrics in half an hour. 'Colwater High' is purely fictitious; it might have been an English single at one time but it was so blatant."

Encouraged by Ronson, in 1975 Hunter had emerged from the ashes of Mott and cut a truly inspired album. *Ian Hunter* achieved a respectable Top Thirty chart placing, but fans began to wonder what peak might have been reached if the record had been eventuated as a Mott the Hoople release. Looking back, Ian realised that his solo debut was the first time that he and Mick had combined "properly" in a studio. The AIR sessions were fun, fresh and exciting, and even with energies depleted *Ian Hunter* was an astonishing achievement.

IH: "After Mott the Hoople split, Buff and Pete got what they wanted. They got Ray Major, they got the name Mott and Buff got to spend a lot of time using me for target practice. I lost two-thirds of my base, as I wasn't Mott the Hoople any longer, but I did put a great album out with a hit single on it. That could have been Mott's next record and it would have been two-thirds bigger with Mott the Hoople's name on it. My first solo album was very good and we had a great time recording it. The album we went into AIR with was not the album that we released, as I started writing even better material in the studio. I don't like doing that; it's expensive but, fortunately, everything worked out great.

"Mick was on top form and was pretty powerful in the mix on *Ian Hunter*. He did a great job on the production and the freedom was fantastic. We were away at last, divorced from Mott. Ronson had pushed for my album as he felt emotion was in the air, and he was right. It's a fuckin' good album. Mick played bass on 'Once Bitten Twice Shy', was a truly amazing arranger and more or less ran my first solo record. After it was done, I went into this room at Columbia Records one day and they all clapped me. I said, 'Well, yeah, thanks, but I have to tell you half of this album is down to Mick Ronson.' There was stunned silence. That's what I got for telling an American label the truth."

Ronson was so special and Ritchie 'The Amp Guy' Fliegler, author of *Amps! The Other Half of Rock 'n' Roll*, once wrote: "When I was much younger and quite confused about what to do with my life, my friend Donnie played me Ian Hunter's first solo album. The guitar playing on that record clarified the whole thing for me; I knew what I had to do. Mick Ronson's arrangements, production and fiery raw sound were the embodiment of true rock 'n' roll."

Joe Elliott still retains a very strong affection for *Ian Hunter* and enthuses that his admiration for Hunter is rooted in Ian's distinctive vocal delivery, his "better-than-Dylan lyrics" and his appearance as a rock star rarity that always seemed accessible: "I was fifteen when the *Ian Hunter* LP came out and I played it to death. To this day it is still one of the best records I've ever heard and production-wise it's great. 'Once Bitten Twice Shy' is a genius piece of music – that's been ruined by other bands; the dynamics are incredible; the way it builds, from the first verse up to the second verse when the guitars kick in, and the great chorus, then a fantastic guitar solo from Mick Ronson. One of the best things Mick ever played in his life is the solo on *'The Truth, The Whole Truth, Nuthin' But the Truth'*. Musically, it's absolutely stunning and a masterclass in feel and restraint, but it's also a great song that I've grown to love more than almost anything Ian has done in his entire career. *Ian Hunter* is an incredible record and there isn't a wasted note, a weak lyric or a bad track on it. Hunter's songwriting has such charm. Regardless of his past track record, the *Ian Hunter* album was Mick Ronson's defining moment and it contains a HUGE amount of Ian's best writing EVER."

In his review of *Ian Hunter*, Paul Nelson of *Rolling Stone* opined that Hunter reached his peak thematically, lyrically and musically on *All the Young Dudes* and *Mott*, "two of the greatest LPs in rock and roll history" – but Nelson added that the star's solo debut contained four near masterpieces, noting that Ian's intelligence had not waned as he continued to mine the vein of his richest subject matter – himself.

Published in 2006, *Classic Rock & Metal Hammer Present 1970s* described *Ian Hunter* as a moving record that was defined by the quality of its songwriting, and rated the album as one of the year's best alongside Dylan's *Blood on the Tracks*, Floyd's *Wish You Were Here* and Springsteen's *Born to Run*. Including the *Ian Hunter* LP artwork in its 'Top Fifty Album Sleeves' of the decade, *Classic Rock & Metal Hammer* also classed the kaleidoscopic cover as a glorious product of its time, venturing that Hunter's hat and scarf on the reverse of the sleeve were later adopted by Tom Baker's Doctor Who!

Jac Holzman, the founder of Elektra Records, once declared that: "Those albums that are 'classic albums', are albums that are perfect – by perfect, I mean, you wouldn't want to change a thing." *Ian Hunter* is a "classic" that could never be improved – an impressive and assured album showcasing vivid rock, emotional balladry, acerbic lyrics, imaginative poetry and some of Ronson's most inspirational musicianship – an ebullient and colourful record, enveloped by bastardised Escher artwork into the bargain. One US review described Hunter's debut as a brilliant display from the man who was Mott the Hoople. And yet, rejecting recognition and repetition, Ian's next project would mark a significant and surprising shift.

Ian Hunter left Mott the Hoople to recalibrate his creativity. He also abandoned the fast-lane pressures of fame and British hero status for a songwriter's life in New York State, not only because he had the opportunity to and could sample the lifestyle, but to write and record what he really wanted.

Nobody noticed at the time, but Ian Hunter was cementing his love–hate relationship with rock 'n' roll stardom.

CHAPTER TWO

The Alien Boy

All-American Alien Boy *was commercial suicide.*

In 1975, Ian Hunter recorded his debut solo album and toured Britain and America with Mick Ronson at his side. Hunter stayed signed to CBS Records and was represented by Fred Heller, while Ronson remained with the RCA label and Tony Defries, but the arrangement caused frustrations. Prevented from recording a Hunter Ronson album, in the end Ian felt that he could no longer collaborate with Mick while he was represented by MainMan Management. The business impasse meant that they would not record together for three years.

> **IH:** "We'd managed to cut a decent deal for *Ian Hunter* but the way it worked out, Mick would have been paid more than me to do the next album and I wasn't having that. RCA wanted some Ronson singles and Mick wanted us to form a band but, in the end, he drifted off. Mick would go away now and again during the years we worked together, because I was a slow writer and he'd have interesting things on offer, or sometimes when I was ready with songs, he'd already be committed to somebody else."

Towards the end of 1975, Ian revealed that his music was becoming more rhythmic as he had spent time with the ever-helpful Bobby Colomby. The drummer's jazz style intrigued Hunter as he always considered "swing" an important musical component, often highlighting the Stones' Charlie Watts as a benchmark. While Ian and Mick remained great friends, they were moving in different directions and Ronson soon accepted a surprise invite to tour with one of Hunter's heroes, Bob Dylan. The pair met the American icon when they went to New York's Bleecker Street to see Bob Neuwirth play a spontaneous gig at The Other End, subsequently re-named The Bitter End club, by owner Paul Colby. On that amazing July night Dylan suggested that Ronson should join a touring collective he was forming and, whilst Mick had never been excited about Bob's vocal style, he agreed to participate. Inspired by a recent Roma gathering witnessed in Southern France, Dylan's concept for a travelling community comprising a loose collection of performers and poets playing small venues became reality in October 1975 when The Rolling Thunder Revue appeared in New England. Mick was surprised when Bob followed up on the collaboration casually suggested in Greenwich Village and Hunter recalls how Ronson's engagement evolved.

> **IH:** "Mick and Suzi used to go to Trude Heller's club in Greenwich Village where Tony Defries held court. It was a 'tranny bar', which was fine, but one night I said I didn't want to go there, so I took them along to The Other End in Bleecker Street. Paul Colby, who ran it, knew us, sat us down and gave us beers. The place was empty but twenty minutes later Bob Dylan walked into the café part with Bob Neuwirth and proceeded to play the *Desire* album, right there and then. The songs seemed quite serious, but Bob was having fun with them. We were sitting a table away from Bob and Mick wasn't even interested, mumbling, 'Fuckin' Yogi Bear', which is what Ronson called Dylan. Suzi Ronson was checking things out with Neuwirth, who I think she knew,

and two hours later the word was out and the place was jammed, but now Mick was drunk. They threw him out three times and Ronson eventually told Colby if he threw him out again, he'd come back in through the window!

"I knew Bob Dylan had a reputation for being an awkward person to talk to, but he was fine with me. That night was the first time we ever met, and he danced down Bleecker Street with one foot on the pavement and the other in the road, singing, 'Mott the Hoople, Mott the Hoople.' I thought he was mocking me but then he turned around and said, 'No man, I dig *Mott the Hoople*; "Half Moon Bay"; "Laugh at Me".' Then I knew he had the record. We'd heard that The Byrds and The Band had *Mott the Hoople* too.

"After that evening at The Other End, over the next few days Bob moved through into the club area and artists started coming in from all over the US. Mick hung out with them because he was living on Hudson Street in Manhattan at the time. Ronson rang me three or four days later in Chappaqua and said, ''Hey, I'm in this band.' 'What fuckin' band?' 'I'm in Bob Dylan's band,' said Ronson. 'I can't figure it out; it's all C, F and G and he never sings the same one twice.' Dylan had got up on stage that first night and it all took off, like a gypsy caravan. Mick asked me to come down, but I didn't want to push it. Mick kept saying, 'Nah, just come down,' and that's exactly what it was; anybody who went along was in because it was so haphazard. I felt strange about going without an 'official' invite, and I never got one, so I didn't go. It still pisses me off because later, I was sitting at home alone while they're having a great time on the road, then, in *Rolling Stone*, they did an article and said I was very good in Dylan's band, and I wasn't even there."

Ronson joined The Rolling Thunder Revue playing a two-leg tour over a period of eight months through to May 1976. Dylan's Neuwirth-led, all-star backing band became known as Guam, named after the Western Pacific US island territory, while the Rolling Thunder derivations included the code for President Nixon's North Vietnamese aerial bombardment campaign and the name of a self-identified medicine man. Fascinated by alternative facts, for the naming of the tour, Dylan claimed he'd simply heard thunder one day, but he also acknowledged Chief Rolling Thunder and learned with delight that the term relates to the tradition of truth-telling in native American culture.

When Mick arrived at New York's SIR rehearsal studio in October 1975 he wasn't familiar with much Dylan material, but Ronson watched, listened and employed his musical awareness as he grew into the mountain of songs to be performed on the road. The situation resonated with the guitarist's baptism on Bowie's early Seventies BBC session work, and Mick later reflected that the Dylan experience was strange and hectic. Bob's "play for the people" sprawling assemblage featured Joan Baez, Roger McGuinn, Bob Neuwirth, Ramblin' Jack Elliott, Kinky Friedman, T Bone Burnett, Arlo Guthrie and assorted musicians and hangers-on. Roughly rehearsed and never routine, the collective performed over 120 different songs at some sixty concerts and the tour highlights are preserved in an amorphous Fellini-esque film, *Renaldo and Clara*, the live albums *Hard Rain* and *Bob Dylan Live 1975*, plus a mammoth 2019 *Rolling Thunder Revue* box set and Martin Scorsese movie. Ronson's presence was deemed the surprising element of the tour; Mick's contributions included a rendition of Roscoe West's 'Is There Life on Mars?' while his electric guitar passages rebooted Dylan's acoustic, country-based numbers and pulled things back into focus when the songs threatened to get "too folky".

Suzi Ronson recalls Mick loving the experience as the only Englishman aboard the caravan, but the guitarist described the set-up as loose and chaotic; one night 'Blowing in the Wind' would be in C, the next night it was in the key of F; song tempos would vary and numbers would stop, suddenly, then start again. Ronson admitted he had never been interested in lyrics but that meeting

Dylan was a "great eye-opener". Bob Neuwirth had heard of Mick's history, while Roger McGuinn was unaware of the guitarist's work until he first met Ronson at SIR.

Bob Neuwirth: "Even though Mick was well known and acknowledged for his musicianship, he was so underrated. I'd seen him briefly in The Spiders from Mars, but I didn't know Mick until 1975 when he came to The Other End with Ian. The band we formed was called Guam. The name was an in-joke, but we later found out that the US B52s had been based in Guam to attack Vietnam and the bombing raids were known locally as Rolling Thunder. Guam included Rob Stoner, David Mansfield and Steven Soles, and then we sent for T Bone Burnett. It was just a lark at first, but Ronson was a great lead player and just jumped into it. I fell in love with his playing on the spot and I asked Mick to stay in the band. He was reluctant at first, but eventually I talked him into it. Ramblin' Jack Smith and Roger McGuinn joined us, the baggage handlers on the tour were famous poets like Allen Ginsberg, and Joni Mitchell came to see a show and never left. Ronson was great every night. There were seven guitarists at one point, but Mick's brilliance was the way he adapted to what everyone else was doing around him. After the tour, Mick and I stayed good friends. I remember he was packing to go back to England for Christmas one year and we had a pint or two and then he sat and played guitar for three hours straight. He played every style of music too – Beck, Hendrix, you name it. Mick Ronson was, quite simply, a tour de force!"

Roger McGuinn: "We did an intense tour of small theatres and Mick and I became good friends on the tour bus. He had the bunk across from me and we were instant drinking buddies. Mick and I visited Bob Dylan's hospitality suite every night and took great advantage of the vodka. Mick was a Vodka Collins man, which was a sort of lemonade with vodka. He was great. I remember running Ronno around the large wooden Belleview-Biltmore Hotel in Belleair, Florida, in a wheelchair. He could walk alright; it was just more fun for him to ride. Mick never talked about Bowie and the

Spiders; he just blended in with everyone else on that tour. We hung out together and jammed. I made a cassette tape on the tour bus, and on it Mick was expounding his music theory, dissecting the structure of a Joni Mitchell song and figuring out the difficult jazz chords: C, B flat, F major 7 with added 6th, C9, to G and into the middle section E flat, F, B flat, C. Allen Ginsberg was on the bus and was truly amazed at Ronson's skill as a musician."

> **IH:** "I saw The Rolling Thunder Revue at New Haven in Connecticut. I didn't like the first half, which was sloppy, and I was ready to go home, but the second half was magic. I just wanted Mick to do well with Dylan. Ronson wasn't that keen on Dylan going into the project but he was a convert when he came out. Later on, I classed Mick as before Dylan and after Dylan. He liked Fender Stratocasters and Telecasters afterwards and became more organic musically. Artistically, The Rolling Thunder Revue was a positive experience. It had a tremendous effect on Mick. Financially, it was typical Ronson though; everybody got paid thousands of dollars but Mick got a bill at the end. He was the worst card player I've ever known."

Rejuvenated by the Dylan experience and recording alongside various Rolling Thunder tour buddies, Ronson produced Roger McGuinn's fourth solo album, *Cardiff Rose*. From the ringing chords of 'Take Me Away' and the pirate sea shanty 'Jolly Roger' to the punky, pre-Clash 'Rock and Roll Time', Mick elevated McGuinn's game, his stamp making the album a stylistically varied surprise. Bassist on the sessions, Rob Stoner, noted that Mick's "no ego" musicianship was like his personality.

Hunter appreciated that his second solo album would now proceed without Ronson's input, and he hinted that the record would be his best piece of work, far removed from his debut LP. Ian had left Britain to reside in the States knowing that it would provide a fresh stimulus for his writing, and he became enraptured by American extremes as he settled down and contemplated a new and different environment. Hunter absorbed round-the-clock television and was fascinated by reports of corruption amongst officials, politicians and business people. He was also enthused by the high-energy, madhouse landscape of New York, describing his arrival in the USA as a great awakening.

> **IH: "I moved to America because I thought England was badly governed. There was nothing happening in the UK and it was apathetic politically. I was also empty of lyrics and that scared me, so I went to New York. It was alive and there was danger and inspiration all around. I needed to be based where the buzz was and it gave me impetus. New ideas came right away. I spent a lot of time writing and the words came faster and heavier than ever."**

Hunter's new project, *All-American Alien Boy*, would be a startling chronology of first impressions and opinions, posing pertinent questions and expressing thought-provoking observations. Ian had always been an artist striving for interest rather than formula and his new material would take an unfamiliar musical direction, emphasising lyricism, eclectic styles and the fun of artistic freedom. Hunter's songs on *Alien Boy* would shine with a maturity unlike anything he had attempted before, but, armed with untypical material, he needed a different band. Having helped Ian when he first re-grouped in America, drummer Bobby Colomby would assist once more, ensuring that Hunter's sessions featured a high-calibre collective of jazz-based players, mixed with musicians from the rock fraternity.

Initially, drummer Dennis Elliott sat in for some demos with Hunter at Bobby's house and former Spooky Tooth guitarist Mick Jones attended a rehearsal. Jones was forming a band with Ian McDonald from King Crimson and US vocalist Lou Gramm; signed to Atlantic Records and originally called Trigger, the "supergroup" would be launched as Foreigner in 1977.

For the *Alien Boy* sessions, Ian would turn to a central core of drummer Aynsley Dunbar, alto saxophonist David Sanborn, guitarist Jerry Weems and keyboard player Chris Stainton. Aynsley was renowned for his work with The Jeff Beck Group and Frank Zappa, and Ronson had suggested him to Bowie as a drummer for *Pin Ups*; Aynsley had also worked on Lou Reed's *Berlin* and Mick's two solo albums. David Sanborn, who had played with Todd Rundgren and The Manhattan Transfer, was fresh from his solo debut, *Taking Off*, and had recently recorded on Paul Simon's *Still Crazy After All These Years*, Bruce Springsteen's *Born to Run* and David Bowie's *Young Americans*.

> IH: "Aynsley was great. He was the first there and the last to leave for every session. He liked to warm up for a while before we started and sometimes I'd watch him utilising both bass drums, playing round the kit until you actually saw a perfect circle. David Sanborn was already well known. I'd heard him on *Young Americans* and I thought he was down in the mix, but I thought he was incredible. He blew me away, so I got him in. A lot of people have worked with me over the years because I give them freedom. If you're going to pick a great musician, you must let him play. I'm choosy, but once they're in, they're in, and they can do what they want. Obviously, something outside the ball park isn't going to work but usually it stays in the park because you pick the right person."

Hunter considered guitarists Les Nicol and Jerry Weems for the *Alien Boy* sessions. Tyneside-born Les Nicol had played in a Sixties Hull group named ABC, alongside Bowie drummer John Cambridge, and in Kala with Peter Arnesen, but Weems was engaged for Ian's album. Reno-born Jerry, wrongly credited as Gerry on Hunter's record, had bridged the gap between Ronnie Montrose and Rick Derringer in The Edgar Winter Group and was a member of Bonaroo.

67

Les Nicol: "I'd joined the Leo Sayer Band through Adam Faith and keyboard player Chris Stainton. I recall that Ronson put me forward as Hunter's guitarist and I went and stayed with Ian for a little while. I didn't really know where his music was coming from at that time and it was not what I expected. I toured with Leo for some years alongside people like Bobby Keyes, Nicky Hopkins and Pete Arnesen but, in the end, it didn't really happen with Ian and me."

> **IH:** "Jerry Weems was a guitarist from Las Vegas. When Ronson went off with Dylan on The Rolling Thunder Revue, I got Jerry to play as he was a classy player. Weems' band Bonaroo had opened for Mick and me on our US tour in 1975. Ronno wasn't keen on Weems, so I knew he was good."

Through Colomby, Hunter encountered *Bitches Brew* drummer Lenny White and Weather Report keyboard player Joe Zawinul, but *All-American Alien Boy* was directly enhanced when Bobby invited Ian back to his house one day to witness a young bass player from Fort Lauderdale. The extraordinary musician was Jaco Pastorius – John Francis Anthony Pastorius III – who had been influenced by an eclectic cocktail of Sinatra, Presley, The Beatles, Sam & Dave, Miles Davis, Herbie Hancock and Stravinsky. Jaco had grown up in Florida and first bought a drum kit but, as a highly competitive individual who had a desire to be "the best", he switched from drums to bass following a football injury. Self-taught, Jaco approached the bass as a solo instrument, applying virtuosity, tone and sophistication to his boundary-stretching eclecticism.

Learning his trade with the likes of Las Olas Brass, Wayne Cochran and The CC Riders and jazz saxophonist Ira Sullivan, Pastorius soon became known for "the Jaco growl", a bass style that involved plucking above the bridge pick-up. Rooted in jazz, R&B, soul and funk, Pastorius played intricate passages, percussive sounds and ringing chords, and brandished "The Bass of Doom", a worn 1962

Fender Jazz that he had de-fretted in order to play resonant notes and slides with an upright bass sound; Jaco considered fret wires to be speed bumps!

After befriending Pastorius in Miami in 1973, jazz guitarist Pat Metheney played alongside Jaco and Paul Bley on a rare "unofficial" album, later retitled *Jaco*, and his debut LP, *Bright Size Life*. Metheney described his first reaction to working with Pastorius as one of shock. The impact of Jaco's individuality was staggering and Sting, of The Police, later described the bassist's instrumentation as revolutionary supernatural miracles that altered the musical landscape to such an extent that nothing was ever the same again.

In 1974 Pastorius met Bobby Colomby, who became his patron; the younger brother of Harry Colomby, who managed jazz pianist and composer Thelonious Monk, the Blood Sweat & Tears drummer had also become a fledgling producer and A&R man, invited to find jazz talent for Epic Records. When Jaco first played for Bobby at Bachelors III nightclub in Fort Lauderdale, Colomby was instantly mesmerised by the thin, pale, five-foot-eleven figure who had the largest hands he'd ever seen. Bobby said he wanted to produce Jaco and, true to his word, he flew Pastorius to New York and signed him. Colomby wanted to unleash Jaco's talent and duly produced his "official" debut album in October 1975, using a crack team of session players. Released after *All-American Alien Boy*, *Jaco Pastorius* would become a breakthrough recording for electric bass, but Jaco was still a relatively unknown talent when he joined Ian. Colomby was good friends with Ian's manager Fred Heller and became godfather to both of Fred's sons, so a Hunter–Pastorius connection was made.

"Bobby produced Jaco's LP for our label, PVT," says Fred Heller. "He was our first artist and Jaco would also tour with Blood Sweat & Tears. In 1975, I asked Colomby to do me a favour and help Hunter. The studio in Bobby's big house in Rockland County was state of the art and BST recorded albums there, when we were on Columbia. Bobby wanted to get the best New York City studio musicians for Ian's sessions and had a great concept to introduce some jazz-rock to the arrangements."

Colomby's intervention would provide *All-American Alien Boy* with musicians from various incarnations of Blood Sweat & Tears, including Dave Bargeron (trombone), Arnie Lawrence (clarinet), Lew Soloff (trumpet) and Charles 'Don' Alias (congas). Bargeron and Soloff would later play on Paul Simon's 'You Can Call Me Al', while Alias had appeared on Miles Davis's *Bitches Brew* and the upcoming *Jaco Pastorius* album alongside Sanborn. Hunter's session list extended to include accordionist Dominic Cortese and Cornell Dupree, an Atlantic Records guitarist who had worked with King Curtis, Robert Palmer and Aretha Franklin.

Bobby's introduction of Pastorius to Hunter's project was inspired. A creative instrumentalist, "jazz punk" and eclectic player-composer, Jaco oozed originality and his technique was astounding. But the intelligent and talented bassist would become a tormented soul. His brashness and hyperactivity were later diagnosed as hypomania, a type of bipolarity, and whilst Pastorius would soon gain wider notoriety alongside Joni Mitchell and shine in the spotlight with Weather Report, he would fly high and ultimately crash hard. Comical and confrontational, Jaco sometimes exhibited daredevil behaviour and ultimately lived on the streets during a distressing period of decline. Tragically, an alcohol-fuelled Pastorius suffered serious head injuries one night when he was ejected from the Midnight Bottle Club in Wilton Manors, Florida, by an employee who had martial arts training. Ten days later Jaco passed away, on 21st September 1987, after he suffered a brain haemorrhage and was taken off life support. He was thirty-five. Years earlier, Pastorius had predicted his death at thirty-four. Jaco's assailant was released following a four-month jail term.

Along with Joni Mitchell, Sting and Robert Trujillo, Ian Hunter would be interviewed for *Jaco*, a 2015 documentary film that reaffirmed Pastorius as bass playing's coolest and most original genius; a striking figure with great spirit who transformed himself

70

from poor Florida boy to family man; a sensational musician who expressed the playfulness, vulnerability and torment inside him, pushing boundaries and leaving shards of his character in many recordings. Joe Zawinul felt that Jaco had a tough life, and whilst he could be a mischievous person, he never had bad intentions. Ian has fond recollections of Jaco from the first time they met at "Camp Colomby". Bobby summoned Ian one day and Hunter took Ronson with him to Colomby's house where the quartet played the beginnings of a new song.

> IH: "Bobby Colomby lived over the Tappan Zee Bridge across the Hudson River and we had the same manager, Fred Heller. Bobby was a jazz freak and didn't really like rock 'n' roll, but he rang me up one day and said I had to see this bass player he'd discovered in Florida. So, I went over with Ronno, who was around at the time, and met Jaco. Bobby had called a lot of people like Joe Zawinul and the jazz-funk drummer Lenny White, who were all popping by to listen. Zawinul thought I was incredible because I was just playing C, F and G, stuff he'd forgotten about when he was a kid. Jaco was like a performing seal and it was a fascinating experience. In England you couldn't get to play with jazz players if you were a rocker; in the US it was different and you could hang out with anybody.
>
> "It transpired that Jaco Pastorius was a Stones fan like me, and he and Bobby liked my lyrics, so *Alien Boy* kind of grew out of that situation. Bobby, Ronno, Jaco and I jammed three chords for something to do that day, and it turned into a seedling version of 'All-American Alien Boy'. We managed to capture a Super 8 cine film of the four of us doing that. Unfortunately, management-wise, we couldn't work it out with Ronson for the *Alien Boy* album. As I was hanging out with Bobby and Jaco they were saying, 'You've got great lyrics. You don't have to do rock 'n' roll. You're better than this' – and I fell for it. Jaco liked jazz, but he also loved rock

'n' roll, and after I played some of my new songs, he asked to do my album. Jaco got fed up with all the brouhaha over at Bobby's and moved in with me and Trudi in Chappaqua."

CBS A&R man Dan Loggins sensed that Hunter was about to make a revolutionary musical step. "In late 1975, I knew that Ian was writing songs at his home in Westchester County," recalls Dan. "As I was in New York for a Columbia CBS meeting, one day I took the train to Chappaqua with Fred Heller's assistant, Sunny Schnier. Ian and Trudi's elegant new house was a modern place in the woods. It was not Shrewsbury or the Archway by any stretch, but Ian appeared grounded and reflective, and seemed to feed off Trudi's quiet strength. Hunter was now working with Bobby Colomby and was really enthused about a new bass player they were teaming up with. Ian sat down at the piano and played the first song for his impending New York sessions. It was called 'Letter to Britannia' and I was blown away. It was incredible and so unexpected, but Ian always had a way with the unexpected. I went back to London and explained to CBS, 'Well, it's a process; it ain't Mott the Hoople and it's not even Hunter Ronson; but it's going to be pretty interesting and possibly great, if you let it.'"

To round off his studio band, Ian was pleased to welcome keyboard player, bassist and renowned session man Chris Stainton, who had formed Joe Cocker and The Grease Band and appeared on the albums *With a Little Help from My Friends* and *Joe Cocker*. Stainton also played on the infamous *Mad Dogs and Englishmen* tour alongside Hunter hero Leon Russell. Without Ronson as a balancing figure, Chris was invited to join Ian's project as musical director and co-arranger, and to play piano, organ and mellotron. Heller knew Stainton when he was with Joe Cocker and Fred always regarded Chris as "a fabulous musician".

IH: "I can't for the life of me remember how Chris Stainton got involved in the *Alien Boy* sessions. He was a wonderful player, but I do recall that I drove him mad, asking him to play like

Leon Russell. I adored Leon and his first album always stayed with me. Ronson nicked my *Leon Russell* LP for a while, but I nicked it back. I tried to get Leon to produce me once and he was going to do it, but he was in litigation with Shelter Records, so he wouldn't have been paid and the deal was off. I would have loved to have worked with Leon Russell."

All-American Alien Boy was recorded at Electric Lady Studios in New York City. Located at 52 West 8th Street and formed within the shell of a defunct nightclub, a who's who of rock had recorded at the famed Greenwich Village facility, including Hendrix, Dylan, Led Zeppelin and The Rolling Stones. It was also the studio where Bowie and Lennon hung out to record part of *Young Americans*. Work started on Hunter's album at the beginning of January 1976 and the sessions took three weeks. Several tracks were first or second takes and all the songs were written, produced and arranged by Ian. A total of twelve numbers were taped but 'Common Disease', 'If the Slipper Don't Fit', 'Whole Lotta Shakin',' and 'A Little Star' were not completed and fell by the wayside. A further week was allocated for Hunter, Stainton and Electric Lady's resident engineer, ex-Amboy Dukes drummer David Palmer, to mix the *Alien Boy* tapes. Heading out to Los Angeles, the trio worked at A&M Studios, located on the site of the former Charlie Chaplin Studios on Hollywood's North La Brea Avenue. Retaining Chaplin's cement footprints as a reminder of the property's heritage, A&M's re-vamped studios had recently captured John Lennon's *Rock 'N' Roll* and George Harrison's *Extra Texture (Read All About It)*.

> IH: "Sometimes you don't have time to get a particular song right and you just have to go on to the next track. 'Common Disease' was written to a formula and just didn't work, and I never recorded the vocal for 'Slipper'. They were a couple of 'rockers' for the *Alien Boy* record, but they were wrong; they didn't fit the mood of the rest of the songs so they were dropped."

Hunter confessed to a degree of trepidation working around a group of greatly gifted players, but he was full of praise for Bobby Colomby. Even though the drummer did not play on the record, the LP artwork would include a special dedication from Ian: *"Bobby Colomby does not appear on this album, but I should like to thank him for his considerable help."*

IH: "After living in America for a while, I met these great jazz people and we worked together really well. You don't have the technical ability of any of the other people, even though you might have something they haven't got in another direction. Bobby Colomby kept telling me how much he liked what I did. I needed that little nudge to do something completely on my own. He was very good for my confidence. Recording and producing the album was a lot of fun, but scary. Why I did it, I've no idea. I'd probably got bored doing the usual rock thing and fancied a change. Jaco was staying with Trudi and me, and our place was about an hour from New York City, so my brother-in-law Kevin Liguori drove me, Jaco and the wonderful Chris Stainton back and forth each day to Electric Lady Studios. We did this for two weeks solid and every day Jaco told filthy jokes all the way down to Manhattan, and all the way back, and he'd never repeat himself once. Admittedly, at the end, the jokes were verging on the totally naff, but I still considered it a sterling achievement.

"Jaco was only twenty-four when he worked and lived with me, and he was fantastic. He'd practise every day from nine in the morning until five at night and it was disconcerting hearing the bass coming through the floor, every day, all day! Jaco had been a drummer, but he'd had to stop after a nasty wrist operation, so then he decided he was going to be the best bass player in the world. He was as fit and strong as a horse at the time of *Alien Boy*, and did not drink, smoke or do drugs. All that happened to him later on when he hit the

West Coast. He had a massive ego but it was a beautiful and uncorrupted one, until he reached Los Angeles. He was as clean as a whistle and into meditation. A few years later he was a mess.

"Jaco pushed me and Bobby around on *All-American Alien Boy*, but, with his love of The Rolling Stones, Jaco had a great rock sensibility and it wasn't as odd a set-up as people thought. He could also identify any chord on the piano. You'd play it and Jaco would name it. He was leaving our basement one day when I slammed my arsenal onto the piano keys – 'E diminished minor 7th' he shouted, as he climbed the stairs – and he was right! I dug Jaco's bass playing and he liked my lyrics. It was just so easy. He could be a flash bastard in the studio, but he would always service the songs and never show off just for the sake of it. I recall for one track I told him to forget everything and play his part imagining he was an old wino. He went out, got two bottles of wine, drank them like bottles of water and sat and played like he was sober. It was astonishing. Jaco was innocent and too clever for dope at twenty-four. He was totally immersed in my record and three months later it was something else. Jaco was a very strange person, but I'll never forget him and our time together."

Before *All-American Alien Boy*'s arrival, CBS Records issued Mott the Hoople's *Greatest Hits* on 27th March. With input from Dale Griffin and Pete Watts, the ten-track LP contained the band's seven Columbia singles plus three album cuts: 'Hymn for the Dudes', 'Ballad of Mott the Hoople' and 'Born Late '58'. With a meagre inlay sheet of miniscule black-and-white photos, the compilation was a predictable affair. It embraced the 'Foxy, Foxy' and 'Saturday Gigs' 45s which had not been issued on LP up to that point, but the collection assumed that even casual listeners knew about the band. A subsequent CD release would add the US single edits of 'Sweet Jane' and 'One of the Boys', even though the medium offered space for more imaginative inclusions. With album art direction by Roslaw Szaybo, featuring comic-strip framing and a glammed-up Mott pose, amazingly, *Greatest Hits* did not chart in Britain and only reached No.206 in the USA. Szaybo recalled: "For the *Greatest Hits* LP I was trying to make an attractive and colourful cover with boxed pictures and different cartoon images conveying 'hits'. The front cover was based on that idea and the strip theme was repeated on the back sleeve but featuring photographs of the band."

A *Sounds* four-star feature titled 'ALL OUR YESTERDUDES' offered an enthusiastic review of Mott the Hoople's *Greatest Hits*, but *NME*'s Charles Shaar Murray let rip about the pettiness of the band's "current incarnation". Describing 'Born Late '58' as "no cultural triumph", 'Hymn for the Dudes' and 'Ballad of Mott the Hoople' as "crucial tracks" and the omitted 'Violence' and 'Sucker' as "far more dynamic pieces", Charles wrote: "'Saturday Gigs' was just tailor-made to be the last track on a Mott the Hoople best of. On a trivia level, however, it would appear from the packaging that various old wounds dating from the Mott/Hunter/Ronson hari-kiri of a year or so back are still more than a little septic. The cover has Hunter, unobtrusively stashed away behind Morgan Fisher, while Pete Watts in all his glory holds sway, front 'n' centre. On the back liner spread and the photo insert there ain't one single pic of Mick Ronson, who was a member of Mott the Hoople. The unfortunate Ronno is simply listed as having played guitar on 'Saturday Gigs'. He's also conspicuous by his absence from any mention in CBS PR chief Dave Sanderson's liner note. It may seem petty to go into all of this, but it was a lot pettier to turn Ministry of Truth and attempt to re-write history like this. Ronno was in Mott so give the dude his due, boys. An album of this nature is supposed to be a picture of what went down, not a means of avenging old grievances. Be British about it, f'Chrissakes!"

On 21st May 1976, CBS Records released Ian Hunter's *All-American Alien Boy*. On 4th July 1976, the United States of America

76

celebrated the bicentenary of the adoption of the Declaration of Independence against a backdrop of civil rights upheaval, a long war in Asia and economic turmoil. During the same month, *All the President's Men*, Alan J. Pakula's brilliant movie of the 1972 Watergate scandal and Richard Nixon's subsequent presidential downfall, hit international cinema screens. In hindsight, the conditions and coincidences surrounding Hunter's album release seemed apposite.

Ian's mature songwriting on *All-American Alien Boy* carried candid views on the standing and mythology of US society, mixed with some personal British reflections. Hunter's uncharacteristic album contained eight jazz-speckled, softer, poetic songs: 'Letter to Britannia from the Union Jack', 'All-American Alien Boy', 'Irene Wilde', 'Restless Youth', 'Rape', 'You Nearly Did Me In', 'Apathy 83' and 'God (Take One)'. The record delighted most music critics, but left many Ian Hunter fans startled.

With a title termed "a play" on Rick Derringer's 1973 LP *All American Boy*, Hunter had shunned commercial expectations and rejected recognised rock templates, delivering an album that marked a refreshing change in direction. Embracing a loosely conceptual feel, the record combined intelligent wordplay and imaginative arrangements, Hunter making forthright observations on Britain, America, young love, the Mafia, rape, drugs, corporate decline, political corruption, rock 'n' roll and God. Ian boldly sang, *"Look out Lennon here I come"* on the title track, and his proclamation was apt, given the stunning songs on offer. Echoing bassist Klaus Voormann's view of the *John Lennon/Plastic Ono Band* album, the aim was for people to "listen to the words, listen to the song and get into the feel". The *"whitey from Blighty"* was taking no prisoners, and with several sensitive topics laid out for dissection, *All-American Alien Boy* remains one of the most potent and insightful records in Hunter's catalogue – a wonderful album that stills deserves attention.

Alien Boy's opening track, 'Letter to Britannia from the Union Jack', originally titled 'To Rule Britannia from Union Jack', was Ian's plea for England to get its act together. With a whisper of national pride for the country he was leaving behind, Hunter was critical of his homeland but he was also sorrowful for the state of Britain as he cleverly depicted the flag talking to the nation.

> **IH:** "My feelings about England are very complicated and that was the only way I could get them down at the time. 'Letter to Britannia' was a comment on the sorry state of Seventies England. It's perfect and exactly the way I felt. I was really proud of that song."

As Hunter bade Britain farewell, he moved to piano for 'All-American Alien Boy', sharing his observations on the new and different habitat that he had discovered. A seven-minute lyrical discourse, the song meshed jazz, blues and a dash of funk with perfect musical embroidery via wailing Weems' guitar and gutsy Sanborn sax. The listener is swiftly propelled from the UK on a transatlantic crossing, Hunter leaving his frustrations *"in the land of rags"*, whilst a flurry of vibrant words conveys hope and inspiration, describing a new environment where *"the buzz is the best"*. Ian's record was an American collage but he mixed in some British images on the title track, referencing the M1 motorway and gigs with his musical cohort Miller Anderson in Sixties England. Crucially, Hunter was now able to write about the USA as a resident rather than a visitor. Ian was humorously confused by grotesque Americana, TV commercials, fast food and guns; the country's history intrigued him too as he referenced numerous Native American chiefs, catalogued authentically and meticulously in the song's outro. The culture shock expressed in Hunter's words showed that, whilst he considered America sophisticated, some of the "dirt" usually covered up in Britain was exposed in the States. US residency, as opposed to occasional touring, had offered Ian a different dimension. 'Alien Boy' was a lyrical gem but it was doubly notable from a musical perspective too, with its jazz-laden brass played by Arnie Lawrence, Dave

Bargeron and Lewis Soloff and an inspired bass interlude from Jaco Pastorius.

> **IH:** "It was my idea for Jaco to do the bass solo, partly because nobody else had done it in my area and partly because if you're working with one of the best bass players in the world – if not the best – then it seems logical to feature him at some point. He was happily surprised when I suggested it and he worked hard at it. We waited for a while before recording 'Alien Boy', as Jaco was putting it together. He laid the solo down in one take having learned the whole thing at our house in Chappaqua. He did return to it a couple of times at Electric Lady, so he tinkered with it a little after the fact as well. For the bass solo I seem to remember he found a better part for the back end, so we went back and dropped him in. We just thought it was Jaco putting down a solo, then, years later, everyone thinks it was magic. The song was just my reflections on being hit by America. I'd toured in America but living there is different. All the chiefs' names at the end of the song are authentic. It took me ages!"

With another British flashback, track three told the tale of a beautiful girl from Hunter's Shrewsbury schooldays. 'Irene Wilde' was a strength-through-adversity autobiographical story of sixteen-year-old Ian Patterson, who ends up heartbroken in the drama of a *"Barker Street bus station non-affair"*. The rendezvous was only a few streets away from the Patterson family home in Swan Hill, and, in his sad confession of lost love, Hunter admits that he *"nearly died"* when Irene began dating other boys, the song's poetic words trembling with the longing that he felt for the girl. Ian's teenage dream rejects him, but his failure to capture Irene's affections would make him more determined to leave his rural surroundings, pushing him towards ambition and success. Written in a less jazzy and more traditional style with poignant piano, and emotionally set in the confessional arena that houses

'Waterlow' and 'I Wish I Was Your Mother', 'Irene Wilde' remains one of Hunter's finest ballads.

> **IH:** "'Irene Wilde' is an entirely truthful song, even down to the name. I always loved what I call the Julie Christie jawline and the first girl I saw with a face like that was Irene Wilde. She was going out with this guy I worked for so I became a go-between – this little schmuck that ran between them with letters. Irene was gorgeous and when you fall in love at that age, it's bad. She went to Shrewsbury High School and snubbed me at the Barker Street bus station where the girls would all meet. She never even noticed me and the rejection did inspire me. It was classic sixteen-year-old angst. I had been going out with a girl called Margaret Oliver and this guy, Brian Poole, who had been hanging around dated her. I remember he had a crimson velvet jacket and I always envied that jacket. Years later I was in Shrewsbury one day and Irene was there. I saw her in the town with her husband and she had twins, but she didn't look at all like the girl I remembered. I never met her since the song was written, but I have reliable information that she did hear the song and liked it, and why not? So, Irene Wilde does know about 'Irene Wilde' and the Barker Street bus station is a car park now. I meant what I wrote in the song. Years later I remembered the snub and all the details clearly. It was quite easy to do, because it was all true and truth is easier to write than fabrication. At one stage 'Irene Wilde' wasn't going to be put on the *Alien Boy* album because I wasn't convinced about the melody. My manager Fred Heller said I was out of my mind and made me put it on. He was right, for once."

The last track on Side One of *All-American Alien Boy* was 'Restless Youth', the album's most robust offering. For once Jerry Weems had a beefy guitar riff to feast on, but the song was still medium-paced and did not spoil the flow or thrust of the record. Chris Stainton played bass and Bob Segarini, from CBS band The Dudes, sang backing vocals as Hunter described the American underworld, referencing Little Italy, gangster Al Capone and corrosive corruption. Ian's child of the city is a gang leader who runs for the hoods, but he doesn't last. The uptight youngster, observing greed and *"legal illegalities"* makes his first hit aged seventeen, but his second is terminal at the hands of a policeman's gun.

> **IH:** "I wasn't born in New York or Brooklyn, but we were having a good time in England along equivalent lines. Good old times with the chaps! The song 'Restless Youth' probably came out of something in the news at the time in the US, but the lyric *'He got Hostile on his school report'* was me. I still have the report."

Hunter's fearless writing continued with 'Rape', a haunting number with a beautiful gospel flavour, telling a terrible story of sexual violation where the hateful perpetrator believes he will escape punishment because he's *"sick, rich and stoned"*. America's casual violence had appalled Ian and he proceeds to impugn the injustice of the legal system; while the knifed victim is dying of grief, Hunter points an accusing finger at the defendant's smiling lawyer, describing the twisted vision that justice is cheap and something to be honed; then, over the song's soaring musical crescendo, Ian gives the final verdict: *"Justice just is... Not."* 'Rape' remains a stand-out song with majestic backing vocals from Ann Sutton, Gail Kantor and Erin Dickens, who had recorded with the Rascals, Bette Midler and The Manhattan Transfer. Hunter's original version of 'Rape' was prefaced by several bars from Gene Kelly's Fifties recording of 'Singin' in the Rain', the inclusion of the musical fragment being a throwback to a violent sexual assault depicted in Stanley Kubrick's dystopian movie *A Clockwork Orange*.

> **IH:** "'Rape' was what I thought about justice and was honest. The song originally started with 'Singin' in the Rain' sung by

Gene Kelly and I'd had the scene from *A Clockwork Orange* in mind. Then Mr Kelly rang my manager Fred Heller and although he understood the sentiment behind my song, he didn't want his associated with 'Rape'. When a CD version of *All-American Alien Boy* was released by Sony Music years later, Gene Kelly had passed away. I thought they had sorted out my original version of 'Rape' on the reissue CD, but I am told that the 'Singin' in the Rain' inclusion was a label mistake."

'You Nearly Did Me In', originally titled 'Weary Anger', stood out boldly and beautifully on Hunter's album, the lyrics conveying another stark American landscape as Ian observed sad broken angels, lost children of the night and silver needles amidst the horrors of addiction. Hunter's voice on 'You Nearly Did Me In' exhibited a new-found confidence and the track brought a potent combination of musical forces into play, but the recording was taken to another level when Freddie Mercury, Roger Taylor and Brian May interposed. Queen's contribution occurred purely by chance, after Trudi Hunter met the band on a 20th January London to New York flight. En route to the USA for pre-tour press promotion, when Queen heard of Ian's recording sessions, they headed to Electric Lady Studios.

IH: "The way that 'You Nearly Did Me In' turned out wasn't planned. Queen got off that plane, came straight down and sat and waited at the studio for an hour before I knew they were there. Then someone told me they were outside, and I found them in the lounge. I was quite amazed. They'd sat there for ages and Freddie said, 'Isn't there *anything* we can do?' So, I had one track that I was going to put girl singers on, and I happened to be working on 'You Nearly Did Me In' and said, 'Well you can do this.' Queen had done some great stuff by this time and they all had amazing voices. The three of them sang the first two backing tracks together for me, then Roger took over for the really high lines and just sang higher and higher on his own. I was quite amazed. The Queenies were fabulous people and wonderful chaps, and I love them all. Fred was the genuine article and is sorely missed. David Bowie was like Freddie Mercury; they weren't really rockers but I did admire them."

Queen drummer Roger Taylor recalls Hunter's influence and the recording of 'You Nearly Did Me In' with modest economy: "That was a fun session – late one night – in New York City – in the crazy Seventies. Mott the Hoople had taken us to America of course and Ian had done it all before. We learned a lot and probably borrowed a few ideas too." Brian May termed Queen's vocal layering technique "Panavision", and the guitarist has fond recollections of Hunter's session: "Ian always has the ability to make the room feel as if it is revolving around him. In this case it was. We had, and have, a very soft spot for him and we went there just for that evening with the intention of giving him a nugget. On 'You Nearly Did Me In', Ian wanted the 'Queen Treatment' on the harmonies, and he got it. It's always great to build up the 'choir' in steps and then the moment comes when you hear it all back. It's magic if you get the parts right and we did know what we were doing. It helped that we really felt the song had big soul. Ian is a great writer. He is one of the greats in the rock 'n' roll river in my opinion. We were an electric combination in that moment. The bass playing is pretty awesome too!"

Some reviewers seemed insistent on drawing dreary parallels with Dylan on some *Alien Boy* tracks, but 'You Nearly Did Me In' possessed little resemblance to Zimmerman. 'Apathy 83' did. A musical departure, featuring accordion and congas, Hunter successfully captured the vigour that once characterised Dylan's work. Ian's song is probably one of the most perceptive pieces ever written about the decaying music scene; he opines that there is no longer any rock 'n' roll and refers to the music of the young and the sickly sound of greed. But there is a worrying outturn – the music of the rich. Hunter's lyrics allude to Richard Nixon and reference American Civil War General Philip Sheridan, but they also "cock a snook" at The Rolling Stones by repeating the phrase *"apathy for the devil"* throughout the song – and there was a notable event behind the inspiration.

> **IH:** "'Apathy 83' was about how rock got messed up. The innocence disappeared and was replaced by coke and corporates. I used the term rock 'n' roll as a substitute for innocence. Rock 'n' roll was Little Richard, not the apathetic bands of the Seventies. After I'd seen The Rolling Stones at Madison Square Garden in 1975, I encountered Dylan in Greenwich Village quite by chance with Ronson, when Bob played unannounced at The Other End club. It was the first time I met him and when Dylan asked what I thought of the Stones' concert, I replied, 'Insipid.' Dylan said, 'Yeah, apathy for the devil.' I simply said that I hadn't liked their concert because they seemed desultory. I've always loved the Stones but, at that time, not so much. 'Apathy 83' got written as Dylan gave me the idea for the song. I wrote it in response to seeing the corporate machinery and its majesty for the first time. It scared the shit out of me."

In 1976 *Rolling Stone* wrote: "Hunter may believe with John Lennon that the dream is over, but he's damned if he'll act like it. He stands up and embodies rock 'n' roll history – it's the spark of all those contradictions that lights the path of the future." Thirty years later, Hunter considered 'Apathy 83' and his Seventies observation that *"there ain't no rock 'n' roll no more"* befitting, because rock music had become the province of profit-focused corporates.

> **IH:** "I think with 'Apathy 83' that I meant things were tightening up in the business even then; and they have; and they continue to. I'd rather have entrepreneurs running music than accountants because there are often situations

84

where a band goes out of profit for one quarter and there's panic at the label. It is laughable, because art doesn't work like that. They should leave music to the mavericks. They're far better at it."

In 2010, former *NME* journalist Nick Kent published *Apathy for the Devil*, a book based around jaunts with The Rolling Stones, Lou Reed and The Sex Pistols. Kent described the Sixties as a period of spirituality and utopianism and the Seventies as vanity-driven and self-centred arrogance. He later opined that The Clash took up exactly where Mott the Hoople left off. Following a 2001 Ian Hunter song, 'Dead Man Walkin'', the working title for Nick's biography had been *Dead Fop Walking*.

Hunter had always admired Dylan's work and admitted that the artist's vocal approach gave him the boost and assurance that he needed to start singing in the Sixties. However, at the time of *All-American Alien Boy*, Ian was tired of the comparisons and boldly lodged his defence.

> **IH:** "I never understood a word of what Dylan was saying. I just had this chill. I got this amazing vibe from Dylan and I knew I couldn't sing properly because people like Paul Rodgers had already informed me of that, so I was aiming at phrasing my vocals. I'm sick of it now. I'm not in awe of the guy. I don't think he's been delivering for a while. I prefer my first solo album to *Blood on the Tracks*. Dylan is a genius and my mentor, but I think I'm lucky enough to be making better records right now. I'm a writer and he's a writer and, at the moment, I think I'm better than he is."

Originally titled 'Advice to a Friend (God)', *Alien Boy*'s final cut, 'God (Take One)', was a witty and thought-provoking dialogue between writer and creator, with God offering explanations about good, evil, faith, superstition and life. Hunter's opening line was killer and the images of planets, bowls of wine, a fortune teller's ball and chess were colourful. Ironically, this was probably the most "Dylan-ish" song on the LP, but it was a deliberate parody.

> **IH:** "I wanted to let people hear how it would sound if I *really* imitated Bob Dylan. 'God' is great and was one of the best things I've written. 'Advice to a Friend' was a version that differs from the original album as it has Jaco on bass and guitar. 'God' was meant to be dry. It's hard to remember the place I was in back then, but I wanted to be careful because you can end up being hurtful, which isn't the idea at all. Songs like 'God' and 'Rape' are dangerous territory. I don't know if there's a God. If there is, he probably thinks a lot of people are making too much money now and using power to scare people out of their wits. The fact is, no one has a clue about God."

Hunter's writing was inspired on *All-American Alien Boy*. At the time of release, he was aware that he had cut an exceptional record, expressing opinions about some delicate subjects in an adept and sensitive style. Ian would later reveal that his writing, particularly 'Letter to Britannia' and 'God', had been fuelled by his manager's supplies of Colombian Red. His first album, *Ian Hunter*, possessed feeling, but he'd tried to have his say on *All-American Alien Boy* and he always felt affection for the record.

> **IH:** "On *Alien Boy* I had a lot to say lyrically and I said it all well, whilst proving I could keep astride with the best session mothers around, even if I had stomach cramps for a month. I'm proud of those lyrics because I went where a lot of people won't go. There aren't many people who can write a lyric about rape and God that you can't stop laughing at."

In a distinct contrast to the *Ian Hunter* cover, *All-American Alien Boy*'s album artwork comprised a stark white sleeve with two loosely styled but wonderfully detailed paintings of Hunter by Philip Hays.

An illustrator of features and advertisements for *Cosmopolitan*, *Rolling Stone* and Coca-Cola, Philip was well regarded for his expressive water colour portraits of Bessie Smith, Billie Holiday, Elvis Presley and Muddy Waters. Hays defined a distinctive type of graphic album art in the Seventies and his *All-American Alien Boy* illustrations echoed that style, capturing a moody-looking subject clad in black leather. The LP's inner sleeve featured portraits of Stainton, Dunbar, Pastorius, Sanborn, Weems and a shades-less Hunter. Before Philip began his *Alien Boy* art commission for Columbia Records, he spent time with Ian and his bandmates so that he could paint based on photographic references. The white LP image was framed in silver with yellow and black lettering in America, a style linked to the cover design of a 1976 US edition of *Diary of a Rock 'n' Roll Star*, re-published by Flash Books as *Reflections of a Rock Star*.

Although Hunter had issues with initial album test pressings and sent different versions of his LP back to Columbia, *All-American Alien Boy* sold 56,000 copies in the first week of US release. With full-page press ads, CBS Records proudly announced: "Hunter's back! With an alien album!" The LP entered the UK album chart at No.47 on 29th May and stayed for four weeks, rising to No.29. In the USA, the record peaked at No.177 on *Billboard* and, with some promotional photographs capturing Hunter minus shades, Columbia proclaimed: "Now you can see what Ian Hunter sees. Since his days with Mott the Hoople, Ian has developed a vision of his own possibilities in music. His new album, *All-American Alien Boy*, invites you to share his vision. It's a risk that other musicians rarely take because Ian Hunter is also showing you part of himself."

Hopes were high at CBS for *All-American Alien Boy* and the press reacted favourably. With the headline 'HUNTER HITS HIS PEAK', *Record Mirror* described Ian's eight songs as: "His most powerful and thoughtful yet, with some knockout lines and tongue-in-cheek references; Altogether a peak album." *NME*'s Charles Shaar Murray wrote: "Hunter unleashes his killer punch on 'Apathy

83' which demonstrates that his ability to slice rock 'n' roll right down the middle is completely undimmed." Barbara Charone in *Sounds* titled her review 'Hunter Turns Up Trumps', describing the adventurous and expansive album as vibrant, alive and inspired; she also highlighted 'Apathy 83' as her favourite track, adding: "Hunter's got no apathy for rock 'n' roll, kids. He's not one of the fat and lazy rockers, content to watch life pass through the confines of a limousine plate glass window. Ian Hunter is still very much of the people and for that I shall be eternally grateful. This is a rock 'n' roll album and Ian Hunter is one of rock's finest."

In America, reviews were less imaginatively titled 'Alien on Main Street' and 'An Exile on Rock & Roll's Main St. …', *Rolling Stone* describing Hunter as a music fan as much as a performer, and his new LP – an almost perfect synthesis of Ian's quest and learning – as his most successful music since *Mott*. Ironically, Mick Ronson would subsequently declare that *All-American Alien Boy* was his favourite of all Hunter albums. Some fans imagined "the Mott that might have been" had Ian's first solo LP been hatched as a Hoople recording, but Mick's revelation also generated grander visions of an already inspired *Alien Boy*, with a recalibrated "post-Dylan" Ronson onboard.

With no live dates planned, CBS issued two singles to promote *All-American Alien Boy*. The first preceded the LP and featured the title track backed with 'Rape', but, for die-hard Hunter fans, the A-side was a shorter alternative cut. Ian had recorded the up-tempo single as a compliment to his session posse because the musicians played the entire seven-minute album version in the style that Hunter wanted. Reviews described the 45 as "pounding" and "gut-shaking", with "important sardonic lyrics". A second CBS single, issued in August, coupled a senseless edited version of 'You Nearly Did Me In' as the A-side with 'Letter to Britannia from the Union Jack'. One British journal exemplified the Apathy '76 that existed at the time with the headline "Hunter Nearly Does It: A slow burner with overwhelming pretensions; everything in the right place but nothing in the charts." Sadly, Britannia didn't rule the airwaves for Ian and both singles died in sales terms, although the discs became collectable via their alternative A-sides.

While fans listened to and digested Hunter's unexpected manifesto, Ian remarked that his new songs were current. He didn't want to wallow in format writing anymore and hoped that people would "come with him" and his output to different places, from album to album. In 1976, Hunter was still astute enough to discern that his new record risked leaving some of his supporters behind.

> **IH:** "If you're a fan, you'll buy it and you'll get off on it, or you won't get off on it, in which case you'll either stay a fan, or you'll not be a fan anymore. The songs were written last autumn and weren't about anything that happened in the past, except for a couple, from my youth. I totally ignored all my band's past. I had a lot of fun with a few subjects that I figured most writers couldn't write about. I like to try and do something that's odd. Like with 'God'. You could make some hideous errors writing a track like that. You could come off sounding like a complete and utter joke and the fact that I got fantastic reviews is great. The subject is a challenge; the same with 'Rape'."

All-American Alien Boy remains one of the most uncommercial records that Ian Hunter ever produced, but it was a coherent, consistent and classy outing from a man who seemed expressive and at ease with himself. Ian would cringe at the term 'concept album' but *Alien Boy* came close. Joni Mitchell's *Hejira*, released six months later, after the Canadian singer-songwriter met Jaco Pastorius, ran parallel. Mitchell's record would be an emotional folk-jazz-rock journey (*Hejira*), while *All-American Alien Boy* had been a profound pilgrimage too, bound by a thread running from homeland Britain into Hunter's new life in the USA.

It may have been a true artistic high, but *All-American Alien Boy* proved to be a costly card in the popularity stakes. Hunter accepted the outcome but felt miffed that the album didn't take off commercially, given the time and effort expended in its creation. He soon branded the record "too intelligent" and "a mile out of its time", but subsequently admired *Alien Boy* because it contained frustrations and ideas that he had harboured for years. Now described as a lost classic, Ian reflects that he confused much of his fan-base and concedes that *All-American Alien Boy* was not a good career move.

> **IH:** "*Alien Boy* was commercial suicide. I knew that when I did it. It was all slow, but it was something I wanted to do. The record royally nose-dived and messed me up totally. I love the album and I'm fully prepared to understand why people wouldn't like it, but, to me, on a personal level, it was a total success. People like to think of me in terms of rock 'n' roll, so I had a chip on my shoulder about slower stuff. I knew I had to get the ballads out of my system, but I thought the record would happen anyway with all these great people playing on it. It comes as quite a shock when it doesn't. Everyone was thinking the album was a piece of art, telling me how I was a genius. They had me fooled. I really thought I'd done something special, but then we went up to Columbia Records. They told me how wonderful it was, but you develop a nose. There's a difference between genuine wonderful and telling you wonderful. I thought I wrote good lyrics, and nobody took a lot of notice of them, but I came out of that album a lot bigger musically. Sometimes it takes people time to catch up. They resist change and they want what they want. The trouble is this can be boring, and I always want to do something different.
>
> "I didn't realise it at the time, but when my followers were confronted with the *Alien Boy* album, they were puzzled. The trouble was, as Joe Elliott of Def Leppard informed me years later, my audience was composed of seventeen- and eighteen-year-old boys who expected another rock record. Joe said to me, 'How could you expect us to get into that?

We were too young!' And he was right. At the time he didn't get it and was totally pissed off when he heard *All-American Alien Boy*. Now he gets it. I couldn't quite understand at the time why I came to a screaming halt after *Alien Boy* but that's seemingly what happened. I liked the record though, and, later on, Ronson said that *Alien Boy* was always his favourite of all my solo albums, even though he wasn't even on it. He was there when I was getting the songs together. Fucking typical Mick! I had so much on my conscience after that turbulent Mott the Hoople period that *All-American Alien Boy* was a relief. It is a reflection of me, at that time. Maybe if it had been put out differently, instead of just another rock 'n' roll album, it might have stood a chance. It's a lyrical album. 'God' is great – one of the best things I've ever written. I was also producing Sanborn, Queen and Jaco. The sessions were incredible.

"I have wondered if *Alien Boy* had been a big hit, would my subsequent career have gone on a different path? Did I blame CBS? Yes. Did I blame my manager? Yes. Was there a grave lack of imagination in the promotion of that record? Yes. Did they get what I was doing? No. They just put it out and left it, and it died. I did feel angry about it at one point because when I do an album like *All-American Alien Boy* it's a year of my life. It was a good record. Am I pissed off? No. I survived and I'm not hard up. Why worry about stuff that happened long ago? You can't do anything about it. Perhaps 'Once Bitten' Mark II would have sold better but I just bumped into a bunch of new people and I was influenced by them. It was new and it was different. I took a dive and sometimes sales really don't matter, but try telling that to Columbia Records. I regretted losing the sales. Now, it's history."

Following the release of *All-American Alien Boy*, Hunter was at a musical crossroads. While Columbia Records fretted that their artist might maintain his latest musical direction, Ian commenced rehearsals in Woodstock with The Fabulous Rhinestones, a soulful, six-piece, funky R&B group that he'd encountered briefly in 1972. Hunter had instantly loved the laid-back band when he first saw them at the Whisky a Go Go in Los Angeles, during Mott's American 'All the Young Dudes' tour, and the prospective partnership was a precursor to possible touring in support of *All-American Alien Boy*. Adored as part of the Connecticut club scene, the Rhinestones featured former Electric Flag, Dylan and Al Kooper bassist Harvey Brooks and guitarist Kal David, while their second album, *Freewheelin'*, had involved Bill Szymczyk, Joe Walsh and David Sanborn. Eric Parker was the Rhinestones' drummer during the rehearsals with Ian Hunter.

"I joined The Fabulous Rhinestones in 1974," recalls Eric. "They were quite the band, with a lot of cool songs and, of course, my playing sounded better than usual with Harvey Brooks around. We rehearsed at Harvey's Bearsville house in his converted garage, which had a funky studio built into it, and one day Ian Hunter showed up with his manager. I liked Ian. My family had moved to London for the summer of 1969 and I saw Mott the Hoople at the Roundhouse and loved them. I bought their record with the Escher cover and played the crap out of that LP until one day I shot it with my BB gun. When I told Ian years later, he got upset. I was just a fourteen-year-old kid at the time and tried to explain. I remember it bugged me that Mott did 'You Really Got Me' as an instrumental track. The Rhinestones rehearsed with Ian but not for long. We played 'All-American Alien Boy' and 'Irene Wilde' and I do remember thinking, 'Holy crap! Aynsley Dunbar, David Sanborn and Jaco Pastorius on an Ian Hunter record?' Ian proposed that we'd be his backing group, but it didn't really work out."

Harvey Brooks' reflections of the sessions with Hunter are patchy and Kal David remembers little of the rehearsals: "I really don't recall much about our time with Ian in 1976 except that 'Ian Hunter and The Rhinestones' didn't happen, for whatever reason. I do recall that Ian was a nice fellow."

IH: "All Columbia wanted to know after *All-American Alien Boy* was, 'Do you want to become this kind of artist full time?' I didn't have an answer, so I started rehearsing with The Fabulous Rhinestones in Woodstock. They were great and I was going to go out on the road with them because I really liked Harvey Brooks, the bass player. We rehearsed *All-American Alien Boy* but after about a week I got cold feet. I was supposed to tour *Alien Boy* with the Rhinestones, but I just didn't think I could hack all those slow tunes live. They were just too quiet. It suddenly hit me. I thought, 'I can't go on stage and do this. I can't play a bunch of slow songs on their own. I have to play rock.' It just didn't feel right without that bit of swagger, so I dropped the rehearsals and was stuck. I didn't do anything."

In 1990, Columbia USA issued Hunter's album on compact disc for the first time, complete with misprinted *All-American Alien Boys* packaging. A 1998 CD on Sony's Rewind imprint featured 'Rape' with the excised 'Singin' in the Rain' introduction, the only situation where the full take was released, other than original American vinyl test pressings and some early LPs issued in Holland. *Q* magazine reviewed the Rewind edition, opining that 'Rape' and 'You Nearly Did Me In' matched Bowie's tragi-soul epiphanies while the title track worked up seven minutes of neurotic joyous funk.

Sony Music released an *All-American Alien Boy* 30th Anniversary Edition CD in 2006, expanded with early versions and different takes of six songs from the Electric Lady sessions. Some of Hunter's preliminary lyrics were intriguing, notably on the title track, where his *"me 'n' the Hoople"* and *"look out Kennedy"* lines pre-dated the Miller Anderson and John Lennon references on the final cut. A pared-down 'Weary Anger' also showcased the stunning song that Hunter had written before Queen and David Sanborn applied additional magic, marking it as one of Ian's finest pieces. *Classic Rock* reappraised Hunter's collection as brave and unusual, noting that he aimed for subtlety and slowish tempos but "stopped off in some very heavy places".

All-American Alien Boy was placed at No.18 in *Classic Rock's* 'Best Reissue' 2006 chart and the publication's special feature on the expanded disc – 'Loving the Alien' – examined a classic record that flew under the radar: "For the follow-up to his stunning debut album, IAN HUNTER moved to America, put together a crack band – including 'the Jimi Hendrix of bass' JACO PASTORIUS – swapped ideas with BOB DYLAN – got QUEEN to sing backing vocals, and set about making the most ambitious, and commercially disastrous, album of his career."

Commerciality never really featured on Ian's musical agenda, and his courageous musical departure and sophisticated lyrics on *All-American Alien Boy* resulted in a startling album. Receiving universal critical acclaim, the record captured attention via its versatility, musicianship and poetic writing, Hunter's radically different style preceding Gerry Rafferty's iconic 'Baker Street' and Sting's 'Englishman in New York'.

Unsurprisingly, *All-American Alien Boy* has attracted renewed praise as the years have passed, one retro-review opining that, whilst Hunter could have taken the easy route and reproduced a facsimile of *Ian Hunter*, he was cleverer than that. He appreciated that if Ian Hunter was to establish himself as a solo artist, he needed to distance himself from preconceptions created in Mott the Hoople. Hunter had to grow and evolve and *All-American Alien Boy* succeeded in that respect.

The *Alien Boy* album became influential with several musicians. The phenomenal Norman Watt-Roy, bassist with Ian Dury and The Blockheads, liked the album and regarded Jaco Pastorius as a hero. Ricky Warwick of The Almighty, Black Star Riders and Thin Lizzy has cited *All-American Alien Boy* as one of his favourite LPs, highlighting 'Letter to Britannia from the Union Jack' as a special song. Tom Semioli, who runs the US website 'Know your bass player', describes the record that introduced Pastorius to rock audiences as an overlooked masterpiece: "Jaco's bold

94

motifs beautified Hunter's intense, introspective, observational verses and melodies. Unlike his time with Joni, Jaco didn't dare outmanoeuvre Hunter. An undeniably captivating marriage of jazz, rock and poetry, no album sounded like this before, and no album has sounded like it since."

The ever-helpful Bobby Colomby reflected recently that, whilst Hunter was from a different musical department, he was an impressive figure: "I wish I could say that I have many stories with juicy titbits about Ian, but actually my recollections are social in nature. I remember Ian as an extremely interesting and bright fellow whose company I enjoyed immensely. Our musical landscapes were completely different, but I found his music much like his personality – intelligent and interesting."

Many rock musicians finally find commercial success but discover there is a contract with the world, and that some of the fine print is not what they had anticipated. To be a rock 'n' roll star, there is often an assumed expectation that the artist must give audiences what they want or expect – but this was never written into Ian Hunter's manifesto. *All-American Alien Boy* arrived from left field and the sales figures and fan response confirmed that his intelligent approach came at a price.

> **IH:** "*All-American Alien Boy* was a problem business-wise. The album took on a lot of topics, but it 'got away', and I do have to blame the record company for that. At the start, Bobby Colomby and Jaco Pastorius were telling me that I wrote great lyrics and that I didn't have to do rock 'n' roll. I wanted respect with *Alien Boy* but, by the end, my fans didn't want that kind of music, few understood it at the time and the record nose-dived. As far as I'm concerned, that was the end of me as a big-time artist. I was very happy with *All-American Alien Boy* and I still am. It was a very good album, but it messed me up totally. People wanted rock 'n' roll – I'd stopped doing rock 'n' roll – they stopped buying it – career ended!"

With a record label confused about Hunter's future artistic aims, amazingly, in 1976, supportive Hunter admirer Martin Richard 'Dick' Asher picked his moment and asked Ian if he would contemplate employment in International Artists and Repertoire at Columbia Records.

> **IH:** "Dick did enquire if I was interested in a job at CBS. I asked him, what would I be expected to do in 'International A&R' at the label? Dick said, 'Well, things like meeting Ray Conniff off his plane.' It didn't take long to politely decline!"

Having exorcised his slower and serious lyrical material, Ian admits that his record company put him under pressure to revert to a more commercial approach. Hunter found that he started to compose harder rock songs again and the inevitable group situation was already on the horizon.

As *All-American Alien Boy* was released, an explosive force started to take British and American music by the throat. Punk rock would redefine the musical landscape for a period of time, and a fashion style evolved too, as glam turned angry with shaved haircuts, bondage clothes and safety-pin body piercings. The Sex Pistols shocked the UK, a Mott-influenced Clash carried punk's political voice and The Ramones led the charge in New York. The music press reacted with the headlines "Rock is Sick and Living in England" and "The Ramones are Punks and will beat you up", while anti-establishment, two-fingered music became de rigueur. The old guard was being pushed aside, but Ian had already given audiences 'Violence' and 'Crash Street Kidds' and had exhibited attitude. Several have-a-go punks had been watching and listening, and it would soon be revealed that Hunter and Mott fans nestled amongst members of The Clash, Stiff Little Fingers and The Sex Pistols, whose brilliant B-side 'Did You No Wrong' reverberated with Mott the Hoople's *Brain Capers* and 'The Moon Upstairs'.

In September 1976, the 100 Club Punk Festival was held in London's jazz-orientated Oxford Street basement venue, featuring eight new bands including the Pistols and The Damned. In the same month Ian was back in Blighty, in nearby Margaret Street, visiting The Speakeasy club where he casually joined Deep Purple guitarist Ritchie Blackmore and The Fabulous Poodles on stage. After their impromptu jam, the Poodles wrote 'The Wrist', reputedly dedicated to Blackmore and Hunter.

> **IH:** "I did 'jam' with Ritchie that night at The Speakeasy. He came over and asked if I wanted to get up, so I did. I've never been a major fan of Blackmore because I don't think he plays with feeling, but when you stand next to him, it is breathtaking."

Hunter had observed the vibrant music scene in London and New York and felt marginally re-energised by the "take no prisoners" attitude of the young emergent groups. Returning to the USA after his September visit, Ian pondered accusations that *"Alien Boy* didn't rock". Soon, Hunter would fly back to Britain to initiate a new band for his next project – an album far removed from *All-American Alien Boy* – a record that *Sounds* would dub "sensational".

CHAPTER THREE

Rough Justice

For a while I was out, until some of the
punks started saying I was great.

Following the lyrical, laid-back *All-American Alien Boy* album, while Columbia Records craved a recognised musical approach from their artist, three strange rumours emerged concerning Ian Hunter – he would be joining Uriah Heep, The Doors, or a reconstituted Mott the Hoople.

Despite riding high on the success of their albums *Demons and Wizards*, *The Magician's Birthday* and *Return to Fantasy*, British hard rock band Uriah Heep had parted company with lead singer David Byron in July 1976. Vocalists linked with the vacant post included David Coverdale and Gary Holton, but Uriah Heep offered Hunter a significant deal to join them on a ten-week American tour. The band's guitarist Mick Box declared himself "a Mott fan", but a Heep–Hunter marriage never seemed feasible and Ian turned the offer down. Jeff Franklin of American Talent International, who had represented The Faces, Badfinger and Deep Purple, acted for Uriah Heep; Franklin also represented The Doors, and Hunter was offered the option of replacing their departed figurehead, Jim Morrison.

IH: "I remember that I was totally skint and sitting in the US after *All-American Alien Boy* had died a horrible death and effectively killed me off. I *was* invited to join Uriah Heep and my reaction wasn't very good. Jeff Franklin, a big-time American booking agent with a big-time agency, called and offered me the Uriah Heep gig and the money, which was great. They sent me albums with the tracks marked that they wanted to do. Then I got another call from their keyboard player, Ken Hensley, but I really didn't like what Uriah Heep did, nor did I see the point in it. I don't believe Ken did after a while. I think they were just looking for a face or somebody who people had heard of. The interesting thing about the Uriah Heep offer was that the money came first, and it was an extraordinary amount. However, I can't do what I don't believe in. Ronson was the same; if you can't do it, you shouldn't do it. In the end, I never 'auditioned' for Uriah Heep; the only 'gig' I ever auditioned for was Mott the Hoople. I also turned Jeff Franklin down on The Doors because you only have to look at Jim Morrison to know that it would never have worked with me. I was a lyricist. I wasn't an oil painting. Jim was a good-looking guy. We didn't match. I also know what I can handle and what I can't."

In 1976, Ian also turned away from the first of many rumoured Mott the Hoople reformations. Stories started to circulate that Hunter might reunite with his former colleagues following the departure of lead singer Nigel Benjamin from Mott, but Ian soon stamped on the speculation. "Hunter Not Rejoining Mott", claimed one press feature, recklessly referencing the band's former vocalist as "Nigel Dempster" before announcing Ian's intended formation of a new group. At the time, Hunter was ready to disclose his feelings about his former band.

IH: "There was a lot stupidity in the ranks of Mott the Hoople and it used to drive me to despair sometimes. I feel sad about where they are now. I worked for that name for six years and I hate to see it slowly go down."

Having plundered a treasure chest of serene material via *All-American Alien Boy*, Ian envisaged a return to energetic rock 'n' roll. He had gone into the Alien sessions never wanting to play a fast song again, but circumstances had changed. As New York City bathed in a post-Warhol void populated by The Ramones, Patti Smith and Television, performing at vogue clubs like The Bottom Line and CBGB, Hunter had noted the scene's new restlessness. He became acquainted with Tuff Darts, one of Manhattan's "first wave" punk groups who had an interesting guitarist in their ranks, Jeff Salen, who had recently replaced Mick Ronson for Sparks' *Big Beat* album sessions. Ian saw Tuff Darts at Max's Kansas City, played with Salen and liked him, but, during his quest for a guitar player, Hunter also met Billy Cross, whose track record included the rock 'n' roll nostalgia group Sha Na Na, the hippie musical *Hair* and two albums recorded with Jobriath.

"I was putting the band Topaz together and Rob Stoner introduced me to Mick Ronson," recalls Billy Cross. "Mick lived on 19th Street and said that he knew of a vacant basement flat. Ronson was an unbelievably lovely and generous man. My wife and I moved in opposite 'The Ronsons' and Mick really adopted us, bringing food over when we were skint. At one point I was unsure about what might happen with Topaz, so Mick said, 'You should meet my friend Ian Hunter.' I did meet Hunter and we got along really well. I stayed at Chappaqua and played guitar on some things with Ian but musically we were not suited. Something wasn't right about it. I had to choose and I opted for Topaz. Ian is a warm, bright and intelligent man. We stayed friends for years and collaborated on 'Crazy Glue', which we wrote at his house one day. Hunter is a great writer who has navigated an incredible path above most people in the rock business."

Almost in parallel with the Salen and Cross options, former Spooky Tooth and Leslie West Band guitarist Mick Jones was interested in teaming up with Hunter. Mick was auditioning prospective players for Foreigner and Ian attended some sessions to see if any candidates might match his expectations.

> **IH:** "I liked Tuff Darts and I helped to get John Morelli into the band on drums. I also liked Jeff Salen; he was a good guitar player and a together guy. Mick Jones had been on at me over the years to get together. Foreigner saw hundreds of people and none of them were any good. Suddenly, I realised that British players needed gigs, so I went to the UK and tried to put my new band together using English musicians."

During his last visit to London, four days prior to "the Speakeasy jam", Hunter reconnected with drummer Simon Phillips for a session at AIR Studios. Simon forgets the project but noted in his diary that Ian was planning recording and that Canadian sessions were a probability in January 1977. Phillips remembers Hunter fondly and enjoyed their short acquaintance.

The Salen-Cross-Jones episode and visits to London resulted in Hunter recruiting keyboard player Peter Oxendale, drummer Mac Poole and bassist Rob Rawlinson as the nucleus of a new band. Poole and Rawlinson had been members of Broken Glass with Miller Anderson, but the group split following the failure of their first album. Malcolm 'Mac' Poole had played in Warhorse and Gong before he joined Rob Rawlinson in Magill. "It was Miller Anderson who recommended me to Ian Hunter as a drummer," recalled Mac. "Miller is one of very few people that I always had incredible respect for in the music industry. He had so much talent as a guitarist, singer and writer. Rob was also a fantastic bass player."

Peter Oxendale was asked to join Hunter's session group as keyboard player, but, echoing Chris Stainton's role on *All-American Alien Boy*, Peter would also act as musical arranger. Oxendale had been a member of Jet and appeared as an auxiliary keyboard player for live shows with Sparks and The Glitter Band. At his Sparks audition, Peter presented a business card listing his qualifications including GRSM, ARCM and LRAM, from the Royal College of Music and the Royal Academy of Music. Sparks enquired if Peter's post-nominal letters meant that he had been knighted, and so "Sir Peter Oxendale" was born. Oxendale later worked with John Cale, Mr Big and Frankie Goes to Hollywood and became a renowned forensic musicologist and expert witness in copyright infringement, acting in over 2,000 legal cases.

Back in New York, Hunter found that his guitar solution lay with twenty-four-year-old Earl Slick, a stunning player, fuelled by Chuck Berry, Howlin' Wolf and Rolling Stones influences and the man hired by David Bowie to replace Mick Ronson. Slick had played on *David Live*, *Young Americans* and *Station to Station*, and had released his own albums *Razor Sharp* and *The Earl Slick Band*; he would later appear on John Lennon's *Double Fantasy* and collaborate with Bowie throughout much of his career.

> **IH:** "The guitar situation in the lead-up to *Overnight Angels* was weird. I'd looked for English guitar players, but they were few and far between. I'd met Jeff Salen and Billy Cross, then Slick rang me up right out of the middle of nowhere, just as I was getting worried. I'd heard him on Bowie's *Station to Station* and I tried Slick out on two of my new songs, 'Golden Opportunity' and 'Shallow Crystals'. Earl was good. He wasn't Bender by any means, but he was another guitar player who'd say, 'What do you want?' He played beautifully."

Earl Slick: "I'm still not sure how Hunter's 'Overnight Angels' all came together, but I know I was excited to be working in a band with Ian, as I was a fan of Mott. It was funny, 'cos when Bowie needed a guitarist after Ronson left, I got the call – then I left, and me and Mick became friends. Mick had worked with Ian, of course – then when he left Hunter, I replaced Ronson, so something was going on. I remember flying to London with Ian to meet the guys – Rob, Peter and Mac – for initial rehearsals."

Hunter was composing harder rock songs following *All-American Alien Boy*, so a 180-degree turn towards a band culture was inevitable. Slick would help bring a harder edge to the proceedings and, by late 1976, preparations for Ian's recording sessions began in earnest at Milner Sound Studios on London's Fulham Road. Hunter had decided that the new album would be titled *Overnight Angels.*

"Slick, Oxendale, Rob and I rehearsed with Ian Hunter in Fulham for about two weeks, before Christmas," said Mac Poole. "The band was already named The Overnight Angels by Ian at that point, which is strange considering what would occur during recording. I remember we played 'Wild n' Free', 'I Think You Made a Mess of His Life', 'Justice of the Peace' and 'Golden Opportunity' at Milner Sound; we also rehearsed 'Irene Wilde' a lot. Ian's album was going to be produced by Roy Thomas Baker and I learned later that Roy had worked with Jet and was big mates with Oxendale. I do remember an altercation though, between Peter and Earl in Ian's hotel suite following one rehearsal. Slick was from Staten Island and his father was a cop, so he could handle himself. We had to pull Slick and Oxendale apart. Suddenly, Peter would be replaced by Jay Ferguson, but after we agreed to Jay being in, Ian said he'd had a word with RTB and we should just forget everything and get on with it. I didn't realise Roy had so much power. You couldn't fault Earl Slick; he was a gentleman and a bloody great guitar player, and it was a real plus to have him in the band. Ian was an excellent songwriter and brilliant company. As far as I could see, Ian took Peter into the group as he'd played in The Glitter Band. Hunter's previous album had not sold well so he was looking for a producer to help reignite his label situation, hence Roy Thomas Baker. Roy seemed to have clout at CBS and whatever RTB said went."

Overnight Angels was recorded in January and February 1977 at Le Studio in the Canadian province of Quebec. Located south of Morin-Heights near Montreal, the studio had been built five years earlier by producer Andre Perry and designer-engineer Nick Blagona. Perry had taped the Plastic Ono Band's 'Give Peace a Chance' during John and Yoko's infamous Montreal bed-in, sweetening the rough hotel room recording for commercial release, and Andre conceived Le Studio as a live-in facility with state-of-the-art equipment in a glorious setting. The new property had a mix of red cedar shingle and expansive glazed façades that contradicted recognised acoustic practices, but the studios offered sweeping views of adjoining Lac Perry and the Laurentian Mountains, a scenic backdrop that was captured in the Rush video 'Tom Sawyer'. Le Studio had recently birthed Nazareth's *Close Enough for Rock 'n' Roll*, possibly their greatest-sounding album.

Andre Perry also owned a five-bedroom, three-storey guest house nearby, and the whole arrangement offered a haunting retreat where artists could enjoy anonymity in a natural setting, remote from the pace and closed-in nature of city recording spaces. Andre would sell his studio in 1998 and "Canada's Abbey Road", known as "The Temple of Sound", became "the shipwreck in the mountains" by the time recording ceased in 2008. The property fell into disrepair, although the Yamaha grand piano and pool table remained in situ for years until 2017, when, following failed sales attempts, Studio Morin-Heights was partially destroyed by fire.

The Canadian location was employed to record *Overnight Angels* because Ian had chosen to collaborate with producer Roy Thomas Baker, who was already familiar with Le Studio. Roy had produced Nazareth, Be-Bop Deluxe, Jet, Hustler and Queen's first four albums, although their recent LP, *A Day at the Races*, was the first without Baker at the helm. Pilot's *Morin Heights*, recorded at Le Studio, featured Oxendale, Baker and engineer Gary Lyons. As RTB (Audio-Visual) Productions Limited, Roy had signed a production deal with CBS Music to record Journey, Ronnie Wood and Ian Hunter.

IH: "I chose Roy Thomas Baker as producer for *Overnight Angels* because I was at the Beverly Wilshire in Los Angeles one day and Roy was in the next room. That night at the hotel, I was very drunk and I ran into Roy and we got more drunk and the next day, when we were sober, we decided to work together. Roy was a Mott fan and thought I'd strayed from the original sound. He liked the *Mott* album and I had wanted to get a new producer. I became fed up with *Alien Boy* because I'd written, arranged, sang and produced it all myself and it was too much to do; you lose your objectivity. I'd also started writing rock 'n' roll songs again and I wasn't sure that I could produce myself doing rock the way I wanted to hear it. I knew Roy could, as he was a huge producer and had loads of hits. He didn't need me; he just wanted to 'have a go' and his humour was second to none."

Hunter and his band headed for Le Studio in January and Peter Oxendale was awed by Ian. "I remember Hunter and me flying, sitting in economy, Ian on the left and me on the right beside him," says Peter. "Hunter was a complete fuckin' hero to me; shades, curly hair, a hard-arsed rock star! To be with Ian in his band was a dream. I'd even got sunglasses and my hair curled like his. I remember on the plane we watched the *Rocky* movie and, at the end, a tear came trickling down my cheek. So, I desperately try to hide this and turn away from Ian slightly, who then tapped my wrist, all emotional and said, 'I know.' I still have a lot of time for Ian and think the world of him."

Overnight Angels would appease Hunter fans as it contained several tougher rock songs, including a hook-laden single, 'Justice of the Peace'. Ian and the Angels commenced recording with Roy Thomas Baker and engineers Gary Lyons and Nick Blagona at Le Studio, but the sessions soon went awry.

Mac Poole: "After good rehearsals in London, when we started recording at Morin-Heights, I suddenly realised that everything I did was now being scrutinised. We taped so many tracks, so many times, then the comments started – 'The drum stool's squeaking; let's take it again' – 'The drum track speeded up; let's do it again.'

They kept putting me through it. After several days of Roy's comments, Ian said to me, 'It's not working, Mac. I don't know why. There's a problem.' So, I said, 'Fine. I'll bow out.' I remember Ian was generous and I got well paid for what I did. I had no animosity towards Ian, but I was gone."

> IH: "We were a few days into the *Overnight Angels* sessions and I got a call to go up and join Roy Thomas Baker in his flat, on the top floor of Perry's guest house. Roy said, 'I'm disappointed in you, Ian. I thought you knew all about drummers?' So, I asked what was wrong and he pointed out that our drummer wasn't playing exactly the way he wanted. That's when we decided to get Dennis Elliott in, who had been fantastic on the *Ian Hunter* album."

Mac Poole went on to play with Mickey Jupp and Screaming Lord Sutch, while Elliott agreed to take a break in Foreigner's schedule and work with Hunter again. Eight weeks from release, Foreigner's eponymous LP would soon reach No.4 on *Billboard* and furnish two hit singles – 'Feels Like the First Time' and 'Cold as Ice'.

> IH: "Dennis Elliott kindly doubled up for my sessions while Foreigner was ready to sky-rocket. I remember us picking Dennis up from the airport and as we drove him to the studio with his drum cases secured on the roof, they worked loose and flew off onto the roadway. I had kittens. That day would turn out to be the first of a few car-related incidents at Morin-Heights. I was in the shit once again, but Dennis was great; he fitted like a glove and really helped me out on *Overnight Angels*."

Hunter sang lead and harmony vocals, and played rhythm guitar and piano on *Overnight Angels* alongside Slick on lead, slide and rhythm guitars and Rawlinson, Oxendale and Elliott on bass, keyboards and drums. The band was eager and expectant but the production of *Overnight Angels* was littered with incident. On their arrival in Montreal, the group's luggage had been lost and chaos would continue with several car crashes in the Quebec snow – but Hunter's project came to a frightening halt on the night of 3rd February when Le Studio's dwelling house caught fire. Fortuitously, Earl Slick was awakened and, in a race against time, the band were alerted and escaped before the property was destroyed. Rob Rawlinson, Gary Lyons and their partners Fay and Michelle were taken to hospital suffering from minor burns and smoke inhalation. The Montreal Police were never able to determine the cause of the house fire while the British press peddled unimaginative "flees naked" headlines and puerile paragraphs suggesting that Ian had been lucky, "after his escape from that eternal deletion rack in the sky".

> **IH:** "The blaze happened around six or seven in the morning. Slick woke up to find his room on fire and raised the alarm. I instinctively reached for my underpants – decorum at all times – and got out of the basement through a back door. Roy jumped from his second storey window into the snow that was six-feet deep and that's how he survived. We all managed to escape before the house was wiped off the face of the earth. Four of us were naked because there had been no time to dress, and although the temperature was four degrees below zero, the house was burning down right in front of us. Nobody was seriously injured, but Rob and his lady had a very close call. I just remember Roy Thomas Baker, naked as the day he was born, trying to get into my 30" Fiorucci's. It wasn't a pretty sight. We also had several car crashes in the snow, so our stay at Morin-Heights seemed cursed."

With all personal belongings and Slick's treasured 1962 Fender Stratocaster lost in the fire, the band was supplied with clothes and shoes donated by neighbours and CBS staff as they moved into the Carriage House hotel nearby. The blaze had been brutal but two figures who were meant to be present that night were absent and missed the drama – Peter Oxendale and Dan Loggins from Columbia Records, who had been "booked into the wrong Montreal airport".

Peter Oxendale: "I wasn't there during the fire or I'd have been killed, no doubt about that. My room was converted to a crater. I had been on tour with The Glitter Band and had flown straight to Montreal from Auckland for Ian's sessions, so by the time I got to Le Studio I was left with the worst room at the guest house; a cell, below ground, with no windows. I'd gone to see a friend in Montreal on the night of the fire and stayed there. Next day, I remember one of our crew, a six-foot-six Texan guy called Cutter, phoning and telling me not to come back as the guest house was destroyed. I thought it was a wind-up. I heard later that when Ian looked at a hole in the ground where my basement room had been, he said, 'Ox's gone!' Then I appeared larger than life, like a ghost and they nearly shit themselves. My room, my belongings and my money from The Glitter Band's tour were gone. We would sometimes have dinner at the Carriage House nearby so, when the house was destroyed, we moved in there. I think Ian was pretty freaked out by the fire and the band was massively traumatised for sure."

The *Overnight Angels* events sheet would become lengthy – replacement drummer; house fire; equipment stolen; Oxendale hospitalised; Slick requiring stitches after a car crash; five vehicle crashes in total, including Baker and Hunter skidding onto a resident's front lawn. Re-housed and undaunted, recording continued at Le Studio and Ian's new songs were given Roy's panoramic stamp, with neat effects all mixed for radio. Some critics described Ian's finished album as overblown, but Baker's productions shone and his style was a known and notable trademark. Rob Rawlinson recalls that the original Morin-Heights takes were incredibly heavy, but he felt that the band's power in the contemporary studio space never came across on record. Ironically, Ian commented before the album was released that he had wanted to discover a more robust approach to recording.

IH: "When I did the *Alien Boy* album, I never thought I'd do a rock album again. The singer-songwriter path was what I wanted then. Now I feel the opposite; I want a group and I want to be on the road. I wanted this album to have very wide sound. I think initially some people may call this album overkill, but the new album has more commercial appeal, I hope. I have done some deliberately commercial songs. I remember doing 'Honaloochie Boogie' only because I desperately wanted a British hit at the time, but I never felt good about that song and I never played it on stage."

Hunter was happy with the outcome of the Canadian sessions, and by March he was back in London laying down additional vocals at the recently opened Utopia Studios in Primrose Hill and Olympic in Barnes, where Mott the Hoople had recorded 'All the Young Dudes'. Mixing of "the Angels tapes" followed at Sarm Studio in London, with Baker and Lyons still suffering the after-effects of the Morin-Heights fire, before the record was mastered at Sterling Sound New York.

CBS announced that Ian's new album would be issued on 20th May 1977 with a single from the LP, 'Miss Silver Dime', planned for 4th May release, but *Overnight Angels* appeared in British record stores on 27th May, featuring nine sparkling songs: 'Golden Opportunity', 'Shallow Crystals', 'Overnight Angels', 'Broadway', 'Justice of the Peace', '(Miss) Silver Dime', 'Wild n' Free', 'The Ballad of Little Star' and 'To Love a Woman'. The LP was preceded by a single on 13th May, but CBS had opted for 'Justice of the Peace', a catchy and memorable track that was highly praised by *Sounds*. All the songs were composed by Hunter, apart from '(Miss) Silver Dime', co-written with Slick. *Overnight Angels* Side One would be promoted with an eight-date UK tour in June, Ian's first British appearances since the Hunter Ronson shows two years before.

Overnight Angels' powerful curtain-raiser, 'Golden Opportunity', commenced with a meandering instrumental overture that slipped neatly into a killer riff, showcasing Slick's guitar, Oxendale's pinpoint staccato piano and impressive bass runs from Rawlinson. It was a feisty musical call to arms but, at the time of release, Hunter emphasised that the song's lyrical content was serious too.

> IH: "'Golden Opportunity' was about England – the stupidity of the country – not the people in it, but the people who run it. I often get angry talking about British politics. You don't have to be sixteen or twenty-five to feel anger and aggression. If you've got hate in you it's not a good thing, but it's there and you should deliver it in a positive way. I did it in music. I still feel that if I hadn't played guitar I'd have been in jail, because everybody I hung around with was, and I would have gone with them."

'Shallow Crystals', originally titled 'I Think You Made a Mess of His Life', was a leisured, acidic piece. The character receiving Hunter's criticism was never declared, but Ian did not deny years later that the subject matter may have been Guy Stevens, David Bowie and Verden Allen in a multi-character setting like 'Boy'. The recording featured beautiful lead guitarwork, and whilst Hunter acknowledged Slick's virtuosity, he recalls that they collaborated to construct the solo.

> IH: "Slick is very capable but on 'Shallow Crystals' we worked out a lot of that solo together in Chappaqua. That happened with Ronson on occasion too. I can hear a solo, but I can't play one. In hindsight, I wasn't really focused for the album and I think 'Shallow Crystals' may simply have been a selection of ideas and words that were attracted to each other. However, I have a better feeling about that track than just about any other on the record."

Merging seamlessly with the conclusion to 'Shallow Crystals', the album's title song was anthemic, but the track was so robust instrumentally that Hunter's voice and lyrics seemed clouded in the mix. *"Can you hear us?"* asked the band in the song's chorus and, at times, it was difficult to decipher the message. Roy Thomas Baker had certainly opted for heavy phasing and production tricks, with a swirling chorus switching between left and right stereo channels, but Hunter's song was still a powerful piece, as dramatic as the blaze that nearly killed the album's inception. 'Overnight Angels' subsequently featured in the soundtrack for *Asphaltnacht*, a grim low-budget German film about a rock musician, conveniently named Angel, searching for songwriting inspiration.

> **IH:** "'Overnight Angels' was fabricated. I liked the sound of the words 'overnight angels' and I was a bit 'metal' at that time – but I repented in leisure! With *All-American Alien Boy*, I had lost sales because there was no rock 'n' roll on that record. *Overnight Angels* was a plastic attempt to get it back."

Angels Side One closed with one of Ian's finest ballads, 'Broadway', a moody reflection on show business traumas that paid homage to Manhattan's famous thirteen-mile street. The track showcased fine piano and voice from Hunter, ascending to a dynamic coda with layered backing vocals; the "Broadway choir" comprised Miller Anderson and CBS A&R man, Howard 'Lem' Lubin, a former member of the bands Unit 4 + 2 and Christie, and ex-tour manager for Argent.

> **IH:** "I happen to think a lot of 'Broadway'. I think it told me I was still capable of writing a good song. To me, at the time, I felt it was probably the best slow thing I'd ever done musically. The music and the verses were great, but they led up to an average hook and that let it down a little. I'm not a fan of the chorus on 'Broadway'. It could have been better, but I think I just ran out of time."

'Justice of the Peace' opened Side Two in rousing style and was classic single material. The humorous lyrics told the tale of a young blood cowering in fear from a girl's father at the prospect of an imminent shotgun marriage. Starting with a section of the Wedding March from Oxendale, the song had power, pace and a great hook, all glazed with production touches that Ian termed "nifty". *Sounds* selected "JP" as their 'Real Single of the Week', describing it as "a natural-born radio hit, layered like expensive pastry to give more bits of half buried weirdness every time you hear it".

> **IH:** "That was another sure-fire hit that missed but, again, it was fabricated. The whole *Overnight Angels* album was recorded too high for my voice. I should have known better. You sit at home and sing high but when you get in the studio at full throttle things can change."

'(Miss) Silver Dime', an ode to Alice, a *"drunken Mona Lisa"* from the hazy past, was based on an Earl Slick guitar lick. Laced with great piano and guitar touches and another attractive melody and chorus, it was claimed the song had been written by Hunter and Slick in ten minutes, during a practice session. Foreigner's manager Bud Prager played percussion on the track and journalist, scenester and early champion of punk Giovanni Dadomo wrote in *Sounds*: "The trouble with 'Justice of the Peace' is that it's *so* good that anything would sound anti-climactic afterwards. All the same, 'Silver Dime' sits well in its allocated place – customised Hunter and one of those songs that manages to have rock 'n' roll in its chorus and *still* come out sounding good."

> **IH:** "Originally, '(Miss) Silver Dime' was going to be the single from the album. It was written naturally and it is nice to write that way, when it just floats into your head. Some people ask if the Alice in the song was the same as the Alice on *The Hoople* album. I don't know who Alice was."

Overnight Angels' final blast of red-hot rock was 'Wild n' Free', a piledriving piece that kicked in with a phased drum intro before an

112

army of guitars and bass took off at a frantic pace. *Record Mirror* liked the manic rocker's "rowdy punch-up attitude" and the song certainly found Ian back in the fast lane, adopting a tough persona based on "memory lane" anger. It almost marked a return to the raw power of *Brain Capers*, but where 'Wild n' Free' proved that Ian could still supply musical frenzy, it also exhibited a literate style of verbal fury seldom achieved by punk rock wannabes. Acrid but eloquent, the track remains a musical highlight for Earl Slick: "It was cool, because 'Wild n' Free' was an up-tempo punk rock thing and it was the sort of solo I would have done on a Bowie record. *Overnight Angels* was recorded not long after *Station to Station*, so I was in the same mode and I even used the same Strat that I used on 'Stay'. It's a really aggressive guitar part on 'Wild n' Free' and it's one of my favourite cuts. Ian was in a good place and we really had a great time making the record."

The energetic squalling guitars and frantic drums of 'Wild n' Free' end in an abrupt snap, before a tranquil merry-go-round keyboard passage prefaces 'The Ballad of Little Star', a song that had been attempted in rudimentary form during the *All-American Alien Boy* sessions. Hunter's narrative concerned a young city hooker of Native American origin and offered reminders of the pain inflicted on her race by *"our fathers civilised"*, as she sold herself and lived a lost life. To conclude *Overnight Angels*, Ian maintained the moderate musical tempo with 'To Love a Woman', a lightweight *"lost and lonely"* love song with more production tricks, multilayered chorus vocals and a style that almost echoed The Fabulous Rhinestones. Quashing possible accusations of Hunter bias, *Sounds* considered that Ian's uncharacteristic number was B-side material, describing the song as a "smooth-soul second cousin".

IH: "'Wild n' Free' was just a track that just came together. It was rather fast, I know that! I do remember that we first started 'A Little Star' during the *Alien Boy* sessions. There is a rough early take, but the vocals were buried way back in the mix and the tape could not be re-mixed. Having shelved the song in 1976, I resurrected it for *Overnight Angels*. I'd been on a reservation in Canada during Mott the Hoople days. They are very depressing places and that event provided inspiration for the song. I still think that Rod Stewart would do a real nice job of 'To Love a Woman'. We never got around to sending it to him, but I think it would suit him. The key was far too high for me, so it sounds more like Rod's territory. I didn't realise how high it was until I had to sing it."

In stark contrast to the restrained fare of *All-American Alien Boy*, Ian had opted for several faster songs with a greater rock emphasis on *Overnight Angels*. Whilst those bolder tracks crackled energetically, some commentators considered the production "thin" and felt that Ian's voice was smothered under much of the music. Creating a zig-zag effect that alternated fast and slow tracks, Hunter and Baker had segued several cuts to create an effective flow for the record, but Ian would later express reservations, remarking that some of his vocal performances were forced. In angrier moments he described *Overnight Angels* as a mistake. Hunter still harbours misgivings but has always confessed that the outcome was his responsibility.

> **IH:** "I'm not fond of *Overnight Angels* and I don't blame anyone but myself. 'Broadway' could have been great, but I never got the chorus right. 'Little Star' is a nice song and '(Miss) Silver Dime' was okay, but it was the rockers I didn't like. *Overnight Angels* was a mediocre attempt at re-rocking after *Alien Boy*. I got it together on the next album, but *Angels* was just where I was – and I was not on top of my game.
>
> "Roy was a lot of fun to be with and we had a good time and got on great as friends. He will tell you that he wants commercial success for you and he's absolutely correct. My

idea of sound is a heavy sort of sound but Roy likes it lighter than that, which worked for The Cars but didn't work for me. One journalist said my record sounded like Mantovani trying to produce Johnny Rotten. I did the songs in the wrong key, so it doesn't sound like me and yet, up until the final mixes, I'd never heard anything like it. The rough mixes were incredible and sounded amazing but Roy had a way of squeezing mixes for radio, which is what most good producers do. I didn't want that, but I didn't fight. Roy gets upset with me when I talk about this, because we have been very good friends over the years, but I can't help the way I feel. It was just a matter of musical differences. I really felt if we'd left the rough mixes on the record and the album had come out, it would have done great. You always go into a studio with the best of intentions and sometimes you come out with something else. I wasn't happy with the songs I wrote on *Overnight Angels*. *All-American Alien Boy* hadn't done well because it wasn't 'a rock album' and it didn't have singles, so I thought I'd just walk in and happily do a rock album for them. It didn't turn out that way. Rock 'n' roll is harder to do for me than that."

Thirty years after the event, Roy Thomas Baker would only comment that there were "selective memories, grandstanding and exaggerations" surrounding *Overnight Angels*, adding that "Ian was happy when the record went down".

Rob Rawlinson: "It's interesting to reflect on how Hunter feels about the production of the album because I remember thinking, when we heard the final mix at Ian's house, how it didn't sound like the record we'd played on. It just seemed overproduced. It should have been remastered at some point, because I know it sounded great in the studio while we were recording. Slick played phenomenal guitar on that album."

Overseen by Roslaw Szaybo at CBS, *Overnight Angels* was presented in a gatefold sleeve, constructed around two images of

Ian by English artist David Oxtoby and Scottish illustrator Wilson McLean. Pop art artist and hard rock fan David Oxtoby devoted his work to portraits of singers, capturing Elton John on the colourful cover of the biography *Elton* and Joe Cocker for his LP *Sheffield Steel*. But while he drew British musicians, David's passion was America and he created pictorial tributes to Otis Redding, Little Richard and Muddy Waters. Like Philip Hays, many of Oxtoby's pencil drawings, watercolours and aquatints were derived from photographs as they allowed David to make up his ideal image. The dark, ink black front cover art for *Overnight Angels* featured Hunter in profile, his hair a mixture of metal coils and feathers.

"I did a few covers for the CBS label," recalls David Oxtoby. "The *Overnight Angels* sleeve was a hell of a drawing and was two-foot-six square originally, although slightly longer in one direction to suit the correct vinyl LP format. I can't remember the original specification but Roslaw Szaybo said it had to have feathers. It took three weeks to draw in pencil and I designed the headshot of Hunter from two or three photographs and combined them into an image that I felt captured his character. I met Ian at the time and liked him very much. He visited my studio in Notting Hill Gate and came back to see my work two or three times. Originally, I drew the *Angels* picture with the edges feathering or fading into white, to mirror the feathers in Ian's hair. This was to give the drawing some softness and flow but when I got the sleeve back from CBS, they had chopped the bloody thing down to eighteen inches square and removed the perimeter, so I needn't have bothered. I drew some of Ian's hair like metallic coils to contrast the lightness of the feathers; the metallic idea was meant to be related to the music. The *Overnight Angels* album cover won a prize and Szaybo toured it for some time with other artwork."

The dramatic inner gatefold for *Overnight Angels* featured Hunter's head again, this time face forward – half-flesh, half-skull – with outstretched black wings repeating the feathers motif. Like Oxtoby, Wilson McLean worked from photographs filtering the most interesting aspects of his subjects, adding creative thoughts and concepts. A jazz lover, music conjured up pictures to McLean and in 1985 he would be selected by the Royal Mail to design British postage stamps illustrating works by classical composers. "On the *Overnight Angels* cover I was working in acrylics and making the transition from dark to light, and one colour to another," says Wilson. "I was also developing a habit of exploring clouds and objects to create surrealistic images, arriving at something slightly unsettling."

Roslaw Szaybo: "For *Overnight Angels,* my idea was to turn some of the curls in Ian's hair into feathers. I decided to have a very strong image of Hunter's head, not as a photographic portrait but painted or drawn by a great English artist. I liked David Oxtoby personally and loved his work, so, behind the concept of him doing this fantastic drawing, I wanted to give him scope to use his talent in a commercial way. Like the US *Mott* and *Live* covers, John Berg at CBS New York tried to change Hunter's sleeve. I liked John and thought he was talented enough not to worry about me taking some of his glory. The cropping and black frame placed around Ian's album artwork was John's idea, as was the inner gatefold. I never spoke with Wilson McLean about his painting and when I saw it, I was astonished because the picture was not the right image for me. I love the front cover and it hasn't dated."

The rear of the *Overnight Angels* sleeve featured colour portrait photographs of Oxendale, Slick, Smith and Rawlinson, but there was no photo of Hunter on the packaging. Acknowledging events surrounding the *Overnight Angels* sessions, the LP cover carried a special credit from Ian: *"Nine of the people on this record narrowly escaped when a fire reduced the house we were sleeping in to a crater. We would like to thank the Jones Family, Yael, The Carriage House Hotel, CBS Montreal and Ernie the Cop for their immediate and most valuable help."*

Released in the UK with punk rock at its zenith, Hunter soon learned that the timing was not good for his record, despite some of its highly charged content. The "new wave" was nothing new as far as Ian was concerned, but the vibrancy of the scene still intrigued him and he confessed he had cut "a rock album" with deliberate intent, as nothing else seemed to move record buyers in Britain at the time.

Most of the UK press embraced *Overnight Angels* warmly. *Sounds* offered a four-star review titled 'Overnight sensation', Giovanni Dadomo describing the album as a "perfectly centred barrage of rock 'n' roll napalm" and enthusing: "I'm delighted to be able to rate 'Overnight Angels' as ample proof that the old dog's balls are in pretty good nick. Great to have you back, killer." Under the headline 'NATURAL BORN ROCKER', *Record Mirror* praised Hunter's record with five stars and proclaimed: "The guvnor's back, doing what comes naturally, rocking hard. This band puts the old Mott in the shade, and the man in the shades back at the top. Pure dynamite. An album that re-establishes Ian as a leading light of the Seventies." In contrast, a punk-friendly *New Musical Express* review called the record "Overweight Angels".

To promote *Overnight Angels*, Ian toured Britain with the musicians who played on the album, apart from Dennis Elliott, who had re-joined Foreigner. When the Angels appeared in concert, the drum stool was occupied by Curly Smith, a former member of Spirit offshoot Jo Jo Gunne, famous for their 1972 hit 'Run, Run, Run'. Rehearsals for the Angels European tour were held at Fred Heller's "funky and chaotic" management offices in Dobbs Ferry, a village located between New York and Ian's Chappaqua home.

In May, Ian featured on the front page of *New Musical Express* and appeared in a double-page centre spread, photographed playing pool and rehearsing with his band at Dobbs Ferry. *NME*'s cover carried the headline 'IAN HUNTER: Cue Album, Cue Tour, Cue Controversial Interview, Cue Balls', Ian prompting Charles Shaar Murray that he would be supporting the Electric Light Orchestra at Earl's Court, but classing them as "completely boring" and casually adding that The Overnight Angels would "kill" Jeff Lynne's band. A week later, ELO manager Don Arden spun an acid letter to *NME*'s letters page, politely denying there was any contract for Hunter's billing and not so politely calling Ian a frustrated loser with a big mouth. The Angels' support slot was cancelled and ELO did not perform any British gigs that year, while Hunter toured England from 3rd to 12th June playing eight shows, including appearances in Newcastle and London.

> **IH:** "I wasn't prepared to go around supporting ELO in England, but I was going to do Earl's Court, as my manager was telling me we had got it. I was having a bit of fun with Charlie that day. I have a lot of respect for ELO; it was just a joke. I think that *Overnight Angels* tour was the last time I played in Norwich; some guy at the university threw a bottle and decked Earl Slick. There's nothing like a good education."

Representing punk insurgency, The Vibrators were drafted in as Hunter's British tour support and the reaction to Ian was interesting, especially when some of the new pretenders professed admiration for musical forebears such as Mott the Hoople and Roxy Music. They had seemingly witnessed Hunter's early desperation and tried to make it their own, but the movement was an attitude with a DIY fashion component, clothes designer Vivienne Westwood admitting in 2016 that "punk" was a fantastic marketing opportunity. Ian had long vocalised strong messages of disillusionment and had forecast an emergent generation of disaffected youth, but his was a cool, literate, straight-shooting presence rather than a rabid, scattershot attack. Hunter's status as an early patron saint of punk was also no mean feat, given that the movement was nominally based on vociferous rejection of the old. Ian later considered punk a smart move, even though it failed to remove established rock acts like The Rolling Stones and The Who.

> **IH:** "I kind of missed Seventies punk rock as I was busy doing *All-American Alien Boy*. I could sense some kind of new wave coming, but I thought punk was the enemy and they'd put me out of business. I went to The Roxy club in London;

119

they kicked Ronson out of there and didn't like him, but I was accepted so then the press had to do an about-turn which was fucking hilarious. Punk turned out to be a great move and because I'd been in a fancy band, the journalists figured the punks would hate me. *Overnight Angels* came out right on top of the new wave–old wave thing and some writers were having a ball with us 'old farts'. Everything went completely anti-flash. For a while I was out, until some of the punks started saying I was great and then I was in. I was a hero again. Never believe what you read in the papers.

"I didn't see The Sex Pistols play although I did meet John Lydon on a plane and we talked our way across the Atlantic once. I remember seeing The Damned in London and going to a session for the first Clash album. I recall punk in America and watching Television, Blondie and The Dead Boys down at CBGB in New York. I saw The Dead Boys with my daughter Tracie, when she was fourteen or fifteen, and one of them tried to hit on her. Cheetah Chrome did fancy Tracie, but I wasn't having any of it. She was very young at the time and I do remember thinking, 'No way; you are not going out with that!' The pot calling the kettle black! Of course, I was a 'that' once, but what's the point of being a rocker if you can't be a hypocrite? I recall Gary Valentine brought Blondie up to my house one night. Chris Stein says I recorded a session that we played downstairs, but I'm not the type that does that. I usually get pissed and have a good time. I remember the night, because I was on piano, right next to Debbie Harry; what a girl and what a looker. I love Clem and the band but I have no tape of us playing.

"I think the Seventies term, new wave, was a very clever invention. Whoever thought of that was a genius. It was designed to wipe us out of the way. By calling the new bands new wave, that meant that people like me were old and that doesn't sound too nice or too fashionable. I'm glad I wasn't living in England then, because the new wave cut off a lot of people by virtue of this huge ageist stigma. Punk was a clever term, but it never quite worked because what they were trying to do was conveniently cut off half and sway public opinion towards the new, which would have worked perfectly had the new been good enough, but it wasn't quite good enough. My punk was Gene Vincent. I remember Elvis Presley happening, and Jerry Lee Lewis and Chuck Berry, and I know what a changeover is. That's a changeover. That took over the world. The punk bands were just not the same.

"Punk was also pretty hypocritical. They were all supposed to be wasted little kids from the streets, but a lot of them weren't. I know one guy whose dad owned half of Brighton and he was in a very famous punk band. He said to me, 'Don't say nuffin' like,' so a lot of it was just bullshit. It was kids who knew C, F and G and had that enthusiasm that I'd had with The Apex in Northampton in the Fifties, jumping around like maniacs. I remember looking at The Damned with Jeff Dexter at The Roxy and I asked him, 'Was that what we were like?' – meaning Mott – and he said, 'Yeah, but you were great.' I thought that The Sex Pistols came in right down the line though and wrote about England as it was in 1977. They were the only band at the time for me, because they made exciting records. I'd been writing 'Crash Street Kidds' and 'Pearl 'n' Roy' three years before, but they were polite. I thought the Pistols had it, but it didn't convert to America and it didn't become a revolution like The Beatles and the Stones."

With a nod to the punk ethic, Mott's 'Violence' was featured in The Overnight Angels live set, alongside songs from the new album. With a taped walk-on intro of 'Broadway', a revitalised Hunter also played 'One of the Boys', 'All the Way from Memphis', 'Letter to Britannia from the Union Jack' and a new number, 'England Rocks'. Some British reviews turned personal, not least another *NME* attack titled, 'Mutton Dressed up as Lamb', but Phil Sutcliffe of *Sounds* said of Ian's Newcastle City Hall gig: 'HUNTER; IT JUST HAD TO BE SPECIAL.' In a live setting, many fans felt that the *Overnight Angels* material rocked with greater power and abandon than the record, but Ian did not regard the shows as successful and matters finally came to a head with his manager at Leicester De Montfort Hall.

> **IH:** "We did the tour of England and I hated the whole mess I was in. I knew I was writing shit, singing shit and playing shit. At Leicester, Fred Heller appeared at the sound desk, two songs from the end of my set, and then came backstage and said he'd enjoyed the show. I told him I'd had enough and things could not continue as they were, so I sacked my manager. Fred took it quite well, but then I was stuck in England with a band and a road crew, and no income. Al Smith of CBS Records brought some guy in who fixed up a few European dates and we went ahead with the final show at Hammersmith to keep the group on the road."

"Ian and I parted company as our relationship had been going downhill," says Fred Heller. "He'd been upset when I delivered the album cover for *All-American Alien Boy*, which I thought was very good and it was at that point that I no longer wanted to manage him. I had his back all through the cancelled Mott the Hoople tour dates and his nervous breakdown; I'd travelled to the UK to see some of his shows; our relationship ended after his Leicester concert."

Although Ian was now in disarray, CBS Records released 'England Rocks' as his next single on 22nd July 1977, paired with 'Wild n' Free'. The A-side had been newly recorded and produced with Bill Price at Wessex Sound in North London. Created in the mid-Sixties inside a Gothic church hall, the studio had been used for pop recordings but, after the first two King Crimson albums were engineered there, Wessex had gravitated towards rock. When the studio was purchased by Chrysalis Records in 1975 along with AIR (London) Studios, Price transferred to Wessex as Chief Engineer and Manager. Bill took the studio out of the doldrums and had recently recorded *Never Mind the Bollocks Here's the Sex Pistols* with Chris Thomas before Hunter's 'England Rocks' session. The Wessex studio environment is captured in the promo video for Queen's 'Somebody to Love', filmed in 1976.

Rainbow bassist Jimmy Bain, who had been an early contender for Hunter's band before Rawlinson, appeared on backing vocals for 'England Rocks'. The single gained attention and alluded to punk with lyrical references to safety pins and the crude, energetic attitude of the new music, but it failed to chart. 'England Rocks' was subsequently covered by Yorkshire band Little Angels in the Eighties and Joe Elliott's Down 'n' Outz, but the anthemic song had first been written by Ian as 'Cleveland Rocks', in honour of the city in Ohio. American actors and writers Pat McCormick and Tim Conway had penned early Seventies material for Merv Griffin and Johnny Carson, who often made fun of Cleveland on their US television shows, but the jibes frustrated Hunter.

IH: "I'd originally written 'England Rocks' as 'Cleveland Rocks' in reaction to the comedy thing that went down at one time. Griffin and Carson made Cleveland a joke town on American TV and we didn't like that in Mott. New York and Los Angeles A&R men might claim they found these great acts in the Seventies, but Cleveland was a heartland and their kids discovered them before they did, especially the British bands. Mott the Hoople, David Bowie and Roxy Music were first accepted in Cleveland, where rock 'n' roll was born.

"I didn't have the faintest idea what I was doing after I fired my manager but CBS Records said they wanted another single from me. I'd written 'Cleveland Rocks' about a year before and we were in Wessex with Bill Price, so I changed Cleveland to England in a panic. It was genuinely written as 'Cleveland Rocks' and I've been defending that ever since. I hadn't written like 'England Rocks' since 'Roll

Away the Stone' and 'All the Way from Memphis', but it was a basic song that had that quasi-classical European chord sequence with the hallelujah chorus at the back end. I was happy to get 'England Rocks', which did nothing of course, until Ronson got hold of it later on."

In addition to their UK dates, The Overnight Angels played some shows in Norway and Sweden but, adding to Hunter's fiscal pain, Columbia Records suddenly refused to release *Overnight Angels* in America. The label suggested they could issue the album when Hunter had new management and some US test pressings were cut, but the LP only appeared in Canada. Given their *Overnight Angels* volte-face, Hunter had become exhausted by Columbia's handling of his work but he became puzzled when the label's American president Bruce Lundvall sent him a complimentary telegram.

IH: "I'd split with my manager Fred Heller after that gig in Leicester and was stuck with a band and no money. I had no means of shifting 40,000 dollars' worth of gear back to the States, plus I had no way of paying the band's wages. Then, *Overnight Angels* was not released in the US because I fired Heller during the English promotional tour, before the record was issued in America. Columbia said they didn't want to release it until I had new management and that dragged on until it became too late. They did use some of *Overnight Angels* later though, for a CBS compilation. I remember I got a telegram from Bruce Lundvall, the president of CBS, telling me, 'This album is amazing. It bewilders me.' That was for *Overnight Angels*, then Columbia never even released *Overnight Angels*. It wasn't until I got off the label that I was able to start writing decent music again. I sometimes think when I'm reviewing the sorry state of my Columbia royalty statements that I should send them back with a note saying, 'If you had pulled only one finger out, I might not owe you anything.'"

Dan Loggins admired Hunter's third album: "*Overnight Angels* had some amazing tracks including 'Golden Opportunity' and 'Justice of the Peace', which should have been a smash. I always felt that *Overnight Angels* could have been a much bigger success as it anticipated a style, a sound and a new direction for Ian. As it turned out, that style would evolve into his next record – and his biggest-selling solo LP."

While Hunter pondered his position, artist manager Don Arden almost came to his rescue. Arden had established Jet Records in 1974 and issued output by Electric Light Orchestra, Lynsey de Paul, Hunter hero Roy Wood and Ariel Bender's band, Widowmaker. The Jet label's first US release was a 1977 Jeff Lynne solo single and Arden was interested in Hunter, even though Ian had mischievously kicked up dust over the prospect of The Overnight Angels supporting ELO at Earl's Court. Hunter had told the *New Musical Express:* "We'll support them because they're completely boring and we'll kill them. They must know that. Having said all this, I'll probably get wiped off the ELO tour, but what can you do?" Ian was "wiped off the ELO tour" and headlined at the Hammersmith Odeon instead, but, at that show, Hunter met Arden.

IH: "I was concerned about that meeting after my bravado with *NME*, but I explained to Don why I'd done the ELO thing and his riposte was, 'Ian, it's business.' We spoke about me joining his label and I nearly went with Jet Records. They were trying to buy my album off Columbia and the story at the time was that they couldn't get it. I then found out years later that Don had secured a six-figure advance from 20th Century Records to release *Overnight Angels* in America, but I never saw that at the time. I met with Don twice in Los Angeles. He flew me out first class and put me up first class, and I remember his greeting was, 'Ian, Ian, what are we going to do with you?' He helped fund things for a short while and after the first meeting he called to say, 'Fire the road crew.' After our second meeting in LA, he called to say, 'Fire the group.' I don't think Don really wanted me. He wanted the *Overnight Angels* album for US release but probably offered too little, while Columbia probably asked too much.

"So, The Overnight Angels was a band for about a year but they didn't carry on because, as usual, I was in a mess. The Angels musicians were great on that album and it was done well by Roy Thomas Baker and Gary Lyons. I just didn't like what I did. I was doing something I shouldn't have done but I did learn from it and that was important to me. However, by the end of 1977, I had no manager, I had no band and I had no money. I also wanted out of the label, because having no US release for *Overnight Angels* was lower than I would want to go. Columbia was great at coming down to sessions and telling you how wonderful everything was and then, the minute you finished, they weren't interested anymore. Like management, it was easy to get out of that. It was Mott the Hoople's label and it had been Mott the Hoople's manager. Technically, I could have done another album for CBS but I knew how it was going to turn out. Finally, I was in a wilderness, which was interesting and frightening. I knew I was in the shit, but now at least I was clear. I also knew I wasn't twenty-one anymore and would anybody want to pick me up?"

During the 'England Rocks' session, the Angels had started to fracture and Rob Rawlinson's departure appeared on the cards. "My involvement with Ian and The Overnight Angels was only about six months," says Rob. "I remember when we did the 'England Rocks' single at Wessex, Jimmy Bain was hanging around, so I said to Ian I'd tour and complete my commitments with him but that he might want to find another bass player." Rawlinson subsequently worked with Climax Blues Band, Freddie Mercury and Alison Moyet and moved into music production. Dennis Elliott once offered Rob a job in Foreigner, but Rawlinson declined.

IH: "Rob Rawlinson was a great bass player and I particularly enjoyed Peter Oxendale's talent and company. He was a brilliant keyboard player, was as mad as a March hare and is on the list of great people that I've worked with. Pete was with Frankie Goes to Hollywood later on. A consummate musician, he once told me he made tons of money doing stuff he hated so he could blow it touring with me. He was an all-round maniac, married a beautiful model with a lovely sense of humour, and, as far as I know, is Britain's premier musicologist. In other words, now he's posh! Peter's idea of keeping fit was standing in a paddling pool with a brandy in one hand and a cigar in the other. Slick did not get on with Oxendale and once dug him a grave; it is true – I was there. We had driven to Slick's house to pick him up and he was in his garden with a spade. We got out of the car and Earl had dug a hole, eight feet long, three feet wide and three feet deep. Pete said to Slick, 'Digging a ditch, Earl, are you?' Earl replied, 'No, I'm diggin' a fuckin' grave, for you.' Slick hated Pete. Fred Heller also knocked Oxendale out cold one night. Pete certainly knew how to wind 'em up. Slick's a great guy and I liked his dad too; his father was a cop, same as mine – old school."

Rob Rawlinson: "I seem to recall that Pete was annoying everyone in those days. The first time Oxendale met Heller, Peter called him a 'See you next Tuesday', and Fred hit him and knocked him out. One night, Pete pissed me off before a gig in Sweden. I received a slap on the back from Oxendale while I was having a drink and it pushed the glass into my mouth, so I delivered a short uppercut. It was just one of those rock 'n' roll moments and I'm not proud of it, although I have to say that I got a 'Fuckin' A' from Earl and Curly."

Peter Oxendale: "I called Earl Slack, as I had a rivalry with guitar players; well two guitarists mainly, and Ronson was one. I remember that Mick came to Chipping Norton Studios when Ian and I were working on a Mr Big album. I said to Ronson that day

127

that he looked like Link Wray, only older, and we had a fight. My other guitar rival was Earl Slick and, yes, he dug a grave for me!"

Earl Slick: "The Overnight Angels were a really good band and should have gone further than the album and one short tour. There are a lot of good songs and performances on the record. I still lean towards the rockers as my faves: 'Golden Opportunity', 'Overnight Angels', 'Wild n' Free', 'England Rocks' and '(Miss) Silver Dime'. Recording at Le Studio with Roy was a trip in itself. I'd never worked with a producer like him before. He had me stack a lot of guitars on top of guitars, which was foreign to me at that time. This method gave my rhythm guitars a more polished sound which I thought was way too perfect and that was my only beef with the record – too polished all round. Luckily that didn't happen on the solos or slide guitars and they were a lot more off the cuff, as I was used to doing. I did the solo for 'Wild n' Free' with stitches and a splint on my right middle finger. I had accidentally put my hand through a window a few days earlier, the night after the mystery house fire. That was the beginning of a slew of weird shit that followed us around, the final straw being Ian's manager getting his ass fired. My input on the record was mostly me embellishing what Ian did, as his songs are pretty much together. '(Miss) Silver Dime' was inspired by a lick that I had and Ian wrote the song around it. It's a real shame the Angels didn't last longer. That was a great band but we were up against some typical business things that didn't help us. Even though it didn't end well, it wasn't the band that wrecked it and I'm really proud of what we achieved."

Curly Smith: "I can honestly say that I probably learned more about showmanship and professionalism from working with Ian Hunter than anyone else I have ever worked with since. Ian has always performed at such a high level and he is still inspiring to me. I always think about those days with fond memories. It was a special time in rock 'n' roll and one of the best, most kick-ass bands I have ever had the privilege to play with."

Whilst the *Overnight Angels* album has never sat comfortably with Hunter, it was popular with many fans, not least Joe Elliott, who covered 'Golden Opportunity', 'Overnight Angels' and 'England Rocks' in 2012 on the Down 'n' Outz' first album, *My ReGeneration* – Ian even made a cameo appearance in the band's promo video for 'England Rocks'. The Overnight Angels' British tour had included a gig in Doncaster, where Joe sidled up to the Gaumont's dressing room door after the show and was greeted by Earl Slick. It was the first time Elliott met Hunter.

"One night during the Angels UK tour a seventeen-year-old kid and his buddy snuck their way up to the dressing room," recalls Earl. "Instead of throwing them out, I invited them in for a pint. The kid was an as yet unknown, budding singer named Joe Elliott. Looking back, *Overnight Angels* is a gem that slipped through the cracks and it still holds up for me. If it weren't for Joe keeping the album alive, it would have disappeared for good."

"When Hunter's 'England Rocks' didn't reach the singles charts in 1977, and songs by The Clash and The Sex Pistols did, I really couldn't get my head around it," says Joe. "It made me angry because it was the perfect summation of that summer, even more than 'God Save the Queen'. I know that Ian doesn't like *Overnight Angels* much because he thinks it's too bombastic, but, to me, it's brilliant."

IH: "After the shock of *Alien Boy*, everybody said, 'You're not supposed to do this, you're a rocker.' So, I said, 'Okay, so I'm a rocker' and I did *Overnight Angels*, but I was never happy with it and it was my fault. My hang-up is that it contained largely fabricated writing and that it was recorded too high for my voice. *Overnight Angels* was probably the most expensive album I made, too – the cheapest ones have been the best ones. Morin-Heights was considered a groovy studio, but I wasn't that keen on it or crazy about the set-up. It was difficult to admire the scenery through all that glazing as we had six feet of snow when we recorded there. I remember Andre got insurance for the house that burned down, then built a bigger one.

"*Overnight Angels* was not a good time for me, and I made some classic mistakes on that record. There was a suggestion once that the album should be remixed, but it can't be remixed – you can see through the two-inch tape! Admittedly, I haven't heard *Overnight Angels* in years, but there's a phoney element to it that sticks in the craw. I don't dislike it *so* much – I'm just not *so* keen on it. It's not the record – it was me. Everyone else was great but people have their off moments and that was one of mine. I was trying to be optimistic but it was a depressing time."

Having opted to sever connections with his manager and record label, The Overnight Angels band folded. The heat of punk was subsiding and a different musical landscape lay ahead. It would take some months to re-group, but the horizon looked brighter when Hunter focused on his next album and contemplated renewed collaboration with Ronson. "I really prefer to work with Mick," admitted Ian.

CHAPTER FOUR

The Outsider

The person who writes the material is a lot more truthful.

Following the *Ian Hunter* sessions in 1975, Mick Ronson became involved in a wide range of collaborations with Bob Dylan, Roger McGuinn, Sparks, David Cassidy, Roger Daltrey and Van Morrison.

In the midst of Dylan's Rolling Thunder gigs, Ronson had recorded at Sundragon in Manhattan's Flat Iron District, a studio that would be utilised by Talking Heads, David Johansen and The Ramones. Mick cut 'Is There Life on Mars?' and a version of David Bowie's 'Soul Love', retitled 'Stone Love', but the Sundragon tapes were shelved. Ronson also helped Kinky Friedman on *Lasso from El Paso* and intended to tour with McGuinn as Guam. The concept was short-lived, so Mick was invited to produce and play on Roger's *Cardiff Rose* – it was McGuinn's hardest-hitting solo album, Ronson providing a framework and musical input as cohesive as The Byrds and as muscular as Mott.

"I don't remember what went wrong with Guam – financing, I think – so I invited Ronson to produce me using Guam as the studio band," says Roger. "That became the *Cardiff Rose* album and it was one of my favourites. Mick did a stunning job as producer, perhaps best illustrated on the song 'Jolly Roger'. He emphasised the downbeat on all the 1s on the 3/4 time, which is a rare time signature in rock; it's really more of a folk music thing. Mick made the track into a great seafaring song. I don't know how, but he went out and found wind sounds and creaking noises for the ship's timbers and assembled the whole thing. He literally was an audio artist – absolutely brilliant! We had a great time working together. Mick was an excellent guitar player and producer and a good friend with a wonderful sense of humour, which made him so much fun to hang out with."

Armed with more faith in himself following the Rolling Thunder experience, Mick set about forming his own band as he felt the solo career thrust upon him by MainMan Management had been an attempt to create "a David Cassidy-type figure". Cassidy he was not, but Ronson was happy to work with the former teen idol, who had starred in the early Seventies US sitcom *The Partridge Family*. David had recently ended a brief exile from live music and, signed to RCA, he sought to write songs and make music on his terms. Cassidy had composed and cut 'When I'm a Rock 'n' Roll Star', a tremendous track that spoke volumes about his new direction, recorded with The Beach Boys' Bruce Johnston and Ricky Fataar. Then David and Mick met in Colorado at the end of Dylan's tour and Ronson played sparkling lead guitar at Caribou Ranch Studios for the power-pop title track on David's final RCA album, *Gettin' It in the Street*.

Cassidy resided for a while at Ronson's Manhattan apartment and the duo rehearsed and considered forming a band, but Mick became unsure of the alliance, and the sudden death of David's father, actor Jack Cassidy, forced him to leave New York for Los Angeles. David had fulsome praise for Mick, years later: "Ronson's soulful guitar playing and vocals contributed greatly to the early Bowie success, but Mick was a far greater musician and a far greater person than anyone was allowed to know. I loved him and admired his uniqueness and was privileged to have worked with him."

132

Immersed in New York, Mick played one-off gigs in the summer of 1976 with the New York Dolls, The Rob Stoner Band and John Cale but he wanted to form The Mick Ronson Band, some of his initial candidates comprising vocalist Mary Hogan, drummer Hilly Michaels and Beckies guitarist Jimmy McAllister. In parallel, Ronson split from RCA and Tony Defries and changed his management representation to Barry Imhoff, Dylan's recent promoter and technical director. Mick and Suzi also moved to Woodstock in upstate New York and set up home, beginning a long affection with the hamlet known as 'The Colony of the Arts', nestled in the borders of Catskill Park. "Like David Cassidy, Mick and I met Barry Imhoff on Dylan's tour," says Suzi. "Mick was still managed by Tony at that point and they didn't get along anymore. Barry got us out of the Defries contract, took us up to Bearsville and started to manage Mick."

Ronson was soon camped in Bearsville Studios, famed for various Todd Rundgren, Jesse Winchester and Foghat recordings. The Mick Ronson Band sessions included drummer Bobby Chen, later to work with Genya Ravan, bassist Jay Davis, who had rehearsed with a fledgling Foreigner, and British guitarist Mick Barakan, who first met Ronson through Dana Gillespie. Barakan, also known as Shane Fontayne, later worked with Ian Hunter and Bryan Adams and formed The New York Yanquis with Ronson.

During September and October 1976, The Mick Ronson Band recorded at Bearsville Studio B with Mick acting as producer alongside engineers John Holbrook and Dennis Ferrante. The session takes included two of Mick's compositions, 'I'd Give Anything to See You' and 'Hard Life', plus 'Just Like This', a cover of Moby Grape's 'Hey Grandma', Ricky Fataar's '(I'm Just a) Junkie for Your Love', 'Crazy Love' by Blondie Chaplin and Jay Davis's 'Takin' a Train'. To create a harder-edged sound, Mick had starting using Mesa Boogie amplification created by Californian engineer Randall Smith, who had built louder, high-gain amps by hot-rodding small Fender units. John Holbrook had never seen a Mesa Boogie before and he and Bobby Chen marvelled at Ronson's musical excellence.

John Holbrook: "I knew of Mick's earlier work but to see him in the studio was a thrill. There was a very good atmosphere. Mick was perfectly charming and we were bowled over by him. We taped the tracks in one hit over the course of a few days. I don't think the recordings were ever intended as a Bearsville Records release – Imhoff probably just got a good deal with the studio – but Mick's guitar sound was incredible."

Bobby Chen: "I looked up to Mick, but I didn't realise how good he was until I sat in front of him and we played a song. You knew he was incredible from the first few notes. Ronson's technique was amazing to me. He would play harmonics then bend the notes from behind the bridge of his Les Paul. You had to be with Mick in the studio to see the skill and all his little tricks. He still had the Gibson that he'd used on his earlier work. I remember the binding was damaged on it. He'd also stripped off the plastic tone and volume knobs and simply twisted the thin metal barrels underneath. He got truly astounding sounds from that guitar. Working with Mick was the epitome of fun, pure and simple. He was just off Dylan's tour and many came to visit. The track 'Just Like This' was a total party. We had anybody in the building come to Studio B and go nuts. It was mayhem, but it was the best of times. The house at Woodstock was wonderful. It was great banging out tunes sitting around this big fire and drinking Smirnoff into the night."

Where Tony Defries had envisaged a David Cassidy image for Mick, guitarist Mick Barakan recalls that Imhoff saw Ronson as the next Peter Frampton, because Barry believed Frampton was the thing to aspire to at that time. "Whilst Mick wanted to be successful, of course, he wanted to do it on his own terms," says Barakan. "He was focused in the studio and would procrastinate and put his lead playing off until the last minute because he was very much a first-take guitarist. He was extremely intuitive, and it was important to him that any engineer understood that and was prepared to press 'RECORD' at ANY time. If you were ready for that moment, you captured pure Ronson magic."

Recording sessions were interrupted when The Mick Ronson Band agreed to play some live dates across New York State and their Buffalo gig was attended by Atlantic Records chairman Ahmet Ertegun. Whilst there was talk of releasing the Woodstock tapes, and although Ronson and Imhoff met with Ertegun, the Atlantic LP never materialised. Barakan recalls that he and Ronson returned to Britain for Christmas but, on their return to America, the group's impetus faltered, even though they taped five more songs in Bearsville's Turtle Creek Barn. The earlier tracks that Mick had captured were amongst his best work, but when the hoped-for Atlantic arrangement flamed out, Ronson's project aborted and the tapes gathered dust.

On 23rd March 1977, Mick and Suzi married in Woodstock and held a reception in a private room of the town's first Chinese restaurant, owned by former Dylan manager Albert Grossman. Suzi was expecting a baby, and on 10th August Lisa Ronson was born. "In Woodstock one day, I literally ran into Mick Ronson and his manager Barry Imhoff in the Bearsville Studios driveway," recalls Mountain drummer Corky Laing. "Mick immediately invited me to his forthcoming wedding party, and I was stunned. I knew Barry through Bill Graham, but Mick went from 'musician stranger' to my new 'best friend' at his wedding dinner. The party seemed to go on magically, for days."

"We stayed in a wooden house in Woodstock with copper baths," says Suzi. "Mick had recently been on The Rolling Thunder Revue with Bob Dylan and was inspired. I became pregnant with our wonderful daughter during this time. We were very happy, still unaware how life can knock you about. The music was great and, for a while, we thought we'd cracked it. Barry Imhoff did a decent job for Mick but he had other business interests. We couldn't pay the Bearsville studio bill, so Mick's recordings were not released."

"The Ronson Bearsville Tapes" eventually surfaced in 1999. Credited to Mick Ronson, *Just Like This* revealed some of the guitarist's finest work and most heart-wrenching playing, exemplified beautifully on 'Crazy Love' and the stellar 'I'd Give

Anything to See You'. In 2018, Easy Action Records issued a seven-track LP on red vinyl, and whilst the songs remain astounding, the quality of The Mick Ronson Band recordings never surprised Hunter.

> **IH:** "In between playing on the road with various people – some who paid him, some who didn't and some who would hand him their bill at the end of a tour – Mick would go back to Woodstock to see Suzi, Lisa and his house on Glasco Turnpike. You never really knew what he was up to in Woodstock, but The Mick Ronson Band tapes had it all – the class, the quality, the emotion and the bits of fun that embodied all of Mick's work."

Ronson's other "post-Dylan" projects included sessions and production with Van Morrison and Dr. John, Philip Rambow, Annette Peacock's *X-Dreams*, Benny Mardones' *Thank God for Girls*, The Rich Kids' *Ghosts of Princes in Towers*, *Storm the Reality Studios* by Dead Fingers Talk and Slaughter and The Dogs. Mick's production of The Rich Kids, a band founded by Sex Pistols' bassist Glen Matlock, proved successful when their debut single charted. Matlock vividly remembers his first encounter with Ronson and Hunter.

"I first came across Mick Ronson when I was working in Malcolm McLaren's shop Let It Rock in the Kings Road," says Glen. "Ian, Mick and Suzi walked in one day and I was chuffed to meet them. Mick was interested in a pair of pink loafers and I had to get every box down in the shop to get the right size as he had tiny size 6 feet. We sorted out a pair that fitted and then Mick thought I was upset at having to pull all the boxes out. I told him I wasn't, but he was straight up the ladder putting all the shoeboxes back with me. He was a lovely bloke from the off. He wore those pink shoes on stage in Dylan's *Renaldo and Clara* movie. Later, when I was getting The Rich Kids together, I invited Mick down and he came with his guitar and ended up producing us."

Jim Rodford, bassist with Argent and later The Kinks, met Ronson at John Kongos' South London Tapestry studio, when Mick produced Hull band Dead Fingers Talk. "I first encountered Ronson in the Seventies when Argent were recording *Counterpoints* and Mick came in and listened to some of our tracks," said Jim. "He was a very charming guy. I met him again when The Kinks were flying, and The Hunter Ronson Band supported us in the USA. I remember Mick coming into the dressing room after their set one night with a Les Paul Gold Top and the headstock was broken off. He really went for it live. Ronson was a no-nonsense, cut-through guitar player and was vital to David Bowie just as Dave Davies was to The Kinks. Mick started something unique with his amazing sound and certainly speeded up Bowie's popularity."

On 23rd December 1977, Ian Hunter joined Pete Watts, Dale Griffin and Morgan Fisher for a British Lions gig at Friars Aylesbury and played 'All the Young Dudes'. Morgan recalls that it gave the band a lift throughout the set, knowing there would be "a cool surprise" at the climax of the show. Former Mott manager Robert Hirschman also re-emerged at this point and asked Ian if he would work with Mr Big, a group who had already scored a harmony-laden hit with 'Romeo' and supported Queen on their *Night at the Opera* tour. Mr Big's vocalist and writer Dicken (Jeff Pain), was another Hunter fan who wanted Ian to work on their third album. At Chipping Norton Studios in Oxfordshire, Hunter produced and added piano, organ and guitar during the sessions, while Peter Oxendale played keyboards. The end result was *Seppuku*, a hard rock assemblage that horrified EMI Records. 'Senora', co-written by Ian, was released as a single but the unreleased album languished in the vaults for over twenty years. A growing sense of disenchantment with the music business fell over Hirschman, but he has always retained admiration for Hunter.

Robert Hirschman: "I got out of the music business in the early Eighties and never had any desire to go back as you can only deal with frenetic people, in a crazy world, for so long. Ian Hunter has always been a terrific performer, though, as far as I'm concerned.

He was frustrated by Mott the Hoople, but he was also strong from an organisational standpoint and he knew how to take charge. With his voice and style, I think he did a brilliant job. Ian has charisma on stage, always has a fascinating point of view and writes interesting songs. Hunter is a very talented guy."

Back in New York, Ian met guitarist Jeff Salen again and made a guest appearance playing electric piano on two tracks for the Bob Clearmountain-produced album *Tuff Darts*, but Hunter felt it was time to re-engage with Ronson. Mick dabbled with forming another band, Rebel of Future, but talked with Ian about joining forces again. Before they recorded Hunter's fourth album, however, more extracurricular activity interposed when Ian agreed to collaborate with Corky Laing. The Mountain drummer had released a solo album, *Makin' It on the Street*, but Steve Wax, president of Elektra Asylum, suggested that Corky should record his next project with a band of "name musicians". Hunter and Laing duly wrote some songs, Bob Ezrin was drafted in as producer at Briarcliff Studios in Westchester and different "superstars" appeared. Initially, the sessions included Alice Cooper guitarist Steve Hunter, keyboard player Lee Michaels and ex-Free bassist Andy Fraser, but the project stalled; Steve went to work with Bette Midler, Lee and Andy left, and Ezrin flew to Britain to produce *The Wall* with Pink Floyd.

Undeterred and attempting to save the embryonic "supergroup", Corky called on 'Buffalo' Bill Gelber, session bassist for Todd Rundgren and The Leslie West Band, and keyboard player George Meyer, who had played in The Asbury Jukes and Laing's touring group. Amidst talk of naming Corky's band Pompeii, Meyer likened the set-up to Foreigner, but although the try-out was good, he recalls that Laing's label did not see him or Gelber as former stars. To prolong the project, Hunter suggested that they should engage Ronson, and Corky was soon observing Mick gracing his album sessions with joy and passion.

"When I was recording with Ian, without much persuasion Hunter got Ronson to play guitar for us," says Corky. "Mick and his inventive, creative, musical world were mysterious, spontaneous, unpredictable, elegant, smooth and unpretentious: all those words summed up Ronson and the notes that flew off his guitar neck, as he puffed away on a cigarette and delivered a bewildering sonic landscape."

Having lured Ronson, former Cream producer and Mountain associate Felix Pappalardi joined in too, Ronson prompting the music press that the foursome *was* forming a band, but *not* Mott the Mountain! Commuting from Chappaqua to the newly constructed Power Station Studio in New York, and later at Bearsville, the quartet taped a new Hunter song, 'The Outsider', plus the Laing–Hunter compositions 'I Ain't No Angel', 'Silent Movie' and 'Easy Money'. Then, amid corporate changes, the loss of Corky's champions at Elektra Asylum and much upset, the unfinished "Mott the Mountain" recordings were shelved until 1999, when they were released as *The Secret Sessions*. A 2018 Record Store Day LP, *Pompeii: The Secret Sessions*, was a further reminder of the chaotic circumstances that circled the project.

> **IH:** "Corky was one of those special guys who often tried to put something together. I'm very fond of him and we had some good times together. *The Secret Sessions* came about because Corky had a tenuous solo deal whereby his label was always telling him to involve as many of his 'notable friends' in projects as possible, so they could sell a few extra records. Corky's a very likeable character so he made it happen. *The Secret Sessions* album flew under the radar for twenty years, then finally appeared."

A second, curious collaboration occurred before Ian's solo sessions when Hunter Ronson played fleetingly with Corky Laing and John Cale, the songwriter and musician revered for his role in The Velvet Underground. Recorded in New York City, on 3rd June 1978, the fascinating "workshop" tapes comprised musical jams and random vocals, and were far more obtuse than *The Secret Sessions*.

IH: "John Cale was going to produce an album with Bob Neuwirth in New York and for some reason Bob got stuck on the West Coast. The Manhattan studio that had been booked was empty, so John invited Mick, Corky and me down for an off-the-cuff session. A lot of drink was imbibed and, as far as I can remember, we mucked around for a couple of days. Nothing was rehearsed and nothing was written down; it was simply free-form and all the lyrics were stream of consciousness. If I get excited enough, I can reel off words without writing them down. It was a great experience and a real guide in how to write a song. We'd jam for ages and suddenly it would turn into something. John would play any instrument or thrash away on some cheapo guitar making an awful din and they'd become songs, somehow. Some of it was pretty good and there were a couple of songs that Mick and I talked about doing, but they were just work-in-progress tapes. I think they were valuable because you see something coming out of nothing and the creative process, to some degree. If you're looking for results, there aren't any. It was looking into nothing for something. I recall one song that had the line *'Queen Elizabeth, you're just a luxury liner'*. I've always found Cale great to work with. John wanted to produce me once, but my label didn't trust him musically."

Some years later, Ronson heard that Cale was contemplating a retrospective release for the "workshop" sessions and Mick was happy for the tapes to be issued. The surviving tracks included: 'Baby Can I Take You Home', 'You Can't Always Get What You Want', 'What's Your Name Jane', 'Donald Duck is Dead', 'Lovin' Your Neighbour's Wife' and 'Slow Jam'. Ronson described the songs as a true rock 'n' roll album and Cale called the recordings world war improvisations, but the tapes remain unreleased.

In 1978, Ian had started writing what he termed "down songs", including 'Standin' in My Light', 'The Outsider' and 'Bastard'.

Ronson rated Hunter's new material and Ian felt the time was right to do something powerful again with Mick. Free from CBS, Hunter penned a new contract with Chrysalis Records, the deal happening by chance following a production request from label director Roy Eldridge. Chrysalis had signed British punk band Generation X and their bassist Tony James, another "Mott fan", proposed Hunter as producer for their second album; originally titled *Intercourse (Old Meets New)*, the album was released as *Valley of the Dolls*. Eldridge visited Hunter in Chappaqua to enquire if he would be willing to produce the group, but during their meeting Ian let Roy hear some new demos. Eldridge was impressed and asked Hunter to send more material to London.

"I'd been a big Mott the Hoople fan and knew Ian a little, having interviewed him when I wrote for *Melody Maker* and *Sounds*," says Roy. "Hunter was very cautious about the Generation X request and said he'd only do it if Mick Ronson would co-produce with him. I couldn't refuse as it seemed like a dream team to me and I knew Billy and Tony of Gen X would love the idea. It worked, but there was some icing on the cake. Talking to Ian that day about songs for the Generation X project he mentioned, almost in passing, that he'd been working on a bunch of new songs for himself and that he was out of his old record contract. He played me some tracks – 'Cleveland Rocks', 'Just Another Night' and 'Ships'. They were great."

IH: "I was pursued by Chrysalis and got flattered into producing Generation X, although I wanted my own new record deal at the time and their offer came when I was willing to take anything. I looked in the papers and saw Gen X were getting a lot of press. The band knew what they wanted and loved rock 'n' roll, but producing Generation X was bloody hard work because they couldn't really play. Der, the guitarist, was great and Billy Idol was singing high then. When Billy took it down an octave later on, things started to happen, big time. I wish I'd thought of that. The drums and vocals were a problem, but I got on with them great and it

141

was enjoyable. They were nice guys but I think I was a little too dominant. Anyway, we got the desired effect and 'King Rocker' was a hit single.

"Around this time Ronson came to stay with me, telling me about The Rich Kids and Dead Fingers Talk and how much he'd been paid for producing them. I freaked, because he was up to his usual stupidity. One night I said, 'You'd go and do anything for people who screw you and the people who help you, you'd shit all over them.' I think that was the first time I ever broke through. For a couple of months, I was on his case, for his own sake. Then with a David Johansen album, he was offered a certain fee and I said, 'Look, that's what they think you're worth, because you do it for these stupid fucking fees!' He got on the phone and told Blue Sky Records what he wanted, and he got very near to it, which was infinitely better than what he'd been getting. I went to David's *In Style* sessions and played a bit on 'Flamingo Road'; I remember that was a beautiful song. I'm a fan of David Johansen; he's always been the real deal, twenty-four hours a day."

David Johansen: "Mick and I enjoyed a cocktail a lot and when Mick moved to New York we'd hang out and he produced *In Style* for me. I would show him something on the organ or guitar and say, 'Let's get someone to play this', and he'd say, 'You're gonna play it.' I'd reply, 'No way!' and he'd say, 'Sure you are.' He was really encouraging. Mick had frosted hair and manicured nails and all that jazz; he was one of the cats. On his birthday I gave him a fine shark-skin suit which was very hip at the time and he asked, 'What do you want me to do with this.' I said, 'Wear it, you'll look good,' and with his thick Hull accent Mick replied, 'I don't give a fook how I look!' To me, that's funny. What a great human being. I dug him like crazy."

Following the Generation X sessions and Chrysalis signing, Ian also agreed a new management arrangement with the organisation that represented Meat Loaf, Jim Steinman and Ellen Foley: the Cleveland Entertainment Company. Operated by Steve Popovich and shareholders Stanford Snyder and Samuel Lederman, Hunter had first met 'Pops' in 1972, during Mott's 'All the Young Dudes' period. Popovich had started his career in the early Sixties stocking warehouse shelves and working his way up through the ranks at Columbia. He helped Epic sign The Jackson Five and was appointed Vice-President of Promotion at Columbia by Clive Davis in 1972, but now Steve had inaugurated the Cleveland International label. Notably, Popovich served up Meat Loaf to the world when no other record companies were hungry, and *Bat Out of Hell* shipped over 40 million copies worldwide. The Cleveland Entertainment Company would be dissolved in 1982, but Popovich maintained the Cleveland International Records imprint and was considered an enthusiastic music maverick and a promotional pusher who worked outside the corporate system. Ian always regarded Sam as a key figure in his career.

> **IH:** "By 1978, I'd become fed up with the surroundings I was in. I was dealing with people who'd always dealt with Mott and me on my own, but they preferred having the group and it got a bit silly, so I figured the only way I could feel fresh was to change things. It was hard to unravel, but I felt if I didn't, I'd regret it. Before my fourth album, Mick and I took a good look at each other and said, 'If we don't do something, we're fucked.' In 1975, Hunter Ronson had been a stupid state of affairs. Mick was under a management contract that made him more money from my records than me and it was very awkward as we were mates, but, eventually, we got it sorted. I signed with Chrysalis Records, run by Chris Wright and Terry Ellis, and found them to be thorough. I was with Roy Eldridge, a stand-up chap, and Chris, who I admire. I never felt pushed with Chrysalis and it was exciting for a while. Steve Popovich was a pretty famous guy within the business, and he heard what I was doing at the same time as

Chrysalis came calling. He had Cleveland International and he wanted to manage me, so, finally, I had management who I liked. That was a nice time, because I felt as though I was in with a shot and that people were really rooting for me. Pops was more than a manager and became one of my all-time heroes. He was a real-deal guy and a true friend, and so different from most people in the industry; a tireless fighter for what he believed in."

Following the Generation X production at Wessex Sound, Ian booked some session time there to kick-start his new Chrysalis album. By now, first-wave punk rock had abated, the new wave was bubbling, and a third-phase new romantic pop culture movement was evolving, all while traditional rock artists were dumped in the outdated file by most critics. The latest new acts included Duran Duran and Spandau Ballet, and some of them were identifying Bowie, Ronson, Mott and Roxy as primary influences. It seemed Ian had been spot on with the sentiments behind 'England Rocks'; he was now mentioned as a "godfather of punk" and The Clash were certainly one band who cited Hunter as an important figure. Apart from his Generation X experience, Ian had largely tracked new wave information via the British music press, while Ronson produced Dead Fingers Talk and The Rich Kids in the UK. Although Hunter felt that the movement didn't teach him anything new, he had observed the spirit, energy and "fuck you" attitude of British punk and was still interested in trying out some of his latest material in London.

The working title for Hunter's fourth LP was *The Outsider*, named after one of the songs attempted during *The Secret Sessions* with Ronson and Laing. *The Outsider* project commenced at Wessex Sound studios with engineer Bill Price, bassist Glen Matlock and former Jethro Tull drummer Clive Bunker, who had been introduced to bolster the Generation X sessions at Ian's suggestion.

"Mick Ronson and I went to Zanzibar's in Covent Garden one evening and Ian walked in," says Glen. "I told Hunter that night

"'Allo!"
Mick and Ian, AIR Studios, London, January 1975
Ian Dickson/Redferns

"The truth, the whole truth"
Ian Hunter and Mick Ronson, Colston Hall, Bristol, 1 April 1975
Michael Putland/Getty Images

"Boy"
Ian Hunter album sessions at AIR Studios,
London, January 1975

"Just a whitey from Blighty"
Zig Zag magazine cover, August 1976

"And this pizza's cheaper than the other"
All-American Alien Boy recording sessions, Electric Lady Studios, New York, January 1976:
Jerry Weems, Jaco Pastorius, Ian Hunter, Kevin Liguori and Philip Hays

"Energy calling me"
Ian during the *Overnight Angels* sessions,
The Coach House, Morin Heights, Canada, January 1977

"Welcome to the Club"
USA, Live 1979
Top: Ian, Tommy 'Mad Dog' Morrongiello and Mick Ronson
Bottom Left: Hunter and Ronson
Bottom Right: Ian Hunter at The Palladium, New York John T. Comerford III/Frank White Photo Agency

Opposite
"Can you hear us?"
Overnight Angels photo session, USA, 11 May 1977:
Rob Rawlinson, Peter Oxendale, Ian Hunter, Earl Slick and Curly Smith
Michael Putland/Getty Images

"We were there for you"
Hunter and Ronson, Paramount Theater, Asbury Park,
New Jersey, 1 August 1979
John T. Comerford III/Frank White Photo Agency

Capitol Theater, Passaic,
New Jersey, 21 October 1979
John T. Comerford III/Frank White Photo Agency

Onstage
The Ian Hunter Band featuring Mick Ronson, Rockpalast, Essen, Germany, 19 April 1980:
Hunter, Martin Briley, Ronson and Tommy Mandel
Laurens Van Houten/Frank White Photo Agency

Backstage
Dr Pepper Music Festival, Central Park, New York, 11 July 1980:
Mick Ronson, Ellen Foley, Mick Jones and Ian Hunter
Ebet Roberts/Redferns

"Theatre of the Absurd"
Short Back n' Sides sessions, The Power Station,
New York City, 13 February 1981:
Hunter, Ronson and Mick Jones of The Clash
Ebet Roberts/Redferns

"From the knees of my heart"
Trudi and Ian, October 1983
Family album photo

that what he really needed was 'a safety-pin band', so he asked me to come down to Wessex. We spent about a week there and recorded a few things with Clive Bunker. I think they had tried to get Simon Kirke from Bad Company originally. I remember we played rough versions of 'Bastard', 'Wild East' and 'Standin' in My Light' – maybe half a dozen tracks – but the material wasn't ready. I said to Ian that he was wasting money working things out in the studio at £40 an hour – that was a lot of cash then – and that he should go home and write songs. Me and my big mouth. He thought about it – and did!"

The Outsider sessions turned out to be brief because Steve Popovich, who knew Bruce Springsteen's pianist Roy Bittan, played some of Hunter's demos to Bittan and he liked what he heard. Ian loved working with former Mott engineer Bill Price and rated him highly, but, after a call from Popovich saying that The E Street Band wanted to record, Hunter Ronson quit Wessex and headed to New York.

> **IH:** "I started recording my fourth album in London, but it didn't feel right. After three or four days in Wessex studios, it wasn't really working and I didn't think it was going to happen. One night, Popovich rang me and asked me if I wanted to go back to New York and start again. He told me that the E Streeters were available and keen to do the record with me, so Ronno and I took the next plane out."

Lavatorial graffiti has been a source of amusement for decades and the art form provided a notable alternative title for Hunter's projected album after Mick Ronson found the slogan "YOU'RE NEVER ALONE WITH A SCHIZOPHRENIC" scrawled on a toilet wall in Wessex Sound studios. Ronson intended to use the phrase but Ian liked it, dropped *The Outsider* and traded the toilet title for a joint writing credit on one of his new songs. It was then ventured that Mick might call his next album *Bat Out of Hull.*

IH: "Mick really did find the *Schizophrenic* title on a bog wall in Wessex when we first started the album there. That tells you a lot about my powers of observation, because I recorded Generation X at Wessex studios for four weeks and never even saw the fucking slogan."

After meanderings with Mountain, Cale and Matlock, work needed to begin in earnest on Hunter's new album and sessions were booked at The Power Station in New York. Located on West 53rd Street in the mid-town West Manhattan area known as Hell's Kitchen, the building was previously an electric power plant that used to drive trams on Ninth Avenue. Subsequently a TV sound stage, the new recording studio featured breakthroughs in acoustics and engineering, including a magnificent wood-panelled live room. Chic and Ian Hunter were among the first artists to record at The Power Station but it soon attracted Lennon, Bowie and Aerosmith and would be the birthplace of The Rolling Stones' *Some Girls*, Duran Duran's *Seven and the Ragged Tiger* and Peter Gabriel's *So*.

Engaging an all-American team for the sessions, Hunter and Ronson would act as co-producers on *Schizophrenic* alongside music mixer and engineer Bob Clearmountain, who subsequently etched his name on Springsteen's *Born in the USA*, Bryan Adams' *Reckless* and Bowie's *Let's Dance*. Three members of The E Street Band were also engaged to provide musical support – pianist 'Professor' Roy Bittan, drummer 'Mighty' Max Weinberg and bassist Garry W. Tallent, who had recorded with Bruce Springsteen on *Greetings from Asbury Park, NJ* and *Born to Run*. Roy would also co-arrange Hunter's record with Ian and Mick.

The songs scheduled for *You're Never Alone with a Schizophrenic* included 'The Other Side of Life', 'Don't Let Go', 'Bastard', 'Standin' in My Light' and 'Cleveland Rocks', but, in two days, Ian adjusted and partially re-wrote seven numbers and rehearsed them with Ronson and the band. The *Schizophrenic* sessions were planned and played around Springsteen's touring schedule so pre-production, arrangements and periodic recordings for Hunter's album eventually spread over three months. This was followed by one energetic week for final recording and three weeks for mixing during January 1979. Ronson also slotted in sessions with Hilly Michaels and Jimmy McAllister for Roger C. Reale's second punk-pop album, *Reptiles in Motion*. When *You're Never Alone with a Schizophrenic* emerged, it was revealed as a beautifully balanced collection featuring surging rock, heartfelt ballads, superb drum sounds and striking production.

> **IH:** "When Mick and I recorded at The Power Station it had recently been used by Chic, who got a great sound. I'd done a couple of demos there, for Corky Laing as I recall, and Bob wanted rock 'n' roll acts to use it and asked me to come in. Clearmountain was fantastic. I remember Max Weinberg had just been to a college to learn more about recording drums and he and Bob argued so much at the beginning of our album. Then we started recording and I couldn't believe the sound we got. I'd wanted to use a rhythm section that was used to each other on *Schizophrenic* and they were great. Max was super and the drums were astonishing. Buffin was never happy with his drum sound in Mott, but Max was in for weeks learning how to tune his kit for the studio and it was amazing. We thought we were on to a good album when we went in, but the sound of The Power Station made it even better."

Released on 23rd April 1979, *You're Never Alone with a Schizophrenic* featured nine songs: 'Just Another Night', 'Wild East', 'Cleveland Rocks', 'Ships', 'When the Daylight Comes', 'Life After Death', 'Standin' in My Light', 'Bastard' and 'The Outsider'. The album title had been fortuitous and was not intended to be wholly serious, but the idiosyncratic reference seemed apt given Hunter's Gemini star sign. More appropriately, the songs on the LP would become almost evenly split, with four rockers and a ballad on Side One and four longer, more introverted tracks on Side Two, showing the other facet of Ian's character. After *Overnight Angels*, Ian had tried to assemble a band and the "down songs" on the second side of the new record came from those collaborations, while the "up songs" were written after Hunter removed himself from former label and management situations and became involved with The E Street Band. Ian knew that his best work was often written in the worst emotional times and that anger and negative emotions were great motivators. He also confessed that the songwriter within him was one facet of his character – an alter ego who was a truthful person, always looking for an idea and a source.

You're Never Alone with a Schizophrenic opened with a punchy drum intro from Max Weinberg, before Ian's spoken count-in and signature piano ignited the singalong, Stones-scented 'Just Another Night'. Described by Hunter as "rustic", the lyrics are based on a night that Ian endured in an Indianapolis city jail during Mott the Hoople's 1973 US tour. After a misunderstanding with an Indiana State policeman at the band's Holiday Inn hotel, Hunter was detained and spent his only free night on Mott's lengthy schedule locked in a cell with a Black Panther staring at him. Mott didn't bail him out, but, freed from court the next morning, after paying a thirty-eight-dollar fine, Hunter thought he could get a song out of the experience. It took five years to write.

IH: "The story behind 'Just Another Night' is true. I was locked up in Indianapolis after an incident in a hotel and I got mouthy with the management, one of whom was an off-duty sergeant. The next thing I knew I was in the communal cage. We were doing sixteen gigs in a row and that was our only night off. I spent it on a piss-stained bench while the esteemed Ariel Bender lay in my bed drinking fine wine that I had bought that morning. The funniest thing was that the cell was beneath the courthouse. At six the following morning people were discussing Mott's appearance but me, minus shades and looking about ninety, went unrecognised."

148

Surviving as a crowd-pleaser in Hunter's live repertoire for years, 'Just Another Night' was presented as "a rocker", but it was first taped as 'The Other Side of Life' in ballad mode, because Ian forgot the original, faster rendition. Several up-tempo takes were recorded at The Power Station, while the shelved ballad version would only be revealed as a bonus track on an anniversary *Schizophrenic* CD thirty years later.

> IH: "I was out of my mind when I wrote 'Just Another Night'. It was fast at first, then we tried to do it slow for two days at The Power Station, but Ronson suggested we try it the original way. I couldn't remember it so Mick showed me how I'd done it. The song was called 'The Other Side of Life' at first and was originally written as a rocker. Mick had a great memory and remembered the song exactly as we first did it. He also had the title from Wessex studios that I wanted, so we traded. It was credited as a Hunter Ronson song but Mick didn't write it with me. Like 'Boy' on the *Ian Hunter* album, I felt obligated to share 'Just Another Night'. I think we might have had a hit if Roy Bittan had got his way with 'Just Another Night'. There was a more commercial arrangement that Roy had worked out and it was good, but we thought it was too Springsteen. I had nothing against the mighty Bruce, but I didn't want a hit that sounded like somebody else. Roy was quite put out."

'Just Another Night' swaggered to a halt but merged seamlessly into the slow-burn groove of 'Wild East', featuring Hoople-style piano chords and blistering sax from George Young and Lew Del Gatto. The song carried slight echoes of Jerry Lee Lewis too, but an E Street strut made 'Wild East' the most underrated track on the album. Mildly energetic and melodic, the lyrics concerned the crazed East Side of New York City. Hunter has never said much about the song other than: "Wild West moved. New York!"

149

'Cleveland Rocks' was placed as track three on *Schizophrenic* and it would be the third UK single to be lifted from the album. After 'England Rocks', Hunter's ode to Ohio's city was now recorded in original form but given added spice by Ronson. The re-arrangement was smart and included a spoken introduction by Alan Freed, the superstar disc jockey credited with coining the phrase "rock 'n' roll". Freed's announcement fragment was taken from an April 1953 archive tape of his *Moondog's Rock 'n' Roll Party* radio show, aired on WJW Cleveland. Almost a natural successor to 'All the Way from Memphis', Ronson's clever guitar embellishments, Freed's radio greeting and the repeat *"Ohio"* effect on the coda made Hunter's track a memorable experience.

In 2018, *Classic Rock* published its 'Top Ten Ian Hunter Songs' and placed 'Cleveland Rocks' at the head of the pile, opining: "It is very difficult for anyone in the music business to write a hit single. It is even more difficult to write an anthem. Not many musicians have written songs that have reached beyond simple pop culture. Queen did it with 'We Will Rock You'. Metallica did it with 'Enter Sandman'. Ian Hunter did it with 'Cleveland Rocks'." Employed as a de facto anthem on Cleveland WMMS radio, Hunter's track found further exposure when it was recorded by alternative rockers The Presidents of the United States of America and was used as a victory song for Cleveland's sports teams and as the theme tune for the TV sitcom *The Drew Carey Show*. Almost an adopted son, on 19th June 1979, Ian was awarded the keys to the City of Cleveland by then mayor and future Democratic Congressman Dennis Kucinich.

> **IH:** "The Presidents of the United States of America covered 'Cleveland Rocks' and Drew Carey put it in his show. I didn't know that they did the Carey theme until I saw it on TV. It was fantastic and financially it was a big help to me. I thought great, that song isn't going anywhere for a while. Drew Carey took me to lunch at Universal one

day and was incredibly funny. We then took a tour of the sound stage but couldn't get in. He told me, 'There are three Careys – Mariah the diva, Jim the genius and Drew the lucky fat bastard.'

"The inspiration for 'Cleveland Rocks' came during Mott days when people used to make fun of the city. They claimed Cleveland was uncool, and LA and New York City were cool, but I didn't see it that way. Cleveland and Memphis were the first American places to embrace Mott the Hoople and Cleveland was the first US city where Mott sold out a gig. Meanwhile Johnny Carson and Mike Douglas were on TV shows, and Cleveland was treated like the Poland of America and I didn't like that. The East and West Coasts had their heads up their arses, but Cleveland was hip to us. I just thought, 'Wait a minute, if this town's such a joke, why are the people picking up on Roxy and Bowie and us? Nobody else is.' Memphis and Cleveland were great for Mott the Hoople. Rock 'n' roll breeds in industrial wasteland.

"After I recorded 'England Rocks' for a CBS single, and then Columbia didn't release it in the US because it was too regional, I re-did it as 'Cleveland Rocks' in honour of Cleveland and Alan Freed. I wrote the line, *'She's livin' in sin with a safety pin'* because there were a lot of punks around at the time; safety pin was my terminology for a punk goddess. The Drew Carey thing was enormous because once songs are out there, people can do them and if it's a hit, fantastic. 'Cleveland Rocks' has been my biggest earner."

The lush 'Ships' was a sentimental ode to Ian's father, largely written around the time of the "workshop" sessions with John Cale, although Hunter had laboured over the song for five years. Originally titled 'Ships That Pass in the Night', Ian composed the ballad for a man he affectionately described as "a bad-tempered sod", who had served his country in the army, police and British Secret Service before a stroke put him out of commission.

IH: "My father had a rough life and I was your typical idiot, so I didn't help matters. We had a terrible time, but the older I got, the more I realised what he'd been up against. He was a character. He was a lot nicer than me in some ways, but a regular bastard in other ways. He always looked at things intellectually. One day I saw some letters that he had written to his sister and he was dissecting my lyrics in the early days, saying, 'I think what he's trying to say is this,' and, 'I think he's driving at that.' My mum and dad always said to me that I was a writer more than a performer.

"I was really the opposite of my dad and 'Ships' is a song about that. I had an intense dislike of my father and he had an intense dislike for me. I felt that I should have perhaps been more patient with him, so I wrote the song and I'm glad I did. We bought my mum and dad a Sheltie dog once. Her name was Kayla and she had three pups and they kept them all. We used to take them for walks by the sea in Bispham on the Fylde coast and that is referenced in the song. My mother, father and brother Bob lived near Blackpool for many years and Dad heard 'Ships' before he passed away at home in Caxton Avenue in Bispham. It was nice that I made my peace with him before he died in 1980. That was important. After his death, my mum moved back to Shropshire. She was made up when I wrote 'Ships' but she was funny, saying, 'Typical. I do all the work, and he gets all the credit. Where's mine?' Mum had great taste in music, loved everything I did and compiled literally dozens of scrapbooks of my stuff, but she couldn't stand the music papers.

"It took me six years to write 'Ships' because I had the verses for a while but no hook. I was sitting with Max Weinberg one night and he happened to say, 'Ships that pass in the night.' That was two years of waiting. Also, if it hadn't been for Steve Popovich and Sam Lederman the song might never have been released. One night in The Power Station,

Pops came by with Sam and we were one track short for the album. So, I started playing and singing, *'We walked to the sea, just my father and me.'* Steve Popovitch loved the first verse, so I finished the song. I completed it quite quickly and it turned into 'Ships'. Sam made me write the chorus and Pops was responsible for it going on the record. Fred Heller had insisted that 'Irene Wilde' was special, and I never wanted 'All the Way from Memphis' out as a Mott single. Sometimes I can be a pretty bad judge of my own work."

Chrysalis Records issued 'Ships' as *Schizophrenic*'s second British single but chart success remained elusive until it was covered by American middle-of-the-road heart-throb Barry Manilow, whereupon his version hit No.9 on *Billboard*.

IH: "Some people have a laugh at Barry Manilow but he's a consummate musician. He was also Bette Midler's arranger so it was clever the way he did 'Ships' and kept changing key to create dramatic tension. Manilow recorded 'Ships' because he felt it encapsulated the relationship between him and his father who had recently died, which is a valid enough reason. Clive Davis was head of Arista at that time and he always liked my material. Barry went into Clive's office, Clive played 'Ships' and Manilow loved it and recorded it. I'm amazed he had such good taste. Financially, that was a great cover because it was not only in the Top Ten singles chart, but it was on an album that went Top Ten, it was on the *Greatest Hits* LP, it was on the live album – the thing goes on forever. Actually, Manilow rang me up and enquired if I could write different lines in the bridges for 'Ships'. I asked him why he wanted to do that. He said, 'Because my audience is comprised of idiots.' I told him I'd try, but I never did. For people who were upset with me for letting Barry do 'Ships', I couldn't stop him. Once a song is out there it's in the public domain. I first heard Manilow's version on a tour bus and all those key changes and modulations were odd; they had never occurred to me. I listened to his recording and my mouth fell open. You like your own songs best because that's the way you envisage them but Mr Manilow's version of 'Ships' was a lesson on how to make a hit. It helped him, and it helped me, because I was skint at the time."

'When the Daylight Comes' closed Side One of *Schizophrenic* and was lifted from the LP as the first British single release, but the song never sat comfortably with Hunter as he believed it sounded contrived. Ian had conceived spectacular hits with Mott the Hoople that he found acceptable, but he felt he could no longer write a single. He also lost interest in 'When the Daylight Comes' during the Power Station sessions, so Ronson, who was more enthusiastic about the song, shared the lead vocal with Hunter.

IH: "By this time, I felt it would be great to have a hit single but with a good song. 'When the Daylight Comes' sounds like a single and when a song sounds like a single, it's the kiss of death. A single is basically something that gives you the chills; it really is as simple as that. I didn't know what a single was anymore. Anyway, Ronson got involved on 'Daylight' and I just let him do what he wanted to do. Mick ended up singing the first two verses because I was talking with Bruce Springsteen and Ronson said, 'Come and do it.' I asked him to hang on a minute, but Mick said, 'Come and do it now, or I'll do it!' I said, 'Okay, you do it then,' and the bugger did. Bruce was a very nice, humble guy. I remember chatting with him and Meat Loaf in The Power Station one day and they asked me about phrasing vocals. I couldn't believe it. I said, 'You tell me – you sell millions of records – I sell a few thousand.' I lost interest in 'Daylight', but Ronson liked it."

Side Two of *Schizophrenic* opened with the dramatic 'Life After Death'. Bouncy and beautifully produced, the track featured

154

staccato piano, an arresting drum sound and another great Ronson guitar solo, while Hunter reflected and posed metaphysical questions about actuality and potentiality. *NME* condemned the song in a caustic review that reprimanded Ian and admonished his album, but Hunter was being tongue-in-cheek and playful. Like 'Wild East', 'Life After Death' is often forgotten and sits in the shadow of *Schizophrenic*'s higher-profile songs, but *Music Week* termed them two of the strongest cuts on the LP.

> IH: "Sometimes this stuff just comes, and you do it. 'Life After Death' was a piano track. I recall that the hook arrived first. I had the hook for a while and then the rest came later. I can't remember the lyric, but I'm sure it was how I was feeling at the time. It's just fun, and fear."

'Life After Death' was a light-hearted and up-tempo entrée to an evocative triptych of Hunter songs that still stand among his finest work. 'Standin' in My Light' is probably the centrepiece of *Schizophrenic* and one of Ian's most significant songs. Beginning with shimmering keyboards and an atmospheric drone, the song builds slowly and compellingly as Hunter gives an account of a new beginning in his life. He could have been addressing an obstructive partner or friend; he might have been targeting himself in another reference to the album's title; but Ian subsequently revealed that his former manager Fred Heller had been the lyrical stimulus and that the song had triggered the entire album when Hunter refocused following *Overnight Angels*.

> IH: "*Schizophrenic* started coming together with 'Standin' in My Light', right in the middle of my 'clear-out'. It was about my manager who was in the way. I've always had a hard time with managers. They want consistency and money. I think consistency is boring and my money should be mine. Never the twain shall meet. I remember they were doing some building work at The Power Station when we were working

on 'Standin' in My Light', so the workmen would all stop and watch when we did a take, and we'd have to stop when the car lift was in use. The track was tailor-made for Ronson as he loved slow, simple songs. Originally, I found the sound on a keyboard and decided that I had to write something around that sound. It turned out as 'Standin' in My Light'. I wrote the line about The New York Dolls as there was much ado with the Dolls and I resented it, because they lacked substance."

Schizophrenic's penultimate cut was an uncharacteristic love song – 'Bastard' – a sinister, brooding chunk of macho funk with a grinding beat, recalling *Black and Blue*-era Rolling Stones but with a crisper, spacey touch. Built on an infectious, gritty guitar riff, pumping percussion and discordant synthesizer lines from John Cale, Ian discharges verbal wrath – but the target was female, not male.

IH: "'Bastard' is a love song, and it is a she. It never runs smooth. There are millions of love songs and they all say the same things, but that was me trying to get a bit real. Sometimes with songs, it's the first line that starts you off. The opening phrase for 'Bastard' came to me on a journey from Woodstock to my house in Katonah with Mick and Suzi Ronson. It stuck with me all the way home. When you get a good first line, everything else gets a bit easier. I wanted John Cale involved as the song has that eerie, ominous thing that he can do so well. There is a musical aura about John and he has a contrary nature which I find fascinating. He's an amazing musician and one of those guys who has music running out of every pore, but you get the sense that John doesn't suffer fools lightly. He was a little nervous on *Schizophrenic* because he loves to work live, and he was overdubbing; he needn't have worried as he immediately captured the mood and enhanced the track. 'Bastard' came to me because I was sick and tired of sloppy love songs. It's

156

a good song and the opposite of most of the pap that's put out about love: a truthful love song as opposed to all the dreck."

Schizophrenic's concluding track, 'The Outsider', was an unusual Hunter composition but another fantastic vehicle for Ronson's swooping instrumentation. Ian's voice was stronger than ever on *Schizophrenic*, paired with beautiful piano on 'The Outsider', while Mick delivered thoughtful guitar configurations, including howling prairie wind sounds. Hunter's Western-style ballad closed the record in dramatic fashion; the production employed arresting echoes on the drum and vocal tracks, while the uncluttered recording created space for the music to breathe, adding clarity and charm.

IH: "Sometimes songs or parts of songs or a lyric line appear in your head from time to time. I often think I get songs that were misdirected to me and 'The Outsider' was one of them. I remember being embarrassed when I wrote it and I thought maybe it should have gone to a more countrified artist. I wasn't Roy Rogers, but some songs just arrive and I'm glad this one did. Everybody types me as a guy that writes hard rock songs, but I've always liked to write ballads. The slow songs on *Schizophrenic* – 'Ships', 'Standin' in My Light' and 'The Outsider' – were three of the best songs I ever wrote."

Ex-Fabulous Rhinestones drummer Eric Parker was subsequently drafted in by Hunter to add to *Schizophrenic* and it started a link that would extend to live work. Eric has fond memories of Ian and the two songs that he worked on: "I was playing with a band called Johnnie Average and The Falcons, and one night at the Joyous Lake, a famous club in Woodstock, Ian Hunter and Mick Ronson were two of maybe twenty-five people there. They approached me about doing some recording at Bearsville Studios and the

157

next day I played on *You're Never Alone with a Schizophrenic*, re-doing some of the drum tracks. I played on 'Ships' and 'When the Daylight Comes' because Ian had a new twist on both songs after he had cut them. Ian said the credits were already locked in for the LP, but he added me to the special thanks on the sleeve. We used Corky Laing's borrowed drum kit at Bearsville, so he got a 'thanks' too.

"Ian was always a gentleman and we would enjoy funny self-deprecating diatribes. He once said with a sly smile, 'Eric, are you taking the piss out of me?' I answered, 'Well, how much piss do you have in you?' He called me Lamb Chop and I still have my tour laminate with that name on it. Ian gave me the nickname as he thought I looked like Shari Lewis's puppet on the kids' TV show. Later, when I grew a thin moustache, he said I looked like a lost RAF pilot. Ian was funny and we often used laughter to break up the seriousness of the work we were doing. We set the bar very high and Ian said to me after one of my first shows, 'You're a great drummer, I don't need to tell you that, but tonight you played for all the drummers out there. Don't. I want you to play for me.' It changed the way I looked at music. It became much easier. In the studio, Ian could always sense when it was starting to get 'special'; that indescribable feeling when the band becomes one organism. Hunter was very tough on himself and his performance. Sometimes we would just play a groove and Ian would sing over it, and riff over it, and have me speed up or slow down to accommodate his vocals or guitar licks for hours. It wasn't just an open 'search' for things; we always found something!"

Springsteen drummer Max Weinberg was equally enthused about Hunter and the sessions: "I had a ball working on *You're Never Alone with a Schizophrenic*. Living legends Ian Hunter and Mick Ronson were fun yet serious and raving it up both in rehearsals and in the studio. Ian knew just what he wanted from the guys from E Street and I think we delivered. It was a great experience."

Close to the conclusion of *Schizophrenic*, Hunter and Ronson were lined up to produce St Louis-born Ellen Foley, Meat Loaf's blonde bombshell backing singer, on her debut album for Epic Records and Cleveland International. Ian agreed to the *Night Out* project to help Mick, but he soon resisted further production requests.

> **IH:** "The *Schizophrenic* album got Ronson a house, but he blew money, so the Ellen Foley production was largely down to Mick needing cash again. Money just came and went with Ronson; I don't know why. Also, people genuinely wanted us to produce their albums because of the first *Ian Hunter* record. In the mid-Seventies, production didn't really teach us anything except the energy level and we always got lumbered with people who couldn't play. It also annoyed me when people asked if I liked being a producer, because it meant they didn't understand me. What I do as a solo artist is good, but it doesn't catch on quick. It has always caught on to a certain extent, but it isn't Fleetwood Mac. I didn't particularly want to be Fleetwood Mac, although I wouldn't have minded their sales."

Meat Loaf's *Bat Out of Hell* had boosted Ellen Foley's profile and she had made some demos backed by Cleveland act The Boyzz, and sang alongside them at the Agora Ballroom with Ian, Mick, Meat Loaf and Karla DeVito for a Cleveland International showcase. When Hunter Ronson entered New York's Media Sound to record *Night Out,* they learned what a powerful vocalist Foley was, so the sessions leaned towards "big production" with Rolling Stones and Spector-flavoured renderings. Ian offered a shelved *Schizophrenic* ballad to Ellen, 'Don't Let Go', and he was pleased with the album production. Foley got on well with Hunter and when Ellen encountered Ronson, she was staggered.

Ellen Foley: "When I first met Mick, I was in awe. It was the Golden God of the Thin White Duke – the man who had the genius notion of recording 'Slaughter on 10th Avenue' on guitar – but as we started pre-production with Mick and Ian on my first album, I was relaxed by Ronno's softness, humour and complete accessibility. As a producer he didn't talk a lot. He worked on his feet with his guitar and played like nobody else. The brilliance that came out of him totally belied his self-deprecating wit. I was inspired by Ian's writing long before I met him and became his avid disciple, so much so that I did a demo of 'All the Way from Memphis' to get my record deal."

> **IH:** "Popovich and Lederman managed me, Mick and Ellen at the time, so the Foley project just happened. Ellen had a big crush on Ronno; this was before she went out with Mick Jones of The Clash, who did her second album. Ellen sold a lot of copies of *Night Out* and there were four or five hit singles on that record in my view. It became a huge album in certain countries. I remember in Holland she had a No.1 and Mick and I got these ridiculous cheques from the Netherlands. We both concentrated on making Ellen 'feel it' more and I think it worked out well. Mick did the subtler tracks and I did the blood-and-thunder bits. Ellen was lovely and easy to work with. I called her 'Effel'. As a singer she was more Broadway-based than rock 'n' roll, so to get her organic you had to get her plastered. You just had to hold Ellen down. She was wild and had a ballsy enormous voice, but she was a great girl and great fun too. I wrote 'Don't Let Go' and it would have gone on *Schizophrenic*, but I gave it to Ellen as I had enough ballads at the time."

Through producer Bob Clearmountain, Hunter also worked on David Werner's self-titled Epic album singing 'High Class Blues', while Ronson assisted Meat Loaf's backing vocalist and MainMan artist Genya Ravan on *And I Mean It*. For the track 'Junkman', Ravan expected to duet with Van Morrison, but Ronson suggested she sing with Ian – and the result was special.

"Mick Ronson was one of the most real people I met in my career," says Genya. "Nothing went to his head. If anyone could have played the 'big shot' card it could have been him. He was not only talented and stunning looking but also the most giving soul on the rock scene. I will never forget how he was always ready to apply himself to anyone who needed him. On 'Junkman', he allowed himself to be a sideman. He let me produce but was so available, pliable and giving. That's why that solo works the way it does. I told him I was waiting for Van Morrison to come off the road to sing the male part on 'Junkman' and he practically begged me to try Ian Hunter, so I did. Mick's vision was clear, and it was great working with Ian on one of my songs. Ian Hunter is a true rocker and there will never be another singer that has his honest approach to music."

You're Never Alone with a Schizophrenic became one of Ian Hunter's most popular releases. The record sold well for Chrysalis Records and was cherished by label director Roy Eldridge, who described it as one of his all-time favourite albums and a wonderful collection of timeless songs. Chrysalis press kits proudly announced: "Ian Hunter is back. One of the most important figures of Seventies rock has returned to the arena after a two-year hiatus. Hunter has come up with an ultra-hot studio sound that marks this as a hit record on first listening" – while the label's advertisements proclaimed: "The critics aren't in two minds about schizophrenics. Get together with yourself and listen. Both of you will be just crazy about Ian Hunter's debut album on Chrysalis Records."

Schizophrenic received rave reviews on both sides of the Atlantic, apart from lone assassins *NME* who slated Ian's work for "creative redundancy". *Sounds* described the record as a triumph, saying: "The album's got a feel of knowing exactly where it's going. It has confidence – you can't mistake this for anything other than a very fine rock and roll album." Simon Frith remarked in *Melody Maker*: "This is a spirited album. Once again (this was the third time) I'd written Ian Hunter off too soon." Peter Coyne penned a five-star review in *Record Mirror*: "Classic, classic, classic. *You're Never Alone with a Schizophrenic* is by far the strongest, most consistent album Ian Hunter has been associated with since the demise of

Mott the Hoople. There are no lows or peaks because like any classic album it has the feeling of continual flow and an aura of malignant lust, all of its own. *Schizophrenic* is a vinyl two fingers to anyone who thought Ian Hunter was finished."

The Guardian described *Schizophrenic* as "an impressive album" while DJ Annie Nightingale wrote in *The Daily Express*: "Rock Star Ian Hunter, rare survivor of the new wave revolution, is back in Britain with a solo LP that is one of the year's best so far." Giovanni Dadomo reflected in *Time Out*: "So Mott fans' younger brothers are far more inclined to buy the echoes of Hunter in the music of The Clash than check out the time estranged source. Pity that. There's four potential hit singles here – not bad by anybody's standards."

Paul Nelson of *Rolling Stone* praised 'Bastard' as an explosive song of venom, adding: "I'm sure M Jagger would cut off his most prized possession to write it these days. *You're Never Alone with a Schizophrenic* is my favourite record so far this year. Somewhat similar to *Street Legal*, it makes Bob Dylan sound sick. Not only do the fast songs here match the great rockers from Hunter's Mott the Hoople days, in some cases, they're probably better." *Hit Line* described *Schizophrenic* as an essential lesson in how to play rock 'n' roll, while *Billboard* considered that Hunter possessed timeless style and some of the most intelligent lyrics around.

IH: "*Schizophrenic* was the best experience, was quite star-studded with Bob Clearmountain, the E Streeters and John Cale, and everybody was serious about it. The only problem was it didn't have a single, although Chrysalis told me at the time it was the best record they ever put out. I wanted to hold it back for a single but the label was so gung-ho they released it. In retrospect, I wish we had held it back. Recording the album was a good experience. I remember that the backing vocalist, Rory Dodd, was a little nervous when we started and he was sitting on a stool with Ronson beside him. Mick observed this and to break the ice he said, 'Rory, do you want a cuddle?' Rory was fine after that. Mick

162

and I kept it simple. We put the tracks down and they would not accept a lot of things that we'd normally do. I was well prepared for the fact that it might not sell, but the way it went 'out of the box' shocked everybody. It shocked me. It was a big turnabout."

Ronson considered that there was good material on *Schizophrenic* but, looking back, he believed the guitar sound could have been a little heavier. Dan Loggins described 'Just Another Night', 'Cleveland Rocks' and 'Ships' as "classics" and felt the LP established Ian Hunter as a genuine rock 'n' roller in his own right. To promote his album, Ian appeared on the Dutch TV show *TopPop*, miming to 'Standin' in My Light', and Chrysalis UK released an edited single version of 'When the Daylight Comes', backed with 'Life After Death'. Presented as a limited pressing on white vinyl, *NME* described Hunter's "moderately animated, slightly chunky milky" disc as positive and purposeful. Chrysalis also issued 'Ships' and the press referenced it as "a near epic single" and "a song with genuine class", but neither 45 charted in Britain. American single releases of 'Just Another Night' and 'When the Daylight Comes' reached No.68 and No.108 on *Billboard*.

You're Never Alone with a Schizophrenic entered the UK LP chart on 5th May and stayed for a total of three weeks, reaching No.49. In the USA *Schizophrenic* hit No.35 on *Billboard* and charted for twenty-four weeks, the record's American success triggering six months of Hunter Ronson touring. As The E Street Band was not available for live work, Ian and Mick called on personnel from Ellen Foley's album, including bassist Martin Briley, keyboard player Tommy Mandel and drummer Hilly Michaels. The band also included guitarist Tommy Morrongiello and George Meyer on keyboards and sax. "I'd met Ian on the Corky Laing project and, some months later, Hunter called and asked me to tour with him behind the *Schizophrenic* album," says George. "Eight days of rehearsal and off we went. Ian and Mick were really good people and the whole band got along very well."

In 1976, Tommy Morrongiello had been the guitarist in Cherry Vanilla and Her Staten Island Band and Hunter had jammed with Vanilla one evening in Manhattan, at Tommy's request. When Cherry's band walked after one night of a week-long residency at Trude Heller's club, a makeshift group was assembled by Morrongiello quickly; Ian "filled in" on bass and Tommy, by then Vanilla's roadie, played guitar and called out the chords for each song on stage.

> **IH:** "I remember Tommy called me one morning and we played that night. I hadn't got a fucking clue what I was doing. A load of people sat at my table and told me how great I was and left me with a bill for 400 dollars at the end of the evening. That's what you get for a favour."

With *Schizophrenic* flying high, "The Ian Hunter Band featuring Mick Ronson" embarked on a mammoth American tour of seventy-nine concerts extending from June to November 1979. At their opening gig in Asbury Park, The E Street Band joined Ian and Mick to reprise 'Just Another Night', and other concerts featured guest appearances from Ellen Foley, Rory Dodd and Meat Loaf. Three shows were recorded by Chrysalis at My Father's Place on Long Island, the Cleveland Agora and the Berkeley Community Theater in California, and track selections were broadcast on FM radio. The Cleveland concert and a September gig at Ryerson College Theatre, Toronto were filmed for television broadcast and the band also appeared on *The Friday Show* and *Midnight Special*.

Hunter's concerts were greeted with absolute acclaim. *Rolling Stone* wrote of one performance: "Ian Hunter couldn't have been upstaged, as he teased, cajoled and badgered his audience into exuberant submission." *The Los Angeles Times* enthused: "Lashing, sneering, going straight for the throat, Hunter benefitted from his keen sense of drama and a deeply ingrained bond with his audience." While *The Oakland Tribune* proclaimed: "After listening to two hours of the best rock and roll music to hit the Bay Area this year, the audience screamed, stomped and cheered its agreement with Hunter." Gigs at the New York Palladium and Cleveland Agora received great reactions and Ian's band were enthused by the tour in a variety of ways, Tommy Mandel describing Mick as the older brother he never had.

Tommy Mandel: "The Hunter Ronson Band was my first professional-level rock touring experience. Having never been a Bowie fan I wasn't hip to Mick's legacy, but it was obvious that he was twice as real as most of the musical directors I'd met to that point. He had this faraway look on his face when he played, as though he never expected to be in that moment, playing that particular song, even if we'd done it fifty times. He'd just plug his guitar into the amp and get all that sound from his fingers on the wood, without overdrive boxes or chorus pedals. After some gigs, the fingers of his left hand would be bleeding at the cuticles from where the sweat-slippery razor-sharp strings slipped and cut into them, from his bending the notes with such force.

"I do remember that Mick really had a thing for hot food. At truck stops he'd order their hottest chilli and then dump packets of pepper and hot sauce on top of it before eagerly downing it. It almost looked like he was preparing a prank for a fellow at school, making atomic fire food to see the lad turn maroon, but Mick would EAT it, like it was nothing special. That can't have been the healthiest thing to do. Working with Ian and Mick was always an electric experience and never, ever dull – well, three Geminis – so that's *at least* six brains! As the first major recording and touring talent to recognise my potential, Ian Hunter changed my life – I'd say firmly, but gently – but that might sound like I was describing Harry Reems sampling grapefruits. In the beginning, I only understood half of what he and Mick were saying, so I just kept saying 'Yes!' Hanging out and sitting in with Hunter is sublime."

Martin Briley: "I first met Mick when I played bass for Ellen Foley and Ronson and Hunter were producing her debut album. I'd worn out my copy of *Hunky Dory* and loved the string parts Mick wrote for 'Life on Mars?' You could tell it was an arrangement done by a guitar player. I confess I was a little in awe of Mick Ronson. Then again, I was easily intimidated by men who wore more mascara than I did. He also had serious rock star hair. Ronson was completely different to what I'd originally expected. He was as unlike a rock star as you could imagine. He was kind, patient, down to earth, respectful, diplomatic and, of course, ridiculously funny. What a great laugh he had. I always looked forward to being with him. I rarely saw him lose his temper. He could also be endearingly humble, sometimes to the annoyance of rock writers. Quite often on the road Mick would be approached by journalists writing for guitar magazines and he was always ready for the obvious and inevitable questions about 'how he got his sound'. With a fairly serious look on his face, he would tell them that someone rents him an amplifier, he plugs in his guitar and that's how he gets his sound."

Tommy Morrongiello: "I remember one night when we were playing up in Portland, Maine, at the Cumberland Civic Center. Somewhere in the show, we're singing away, and Mick's guitar is singing too. He bends down to the crowd, allowing them to strum his Les Paul. One hyper-excited fan grabs the strings and yanks a bit too hard and the guitar's headstock breaks clean off its neck. The fan is appalled but Mick is amused. He swaps over to his Telecaster and we complete the show. The next day, Ian takes Mick down to a music store where Mick points to a guitar up on a wall and says, 'I'll have that one.' Ian says, 'Aren't you going to PLAY it first.' Mick replies, 'Why? It's just a piece of wood with six strings on it.' So, the days and shows go by and at one soundcheck Ian finds Mick dejected-looking, sitting on the edge of the drum riser. Ian enquired, 'What's wrong, Mick?' – and Ronson said, 'I can't play me guitar.' Ian replied, 'Why not? It's just a piece of wood with six strings on it!' They had a relationship that was fun to watch – and great music came out of it."

IH: "Ronson was classically trained – a violinist and pianist. The quality of what he could play was amazing. Mick was always in or around his amp checking what he could get

out of it in terms of sustained feedback, but he also used a strange finger configuration whereby he didn't stretch two or three strings at once, only the one he wanted. His little finger was flat, and the nail distorted so that he would bend beneath the other strings. Why pull them all when you only want one. He was also a strange player. He would think out a solo before he played it and he wasn't that fast as a player, which I thought was a good thing. He would imagine the complete solo, so you would write a song and he would write the solo before he picked up the guitar. Then when he picked up the guitar, it would often sound revolting, because he was trying to get from his head to his hands. Sometimes I've walked out of the room and then, all of a sudden, you start hearing this pure thing coming out. Sometimes it took an hour, sometimes more. It was often funny on sessions for other people because they didn't know what he was doing. I remember Meat Loaf saying, 'What the fuck's he doin'?' – but Mick wrote the solo in his head and then converted it to the melody that he would play. So, he always had a song within a song, which to me is a great idea."

By August, drummer Hilly Michaels left Ian's band to pursue a solo career and was replaced by Eric Parker, who had toured for six months with guitarist John Hall, opening for Little Feat. Eric recalls Ian inviting him to an audition, termed "a formality", at Full Tilt Rehearsal in New York; he also remembers fantastic times touring with Hunter Ronson.

You're Never Alone with a Schizophrenic first appeared on compact disc in 1993, when New York label Razor & Tie released the album as "a heavily requested reissue". This was followed by a Chrysalis Records limited edition long box (1994) and an EMI *Classic Rock Series* CD (1999). In September 2009, EMI Chrysalis marked *Schizophrenic*'s thirtieth anniversary with a special package containing the original album, studio bonus tracks and a second CD of live cuts compiled from three concerts. The previously unreleased studio takes on Disc One included 'The Other Side of Life' that Hunter had considered "too Bruce", Ian at the piano demoing 'Don't Let Go', and early versions of 'Daylight' and 'Ships'. A subsequent EMI Chrysalis compilation would feature 'Alibi' from the *Schizophrenic* sessions, which Hunter had forgotten he'd recorded, and an alternative version of 'Just Another Night'.

1979 had been an astonishing year for Ian and *You're Never Alone with a Schizophrenic* will always stand tall as an exceptional rock record. The album re-affirmed that Hunter reached stellar heights when his work was underpinned by Ronson's guitar and creative arrangements, and Ian has always remained enthusiastic about the *Schizophrenic* era.

> **IH:** "*You're Never Alone with a Schizophrenic* was one of the best solo albums I ever did but it was panned by the English rock critics because I was a US resident – very small-minded. The album was people getting down to business and really working hard. Bob Clearmountain was just about to take off and we had Cale coming in for odd sorts of things like 'Bastard'. The E Streeters were all extremely nice people and nothing was too much trouble. Roy Bittan argued with me passionately over a couple of things and was totally committed, and so were Garry and Max. I've seldom heard a better band. Working with Ronno and John Cale made *Schizophrenic* a much better album. Mick was full on, and it was one of the earliest albums ever recorded at The Power Station.
>
> "Only once in my entire career did I feel that I had the whole set-up right and that was *You're Never Alone with a Schizophrenic*. Management was right – label was right – the rest of the time it was a matter of no management to speak of – and no record label. *Schizophrenic* was one of the more positive experiences. All the songs were good and it was done well. Good albums are fluky. *You're Never Alone with a Schizophrenic* was a combination of good musicians, good

studio, good engineer, good co-producer and a few good songs I'd put together while Mick was away. Fluky!"

After a two-year hiatus, Hunter had struck back with one of the hottest albums of his career. Now, commercial opportunity was back on the agenda at Chrysalis Records.

CHAPTER FIVE

From the Knees of My Heart

So, you're back in the big league again.

Following the excellent critical and public reaction to *You're Never Alone with a Schizophrenic*, there was inevitable discussion between Ian Hunter and his label about delivering another studio album – swiftly! Chrysalis Records sought to capitalise on Hunter's chart success, but Ian rarely wrote on the road and had few new songs prepared. Eager to maintain the momentum that had been generated, Chrysalis and Cleveland International convinced their artist to record a live album instead. Ian remarked at the time that his manager, Steve Popovich, had pushed for "some kind of collection"; however, whilst he succumbed, Hunter wasn't particularly excited as he always received a greater kick from new songs. Ian was actually more intrigued about how his next studio album might sound but a live record would put Hunter's musical past in focus as the preface to a new decade and offer fans an impressive memento of a memorable tour.

IH: "Because *Schizophrenic* had done so well, Chrysalis wanted another LP. Such is life in the record biz. Of course,

I had nothing in the can and was empty in terms of songs, so the decision was taken to do a live album but with one side of new material, live in the studio. I didn't want to put a live record out in the first place because I wanted another one like *Schizophrenic*, only better. I probably could have gone into the studio again around October but they wanted to keep my name going."

Chrysalis duly captured "Ian Hunter Live", employing Le Mobile studio and engaging recording engineer Harvey Goldberg, who had worked with Mick and Ian on the recent David Johansen and Ellen Foley sessions. Following seven days of rehearsals in San Diego and two gigs at the Old Waldorf in San Francisco, Hunter Ronson "Rocked the Roxy", playing a week of sold-out shows at the West Hollywood venue where Frank Zappa had recently recorded most of his live album, *Roxy & Elsewhere*. Chrysalis taped six sets from Monday 5th to Sunday 11th November 1979, Hunter's run breaking the record for the most consecutive nights booked at Sunset Boulevard's world-famous club. Ian's upcoming live album was first announced as *From the Knees of My Heart*, one of his more striking titles, but it would be released as *Welcome to the Club*.

IH: "The Roxy week was good fun. I remember fans sitting on the street all day, every day, outside the club and we dropped by to say hello. We had the Scottish comedian Billy Connolly there as support and he was supposed to open for us all week, but he left after the first night because nobody would listen to him. Billy was headlining in Toronto the following week and was worried about losing his confidence. It must have been the accent. He never had a problem on the East Coast, but they just couldn't get it in LA, and the audience kept talking and drinking throughout his act. It was a bummer, because I liked the guy and was really looking forward to meeting him. I remember Jack Nicholson was

171

hanging out with the owner upstairs. I was also told that Cher walked out on us one night after we played 'Laugh at Me'."

British fans received only one opportunity to witness Hunter Ronson in concert when the duo played a sold-out show at London's Hammersmith Odeon on 22nd November. Some followers mingled with their heroes the day before the gig, when Ian and Mick participated in a signing session at Our Price record store in Kensington, an event attended by Steve Hyams, a friend of Hunter's from the early days of Mott the Hoople.

"I was wandering down Kensington High Street and noticed people lined up outside a record shop," recalled Steve. "Ian and Mick were doing an excellent PR job, signing albums and photos, and fielding questions… 'Are you going to reform Mott?'… 'When are you going to play with Bowie again?'… all received with laconic thanks and tired smiles. They asked me to hang on for a little while and when they had finished their signing session we went off for lunch. We had a good old chat and Mick, as always, was cheeriness and politeness itself. I loved the way Ronson phrased his guitar playing; not too many notes but always in the right places. I think he was an instinctive player. Whenever I heard Mick's name, I always recalled his guitar on 'The Jean Genie'. He was spot on!"

To coincide with Hunter's Hammersmith concert, Chrysalis released a third British single from *Schizophrenic*, 'Cleveland Rocks' backed with 'Bastard', but it didn't threaten the charts. During their London visit, Ronson denied that he had plans to form a new Mick Ronson Band. The press and posters for the Hammersmith show advertised 'The Ian Hunter Band featuring Mick Ronson' but the guitarist said: "That might help to sell a few tickets, which is fine, but for me to start doing my songs on Ian's albums would be wrong. I want to play but I don't have any great ambitions to see my name in lights. I don't particularly want to be a big star. I'm past all that. I'm quite happy the way I am."

Hunter's stunning Hammersmith performance was recorded by Chrysalis Records to secure further source material for Ian's projected live album and an edited tape from the show was broadcast on BBC Radio One as a sixty-minute *In Concert* programme. The London set featured 'Laugh at Me', 'The Golden Age of Rock 'n' Roll' and 'Life After Death', while die-hard fans wryly noted Ian's reference to *Brain Capers* and his affectionate dedication to Mott mentor Guy Stevens prior to 'Sweet Angeline'. The Hammersmith gig was attended by Mott drummer Dale Griffin, although he subsequently denied being there.

Following "the second coming", as one journalist described Ian's concert appearance, luminaries accompanied Hunter Ronson to a Mayfair hotel, the aftershow celebration involving Mick Ralphs, Dale Griffin, Mick Jones, Ellen Foley, The Skids, The Pretenders, Kirsty McColl, Philip Rambow, Pete Townshend and Ian's mum. When a cameraman doused the party with a fire extinguisher and a massive floral arrangement was destroyed, Hunter Ronson's entourage left. The Who's infamous guitarist followed to Ian's hotel and, when Townshend was denied access, Hunter intervened.

> **IH:** "That after-gig event was another dose of the fucking stupidity that confronts bands in British hotels. I remember doing an interview with Anne Nightingale for *The Old Grey Whistle Test* show at that godawful hotel and that was the night I had to fish Pete Townshend out of a police car! Keith Moon had passed away a year before and I suggested to Pete that night that The Who should go for Aynsley Dunbar; he didn't listen. At the Hammersmith Odeon show I gave my guitar away to a guy in the crowd, then the roadies got it back but I promptly gave it away again. It was the smoky grey Les Paul featured in the picture inside the *Welcome to the Club* sleeve. It's hard to give a guitar away, so I must have wanted to give something back. Eventually the kid got it but other kids wanted pieces of it, so it got torn apart. I meant

173

well, but really it was a dumb thing to do. I had two of those Silverburst Limited Edition Les Paul Customs from Manny's guitar shop in New York. They were two of only five very solid exotic rosewoods built for some exhibition and they sounded great, but were much heavier than a normal Les Paul, which I could handle. I couldn't be bothered with the Silverbursts and got fed up lugging them about. I remember trading one to Earl Slick for one of the first Steinbergers ever made, a prototype of the sled design guitar."

The live reviews for Hunter's Hammersmith show were magnificent, *Record Mirror* describing it as the best gig of the year. *Music Week* enthused: "This was rock 'n' roll my dear brethren. At a triumphant sell-out, one-off concert at Hammersmith Odeon, Hunter hurled musical hellfire and brimstone from the pulpit. All in all, it was a thundering great performance. This was a night to remember." *The Guardian* called Ian's performance: "A memorable rousing exhilarating show and evidence that there is still life in the old wave yet; an immaculate set of timeless-sounding mainstream rock." Even the *NME* enthused; having damned *Schizophrenic* they highlighted 'Standin' in My Light' as the finest moment and "a perfect statement of intent", noting: "Hunter harangued repeatedly on the song's title, striking out at the auditorium, informing them in no uncertain terms that he will not lie down and disappear – that he can take on the youngbloods if they choose to fire the first salvo!" During his London visit Hunter was presented with a gold disc for sales of *You're Never Alone with a Schizophrenic* and spoke of his working relationship with Ronson.

> **IH:** "We just seem to take it one stage at a time. Initially we were only going to tour for a month. That turned into five months, which turned into a live album and that'll turn into something else. I think it's better for us both if we don't know exactly what we're going to do. When we don't know what's happening, we work harder."

After his London conquest, Ian returned to America to rehearse a new live set with a potential six-date UK tour anticipated for April 1980. Before he left Britain, he starred on Radio One's *Roundtable* review programme and *Star Special*, where he indulged in playing records by Jerry Lee Lewis, Little Richard, The Rolling Stones and Roy Wood. At the time, Ian was also considering moving away from New York.

> **IH:** "I came out of the sticks to London and it was a big change for me. I went from London to New York and it was a big change for me. Now I'm looking at Mexico. It's dangerous to stay in one country all your life. I like moving around."

Ian and Mick had played six-week treks before, but never six months, so, following some Christmas recuperation, after their longest ever tour, Hunter, Ronson and Goldberg convened at New York's Media Sound Studios to mix the Roxy live tapes. Harvey Goldberg had commenced his engineering career at Media Sound, an ambient West 57th Street studio constructed in a former Baptist church and a hit machine through the birth of Seventies disco. On 10th and 11th January, Ian and his band taped three songs at "The Church", aimed at meeting the Chrysalis Records mandate that Side Four of the forthcoming live album would feature new songs, billed as "Live in the Studio" – music-biz parlance for organically edited and mixed songs without any artificial overdubs. "I never like live albums," remarked Hunter at the time. "It's hard mixing them because you've heard it all before."

At Media Sound, Hunter Ronson also assisted Cleveland International act the Iron City Houserockers, when Mick co-produced and arranged *Have a Good Time But Get Out Alive!*, Ian contributing some instrumentation, backing vocals and production on two tracks. Mick also guested on The Johnny Average Band album *Some People*, while Ian produced 'Dangerous Eyes' at Media Sound, a single for New Jersey group Sam the Band, who were known to Tommy Morrongiello.

Immediately prior to the issue of Hunter's live album, his former label decided to capitalise on the success of *Schizophrenic* with a double LP set, titled *Shades of Ian Hunter: The Ballad of Ian Hunter & Mott the Hoople*. Compiled in 1979 and released in February 1980, Columbia devised one disc devoted to Mott with a second reflecting Hunter's three CBS solo albums, including five *Overnight Angels* tracks that were previously unavailable in America. The Mott disc included the band's exceptional B-sides 'Rose', 'Where Do You All Come From' and 'Rest in Peace', American single edits of 'One of the Boys', 'Sweet Jane' and 'All the Way from Memphis', and a 1974 Broadway recording of 'Marionette' omitted from *Mott the Hoople Live*. David Gahr's grainy 1975 monochrome portrait photographs for *Shades of Ian Hunter* suited the moody gatefold artwork, but the sleeve notes were minimal. *Record Mirror* contemptuously described the compilation as: "CBS milking the man and the Mott. A nifty collection though CBS, bearing in mind the fact that they slung out a Mott greatest hits not so many years back, do seem to be punishing the lad for his recent move to Chrysalis. I'm sure he'll refuse the royalty cheques." American writer Robert Christgau described the *Shades of Ian Hunter* album as exemplary and a genuinely obsessive compilation.

> **IH:** "*Shades* was something Columbia put out because *Schizophrenic* was doing well and they wanted a piece of the action – jolly unsportsmanlike if you ask me. It was well compiled but fortunately they didn't spend much on promoting it, which was fine, because the idea of two double albums coming out within four or five months of each other, containing some of the same songs, sounded like a rip-off."

Originally scheduled for March release, Hunter's live album was issued by Chrysalis on 4th April 1980 to cushion the clash with Columbia's hybrid collection. Ian had opened his Roxy sets with the audience greeting "Welcome to the club" – and closed proceedings with "I would like to thank you, from the knees of my heart." Sadly, the original and imaginative *From the Knees of My Heart* title was dropped, and the LP hit record shelves as *Welcome to the Club*. The front cover boasted bold graphics in bright primary colours, while the inner gatefold housed an array of live photographs, capturing the band on stage with Ian amidst the invading Roxy audience. The rear of the album sleeve featured a Hunter Ronson image and carried a simple instruction, PLAY IT LOUD! Ian's shows, and therefore the live album, opened with Mick's trenchant guitar on a vibrant version of Peter Gormley's 1961 instrumental 'FBI'.

> **IH:** "That was originally a Shadows song that featured Hank Marvin on lead, and he was to have a major influence on British guitarists. Mick changed 'FBI' around a bit and it was our opening tune for several years. Ronson loved The Shadows, a fact that I always took the piss out of him for, at every opportunity."

Sides One to Three of *Welcome to the Club* featured sparkling renditions of classic Hunter material, while Side Four housed four new tracks, albeit 'Sons and Daughters' and 'Silver Needles' had originated some years before. 'We Gotta Get Out of Here', featuring Ellen Foley and Suzi Ronson, was a melodramatic slice of pop rock with a spoken section from Ellen and lyrics that mocked disco music. The genre, led by Studio 54 – a nightclub located in a former Broadway theatre once purchased by CBS – was reaching a commercial peak and it was ripe for satire. Unimpressed with the dancing and music trend, in most live settings Hunter altered his chorus lyric on 'Cleveland Rocks' to *"Disco sucks"*.

> **IH:** "'Disco sucks' on *Welcome to the Club* may have been based on Studio 54. I only went there once, by invitation, and passed the sorry line of hopefuls outside. There was a half-empty room full of stupid flashing lights, lawyers, accountants, hookers, weekenders and lousy music. Donna Summer was the only one to come out of that. Most of those

disco singers deny they ever sang it. What a fucking joke! 'We Gotta Get Out of Here' was a nod to what was going on at the time and a not too successful stab at a single, so I'm not fond of the song in retrospect."

'Silver Needles' was Hunter's moving lament for a deceased rock star. Reviewers assumed the piece was an expression across the ether to notorious Sex Pistol Sid Vicious, who had died in New York in February 1979, but an embryonic portion of the song had been rehearsed with Mott the Hoople in 1973. Ian mentioned that the lyric was inspired by Sid's decline and fall from grace but there were other influences in play, including Tommy Bolin. Like 'Boy', 'Silver Needles' was another composite account.

> **IH:** "Apparently, I signed a book for Deep Purple guitarist Tommy Bolin once and gave him some advice he unfortunately didn't heed. I can't help thinking 'Silver Needles' is loosely based on Tommy and a lot of other victims of that era, but the song included Sid Vicious to the best of my recollection. It was also me trying to write about somebody who died that believed the press. I've always believed that the press should mirror, not lead, music."

'Man O'War', a confident, tongue-in-cheek, twelve-bar, Stones-style rocker, was written by Hunter and Ronson. Following the Dylan experience, Mick had become more open musically and, having employed Fender Telecasters and a Stratocaster on the *Schizophrenic* sessions, for the Media Sound tracks he used a guitar offered by Harvey Goldberg. 'Man O'War' carried a musical kick and sounded great, but Chrysalis Records was concerned that the song had "unsuitable airplay lyrics", while Ian was never enthusiastic about the track.

> **IH:** "Mick and I weren't keen on 'Man O'War'. It was a last-minute-put-together effort because I was empty after so

much touring, but the decision had been taken to do the live album with a side of new material. They had me playing live all the time after *Schizophrenic* and I can't write on the road, so I pretty much dried up. In preparation for the fourth side, I was trying desperately to write new stuff in San Diego where we were rehearsing for the Roxy week. Nothing!"

A live recording of 'Sons and Daughters' closed Side Four of *Welcome to the Club*, Hunter's suburban country-style ballad echoing the lyrical content of Mott the Hoople's 'Waterlow'. Another autobiographical tale, the song referenced London's Archway, alluded to Ian's divorce from Diane in the early Seventies and lamented the separation from his two children, Stephen and Tracie. Hunter revealed regret, but also disdain for the allure and trappings of showbusiness, with references that bemoaned stardom.

> IH: "'Sons and Daughters' was a song about a long divorce, and guilt and pain and you can never put it right again; a true story."

Hunter's three new studio songs had been attempted on stage two days before the Media Sound sessions, when the band recorded their 8th January gig at My Father's Place on Long Island. 'We Gotta Get Out of Here,' 'Silver Needles' and 'Man O'War' were played twice during the set to try to add genuine "live" songs to the upcoming album, but Ian was unwell on the night and was not happy.

> IH: "We went to My Father's Place and tried to do those songs. At that time, we had been off the road for six weeks and the band just didn't get it, so we couldn't use them and recorded live in the studio instead. We'd played the Roxy for seven nights and recorded each night, but the live LP is mainly from the Sunday night, the last show. It had to be edited, which is a drag because we could only put

179

live stuff on three sides – maybe sixty minutes – but we had 106 minutes of solid material. We had to take 'One of the Boys' off and cut a lot of the crowd responses; there's always a fucking compromise. Like *You're Never Alone with a Schizophrenic*, Chrysalis came up with the cover for the live album. I thought the *Schizophrenic* artwork was very good; I thought the cover was very average for *Welcome to the Club*, but that was a good live album."

Chrysalis Records' press kit and adverts for the record declared: "Ian Hunter proves he puts on the hottest show in town on this double live album. It's all here on *Welcome to the Club*. If you thought all ballads were wimpy, or all heavy rockers were just noise, you haven't heard a master like Ian Hunter at work. Recorded live with no overdubbing, Side Four contains a quartet of brand-new Hunter classics. One Warning: Don't be surprised when *Welcome to the Club* rattles the windows and shakes the floors. Everything you really need to know is right there in the grooves."

Welcome to the Club entered the British chart on 26th April and stayed for two weeks, peaking at No.61, as it hit No.69 in America. The collection remains a remarkable live representation of Ian's Seventies repertoire, capturing a full-blooded set as Hunter seamlessly blends Mott and solo classics, applying blistering twists to older songs like 'Angeline'. On a dusted-down, light-footed version of 'Laugh at Me' from *Mott the Hoople*, Ian toys with the audience, saying, "This is an old song, done a new way. It may not be the best way, but it's the latest way." *Welcome to the Club* was an exciting live album; it successfully bottled the explosive energy of Hunter Ronson in concert and was charming, not just for the depth of the songs but also for the delivery and connection between Ian, his band and his audience. Chrysalis was happy and Roy Eldridge, who had signed Hunter to the label, marvelled at a passionate and powerful live act.

"Ian and Mick toured together with one of the hottest rock bands I've ever heard," says Roy. "They seemed to give each other strength and confidence, not that they should have needed it. Everyone from Billy Idol, Tony James and The Clash's Mick Jones to The E Street Band who played on *Schizophrenic* had the utmost respect for them as musicians and producers. Mick was a quiet, shy guy off stage, but on stage or in the studio he was an absolute musical giant. Hunter and Ronson were a dream team."

In a review of *Welcome to the Club* headed 'IAN ROCKS', *Record Mirror* noted the reaction of the "hysterical LA Roxy audience" and mischievously opined: "Chrysalis see a new act with a past and sign him, put out an excellent studio work, then have their boy do a live set and – shazam – they too have a back catalogue at a stroke." An *NME* feature included the headline 'A shade of his old self' and deemed the live recordings bloated and bombastic and the album cover an ugly monstrosity, but Charles Shaar Murray acknowledged that 'Silver Needles' and 'Sons and Daughters' sat with Ian's best work, describing the latter as: "A confessional song in the grand manner – a 'shades off' tour de force that escapes sounding mawkish because of the quiet strength of Hunter's delivery and his unwillingness to blame others for the consequences of his own actions." In *Melody Maker,* the astute and likeable David Hepworth was positive in his assessment, titled 'Sid's death: an older (and wiser) man's view' – Hepworth described Ronson as a "ramrod", awarded the album four stars and noted: "*Welcome to the Club* finds Hunter more or less reconciled to himself, taking a healthy swing through the war zones of his past with verve, nerve and the stuff that can only be called spirit. This is the work of a man of substance."

Welcome to the Club was promoted in Britain with a limited edition "double-pack" single featuring 'We Gotta Get Out of Here' as the lead track. Released on 30th May, the gatefold set also contained 'Sons and Daughters', an edited and specially constructed 'Live Medley' plus an exclusive live version of 'One of the Boys'. 'We Gotta Get Out of Here' was issued as a single internationally and scraped America's Top 100 chart.

Ian filmed a three-track Chrysalis video to promote *Welcome to the Club*. Featuring Ellen Foley and with a loosely devised theme, the film finds Hunter spotting Foley in a New York City clothes store, the pair entering a club, Ian and his band performing 'Irene Wilde' and 'Once Bitten Twice Shy' at the venue and Ellen sparring with Hunter on 'We Gotta Get Out of Here', before they stroll down a Manhattan backstreet to the strains of 'Slaughter on 10th Avenue'.

Hunter Ronson's two-hour live set was adjusted in April 1980 when the band played on *Rockpalast*, West Germany's TV music showcase. Sharing the bill with ZZ Top, Ian's set was recorded on 19th April at Grugahalle arena in Essen, while two concerts followed at Pavillon Baltard and the Empire Theatre in Paris.

> **IH:** "After the Hammersmith Odeon show, Mick and I did *Rockpalast* in Germany and it was put together extremely well. We were there for a week and they gave us a large boat, full of booze, so we could swan it on the local lake. We also had our own studio backstage to warm up in, before we went on. The concert was filmed and went out late at night on most European TV stations, so it would be the only programme left on air. It had 21 million television viewers, with nearly ten thousand in the live audience; it was quite a big deal at the time, when most Euro rock shows were pathetic. My record sales jumped dramatically in Germany after that one gig. I realised that having done *Alien Boy*, I missed rock 'n' roll, and that band with Ronson rocked. I'd tried to be Gordon Lightfoot and it didn't work. As for France, every time I've played there, people stand and look at me – and don't get it!"

Hunter Ronson embarked on a further American tour in May and June, including a revisit to the LA Roxy. 'Who Do You Love', 'The Truth, the Whole Truth, Nuthin' But the Truth' and 'Man O'War' were introduced to the set, and Ellen Foley joined Ian on stage in New York to duet on 'We Gotta Get Out of Here' for the US television show *Fridays*. Hunter follower and Def Leppard vocalist

Joe Elliott finally met his guitar hero in 1980. "The first time I met Ronno was in New York," says Joe. "I'd met Hunter as a fan after the Overnight Angels' show in Doncaster, but The Ritz was when I met Ian and Mick properly. I remember the first words out of Mick's mouth when we were introduced were, 'Ay up lad,' a very Yorkshire phrase but not really what I expected from the dude who played *that* solo on 'Moonage Daydream', that *other* solo on 'The Truth, the Whole Truth, Nuthin' But the Truth' and the icon I'd seen on the first Hunter Ronson tour."

During promotion for *Welcome to the Club*, Ian remarked that Hunter Ronson operated contrary to music business norms as the duo never had any "plan" for what they did; taking things as they come, Ian noted that they were simply having a great time and imagined that they wouldn't continue if the fun stopped. All seemed well with The Hunter Ronson Band, but, prior to their 11th July Dr Pepper concert in Central Park, Mick announced that he had decided to leave the group. Twenty-five dates plus an August appearance at the Reading Festival in England were scrapped and the band folded. Hunter returned to writing material and offered a song entitled 'Lullaby' to Tommy Mandel for Cleveland International's charity album, *Children of the World*. In an interview from the period, Ian admitted that the former members of Mott the Hoople had been talking about a retrospective project but he possessed no desire for any re-formation, Hunter noting that some of the band had not seen each other since 1974.

> **IH:** "We met three weeks ago but we're not reforming. We were talking about a video project and footage. We'd like to put Mott into perspective. There's some good German film but some stuff belongs to the BBC, which is unfortunate as they won't let you have it."

In October, Ian agreed to play twelve charity concerts with Todd Rundgren in support of Congressman John Anderson, who was running as an independent candidate in the 1980 US presidential election. Hunter decided to participate in the benefit shows for fun, the band comprising Tommy Mandel, Roger Powell from Utopia, Santana drummer Michael Shrieve and Hall and Oates bassist Stephen Dees. Billed as 'An Evening with Todd Rundgren and Ian Hunter', the live set included several of Ian's songs plus covers of 'Eight Days a Week', 'Do Ya', 'Needles and Pins' and 'Cathy's Clown'. Rundgren described the liaison with Hunter as an interesting non-merging of two styles, and Ronson joined in for one concert in Cleveland. Hunter also appeared in a party scene for a ninety-minute Rundgren film, *The Ever Popular Tortured Artist Effect*. Todd invited people he knew for a section that recreated Max's Kansas City New York club, particularly individuals who had been there, and his guest list included Rick Derringer, Suzi Ronson and Hunter.

IH: "I think the first time I met Todd was backstage at a Mott gig at The Felt Forum in New York. I met Todd properly when Ronson had his house in Woodstock. Todd lived in Woodstock too and Mick and I had messed around with him for a while with Corky Laing before we did *Schizophrenic*. Then, one day, Todd just rang me up out of the blue and asked if I wanted to go on the road and do those gigs. I toured with him not for political reasons, but because I was sitting around and because Todd's a lovely guy. He got Mick and me into a Stones rehearsal once because he remembered we liked them. I liked the idea of touring with Todd, but I knew fuck all about John Anderson. Todd bypassed all of his trickery and played straight from the amp. We opened with The Move's 'Do Ya' and did a great version of The Beatles' 'Eight Days a Week', or so I thought. We also formed a band for a benefit for Vietnam Vets with John Cale, Paul Butterfield, Michael, Todd and me. These gigs were Todd's idea – one of millions. He's a legend and he has got frightening intelligence. I think it's very difficult for Todd to get on with anybody because he's got so much brain in his head."

Chrysalis Records was delighted that Hunter was back under the spotlight with his first studio outing for the label. *You're Never Alone with a Schizophrenic* had been successful and proved that Ian had lost none of his cutting edge, an observation reinforced by a formidable live album.

Welcome to the Club was reissued in 1983 by Pair Records of America as a 2LP set, retitled *Ian Hunter Live*, but Ian was pleased when Chrysalis enhanced the album in 1994. Originally forced to adopt sacrificial tactics, with 'Roxy' cuts crammed onto three sides of *Welcome to the Club* vinyl, the new double CD accommodated previously unreleased live takes of 'The Golden Age of Rock 'n' Roll' and 'One of the Boys', as well as a "bluesy" ten-minute-plus extended version of 'When the Daylight Comes'. Collectors are sometimes unenthusiastic about exhumed cuts and there is often a reason for discarded songs staying buried, but *Welcome to the Club*'s extras were worthy additions. On 'The Golden Age of Rock 'n' Roll', Hunter's band burns rubber through the verses and choruses but the breathtaking pace is relieved with a fun doo-wop middle eight and introductory a cappella section, Ian describing the entrée as "a little bit of New York City toilet music". In 2007, American Beat repackaged *Welcome to the Club*, *Mojo* rating the set highly and opining: "It makes up for the fact that Mott never released a decent live album."

Hunter's 1980 Essen gig circulated as a bootleg recording for years until *Live at Rockpalast: The Ian Hunter Band featuring Mick Ronson* appeared in 2012 as an official MIG Music CD and DVD release. Notable for the rare in-concert version of 'We Gotta Get Out of Here', a 2LP gatefold vinyl set soon followed. *Classic Rock* described the *Rockpalast* album as: "Just another night for the guys, but one worth savouring – as the Seventies dream team – embraced by punk and armed with killer songs – was preserved in action before the Eighties bit."

IH: *"You're Never Alone with a Schizophrenic* **brought me back and did a lot in the States, but then they had me on**

185

the road all the time and I can't write on the road. So, you're back in the big league again, and you're supposed to write an album each year and continue to tour, and I can't do that either. *Welcome to the Club* could have been smoother, but the whole purpose of doing a live album is to do a LIVE album, cock-ups and all. The live record was a good record and, of course, Mick Ronson was at the top of his game – again!"

You're Never Alone with a Schizophrenic and *Welcome to the Club* proved that Ian Hunter deserved to be celebrated alongside rock's biggest names, so, predictably, Chrysalis Records craved fresh studio product. The insatiable label got their wish when Ian Hunter started recording his next album in late 1980. Tentatively titled *Theatre of the Absurd,* the new record would surprise everyone – and shock Chrysalis to the core.

CHAPTER SIX
Noises

I don't like doing things that people expect.

In 1981, Ian Hunter released his fifth studio LP, the fan- and critic-polarising *Short Back n' Sides*. The year also became notable for the birth of Ian and Trudi's son, John Jesse Hunter Patterson. Defying the music business axiom that you run a successful formula like the *Schizophrenic* album into the ground, Hunter turned through 180 degrees for *Short Back n' Sides*. Always avoiding predictability and any "stuck-in-a-rut" syndrome, Ian would take chances from time to time, as exemplified by *All-American Alien Boy*. Now, he would spring another slick surprise. The public perception of what Ian Hunter *should* be was about to be thrown through the window.

Adopting *Theatre of the Absurd* as a working title, Hunter and Ronson commenced Ian's new album at The Power Station, New York, in December 1980. Most tracks featured Martin Briley, Tommy Mandel, Tommy Morrongiello, Eric Parker and George Meyer, but Todd Rundgren and players from his group Utopia and Bearsville Studios' "house band" appeared on two songs. Additional recording took place at Electric Lady, Wizard Recording and

Wessex Studios, with sessions running through to February, prior to final mixing at Bearsville and Utopia Sound. Ronson started the production of Hunter's record but the duo experienced problems with one untypical song; they needed inspiration and ideas for the title track, so they decided to invite former Mott fan, Mick Jones of The Clash, to assist.

> **IH:** "*Short Back n' Sides* was Ronson and me at a low ebb: short on material, short on enthusiasm and feeling lazy. We were contractually obligated to record another album but we'd been working hard, we'd toured too much and we didn't have much energy left. *Short Back* came far too soon after my previous record. It turned out different, but it did not go down well with my label or management. It was fun to do and it widened the horizon, but widening horizons is not good for business. People don't like it when you pop off up some side alley but I've done it a couple of times because I get bored doing the same sort of thing. It has cost me, but what can you do?
>
> "Mick Jones of The Clash saved us and salvaged *Short Back n' Sides* when there really was very little there. Mick had been a Brixton boy – half reggae, half rock – and that's basically what The Clash was. During *Short Back*, Ronson and I were disenchanted and it was one of those spells where we didn't know what to do; we needed somebody. Mick Jones had followed Mott the Hoople around and knew reggae, and we were doing a song called 'Theatre of the Absurd', which, unusually for us, was reggae-based. Ronno and I weren't too sure how to approach it, so we got Jones in, but only on that track. I rang him up and said, 'You'd better come down here because we're in trouble.' So, Jones came to The Power Station for a night just before Christmas, stayed for a month and things progressed from there, on the entire album. We just let him have his way."

Jones was fresh from recording *Sandinista!* when he worked with Hunter. Released in December 1980, The Clash's monster thirty-six-track triple album contained a plethora of styles, including gospel, rockabilly, dub, calypso, rap and reggae, and Mick's eclectic interests had a strong influence on Ian's sessions. Finding himself at another musical crossroads, Hunter was open to ideas. Ian was always prepared to test himself, but *Short Back n' Sides* would soon test his audience. Having helped with 'Theatre of the Absurd', Jones played guitar on some other numbers, stayed to co-produce with Ronson, and introduced Clash drummer Nicky 'Topper' Headon and violinist Tymon Dogg.

Mick Jones: "In the early Seventies there was a small group of us, all from the same school – Strand Grammar in Brixton Hill – and we had somehow found OUR band, Mott the Hoople. Sitting around the school blues club, scanning the upcoming gigs ads in *Melody Maker*, we would go to Mott's shows whenever we could in London and the surrounding areas. The furthest I went was one Saturday gig in Liverpool. We would try and bunk the trains as one of our group's dad worked for the railways. He had a concession card, and boy did we work that card, hiding in the toilets and passing it between ourselves. As the train came into the station, we would all jump off as it slowed down and leap over the fence alongside. We all had fairly long hair, platform boots and flared trousers. One time, Simon Rodgers in our group got his hair caught on the barbed wire fence: it was like *The Great Escape*. Without the kindness that Mott the Hoople showed to us in those early days, I don't think I would have got anywhere.

"In 1980 I was in New York with Ellen Foley, spending most of my time at her Upper West Side apartment and running around the reservoir on Central Park – really! One day we went over to visit Ian at the studio where he was just starting on his new record. Ellen and I both had a connection; Ian and Mick had produced her first album and I had followed Hunter's career since the Mott days. Ian invited me into the studio and I did something on 'Theatre of the Absurd' and some backing vocals on 'Noises', as I recall."

Ronson was content to retreat on guitar as Jones set about producing Hunter's album, and the record soon became watermarked by Mick's style. Ian was impressed by the Clash guitarist, but was troubled that he had retained his fanaticism about him and Mott the Hoople. The situation made Ian increasingly cautious around other musicians who cited him as influential.

IH: "I'd heard what Jones had done on Ellen's *Spirit of St. Louis* and I liked the Clash's *Sandinista!,* so I knew Mick was good with sound. When he played on 'Theatre of the Absurd' we liked it straightaway. Topper Headon was great on those sessions too. He came in, he did his job, he made comments and he changed things. Apparently, he was under the influence, but I didn't know. I thought he was a brilliant guy and he told some great stories too. We had a good time.

"Mick Jones had all kinds of ideas and used the mixing board like a musician. I only asked him to overdub on one track, but he took over. I couldn't argue with him – very strong personality in the studio – stronger than me – most upsetting. I became wary though, because Mick had thought I was God when I first met him. That was in 1977, when Dan Loggins asked me to have a listen to The Clash at CBS Studios in Whitfield Street one day. So, I went down and walked into this session and the whole place went still. Then Mick Jones turned to somebody and said, 'Play him that track.' I listened to this song and he asked me what I thought, and I said, 'Yeah, it's fine,' and he turned around to the others and said, 'It's the blessing.' I thought, here we go. Now anything out of my mind, less than God, is going to be a let-down, and it was. I was now put on this podium by Mick and he was upset apparently, because I was supposed to be this person from another planet and because I hadn't said more about the track they'd played. He found out I was just a normal guy.

190

"The trouble is people don't understand that it's a different person who walks on stage, and it's a different person who writes the songs, just as I'm a different person day to day. I can't walk round like fucking Job all my life just to please people. It was because of Mick Jones, when Joe Elliott and Def Leppard wanted to meet me so badly that I didn't want to meet them, because I thought these people obviously think I'm something that I'm not. I was wary but, when I eventually met Joe, he turned out to be just a powerful guy with so much energy. He's also the most honest bloke I know in the business."

Hunter may not have welcomed the hero status accorded him by The Clash and Def Leppard, but the assassination of one of rock's greatest legends, nineteen blocks from the Manhattan studio where Ian was recording, brought unprecedented shock to the *Short Back* sessions and the world on 8th December 1980.

IH: "John Lennon died the night we started recording 'Old Records Never Die' and I guess every session in the world stopped that night. There's an aura on *Short Back n' Sides* on several tracks. The songs weren't about John Lennon, of course, but they assumed a different aura because of that incident."

Short Back n' Sides contained ten new tracks: 'Central Park n' West', 'Lisa Likes Rock n' Roll', 'I Need Your Love', 'Old Records Never Die', 'Noises', 'Rain', 'Gun Control', 'Theatre of the Absurd', 'Leave Me Alone' and 'Keep on Burning'. Nine of the songs were written by Ian, with one co-write and a running order selected from a final shortlist of twelve tracks.

Short Back n' Sides' title and artwork suggested a significant change of style, and here it was – Ian Hunter captured in Lynn Goldsmith photographs, cigarette in hand, shorn of trademark "barnet", parading a new rocker hairstyle greased back with fixative. Even the music press ads and promo photos for *Short Back n' Sides* featured Hunter in sharp houndstooth suit and narrow tie. The diverse new style was also echoed in the vinyl, with experimentation on 'Noises', odd sound effects applied to 'Lisa Likes Rock n' Roll' and a dynamic departure towards reggae in 'Theatre of the Absurd'. Ian always sought to avoid repetition and, like *All-American Alien Boy*, *Short Back n' Sides* was an unexpected bolt from the blue. Hunter casually described the record as his "garage" album, but it was actually an audacious and significant departure. Mick Jones was alive to fresh influences and had gradually been edging The Clash towards new soundscapes, *Sandinista!* being a radical challenge. Similarly, Jones brought foreign ideas and techniques to *Short Back n' Sides*, shaping a different direction for Hunter. The reception to Ian's record was decidedly mixed. Some fans regarded it as too right-angled. The powers that be at Chrysalis Records were ashen-faced!

> **IH:** "*Short Back n' Sides* splits fans and it splits me too. My label hated it, but I think it's an interesting album, so I wouldn't put it down. I think I've written better songs, but Ronson and I were at a dead end, so Mick Jones came in to help. We were ripe for the taking and Jones took us. Having said that, I loved the way he would record anything that sounded good to him – taps, door handles – if a radiator sounded good, on it went. I liked the width of his imagination. I also thought he was great with the sound end of things and found it really interesting. Jones' personality needed re-adjusting from time to time but he eventually relaxed and became himself, a really nice chap. As I recall, the album sleeve was Mick Jones' idea too, and I'm even wearing his clothes on the cover. I don't like doing things that people expect and *Short Back n' Sides* was totally different to the way I normally sounded."

Drummer Eric Parker retains fond memories of Ian's album and thought that Hunter and the group produced a groundbreaking record: "Mick Jones and I were playing radiators with hammers and he even played a toy guitar. We really got into a strange mix and sound ideas, with Bob Clearmountain and Neil Dorfsman recording *all* of it."

Ian had created the most varied, diverse and experimental record he had ever attempted and the LP opened with two tracks that reflected the new musical palette: 'Central Park n' West' originated as a poem and was a mythologising accolade to New York City that carried genuine sentiment amidst all the instrumental stomp; while 'Lisa Likes Rock n' Roll' saluted Ronson's four-year-old daughter and was an inventive piece, described as carrying the "radiator and tin-can rattle of Bo Diddley".

IH: "Ronson and I lived in The Mayflower Hotel for six months, next to the Gulf & Western building on the south-west corner of Central Park. At that time, I remember reading bad stuff about New York in the English papers and I just wanted to say something good about it. I was looking out of the ninth-floor window from The Mayflower one night with Mick and the words just arrived. I wrote the lyrics to 'Central Park n' West' as a poem at first. I always had a few poems stashed away. Mick Jones read it and came in with some chords on a bit of paper and off we went, we had a song. I like it because there are sounds on the track that I'd never have thought of. It's a little off the norm.

"The Ronsons – Mick, Suzi and Lisa – lived with us for a while. I wrote a song for Lisa, who was little and gorgeous; now she's grown up and gorgeous. I always loved Lisa. If anything had happened to Mick and Suzi, Trudi and I would have looked after Lisa. She would have been about four or five at the time we did this, and I just wanted to write a kid's song for her. We had a hell of a job getting her to say 'Here's my Daddy', but she did it in the end. I can't remember what the deal was. It was just a fun little song about a little girl. The Stones could have fun because they'd got the weight to have fun, but with a borderline artist like me it was very difficult to take a chance."

Hunter worked with Todd Rundgren on *Short Back's* third track, 'I Need Your Love'. Rundgren took care of the mixing, engineering, bass and backing vocals, and introduced Gary Windo on sax and Roger Powell on backing vocals, from his band Utopia. Ian felt unsure of the original recording and an alternative version was taped with Mick Jones.

> **IH:** "'I Need Your Love' was a great pop song and could have been a hit, but I think it turned out lame. It was done at the back end of the sessions and was a one-off. There was a day where the song worked, but 'I Need Your Love' became dreary and it's my fault because I persisted with it. The drums and the bass have no spark and we didn't get it right – either that or the song wasn't up to it. It was a major disappointment to me as I never captured the track how I heard it in my head, but Chrysalis released it as a single and it charted. Todd had asked if I would like him to produce me on one occasion, but I thought we were too different for that. We were like beauty and the beast. Todd has a definite way of doing things and is quite an artist. His songs sound simple but there are millions of chords in them. He's always up to something, has an unbelievable mind and gets terribly bored pretty quick. Mr Busy, they call him."

'Old Records Never Die' was inevitably transformed when the first session for Hunter's song coincided with the night of John Lennon's murder. It was later claimed that assassin Mark Chapman had obsessed over the music of Todd Rundgren and that he contemplated killing other notable figures, including Paul McCartney, before he shot Lennon. When he was arrested at The Dakota in New York, Chapman was wearing a Todd Rundgren *Hermit of Mink Hollow* T-shirt.

IH: "The night John was shot, I was in The Power Station, in Hell's Kitchen, doing 'Old Records Never Die'. I went out to the street at one point and saw this guy from Channel 7 that I knew. People were running around all over the place screaming, 'It's not true! It's not true!' Americans react instantly to this kind of thing but, with British people, it's three days before it hits. That night, my first instinct was, 'Use it!' Bob Clearmountain and the musicians just dissolved and had to stop playing, and the atmosphere in the studio was bad. To me it was tragic but it was inspiration in reverse. I'd written 'Old Records Never Die' because Elvis Presley had died, but as the Lennon shooting happened it became relevant to John. His death was so stupid, but then lots of things in life are stupid. Sadly, by the time 'Old Records Never Die' was finished, it sounded like I'd sung it too much. The song has a good hook, but it should have had harmonies on the hook. It could have been better and could have been a hit single for somebody. Tommy Mandel was great on that track."

Side One of *Short Back* closed with 'Noises', credited as a Hunter-Morrongiello composition but another of Ian's poems set to music at Mick Jones' insistence.

IH: "I don't think this would ever have got on to vinyl if Jones hadn't been around. He was responsible for the stop-start stuff at the beginning. I wrote 'Noises' with Mad Dog Morrongiello and it was a lot of fun. I remember Guy Stevens, not in the best of shape, wanted us to 'lop the intro off'. He said it was pretentious."

'Rain' was a peaceful, rolling, hypnotic ballad recalling Ian's youth and naming several friends and personalities from his early years in Northampton. The song referenced figures that Hunter always remembered with affection including Barry Parkes, Johnny Facer, Tony Perrett and Alan Manship.

IH: "'Rain' gets a bad rap because it's a little like misery in a way. I lived in Northampton between the ages of sixteen and twenty-seven. I had some good friends. Some of them are still around and some of them are not – Tony, Alan, Barry and Biddy, who was 'one of the chaps' and did die when he was twenty-three. I wrote 'Rain' about all those mates in Northampton, which was a great place at the time. We had nothing and it was hard back then, but the town was full of life with bands playing all over the place and it had spirit. My friends were great, when I was on the right side of them. It's a pity you have to leave those years behind. I still think of them and they are very much part of me."

For the musically upbeat 'Gun Control', Hunter employed sharp satire aimed at the US government and the National Rifle Association, as he addressed the divisive dilemma of the country's right to keep and bear arms. Ironically, one of several American gun horrors would occur close to Ian's home thirty years later when a mass shooting occurred at Sandy Hook Elementary School in Newtown, Connecticut. Recorded at Bearsville Studios with guitarist Mick Barakan, drummer Wells Kelly and bassist John Holbrook, the sarcastic *"viva macho"* 'Gun Control' followed hot on the heels of John Lennon's murder and an assassination attempt on President Ronald Reagan. Hunter captured the atmosphere of the times singing *"assassinate presidents"*, but the irony and caricature didn't stop there; the lyrics targeted almost anyone, irrespective of age or station, if they tried to restrict gun ownership. To emphasise the perverse message, Ian had adopted the persona of a weapons-crazy psychopath, but one learned journalist missed the parody and called the song irresponsible. *Sounds* termed 'Gun Control' "the best Clash song since the first Clash album".

IH: "I made my anger about guns and the NRA known with 'Gun Control'. I still feel very strongly about gun control and always have done. It's not political, just anti-stupidity.

The song was written as a piss-take of all the gun freaks. It really would be hilarious if it wasn't so sad. The single most heinous, barbaric error American politicians make is their weak-kneed obeisance to the gun lobby. Every year kids pick up their dads' guns and kill themselves or each other. Now we have classes full of school kids being murdered."

'Theatre of the Absurd' was Hunter's first and only attempt at a reggae-flavoured track. The song was inspired by Ellen Foley's *Spirit of St. Louis* album, a discussion with Mick Jones and walks that Ian used to take around Shepherd's Bush market in London during the early Seventies, observing the youth community and their music.

IH: "Black kids listening to white kids' music – white kids listening to black kids' music – you could see they were going to come together. The first night I met Mick Jones round at his place was the first time I heard 'reggae rock' and I said to Mick that it was 'Brixton Rock'. 'Theatre of the Absurd' was another poem and it was just about meeting Jones. It's a story about the Brixton section of London and the combination of rock and reggae that began to take shape there. The sound of The Clash was Brixton Rock, exactly the kind of music I had seen coming as early as 1973. 'Theatre of the Absurd' is about a conversation Mick Jones and I had concerning rock 'n' roll. The theatre of the absurd is my rock 'n' roll and when I say, *'your theatre of the absurd'*, I'm talking about his rock 'n' roll. There were a few mixes of this song, all of them good. It was great watching Jones and Bill Price messing with sounds. It's a good song, but 'Brixton Power' would have been a better title. I remember when I was taken to that early Clash session and they played me some songs, I said what I thought and called it Brixton Rock. This went down rather well, so I guess that's where I got the *'Brixton power'* line from."

197

Short Back n' Sides closed with two unusual love songs, but Hunter was never satisfied with the pairing. 'Leave Me Alone' spoke of young romance, and whilst Ian considered, in hindsight, that the song exhibited an alarming lack of taste, he believed it might have originated for fun. 'Keep on Burning', initially titled 'Burning Bridges', was a reflection on current love, Hunter exhibiting deep-seated Leon Russell and gospel music influences.

> **IH:** "'Leave Me Alone' and 'To Love a Woman' on *Overnight Angels* were both written for airplay. Well, they weren't specifically written for airplay, but they did seem like singles. I remember 'Leave Me Alone' left me alone. I wish I'd never written it because again, I never did get it right. Everybody's allowed to fuck up now and again and I did with 'Leave Me Alone'. Maybe it was a piss-take, but even if it was, it doesn't come off. The band plays 'Keep on Burning' great, but it was another odd song and I wasn't sure about it. There is a heavy Leon influence at the end because I loved the guy."

Short Back n' Sides was first scheduled for April 1981 release but eventually appeared in August; the album hit No.79 on the UK chart and spent eleven weeks on *Billboard* in America, reaching No.62. To promote the LP Chrysalis UK issued one single, 'Lisa Likes Rock n' Roll' backed with 'Noises', as a clear vinyl pressing. 'Central Park n' West' and 'I Need Your Love' were released variously as A-sides in Europe and America, the latter reaching No.47 on one US chart. *Melody Maker* noted Hunter's rock 'n' roll spirit and described 'Lisa Likes Rock n' Roll' as "lively and vital", while *Sounds* wrote of the single: "Odd but charming. File under nerve!"

All the puns came out for Chrysalis Records' album ads: "SHORT BACK N' SIDES. A CUT ABOVE THE REST. No one knows how to rock quite like Ian Hunter. A legend whose exuberant music refuses to be upstaged by anyone. Groomed for success, Ian's album has all the style you'd expect. It's good old rock 'n' roll re-styled for right now."

Despite an apparent brain freeze among label promotional staff, *Short Back n' Sides* received excellent reviews, including a five-star rating from *Sounds*, who felt that the record had context and a sassy drum sound. Under the headline 'AGEISM AXED', Dave McCullough wrote: "Hunter is perspicacious. He has the skill of a short story writer, his medium never failing him. *Short Back n' Sides* delivers against all the odds. Ian Hunter has made the best old rock album of the year thus far. It's a lovely, silly surprise." *Record Mirror* awarded four stars and remarked that the LP had purpose.

In America, *Creem* considered that *Short Back n' Sides* was full of "fine pop melodies and diversified rock styles" – while Circus wrote: "*Short Back n' Sides* drifts back and forth from style to style as Hunter busily switches masks while he goes along. The record is a startling project, using almost every studio sound imaginable to rock." *Muzik Magazine* described 'Rain' as a masterpiece, while *Whoot* wrote: "Though there aren't any butt-kickers on *Short Back n' Sides,* a change of plan and scenery does give a creative lift – and the change works rather nicely."

Mick Jones' influence on Hunter's recording sessions shone through in *Short Back n' Sides'* trick fade-outs, odd percussion, weird sounds and liberal echo. Described by one US reviewer as a stylistic smorgasbord, for many fans this was Ian's least approachable LP and Hunter admitted that, whilst the record was ambitious, it was unfocused and contained more styles than any album should.

IH: "*Short Back* was very different from a production point of view, but all my albums tend to vary because I like a change now and again. I don't like doing things that people expect and it can take me two years to do an album, so your tastes change. When I did *Schizophrenic,* I was very heavy on bass and drums. When I did *Short Back n' Sides,* I didn't care. A lot of the songs were demos and they sounded okay, so we put them on it. It *was* much more like a garage album; it wasn't like a studio album so it was an interesting record to do. It was recorded quickly, some of the tracks in one take, and we wrote a lot in the studio. I met a lot of interesting people and had fun, but I was right up the fucking creek. My mind and Ronson's were on different things and, in fact, I don't know why we were in there. Trudi was pregnant at the time and I was extremely worried about that and was convinced that she was going to have trouble. The material on *Short Back n' Sides* took a bit of time to catch on with the public but I thought it was interesting. After we'd completed the record, my manager didn't phone me for a month."

From Mott devotee to Hunter co-producer, Jones' studio contributions were great, but he also thinks Ian made a very bold play. The two characters were a generation apart and it was perhaps inevitable that the combination would create a surprising record.

Mick Jones: "*Short Back n' Sides* was very much through the lens of then, of its time. New York was an exciting place to be in the early Eighties and I was certainly captivated in those days by the thrill of the new. Ian had liked what I'd done and asked me to come on board to co-produce his record with Mick Ronson, and I naturally jumped at the chance. Relatively inexperienced, it was a great opportunity for me to work with two people that I greatly admired. It was a brave move on Ian's part and the album turned out quite different to the rest of his work, but that's good! When the criticism came, much of it, I felt at the time, was laid at my doorstep, but Ian fiercely defended me till the end, which is another reason why I love him. My favourite songs on *Short Back n' Sides* are 'Leave Me Alone' and 'Central Park n' West'."

Several other tracks were attempted during the *Short Back* sessions, including 'Detroit', an abstract picture of the Mid-Western city and an ode to America's automotive industry heartland losing out to car Japanese production. Ian persevered with 'Detroit' but dropped it, although his song was reputedly recorded and shelved by fellow Chrysalis artist John Waite. 'Na Na Na' was another *Short*

Back cut that had first kicked around during the *Schizophrenic* sessions; a sax-laden Fifties-style romp, Hunter thought the song would have been great for Little Richard. Ian described the other *Short Back n' Sides* outtakes, including 'I Believe in You', 'You Stepped into My Dreams', 'Listen to the Eight Track' and 'China', as "strictly work demos".

> **IH:** "I remember I eventually wrote some words for 'Na Na Na' and they were good. That song would have been great for Little Richard – the Governor – there was nobody better. 'Detroit' was okay and there were things like 'I Believe in You' that was rough, 'Venus in the Bathtub' where the band didn't get it and 'You Stepped into My Dreams' which was pretty good and could have made an album. We got Ronson to sing 'China' because it's a trawler boat song and he was from Hull. 'Listen to the Eight Track' only happened once; it had stream of consciousness lyrics and it sounds like we were out of it – well out of it."

In 1994 Chrysalis reissued *Short Back n' Sides* with a bonus CD of alternative and unreleased cuts titled *Long Odds n' Outtakes*. For many listeners *Short Back* had been a case of too many producers, too many ideas and perhaps a semi-contrived attempt to entice too wide an audience. The album was a fascinating experiment though and many of the mixes on the *Long Odds* disc possessed something that was possibly lost on the final record. *Kerrang!* wrote of the reissue: "*Short Back n' Sides* finds the experimental input of Clash-B.A.D. man Mick Jones leadin' our Ian round some streets he's unfamiliar with, then leavin' the bugger there to find his own way home." Mick Jones had asserted much of his musical personality on Hunter's album and it was exciting. Ian felt that some faults lay with his depleted creativity during the period and Ronson's lesser input was probably crucial too, but Mick had become jaded playing guitar and declared that he didn't want to keep performing 'All the Young Dudes' every night.

201

IH: "*Short Back n' Sides* wasn't me. It had a bit of everything and I loved it in that sense, but my manager and Chrysalis hated it! While the album began well, it ended up pretty bad and I guess Jones and I finished up having less respect for each other, largely due to him finding out that I was a normal guy. I loved the way he worked though. He loved freedom and he liked to do anything and use anything. He was good on the record and didn't give a shit in the studio. Mick Jones is very persistent in what he wants and it's actually very difficult doing a record with someone like that, because you're paying for it and if the guy doesn't get it where you want, you end up saying 'Fine', because you must get the record done. Then they'll turn it round and accuse you of backing off, which is unfair. I'd played the game ten years before. I guess I have some difficulty with being told what to do."

According to Hunter, Ronson "was there, but not really there" for the *Short Back* sessions and the guitarist soon departed to work on other projects and play on individual tracks, including 'More Than You Deserve' for Meat Loaf's *Deadringer* LP. Back in Woodstock, Mick worked with The Johnny Average Band; also known as The Falcons, some group members adopted aliases and included Mick Hodgkinson (aka Johnny Average), Frank Campbell (Brian Briggs), John Holbrook, Wells Kelly and Mick Barakan (Shayne Fontayne). With members of The Falcons, Ronson formed The New York Yanquis, so spelt to pre-empt any legal challenge, and the band played several shows with a repertoire that included 'FBI', tracks from Mick's shelved 1976 Bearsville album and an unreleased Ronson song, 'Time Bomb'. The New York Yanquis helped Lisa Bade on her 1982 album *Suspicion* and Mick also worked with Stanley Frank, The Proof, Los Illegals, Les Fradkin, The Mundanes, Visible Targets and Canadian band Lennex, who later became Perfect Affair, fronted by Rick Rose.

Rick Rose: "Growing up in Niagara Falls in the early Seventies, we were into Mott the Hoople and David Bowie, but most of all it was Mick Ronson who stood out for me. He was the ultimate rock star and God could he play guitar. I met Mick in Connecticut when my band Lennex with Johnnie Dee, later of Honeymoon Suite, opened up for Ronson's group one night in Hartford. Then I started to work with him on my recording career and that was when I realised Mick was unique. I had been shot down and rejected in the business, but Mick said, 'Rick, don't let anyone tell you that you don't have what it takes. Just work hard, stay focused and follow your heart.' Ronson found the time to give you words of encouragement."

Johnnie Dee: "I have to thank Ian Hunter for thirty years of inspiration. I formed Honeymoon Suite in the early Eighties. I sent out set lists to promoters and clubs. I got hired, then most times I got fired. I played some original songs. Then I did two great covers that got us attention; 'Bastard' and 'Standin' in My Light'. The latter remains one of my favourite songs of all time."

Following Ronson's departure, to promote *Short Back n' Sides* live, Hunter assembled a completely new group comprising Tommy Mandel on keyboards, drummer Mark Kaufman, guitarist Robbie Alter and bass player Mark Clarke, a former member of Colosseum, Uriah Heep and Rainbow. Ian spoke of Mick and commended the new band members at the time.

> IH: "Mick Ronson is a very complex character. We do play together now and again. So far, we've played together twice, and we've not played together twice. At the moment, we're not playing together. The old band got to know me too well. Some of the others came to me and wanted to do the tour, but three new people were around and were really keen. Somehow Mandel was still there; he was always around. The great thing is that this new band can think independently of me and musicians like that are hard to find."

Alter first met Hunter when he played a gig at an uptown record industry club on Manhattan's West 72nd Street, where The Rolling

Stones were sometimes patrons. Twenty-four hours later, Robbie auditioned at a recording studio to replace Ronson as lead guitarist in The Ian Hunter Band. Hunter could see that it was the first group of any note for Kaufman, and Alter seemed visibly nervous standing in Ronson's place, but Ian was proud of them pulling together quickly when he needed it.

Robbie Alter: "If I had to pick just one word for Ian it would be 'distinctive'. They say in this business that you've got to have your own 'voice' or else you're just an also-ran. I'd been a Hunter fan before I ever met him. I heard the records – saw him in concert. Who's the bloke with the ginger wavy locks falling in ringlets when everyone else has got 'em dark, straight and lank – and what about the shades? Cool. He sings, and it doesn't sound like anyone else I've heard. Maybe a little like Dylan – maybe. The first three notes and you know it's him – and what about the piano – hard-charging, barrel-house style, killing it with the low end – steady thumping rhythm – *WTF is that*? One off! I can't make out what's happening there – but I dig it whatever it is.

"I first met Ian Hunter at a nightclub in New York; Trax, it was. I'm gigging there one night and the very next day I'm auditioning at a recording studio for the spot in his band to replace Mick Ronson as guitarist, as the guys were taking a chill pill. We're gonna play some – so Ian sits down on the glossy bench at this massive black grand piano – I'm standing over his shoulder watching him as he starts hammering away – 'All the Way from Memphis' I think it was. Out comes this thundering sound and whoa – there IT is – up close and personal this time – 'That Sound'. I gotta ask, because it's been a curious mystery to me for quite some time. Now's my chance to get the definitive answer, straight from the source! 'What's that you're playing there with your left hand? Sounds amazing,' says I, scratching my head thoughtfully. Finally, the riddle will be resolved as I anticipate the erudite musicological explanation that has had me perplexed since I first heard his recordings. Diminished triads? Flatted clusters of minor seconds? Pixilated augmented semi-quavers – *WHAT*? Honestly, I don't remember Ian's exact words, since I was blown away by the reply, but it came back something like, 'Nah, I don't know, I'm just mashing down with me palm on the keys in time. It helps keep the beat.' It cracked me up and I've loved him ever since. Distinctive!"

With a new band in place, Hunter travelled to Britain for one gig in 1981, appearing at the Milton Keynes Bowl on 8th August alongside Phil Lynott's Thin Lizzy, Judie Tzuke and Paul Young's Q-Tips.

> **IH:** "Phil was a sweetheart of a guy. I remember at Milton Keynes we didn't have a babysitter, so Phil sat with Jesse while I was on stage. I met some of my mates from nearby Northampton at that gig; some of the others were doing lengthy time. I told them about 'Rain' on *Short Back n' Sides* and that they were name-checked on the album, but they were all scrap dealers; they weren't going to buy a record."

After his Milton Keynes performance, Ian played a surprise set at Battersea's tiny 101 Club in South London. In a crammed basement crowd, barely numbering one hundred people, Jake Burns from punk band Stiff Little Fingers cheered, played air guitar and sang along to almost every Hunter song.

Having stepped bravely into the new decade with a very different album, a fresh attack and a new band, Ian's activities were suddenly interrupted with news of Mott the Hoople's original mentor, Guy Stevens. After producing The Clash's acclaimed 1979 album *London Calling*, the signs were that there might be a Stevens renaissance but, on 29th August 1981, like Who drummer Keith Moon before him, Guy died from an accidental overdose of a drug prescribed to help him beat his alcohol dependency. Hunter had been flattered that Stevens paid so much attention to him in Mott the Hoople and had tried to make him more confident. Ian faced psychological barriers in his early days – he had been told he was no good and he was advised to forget about music – but Guy Stevens made Ian Hunter Patterson believe in himself.

IH: "I'd never met anyone like Guy then, and I've never met anyone like him since. He was the first person to look me in the eye and tell me I had something. This can be pivotal in a young man's career. Insecurity was one of my strong points and without Guy I'd probably have got nowhere in this business. He couldn't play or sing to get across what he wanted, even though music was coming out of every pore in his body, but Guy was amazing. He had musical taste, he had the right records and he believed in passion and rage. When Mott was in the studio, Guy became frantic and the sessions were like a mad gig. His stock in trade was to create situations where you'd become frustrated. His extreme idea of 'production' was to stop you playing at first, to drive you up the wall with alarming chat that went on and on, and then, suddenly, he would let you play. You were like a dog unleashed and you got to explode, Guy having taken you on a flight of fancy to the point where you'd play harder than normal. He tried to create an atmosphere away from reality and sometimes it worked.

"I remember Mott were travelling in a car down to Olympic Studios one day and Guy turned to me and said, 'Here, hold this a minute,' and it was a wooden box. Suddenly, we got stopped by the police and Guy got out and spoke to them, then got back in our car and took the box back. Guy had done two stretches for possession and you never knew what to expect with him, but I was too ignorant to know what was going on in those early days, or what was in the box that he'd passed to me.

"Guy was a destructive figure. One day he locked himself in his flat in London and I went down there with Trudi and the place was wrecked. Next to the front door there was a toilet, but it was now a hole in the floor. In the apartment everything was burnt. His bed had gone, the baize and slate were missing from his snooker table and the place was knee-deep in porn. You never could tell which way

Guy would go. He loved beginnings but wasn't very good at endings. If Guy could have taken himself a little more seriously, he might still be with us. He was crazy but had amazing taste in literature and music. Bipolar would be as near as you could get but Guy's main problems were amphetamines and drink. He became a drug addict and did have psychological issues and problems with his family. He died of a heart attack precipitated by an overdose, but he really died of a death wish. Sadly, at the end, he was in very bad shape. His talent was exploited and he suffered from his own self-destructive nature, but his assets were his enthusiasm, his knowledge and his humour. We all loved him, but he grew sadder as the years rolled by, and, in truth, he was waiting for an exit. It's difficult to explain Guy because he had too many contradictions, but believers like him were so important. Mott had little confidence, but he boosted us and he guided us. He was pivotal, but it turned out he screwed me royally on the money. I called him the glorious hypocrite."

When his involvement with Mott the Hoople ended after *Brain Capers* in 1971, Guy Stevens' Island career had waned, as he tested the label's patience to the limit. At one A&R meeting, having witnessed Virgin Records' success with Mike Oldfield's *Tubular Bells* album, Chris Blackwell proposed a subsidiary Island label to release mood-laden, avant-garde music. Guy killed the boss's brainwave by suggesting they call it "Lukewarm Fucking Records". Following increased binges and rows between Stevens and the Island organisation, Guy's position became untenable. Trevor Wyatt remembers joining Island prior to Stevens' departure and the "Special Brew lunches" that Guy consumed most days with Chris Wood and Reebop Kwaku Baah of Traffic. Mick Ralphs, meanwhile, felt that his former producer was still on the button with his musical opinions, but Guy's outbursts and unreliability meant that his days at the label were numbered.

Mick Ralphs: "After Mott, I was working with Paul Rodgers to get Bad Company together and Guy came around to hear what we'd being doing. We'd just done a version of 'Can't Get Enough' and, as soon as Guy heard it, he was jumping up and down shouting, 'Yes that's it! That's going to be a smash hit!' I couldn't really see it. I thought it was alright, not that great, but Guy said, 'Oh yes, that's the one. That's going to be big.' And he was right."

Through the Seventies, Stevens' drug and alcohol consumption impaired his abilities and fewer artists considered engaging him. He worked briefly at Warner Brothers A&R then produced Philip Rambow's great band, The Winkies, at Olympic Studios, alongside *All the Young Dudes* engineer Keith Harwood. Mick Jones once referenced *The Winkies* as his third-favourite British album of all time and Rambow termed Stevens a wonderful, mad genius. "Guy was a great producer and larger than life person but he was victimised sometimes," says Philip. "Many people thought Guy was 'weird' or 'out of it', so some people would pick on him and he was mugged more than once. When we recorded *The Winkies*, though, he was absolutely in control. He did a great job. I loved Guy."

Stevens turned creator again at AIR Studios with Little Queenie, a band that included Mick Jones and Eunan Brady. Guy would mentor a new Mott for Warner Brothers and he invited Verden Allen to guest on keyboards. Re-naming the group Violent Luck, they recorded three tracks including a re-make of Mott the Hoople's 'No Wheels to Ride' and Allen noticed Stevens, as eccentric as ever, bringing toy money into the studio to pay for the session. Eunan Brady recalled that Guy was given £100 a week by Warner Brothers just to stay away from their offices, and against a backdrop of binges, booze and frantic calls to Warner boss Mo Ostin, the Violent Luck deal was downed. Brady described Stevens' Swiss Cottage flat as a magazine feature from hell, with thick dust everywhere, a fridge full of empty beer cans and a fully inflated life raft in the bedroom. Veering from hysterical laugher to manic depression in once sentence, Guy was dangerous to know. By late

1975, the boundless plans for Violent Luck fizzled out as Stevens sought refuge in a river of alcohol.

A year later, Guy perceived that rock 'n' roll was finished, saying of Led Zeppelin's movie *The Song Remains the Same*: "I went to see the Led Zeppelin film last week – and Peter Grant can beat me up – but I fell asleep, four rows from the front. It's a different ball game now. It's all over!" Unflinching and contrary to his dramatic prediction, Guy was soon back connecting with The Clash as their manager Bernie Rhodes, a former Scene patron, thought that Stevens would understand the group's energy. Guy was meant to produce the first Clash album but the partnership did not last. *The Clash* was produced by Mickey Foote but a subsequent retrospective featured an unreleased outtake, 'Midnight to Stevens'.

Guy re-surfaced at Island when Chris Blackwell asked director Tim Clark to take Stevens back as a roving A&R man. "Chris was always ready to give it another shot," says Tim. "Guy sat and said, 'Look, I've been working in Woolworths. My talent is going to waste. I've got to get back into the business.' We welcomed him back. We knew that he wasn't taking drugs particularly. What we hadn't realised was that alcohol was now the bugbear. He kept disappearing and you wouldn't see him for two or three days. He was too unreliable. In the end he disappeared to America and told Chris about how awful the company was, and then broke up his hotel room in New York. He was, in the end, a rather desperate figure."

In 1979, Stevens was given a second chance to produce The Clash, to the dismay of CBS Records. *Guy Stevens' Testament of Rock and Roll* had been one of the producer's Island compilation LPs in the Sixties and, ironically, the working title for The Clash album was *The Last Testament*. The band's double LP was released as *London Calling* and it became one of rock's most revered records. It also marked a triumphant comeback for Guy, but the project would be his swansong. CBS had demanded a name producer for *London Calling* but the group opted for Guy, partly for his inspiration but also because they could do what they wanted while Stevens passed out under the mixing desk. Guy was still idiosyncratic but inspiring, still echoing spontaneous Fifties records by describing wrong takes as "fine" and "just right", and still screaming out rock 'n' rollers' names at the band as they played. The Guy Stevens Production Manual had been opened once more, but where Mott's *Brain Capers* had been cut in only five days, *London Calling* took five weeks. Stevens would telephone Hunter in America for pep talks, claiming that he couldn't continue with the project, but Ian could see that Guy was now oscillating between drugs and alcohol, using one to supress the other in a slow downward spiral.

> **IH:** "Drugs take away guilt. Guilt is a very big thing. Guy felt his mother didn't like him, which gave him a tremendous inferiority complex. He really had great difficulty simply living. Guy may have looked secure but he was one of the most insecure men I've ever known. When he was producing The Clash in Wessex, he would ring me a lot and panic – it wasn't the same – he couldn't do it – they didn't understand him – they didn't get it. He went on and on and on. I just kept saying, 'You can do it.' I didn't know if he could, but I kept telling him he could. For one reason or another he wanted out, but I told him to stay put and get on with it. I loved him, but he was a pain and I'm sure The Clash got fed up with him from time to time. I know he stretched my patience and the rest of Mott's too. He could get a little rowdy, but he was trying to create live magic in a studio and it's not an easy thing to accomplish. He was this mad, one-man, 2,000-seater audience, broken seats and all."

During the *London Calling* sessions, Stevens alighted on a Clash fan who was an Arsenal Football Club employee, bribing the lad with music goodies to gain access to the stadium. During journeys to Wessex Studios, Guy would instruct his cab driver to stop off at Highbury Stadium so that he could kneel in the centre of the pitch, glassy-eyed, in homage to Gunners legend Liam Brady. Bill

Price made many of the production decisions on *London Calling* but Mick Jones spoke highly of Guy as a driving force and catalyst, and the group got on well with their producer. Topper Headon saw their third album as a peak and described Bill Price as a fantastic engineer, while Stevens kept the whole thing live. During a run-through of 'Brand New Cadillac', the band didn't know it was being recorded until Guy exclaimed, "That's it!" With echoes of Mott's 'Sweet Angeline', The Clash pleaded that they couldn't keep 'Brand New Cadillac' as it speeded up too much, but Stevens screamed, "Great! All rock 'n' roll speeds up. Take!"

As his alcohol intake accelerated, unhappiness and petulance increased, and Guy often passed out in the Wessex control room or slept off his imbibing in the tech room. The *London Calling* sessions were littered with incident and really did echo Mott's *Brain Capers* as Guy trashed chairs, poured red wine into a piano and threw a set of stepladders around. Strummer felt Stevens gave a crazed edge to proceedings and drew performances out of the band, but Guy had become a liability. Some grainy film footage included on a *London Calling* anniversary DVD captured some of Stevens' studio antics, but the release did him few favours.

Guy soon reconnected with his former Woolverstone schoolfriend Alan Baguste, arriving like a whirling dervish at Alan's office one day. Guy said he needed a break after working with The Clash, so Alan drove him to Hadleigh in Suffolk for a few days, Stevens bringing a two-litre bottle of cheap white wine and a bottle of vodka along, just for the journey. While *London Calling* hit the Top Ten in the UK and the US Top Thirty, industry resistance to working with Guy solidified. He became isolated and often did not know where he was or what was happening. Nor did he care. In one of his final interviews, Guy reflected on his life's work and opined that he never really recovered from working with Mott the Hoople. "The real trouble with Ian is that he takes himself so seriously," Stevens claimed.

Guy separated from his wife Diane and his Fairfax Road flat became crammed with old records, bottles and the life raft, "just in case". Stevens had also hung two pictures in the bathroom: Bob Dylan and Adolf Hitler. Close to the final curtain, Guy moved to live with his mother in a second-floor maisonette at Perry Rise in Forest Hill, London. Manically enthusiastic, when he played a favourite record, Stevens would take out a hammer from a chest of drawers to replicate the beat on the floor, walls or furniture. His mother would order him to cease the blows for the sake of the neighbours and her sanity, and the rock 'n' roll wild man became a chastised infant who put his toy back in the box.

In a final fling, Stevens was lined up to produce his hero Jerry Lee Lewis and a comeback album with Twinkle (Lynn Annette Ripley), the Sixties' singer who achieved fleeting fame with the teenage tragedy hit 'Terry'. But time was running out. Looking older than his years and exhibiting signs of physical deterioration, life's excesses finally caught up with Guy when he passed away at his mother's home. The cause of death was reported as a mistaken intake of prescribed drugs that Guy had been using to reduce his alcohol dependency, which in turn caused a heart attack. Described as serious medication, members of The Clash had shared some of Guy's pills during a car journey one day and suffered severe headaches.

Guy Stevens' funeral at Honor Oak Crematorium, Forest Hill was attended by Diane, Lillian and Roger Stevens, Dale Griffin, Pete Watts, Verden Allen, Philip Rambow, The Clash, various Island Records personnel and Alan Baguste, who noted that Guy's wife, mother and brother were very composed. The Clash arrived in a pink Cadillac and Watts remembered the band members distraught and ashen. "Guy was such a big figure, and yet the funeral was a small affair," said Pete. "They played 'A Whiter Shade of Pale' and Dylan's 'Visions of Johanna' at such a low volume and I could visualise Guy screaming, 'Turn it up!' It was a sad occasion. There were absurdities too, Guy's mother saying to Twinkle, 'So you were working on a record with Guy? Well, he can't finish it now. He's dead.'"

Mick Jones, who picked Guy as his all-time hero, was later saddened that *London Calling* was voted 'Best Album of the

Eighties' by *Rolling Stone* but Stevens didn't live to witness it. Hunter had seen Guy a few weeks before his death and he realised that the end was near.

> IH: "You just knew Guy was going to go. You couldn't understand what he was saying. A lot of people shed a tear when Guy went. It wasn't totally unexpected, but we were shattered because he was never happy. By any normal standard Guy was a fool, but he wasn't. He knew about rock 'n' roll and was one of those fascinating people you only meet once in a lifetime. The fondest memories of Guy are invisible and that was his whole problem. His talent was invisible and it frustrated the shit out of him. When he sang it was like a horse in trouble and it was awful when he tried to get his point across at times. Guy, like me, did not have any apparent talent on the surface. You had to dig down and he dug down into me. Until he paid me that enormous compliment of talking to me, about me, I never really knew I existed. That was Guy's genius – finding things in people. Somebody like me would have no chance nowadays, absolutely no chance at all. I found out afterwards what Guy had been looking for in Mott. When I got in the band Guy thought I would do for now, but the band didn't want me. Then when Guy didn't want me in, the band did want me, so someone was on my side on both occasions. He kept Mott going through four stiff albums at Island and I still appreciate that.
>
> "Guy always drove his car slow if the song he was playing was slow, and he always drove his car fast if the song was fast. We were at a pub in Hampstead Heath one night and I made the mistake of getting in his Beetle when we were listening to 'Half Moon Bay' from *Mott the Hoople*, a track that went slow and fast. Guy never had much regard for roads. He just drove! We were on the heath in the middle of the night and it was misty. We could have hit somebody

quite easily as Guy was driving all over the park, screaming about this track. He was so madly enthused about the quiet bit and then, suddenly, the quick bit came and you were off at high speed, and then the track would go slow again and he'd screech on the brakes. This is what life with Guy was like."

Observers around Mott perceived that, from the outset, Stevens had "got" Hunter and saw something important "underneath". Guy also realised that he could express himself through Mott the Hoople. He made the group members feel good by telling them they were going to be the greatest band in the world, but Ian knew that Guy was not a record producer in the true sense of the word; his methods were completely unorthodox.

> **IH:** "Guy wasn't the slightest bit interested in production. Guy was called a producer but people found out what he was, to their cost, when they tried to emulate us later on. A lot of people wouldn't work with him and he was an acquired taste as a producer. He wasn't interested in notes. To Guy, it was all about performance."

Hunter would soon write 'Guy Stevens Poem' and include the verse in the artwork for his next album, while Patrick Campbell-Lyons of Island group Nirvana, who knew Stevens in the Sixties, also recorded a spoken tribute, 'The Indiscreet Harlequin'. Patrick had attended the launch party for *London Calling* where he discovered that Guy's former smile had frighteningly become a manic grin; he also recalled his final sighting of Stevens, slumped on a bench near Swiss Cottage, which was a sad and shocking experience for him.

The Mott the Hoople band members had valued Guy's enthusiasm and motivation. "During the difficulties of the early days," said Dale Griffin, "Guy Stevens would tell us over and over, 'You ARE The Rolling Stones. You ARE Bob Dylan. YOU

214

are up there with them. YOU are better than them.' We believed him after a while. There was no alternative. Guy was beyond normality."

Mick Ralphs: "I loved Guy. He was a genius, but, of course, like all geniuses he was wracked with pain and was a tortured soul. He was a wonderful man though and very passionate about what he did. If he believed in something, he would do anything for it. He had great ideas and was the catalyst for Mott the Hoople. He instigated our wildness, although it was probably in there and he encouraged it."

Pete Watts recalled: "Guy was tone deaf, totally unmusical, couldn't sing in tune or hear a mistake on tape and really had no sense of rhythm but, God, did he make up for it in other departments. He used to motivate the group by screaming things at us like 'You make The Rolling Stones sound like shit!' Lots of people have got something special buried in them, but they haven't got the courage to let it out. Guy gave us that courage. We were timid tigers in a cage, and Guy opened the door and let us out at everybody's throats."

Diane Stevens remained intensely loyal to Guy. Separated in 1981, but not divorced, she remembered her final discussion with Guy one Friday evening. It was optimistic and "up". He was trying to avoid alcohol, he intended to move out of his mother's flat and he was going to re-launch the Sue label, so the Sunday telephone call from Guy's mother was all the more devastating. Named and nurtured by Guy, Diane believed that Mott the Hoople's music was "real rock 'n' roll, warts and all", and that everybody was so affected by what Guy did. "That was what was sad about it," said Diane. "All those records that Guy imported, all the things he tried to do with Mott the Hoople, they all live on; but at the time, people don't really appreciate that."

Agent provocateur for The Clash and Ian Dury, Kosmo Vinyl was friends with Diane Stevens until she died in 2012; she had contracted cancer but did not share the details of her illness. "I didn't know Diane had taken a serious downturn until after it was all over," says Kosmo. "I got a call about a funeral. It was a sad ending to a mostly sad life."

Schoolmate Alan Baguste knew Guy from a different, non-musical standpoint and got to know him again before he died. "Guy was a contemporary of mine and we remained in contact until his death," says Alan, "albeit they were random meetings throughout the years until the last two years of his frantic life when we met on several occasions. He was not in a good place by that time. I remember Guy as fun-loving. He would sit on a Tube train with a broadsheet newspaper, set it alight and pretend he didn't know the paper was on fire – or cut out a square from the middle of newspapers and 'read them', but look through the hole persistently at the other passengers. I recall my wife and I meeting Guy and Diane, quite by chance one weekend in Soho. Guy insisted that we hop into his yellow Beetle and we ended up back at his flat on Marylebone Road. The apartment was almost empty except for piles of records. He played me an album by Cream that day and was wildly enthused by the band, pressing his face up to mine and saying that I had to like it, and if I didn't like it, then he didn't understand me anymore."

During Island Records' 50th Anniversary celebrations in 2009, Chris Blackwell described Guy Stevens as the most talented person he'd ever met in the music industry. Ian Hunter knew why.

IH: "Guy was right up there in the lunatic echelons and I have known a few lunatics. He was through the roof. His thing didn't have much to do with music; it was more about motivating you out of your brain. His sole contribution to the sound was maybe pouring a few beers into the faders or setting fire to something. He would rev you up, then suddenly you'd start to play and it was like the Charge of the Light Brigade. Guy was glorious, insightful and a fucking maniac. He really was the first person who ever took a blind bit of interest in me and dragged things out of me. I didn't think I was up to much, but then there's a lot of insecurity in the music biz. You're kind of an introvert and an extrovert. You're scared to go out and do it, but you know you can if given the chance. I guess Guy was my chance, him being an extrovert and an introvert, and everything else in between. He used to say to me that I took myself too seriously, but you have to take yourself seriously – if you're going to survive."

Guy Stevens Poem

Guy, what am I supposed to say about you?
Crazy, restless, on the move
You found a me I never knew
And you loved me, and I loved you

So off we went, the beginning of me
Wrote a few songs into history
Most never knew the gift you sent
But then most people ain't one hundred percent

I had to do something just for you
I wasn't lazy, and I've tried to be true
You were my father, you were my son
Maybe you felt your work was done

For you dealt in beginnings, never in ends
You dealt in magic, so you had few friends
I watched your vivid colours fade
As you had to face the corporate jade

To you the best was all that matters
You screamed, you cried, put down 'n' flattered
And they never did give you much respect
Your talent was too indirect

Don't rest in peace, insult me on!
Or nothing will change because you're gone
Thanks a lot for believing in me
You know how I feel privately

Some tears were shed in the world tonight
For the man who never got living right
A friend got off the phone just now
I gotta get to sleep somehow

I'll be rehearsing tomorrow at S.I.R.
Still trying to be your superstar
'N' if I don't make it, when we're through
Don't worry 'bout me, I'll be blaming you

I remember the guy with the electric hair
At that first rehearsal standing there
You gave your heart, you gave your soul
God bless you Guy, Rock 'N' Roll!

Ian Hunter (1981)

CHAPTER SEVEN

Staring at Your Wilderness

I didn't know what to do in the Eighties.

After Guy Stevens' passing, rumours started to circulate that Mott the Hoople might reunite to pay tribute to the man who first formed and mentored them. Ian Hunter admitted in late 1981 that he had spoken with Mick Ralphs, Pete Watts and Dale Griffin about recording a new album and that his label, Chrysalis Records, wanted the reformation to happen, assuming "all the red tape" could be resolved.

> **IH:** "Apart from Ralphs, I haven't played with them for years. It would be interesting to see where they're at now. The music would probably be totally different. My suggestion was that we left two months out of our schedules to do that and then no one would go in with any preconceived ideas. It would just be Mott the Hoople now, rather than trying to do something that we did a long time ago."

During a visit to London, Hunter met Ralphs, Watts, Griffin, Morgan Fisher and Scorpions' guitarist Michael Schenker to discuss potential recording sessions. Dale recalled a great convivial evening and late-night talk of finding a studio after a huge amount of champagne had been consumed; he also considered there was an informal agreement that, having stopped, Mott the Hoople would re-convene at some juncture and he intimated moves were made for the band to reunite on a British television show. "What it actually came down to was a three-minute slot," claimed Griffin. "The producer said, 'Can you do a medley of three of your hits,' at which point I told her to fuck off. The show turned out to be so piss-poor and small-time that I pulled us out. I think the perception of Mott's success is much greater than the reality. People thought we were much more successful than we actually were. The only problem with getting Mott the Hoople back together again is the possibility of ruining the rosy memories people have of those days, not least of all our own."

During his *Short Back n' Sides* tour, on 11th September 1981 Hunter made a televised appearance at New York's Dr Pepper Festival, an event that had been held annually in Central Park but was now moved to Pier 84 on Manhattan's West Side to pacify residents around the city's urban landmark. *Circus* considered Hunter "one of the few geniuses in rock & roll", as he delivered "a perfectly paced show that ranged from the blistering ('Bastard') to the classic ('Ships')". Ian's filmed performance was later released as *Ian Hunter Rocks*.

> **IH:** "That night was most enjoyable, but I remember it was very, very hot. There was no air. I could hardly breathe at one point and my knees nearly gave way. I walked off stage to try and get some air. Great, when it's being televised."

Hunter also appeared at New York's Palladium Theatre on 13th September with Rick Derringer, Todd Rundgren, Hall and Oates, Ellen Foley, Southside Johnny and Edgar Winter. The charity concert had been arranged to raise funds for Derringer after the theft of music equipment worth 100,000 dollars. Known as "The Party at the Palladium", the two songs played by Ian appeared on

221

a 1998 album, *King Biscuit Flower Hour presents Rick Derringer and Friends in Concert*. One reviewer wrote of the event: "The surprises are reserved for the encores where Rick is joined on stage by Ian Hunter who delivers a great version of 'Just Another Night'. Ian then delivers the knockout blow with a medley of 'All the Young Dudes', 'Roll Away the Stone' and 'Ships' – quite simply, brilliant!"

The Ian Hunter Band played gigs in Europe and America through to January 1982 including shows at Cobo Hall, Detroit and three October appearances at the Old Waldorf in San Francisco, where one concert was recorded and broadcast by the Westwood One radio network. Hunter also featured on *Don Kirshner's Rock Concert* television show, where his set included a cover of 'Is Your Love in Vain' from Bob Dylan's recent album *Street Legal*. Ian had toured to promote *Short Back n' Sides* minus Ronson, engaging Tommy Mandel to bring some discipline to the proceedings, but Mick reappeared in October, taking over Mandel's role when the keyboard player was hospitalised in a Cleveland clinic with a brain aneurysm.

Tommy Mandel: "The night before my brain surgery Mick Ronson called me up from Woodstock and asked me one thousand questions about what synth patches I was using on which song and other performance details about the set. He was about to fly out to 'fill in' for me on the tour, on keyboards. Ronson was a wonderful pianist but I think he was doing that to calm me down and focus me too. While I was going over something that I knew very well, I had no time to be nervous about the next day's operation. And my brain was doing some good pre-op exercise as well. I was so grateful to Mick for that."

IH: "When Mick stepped in on keyboards, he made some horrible mistakes now and again. He joined us in Austin and was drunk when he got off the plane and I thought he was burned out, but he sat down at the soundcheck, was still there six hours later and got the hang of it. Mick sobered up and was fine."

222

Further Hunter concerts included two gigs at The Ritz in New York, but in Cleveland Ian had gone from headlining a packed 10,000-seater Richfield Coliseum in September 1979 to the 1,800 capacity Agora in April 1982. It would be Hunter's last tour for four years as he split his band and left Chrysalis Records, Cleveland International and his manager Steve Popovich. The commercial and critical reaction to the *Short Back n' Sides* album had been mixed, but Ian was pragmatic and had good memories of the period.

During another Hunter Ronson recess, Mick worked with John Mellencamp on *American Fool*, transforming one of the singer's discarded songs into a hit. "I owe Mick Ronson the song 'Jack and Diane'," admitted Mellencamp. "Mick was very instrumental in helping me arrange that. I'd thrown that song on the junk heap and we were down in Miami making that record, and Ronson came down and worked on *American Fool* for about four or five weeks. With 'Jack and Diane', he came in and suggested putting percussion on there and then he sang the part, *'let it rock, let it roll'* as a choir-type thing. It was Mick's idea and that's the part everybody remembered. All of a sudden, the song worked."

In 1982, Hunter participated in the 'Concert for Vietnam Veterans Agent Orange Victims' at New York's Pier 84; joined by Todd Rundgren, Paul Butterfield, John Cale and Al Kooper, the set included 'Irene Wilde' and 'Like a Rolling Stone'. Ian also accepted 'The Musical Syndrome Award' from the students of Ohio State University in appreciation of his creative career in rock music. During this period, Hunter was working on new songs including 'Absent Friends' and 'You're Messin' with the King of Rock 'n' Roll', the latter written in response to author Albert Goldman's controversial biography *Elvis*.

> **IH:** "I hated Albert Goldman's book. He was a twerp who waited until Elvis died and then made a fortune out of exposing all the crap. My song included the line, *'You made your money on a dead man's grave.'* It was a good song, in a rockabilly style, like Queen's 'Crazy Little Thing Called

Love', but more of a flat-out rocker. 'You're Messin' with the King of Rock 'n' Roll' was supposed to have been on my next album. I guess it wasn't performed well enough, or I didn't finish the lyrics to my satisfaction, or it didn't record well enough, again. It eventually saw the light of day on a compilation."

In the early Eighties, two more Mott the Hoople collections appeared: *All the Way from Memphis* on British budget label Hallmark and a German CBS LP, *Rock Giants*, with an imaginative track selection that included 'Sea Diver', 'Alice' and 'Pearl 'n' Roy (England)'. But, by the winter of 1982, Ian was focused on his next album – *All of the Good Ones Are Taken.* Hunter had been courted by three different record labels but his sixth solo project reunited him with Mott's former CBS liaison man, Dick Asher, who had re-signed with Columbia. Commencing sessions at Wizard Sound Studios in Briarcliff Manor, New York State, Ian collaborated with Max Norman, a hard rock producer and engineer who had recently completed albums by The Tubes, Ozzy Osbourne and Bad Company. It seemed a strange choice, but Norman was credited as producing *All of the Good Ones Are Taken* "In Association" with Hunter. Ian engaged Mandel, Alter, Michaels and Clarke for the sessions and Mick Ronson also appeared, but only on one track. Hunter spoke positively of Max Norman.

IH: "Max was great and hung in twenty-four hours a day. He produced more hard rock stuff than me, but he did a great job on my record. Max was producing Ozzy Osbourne and thought he could do the trick for me. I just about did him in."

Released in July 1983, *All of the Good Ones Are Taken* featured ten tracks: 'All of the Good Ones Are Taken', 'Every Step of the Way', 'Fun', 'Speechless', 'Death 'n' Glory Boys', 'That Girl Is Rock 'n' Roll', 'Somethin's Goin' On', 'Captain Void 'n' the Video Jets', 'Seeing

Double' and 'All of the Good Ones Are Taken (Slow Version)'. The songs were all new Hunter compositions except for two co-writes involving Mark Clarke and Hilly Michaels. In similar vein to *All-American Alien Boy*, Ian's songs addressed some offbeat topics, including the fear of nuclear missiles and the Falklands War, but with a radically different musical touch. Employing forty-eight-track recording and some of the patterns and conventions of the time, like many Eighties' renderings, Hunter's album sounded sharp and polished. *All of the Good Ones Are Taken* was lighter, brighter and vaguely commercial too, *Hit Parader* describing the collection as a danceable and upbeat album!

The opening track, 'All of the Good Ones Are Taken', was one of Ian's most attractive songs, featuring an infectious chorus and heartful sax from Clarence 'The Big Man' Clemons of The E Street Band. Continuing Hunter's former Springsteen link, the song was recorded as a fast and slow version, mirroring the dilemma that had surrounded 'Just Another Night' and 'The Other Side of Life' on *You're Never Alone with a Schizophrenic*. The contrasting 'Good Ones' takes bookended Hunter's album nicely, the first cut on the LP being the lively, up-tempo version. At the time, Ian considered the song was one of his best and he viewed it as a potential link to renewed success. Like 'Justice of the Peace', it should have been a hit.

> **IH:** "The 'All of the Good Ones Are Taken' title was just an expression and a sort of cliché that I latched onto – something people say at odd moments. Lines like that often spark a song for me, like 'once bitten twice shy'. The feeling is bittersweet, lost love – the feeling you get at the end of a romance. I originally did the slow version for the album and that was the one I wanted to release. CBS would not have it as a single though, so they asked me to record a fast version, which I did – like a fucking idiot; even Trudi warned me. Max Norman liked the fast take and since there were a couple of other songs that weren't working out, we compromised

and put both versions on the record. It was originally written fast, but I lost the tape of that session and I could never get the groove back or figure out what the original mood was. It only worked as a ballad for me after that. For ages it was one track that I'd always wanted to do again. Years later, on a live album, I did re-do it and I think I captured the best version. It took me twenty years to get the original groove."

Two unusual and untypical cuts followed the album's title track. 'Every Step of the Way', composed by Ian and Mark Clarke, was a simple love song with basic beat and rhythm driving direct verses alongside a rolling wash of pop-styled, synth-based choruses; the song was subsequently covered by The Monkees on their 1987 album *Pool It!* 'Fun' was co-written by Hunter, Clarke and Hilly Michaels and it was an odd piece: intricate, jumpy and confused, the song's guitar riffs, horn sounds and cute spoken middle eight, were all mixed, shaken and stirred in a single shot. Tracks Two and Three were not the Ian Hunter that everyone knew and one recent retro-review rightly ponders whether the songs were honest rockers or, in hindsight, merely sad relics of the times.

> **IH:** "'Every Step of the Way' was a smutty, dumb, love song, but good dumb. That's the rhythmic feel I wanted. I usually have one song like that on my albums. With 'Fun' there was a kind of desperation about the song. I was just thinking in general that fun didn't seem to be what it used to be."

'Speechless', featuring Dan Hartman of Edgar Winter Group and 'Instant Replay' fame on bass, was an effective satirical take on obsession and the absurdity of television. Lyrically it seemed that Ian was addressing somebody and expressing surprise; musically his voice sounded thinner and higher than some of the *Overnight Angels* tracks that had caused such frustration five years before. Hunter *was* surprised when 'Speechless' was covered by Status Quo on their hit album *In the Army Now*, but he enjoyed the band's version. Quo's Francis Rossi liked the song, as Ian was seemingly distancing himself from Mott the Hoople and being more Eighties, but Rossi later admitted he was baffled by 'Speechless' and that Status Quo's take sounded like a faxed copy of Hunter's original, only more contrived.

> **IH:** "'Speechless' and 'Every Step of the Way' wouldn't have happened without the band because sometimes a guy contributes a lick that will turn a song around. 'Speechless' was written as though it's sung to a person you're fed up with and there's a nice sort of ambiguity in there which I like, so it could go either way, but I was thinking of TV when I wrote and sang it. The words just came from noticing how much time people, kids included, spend sitting passive, in front of televisions. TV – the medium of our age – dumbed down millions. I wish it had never happened; it's worse than gross. I actually loved Status Quo's cover of 'Speechless'. Our version was colourful, while Quo just went for it. It really made me smile."

The story behind 'Death 'n' Glory Boys' depicted Ian's reflections on the recent Falklands War. In line with military theorist Carl von Clausewitz's famous aphorism – that war is the continuation of politics by other means – the 1982 South Atlantic islands conflict between Britain and Argentina had occurred as Prime Minister Margaret Thatcher's mid-term political popularity had started to diminish. The rousing track featured one of Hunter's best vocals on the record and, inevitably, for his singular appearance, Ronson contributed earth-shattering lead guitar in his own inimitable style.

> **IH:** "The Falklands War was like a mini-Vietnam and should never have happened. The Islands cost a fortune to defend and it also cost a fortune in young lives lost. I had a seventeen-year-old daughter then and it was frightening that a kid can be killed that young. I'm apolitical but I don't

227

like stupidity. Ronno did play his ass off on that track and I still remember the night that he played it. I wasn't working with Mick at the time, but he just dropped by one day and did 'Death 'n' Glory Boys' and it was brilliant guitar playing. I was sitting next to him and off he went, soaring like an angel with a look of blind panic on his face. He'd forgotten the chords, as usual, and was winging it. He stayed where he was, but it was pure magic and it worked perfectly. I said to him afterwards that I saw him freeze. He said, 'Well, if you're lost, you might as well stay where you are.' Priceless!"

Lyrically, 'That Girl Is Rock 'n' Roll' left little to the imagination; musically, it sounded slightly rougher round the edges than the rest of the tracks on *All of the Good Ones Are Taken*, and Hunter's song was all the better for it. The light-hearted respite was timely, as 'Somethin's Goin' On' was serious matter. Likening the world to a subway, labelling the human race an endangered species, and describing international leaders as muggers, Ian observed the aura of war around us, surveyed the prospect of nuclear confrontation and expressed distrust of the political elite.

IH: "'That Girl Is Rock 'n' Roll was obvious and it speaks for itself; some girls just are, most girls aren't! 'Somethin's Goin' On' was just what the average guy on the street thinks after reading the papers, trying to figure out why things happen the way they do and then giving up and getting disgusted by it all. It may have been cynical but a lot of people feel that way."

Hunter addressed the ridiculousness of television for a second time in 'Captain Void 'n' the Video Jets', but in a fanciful and comical mood – while 'Seeing Double' was possibly the album's standout track, Hunter's hazy reverie bolstered by Peter Frampton band member Bob Mayo and a further appearance from Clarence Clemons.

228

IH: "'Captain Void' was another comment on the power TV has over people, only here it's a funny sort of fantasy where the aliens land and take us over through our television screens. I've always had a soft spot for 'Seeing Double'. It's like 'All of the Good Ones Are Taken' – a sad little song about when you feel you're at the end of your rope. It was improvised and recorded live in the studio. We'd been doing some other song, and I got the chords wrong and it led into 'Seeing Double'. It was funny, because Bob Mayo, the keyboard player, thought that we were still doing the other song and kept giving me these desperate looks. Clarence came in, did his bit and went. I didn't guide him and just let him do what he heard. He had got the most beautiful tone. I loved the way in Bruce's shows that you didn't hear Clarence for a while, then he appeared and that awesome tone filled the arena. I really liked Bob Mayo; his playing was very organic and 'Seeing Double' was the same."

Hunter's LP closed with his second melancholy re-reading of the title track and, in line with public expectation, when *All of the Good Ones Are Taken* was released, Ian described the album as the best he'd ever recorded.

IH: "I worked harder on this album than any other I've ever done, mainly because it's the first time I've had to sit down and do all the arranging myself as well as being associate producer. I've been used to collaborating with people in the past and that tended to bring out my lazy side. Not this time. The album involved a lot of persistence and song-wise it's strong."

All of the Good Ones Are Taken was unlike any other Hunter record and Columbia's artwork was different too. The ice-white front sleeve featured Ian minus shades, while a colourful headshot framed by distorted yellow and green screen interference offered a contrasting image on the rear. The package also contained a lyric sheet that included Ian's personal tribute, 'Guy Stevens Poem'.

Sounds awarded *All of the Good Ones Are Taken* four stars; describing the title track as a sombre, sobering song of lonely desperation, they considered the record a triumph because it was based on Hunter's two major strengths – talent and experience. New York's *Daily News* wrote that Ian possessed a deft understanding of the intricacies, aesthetics and business of rock, admiring the slow funeral-like projection of 'Death 'n' Glory Boys'; they also considered that 'Speechless' was coloured by Australian-inspired rhythms and that some tracks were too commercial. *Creem* opined, aimlessly, that "some of the good ones are still kicking", while *Kerrang!* wrote: "Die Hard the Hunter; 'All of the Good Ones Are Taken' really is in that classic McCartney mould."

Ian's LP did not chart in Britain and it wasn't helpful that there was limited press coverage for the record; one ridiculous UK review even listed the CBS album as a Chrysalis Records release. In America, *All of the Good Ones Are Taken* peaked at No.125 on *Billboard*, spending eleven weeks on the chart. Columbia and CBS issued two singles. The first, released internationally in August, featured the fast version of the title track as the A-side, backed with 'Death 'n' Glory Boys', and it reached No.25 on *Billboard*'s Mainstream Rock Songs chart. A second British single, 'Somethin's Goin' On', was issued in October, while America opted for 'That Girl Is Rock 'n' Roll'.

A limited edition 'All of the Good Ones Are Taken' twelve-inch disc was pressed in the UK containing a non-LP track, 'Traitor', written by Hunter with input from Robbie Alter. Up-tempo, featuring a call-and-response lyric and glorious glissando piano from Tommy Mandel, the song's treated back-end vocals and instrumental sound effects were reminiscent of *Short Back n' Sides*. Mirroring Mott's generosity and their former B-sides, 'Rose' and 'Rest in Peace', Hunter had given fans a nugget with 'Traitor' – a track that was as strong as anything on the new album.

IH: "I can't remember much about 'Traitor' other than it was a purely manufactured lyric to go with the music. I wasn't writing that well at the time. One journalist speculated about the song; it certainly was *not* about Mick Ronson!"

Hunter's 'All of the Good Ones Are Taken' single was promoted with an acclaimed video that lampooned the rock star image and spoofed the 1981 Dudley Moore comedy *Arthur*. Playing the part of a pining-for-his-girl rocker, Ian's film featured numerous parallels to the movie's billionaire scamp Arthur Bach, the story set variously in New York's Central Park, a mansion building on 14th Street and Second Avenue, and a Brooklyn diner. Directed by Martin Kahan, who shot videos for Kiss and Bon Jovi, and with guest appearances from Arthur 'Captain' Haggerty, Kahan's girlfriend and New York DJ Carol Miller, the 'All of the Good Ones Are Taken' promo has been termed a lost gem and "the most underrated video of all time" by The Golden Age of Music Video.com. Inspired by the earth-shattering onset of Fifties rock 'n' roll music as a teenager, the medium of "promo video" never carried much importance for Ian, but Columbia's project appealed, Hunter saying that acting gave him the same kick and chill that playing music had done in his early years. The 'All of the Good Ones Are Taken' video was superb and successfully converted Hollywood movie storytelling and scripting into a charming three-minute musical expression.

IH: "Videos became a necessary evil in the rock business. They involve too much 'hanging about', but the 'All of the Good Ones Are Taken' film was fun to do. The theme was loosely based on *Arthur* – very loosely. I was worried going into it as Marty Kahan said, 'You've got to be funny.' The big guy in the film, the late Captain Haggerty, coached me enthusiastically. He was great. He'd been a character actor and dog trainer for years, ran Captain Haggerty's School for Dogs in Manhattan and portrayed Mr Clean in TV commercials. He weighed 385lbs and became the butler in my video. For the scene on the Central Park lake, there was a cassette player in the bottom of the boat so that I could lip-synch to the track, but the boat was sinking with the big man's weight. I had to stand up while the player was going under. Our feet were covered in water, the cassette got waterlogged and it really was a fight against time before it packed up. I remember being nearly drowned and soaked to the skin. I also recall filming in the diner with the girls, at 4am, so they could open for regular business. It's not easy being a video star but it all worked out well. I think video helped some people's careers and it hurt others. It depends if you can act. I don't know how good I was, but I loved it. The 'Good Ones' film was great – my first proper video – but the song was another so-called hit that missed!"

All of the Good Ones Are Taken failed to capture the attention of a music audience that was mired in a confused mix of synth-pop, hard rock, hip-hop, post punk, heavy metal, MTV and the arrival of Madonna. Although Mick Ronson made a welcome appearance and the title cut, 'Death 'n' Glory Boys' and 'Seeing Double' are great tracks, the album embraced elements of Eighties production that didn't suit Hunter. No live dates were planned or played to promote *All of the Good Ones Are Taken* and, in retrospect, Ian has mixed feelings about the record.

> **IH:** "Unfortunately, 'Seeing Double' was the only organic song on *All of the Good Ones Are Taken*. Ronson was great on 'Death 'n' Glory Boys', Mark Clarke did some fine harmonies and Robbie Alter was excellent on guitar. There was another song called 'Bluebirds' that I always liked very much, but Steve Popovich wasn't keen on it at the time so we dropped it from the album. I kind of liked 'Captain Void' but, overall, I'm not too keen on the album or most of the songs on it. *All of the Good Ones Are Taken* was a bit like *Overnight Angels*, not musically, but in the sense that it

didn't really mean anything. There were some good songs on those records though. *Overnight Angels* was just a rock album, but my label destroyed it. *All of the Good Ones* was just a bunch of songs, but my label still managed to destroy it."

All of the Good Ones Are Taken was reissued briefly on compact disc by CBS Europe in 1990, and a 2007 American Beat release added the exceptional 'Traitor' as a first-time CD track. In a 4/10 review of the American Beat edition, *Classic Rock* reflected: "Not Hunter's finest moment by any means. The record really hasn't dated well. As for the Michael Bolton-esque picture on the cover, the less said the better."

Having witnessed the reaction to *All of the Good Ones Are Taken,* Ian realised that he was entering a musical wilderness. Hunter effectively began an extended musical hiatus and would not release a new studio album for six years. He soon left Columbia Records for a second time following unexpected upheaval at the label, when long-time ally Richard Asher was effectively forced to resign following a political struggle with Walter Yetnikoff. In 1981, Bruce Lundvall had left Columbia and Dick Asher, who had gained a reputation for loyalty and integrity, became deputy president of the records division. Ironically, Hunter had re-signed with Columbia Records because Asher was there. Ian felt that Dick would press the right buttons at the label. By 1983, Asher was gone.

IH: "That was one of the worst days of my life. When *All of the Good Ones Are Taken* came out, they didn't do anything to push it. They shoved it out the back door as if they were embarrassed and then asked me to do another album. That suggestion was crazy because I wasn't signed to do another record and I couldn't understand why they'd want me to do that. I had no good songs and they hadn't done anything with the ones I'd just given them. So, rather than do another album, I got my manager to try and get me a situation where

233

I could experiment. They did offer me money to build a sixteen-track studio, so I got that together – then spent two years trying to figure out what to do with it – then I found out that I couldn't write songs anymore."

While Hunter's Columbia Records contract ran out, the small domestic studio set-up became his focus as he started working on demos. His band had split, but Ian kept in touch with guitarist Robbie Alter, who has always retained admiration for Hunter's talent.

Robbie Alter: "I've always respected Ian's work ethic and approach to his songwriting craft. He's not lazy but, by the same token, you have to manage your creative expenditures or you will burn out. It can be hard work to tickle ideas and songs out of the nothingness of thin ether, but Ian's brave enough to have his opinions and expose them. He's not one of those vacuous lyricists of the Eighties who revelled in the celebrity of being a rock star. I was slightly embarrassed by those self-indulgent songs and the 'hair bands' of the Eighties. The thing I appreciated about my professional relationship with Ian was the fact that we reset it after it had been 'employer' and 'employee'. When I quit the business and the dust settled, he and I made a more productive team; more like peers. There was less pressure and it needn't have happened as I think he was fairly upset about the *Good Ones* record and the way it all went down. But when Ian moved back into New York City, close by where I was living, I helped him move in and we started hanging out together. For me it was good fun as I had no musical outlet at that time, so we'd just do some work at his home studio."

Hunter was now a more relaxed figure and a New York Yankees baseball fan, an interest that provided helpful release while he thought about and re-tooled his songwriting. Ian wanted to play in a band but felt he was too bossy for a group situation. This was exemplified when he met Mott's former members to talk about a possible commercial release of Mott the Hoople videos and TV clips with new interviews, whereupon Hunter felt "the old antagonism" rising again. Mick Ralphs liked to run things and so did Ian. It would have been hard for Hunter to revert to a group structure.

In December 1983, Ian attended one of Ronnie Lane's Appeal for ARMS concerts at Madison Square Garden in New York, where Clapton, Beck and Page appeared as part of an all-star show. Although Hunter's musical direction was clouded, there were rumours of movie opportunities and one report in London read: "Ian Hunter, known for his hell-raising days fronting Mott the Hoople, is to become wheelchair bound. But it's not for reasons of health. Hunter has landed his first film role. He is to play two parts, in a horror tale called *The Graduation*, as a fifty-three-year-old paralysed professor, with a nasty habit of doing away with people, and a rock and roll musician. The film, his first stab at acting, is a small-scale affair by Hollywood standards, with a budget of £1,600,000."

> **IH:** "I got offered a few film parts and scores, but it was always some dumb movie about groupies and cocaine. I remember one movie opportunity after 'All of the Good Ones Are Taken'. A guy in Chicago wanted me to do it but I said, 'I can't act, well maybe I can, but you're taking a chance here.' They said, 'No, we just want you to do what you did in that video.' It was all looking good, until it came to the financing. The woman who produced the 1982 *Eating Raoul* movie, Anne Kimmel, had seen the 'All of the Good Ones Are Taken' video and liked it, so I was going to get a similar role in her film. I thought that was fine because my video wasn't hard to do. She was a ballsy lady and she fought and fought, and ran around, and tried to get finance, but couldn't. Mick Ronson and I got offered movie ideas over the years, but nothing ever seemed to materialise."

Ian's son Jess would later appear in the Oscar-nominated film *Sleepers*. Directed by Barry Levinson and based on Lorenzo

235

Carcaterra's book about a reform school, the movie was shot around New York and in Newtown, Connecticut, near Hunter's home.

> **IH:** "Jess phoned one day and told me he was in this movie. I said, 'Who's in it?' – thinking it was a school movie – and he said, 'Kevin Bacon, some guy De Niro, and who's the bloke in *The Graduate*?' I said, 'Dustin Hoffman. What the hell are you talking about?'"

Hunter attended a ceremony held at New York's Radio City Music Hall on 14th September 1984 when 'All of the Good Ones Are Taken' was nominated at the first-ever MTV Video Music Awards. Other nominees for 'Best Direction in a Video' alongside Hunter included The Police, Cyndi Lauper and ZZ Top. With hundreds of photographers in attendance, sitting in front of Quincy Jones and Diana Ross, Ian rapidly became aware that what he'd perceived as a small affair was something much greater, especially after stage performances by Rod Stewart and Madonna, and a speech from Phil Collins.

> **IH:** "I was shitting myself that night and wondering what the hell was going on. I went into the toilet and the director said, 'We're gonna win! We're gonna win!' In the hall I was sitting in the third row from the front, on the alleyway. I had a camera in my face and another camera down at my knees, and I have no speech written. Then, suddenly, ZZ Top has won. It was the biggest relief of my life. I *was* dying!"

In the early Eighties, Ronson worked with The Mamas and the Papas and appeared at California's 'Peace Sunday' anti-nuclear concert, held in Pasadena's Rose Bowl. Mick commented that he and Ian always remained friends, but admitted they sometimes had musical differences. Ronson wanted to try other projects occasionally and, alongside Hunter, he felt he sometimes couldn't express what he wanted to say musically on Ian's material. Mick contemplated a third solo album, but joked that nobody wanted to put one out. He also claimed that he had developed some hesitancy in singing vocals, but he was soon playing in T Bone Burnett's band, supporting The Who on their 1982 US Tour. Burnett invited Ronson at short notice, Mick having turned down a more lucrative offer from Bob Seger. Hunter marvelled at Ronson's integrity.

> **IH:** "Mick went on tour with T Bone for 100 dollars a week, sleeping on people's floors. The alternative was 2,500 dollars a week and hotels with Bob Seger, but Mick didn't like the music much and didn't want to play C, F and G chords. So Ronson went with T Bone. I really admired him for that. Suzi had a fit!"

"Mick didn't have a formula," says T Bone. "That's the trick. He just had the touch and was courageous. Any time the audience would start chanting for The Who, I would just look over at Ronson and let him rip. He would do great guitar solos, always the best received part of our show. It just sounded like the building was falling down."

Ronson's production CV extended further with two acclaimed albums for Vancouver post-punk band The Payola$, led by Paul Hyde and Bob Rock. Hunter sang on 'I'll Find Another (Who Can Do It Right)' for the group's 1983 LP *Hammer on a Drum*, Mick contributing keyboards and backing vocals. British-born Paul Hyde had moved to Canada with his family in 1969 but returned to England in the early Seventies with a group. Unprepared to attack the UK music scene, his bandmates retreated to Vancouver, but Paul stayed and worked as a groundkeeper at Leeds University; he attended two Mott the Hoople concerts during his stay.

Paul Hyde: "One day in the studio, Bob Rock and Mick Ronson announced that they'd intended to surprise me but couldn't keep the secret anymore. Ian Hunter was going to sing on the Payola$ record! It was a dream come true. One of our songs was 'I'll Find Another' and it was tailor-made for Hunter, so, once I found out he was coming, I changed it so there was a section that we could sing together. As a teenager I was heavily influenced by Mott the Hoople, and Ian Hunter is one of the great lyricists of rock 'n' roll. He can rock out, but he's also the king of the compassionate ballad. I copied his singing style until I found my own voice. Recording with him was like winning a lottery."

Bob Rock: "It's rare when you get to meet one of your idols, let alone work with them and write a song with them. My partner in music, Paul Hyde, played me *Brain Capers* one day, a record he'd brought back from England. I was immediately hooked. Mott the Hoople were a huge influence for their sound, their look, their attitude and, of course, the songs. Ian Hunter has always been an inspiration for his lyrics and view on the world: the working man's rock star. The time I spent with Ronno and the few days with Ian were really the basis of my style of production and making records; 'Serve the song and rock!' When The Payola$ recorded *Hammer on a Drum*, Ian Hunter was every bit the mysterious star that I'd imagined, and he was a true gent. I played a guitar solo on 'I'll Find Another', with Ian and Ronno staring at me. It was terrifying, but they were the best days – my golden age of rock 'n' roll."

Mick collaborated further with T Bone Burnett on *Proof through the Night*, and there was also a brief Bowie–Ronson reunion in 1983, when Mick played guitar on 'The Jean Genie' at Toronto's CNE during David's *Serious Moonlight* tour. Ian Thomas, XDavis and Lisa Dalbello also received Ronson's collaborative attentions; Dalbello's *Whomanfoursays* was a dazzling and daring album and, during European promotional work for the LP, Sami Yaffa of Hanoi Rocks encountered Mick in Germany.

"I met Mick Ronson in Frankfurt on my 21st birthday in September 1984," says Sami. "Mick was playing with Dalbello, and he was an absolute gentleman and funny as hell. After a TV show both bands retreated to a tavern. As I was waiting for my beer at the bar, I turned around to have a chat with someone but when I turned back there was a bucket containing Moët et Chandon champagne instead. The barmaid said it was a birthday gift from the gentleman along the bar, and there was Ronno, grinning and mouthing 'Happy Birthday'. Mick Ronson: down to earth, non-pretentious and a great talent."

The Dalbello record had been cut for Capitol Records and Ronson was soon approached by the label about working with another of their new signings – the legendary Tina Turner. The proposed album, *Private Dancer,* slated to include versions of David Bowie's '1984', Al Green's 'Let's Stay Together' and The Beatles' 'Help', was an important production aimed at rejuvenating Turner's career.

> **IH:** "I remember going up to the Capitol building in Hollywood with Ronson to see Tina Turner and the label people. Mick got on great with Tina at that meeting, so much so that at one point she mentioned she had a corn on her foot and suddenly Ronson had his shoes off, showing her a bunion that he had on his toe. They eventually got Mick to stop rambling and play some of his tapes, so he fumbled with the stereo system in the boardroom playing short bits and pieces, and repeatedly changed the cassettes. I thought it was a disaster. We left Capitol that day and heard no more. Tina Turner's album went five times platinum and sold 20 million copies."

With Ronson playing and producing on various fronts, Hunter entered a fairly barren phase where he would only work on ad hoc movie music commissions and extracurricular collaborations. With Blue Öyster Cult's Eric Bloom and Donald Roeser, Ian co-wrote 'Let Go' and 'Goin' Through the Motions', the latter covered by Bonnie Tyler. Hunter also assisted Hanoi Rocks with some tracks that appeared on the band's *Two Steps from the Move* album.

> **IH:** "I played on the same bill with Eric Bloom once and then met him at a New York City gig. He came out of the shadows backstage and said, 'Remember me? I'm Eric the Oyster.' Eric

was a small bloke with a small house and a small basement and a small tape recorder – he was a lovely guy who knows his stuff and we wrote 'Goin' Through the Motions' in an afternoon. I'm not keen on co-writing, but Bonnie Tyler wound up recording 'Goin' Through the Motions' because Jim Steinman was the producer and he was very fond of some of my material. Jim also tried to get someone to do a song of mine called 'The Jar' for ages.

"Hanoi Rocks and Bob Ezrin was a strange combination. The band needed lyrics so Ezrin asked them who could write them and the only lyricist they would use was me. Bob phoned me up and invited me down to the studio. I remember Jack Bruce was there for some reason and I was given some music demos, so I took them home and wrote three sets of lyrics the following day. I sent them back and they used them. I always liked their singer, Michael Monroe. He came to my apartment at three o'clock in the afternoon one day, in all his finery. Michael is the genuine article."

"We were big fans of Mott the Hoople, one of the greatest bands ever," admitted Michael Monroe. "I love Ian and his first solo album is still my favourite; he's a great songwriter. When I was a kid, I always thought, 'That's a rock 'n' roll star!' Hanoi Rocks played 'Boulevard of Broken Dreams' and Hunter worked on the chorus and put it together. What a genius. It was great to meet him. It's a tough business, and it's easy to lose it, but Ian is really down to earth."

Hunter also appeared on Mountain's *Go for Your Life* and Ian and Mick collaborated briefly with Duran Duran's John and Andy Taylor and drummer Tony Thompson, who were to be the nucleus of a "supergroup" with revolving guest singers and players, including Mars Williams from Psychedelic Furs; the band concept never flew, but the initiative became a precursor for The Power Station, which was soon cemented with Robert Palmer.

Hunter Ronson undertook their last joint production for Urgent, a New York band featuring vocalist Donnie Kehr. Ian co-wrote four tracks for *Cast the First Stone* and their single 'Running Back' hit No.87 on *Billboard*, but the sessions were a soulless experience for Hunter. He had become jaded by the Eighties, apart from the music of Prince, who he regarded as a viable artist. Ian certainly considered that record companies and radio had become closed books.

> **IH:** "Ronson and I got together and produced an album for Urgent in Los Angeles. Mick was usually skint and was looking for money again, and that project, if we both did it, was 30,000 dollars. I agreed because he wanted to do it, so I just sat there and let him. That way he was happy, and I'd make a few dollars as well. I found producing extremely boring though; you'd get none of the credit if the band made it, and all of the flak if they didn't. Ronno and I sometimes worked as 'The Slimmer Twins' when we produced outside stuff – that was just our affectionate take on 'The Glimmer Twins' – Mick 'n' Keef. I remember Ronson and I were in The Village Recorder in Los Angeles and Jimmy Iovine was next door recording Stevie Nicks from Fleetwood Mac. He was also doing The Cars in New York and was travelling back and forth. One day I asked Jimmy, 'How's it going?' – and he said he was tired, adding, 'Stevie takes an hour to do her make-up before she's ready to record.' I said, 'You're lucky – it takes Ronson two.'"

Having disappeared from view, between 1984 and 1987 Ian wrote and recorded material at home. Some songs would be developed for his next album, a few were covered by other artists and some appeared in movie soundtracks. Several Hunter compositions were never released, including 'Don't Throw Your Life Away', 'Mad at the World', 'You Got What It Takes', 'I Can't Find You', 'Boys 'R' Us', 'Mean Streets', 'Read Me Like a Book', 'If You Need

Somebody', 'Someone Else's Girl', 'Danny', 'It Must Be Love', 'Girl Shy', 'Perfect', 'Lonely Kids', 'Beat of My Heart', 'Chains', 'Slave', 'Hell' and 'Love Bug'. Ian used his domestic studio as a learning experience and admits that he was fraught and frustrated by the industry. There had always been a patriarchal structure to rock music and the late Sixties and early Seventies had witnessed some casualties, but the Eighties – "the cocaine decade" – created an arrogant corporate landscape. Ever astute, Ian steered clear of the industry's idiosyncrasies.

> **IH:** "In the arts, if you're any way successful, drugs are always around. The question of whether you take them is another thing altogether. In the Mott days we toured endlessly and I gravitated to some downs. I didn't like speed because it made no sense. The body's an engine and if you want to overload it, it's going to pack in quicker. You have a lifespan and if you speed it up, you live less. I'd rather live longer. Mandrax, as a sedative, used properly, were non-barbiturates that gave you instant sleep with no hangovers. You'd get a day off on the road but often couldn't sleep with all the adrenalin, so you'd go to Doctor Robert, fabled by The Beatles, and the faces you'd see in his Harley Street office on a Monday morning was like 'Sunday Night at the London Palladium'.
>
> "I always want to be in full control at a gig. I won't take a beer before a show as it bloats me, but a glass of champagne seldom comes amiss. For the life of me I don't see the connotations with cocaine. It's a singularly stupid drug favoured by shallow people lacking in personality. I haven't taken acid or the dumbest drug of all, heroin. Mott had a so-called 'drug incident' in New York, which happened because Buffin found prune juice for the first time in America and immediately drank two bottles of it, because he liked it so much. The brand may have been *Mott's* prune juice. With Buff's butt cemented to the bog, I had to inform a few

242

thousand booing fans that we wouldn't be performing as our drummer had OD'd on prune juice. By the time the news reached Detroit, Buff had overdosed and was dead. Typical media bullshit – but fun.

"The Eighties were terrible without a doubt; the beginning of corporate labels and corporate radio stations. Nothing got me off at that time. Funnily enough, I liked Bruce Springsteen in the Seventies and the Nineties, but not in the Eighties. I liked Prince, but that was in another neck of the woods, so I didn't know what the fuck to do. I'd tried all these demos at home, but most of my Eighties material I never put out. Some would eventually come out on a box set thirty years later, but I've got stuff that will never see the light of day. They were interesting tapes but they were sounds really, rather than Ian Hunter songs. I'd work most afternoons, trying things out, but I almost stopped for five years as the whole industry was so depressing. In 1985, I got a place in England and just sat around on the South Coast with my kids, doing what people do. Our mates Miller and Fiona Anderson lived in Shoreham, so we moved nearby and bought an apartment with a sun deck, right on the Worthing seafront."

The Hunters' top-floor Worthing penthouse was in a Grade II listed building named Beach House, and it had a rich history: Edward VII and the writers J.B. Priestley and Arnold Bennett had all been visitors to a home whose former owners included Sir Frederick Adair Roe, head of the Bow Street Runners in the 19th century, and playwright Edward Knoblock, author of *Kismet*.

IH: "Worthing was great in the summer with the kids. The rest of the year it was expensive and empty. But music plagues me, so in the end I had to come back to America. I'd written best in the filth and small surroundings of New York. That was good for me; it wasn't good for the wife, but it worked for me. I really didn't like the Eighties, I really didn't

243

try in the Eighties, and I wasn't very good in the Eighties. I was battling here, there and everywhere, so I started writing songs for movies, which wasn't much fun but it paid the bills. I would work in my home studio because having missed my first two kids growing up, I was determined to be with Jess until he was five. It wasn't until 1986 that I really got back into being Ian Hunter again."

Hunter was writing, but with a leniency that he would not normally allow. The well was fairly dry, but the briefs and commissions for soundtrack songs were manageable and offered some direction and income. Ian's first movie composition, '(I'm the) Teacher', was commissioned by United Artists Pictures for the 1984 comedy drama *Teachers*, starring Nick Nolte. Former collaborator Bobby Colomby was involved with the project and Hunter was asked by Sandy Gibson, the film's music supervisor, if he would write one song. The track, recorded at The Power Station, was co-written by Ian and Mick, produced by Ronson, arranged by Hunter and mixed by Bob Clearmountain.

> **IH:** "'(I'm the) Teacher' was commissioned for a movie but it's one of my best lyrics. Somebody rang me up, as the film's producer was a fan. I had this lyric… *'The question's arisen, is this a prison, some say it is, some say it isn't.'* I liked that first line and it was all over in five minutes. Then the producer came back and said, 'I love the lyric but the song's so slow, like a death march.' So, we revved it up. Mick changed my original idea around completely. He was a truly great arranger. We got a gold record for that."

Hunter also wrote a song for Orion Pictures' college comedy movie *Up the Creek*. Recorded in Hollywood with Virgin Records' rock act Shooting Star, 'Great Expectations (You Never Know What to Expect)' was partly inspired by Ian's daughter, Tracie, and was tongue-in-cheek. Hunter and Ronson also covered 'Good Man in a Bad Time', written by Marc Tanner and Jon Reede for the 1985 Columbia horror movie *Fright Night*. Ian was happy to tackle single song remits, but not full soundtrack albums, so he cut 'Wake-up Call', composed by Arthur Baker, Tina B and Tommy Mandel, featured in the sci-fi film *The Wraith*, starring Charlie Sheen. Hunter has remained pragmatic about "the soundtrack years".

> **IH:** "For the 'Great Expectations' session I turned up at Pasha Music in LA and they had this heavy metal band there that couldn't really play it. Like all my stuff, it sounds simple, but it's a little more sophisticated than that when you get down to it. 'Great Expectations' *was*, loosely, Tracie. I did three things in the Eighties for the producer and DJ Arthur Baker. He came out of the woodwork and liked my voice. I recorded 'Good Man in a Bad Time' in his Manhattan studio and it was used in *Fright Night*. Then he rang me up out of the blue and asked if I would do a vocal on 'Wake-up Call'. We did the song in a day in New York, starting at six in the evening and finishing about four in the morning. I worked with Arthur for a week and we got on well. We also did a demo of a song called 'Professional Lover' for Tina Turner, which I thought was great, but I don't think Arthur pursued it. I liked the sound Arthur got. The one-track film was great for me. You'd put all your energies into one song and you'd be in and out in two days."

Other Hunter songs featured in film soundtracks, but not specifically written for movie projects, included 'We Gotta Get Out of Here' in *Up the Academy* and 'Cleveland Rocks' for *Light of Day*, both lifted from *Welcome to the Club*. 'Standin' in My Light' was recorded by Sam Brown and Tom Van Landuyt for *Ad Fundum*, Mott's 'All the Way from Memphis' had featured in *Alice Doesn't Live Here Anymore* and Hunter's 'Overnight Angels' was used in *Asphaltnacht*. 'All the Young Dudes' has also appeared in several films, including *The Last of the High Kings*, *Amongst Friends* and *Juno*.

IH: "My early Eighties writing had been eclectic. In 1984, I'd got my home studio together and after a while I started to write again, but I found out that the writing was pretty poor. I realised it was probably something to do with the fact that I lived in upstate New York, so I sold my house and we moved into a rabbit hutch on 23rd Street in New York City around 1985. The writing started to improve as I'd slipped a long way in the preceding five years, and a lot further than I thought I had. I know, because coming back was a long haul. You can't just skip back into the business. I was doing occasional gigs and getting an average reaction to things I thought were great, so I had to make even more of an effort. I set up the sixteen-track studio in our Manhattan apartment, all in my bedroom, in a ten by six area overlooking the river. I remember I had to write in the afternoons because they used to bang on the walls after 6pm. I liked writing there but we didn't stay in New York City for too long. We left because one day I was with Jess, who was four at the time, and we were on a bus and saw a guy shot in the face. I turned Jess's head away, but he still saw it."

On 13th November 1985, CBS celebrated Bob Dylan's twenty-five-year career and cumulated sales of over thirty-five million records at a star-studded ceremony in the Whitney Museum of American Art on Manhattan's Madison Avenue. As banks of video screens beamed out illuminated career images of the star, the guest list constituted a who's who in music and included Roger McGuinn, Judy Collins, Arlo Guthrie, Roy Orbison, The Band, Lou Reed, John Cale, Iggy Pop, David Bowie, Pete Townshend, Yoko Ono, The E Street Band, Billy Joel, and Ian and Trudi. Invitees from the world of film included Martin Scorsese, Harvey Keitel and Robert De Niro. Ian was photographed with Bob at the Whitney and Hunter commented on the night that everyone there owed Dylan thanks for something.

In the mid- to late Eighties Karla DeVito recorded Hunter–Mandel's 'Money Can't Buy Love' for *Wake 'Em Up In Tokyo*, Billy

Cross co-wrote 'Crazy Glue' with Ian, and Scott Fulsom recorded 'Red Letter Day' and 'White on White'. Whilst Hunter Ronson declined an invitation to produce Urgent's second album, *Thinking Out Loud*, Ian co-wrote 'If This Is Love', 'Inch by Inch' and 'Pain (Love Is a Victim)' for the band. Then Hunter's renaissance really took root when he played a series of Canadian and American gigs in late 1986 with The Roy Young Band.

British singer and keyboard player Roy Young's track record included experiences in Sixties' Germany alongside The Beatles, Little Richard and Jerry Lee Lewis. Roy had been a booker for The Star-Club in Hamburg and had played with Chuck Berry, Ray Charles and Fats Domino. Returning to Britain, he joined Cliff Bennett and The Rebel Rousers, formed The Roy Young Band and later worked with Long John Baldry, Nicol Williamson and David Bowie. When he met Ian, Roy was a resident of Toronto, where he'd assembled an impressive group of musicians. Through his friendship with drummer Dennis Elliott, Young agreed to support Hunter on some live dates.

Roy Young: "Dennis asked me one day if I would mind him inviting Ian over to his house, as Hunter wanted to meet me. So, Ian arrived and started telling me that in his early days he would watch TV shows just to catch my performances. During that visit we all had dinner and got talking down in the basement studio about working, and said we'd like to play together. I already had a big band with a horn section in Canada that I was touring with. This excited Ian and several months later I invited him to join us for a tour, which extended into two tours. For me it was a big thing to go out and work with Ian Hunter. I was very proud of being able to do that."

> IH: "Back in the Sixties, this blonde-headed kid used to hammer an upright piano on TV shows called *Drumbeat* and *Oh, Boy!* Roy was the only English guy who could do Little Richard and the music seemed to carry him out of the building. Roy told me he was asked to join The Beatles in Hamburg.

He used to book bands for The Star-Club and played with The Beatles twice. McCartney had wanted Roy in the band, but he turned them down because he had such a good gig at The Star-Club and didn't really know if they'd make it. I asked him once how he felt about that. He said every day when he got out of bed, he banged his head against a wall, but other than that he was okay. I particularly wanted to get better as a singer and with Roy I learned what made my vocal work. Roy was telling me to go up instead of down and, using his band in Canada, I found that certain songs I was writing weren't going to cross over to record. I had to knock a lot of songs on the head. By this time Roy was more into Ray Charles and jazzier stuff but we hit it off. We were both at a loose end, so it was real fun. Roy was a big hero of mine in the Sixties so it was a real honour to work with him."

Young's nine-piece band included three horn players, drummer Shawn Eisenberg and guitarist Papa John King, who had worked with Long John Baldry. Roy had also recruited a twenty-one-year-old Canadian named Pat Kilbride, a prodigious bassist and a huge Jaco Pastorius fan who would bring flashes of sophistication to Ian's repertoire. Touring the East and West Coasts of North America in late 1986, The Roy Young Band prefaced Hunter's set each night playing traditional rock 'n' roll standards including 'Great Balls of Fire' and 'Dizzy Miss Lizzy'. Ian was enthused.

IH: "I liked Roy's band so much and always knew it would be a great group as Roy had an innate sense of rhythm. He wouldn't play with people who weren't good, so that was one of the reasons I did the gigs. I originally signed up for a month, but it carried on from there. I was along for the ride in his band, but it developed into two separate shows. We were only going to play in Canada, but then I thought the band was so good that maybe we should do some American dates. It was a real buzz."

248

Hunter utilised his gigs with Roy Young to try out material as he advanced preparatory work for his next album. He noted that he had five songs but they were eclectic. Lyrics were now harder to write given the subject matter that Ian had covered over a fifteen-year period and he admitted it was difficult creating a new body of songs that matched, and frustrating that it took time. Hunter had written one simple song called 'The Other Man' but didn't know about recording his next record with Ronson as he felt he got on better with Mick when they were not working together. On the question of songwriting, Hunter remained modest.

> **IH:** "There's no talent involved at all in songwriting. You're just blessed. Everybody has a gift of some kind. I have an aerial and waves come in. I don't go looking for it and I've never sat down and passed examinations, I'm just lucky. When I write, titles are important to me and the more vivid the title, the more vivid the lyric and the better the story. The great songs are the ones that come together at once – words and music – beginning and end. Perhaps if I'd been a little more conscientious, I would have written a lot more and maybe been a lot more prolific."

As he toured alongside Roy Young, Hunter commented once more on his former Mott the Hoople colleagues.

> **IH:** "I was with Mott's bass player a few months ago, in July. He has a big shop full of weird stuff; Pete always wanted that. Buff's a producer with the BBC, Mick Ralphs has got another Bad Company album out, and one of them is in a halfway home and he's probably better off now than he ever was. I felt really bad about the Mott split but there was not that much I could do. I was sick of the name, not because of the name itself but because of the trouble that we'd been in. I also felt that the bass player and drummer wanted the Mott name. The only chance they had was to

keep it. I was unhappy when those Mott records came out though, because Mott the Hoople was very near and dear to me. For it to be given to people who were no part of it was somewhat demeaning, I thought."

In 1987, Ian played piano on four tracks for Michael Monroe's *Nights Are So Long* album but, crucially, Hunter was collaborating with John Jansen on the production of his latest demos. Jansen had worked with Blue Öyster Cult, Lou Reed and Karla DeVito, and had recently co-produced English pop-rock band Cutting Crew, who found huge success with their hit single '(I Just) Died in Your Arms'. Ian's first encounter with John had been during the early Eighties when Jansen was working with Jim Steinman, and they mixed and added some percussion overdubs to a version of Hunter's 'All of the Good Ones Are Taken'. John later assisted on a track called 'Abnormal' for Ian, with New Jersey guitar player Bruce Gatewood. Jansen and Hunter worked well together.

> **IH:** "I got on with John really well but we never actually made a record together. It's not that I chose him; he just came around one day and didn't destroy my stuff like a lot of people did. John didn't really want to spend too much time overdoing it, which was great, because I'd been through all of that."

"In the Eighties, Ian had an apartment on 23rd Street in Manhattan and we worked together and did some tracks at A&M in New Jersey," recalls John Jansen. "Hunter had a song that I thought was going to be such a big hit – 'American Music'. Working with Ian was a pleasure. He had patience for any suggestion or observation and was very focused and professional. On the occasions I visited Ian and Trudi they were always gracious."

Hunter soon had ten songs drafted for a new album and was in a strong position, having travelled down different alleyways. He was confident of securing a record deal but it had to be the right one. Ian appreciated that John Jansen would not have become involved musically unless he believed the new material was special. Hunter's favoured songs included 'Sign of Affection', 'Angel', 'National Holiday', 'Give Me Back My Wings', 'Red Letter Day', 'My Love', 'Someone Else's Girl', 'American Music' and 'The Loner'.

Ian played more North American dates in November 1987 with The Roy Young Band, continuing to try out material in a live setting, but whilst he was offered two record deals, he declined them. Hunter had experienced publishing success via covers by Barry Manilow, Blue Öyster Cult and The Pointer Sisters and registered three publishing companies: Jesse John Music, Ian Hunter Music and Spiv Music.

Interest in Hunter increased further when Greendow Productions, run by Joy Division and Magazine producer Martin Hannett, announced their intention to make a television documentary. In bizarre press features headed 'Morrissey and Noddy join Mott-ly crew' and 'Ian Hunter: TV Eyes', it was reported that the former Smiths and Slade frontmen were the first stars lined up to pay tribute to "the former Mott the Hoople main man". Other artists approached to take part included Bryan Ferry, Queen, Mick Jones and Status Quo, and Greendow claimed that their proposed film would not be an obvious accolade to Ian, rather a reflection on Hunter in the present with "an eye to the future". They intended to record part of the documentary in Ireland with Ian and an "all-star" band supporting Def Leppard, but the Greendow film was never commenced and Joe Elliott was unaware of the plans. "No one ever approached me or Def Leppard about an Ian Hunter documentary," says Joe. "Trust me. I would remember."

> IH: "Martin Hannett was a big underground producer and I agreed to do the film because it was him. However, they'd got a movie to do beforehand which was about independent producers, so they spent their money doing this programme about independent producers – which I think is a pretty boring subject – and they couldn't flog it. Then they couldn't

251

get the money together to get mine going and it was sad, because they'd already got one backer, MTV Europe, who were willing to go in. They rang me up and asked if I'd do it and I said yes, because I was completely off the roll. I didn't know what to do at that time. I thought the film might set the ball rolling again for me, but Mick Ronson and I got back together and that started the roll in other ways. By then, the documentary no longer appealed to me anyway."

In February 1988, British imprint Castle Records issued *Mott the Hoople featuring Ian Hunter: The Collection,* notable for an unheard full-length version of 'Walkin' with a Mountain' that had been slashed and savaged for *Mott the Hoople Live,* plus a peculiar edited fragment of 'Crash Street Kidds'. Chrysalis also released *Shades of Ian Hunter* in America, placing previously released solo tracks on compact disc for the first time. Many Mott and Hunter recordings had been deleted, and whilst Warner Brothers contacted Ian about back catalogue material, Hunter considered in 1988 that past albums deserved enhancement rather than simple transfer to CD.

IH: "When I hear Mott's recordings, the songs and words aren't dated but I think that some of the sounds and the speeds are a little bit duff. I don't think they should be re-released as they are. If I had my way somebody would ring me up and say let's remix these and put them out, because there is equipment to do it now. I think the songs still stand up though. Chrysalis owns the licensing on my solo albums, and they are doing a reissue and it is funny because they don't particularly like my new stuff and yet, to me, the new stuff is about ten times better than some of the things on their compilation."

Since Ronson played with Hunter on 'Death 'n' Glory Boys' in 1983, he had spent more time in England than usual but had also worked in Canada, Italy, France, Holland and Switzerland, collaborating with Sandy Dillon, One the Juggler, Midge Ure, Kiss That, Lisa Dominique, Andy Sex Gang, Cody Melville, Rick Rose, Marie Laure et Lui and Steve Harley.

Steve Harley: "I produced an unreleased song called 'Lucky Man' featuring Mick on electric guitar. You couldn't wish to meet a nicer, more generous man and musician, but I was in awe of him, even though we had socialised somewhat and shared a mutual respect. Mick was an arranger from the top drawer and an inspired guitarist. He played piano well enough to pass most rock band auditions, so there was the musical brilliance, and what with the stone-carved bones and the earthy attitude, Mick had it all really. Mick Ronson fired up the embryonic David Bowie's career and life. He was that good. It must have been like having Stravinsky in your band."

Feeling lost and having ditched his guitar, Ronson questioned whether he was being honest with himself and considered quitting music at one stage. He thought about going to college and becoming a chef; he didn't want to be known as "just a guitar player" for the rest of his life. Then, in 1987, Ronson headed to Nashville to produce a country album for David Lynn Jones at the behest of Steve Popovich, who was now employed by Mercury Records in Tennessee. Mick could have secured considerable work in Nashville and although he felt that record production was beginning to feel like retirement, he collaborated with Funhouse, The Phantoms, Fatal Flowers and The Toll. He also assembled a short-lived Mick Ronson Band with Sham Morris – Rokko Lee of One the Juggler – playing gigs around New York State. Hunter Ronson met The Fentons in Toronto and Mick produced the band at Nevessa Studios in Woodstock, Ian noting that Mick still caused artists to sweat over studio time as he asked for tapes to be played over and over again while he "devised" his part.

IH: "Ronson was still hilarious on sessions. All these serious people would wander around, looking at Mick as he asked for repeated playbacks. They were fretting and wondering

253

what the hell Ronson was doing. I knew. He was listening and forming the solo in his mind; then there was a mess, as he tried to get it out of his head and through the guitar; and then when they were ready to give up, 'Bang' – it was brilliant."

Although Ronson had worked globally, he maintained contact with Ian and sometimes cooked barbecues at the Hunter's home, where he was known as 'The Great Marinator'. Central to Mick was the fact that he and Ian always remained great friends, whether they wanted to work together or not. Ronson had undertaken record production widely, living from pay cheque to pay cheque but, by May 1988, he felt revitalised. "I rang up Ian," Mick would recall, "who I always talk to whether we're working together or not, and said, 'Look, I've got to do something. I want to play the guitar again and get out there.'"

Ian Hunter's new songs and recent gigs had proven that he still possessed musical muscle and substance. Mick Ronson was re-energised and eager to play. With a new sense of enthusiasm, the stage was set one more time for The Slimmer Twins.

CHAPTER EIGHT

Balance

This is not the end – this is a beginning.

In 1989, Ian and Mick released an album as 'Hunter Ronson' and the songs and recordings capped a triumphant comeback. Both artists had become musically frustrated during the Eighties and the muse had deserted Ronson, but in 1988 Mick yearned to play guitar again.

> **IH:** "Mick and I had lost ourselves for about six years. We hated that period of music and the corporate takeover bands with hair extensions and lipstick. It was fucking stupid and so disenchanting. We had to keep our mouths shut, of course, because commercially we were nothing compared to them. We couldn't say anything then, because they'd say, 'Well you're not selling records,' but we hated the Eighties – Loverboy and all that crap – Poison and all those hairy people. That period of music was a joke, but it fooled people. Ronno and I had done production projects together but by the mid-Eighties I tried not to produce, mainly because when we did it, we always got lumbered with people who couldn't play.

255

Slowly my career was disappearing. In the end I was gigging to make a few bucks and generally not writing. Everybody has a period where things go off the rails in their life, and I knew I was off and that I had to do something. I got rid of my manager and the songs got better, then Mick rang me up and we hit the road with The Roy Young Band. One of the reasons I came back was because I'd lie on the bed and watch *MTV* and whine at everything I saw, until Trudi turned around one day and said, 'Well why don't you go out and do something about it, instead of just moaning?' Mick was in Nashville and he'd had some success there as a producer. I happened to mention that I was going off on a two-week tour of Canadian clubs and he said, 'I want to play guitar. I want to come too.'"

Mirroring the lead-in to *You're Never Alone with a Schizophrenic*, Hunter realised that his new material intrigued Ronson. 'Look Before You Leap', 'Ill Wind', 'The Loner' and 'American Music' were strong and the latter two songs were first aired during Canadian live dates in a set that included '(I'm the) Teacher', a re-working of The Beatles' 'Day Tripper' and a beautiful Ronson instrumental, 'Sweet Dreams'. Ian also nailed an attention-grabbing version of 'While You Were Looking at Me', written by E Street Band guitarist Steven Van Zandt, but Michael Monroe beat Hunter to the punch and placed the song on *Not Fakin' It*, an album that would feature Ian on one track.

Hunter, Ronson and Roy Young toured Ontario in June 1988, playing nine club gigs including London, Mississauga and Windsor. The band comprised Pat Kilbride, John King, backing singer Carmela Long and drummer Shawn Eisenberg, who considered Ian a brilliant songsmith with a gift for writing refreshingly relevant lyrics. Hunter's concise comeback ended with a packed show at Rock 'n' Roll Heaven in Toronto where Joe Elliott appeared on stage, the first of many "Hunter leap-ons". Def Leppard were touring the globe promoting their mammoth *Hysteria* album and following a sell-out gig at the Toronto Blue Jays' baseball stadium, Elliott ached to dash across the city and join his heroes. "After their set, Ian asked if I wanted to join him on an encore of 'Cleveland Rocks'," recalls Joe. "So, we did it, but there was a power cut halfway through the song and we did it again. I'm still the only guy that played 'Cleveland Rocks' one and a half times with Hunter Ronson."

> **IH:** "On that Canadian tour we did a great take of The Beatles' 'Day Tripper' that was a little like Free. Just like 'FBI', 'Day Tripper' was Mick's idea. He'd developed 'FBI' on his own, but I was there for the birth of 'Day Tripper'. We'd been working on something else in my apartment and suddenly, just for a break, he started playing a riff. I loved the speed and immediately started singing the song, and we just kept at it. He got a middle bit and I was very excited. We demoed 'Day Tripper' but never recorded it properly in the studio. We also played a live version of 'While You Were Looking at Me' in Canada, and it was fucking great. I would have recorded it but Little Steven gave it to Michael Monroe for his album. I knew Michael well and he came around one day and said, 'Cop this!' It was 'While You Were Looking at Me'. Hunter Ronson did it live because it was such a good song. I loved that number."

Mick enjoyed the Canadian tour because he *wanted* to play, but as he and Ian travelled, the guitarist was often probed about "the Bowie years" and was asked how he felt about a lack of recognition for his contributions. Mick didn't feel bitter about the past, the money or David's departure, noting with grace: "I have two arms and two legs, and can still play."

"I played with some of the finest guitar players, including Eric Clapton, Jeff Beck and Albert Lee, but Mick Ronson's unique style stood out amongst all the greats," recalled Roy Young. "Being on stage with Ronson was electrifying. He became a great companion and a fun person to be around who got us into some sticky situations. One time, on tour with Ian, flying in a private plane to our next destination, we got into an early morning laughing fit while suffering hangovers from the night before. With Mick's wit we were soon in hysterics, unable to stop the pattern; Ian even got up and changed seats. It was all capped off when the captain threatened to throw us off the plane and the hilarity became even worse. I wish I'd met Mick Ronson earlier."

The new Hunter Ronson band were welcomed warmly in Canada and audience reactions triggered fresh management support. Bob Ringe of Variety Artists in Los Angeles had worked at RCA Records and brought David Bowie, Lou Reed and Annette Peacock to the label in the early Seventies. Now, Bob offered to put together an American tour for Hunter Ronson, to Ian's absolute amazement.

> **IH:** "Ronson and I got together to decide if we wanted to play together again. It was weird for the first two or three days on the road in Canada. I don't know what we had between us, but it wasn't there at first. Then, all of a sudden, it started clicking in. When it was still there, Ronson and I got excited. Then Bob Ringe phoned us up from LA and said he wanted to do a tour. I couldn't believe it when it became a nine-week tour; I'd figured two weeks at most. Bob was enthusiastic about managing the pair of us, and polishing up our tarnished images and putting us back where we were supposed to be."

During their North American shows Ian's new songs received favourable reactions from crowds, press and several record companies. Now there was a contemporary Hunter Ronson partnership and an edict for touring, finding a record label and producer, and making another exceptional album. Conscious that the pair had not played together in seven years, Ian explained their comeback strategy.

> **IH:** "Ian Hunter hasn't been around since 1979. I disappeared on myself for a while. The people around me weren't

motivating, so I got re-organised in Manhattan, wrote material, played it to Mick and now it's great. We think of this tour in terms of the first stage and there's a very definite plan in our minds which will take over a year. Mick and I are not starving. We don't have to do this. We're coming at this for the right reasons, but we want a label that's really blown away by the band. It's hard getting a record deal when you're an old warrior, because ageism is rampant in this game and it makes life very difficult. What matters now is that we write some really good songs and put out a *great* record. I've not been in this mood for years. It's pleasurable and in a couple of years' time I think we'll be major."

With their band name informally abbreviated to 'HRB', between 27th September and 4th December 1988, Ian and Mick played a grinding coast-to-coast North American tour, comprising over sixty shows. One concert reviewer described Hunter Ronson as one of the most underrated collaborations in rock 'n' roll, while another praised their older songs including a mesmerising version of 'Standin' in My Light' and a nasty rendition of 'Bastard'. A *Los Angeles Times* feature on their San Juan Capistrano gig noted: "If Ronson and Hunter have a record deal, the forthcoming album should be one hot item; if they don't, some smart, adventurous A&R guy should sign them today." Hunter was in his late forties – an older man in a younger man's world – but he was happy, was enthused about the musicians around him and was considering calling his next album *Balance*.

IH: "I think the 1975 Hunter Ronson band was a great band musically and, had the group been given a chance, Mick and I could have been huge. So, we're coming back with a vengeance now. The new band sounds terrific, the set's got nine new songs and it's more than two hours long. It's less body and more head, and not what I thought it would be. I'm more balanced and a lot more confident now. I never used to be able to talk about the studio with Mick on the same level, but having had my home studio, it has helped. Now we're better as players, we know more, we're older and we're able to put up with each other more than we used to."

Hunter Ronson's live shows were heralded with Ian's taped recitation of 'A Sane Revolution' – the D.H. Lawrence poem emblazoned on the *Mott* album – and their streamlined group now comprised the Canadian trio of drummer Shawn Eisenberg, bassist Pat Kilbride and keyboard player Howard Helm, who had recorded with Zon and Refugee for CBS, Chrysalis and PolyGram. Musically, Hunter likened Kilbride to Pastorius and Pat could *really* play; he could also deliver uncanny Ronson impressions, in front of Mick, until the pair often ended up wrestling on the floor. With a band reduced to five players, Ian's songs took on a tougher edge and Mick hit his stride. Ronson said of the group: "I think it's your basic kind of rock 'n' roll band, without all your horn sections and backing singers and all that business. Back to basics! Straight rock 'n' roll. I've kind of missed that. I always enjoyed playing with a three-piece band. You can feel the power more. I think you can express yourself more with less."

Mick felt the songs that Ian had written were his strongest since 1979, and Hunter Ronson was aimed at convincing people of their musical rejuvenation. Looking back on the concerts, Ian considered it was one of the few times in his career when things worked out the way he had hoped. The live shows were impressive, record companies hovered and Hunter Ronson soon penned a worldwide contract with PolyGram International, who signed the duo after witnessing gigs in New York and Indianapolis. Ian and Mick's new album would appear on Mercury Records, a label that included Rush and Def Leppard, and an imprint where Dick Asher and Steve Popovich were now employed.

> **IH:** "Mick had changed a lot by 1988 and it was the first time that he had instigated anything which was interesting to me. He'd stopped drinking too, so I said, 'Why don't we

go partners, right down the middle?' I got an offer for a deal in Scandinavia that was pretty good, but not on the level of a worldwide American. The next offer I got was from CBS, but I had to move back to England to do it. Then, on the tour, people from RCA, PolyGram and Epic started turning up. PolyGram came to see us a couple of times and offered us the deal in Indianapolis. I thought it was a good label because Mercury didn't have many acts but they did sell records. PolyGram also had Dick Asher and I'd always been a fan of his."

By early 1989 Hunter Ronson was represented by Bob Ringe and Greg Lewerke of Vault Management and they embarked on European live dates, including two concerts at London's Dominion Theatre. Homing in on the right record producer, their live set featured seven new songs: '(Give Me Back My) Wings', 'How Much More Can I Take', 'You're Never Too Small to Hit the Big Time', 'Beg a Little Love', 'Following in Your Footsteps', 'The Loner' and 'Sweet Dreamer'. At the Dominion, Joe Elliott joined in for one encore and Hunter closed proceedings with a message of triumph and clarification, saying that whilst a lot of people expected this to be the end, it was in fact a beginning. Ronson remained as composed as ever, though his iconic maple Gibson Les Paul had been replaced by a Pacific Blue Fender Telecaster. Mick claimed he had never owned a decent acoustic guitar and that he'd played a 100-dollar Akai on Mellencamp's 'Jack and Diane'; for bottleneck he still liked the Les Paul for sustain, while he used a Tomasio and a BIC cigarette lighter for slide.

> **IH:** "Ronno's favourite guitar was now a mildly metallic blue Telecaster. I wanted him back on a Gibson Les Paul but on the Fender Telecaster he stayed, probably just to spite me."

Kilbride and Helm remained in Hunter Ronson for the European gigs, but drumming duties were now fulfilled by Londoner Steve

Holley who had worked with Kiki Dee and had been invited, simultaneously, to join Elton John and Paul McCartney and Wings. Steve opted for the Wings drum stool and played on the band's vastly underrated 1979 album *Back to the Egg*. Moving to New York in 1981, Holley worked with a range of artists including Julian Lennon, but he joined Ian and Mick following discussions at a Musicians' Assistance Program benefit concert at the New York Ritz.

Steve Holley: "It was so much fun playing with Hunter Ronson and the European tour in 1989 remains one of my career favourites. 'Following in Your Footsteps' was one of the highlights of the show for me, a powerful song with sensitive and intelligent lyrics. Mick was a treasure. People know he was great, but I don't think they really realise just how good he was. His understanding of dynamics within any song and his choice of notes and arrangements were sublime. He was unlike anybody I ever worked with. Mick was a tour de force in terms of understanding musicians and music. He was a genius and so humble."

> **IH:** "I've always liked drummers who are slightly behind on the snare. Charlie Watts comes to mind and Levon Helm was amazing. Steve Holley likes it 'back' a little too. I'm not keen on drummers who come to drum. The same goes for guitar players who come to solo. The song must come first and Steve knows that. Holley is one of the very best."

Howard Helm: "After completing the first HRB tour in the fall of 1988, I was thrilled that we went to Europe in early '89. Ian and Mick had not toured there for ten years so the reaction was amazing and every show was sold out. Each night on stage was a very moving experience. To observe Ian's control over an audience and feel his stage persona was incredible. Mick played beautiful lead guitar solos that could move you to tears and I have spoken to several guitarists since then who credit him as one of their greatest influences. Hunter Ronson were real rock stars on stage, but off stage we had a lot of fun. Mick was a foodie, before foodies were in fashion. I remember sitting in many restaurants and when we got the menus Mick would read them out loud, from top to bottom, every page, reciting the description of each dish. It was so hilarious that sometimes we ordered according to Mick's excitement about a particular item.

"I have fond memories of Ian too. I spent the day walking around Hamburg with him once and it was an amazing musical history lesson. Ian showed me where The Star-Club used to be and told me about the times, back in Sixties; what he knew about The Beatles early days in Germany; how he played there with Freddie Fingers Lee; the brutal schedules and living conditions. Late-night card games on the Hunter Ronson bus were another way that I got to know Ian better. He was a wealth of information about so many things. Whenever the guys would start talking about all the different influential shows they might have seen over the years, usually on a long bus ride, Ian would listen from the front lounge until he was tired of it all, and stand up and say, 'Well that's all well and good, but everybody who's seen Buddy Holly live, put your hand up.' There was dead silence. Ian's hand was, of course, the only one raised and we all went back to doing something else."

Hunter Ronson's London appearances were warmly received with optimistic press headlines, including 'Night of the Hunter' and 'Still in the Hunt', and one journalist enthused: "The truculent manner and magnificent moodiness of Hunter's stage persona is evidently more than skin deep and, what is more, has not been diminished one jot by the passage of time. If he can harness the new material and a show as good as this to the emergent trend in favour of adult rock 'n' roll, the Ian Hunter story is far from finished." Over two sparkling nights, Ian daringly pushed new material, based on an awareness that the songs were great, and he even had the nerve to close proceedings with a ballad – the perennial 'Irene Wilde'. Paul Hyde and Bob Rock of The Payola$ went to see the reunited Hunter Ronson in London, Paul admitting that he watched through tears of joy.

The first Dominion show was filmed and recorded by PolyGram, and an edited sixty-minute audio programme was broadcast on BBC Radio. In 1995, Windsong released *The Hunter Ronson Band: BBC Live in Concert* and reviews praised Hunter's "redoubtable songwriting skills and idiosyncratic vocals", "the snap, crackle and flash of Ronson's guitar playing" and the "rabid, tear-'em-up rockers 'Once Bitten Twice Shy', 'All the Way from Memphis' and 'Just Another Night', rocking London's Dominion to its very foundations". The live disc became notable for the inclusion of '(Give Me Back My) Wings' as the song would not be included on Hunter Ronson's forthcoming studio album.

> **IH:** "I originally wrote 'Wings' when I was working with Robbie Alter and I loved his stunning guitar lines running through the demo that we did. '(Give Me Back My) Wings' was a good song, but sometimes even good songs fall through the cracks. The lyric was good. When you're married and maybe a little selfish about your art, it's hard, and it can be tough on the person who doesn't play a direct part in the writing scenario. I didn't really like family around me sometimes when I was 'Ian Hunter' because, when things go wrong musically, you can get very frustrated. We went through some dramas over the years. I'm glad a version of 'Wings' made it onto the live CD that came out, because that was a great band. Mick and I really enjoyed that tour."

At the time of the London shows, Hunter Ronson's PolyGram deal had been signed, material was ready and the only delay was deciding on a producer. Ronson pondered over production suggestions but knew he could always offer Hunter an honest opinion; whilst they could both be opinionated, they worked things out for the greater good of both parties, their unique union being based on the productive chemistry between them. Hunter weighed up different working titles for their new record including *Balance* and *Wish,* and the US press first announced the upcoming album as *American Music*, but it would be presented as *YUI Orta*. The title was an adaptation of *"Why you I oughta…,"* a comedy phrase used by America's masters of slapstick and wise-crack dialogue The Three Stooges, who had slayed audiences via countless classic black and white films. The pronunciation of *YUI Orta* would *"soitently"* confuse several DJs and radio hosts. By May it was confirmed that Hunter Ronson would record at New York's Power Station, where they had cast *Schizophrenic* ten years before, and that the *YUI Orta* sessions would include Chic's bass player Bernard Edwards, who had produced *The Power Station*, Robert Palmer's *Riptide* and Duran Duran's hit single 'A View to a Kill'.

> IH: "I loved *The Power Station* album. I think that record was the only Eighties rock 'n' roll that made any ground sound-wise. I'd liked The Power Station – Robert Palmer and the Duran Duran guys – and their album had been produced by Bernard Edwards. We did *YUI Orta* with him because I craved that Power Station kind of sound and Bernard had originally got this great ambience and snare sound in a garage at the studio. So, we arrived and got in there and the first thing Bernard said was, 'Well, we can't do that, because the garage where we recorded before is a mixing room now.' They had got Tony Thompson's drum sound in the garage and the fucking garage was gone. We found this out on the first day, and that was the main reason I'd got Bernard in."

As Hunter Ronson focused on recording, American hard rock band Great White released a cover version of Ian's classic 'Once Bitten Twice Shy'. Taken from their album *Twice Shy*, the single hit No.5 in America and became Great White's biggest hit. In another flashback, Hunter assisted Mick Jones of Foreigner on his eponymous solo album, re-vamping the song 'Just Wanna Hold'. Ultimately credited to M. Jones, I. Hunter and M. Phillips, Michael

Philip Jagger had assisted on an early demo tape while Ian played piano on the recording, co-produced the track and appeared in Mick's promo video for the song.

> IH: "I'd known Mick Jones since Island Records and Spooky Tooth, and he always wanted to write with me. He's a really nice man and he invited me to help him complete a song he was having trouble with. He didn't write 'Just Wanna Hold' with Jagger. Mick Jagger was jamming vocally on a cassette that Mick Jones had, and he'd tried to add to it. The tape had various bits on it and Jagger had ignored the bits and concentrated, quite correctly in my view, on the main riff, which was great. Mick played it to me with Jagger warbling over the riff, so I said, 'What you should do is forget about all the other stuff and use the riff.' I just took it back to basics. We had to do a lot of editing. M. Jones wrote some of it, I wrote some of it and M. Jagger wrote some of it too. I put a new middle to it and wrote the words around Jagger's phrasing. We did it in one night with me producing and Mick Jones kept asking, 'What's it like?' I said, 'Fucking terrible.' I like Mick, so I helped out on the video shoot for the single too with Billy Joel, Christie Brinkley and Dennis Elliott. I took a day off, on my fiftieth birthday, and we filmed up on Long Island. When I turned up, Billy was already there and playing a gorgeous operatic version of 'Dudes' when I walked in. I remember his wife dancing on the piano. Billy Joel is an incredible musician and a brilliant pianist. He can play anything instantly."

Hunter Ronson's Power Station sessions were held during June and July. Pat Kilbride joined Ian and Mick in the studio, but Steve Holley had accepted gigs offered by Joe Cocker, so drummer Mickey Curry was engaged alongside keyboard player Tommy Mandel, the pair having combined on Bryan Adams' *Cuts Like a Knife*, *Reckless* and *Into the Fire*. Backing vocalists included Robbie Alter, Donnie

Kehr of Urgent, Carola Westerlund and Carmela Long, who was thrilled to sing with Hunter: "Ian is such a legend. Behind the dark glasses is a great songwriter and storyteller being true to himself and to his music, worthy of ultimate respect." Ian and Mick were charged from the spirit and momentum built up during months of touring, and their road test of new material became essential to the album's success. After the New York sessions, Ian explained he had been devoted to the preparation of songs for three years, but that Hunter Ronson's recording at The Power Station had been swift.

> **IH:** "It's been a long process but, in the end, we were in and out of the studio in forty days, six hours a day. And I'm glad we were, because we demoed several songs first and that can be fatal. It's something that happens all the time now, because to get a deal you've got to have thirty-six-track demos perfected, then you try and make a record and it sounds half as good as the demos. Records take such a long time these days. It used to be you put them out and it died, or it went. Now it takes nine months before records kick off. I guess it's progress."

YUI Orta contained thirteen tracks: 'American Music', 'The Loner', 'Women's Intuition', 'Tell It Like It Is', 'Livin' in a Heart', 'Big Time', 'Cool', 'Beg a Little Love', 'Following in Your Footsteps', 'Sons 'n' Lovers', 'Pain', 'How Much More Can I Take' and 'Sweet Dreamer'. The songs were written largely by Ian with four Hunter–Ronson compositions and two co-writes, 'Beg a Little Love' and 'Pain'.

'American Music' was Hunter's ode to the arrival, power and influence of rock 'n' roll during his youth. With a nod to the musical nerve centres of Nashville, Memphis, Chicago and Harlem, and references to 'Whole Lotta Shakin'' and 'Dock of the Bay', Ian openly declared his love of the early rock 'n' roll records he'd first heard on radio as a teenager. The music was inspirational but the poetic names of America's cities had enraptured Hunter too.

267

IH: "We were listening to *The Light Programme* on the BBC in the Fifties and it had light music on it. Then twice a week they'd play 'Whole Lotta Shakin'' or 'Hound Dog'. You never knew when these songs were going to come on so you had to listen to crap, all week long, just to hear these great songs. They were like a letter from a friend and what it did to me was amazing. American cities do have poetry in their names. I remember when I wrote 'All the Way from Memphis', some idiot in *Melody Maker* wrote, 'Why didn't he call it All the Way from Wigan or Oxford?' It doesn't have the same poetic rhythm. Put American names in a song and they sound great. I didn't want to call the song 'American Music' but it just came that way. I tried to change it; I wrote another verse; I messed around with that song for three months. In the end I just gave up."

'The Loner' successfully conveyed another image of Ian Patterson in his early life, but as an isolated and troubled youngster. Hunter would admit that he was "a down person" ever since he was a kid; he never felt part of anything, he never belonged to any religion and he never liked the herd mentality. Ian had often closed Mott's live shows with the plea "think for yourselves" because he favoured truthfulness and believed there were only two truths – himself and the audience. Ronson's fuzzed-up, slow-burning guitar riff on 'The Loner' was sublime. Hunter described the song as strange but simple, and a story about "somebody who doesn't like anybody".

IH: "Mick loved 'The Loner'. When he first heard it, he knew I was back on form. The song was about my early days living in Shrewsbury, where I had no friends. You couldn't get much in the way of rock 'n' roll, but my friends became those late Fifties rock 'n' roll songs. I really liked 'The Loner' too. It's like something Free would have done and I couldn't believe it when I wrote that. It put the chills in me for a long time. I just got up one morning and wrote it on an acoustic guitar

268

and thought I should get the thing down quickly, because I have a great deal of difficulty with 'rockers'; they don't come that often. I always thought the song was up there with my best, but it never seemed to get noticed. A big heavy metal band in America asked me for 'a rocker' once and I offered 'The Loner'. They never got back to me."

'Women's Intuition', written by Ian and Mick, was a resonant rock song in Open-G tuning, Keith Richards-style. One of the last tracks assembled for the album, Bernard Edwards played bass on the session and Hunter was happy to openly acknowledge another of his important musical influences. One reviewer noticed, saying; "If only the Stones could still sound this good in the studio." 'Tell It Like It Is' was also a Hunter–Ronson composition, Mick's guitar riff cheekily refracting 'Get It On', T. Rex's chart-topping Seventies single that in turn paid homage to Chuck Berry's 'Little Queenie'.

> **IH:** "'Women's Intuition' was directed at girls who say to musicians, 'It's me or the band.' Mick and I just wrote the song about girls who rip groups apart. It's to do with fighting to be happy – men and women – aggression versus possession. 'Tell It Like It Is' was simply a happy little song and we managed to get a bit of Johnny Kidd's 'Shakin' All Over' in there too, which was good."

The autobiographical 'Livin' in a Heart', first titled 'Angel', was a classic Hunter ballad, referencing Ian's marital break-up during the early days of Mott the Hoople and sitting in the same lyrical territory as 'Waterlow'. Musically, 'Big Time' was an optimistic piano-based boogie in the style of 'Once Bitten Twice Shy', while 'Cool' featured kicking drum beats, wah-wah guitar and synthesised brass, the punchy song sending up all things trendy.

> **IH:** "Your own family is more important than anything else and I've been guilty of putting music before everything,

269

which has caused a lot of grief in some circles. 'Livin' in a Heart' is about atonement and was basically an apology for a mistake I made many years ago. 'Big Time' was good fun. The minute I moved back to New York City I really started working again. I wrote 'Big Time' after a couple of months and I remember thinking that if I could get a few more songs like that, then it would be a good record. It was the first song that made sense in a long time. It deals with hope. You should play this in the morning on your way to work, if you're not doing much with your career. It's about what happens when you get very single-minded. If you will things to go your way, anything can happen. Cool was originally called 'Cool Jerk' and was about the herd mentality: the hipster who comes in with a preconceived idea and won't change their mind."

YUI Orta's epic cut was undoubtedly 'Beg a Little Love', co-written by Hunter and R. McNasty, a pseudonym for Robbie Alter. Dramatic and personal, Ian reflects on life's *"years, fears, dreams and screams"*, over galloping drum patterns and twisting Ronson guitar lines. Before the song's tense coda, the band cools down for several bars, Hunter finding breathing space in a *Mad Shadows* flashback, reciting lyrical fragments from Mott's 'When My Mind's Gone'.

IH: "It's a funny thing that no matter how advanced in years you become, a lot of you still wants the same things. 'Beg a Little Love' isn't about me to anybody else; it's about me to me. I really liked the lyric a lot. It's the diary of a guy floundering in the middle of his life. I thought that was the best lyric on the record."

Like 'Livin' in a Heart', 'Following in Your Footsteps' and 'Sons 'n' Lovers' continued Hunter's relationships theme, both of the songs being moving compositions concerning heredity and genetics.

270

IH: "'Following in Your Footsteps' is about not wanting to be like your father, but being like him, and the older you get the more you realise the inevitability of the genes. I loved the way the lyric turned out. My dad's more important to me now than when he should have been. With 'Sons 'n' Lovers' I was reflecting that I had an eight-year-old son at the time and I was watching the relationship between mother and son, and thinking about myself with my mother and the jealousies that kids have. They want to marry their mothers because there's nobody as beautiful, and then it all changes and the mother gets left behind; it's almost like she loses the guy she loves. 'Sons 'n' Lovers' is an odd subject, but I believe I said what I wanted to say in the song."

'Pain', one of the more forceful tracks on *YUI Orta*, was a tale of betrayal that Ian had written with Donnie Kehr for Urgent's album *Thinking Out Loud*. Originally titled 'Pain (Love Is a Victim)', Hunter Ronson's version featured fine piano from Tommy Mandel, but Mick's muscular guitarwork was a key component. Ronson's stabbing chords shored up the verses and choruses delightfully, but his spikey solo, riddled with controlled feedback, was superb. 'How Much More Can I Take' was also memorable and snappy, and another Hunter relationships lyric where the protagonist is unable to tolerate love and rejects it, then yearns for the unattainable.

IH: "Mick and I produced the Kehr guys in a band called Urgent. Donnie Kehr became a successful actor and I knew him very well for a while. They were good singers and 'Pain' was from their second album. I can't remember much about 'How Much More Can I Take', other than it was too fast!"

YUI Orta's closing cut, 'Sweet Dreamer', was Ronson's reinterpretation of Don Gibson's 'Sweet Dreams' – a Fifties vocal hit for Faron Young, a Patsy Cline Sixties classic and an early Seventies instrumental by American bluesman Roy Buchanan. Ian and Mick had been playing Porter Wagoner and Patsy Cline tapes on their tour bus, but Ronson's take was based on Buchanan's arrangement. Mick's rendition illustrated why he was such an influential guitarist: a special musician who could apply his passionate imprint, expression and individuality to any song. Carrying the same poignancy as 'Slaughter on 10th Avenue', 'Sweet Dreamer' was a breathtaking crash course in Ronson's style, a masterclass in electric lead guitar applied to a country standard, and an outpouring of sad and triumphant playing. "Mostly, it's simple," said Mick modestly. "I got tired of seeing all these guys on the telly playing a million notes a minute for no reason at all. I thought that trend would only last a while, but it's been going on for years."

> **IH:** "Mick loved slow and simple songs like Patsy Cline's 'Sweet Dreams', so he would take it, expand upon it and develop it into something very special. It grew to about thirteen minutes long, and I finally figured out a way to infiltrate a bit of gospel piano, and he let me do it. 'Sweet Dreamer' remains my all-time favourite Ronson solo. I thought Mick did it better live than in the studio. Some nights it was so emotional that I just wanted to walk offstage and cry. It's very emotional when you hear something so tone perfect. I got the same feeling with David Sanborn on 'You Nearly Did Me In'."

YUI Orta was issued by Mercury Records in America on 3rd October 1989 and 22nd January 1990 in Britain. The LP release featured ten songs, while three extra tracks were added to the CD – 'Following in Your Footsteps', 'Pain' and 'How Much More Can I Take' – arguably three of the strongest songs from the sessions. Photographs for Martin Kanner's album artwork were taken by Mick Rock: "My favourite photographs of Ian happen to have been taken by me for the *YUI Orta* album. I'm sure that had a lot to do with Mick's presence. I originally had a meeting with Ian and Mick

272

"Noises"
Chrysalis Records
promotional photograph,
1981

Short Back n' Sides album cover photo session outtake
Lynn Goldsmith/Corbis/VCG via Getty Images

Ian Hunter Rocks
Dr Pepper Music Festival, Pier 84, New York City, 11 September 1981
John T. Comerford III/Frank White Photo Agency

Royal Manor, North Brunswick, New Jersey, 19 January 1982
John T. Comerford III/Frank White Photo Agency

"A Little Rock 'n' Roll"
Queen Party at Danceteria, New York City, 9 August 1982:
Freddie Mercury, Ian Hunter and Brian May
Ron Galella/Getty Images

Todd Rundgren with Hunter, 1983
Lynn Goldsmith/Corbis/VCG via Getty Images

Ian with Pete Townshend, Ronnie Lane ARMS
Benefit Concert, Madison Square Garden,
New York, 9 December 1983
Ebet Roberts/Redferns

"Anyone who doesn't understand Bob Dylan, doesn't understand rock 'n' roll"
Hunter and Dylan, Whitney Museum, New York City, 13 November 1985

"Staring at your wilderness"
Ian at California's Musical Roadhouse,
Windsor, Ontario, Canada, 5 October 1986
Alan Smith

"A genuine camaraderie"
Mick and Ian, *YUI Orta* photo session, New York, 1989
© Mick Rock, 1989, 2020

"Dudes reunited"
Hunter and Bowie performing 'All the Young Dudes' at The Freddie Mercury Tribute Concert,
Wembley Stadium, London, 20 April 1992

The Gringo Starrs
Ian Hunter's Dirty Laundry 1995:
Glen Matlock, Honest John Plain, Ian Hunter, Darrell Bath, Vom and Casino Steel

"To Hull and Back"
Backstage at The Mick Ronson Memorial Concert II, Hull Arena, 9 August 1997:
Paul Francis, Darrell Bath, Ian Gibbons, Ian Hunter, Paul Cuddeford and Alan Young
Ian Dickson/Redferns

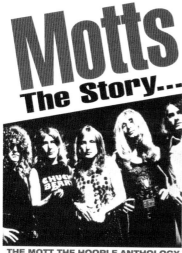

Mott's the Story
Original unused concept for Sony
Anthology box set, 1998

"The Prongs"
Andy York and Ian Hunter, The Bowery Ballroom,
New York, 2 June 2000
Justin Purington

"Screaming at the sky"
Promotional shot for the *Rant* album, 2001

at the Hunters' apartment in Manhattan to talk about the concept, and we shot a lot of stuff at my Soho studio in New York. I think I was using daylight film with photo-floods to get the orange effect. The dual headshot on the sleeve was my idea and I really liked the cover. I got a lot of great pics that day. I especially love the photo inside the album with Ian's hand on Mick's shoulder; that really caught their genuine camaraderie – a beautiful friendship."

Many music critics admired *YUI Orta* but some seemed unconvinced about a record that was loosely described as "Americanised". *Rolling Stone* wrote: "Like Lennon before him, Hunter is the hard guy whose shades hide tears; the soul-bearing comes strong and tender in 'Beg a Little Love' and 'Sons 'n' Lovers'; the time may be right for the genuine old master. As Hunter and Ronson progress from swagger to maturity, their rock seems not only solid but refined by the polish of hard time and tried faith." *Kerrang!* proclaimed: "YU ORTA BUY IT." *The Guardian* declared that "anyone looking for a shot of straightforward rock 'n' roll will be unable to live without *YUI Orta*", while *The Times* noted that Ronson was possibly rock's most underrated guitarist. The album hit No.157 on *Billboard* but didn't chart in Britain, Hunter saying he was convinced the record would only be truly recognised in the future.

Mercury Records' promotional material for Hunter Ronson's album declared "Two Rock Legends Whose Time Has Come Again" – the label issuing 'American Music' as a worldwide single backed with 'Tell It Like It Is' and 'Sweet Dreamer', depending on CD, cassette or vinyl formats. In the USA, a second single was released: an edited mix of 'Women's Intuition' coupled with 'Following in Your Footsteps'. PolyGram also produced a promo video for 'American Music', directed by Michael Patterson, who had animated the MTV hit 'Take on Me' for A-ha. Hunter Ronson's film, shot around Russell Square in London and a dilapidated mental hospital in Teddington, was presented predominantly in monochrome. Juxtaposing Ian and Mick playing the song, Hunter's story was visualised via a boy–girl schooldays theme amidst images of instruments, Fifties-style radios and iconic pictures of Jerry Lee Lewis, Muddy Waters, Little Richard and Chuck Berry. Ian spoke about the album and single after their release.

> **IH:** "'American Music' was the record company's choice for a first single. Now they're going with 'Women's Intuition' which was our choice. They want to put out two more after that. It's a long, deep album and it'll take nine months to work it. It's as good as anything that's gone before it, if not better. When I first played 'All the Way from Memphis' people wanted to hear *Brain Capers*, and when I first played 'Cleveland Rocks' people wanted 'Memphis'. If we're still around in ten years from now, people are going to want to hear 'The Loner'. We wanted *YUI Orta* to give a certain feel, starkness and groove. Bernard is one of the big guys and I've got nothing but respect for him."

Ronson explained that Hunter and the band had recorded most of the album tracks in one or two takes, avoiding analysis and without Edwards' interference. Ian had written other songs that had been contenders for the record but 'Look Before You Leap', '(Give Me Back My) Wings' and 'Ill Wind' became shelved demos.

> **IH:** "It got to the point where we had fifteen tracks for *YUI Orta.* There were certain songs that we didn't want to lose but we couldn't do everything. We got to 'Wings', which ironically enough was the first song I played to Bernard Edwards, and whilst we didn't want to knock it on the head, there just didn't seem any point in doing it. I originally did 'Wings' with Robbie Alter as a ballad, but, later on, David Letterman's drummer, Anton Fig, came up to my house in Katonah one day and re-arranged it. I liked our live version that came out on the Dominion CD, but the trouble is I'm always on to new stuff. 'Wings' was really good; maybe I wrote it too soon."

Hunter Ronson's American promotional concerts in late 1989 included a 4th November show at Cleveland Music Hall, to benefit the Rock and Roll Hall of Fame and Museum. Ian and Mick donated the proceeds from their 'Cleveland Rocks' appearance to boost the construction project fund and the Mayor of Cleveland, George Voinovich, presented the duo with keys to the city. Sex Pistols guitarist Steve Jones and Joe Elliott joined Hunter Ronson on stage in Cleveland for a cover of Bowie's 'Suffragette City', but a guest appearance by Axl Rose and Slash from Guns N' Roses, playing 'White Light/White Heat' at the Hollywood Palace nine days later, proved to be an awakening for Ian.

> **IH:** "I didn't do that Music Hall gig for the corporate Hall of Fame; I did it for the people of Cleveland. There was a heated debate as to the location of the Hall of Fame and we thought it should be in Cleveland. When Mick and I played at the Palace in Los Angeles a few days later, Axl and Slash jumped up with us. The next day, the *Hollywood Reporter* wrote that Guns N' Roses weren't fit to be on the same stage as Hunter Ronson. We were stunned. Mick and I suddenly realised that we'd gone prissy and had been blowing it for years. Guns N' Roses actually helped me to re-focus and made me see some light at the end of the tunnel, because their attitude was incredible. Nirvana helped to perk me up too, because when the corporates took over, I thought there would be no more craziness – and craziness is what you need in rock 'n' roll."

Through January and February 1990, Hunter Ronson played nineteen European concerts and seven dates in England, including London's Hammersmith Odeon, while further shows were planned for Tokyo during May. Drummer Moe Potts, a friend of Mickey Curry, was added to the line-up and bassist Pat Kilbride remained appreciative, sharing the stage with Hunter Ronson: "I was quite young when I played with Ian and Mick, but it was an unforgettable experience. Ian's music has a unique mix of intelligent lyrics and raw but melodic rock 'n' roll power. On the road Hunter was always the epitome of cool and he's a rare artist who has been able to have a lengthy career, while always staying fresh and maintaining integrity."

Audience responses to Hunter Ronson were glorious, but several members of the esteemed press flaunted further ageism with some sad headlines: 'All the (Not So) Young Dudes', 'The Golden Aged of Rock 'n' Roll', 'All the Old Dudes' and 'The Artful Codgers'. Creative redundancy had reached a new nadir, but Ian's old foe, *Melody Maker,* had changed tack. In a 3rd February article, 'Hunter Ronson Holding Back the Years', Carol Clerk enthused: "Guns N' Roses adore them, Michael Monroe reveres them, Great White covered them, but the press has always slagged them off as ageing rockers. I want to tell Ian Hunter that I'd rather shake his hand than stab his back – that I'd rather get his autograph than stitch him up – and that I'm in love with the new Hunter Ronson LP, *YUI Orta.*" The publicity was great, but Ian was annoyed with *Melody Maker.* In early 1989, following his Dominion comeback concerts, Ian's mother Freda Patterson passed away. A year on, Hunter remained upset over the paper's comments about his London shows with Ronson, especially as he considered them two of the most memorable gigs in his storied career.

> **IH:** "My mum's funeral really affected me. When your mum dies, that's the unconditional love gone. Some of that stuff in the papers was pretty vicious. 'Senile' was brought up more than once in *Melody Maker.* It upset me because as soon as I saw the live review in *The Times*, which was amazing, I knew what the Lefties were going to do. It's almost premeditated. We sell places out, but that doesn't seem to have much bearing on anything. My mother was very ill at the time. She got the papers and she looked at them and it was upsetting to her. She died about a month later. It pissed me off."

For their 1990 dates, Hunter Ronson's live set included 'Central Park n' West' and Mick delivered 'White Light/White Heat' and an extended version of 'Slaughter on 10th Avenue'. He also performed 'Darling, Let's Have Another Baby', one of punk rock's DIY love songs, first recorded in the Seventies by Johnny Moped. Mick's nightly introduction for 'Darling' was classic Ronson: "I think this was the first punk song ever written, so fuck off!"

> **IH:** "I remember Ronno doing 'Darling' in Helsinki and they all got off on it. Half the equipment blew up, so Mick stepped forward and delivered it perfectly. Then, buoyed on by the rapturous applause, he proceeded to tell two of the most hackneyed jokes I've ever heard; they were both awful but they brought the house down. I do remember most of Ronson's jokes and if they weren't bad to begin with, after repeated airings, up to three times a day over a three-month period, they became intensely boring. Obviously not to the people we met just once, but we did suffer. He had this horrible one about bacon and eggs, and it went down a storm in Helsinki too. I think it was the delivery."

On tour, Ronson was asked how troublesome record deals and management situations occurred in the business and Mick confessed he had always been driven totally by musical enthusiasm: "I was just so glad to be able to do what I was doing. I didn't want to know about bits of paper and contracts. I wanted to be a musician, but then you find out later that you have to be able to take care of that."

> **IH:** "You could agree to some ridiculous things in those days and it was usually put in front of you just before you went on to do a gig. There would be a lot of people there and they would stick a piece of paper in front of your face. 'Sign this.' 'What's it about?' 'Don't worry. We'll sort it out later.' Yeah! Sort it out later – ten years later."

On 16th February 1990, Ian was back prowling the Hammersmith Odeon stage that he had stormed in 1973 and 1979, still looking every inch the rock star. Hunter Ronson was a refreshing, no-nonsense, stripped-down rock 'n' roll band – the stage devoid of paraphernalia and backdrops – just amplification, instrumentation, three superb musicians and two heroes. 'All the Young Dudes' remained anthemic, climaxing a performance that lasted two hours, and Brian May of Queen guested during a seismic finale.

Brian May: "I thought it would be great to play 'All the Way from Memphis', so when Ian said would you like to come along, I said that I'd like to play that because it's a great memory from the Mott/Queen days, and because it's a great song. That was the first time I'd gone on stage with Mick and he was great; he didn't just play, he originated."

Ignited by Hunter's musical rebirth there was renewed speculation surrounding a Mott the Hoople reunion, underpinned by interest from a significant American record label. Conversations took place between Hunter, Ralphs, Watts and Griffin at Ian's Worthing home, but whilst Ralphs was prepared to consider recording work, he was unwilling to commit to live work in a reunited Mott. Dale later claimed that he and Watts offered an option of reforming Mott the Hoople with Ronson in the line-up, but the debate died.

Island Records, now part of PolyGram, surfed in on Hunter Ronson's reincarnation issuing *Walkin' with a Mountain: The Best of Mott the Hoople, 1969–1972*, a CD compilation of the band's dawning featuring sleeve notes by Dale Griffin. *Kerrang!*'s Ray Zell, in a five-star review headed 'DIE HARD THE HUNTER', noted the omission of 'Laugh at Me' and 'Sweet Angeline' and described the Island era as "Mott's reckless years, when Britain's greatest-ever rock band bounced from magic to tragic". In January 1991, Atlantic Records also released Mott's five Island albums on compact disc for the first time. Sadly, the American CDs of *Mott the Hoople*, *Mad Shadows*, *Wildlife*, *Brain Capers* and *Rock and Roll Queen* were not remastered, and no bonus tracks or rare material was added.

After a successful *YUI Orta* tour, Ian and Mick made tentative plans to record another album at Joe Elliott's studio in Ireland. Ronson ventured that the next project would be a harder rock record and that '(Give Me Back My) Wings' would probably be included. Ian was happy how things had turned out and was looking forward to further recording, saying it would be more united and that Bernard Edwards had agreed to work with them again. Suddenly, the proposed studio sessions, two Tokyo concerts and potential Australian live dates were scuppered when PolyGram opted to pass on a further Hunter Ronson album, a label spokesman commenting that sales of *YUI Orta* had failed to meet expectations.

Following Richard Asher's appointment as CEO in 1985, PolyGram had acquired Island Records and A&M Records but, by mid-1990, *The Los Angeles Times* reported that the label had a lower than expected album count on *Billboard*, that they were experiencing delays in issuing and distributing new releases, and that PolyGram was dropping several acts to slash their artists roster. Ian considered that Mercury's Hunter Ronson volte-face occurred after Dick Asher's departure from PolyGram and a resultant series of label management changes, centred between the US and UK release dates for *YUI Orta*.

> **IH:** "The man who signed us to Mercury, Dick Asher, was an excellent record guy but he got fired just as *YUI Orta* was released. This has happened to a lot of people. It's happened to me three times and it's a drag, because the people that this guy's employed are now out of work, so the last thing on their mind is my album coming out. Dick had agreed a deal on percentages and as PolyGram had a huge turnaround, at the end of the year Dick was apparently owed millions of dollars. So PolyGram said, 'Well, we aren't paying you millions,' and Dick said, 'Well, you are because I have a contract.' Then the shit hit the fan, Dick left and my album disappeared. So that left us without promotion. The record didn't do anything because of the label mess; we couldn't do anything about that and we only managed a few dates to tour the album. It was a shame as it was a good record, but you can't survive that kind of upheaval."

Howard Helm: "One of my greatest career disappointments was when Ian phoned and told me that the Hunter Ronson tour of Japan and Australia had to be cancelled. The band was great and I wish we could have made that tour. I loved playing with our drummers, Steve Holley and Moe Potts – different styles, but solid as a rock – and Pat Kilbride, one of the greatest bass players ever. In those days Pat was doing his utmost to literally re-live the life of his idol, Jaco Pastorius. The greatest Hunter Ronson moment for me was playing at the Hammersmith Odeon. Brian May and Roger Taylor from Queen were there and Brian playing his solo on 'All the Way from Memphis', back to back with me on my riser, was special. I'll never forget my time with Ian and Mick."

Overlooked and ill-fated, *YUI Orta* was a passionate record – a fine album that generated excitement via a striking cache of varied songs – and an absolute object lesson in rock 'n' roll as a source of self-renewal. In retrospect, Hunter has mixed feelings.

> **IH:** "I'm not completely keen on *YUI Orta* but there is some good stuff on it. I put a lot of songs on the album at the last minute because of Bernard Edwards, and because of the kind of vibe that we thought it would be. In hindsight, we chose the wrong producer. Mick didn't really want Bernard. I did. Ronson was right. I liked 'Following in Your Footsteps' and 'Sweet Dreamer' is beautiful. *YUI Orta* is alright. It's not a bad record, but I think the sound lacks personality. It was a good sound, but I guess it didn't sound like us."

Hunter had signed with PolyGram Records in 1989 because Dick Asher was their president, but before fans could devour *YUI Orta*, Asher was gone and Ian's record deal proved short-lived. As *YUI Orta* sank, the new partnership that Ian and Mick had always craved was over, almost before it began. Hunter was no stranger to artistic injustice within the music business, but as he defiantly pointed out at the time, "There's nothing out there like me. Maybe there shouldn't be, but I just feel there should be."

In 2003 Lemon Records reissued *YUI Orta*, adding '4th Hour of My Sleep' and 'Powers of Darkness', two out-of-place bonus tracks, originated in 1971 by Mick's short-lived band Ronno. To Hunter this was more label stupidity and a let-down; historic experiences and difficulties with record companies, and the virtual abandonment of *YUI Orta*, frustrated him.

> **IH:** "Every time I get a label statement showing how much I am in the hole to them, it annoys me. They are a record company. They made no effort to sell my album or retrieve it later. To them it's gone, and with it five years of my life."

CHAPTER NINE

Michael Picasso

*Mick Ronson was absolutely unique
because he came from the song.*

Following the release of *YUI Orta* and a torpedoed PolyGram record deal, Mick Ronson settled in Stockholm. The guitarist had seldom found a stable base where he lived for any length of time, as he often travelled to undertake production for a wide selection of artists.

> **IH:** "In the early Nineties, Mick and I were bored out of our minds again as the music industry was even more corporate than the Eighties. We'd let things slide to the point of extinction. I couldn't get arrested. Mick was doing alright on the production side of things, but I went right off the radar; no deals – no management – no nothing."

Based in Sweden, Ronson worked with EC2, a short-lived duo that featured Estelle Milburne and Carola Westerlund. Mick was in a relationship with Carola and in 1990 they had a son, Joakim, Ronson's third child. Mick produced three singles for EC2, worked on Secret

Mission's *Strange Afternoon* and collaborated with Stockholm-born musician Johan Wahlstrom. Currently an accomplished painter of social critique art, Wahlstrom invited Ronson and Hunter to join him, Mats Ronander and his band, Johan Wahlstrom and The Yobs, on a Swedish tour. Billed as 'Klubb Rock', Mick previewed two songs, 'Take a Long Line' and 'Trouble with Me', that would ultimately appear on record. Mick stayed with Johan after he split with Carola, and Hunter, Ronson and Wahlstrom played more Scandinavian concerts under the banner 'Park Rock'.

Johan Wahlstrom: "I met Mick in late 1990 in Stockholm, and he moved into my apartment before we embarked on the Klubb Rock tour. The idea was to bring together several top artists and play long concerts, and the tour sold out. Ian Hunter joined us in 1991 performing Mott hits and solo songs, and the audiences loved him. I remember we played Lulea, above the polar circle, and it was 25th May, so after the concert, when the clock passed midnight, we presented a big birthday cake with 'Mick Ronson Rebel of the Future' on it."

Mats Ronander: "I first met Ian through Johan's great band. I invited 'Mr Hunter' to my flat for dinner one night, to discuss the songs we would like to play. I nervously thought I'd meet a figure in black leather, with rock 'n' roll shades, but Ian wore jogging clothes and had no sunglasses, but he brought a lovely gift for my new-born daughter. We became good friends and it was a pleasure playing great tunes from Ian's albums. Ronson became a great friend too and was a wonderful guitar player with his own sound. I played with ABBA, Mick Taylor and Peter Green, but working with Ian and Mick was the best."

After the Klubb Rock tour, Ronson wrote material for a solo project, planned live work with Lisa Dalbello, Dan Reed and Graham Parker, and worked with The Leather Nun and Dag Finn. Mick also recorded with Norwegian keyboard player Casino Steel, who had started out in a school band with Bjørn Nessjø, now a record producer. 'Cas' had moved to London in 1971, where he met Canadian Andrew Matheson and formed The Queen, who

283

became The Hollywood Brats. Steel later joined London SS with Matt Dangerfield and recorded four albums with Heavy Metal Kids and *Auf Wiedersehen, Pet* star Gary Holton.

"I did a TV show in Stockholm and suggested to Mick that we record together," says Casino Steel. "Ronson was an extremely nice guy, a superstar and such a gentleman. During our sessions for *Casino Steel and The Bandits Featuring Mick Ronson*, Mick refused to live in a hotel I had booked. He stayed at my place listening to records, watching TV and playing with my little daughter, while my wife made him great curries."

In August 1991, Ronson worked with Randy Vanwarmer and Shane Fontayne at Bearsville Studios, on sessions that were later issued as *The Vital Spark*. During recording, Mick experienced back pains and felt weak and, although eager to rest, he returned to London where he was persuaded by his sister, Maggi, to visit a doctor. Within two days Mick's world fell apart when it was confirmed that he was suffering from carcinoma of the liver.

Maggi Ronson: "I could tell Michael wasn't well. He had a lot of pain in his back, neck and the right side of his body. One doctor diagnosed pleurisy and gave him antibiotics, then Michael noticed a lump. A friend arranged a scan and the hospital told me they'd found three tumours on his liver. The consultant advised that nothing could be done. I just couldn't tell Michael. As we drove to his hospital appointment the next day, he was so cheerful. When they told him, I think he was angry at first, then he started to take a really positive attitude. He fought it all the way. He had chemotherapy but changed to a super healthy diet and alternative healing. He kept making plans and never talked about not getting better. Michael was told that he had three months left."

Although shattered by the news, Ronson was determined to beat his illness. "I'm going to get rid of this," said Mick defiantly. "The doctors say it's incurable, but I don't believe anything is. I'm looking forward to fighting it and getting on with my life again. There comes a point where you have to change your life and now is as good a time as any."

IH: "I'll never forget when Mick called me and said, 'I've got cancer, and it's incurable.' Then insane optimism took over. I remember before he got sick, he was coughing up blood in Arizona one day. He was in a hospital all day, but got the all-clear. I was worried and told him that if anything happened, I'd be there for him. His reply – 'Don't be so fucking stupid' – was typical Mick. It was as near as you got. You could never talk to him seriously about anything."

"Mick continued to enjoy life as much as possible, even during the hard time that he received treatment," recalls Johan. "I remember all our discussions about music, relationships, kids, people, death, life, God, heaven and hell. Before he found out about the cancer, we usually had quite a few beers during those 'kitchen sessions'. After he found out about his illness, healthy teas and juices were in, but the talks remained deep and interesting."

Eventually, Mick moved back from Stockholm to London for specialist care and worked on his intended album, recording with various artists. Ian Hunter and Joe Elliott pledged support and Def Leppard decided to record Ronson's guitar-laden 'Only After Dark' from *Slaughter on 10th Avenue* as the B-side of their 'Let's Get Rocked' single. "We had high hopes it would sell well," says Joe. "Mick was genuinely grateful, if not a little embarrassed at the fuss this was creating. Ian told me when Mick first let it be known he was ill, he said, 'Hey, I've got cancer!' as if he'd won the Lotto! That was the kind of guy Mick was."

As his illness took hold, Ronson halted work with Swedish group Sonic Walthers and cancelled live dates with Lisa Dalbello, Dan Reed and Casino Steel. "We had a whole Scandinavian tour booked," says Cas, "but, the week before we were due to go, he called me up and told me he had cancer. When I met him in London, he actually apologised to me for having got cancer." Playing on stage was not good for Ronson's health but he fulfilled gigs with Graham Parker and Johan Wahlstrom, featuring more new songs – 'Take Me Away', 'Don't Look Down' – and two numbers by Australian

285

band The Angels – 'Take a Long Line' and 'Marseilles'. It would be Mick's last tour.

Graham Parker: "The idea of having Ronson playing my songs was too tempting to resist. The tour lasted about three weeks. Mick's illness had really begun to kick in and, as I recall, we took every Tuesday off so that Mick could fly over to England for chemotherapy. Ronson would return the next day unruffled, uncomplaining and with that marvellous head of rock star hair still intact. He was one of the most down-to-earth people I've ever met. I remember one day, after checking into one of those silly hotels with rooms the size of a dustbin, complaining to Mick about how my room was so small. Mick just said, 'What's up? It's got a bed.' And he wasn't joking. That's the kind of guy he was. Turning my head every night to see him blasting out wicked solos on my songs was something I'll never forget."

Packing in as much work as his failing health would allow, Mick produced Morrissey's *Your Arsenal*, an album that rocked harder than anything the singer had ever recorded. Oozing Ronson toughness, squalling guitars and polish, Morrissey guitarist Boz Boorer said that Mick seemed like a master at work and described him as a humble man, taking out *The Racing Post* as they placed their bets each morning. Guitarist and songwriter Alain Whyte remarked that the greatest thing about Ronson was his spiritual personality because he knew he had a limited amount of time left and yet wanted to do as much as possible every day.

> **IH: "I remember going to one of Ronson's Morrissey sessions. I asked Morrissey, 'What's it like working with Mick?' He said one word: 'Perfect.'"**

Plans to cut a second LP with Morrissey were aborted, but Ronson helped David Bowie on *Black Tie, White Noise*, recording Cream's 'I Feel Free', a song that they had played live in the early days of Ziggy Stardust. Mick was ebbing and with his power depleted the session was tough. "It was really very poignant," said David. "He turned up and played his usual breathtaking solo. Extraordinary man – extraordinary guitar player."

Mick Ronson made his last live appearance at the Freddie Mercury Tribute Concert for AIDS Awareness at Wembley Stadium on 20th April 1992. Held on Easter Monday, the event was televised globally to launch the Mercury Phoenix Trust, an AIDS charity organisation, following the Queen star's passing in 1991. Mick rested on a dressing room couch prior to his appearance but took to the stage, battled on and played brilliantly. For most of the stadium crowd and television viewers worldwide, one of the Mercury Tribute highpoints was 'All the Young Dudes', performed by Hunter Ronson, joined by Bowie on sax and backed by members of Queen and Def Leppard. Mick also played a robust version of 'Heroes' with David and one reviewer wrote of the day: "The highlight? Ian Hunter doing 'All the Young Dudes' with such gusto, he's clearly at a different event to everyone else."

Joe Elliott and Phil Collen helped out on backing vocals on 'All the Young Dudes'. "We were like a couple of kids who had won the pools that day," says Joe. "You've got Queen as the backing band and you've got Bowie, Ronson and Ian Hunter all on stage in front of a billion and a half people. It was just like the ultimate three minutes of your life."

Ronson remarked of the Wembley concert: "It was pretty hectic. The whole event was wonderful. It was a magical sort of day. Everybody was smiling and that made me very happy. I didn't know Freddie Mercury, but I know he brought a lot of happiness into people's lives and to bring happiness into people's lives is a great thing."

IH: "That gig was tremendous for Mick and he was thrilled to bits to be there. Freddie's tribute was well organised, and it was huge – a billion people watching on TV in seventy-six countries, 72,000 people in the stadium, twenty-one televisions in a room backstage and 3,000 crew and staff. That's a gig! To many, it topped Live Aid. People were so nervous, but Mick and I were fine. We were thinking, 'Big stage? We can show off up here, no problem.' There is, of course, a lot of camaraderie at a gig like that. The rehearsals lasted a week and that was fabulous. I saw all sorts of people I hadn't seen for years. Roxy Music was there, Nick Faldo, footballers – Britain, all in this film studio, in Bray. 'Dudes' got applauded at rehearsals when we played it, which was great. I remember on the big day, watching the first half at Wembley from the royal box. It went by really quickly and, of course, it was bittersweet in several ways, but everything worked and we thoroughly enjoyed it. The crowd was great and went on as far as the eye could see. Following the Mercury tribute, I recall Simple Minds' management, in partnership with Elton John's manager, wanted to hear some of my songs, but I didn't have enough new material at the time."

Hunter had planned a Scandinavian summer tour with Johan Wahlstrom and Ronson wanted to join them, but he was discouraged on medical grounds. Ian played around twenty concerts with The Mats Ronander Band and Swedish covers group The Few, Hunter including 'Speechless' in his set, an up-tempo version of 'I Wish I Was Your Mother' in the style of 'Brown Sugar', plus a new song, 'Now Is the Time', written with Freddie Mercury in mind around the time of the Wembley tribute concert.

Ronson's new solo album now became his remaining lifeblood. Originally planned as *To Hull and Back*, the final title for the LP, chosen by Mick, would be *Heaven and Hull*. When Steve Popovich heard that Ronson had cancer he intervened and former MainMan employee Marc Coker recalled how Tony Defries lent Mick his house to stay in, at Hasker Street in Knightsbridge.

"Mick mentioned that he would love to make an album," said Steve Popovich, "So I called an old friend, Tony Martell, who was a vice president at Sony. He was also founder of the music industry's number one fundraiser for leukaemia research, the T.J. Martell Fund, named in memory of Tony's son who had died at the age of

288

eighteen. Tony, Epic president Richard Griffith and Sam Lederman were instrumental in getting Mick's project to market. The *Heaven and Hull* album turned out amazing with brilliant performances, vocally and instrumentally, from a much pained and weakened Mick."

"The MainMan house was fantastic, except that no one had lived there for years and the place was an absolute wreck," recalls Marc Coker. "MainMan and friends set about restoring the place into a home fit for heroes. I happened to be there one day with Mick, admiring the freshly painted rococo surrounds, when Lou Reed's 'Perfect Day' from *Transformer* blasted out on the radio. 'There you go Mick, another fifty quid in the bank,' I volunteered. 'Not likely,' he replied. 'When we did it, I was on less than fifty quid a day and when we finished, that was it.' I've always remembered that."

"Tony Martell gave Mick his last record deal and it made the last three years of his life liveable," says Suzi Ronson. "He got lost in his music. The only time he forgot about it was when he was playing. He was fine if I could get him in the car and to the studio and sit him in front of a keyboard."

Throughout the remainder of 1992 and early 1993, Mick continued working on his album and contacted various people to assist, including John Mellencamp, Chrissie Hynde and Joe Elliott. At one stage Ronson's cancer appeared to have gone into remission, but his decline became marked again and he would often tire easily. During February, Mick was admitted to hospital and given forty-eight hours to live but he rallied and went back to work in the studio. One of Ronson's last sessions was a Wildhearts' track for their album *Earth Versus the Wildhearts*; Mick played astounding slide guitar at Wessex Studios that day and it was a memorable moment for the band's founding member.

"Mick turned up with his guitar case," recalls Ginger Wildheart. "We expected him to open it and reveal the beautiful, famous Les Paul, but instead he pulled out this battered blue Telecaster. We were a little shocked when he told us he didn't have a Gibson endorsement like we had. We decided that we would all play our solos using CJ's Les Paul Standard. Mick made that guitar sound fantastic. He played the best solo I've ever heard in my life with a bottleneck and wah-wah pedal, and made it cry and wail, while we fumbled around with our Chuck Berry licks. We all fell in love with Mick and his down-to-earth nature. He projected nothing but warmth. He didn't live long after that. We didn't think he would be gone that quickly. If we'd known, we would have paid more attention."

Marty Kristian from The New Seekers recalls his final meeting with Ronson, filming an interview about his time with David Bowie: "The thing that struck me about Mick was his kind, open-hearted spirit. He could only see the positive side of people and would give anyone the benefit of the doubt, even those who may have done him wrong. He was a great guitarist with his own distinctive style and sound. If you made a friend of Mick Ronson, you made a friend for life."

Dana Gillespie had stayed acquainted with Ronson since MainMan days in the Seventies: "Mick and I always had lots of laughs. I was helping the League of Friends at London's Royal Marsden Hospital in the Nineties. I learned that carrot juice helped people with stomach cancer and digestive problems and told Mick about this. So, we went to Peter Jones store together to buy a carrot-juicing machine. It was sad, because Mick told me then that when David moved on in 1973 and didn't talk to him for all those years, he was very hurt by that. He experienced great loss and felt that a good friendship had gone. You see, Mick Ronson was one of the really good guys in the music business and, let's face it, good guys in this industry are as rare as rocking horse shit!"

Drummer John Cambridge and producer Tony Visconti reconnected with Ronson in his final months. John spoke to Mick on the phone three weeks before he died, for the first time in twenty years. "Maggi told me that Mick would like to come back to Hull to do a couple of tracks at Fairview Studios with The Rats," says John. "That would have been nice. Even if it had taken place, we would have sat there laughing and reminiscing all the way through the session. Nothing would have got done, but it would have made one hell of a bonus track."

"I met up with Mick at a barbecue about three months before he died, and he looked tanned and very well," recalls Tony Visconti. "He knew he had cancer, but he was very optimistic about getting over it. He was on a macrobiotic diet and receiving a lot of acupuncture treatment. He was thrilled that Bowie was going to sing 'Like a Rolling Stone' on his solo album. I actually thought he was going to make it."

Mick's driving ambition to complete his third solo record was relentless, and he and Suzi spent a few days during the last month of his life at Joe Elliott's studio. "I had been a fan of Ronson's for twenty years and now had a chance to see how it would be to work with someone who I absolutely respected 100 per cent musically," says Joe. "We got together in a house in Hasker Street, later immortalised by Ian in song, where Ronson had an insatiable appetite for Hobnob biscuits and tea. Mick suggested I duet with him on 'Don't Look Down'. He was pretty stoked about it and it was hard not to go with his instinct. I suggested recording in Ireland, so I met them at Dublin Airport and Mick was gaunt. He'd always been wiry, but I could really see the difference and the change in his appearance was dramatic. His positive attitude to life, though, his humour and honesty were just the same. My wife cooked him Yorkshire food and we went to the studio and worked our butts off to get this thing finished. He was painfully thin but in great spirits. He was taking all the prescription drugs that he was being given and they were basically bearing him out as best they could. We had three wonderful evenings where I played Mick a bunch of bootlegs and other stuff that he'd forgotten he'd performed on. He asked me to make him tapes of some of it. A few months later Suzi told me she knew right then that he was close to the end, because he *never* listened to himself and *never* kept anything."

Ian heard from Mick on a regular basis and was always amazed to find his spirits higher than those around him.

> **IH:** "The only calls I ever liked was when he rang me – because this was Mick – if he was sick for twenty-three hours a day, then the other hour he'd be on the phone telling everybody how wonderful he felt. But then, when I moved in with him, towards the end, I saw what he was doing. The morphine would come down to a point where he'd be totally sane and then he would pick up the phone, and he was telling everybody how wonderful he felt. He wanted everyone not to worry about him. The first thing out of his mouth was, 'How are you?' Mick was incredible. We were out in a car, two days before the end. He would not lie down."

Despite incredible spirit, Mick's strength was diminishing. The original plan had been to release *Heaven and Hull* in 1992, but that was postponed when Ronson recorded some of the songs he had previewed live in Scandinavia. Additional sessions with Bryan Adams, Morrissey and Meat Loaf, and a further track with Ian Hunter, were unfulfilled and the *Heaven and Hull* album was not completed. Mick spent his final days in 34 Hasker Street, Tony Defries's four-storey Chelsea townhouse where his ex-wife, Melanie McDonald, had died from cancer in 1989. Ronson worked on his solo album until three days before his death. Hunter had flown in from New York to record with Mick.

> **IH:** "There was a track that Mick wanted to do in a 'Once Bitten' kind of groove, then he changed his mind. Those type of songs are not easy to do, contrary to what people think, and I believe he was looking for something simpler. I remember meeting Johnny Lydon on the plane when I flew over and we talked across the Atlantic. I asked him to visit Ronson at Hasker Street."

"On 26th April Michael came to see me and I just knew he had reached the end of the road," says Maggi Ronson. "Even then he was making lists of people to call and things to do. Next day, the doctor said we should get him to hospital, but when we did, there was nothing they could do. It was heart-breaking taking him home in the ambulance, knowing he was going home to die. Even then, he kept waking up and smiling, and asking if I was alright."

Mick Ronson passed away on 29th April 1993, one month short of his forty-seventh birthday. He was survived by his wife Suzi and his three children Nicholas, Lisa and Kym. A memorial service was held in the Church of Jesus Christ of Latter-Day Saints in South Kensington on 6th May. The Ronson family, Ian and Trudi Hunter, Chrissie Hynde, Annette Peacock, Martin Chambers and Trevor Bolder attended the service, which included playbacks of 'Love Me Tender' and 'Sweet Dreamer'. Ian addressed the congregation and remarked that his long-time friend didn't make a fortune, but he died rich in the knowledge that he was an innovator and a kind and gifted man. Mick Ronson was buried the following day at Eastern Cemetery in his home town of Hull and a tree-planting ceremony was held at Wilson State Park in Woodstock, where he had lived periodically for nearly twenty years. The music world mourned and the tributes flowed. Ironically, during his recent collaboration with Ian, Mick had opined that he was "just starting out". Hunter found it difficult to talk about Ronson's passing and the loss remained painful for a long time.

> IH: "Mick died from 1991 to 1993. He simply called me up one day and said, 'I'm on the way out.' Throughout the next two years Trudi and I were dealing with that. Mick was really dealing with it, but I was with him when he died and it was a big relief, because you live with the dying and grieve for two years. One of the most horrible things was having to lie, because I'm not a good liar. I remember he was coming back to our house in the States on the day he died, and we had to go through the moves of booking the seats and everything else because one false move and he'd know. Mick would not acknowledge the fact that anything was going to happen. He was brilliant; he was in Ireland, he

produced Morrissey, he did his album for Epic. What a way to deal with it.

"Mick was always an optimist. I couldn't have done it. He said to me the night he died, 'I love to tour, because you just get better as a musician.' His thing was always about working and improving, not about making lots of money. On a personal level he was so kind and full of life. It's like a lot of people, when they die; you realise how good they were. He was just forty-six and had so much life ahead of him. Mick was amazingly positive and unreal at times. He'd come back from the hospital and say, 'There are seven-year-old kids with it. What right do I have to complain?' To be next to somebody, to be that close, and they've got cancer, and you haven't and there's nothing you can do about it – it was so sad. Mick was cooking at that time and had just got a deal with Epic Records so there was no reason on earth for him to leave the building. This was like my brother dying – it was that close. I didn't expect anything like that, ever. Yes, he was a bit of a character, but not that crazy. Mick wasn't just a bandmate in Mott the Hoople and Hunter Ronson – he was my mate. Our wives and kids were mates too. I remember when we were at CHUM TV in Canada once, I happened to mention that I only had two real close friends. Mick said, 'Who are they?' I miss him so much. Losing Mick was a kick in my ass – big time."

Ronson was remembered with huge affection by many friends and musicians. David Bowie termed Mick's demise a lesson in dignity and the perseverance of the human spirit, whilst pianist Mike Garson said there was no one who had a better sense for melody in rock. Angie Bowie praised Ronson as a musical force, a talented player, an inspired arranger and a seductive performer who could coax joy, anxiety, passion or grief from his thrilling guitar playing. Mick Rock described 'Ronno' as Ziggy Stardust's anchor and a very unspoiled man who never showed any interest in stardom, while

John Mellencamp felt that Ronson hadn't cared about credit and that, musically, he was a force of nature. Recording and mixing engineer George Cowan described Ronson as a rare genius and remembered Benny Mardones telling him, "Never trust someone who doesn't like puppies, children or Mick Ronson." Marco Pirroni of Adam and The Ants called Mick his guitar hero and, in 2018, Glen Matlock picked the "superlative guitarist and arranger" as his "Rock God" on BBC radio. The anecdotes about Mick were invariably humorous.

Glen Matlock: "It was impossible not to like Mick. I used to go to the Walthamstow dog track with him. In the studio, he'd stroll in and wonder how things were going. I'd say things were good, that Steve had done his guitar track and the drums were right, but Mick would say, 'No, not the music. I've got a horse running in the 3.30!'"

John Taylor: "Around the time of the Power Station project with Robert Palmer, I met a sax player named Mars Williams who knew Mick Ronson and wanted to set up a super-session, so we rented a rehearsal room in Manhattan. We were all in our full-on legends of rock drag and could not get our heads around turning down. After some free-form jamming, Mick said he was wasting his time. Mick and I ended up at Bebop, our favoured watering hole in the Village and we talked. I honestly don't remember what about. I wish I did. I wish I'd had the humility that evening to take the spotlight off myself and put it on Mick. I wish I had taken the time out to tell him just how great he was."

Steve Holley: "Mick Ronson was truly an inspiration. Immediately engaging in person, he taught me so much, probably without realising, about dynamics and blending with the musicians around you, especially within the music of Ian Hunter. His insight remains with me to this day and I pass it on to anyone who is willing to listen, as often as I can."

Tracie Hunter: "Mick was one of the finest guitar players I've ever heard. He had a truly unmistakable and unique sound all of his own. The first time I heard him play 'Sweet Dreamer' it made me

ROCK 'N' ROLL SWEEPSTAKES

cry. It's just so beautiful. Mick was funny and gorgeous, and one of the most 'gentle men' I ever met in my life. He made the best chilli and told the most crap jokes. He had the worst yellow mackintosh I ever saw and the most optimism I have ever seen, right to the very end."

Jesse Patterson: "Finding words that do justice to Mick Ronson is hard. I only knew Mick in the later days, but to me, he was a care-free, kind soul who cared passionately about music. My dad used to say he could tell Mick's playing from any amp, any guitar, the second he picked it up. It was his sound, bent to his will. Growing up around someone like this is humbling."

Mick Ronson passed before his solo album was completed, but mixing and mastering was arranged in Los Angeles for an Epic Records release. Held back to coincide with a memorial event, *Heaven and Hull* was issued on 3rd May 1994 and it was a sublime record. Ronson had shot life into 'White Light/White Heat' on *Play Don't Worry* and he did the same with 'Like a Rolling Stone', adding to a 1988 session recording of Bowie backed by Bryan Adams' band. Mick's earlier production of One the Juggler's *Some Strange Fashion* led to a link with Rokko Lee – Sham Morris – and the duo co-wrote four songs for Ronson's record: the warm and atmospheric 'When the World Falls Down', 'Trouble with Me' featuring Chrissie Hynde, 'Life's A River', cut with Hunter before Mellencamp sang lead, and 'Colour Me' – the latter song was inspired by an alternative holistic therapy that Mick had embraced and, ironically, the recording was completed five days before Ronson's death. 'You and Me', originally titled 'Maria', was a delicate acoustic instrumental and Mick included an emotional cover of Giorgio Moroder's 'Midnight Love', which he'd intended to develop with Woody Woodmansey and Trevor Bolder before time ran out.

One of Ronson's best cuts was his rendition of The Angels' 'Take a Long Line'. Retaining the Australian band's powerful, grimy lyric that had been inspired by homeless derelicts in Sydney, with Joe Elliott and Ian Hunter sharing vocal duties, Mick took the song to new heights. *Heaven and Hull* also included 'Don't Look Down', recorded with Joe, and, fittingly, the final track on Ronson's swansong album was his last live performance – 'All the Young Dudes' from the Freddie Mercury Tribute Concert. With the help of some friends and rock luminaries, *Heaven and Hull* had captured Mick's magical flame before it expired. Q magazine considered the record a timely reminder that Ronson had touch and grace, as well as power and flash.

Two other songs that Mick wanted to include on his album, 'Indian Summer' and 'Just Like This', were dropped. Frankie LaRocka, A&R director of Epic Records, recalled how the unfinished project was concluded: "There were a couple more songs that Mick was supposed to do, one by himself, one with Morrissey and one with Bryan Adams, but he never got around to them. All the other stuff was practically finished. Mick did my second record when I was with The David Johansen Group back in 1979. I knew how Mick worked, just from watching him back then. He left a rough mix of the album so we took that and enhanced it a bit."

> **IH:** "Everyone helped willingly on that record because they really wanted to. Putting Mick's album out was great because to be able to make music, especially his own album, just filled his whole head. To a large extent, he managed to minimise the discomfort from the cancer, which was really bad at times and it probably put six months on his life. That record was a success before it even started."

Following his passing, Mick Ronson's two Seventies RCA albums, *Slaughter on 10th Avenue* and *Play Don't Worry*, finally appeared on compact disc; Trident issued a 2CD compilation, *Only After Dark*; and Tenth Planet Records produced a retrospective Rats LP, *The Rise and Fall of Bernie Gripplestone and the Rats from Hull*. Fans were also favoured with three retrospective NMC releases: The Mick Ronson Band Bearsville sessions, *Just Like This,* and a live collection, *Showtime*, were issued with limited edition bonus discs of extra tracks, while *Indian Summer* comprised more unreleased studio songs and instrumentals including 'Tinker Street', 'Satellite' and 'Plane to England'. *Indian Summer* was promoted as a soundtrack from an unreleased movie with a second disc of "screen test dialogue", but there never was any original film or even a proposal; the presentation was a spoof to present obscure and important Ronson material in a fun way, and it fooled everyone.

> **IH:** "Mick was highly talented and great fun. He was an amazing player and arranger and did so much for Bowie, because David was basically a folk singer when Ronno joined him. There will always be guitar players out there copying Mick because someone will tell them to check it out. I remember Andy Taylor from Duran Duran talking about him, and Phil from Def Leppard and Bernard from Suede. They're all fanatics. At times, it kept Ronson and me going, because we'd never been big artists and yet we survived for twenty years. It certainly wasn't the media that kept our names alive – it was the bands that liked us."

Mick's inspiration on younger musicians was wonderfully encapsulated in the tribute 'Mr Fuzzy Fingers', written and recorded by Australian John Justin 'J.J.' Stewart – a stunning song with fantastic facsimile Ronson guitar playing, mixed by Robin Mayhew who had worked with Bowie. Inexplicably, this endearing track remains unreleased. J.J. has also contributed guitar for Oasis and Grace Jones. "In the early Nineties, with a 'fuzz-builder' named David Main, I set out to discover more about Mick's sound, which largely remained a mystery back then," recalls J.J. "We found out by looking at many photos and contacting several people, including Robin, that Ronno's fuzz was a MK I Sola Sound tone bender, and so the huge demand for owning a MK I replica began. Mick Ronson remains my main guitar inspiration to this very day."

As for Ronson's emblematic stripped 1968 Gibson Custom, during the Eighties the headstock was broken off and a new partial upper neck and non-matching headstock were spliced on, before the entire guitar was sanded to natural. In the early Eighties, Mick donated his iconic Les Paul to the Hard Rock Café in Sydney, Australia, and in 2001 Rick Tedesco of Guitar Hangar in Connecticut traded and acquired the Gibson. Loaned to the Rock and Roll Hall of Fame for two years, played by Def Leppard guitarist Phil Collen and The Dennis Dunaway Project, and used by Tedesco for gigging and recording, in 2014 the "Ronson maple top" was sold to British entrepreneur and race car driver Simon Dolan for a reputed 200,000 dollars.

Perhaps one of the most poignant Ronson observations came from Bob Harris. Reflecting on his first meeting with David Bowie in 1968, and his involvement on the early Ziggy Stardust concerts as compere, Bob remarked in liner notes for a Bowie BBC Sessions project: "It's an odd thing. At no time did I remotely get to know him. He had his direction. These days we would call him 'focused'. I don't begrudge David his self-obsession. It is the prerequisite of superstardom. I just wish he'd given Mick Ronson the credit he deserved."

Mick transformed Bowie's lyrical acoustic material majestically, applying his burning guitar technique, astonishing arrangement skills and collaborative creativity. 'Moonage Daydream', 'Cracked Actor' and 'Panic in Detroit' shone when Ronson, glam's best musician, brought muscle to the genre's glitter. Mick's passionate, tiger-let-loose guitar playing on tracks like 'The Truth, the Whole Truth, Nuthin' But the Truth', 'I'd Give Anything to See You' and 'Sweet Dreamer' was also remarkable. It was his classical grounding and natural intuition that enabled Ronson to devise astonishing solos and arrangements before touching a fretboard, and those attributes, fused with innovation and emotion, gave us a special and irreplaceable musician. Mick Ronson had been voted second best guitarist in *Creem*'s 1974 'Readers' Poll', placed between Jimmy Page and Eric Clapton; in 2003 he was also included in the

'Greatest Guitarist of All Time' listing by *Rolling Stone* and placed at No.41 in the publication's 2012 'Top 100 Guitarists' chart.

The most heartfelt reflections of Mick come from his family and his longest-standing musical partner.

Maggi Ronson: "I have great memories of Mick's life – the performances at local churches, the Hull Parks free concerts, sitting cross-legged around Michael Chapman's 'low' table, Iggy Pop's house in London with his Swedish chef-ess, Liza Minnelli at The Ritz, days and nights at Trident Studios, the *Slaughter* tour and the Bowie days. Also, the Freddie Mercury tribute, Morrissey's *Your Arsenal* album and *Heaven and Hull*, all when Mick was in a significant amount of pain. Mick never made any royalties. He didn't bother with product endorsement. At the Freddie Mercury tribute concert Guns N' Roses said to him, 'Don't you get guitars from all these different companies?' Michael wasn't into doing that. His last car was a Toyota Corolla that sounded like a hairdryer. Mick was and always will be my hero."

Suzi Ronson: "Mick was loveable, kind, gentle and breathtakingly handsome. He loved to look good and took a lot of pride in his appearance, but the thing he excelled at was his sense of humour. When he told a joke, he would be laughing so much that before he finished it everyone would be laughing with him. His one-liners were exceptional. When Ian and Trudi's new puppy shit in their living room, Mick's answer was – 'Keeps flies out the kitchen.' He was the eternal optimist!"

Lisa Ronson: "I miss my dad very much and I think about him every day and often wonder how life would be if he was still around. He has been a huge influence in many lives, but I think he influenced me more than most. He taught me to be strong and courageous, but most of all he taught me to be kind. To this day I continue to meet people who met him and they tell me stories of how kind he was to them. If ever someone felt out of place or unsure of themselves, he would always find that person and make them feel loved and accepted just as they were. He never wanted much but would go out of his way to help someone else. My dad once said to me, 'It's nice to be important, but it's more important to be nice.'"

> **IH:** "My fondest memories of Mick are the nine months we lived together in Chappaqua. Lisa was little, and he'd always be singing daft songs to the kids and cooking incredible meals. Mick never made a mess of anything but often broke things, by accident, when he stayed with us; he fell through a table tennis table once and knocked over our mailbox with his car one day and blamed the driveway because it wasn't straight. He'd also wait until he was leaving to tell you about the table or the mailbox. Ronson was unbelievable.
>
> "When Mick was alive, 'Sweet Dreamer' used to make me tear up a bit – now, I can't listen to it. He had the most beautiful guitar tone – it was kind of pure and childlike. I hung out with Mick for twenty years and we never talked about careers. We had fun. He was just a great bloke. When we used to share a hotel room on the road, I'd wake up to Ronson finishing off the previous night's wine and arguing with the contestants on *The Price is Right*. He was a nutcase, but his legacy is pure class. After he passed, Mick's mum, Minnie, said I was his best mate, and that's how I like to remember him."

Hunter would soon pay the ultimate tribute to his friend and musical partner with a stunning song.

Michael Picasso

Once upon a time, not so long ago
People used to stand and stare
At the Spider with the platinum hair
They thought you were immortal

We had our ups and downs, like brothers often do
But I was there for him
He was always there for me
And we were there for you

How can I put into words what my heart feels?
It's the deepest thing, when somebody you love dies
I just wanted, to give something back to you, gift to gift
Michael, Michael Picasso, Goodnight

You used to love our house, you said it was relaxing
Now I walk in the places you walked
I talk in all the spaces you talked
It still hasn't sunk in

Are the words real, that come into my head on a morning walk?
Do the shadows, play tricks with my mind?
For it feels like, nothing has changed but I know it has
Michael, Michael Picasso, Goodnight

Heal me, won't you, heal me
Nothing lasts forever, let it be
Heal me, won't you, heal me
I'm the one who's left here, heal me

You turned into a ghost, surrounded by your pain
And the thing that I liked the least
Was sittin' round Hasker Street
Lying about the future

And we all sit, in a room full of flowers, on a windy day
And I look down, but none of these words seem right
I just wanted, to give something back to you, gift to gift
Michael, Michael Picasso, Goodnight

Ian Hunter (1993)

CHAPTER TEN

Life, Get One!

I thought you knew what to do with records.

Mick Ronson's death was one the toughest tragedies that Ian Hunter faced in his life.

IH: "Mick's last year was painful, and it was just awful when he died. I've had bad stomach symptoms during my life and after Ronson's passing it hit me very badly. I was taking tablets, but it took months to settle. I often wonder about Kurt Cobain as I know he had stomach problems and I think pressure can manifest itself in different ways. I think Mick's funeral was part of the problem for me. I gave the memorial speech at the funeral and I'd expected that his coffin would be in another room while I was delivering it. It wasn't. It was there, right next to me. I managed to get through it but about a week later, it hit me, and it hit me hard. Mick's death was enormous. He was only forty-six, he had the world at his feet and his passing was so sad.

"After Mick died, I just stayed at home and became a bit reclusive. I was getting calls, but I didn't want to do anything.

I'd had no respect for music for years, so I thought I'd have a good time and just join up again when I felt like it. Suddenly, Ronson's passing gave me a hell of a wake-up call. I realised life is short, that I'd been given a gift and that I wasn't using it. It dawned on me that we had been lazy people who could sit around all day and not touch a guitar, so I had to start 'meaning it' again. People forget who you are quickly and I'd been off the roll, but Mick became the motivation to get back on track and it was a gradual comeback. I also thought to myself, you'd better do it properly because what you're doing at the moment is bullshit. I just thought, from now on if anybody rings, I'm going. That's what I did. For the first time in years I put music first again."

In 1993, Columbia Legacy released *The Ballad of Mott: A Retrospective*, a 2CD compilation comprising thirty-three tracks including Mott the Hoople's unreleased take of 'Lounge Lizard' and a *Dudes*-era demo, 'Henry and the H-Bomb'. Columbia's promotional material proclaimed Mott as a band that defined Seventies rock 'n' roll, but Ian was hurt to discover that the release included the "profanity take" of 'Through the Looking Glass' that the group assembled in 1974 to tease CBS record executives. The tape had been a private prank, never intended for public consumption, but, inexplicably, the shelved version was exhumed to Hunter's chagrin and utter dismay. The culprit who proposed its inclusion on the Columbia compilation was never identified.

> IH: "I don't like the invective at the end of 'Through the Looking Glass'. It was done purely as an inside joke to freak out our A&R guy. I just wanted to see his reaction about our suggested inclusion of all the swearing. Dan Loggins was our benefactor and you could do things like that in the studio and play it back and watch for the record company response. So, we did it and replayed it straight-faced, as if that was the version for the record, just to get Dan going.

He didn't do anything, bless him, until a few days later when he phoned in a panic about the ending. I then explained that we were pulling his leg. Obviously, it was dropped in 1974 but somebody had the brilliant idea that it should come out in 1993 and put it on a reissue, and I didn't know until it was too late. I was pissed off. It fulfils absolutely no purpose and was strictly for the studio. You can't do anything, it seems, without it being flogged publicly. That tape was just a bit of fun and was never meant for release but, of course, some bright bastard leaked it. Embarrassing to say the least. Still, I got it off my chest!"

Dan Loggins: "I recall the 'Looking Glass' playback; I think it was at Advision Studios. It was a joke Mott wanted to play on me and Clive Davis. It was supposed to freak us out and I was sitting listening to all this swearing and thinking, 'What *is* this?' I never saw the *Ballad of Mott* years later. It might have been some Columbia compilation producer or staffer who found the profane-laced track. We'll never know if Dale Griffin, as the Mott 'overseer' at that time, gave any green light."

Griffin and Watts once related that Mott had played the same kind of trick on Dan Loggins twice before. One incident was during the band's 'All the Way from Memphis' vocals and sax dubbing sessions, while the other episode followed Verden Allen's departure in early 1973, when CBS Records was nervously bankrolling the band. The scene at Abbey Road Studios was over money and a situation was devised where Watts would ask for more cash as his Cadillac needed repairing, and the butcher was threatening to repossess the meat in Pete's freezer. Watts did a grand acting job and engineer John Leckie recorded the event, with Dan Loggins protesting about all the money that CBS had spent on Mott the Hoople.

Hunter put music first again in August 1993 when he performed British and Scandinavian gigs with Johan Wahlstrom and Ricky Byrd, a New York guitarist who had worked with Joan Jett and

Roger Daltrey. Inspired as a youngster by The Rolling Stones, The Faces and Mott the Hoople, Ricky had been a fan of Ian from the age of fourteen. He remembers standing behind Hunter at the famous large round table in the back room at Max's Kansas City following a Mott show. In the Seventies, young Ricky had also worn "faux-British clothing" that he'd created after studying the group in *Circus* magazine. Now, twenty years later, he was treading the stage with Hunter.

Ricky Byrd: "What I learned from Ian Hunter is that you can be a rock 'n' roll animal and still be a gentleman. I also learned how to write intelligent lyrics like 'Saturday Gigs' – and 'Hymn for the Dudes' – where Ian's words totally encapsulate the whole rock business – in a nutshell!"

Hunter was scheduled to perform in Scandinavia on the 1993 Hamn Rock (Harbour Rock) tour, a series of concerts played from a boat called *Rockvågen*, taken around different Swedish ports. Only six of twenty planned gigs were played, Johan Wahlstrom describing the tour as a fiasco. Ian and Ricky appeared at some shows as guests of The Mats Ronander Band and played at the televised Stockholm Water Festival and the city's Melody Club, where Hunter dedicated a new song, 'Michael Picasso', to Carola Westerlund. Then, with Ricky and Johan, Ian played three British live dates during August, the shows comprising a 'greatest hits' set. After Hunter's gig at The Forum in London, Maggi Ronson announced that she wanted to organise a memorial concert for Mick and Ian was the first to offer support.

During September, Hunter joined Michael Monroe at a show in New York playing 'Roll Away the Stone' and a month later Def Leppard released a rarities compilation, *Retroactive*, including Ronson's 'Only After Dark' and a re-recording of 'Ride into the Sun' featuring Ian, as 'Honky Tonk Messiah', on piano. In 2006, Leppard would include Hunter vocalising the introduction to 'The Golden Age of Rock 'n' Roll' on their covers album, *Yeah!*

A year after his passing, on 29th April 1994, the Mick Ronson Memorial Concert was staged at a sold-out Hammersmith Odeon in London. In the run-up to the event, Hunter and his musicians rehearsed at Milhanger, the Surrey mansion, mill house and estate owned by Queen drummer Roger Taylor. Bob Harris acted as compere for Mick's memorial and the stars paying tribute included The Rats, Dana Gillespie, Glen Matlock, Big Audio Dynamite, Gary Brooker, Bill Wyman, The Spiders – comprising Trevor Bolder, Mick Woodmansey, Billy Rankin of Nazareth, Bill Nelson, Joe Elliott and Phil Collen – Steve Harley, Roger Taylor and Roger Daltrey. Late rumours of appearances by Morrissey and Bowie proved unfounded and some of the Hammersmith audience were upset by David's no-show.

> **IH:** "At Mick's tribute we had a great time because that's what you're supposed to do. What else can you do? The evening was sad, but it was a great gig. There were a lot of people there. A couple of people weren't there who should have been. Bowie wasn't there."

The spotlight at Hammersmith was rightly reserved for Hunter. Backed by Morgan Fisher and Robbie Alter, alongside Roger Taylor and his band The Cross, Ian played 'Once Bitten Twice Shy' and two new songs – 'Resurrection Mary' ("because Mick always liked new songs") and a poignant tribute to his musical partner, 'Michael Picasso' ("dedicated to Suzi, Maggi and Minnie Ronson, Mick's mum"). A timeless finale of 'All the Young Dudes' featured the entire cast led by Ian and included Geoff Appleby from the original Hunter Ronson band. It was difficult to find a dry eye in the house and one journalist encapsulated the emotion in a single line: "The show went straight for the heart and hit a bullseye."

Proceeds from the Hammersmith concert were used to build the Mick Ronson Memorial Stage at Queen's Gardens in Hull, where Mick had worked as a council gardener, and to help fund a children's cancer charity holiday home. Another memorial event, 'Ronson, Play Don't Worry in Heaven', was held on 15th May in Tokyo; the concert was led by Japanese band The Yellow

Monkey, with special guest Morgan Fisher, who always admired Mick, contrary to several inaccurate reports surrounding the 1974 Hunter–Hoople split: "After Mott the Hoople broke up, I was constantly referred to as one of the team that didn't like Ronson and that is bollocks. I don't like taking sides and I always felt caught between two opposing teams: Ian and Ronno, and Pete and Buff. I was a fan of Mick and really liked him. I visited his place several times and taught him all our Mott songs. I had great hopes for our musical collaborations to come. Sadly, it wasn't to be."

American journalist Robert Christgau once wrote of Hunter: "Ian should remember that it's a mighty long way down rock and roll, because as your name gets hot, your heart gets cold. Then your name gets cold." But, following the loss of Ronson, Hunter's musical heart was reignited and his fortitude would soon regenerate his standing. During his visit to Sweden in 1993, Ian had been approached by Casino Steel with a suggestion that they work together. Cas had collaborated with producer Bjørn Nessjø and Mick Ronson, and he invited Hunter to join a project called *The Gringo Starrs* at sessions in London.

> **IH:** "When Mick died, I vowed that life was too short and I was going to start moving again. This entailed saying 'yes' to a couple of things that you might normally say 'no' to. So, the first thing that came along was Abbey Road Studios and Mexican folk songs! They wanted to pay me an alarming amount of money to sing songs and I didn't have to write them; all I had to do was sing them. Casino Steel, who Mick had worked with, said he wanted me to sing on the project and enquired did I want to record at Abbey Road. It sounded like a mad idea, so I agreed."

Casino Steel: "I've always been a fan of Ian Hunter. I saw Mott the Hoople at The Royal Albert Hall in 1971 and, to this day, that is probably the best gig I ever witnessed. Mick had introduced me to Ian, and I went to Stockholm when Hunter was touring and asked

309

if we could record together. Ian Hunter is one of the few giants of rock 'n' roll, so it was one of my lifetime ambitions. Ian agreed, and I invited Bjørn Nessjø as producer."

Hunter demoed new material for his next solo album with guitarist Robbie Alter in the US, before *The Gringo Starrs* sessions commenced at Abbey Road in July 1994. Alongside Cas, "The Gringos" included Honest John Plain and Darrell Bath, two very charismatic guitarists who had formed The Crybabys. Honest John Plain had played in pre-punk prophets The Hollywood Brats with Andrew Matheson, The Boys with Casino Steel and The Lurkers. John Splain acquired the name "Plain" from a journalistic misspelling and the "Honest" tag from The Boys, after he used the band's NEMS Records advance to back a horse. Darrell Bath, who was musically inspired by Paul Kossoff and Ronnie Wood, had featured in The Tower Block Rockers, UK Subs and Dogs D'Amour. Darrell recalls that the name Gringo Starrs had kicked around before The Crybabys because of a fondness for Texas, cowboys and mandolins.

The band for the Abbey Road sessions was completed with the addition of Doctor and The Medics and Crybabys drummer Steve 'Vom' Ritchie and bassist Glen Matlock. With such a gathering of punk demi-legends, the *Gringo Starrs* project swiftly changed direction and ultimately became *Ian Hunter's Dirty Laundry*. Twenty songs, including two cover versions, were first slated for the sessions, but eighteen tracks were taped in eleven days with fourteen cuts originally listed for the album. Importantly, the project had merged Bath with Hunter, who soon realised he'd found a guitar partner that he was comfortable with. Ian would collaborate with Darrell for the next five years.

IH: "*Ian Hunter's Dirty Laundry* wasn't really one of my records, it was Dirty Laundry. They had agreed to put me up in the apartment next to Abbey Road Studios, which was good, and the money was good too. I came into the project last, but when I got there, I had to tell them that

I just couldn't get my head into the intended album of Mexican folk songs. We had to do something to pay the Abbey Road bills when 'Mexico' went out the window, so we decided we'd just do what came naturally to us – rock 'n' roll. We agreed to write an album there and then, and record it on the spot. We did that and the whole project just took off on its own, in a completely different direction. At the start, I gave Honest John money to get fifty quid's worth of stuff to smoke and the album was done in a few days. We had great fun and it changed into this really raucous record which came out sounding like '62-era Stones. An amazing guy from Norway, Bjørn Nessjø, produced the album, but the thing was I'd never worked with people like this before. They were a right bunch of unsavoury characters and I loved every minute of it.

"The Dirty Laundry band included Darrell Bath, who could replace Keith Richards and the Stones would be just as good as they ever were. Darrell *is* on a parallel with Keith and I loved his totally organic playing style. The other guitarist, Honest John Plain, was one of those unsung heroes of punk. A brilliant guy, he played tennis for two hours every morning then tried to kill himself every evening. The dichotomy was amazing. Then there was Vom, the drummer, who fell down a manhole at the studio one day; Vom was three foot six inches tall with green hair and the girl that he was with was six foot two and a German dominatrix. So, I was looking at this band at Abbey Road thinking this isn't going to work, but it did. We were barely aware of what we were doing so we just started making things up. We wrote some good stuff."

Darrell Bath: "I first met Ian at The Forum in London. I was a bit apprehensive and I couldn't work out why. Anyway, John and me went to see Hunter at his hotel the next day. Ian had such a great repertoire and it was a real high point playing with him. My favourite memories of the Abbey Road sessions are the times when the band started to gel and good performances were stumbled upon – 'Dancing on the Moon' being an example – and finishing writing 'Scars' by committee, line by line – it was creative stuff."

Honest John Plain: "I didn't live too far from the studios where we recorded *Dirty Laundry*. My girlfriend at the time owned a bike, which I used to borrow to travel back and forth to the sessions. On the day we were due to meet Ian at Abbey Road for the first time, I enjoyed lunch with my old mate Vom Ritchie, who was to play drums on the new album. The bicycle had a basket on the front so, after our liquid lunch, Vom sat in the basket as I rode to the home of The Beatles where I parked our bike alongside the expensive sports cars. I spied Ian Hunter looking out of the window, laughing at us hysterically, not realising that we were to be his band. In the evening I recall we went to see Darrell playing; Vom and I were not in good shape and Hunter was already in the venue with some important record company people. They came outside and I recall Vom sprawling on the pavement while Ian introduced us: 'This is Honest John Plain, my guitarist; and that thing on the floor is Vom, my drummer.' I don't think we made a good impression. I remember one evening we went out to the pub after one of the Abbey Road sessions. Everyone was swarming on Hunter that night, wanting his autograph, and I'm thinking, 'He's still massive!' As soon as we'd recorded all the tracks, Bjørn Nessjø only wanted the record released in Scandinavia, and that was a great pity because I think it's a really good album."

Ian Hunter's Dirty Laundry finally featured twelve songs, seven of them penned or co-written by Hunter: 'Dancing on the Moon', 'Another Fine Mess', 'Scars', 'Never Trust a Blonde', 'Psycho Girl', 'My Revolution', 'Good Girls', 'Red Letter Day', 'Invisible Strings', 'Everyone's a Fool', 'Junkee Love' and 'The Other Man'. The backing tracks and guide vocals were all taped at Abbey Road with final vocals added at Nidaros Studios in Trondheim, Norway. Overdubbing was completed at Right Track Studios and The Power Station in New York, and at Oslo's Ambience Studios.

312

IH: "I have never written so much in the studio as we did for *Dirty Laundry* and, in this case, it was a great way to do it. Some of the tracks, such as 'Scars', took about an hour or less, and Darrell and I wrote three or four songs in one day. We recorded lots of Stones and Dylan references, something I've always enjoyed doing, and it was all very interesting and a pleasant surprise. I was as low as I could get after Mick Ronson's passing and I had no record deal at the time, so the album was great for me. It came out on a Norwegian label and sold about two copies, but it is a really good record and it still seems to sneak its way around. Bjørn helped an awful lot and by the end of the sessions I really rated him. I liked the way Bjørn did the album and it helped me personally too, because I didn't have anybody else. When Mick went, I lost my friend, my producer and my arranger. I didn't have that anymore, but I really had started to put music first."

Hunter co-wrote the opening three cuts on *Dirty Laundry* with Bath and Plain: 'Dancing on the Moon', 'Another Fine Mess' – a humorous Hunter Ronson ode from the road – and 'Scars', featuring beautiful keyboard touches played by Blue Weaver. 'Another Fine Mess' referenced Hollywood comedy duo Laurel and Hardy and one of Ollie's most renowned catchphrases – a nice comedic parallel to The Three Stooges title that had inspired *YUI Orta*. In a flashback to the *Mott* album, and referencing the idea of "a revolution for fun", 'My Revolution' was co-written by Casino, Ian and Matt Dangerfield. The remaining Hunter-penned songs on *Dirty Laundry* were 'Red Letter Day', 'Invisible Strings' and 'The Other Man'.

IH: "Casino Steel was mostly responsible for 'My Revolution'. It was his idea, if I remember correctly. He liked Mott the Hoople a lot. 'Dancing on the Moon' was written in the studio and the band didn't know what they were doing at all. The drummer kind of keeps time because he doesn't know

313

where to roll, as I keep on changing the chords. The band were just following me and it wasn't really a song; it was just something that happened when we were in there. 'Another Fine Mess' was about Mick and me, on the road in 1988, and I'd already written 'The Other Man' before the Abbey Road sessions. As I heard it from two lawyers, we pulled 'The Other Man' from an Everly Brothers album because we were told that Willie Nelson was doing it. Willie was then reputed to have recorded it twice, once as a duet. I asked my manager at that time, Sam Lederman, what happened and he said Nelson did do it, but neither track was released, so 'The Other Man' went on *Dirty Laundry*. 'Red Letter Day' was one of my wife's favourites – Trudi loved that song – and 'Invisible Strings' was good, but too wordy to play live unfortunately. It's a real conversation!"

Exceeding expectations, the original Gringo Starrs project was retitled *Ian Hunter's Dirty Laundry* at the record label's request and, deferring the scheduled release date by five months, the album was issued by Norsk Plateproduksjon in March 1995. The Norwegian label, owned by Ivar Dyrhaug, had been established in 1988 and would be taken over by Sony BMG in 1996, but discontinued shortly afterwards. After releasing a promo disc of 'Red Letter Day' and having considered 'Scars', 'My Revolution' was issued as the album's single, Hunter and the band promoting the song with a live television performance in Oslo, on NRK TV's entertainment show *Rondo*. Steve Popovich's Cleveland International label issued the album in America and the track 'Good Girls' scored highly on several US radio charts.

Ian Hunter's Dirty Laundry received low-key press coverage but positive appraisal. *Kerrang!* awarded four Ks to "a cool and listenable record" and *Mojo* noted: "*Ian Hunter's Dirty Laundry*, his first band project since leaving Mott the Hoople in 1974, finds the leather-lunged rocker in fine form, boasting unusually strong songs. You get 45 minutes of first-rate rock and roll delivered with considerable panache and savvily produced by Bjørn Nessjø. In a perfect world, we would hear more from pros like Ian Hunter and less from too many younger, lesser talents with too little to say."

Rejuvenated by the *Dirty Laundry* experience, Hunter commenced sessions for his next solo album in May 1995. Collaborating with producer Bjørn Nessjø again, the project commenced at Time Machine Studios in Vermont, before the bulk of the recording and mixing was completed at Nidaros Studios in Trondheim. Originally titled *Life, Get One* – then *Pilgrim's Progress* – and finally *The Artful Dodger*, the album became an important milestone and marked the beginning of an astonishing revival.

The Artful Dodger featured eleven new tracks: 'Too Much', 'Now Is the Time', 'Something to Believe In', 'Resurrection Mary', 'Walk on Water', '23a Swan Hill', 'Michael Picasso', 'Open My Eyes', 'The Artful Dodger', 'Skeletons (In Your Closet)' and 'Still the Same'. All the songs were composed by Ian with three "co-writes" but a further four tracks were recorded and shelved – 'Fuck It Up', 'Ain't No Way to Treat a Lady', 'A Little Rock 'n' Roll' and 'Testosterone'. The musicians on *The Artful Dodger* sessions included guitarists Darrell Bath, Robbie Alter, Frode Alnaes and Torstein Flakne, drummer Per Lindvall, Kjetil Bjerkestrand on keyboards and bassist Sven Lindvall. There were also fleeting appearances from former Hunter Ronson players Dennis Elliott on 'Something to Believe In' and Pat Kilbride on 'Skeletons'.

IH: "After *Dirty Laundry*, Bjørn Nessjø said that I should come back to Norway and do a solo album with him. He had a lot of heavy rock hits in the Eighties and owned a studio that was state of the art. Nobody else was permitted to use it and if he wasn't there then it was locked. Norway is a great country and a really nice place. People asked why I recorded there, and I'd say, 'Nip out and look at it.' The Norwegian people treat you extremely well and they're quite old-fashioned too. Norway's not far away from Scotland and, like the Scots, Norwegians love music. *The Artful Dodger*

315

featured very creative people; one had worked with ABBA. Bjørn did things for the soul and things for money; he did rock; he also recorded a violinist and a trumpet player; he liked the Stones, so he'd wanted to do the *Dirty Laundry* album. The money and the clock were totally irrelevant to him. When we went to Vermont to do *The Artful Dodger* and it didn't work, it cost about fifty grand's worth of Bjørn's money. I felt embarrassed but he said, 'Look, if we didn't do that, we wouldn't be here.' He had a great attitude. The *Dodger* sessions were good, but it took four guitar players to replace Ronson!"

The Artful Dodger referenced a wide range of themes: Hunter's parents, his youth, New York City, the gutter press, the after-life and religion. There were also acknowledgements to figures departed on 'Michael Picasso', 'Walk on Water' and 'Now Is the Time', three of the record's strongest tracks. The album opened in uncharacteristic fashion with a beautifully low-key and alluring love song, 'Too Much', before Ian played an ace with 'Now Is the Time', a song from the heart, partly inspired by Queen's inimitable frontman.

IH: "'Too Much' is a pretty song. I love the mood and it's very atmospheric. The song is easy but somehow it never gets played live because it's so slow, and that's a pity because I really like the track a lot. 'Now Is the Time' was when I got serious about writing again. The trouble was nobody was particularly interested, as I was out of favour. Bjørn put up with me as I began to find myself again and 'Now Is the Time' was the first decent song I'd written in a while after the Eighties. It was a real 'Yes!' moment. I had 'Now Is the Time' when I played the Freddie Mercury Tribute and I remember talking to the Queenies about it at Wembley. Ronson knew about that song and I was very excited about it. The song was kind of written about Freddie because he was in my mind at the time. Fred was very nice and crazy as

316

a loon – the archetypal rock star. He was shy, but when you knew him, you could see that people aspired to be what Fred naturally was. People show off and pretend in front of the media, but Fred was the real thing. He was a natural giant, outrageously great morning, noon and night, and it wasn't put on. Queen were lovely blokes and it really upset me when Fred died, even though I hadn't seen him for a while – so I wrote 'Now Is the Time'."

The philosophical 'Something to Believe In' expressed some scepticism about religion, but acknowledged that one man's God is as good as any other, and that everybody needs to place faith in something. Hunter sings of earthquakes, mudslides and the shallowness of faith, but whilst the song is founded on a different tempo, in many respects it is a companion piece to 'God (Take One)'.

IH: "Believing in God is illogical – and not believing in God is illogical too. The point is that nobody knows. 'Something to Believe In' was a general opinion at the time, on various subjects. It has a lot of verses and is a pain in the ass to learn, but if you do, it's good live!"

'Resurrection Mary' was also other-worldly, Hunter finding inspiration in an *Unsolved Mysteries* television documentary concerning the urban legend of Resurrection Cemetery in Justice, a district in Chicago's southwest side. According to myth, a ghostly hitchhiker walks occasionally on Archer Avenue, outside the walls of the Illinois graveyard. The elusive spectral girl with the "*incandescent glow*" was the victim of a Thirties hit-and-run incident. Mary was buried in Resurrection wearing her white dancing dress and shoes, but she was "disturbed" when her remains were moved to an unmarked grave in the Seventies.

IH: "Somebody once said this was one of the best songs I'd ever written and I'm glad somebody figured it out – I agree.

317

I saw a short documentary about the legend of Resurrection Mary who was run over by a car and is supposed to have been picked up by several taxi drivers every once in a while. When I saw the documentary, I was in writer mode and the antenna was up. The words just kept coming to me – Resurrection, Justice, Cicero, Mickey Finn – I loved all that. It fascinated me. Somehow, I took it into Big Jim Colosimo land, mob towns and the Mafia. I got maps out and spent hours poring over details of Chicago, inserting Mafia chaps and backdating to 1935. It was a lot of research and the lyric took months. I rang the cemetery and they admitted Mary is buried there, but they weren't allowed to comment on the legend. The song's all factually correct and it is a proper story. I loved 'Resurrection Mary' as a title. Unfortunately, the song was on an album that no American company would take."

'Walk on Water', co-written by Hunter and Robbie Alter, was another of Ian's oblique narratives, offering a cryptic tale in the style of 'Shallow Crystals' and 'Silver Needles'. Describing a tormented soul who gets lost in rock 'n' roll and does not come out alive, Ian laments the character's demise. Hunter did not deny that the spirit of Guy Stevens hovered above the song, but the inspiration for the lyric included Kurt Cobain, who died in April 1994. '23a Swan Hill' was the address of the Patterson family's Shrewsbury residence where Hunter grew up as a teenager and, once more, up-tempo music is used as a contrast to a sad tale of parental discord and home-town constraints.

IH: "I can't remember who 'Walk on Water' is about. I always think that anonymity is really part of the fun but the song is not a favourite of mine. '23a Swan Hill' was where my teenage years came to a head. My father was a police sergeant, and the house was free. They never paid coppers much but gave them free housing, electricity and coal. The idea was you didn't have enough money to live, but you lived well; kind of like MainMan and Motown. My Dad and I had a tough relationship that made life hell and I left home when I was sixteen. I wrote the song about those troubled early days. I have been back to the house in Shrewsbury and the owners were great; they showed me round and the old piano was still there. People visit 23a now and again, so the occupants told me."

'Michael Picasso' – Ian's reflective, touching tribute to Mick Ronson – remains one of his finest songs, his earlier live treatment now beautifully transposed in a studio setting, featuring only lead voice, soft guitars and light orchestration. It remains a glorious piece of writing and an emotional eulogy to a talented man and a cherished friend.

IH: "When I think of Ronno, one word comes to mind: artistry. Picasso was a great artist and Mick could paint with the best of them. I just approached the subject carefully as a song. I wanted simplicity. I wanted truth. I just tried to get the words right because I knew all of his folks. It wasn't written before Mick died – I could never have done that – but certain lines were in my head from seeing him change and I used them afterwards. When you sing it, you don't think about it, otherwise it's impossible to do. It took me three and a half days to get a take that we liked. The studio can be like a doctor's waiting room. It became easier to play 'Michael Picasso' on stage in later years; at first, I used to announce that I was doing it, to give a few people time to get out of the room. When you sing a song like that, you have to zone out. If you dwell on it, it's not good."

Hunter's Abbey Road encounter with Bath and Plain resulted in two unused songs that blended into *The Artful Dodger* sessions: 'Skeletons (In Your Closet)' and the title track, inspired by Darrell Bath. Unusually, the *Dodger* album booklet featured a single picture of the guitarist and some of his classic lines:

> *"Whilst leggin' it home from work one day – as I entered the grim portals of my terraced abode – I could not help but notice Dame Vera Lynn gargling in my bathroom. 6 years and 16 stitches later – having run it up and down the flagpole a few times and given it a good old rub down with the Sporting Life – I have come to the conclusion that there is more to life than Breakin' and Enterin'." A Bathism – 95.*

The stuttering social satire of 'Skeletons (In Your Closet)' was a critique of invasive television shows and journalism. Written and sung by Hunter, Bath and Plain, the light-hearted vocals conveyed serious undertones and scandalous situations: innuendo, private conversations, sexual predilections, lurid tales and intrusion, all adored and feverously pursued by the insatiable gutter press.

> **IH:** "The verse on *The Artful Dodger* liner notes about running it up and down the flagpole were classic Darrell. He just came out with that one day and I said to him, 'What did you say? Say that again.' So, he did, verbatim, and I wrote it down. Darrell is a wonderful character – a rocker through and through – with a lovely turn of phrase to boot. Darrell Bath was the Artful Dodger. 'Skeletons (In Your Closet)' was good humoured. In America every morning, there are sick, mindless TV shows with people snooping into other people's lives. Britain has it with tabloid journalism. The lyric to 'Skeletons' was quite serious, if you get past the fun of it."

Two of Hunter's fine ballads were wrapped around and contrasted distinctly with 'The Artful Dodger' and 'Skeletons'. 'Open My Eyes' reflected on New York viewed from the Hunters' ninth-floor waterside home on Kips Bay, overlooking the East River. Ian's beautiful song captured the panoramic light and sinister dark of the city, brilliantly bookended by poignant references to the avenue of dead umbrellas and a brolly salesman on 23rd and Second Avenue. It has to be one of Ian Hunter's most underrated songs because, amid the gentle musical atmosphere and emotional vocal, the listener can virtually smell the morning coffee in *"funky town"* and enjoy DJ Don Imus's WFAN radio show. In 'Still the Same', Hunter lamented love in another tender musical setting, but 'The Artful Dodger' and 'Skeletons' intervened sharply. Ian accepts that the rollover rockers from *Dirty Laundry* did interrupt the overall pace and flow of the record.

IH: "'Open My Eyes' was written in our apartment on the East Side, observing Manhattan. I remember the refrain in 'Still the Same'. It's a good lyric, but just a love song. 'The Artful Dodger' and 'Skeletons' were two tracks from the back end of *Dirty Laundry* that sneaked onto the next record. They are kind of at odds on *The Artful Dodger*, which pisses me off a bit, but, although I think the album is flawed, I was pleased with it. 'Something to Believe In' was a step in the right direction. I was aiming for a complete journey, like Dylan's *Oh Mercy* album. That's what I wanted to do – a complete record, where you sit down, and you're never taken out of the mood. I just missed it with *The Artful Dodger*. My idea of success is when you write an album that hangs together as one piece. Obviously, this doesn't always happen, but you go in with good intentions.

"Writing is therapy. I have to do it. I'm lost without it. Writing songs is difficult and there are no set rules for me. I had two huge hits in America: 'Ships' took six years to write; 'Once Bitten Twice Shy' took ten hours. Some people can write lyrics and music at the same time, but for me it's usually music first, because I do have a terrible time with lyrics. I'm a big one for the first line – and you can wait forever, so you enjoy it when it comes. I've done albums that sold a lot of records, then they've wanted me straight back in the studio, but I find after touring that it takes at least a year to get the muscle back, and then another year to write. When I worked with the E Streeters they said Springsteen carries five new songs in his head all the time, which astonished me, but now I know it's possible."

Following interest from John Reid Management, at one point it seemed that Hunter might align with talent manager David Spero, who represented Joe Walsh and The Eagles, but Ian was aided by Kris Gray, a tour agent and musician who played bass for Cliff Bennett, Maggie Bell and Miller Anderson. "I first became involved with Ian Hunter in 1993 when a Norwegian promoter suggested a UK tour and I booked three dates," recalls Kris. "I met up with Ian again when he came over for the Mick Ronson Memorial Concert. When he was looking for a deal for *The Artful Dodger*, I shopped around for Ian, but I was getting involved with a new label, Citadel Records, with ex-RCA A&R man Bill Kimber; we signed the album for the UK and engaged the ailing Tony Brainsby for PR and, while the music press seemed less interested in Ian than of old, we got some mainline features."

> IH: "David Spero was a guy I knew in Cleveland. I don't think he wanted to manage me – I'm unmanageable anyway. Kris Gray never 'managed' me, but helped get me going again in the UK when nobody else was interested, pulling shows together as I was making my way back."

In 1996, Independent Music Press re-published *Diary of a Rock 'n' Roll Star*, and whilst the first reprint sold out swiftly, Hunter still pondered why the book had been withdrawn in the first place.

> IH: "Originally the diary sold out two editions and then they just stopped publishing, so it was difficult to find. I could never figure that out. I think people still buy the diary because it's interestingly historical. We never heard from anybody about that book for twenty years and then I got two offers in a row. I had wanted to call the original book *Rock 'n' Roll Sweepstakes* but the publishers said that to

sell it in airports, it had to be *Diary of a Rock 'n' Roll Star*. It still seems to me, if you're not sucking somebody's toes in a book or it's not Danielle Steel, they won't have it: the tabloid mentality. I only wrote the diary in 1972 because I'd just got married and didn't want to get involved on the road. Much has changed since then. It was venereal disease before us and AIDS reared its ugly head afterwards, so we were lucky. Touring, sound, travel and hotels are better these days; we used to get stuck in a single bed with a winceyette sheet and a radio.

"On the corporate side it's worse, because music labels have disappeared up their own arses. Trying to go forwards, they've gone backwards, over-pressurising bands, putting too much money into too few baskets and generally fucking up the golden goose. There are also too many people involved in music who don't know enough about it. It used to be you were mad on records and you'd work in a shop, then become a tea boy at a record company and work your way up. Now, you have to come out of a business school and speak the corporate language, because they're the people you need to pacify. They over-market bands until people get bored with them and the life of groups is shorter. Mott the Hoople had four stiff albums at Island Records. Now, we'd be out of there and gone. I remember a band that sold 1.3 million records with a Top Five single in America and they were in debt. Mott was given time to grow, but now it all costs too much. Kids realise they've only got one shot and fans have shorter concentration spans and move from one fad to another. Marketing puts too much pressure on youngsters, then they start acting up and the tabloids kill them. They're not blessed with wonderful intelligence. They just happen to play music. If you had any brains, you wouldn't do it."

The Artful Dodger album was issued in September 1996 by Polydor Records, but only in Norway, as Ian believed he needed major management to bolster an international release. The Polydor set included a poster-style lyric booklet containing Darrell Bath's "mission statement" and a dedication from Ian: *"I would like to thank the musicians for more than playing, to the Maddog for lending me a guitar to write the tunes on and my wife Trudi for putting up with the usual. IHP."* Seven months later, Citadel Records issued *The Artful Dodger* as a picture disc CD in Britain, followed by a box set containing a gatefold LP and *Diary of a Rock 'n' Roll Star* presented as a cloth-bound 1972 desk diary. 'Michael Picasso' and 'The Artful Dodger' also appeared as Citadel singles, the latter featuring the "non-album" 'Fuck it Up', inspired by P.J. Proby and written by Hunter after he read a newspaper feature about the controversial Texan-born pop star. Ian regarded P.J. as a wonderful character and enjoyed the absolute nerve of Proby's Top Ten hit 'Somewhere'.

> **IH:** "I loved P.J. Proby. In the Sixties, I bored every pub stupid in Northampton playing 'Somewhere' on all the jukeboxes, over and over again. I did meet P.J. once, in a large gathering of leather-clad rockers, and they all loved him to death. Proby was a one-off who really enjoyed shooting himself in the foot on a regular basis, which I kind of admired. He didn't play the game."

Hunter had been off the radar in recent years, so press reviews for *The Artful Dodger* were few, but *Q* highlighted 'Michael Picasso' as impassioned and wrote: "Ian Hunter's perennial Englishness is probably more voguish now than it's ever been and his vocal and lyrical nous remain a constant. The excellent 'Too Much' and 'Still the Same' cast Hunter as a winsome old trouper admitting his foibles with unflinching candour."

Reunited with former Mott publicist Tony Brainsby after more than twenty years, a British tour was set up to promote *The Artful Dodger*, including a sold-out show at London's Shepherd's Bush Empire. Guests at Ian's gigs included Roger Taylor, Joe Elliott, Dicken and Verden Allen, while the British touring band now

324

comprised drummer Alan Young from Alvin Lee's group, Kinks keyboard player Ian Gibbons, guitarists Paul Cuddeford and Darrell Bath, and Steve Hillage bass player Paul Francis.

"It's a shame there really aren't many rock 'n' roll heroes anymore," reflects Paul Francis. "It was a different story when I was growing up. The music of David Bowie, The Faces and Mott the Hoople filled the airwaves. Then, when I listened to *All-American Alien Boy,* with Jaco Pastorius, it was like another moment in time. Unfortunately, it would take twenty years for my and Ian's paths to cross. That happened one night at the Roadhouse in London's Covent Garden. Ian was there with a guy who I had known previously as the bass player for Maggie Bell and Chris Farlowe, and the conversation sort of went: 'Ian's looking for a bass player. Are you looking for a gig?' 'Fuck me mate, yeah!' Now I had grown up as an adolescent in the Seventies with a deep affection for the music and the fashion, but it wasn't until I got to work with Ian Hunter, performing many of those great tunes – 'Saturday Gigs', 'Bastard', 'Boy' and 'All the Way from Memphis' – that I truly realised how fundamental he'd been to the history of rock 'n' roll as a writer, as a performer and more importantly as a human being."

Uncut's review of Ian's Shepherd's Bush Empire show adopted a tired and tainted 'All the old dudes' headline, but their four-star review had to acknowledge that Hunter had mapped out an extraordinarily lengthy career – and it was still the Nineties. Reviewer Tony Horkins noted that Ian had been many things to many people: at Island he flirted with the notion of serious rock star, after 'Dudes' he was officially a pop star and he could also be defined as an author, solo artist and one of the "Class of '77" godfathers of punk, a status authenticated by the Clash. Horkins wrote: "These days Ian Hunter is either a cult hero of near-mythical proportions or that bloke with the dodgy barnet and shades that used to be famous, depending on your record collection. Why he's decided to tread the boards again after an eight-year hiatus is anyone's guess, but all tonight's audience want to do is roll away the stone and reminisce."

"I put together a thirty-date British tour to promote *The Artful Dodger* from April to June 1997," recalls Kris Gray. "Shepherd's Bush Empire was a great concert. The worst gig was probably Cork, where the drunken audience only wanted to hear 'Dudes'; they had billed Hunter's appearance as Mott the Hoople, and Ian was understandably livid and refused to play the hit song. We did a session for the fledgling MTV and I was also trying to get Ian on a mainstream British television show; the TV producer was going to come to a Hunter gig but said he couldn't find it; it was an old cinema on the main road in Rayners Lane; to miss it you'd have to be blind – or not bothered." The music business still involved episodes of desperation but Hunter confessed that live performance remained enjoyable.

> **IH:** "I like doing albums and I like doing gigs, but the in-between bits are a drag. Touring varies, because whilst hotels are better nowadays, getting there is bad. Roads are a mess with too much traffic and airports are a nightmare, but the shows are great. If a hall is full of people who love you, and I've had a fair few loyal fans over the years, you can have some great times. I never liked the 20,000-seater syndrome in Mott because it didn't make any sense. You hear 20,000 people roaring the group's name when you come on, but then it's so isolated. I much prefer clubs and I like 500-seaters because you can see people. To me, the industry was a lot better when it was less corporate, but I wouldn't change anything. If you don't experience the bad, then you never recognise the good."

Hunter's rejuvenation gathered more momentum with three VH1 television appearances during May. On the channel's *My Top Ten*, Ian introduced some of his favourite songs, this time focused on more recent material and videos. Prefaced by Mott the Hoople's 'The Golden Age of Rock 'n' Roll' promo film, his selection included Aerosmith, Robert Palmer, Cyndi Lauper, Bob Dylan, The

Waterboys, Prince, Keith Richards, The Police and Chuck Berry. For *Take It to the Bridge*, Hunter recorded 'Michael Picasso' and 'Irene Wilde' at VH1's Bridge Studios in London, and the live film was aired in separate episodes of the TV show. "The VH1 performance was a classic case of taking advice from a more experienced person, or rather not taking advice, about my Fender XII," recalls Darrell Bath. "At the session, Gibbo said to me, 'Don't tune it up – it'll still be in tune from the last gig.' Anyway, I got hold of a tuner – it's a bit out on that TV appearance!"

During his summer tour, on 4th June, Ian played a gig in Dublin then visited Joe Elliott's Bow Lane Studios. "I remember I was mixing the Mick Ronson Memorial tapes," says Joe. "Ian listened to and approved of his set from Hammersmith and he'd brought his band with him, so they set up and played a couple of up-tempo rockers: no vocals, just music. We spent an hour messing around, but I'm not sure it turned into anything. After that we just hung out and had one drink."

On 9th August 1997, the Mick Ronson Memorial Concert 2 was staged at Hull Arena. Hunter headlined a bill that included Michael Chapman, The Rats, Glen Matlock, Mick Jones, Steve Harley and The Spiders from Mars. The Yellow Monkey also appeared and brought 600 devoted fans from Japan. The opening of the Mick Ronson Memorial Stage took place in Queen's Gardens the following day, Ian playing at the open-air celebration as "Jim Spader".

Hunter's jetting to and from America continued with British and European live dates from September to November. In Hof, Germany, Ian taped a "trio" session for the Bavarian radio station HOT-FM, playing 'Resurrection Mary', 'Something to Believe In' and 'Waterlow', while his live performances included renditions of '3,000 Miles from Here' and 'Red Letter Day'. There were also occasional concert previews of 'Salvation' and Ian spoke of his new song and its importance at the time.

> **IH:** "There are some songs that I ditch and there's a reason why I didn't record them. There are a couple of exceptions,

327

one of which is 'Salvation'. I'm saving that as the last track for my last CD."

Optimism had been high for *The Artful Dodger* album but, mirroring *Ian Hunter's Dirty Laundry*, scattered sales on different labels proved fatal. Ian confessed that, whereas record companies had sought his signature in the Eighties when he was musically dry and busking with movie soundtrack songs, now he was armed with some of his strongest material but he had no worldwide record deal. Hunter would not release a follow-up to *The Artful Dodger* for nearly five years.

> **IH:** "*The Artful Dodger* was a really good record. We just couldn't get anybody in the industry interested in it. One major label said, 'What would we do with it?' I said, 'I don't know what you do with it. You're the record company. I thought you knew what to do with records.' Some labels know so little about music now that they have to hire consultants to tell them if the music's good or bad, and how they might handle it. That's what you have to deal with. It is a business that has caused a lot of problems for a lot of people, me included. It's very difficult to be in this industry if you're not as tough as old boots, and, of course, many of us aren't. Managers make a big difference as they can shield you from the idiocies of record labels, but good honest managers don't grow on trees and are usually overloaded with people who want them. Bad managers, as in the case of Badfinger, can tip somebody over the edge. You have no protection. It happened to me. I know what it's like."

Darrell Bath was enamoured with the outcome of the *Dodger* and Hunter's approach to music: "Ian's a great guy. He encourages you and looks for things and brings out the best in people. *Dodger* was done up in the hills in Vermont, then Trondheim. I don't think the Vermont tapes were dumped entirely; perhaps a couple of outtakes were, but mainly the drum tracks got replaced. 'Open My Eyes' was found on a tape that I'd been checking of jams at Ian's house, so it was sorted out a bit and put down in one hit by myself, including the lead part. A great guitar sound can take you anywhere, so that is one of my faves on *Dodger*. I love it. It's a classic album. I toured Britain with Hunter from 1997 to 2000, then me and Paul Francis were in Dan Baird's band. Ian is a pretty understanding person – and he's cool."

Hunter realised that a reformed Mott the Hoople would still interest international record labels and two interesting Mott projects soon followed. Morgan Fisher, who remained resident in Tokyo, collated a tribute album comprising new versions of Mott the Hoople songs by other artists, including Brian May and drummer Cozy Powell. Fisher originally sketched out his plan and consulted Queen, Aerosmith, REM and Robert Fripp, who all seemed willing to contribute, but the concept and cost of dealing with multiple management companies proved difficult. Finally, the first Mick Ronson Memorial Concert in Japan had created a springboard for the project.

Moth Poet Hotel – a Fisher-inspired anagram of Mott the Hoople – was released on Nippon Columbia's sub-label Triad. Morgan considered the album title apt as "moths come out at night like rock stars, hotels were where bands lived and Ian Hunter is a poet". The collection contained ten tracks, most notably a wonderful re-working of 'Honaloochie Boogie' by The Yellow Monkey and Fisher's clever title piece, featuring historic live fragments of Ian Hunter introducing Mott songs and a spoken message from Hoople admirer Frank Zappa mixed in with Morgan's music. Brian May wanted his version of 'All the Way from Memphis' to appear on a solo album, so *Moth Poet Hotel* was only sold in Japan.

Morgan Fisher: "Some famous Japanese friends wanted to play on the Mott the Hoople tribute album and it was very effortless and a pleasant recording experience. Mott gave me some of the most fun-filled years of my music career but also a lot of heart and a lot of humanity. When I look at Ian's lyrics now, I see that he likes

329

to write about the common people – the ordinary people – the whore on 42nd Street. He also writes about himself very honestly and very frankly and I wish I'd realised that at the time. I wish we all had, because I think we might still be together. Somehow, he couldn't communicate it to us directly; he just did it through his songs, which was quite enough. Why should we expect any more?"

> **IH:** "The Japanese tribute album to Mott the Hoople was great. It was put together by Morgan Fisher, he of the never-ending intellect. I thought he did great and it sold a lot of copies too."

The Nineties involved a further flurry of Hunter and Mott releases by Castle, Columbia and Rhino Records, including *Ian Hunter: The Collection, The Very Best of Ian Hunter, London To Memphis, The Ballad of Mott* and *Backsliding Fearlessly: The Early Years.* Chrysalis Records celebrated their twenty-fifth anniversary with embossed special editions of twenty-five classic albums including *You're Never Alone with a Schizophrenic*; the label also reissued *Welcome to the Club* with four bonus tracks and *Short Back n' Sides* accompanied by a limited-edition disc of previously unissued material – *Long Odds n' Outtakes.* In 1995, Windsong released *The Hunter Ronson Band: BBC Live in Concert*, a tremendous testament to Ian and Mick's live prowess, followed by a compilation of Mott the Hoople's surviving BBC recordings, *Original Mixed-Up Kids.* Featuring five studio session takes and six live tracks from Mott's final *In Concert* performance in December 1971, the renditions were saved by Transcription Services, part of the BBC's World Service, which had compiled programmes for export to overseas radio stations. *Original Mixed-Up Kids: The BBC Recordings* received positive reviews, one commentator noting that the versions of 'Darkness, Darkness' and 'The Moon Upstairs' were almost apocalyptic in their power, radiating a desperation that *Brain Capers* only hinted at.

Collections fell like confetti but, in 1996, budget label K-Tel released a shocker, *The Best of Mott the Hoople.* Said to contain songs that had been re-recorded by Mott, the bogus album with laughable liner notes claimed that Hunter Ronson had reformed Mott the Hoople in 1993 to re-create their greatest hits. The disc also featured five new songs written by music promoter Gerry Chapman and Danny McCulloch, a former bass player with Screaming Lord Sutch, The Plebs and The New Animals. In a March 1998 court hearing, K-Tel was fined under the Trade Descriptions Act over the fake recordings and ordered to pay costs by magistrates in Hampshire. K-Tel's defence lawyer told the court that the Mott material was purchased by the label from America and, following industry procedures, the company was happy with the authenticity of the songs, having dealt successfully with McCulloch in the past. Astonishingly, the court heard that Hunter's voice had been remixed with "a sound-a-like" to strengthen it, and it was claimed this was done with his knowledge and permission. Because the label admitted guilt, Ian did not appear in court, but a written statement was presented, confirming that Hunter Ronson had not recorded together since 1989. The court case over "The Misrepresented Mott the Hoople" recordings was covered by *The Times* and *The Daily Mail,* but the K-Tel judgment did not stop eight different releases appearing across Europe, dropping the Hunter Ronson reference but still presenting Mott recordings. Dale Griffin was furious with the erroneous *Best of Mott the Hoople* release and liner notes that claimed the tracks were the last work of a fading Ronson. Dale said at the time: "In a business where chicanery and reprehensible behaviour are commonplace, they even have the gall to dedicate the project to Mick Ronson's memory."

> **IH:** "I picked up on the bogus recordings on the web, when some of the people who bought it were discussing it. I couldn't really believe it, because it was so blatant. Deception's a big thing. If Mott had re-formed and re-done their hits, they would have been offered a lot of money. That CD was like a £500 job on a Saturday afternoon, but I'm told they got 75,000 dollars for the tapes! We had to twiddle our thumbs

while people went out and bought that shit and were conned. These sorts of people pillage and steal, and their reaction is the same: 'So? Sue us!' The expense and the time involved stops a lot of people going after them. We got them once, but it didn't stop people doing it again. How do you sleep, when your sole contribution to life is stealing other people's work? I guess it's worth a few quid to be worth nothing."

In September 1998, Sony Music UK issued *All the Young Dudes: The Anthology*. Three years in the making – with the original working title *Mott's the Story* – the limited-edition three CD box set contained sixty-two songs, including the unreleased rarities 'Ohio', 'The Hunchback Fish', 'Moonbus' and 'Find Your Way'. The set also became notable for a version of 'All the Young Dudes' that mixed Bowie and Hunter vocal takes, DJ Bob Harris describing the "Dudes audiomorph" as brilliant. The *Anthology* discs were subtitled 'The Twilight of Pain through Doubt (Three Years on Treasure Island) (1969–1972)', 'Temptations of the Flash (Columbia Hitts & Hottrax) (1972–1974)' and 'Blistered Psalms (Demos & Rarities) (1968–1978)'. Once again, Island Records instigated parallel Mott product with *The Best of Mott the Hoople: The Island Years 1969–1972*, a Spectrum Music release that simply duplicated 1990's *Walkin' with a Mountain* compilation.

Maxim magazine wrote of *All the Young Dudes: The Anthology*: "Forget *Velvet Goldmine*, this is the real, big-haired, glam McCoy" – while under the headline 'HUNTER'S HEROES', *Mojo* welcomed the "triple-decker sandwich of hot Mott", referencing the band as "the mob who embodied Seventies rock". *The Times* admired the "painstakingly annotated and lavishly illustrated" *Anthology* and termed the "garish, loutish and endearing" Mott as "the quintessential rock and roll band of the 1970s". *Classic Rock* described the "impressive" box set as a "worthy and well thought out package". In 1998's 'Best Box Set' charts, *All the Young Dudes: The Anthology* was placed seventh and fourteenth by *Uncut* and *Record Collector*.

The Sony set was issued as a companion piece to *All the Young Dudes: The Biography*, published by Cherry Red. Morgan Fisher described the book as a monumental effort and *Mojo* wrote: "The story crackles with drunken debauchery, clashing egos and seemingly constant friction, not to mention a little pathos." *Metal Hammer*'s Valerie Potter enthused: "There's something new for the MTH fan to discover on almost every page of this excellent official biography of the band. It's a magnificent achievement and, when laid next to Hunter's classic *Diary of a Rock 'n' Roll Star*, tells you all you'd ever need to know about one of Britain's most influential, yet underrated, rock bands (10/10)."

During preparation of the Sony *Anthology*, Dale Griffin advised Sony Music that Mott the Hoople had reached an in-principle agreement to spend 2nd November 1997 in a London studio, recording 'Like a Rolling Stone' as a box set bonus track; the session was never booked. Encouraged by Dale, Sony arranged a signing session for the box and biography at Virgin's Megastore in London, advertising that Mott would play an acoustic set at the event. Watts, who claimed he was not comfortable with recognition and had declined the 'Like a Rolling Stone' session, avoided the Virgin event; Griffin withdrew on the eve of the signing. Hunter, Ralphs, Verden Allen and Blue Weaver appeared at Oxford Street's flagship music store and, amid the unnecessary drama, Ian was happy.

> **IH:** "When I heard about the Mott the Hoople box set coming out, I thought it would be the normal course of events; that they'd get old catalogue out and bung a little piece of paper around it. The project was suggested to Sony by a longstanding fan and it developed. The label really got behind it, which surprised me. Then, when I saw the artwork and the quality of the CDs, I thought it was great. I couldn't believe it. Sony's 'Mott performance' in London was a fiasco though. Ralpher went to the wrong Virgin store on the night and then had to walk because he couldn't get a cab! Phally was there and Blue Weaver turned up to say hello, so we

333

dragged him in. In the end it was a typical fucking Mott the Hoople event. How Sony ever thought we were going to play was beyond me. Still, Ralpher found us and lots of people were there. I was told that the queue for the Mott box and book was longer than the queue that week for Sir Richard Branson's biography, which was fantastic."

In 1998, a contrary and incongruous Pete Watts bemoaned most of Mott the Hoople's recorded work and was scathing of the band's output: "We hardly made a decent record. 'All the Way from Memphis' was a great song, but our take is insipid and the production is awful. 'The Golden Age of Rock 'n' Roll' was another classic; a great idea for a lyric, but we didn't know what we were doing musically when we recorded it. In the later period of Mott, Hunter tended to like brass and saxes, harping back to old rock 'n' roll. He liked Leon Russell and *Mad Dogs and Englishmen*, and I couldn't stand any of that. Ian always wanted to get girl singers and sax players in, while I kept thinking, 'Why can't we just be fucking Mott the Hoople?' There were many wrangles in Mott about our direction. Travelling to gigs, the car often got stopped in a lay-by for a fight, but someone would hold two of us apart. There would be lots of shouting, like on 'Violence', but never quite a punch-up. The arguments could be over a song, or someone's playing, or politics, which was always a group favourite. We often had arguments and yet, when we played, we were totally together and focused. On the *Anthology* tapes there are one or two demos that have got the electricity that none of our original releases ever had – like 'Moonbus', where we were just jamming. That was great because it has the electric tension that we used to get live. Maybe 'Moonbus' is an example of what we really had? Ian had lived a life before Mott. He had experience and understood things and had seen poverty. I'd always had a reasonably easy life and all I was interested in was playing music and meeting girls. Ian cared much more about things and took them to heart. He was a level-headed guy and very down to earth."

Under the celebratory spotlight of the Sony anthology, when asked if Mott the Hoople should reunite, Ian Hunter remained frank and honest.

> **IH:** "Mott was a totally democratic band and I've been a solo artist for a long time, so I don't know if there could be a Mott the Hoople now, especially with Guy no longer around. If somebody made it extremely easy, something might be done, but I can't see us getting together, not without somebody in between us to sort it out. Maybe it's better to let sleeping dogs lie. I don't think it's a big deal, although I know a couple of record companies have approached us over the years, one as recently as 1994. However, to reform Mott the Hoople would mean taking the personalities into account all over again and I don't know if I could do that. I would find a band very hard now. I'm naturally dominant and I don't like aggravation so it's hard for me to be a part of something. Everything seemed to be very intense and dramatic in Mott. People look back with rose-tinted glasses and the reality might not be quite what they think.
>
> "I think Mott has died once and for all. We did it, but it's gone. I know it may be a duff attitude, but that's the way I feel. I find it hard to listen to anything I've done with the band because I always remember what went on and can't enjoy it for itself. I look back and I don't feel a thing. I'm not in the slightest bit interested. Neither was Ronson. We never sat around listening to old records like people seem to think you do. Mick, like me, never really wanted to be huge. He just wanted to have a good time, which we did, on a daily basis. He did what he wanted to do and I've done what I wanted to do. If a situation went a bit funny, then I've left that situation. That's how we both felt. We left each other often for that reason, but somehow we survived."

As the band was celebrated with their *Anthology* release, it was claimed that the novel *Mott the Hoople* and the story of Norman

Mott might be captured on film, but author Willard Manus remained doubtful about the prospect: "Mott the novel has been optioned six or seven different times by Hollywood producers, but to date the film version has obviously not been made. One of the guys who had formerly optioned it called to ask if the rights were still available. He'd actually written a screen adaptation of the book. I read it a few years ago and it wasn't bad, though he envisaged cutting down my Rabelaisian, bigger-than-life character of Norman Mott to Dustin Hoffman size. I have my doubts about the book ever being turned into a movie. It's such a Sixties novel, but you never know. As with just about everything else in life, I have hope but no faith."

Despite misty-eyed reflections on Mott the Hoople, Hunter was developing material for his next album, writing songs as "a kickback" to *The Artful Dodger*. Ian had penned 'Salvation', 'Morons' and 'It's Alright with Me', and had commenced another diary.

Following the success of the Sony *Anthology*, during Hunter's UK tour, a Mott the Hoople convention was held on 17th April 1999 in Bilston near Wolverhampton. The afternoon event included live sets from Steve Hyams, Ray Major, John Fiddler and Verden Allen's Flat Out, before Ian's evening concert where he was joined on stage by Joe Elliott and Luther Grosvenor. Darrell Bath regarded Hunter's convention show as the mega-gig of his career: "The great fucking Ariel Bender appeared and Verden Allen was there, so it was a mini-Mott reunion. Luther got up and it was out of control because he used Ian's Stratocaster, which was in open-tuning, which Luther didn't know."

Hunter's website launched a forum in April 2000, *The Horse's Mouth*, where Ian could answer fans' questions, but his first posting revealed technophobia.

IH: "So here I am, dragged kicking and screaming into the new world of the internet. I must admit I don't like computers. They look horrible – all dirty cream and keyboardy. I learned Pitman when I was 16, but I was fired after three months and that was that. One could say that I am computer hostile, so Trudi will be pressing the buttons."

In June, Burning Airlines issued *Missing in Action*, a selection of live tracks culled from 1979 to 1989 concert performances in Long Island, Chicago, Essen, Toronto and San Jose. The sound quality varied given the multiple recording sources, but, importantly, the album contained rare live versions of 'While You Were Looking at Me', 'Na Na Na', 'Wild East' and 'Day Tripper'. Initial copies of *Missing in Action* contained a bonus CD, *Collateral Damage*, featuring live tracks from the *Welcome to the Club* era. The Burning Airlines album was later re-packaged as *Standing in the Light*.

Stimulated by the success of *All the Young Dudes: The Anthology*, in August 2000 Sony Music released *Once Bitten Twice Shy*, featuring thirty-eight Ian Hunter tracks on two discs subtitled 'Rockers' and 'Ballads'. Eighteen recordings were rare or previously unreleased cuts and included 'Colwater High', 'One Fine Day', '(God) Advice to a Friend', 'Ill Wind', 'Bluebirds', 'All is Forgiven', 'Sunshine Eyes' and 'Ain't No Way to Treat a Lady'.

> **IH:** "Sony wanted some demos for *Once Bitten Twice Shy* but most of the ones I still had were from the Eighties. That was quite an eclectic decade for me so I rooted around and found a few rare items. The fast and slow CDs were my idea – one mood or the other – whichever one you're in. 'Ill Wind' was me and Robbie Alter in my bedroom studio in New York City around 1988 – one-take Robbie, a great guitar player. 'Ill Wind' was not 'Ill Wind Blowing', an old Mott song I'd forgotten about; it was my gospel blues song, about a guy in the Twenties who was working in the cottonfields all morning, went in to make a record in the afternoon and got nothing for it. I think 'Ill Wind' was floating around and landed in the wrong head.
>
> "'All is Forgiven' was for my mum and 'Sunshine Eyes' was written for Jesse, when he was a toddler. I like the song a

lot and it still gets me emotionally. It's just me and a crappy organ, playing in our apartment and featuring an Oberheim drum machine; the snares were pretty wimpy but somebody gave me a load of them and that take was the strongest version. I could have remixed 'Sunshine Eyes' but I kind of liked it the way it was. 'Ain't No Way to Treat a Lady' was an outtake from *The Artful Dodger*. I liked the lyric but somehow the recording didn't quite make it for me."

Hunter had participated in *Once Bitten Twice Shy*, selecting historic demos, but he also wrote lyrics and recorded new vocals at Riverside Studios in London for two *Ian Hunter* outtakes – 'One Fine Day' and 'Colwater High' – songs that Ian had first conceived as potential Mott the Hoople singles. Hunter dedicated *Once Bitten Twice Shy* to "the people who are dedicated to me" and offered the following reflection in his liner note.

IH: "I left England in 1975 and when I periodically return people say, 'What have you done since then?' *Once Bitten Twice Shy* should go a long way towards solving that problem. For those of you who have been loyal over the years, it's much appreciated. Thanks for hanging in. I'm a lazy sod, but in my own way I've tried my best to spit it out and thankfully you've got it. Millions didn't! Well, I'm supposed to die now (some labels will do anything to boost sales). Is it over? Not by a long chalk on a short board. The muse is still upon me now and again just as it always has been, and I am immensely grateful to receive it. So, this is what I do – hope you like it."

Once Bitten Twice Shy was never intended as routine greatest hits fare because it specifically sought to assemble hard-to-find tracks, unreleased songs and some unexpected surprises. Described as "a slice of incredible unique music history", *Record Collector* termed *Once Bitten Twice Shy* a collection worthy of a mighty and criminally undervalued rocker, while America's *Entertainment Weekly* considered that Ian's sly anthems and forthright ballads affirmed the "unshakeable humanity and integrity of a true rock and roll believer". Hunter toured Britain playing six gigs to promote *Once Bitten Twice Shy* but was at pains to point out that the collection was not an anthology; it represented only a part of his legacy, but Ian acknowledged that it was a valuable illustration of his solo work.

> **IH:** "*Once Bitten Twice Shy* was a great collection because there were a lot of people out there who hadn't got a clue who I was. When we played those live dates in 2000, Joe Elliott came on stage with us again in Leeds and sang 'Through the Looking Glass' from *The Hoople*. In fact, I thought it was a track from *Overnight Angels*. Joe would have got away with it if it hadn't been for the ninety-seven chords involved. What a bloke."

Once Bitten Twice Shy featured an unreleased live version of 'All the Young Dudes' recorded with Def Leppard in 1996 during their *Slang* tour; Ian had joined the band on stage at Orange County Fair in Middletown, New York State, and he also appeared with Leppard at Jones Beach Theater, Wantagh, NY in 2000, when they promoted *Euphoria*. Sony's Hunter collection was warmly received, but Ian was already focused on his next studio album – a project that would adopt a powerful and controversial slant. British politics had frustrated Hunter for years and, as he toured in 2000, it seemed little had changed since his 'Letter to Britannia' plea.

> **IH:** "Britain is a gorgeous country to traverse but it's still the same. It costs about 3,000 dollars to fill up your car and I always encounter one of England's road works management snafus on my tours; this consists of two lanes merging into one causing a two-mile tailback; you are then in two lanes with bollards occupying the third. Unfortunately, the

bollards are the only thing inhabiting the lane – no work being done, no workmen in sight, no vehicles – just bollards for two miles; and then three lanes again."

Hunter's two Nineties studio albums evaded commercial recognition and reward, but both were critically acclaimed. Importantly, after the loss of Ronson, Ian felt ready for a new phase in a new millennium. With Darrell Bath, he had also discovered another talented and collaborative guitar partner.

IH: "*The Artful Dodger* and *Dirty Laundry* were both great albums and, in my opinion, much overlooked. Those two records were important to me. Even though they were on European labels and I think the *Laundry* label went bust, I'd met Bjørn Nessjø and was finding my legitimate feet again after a few years of indifference. I played with some great people on *Dirty Laundry* and had some good times. It was quick and not altogether serious, but it helped me sort my head out after Mick's death. In the end, we made a great, grubby rock 'n' roll record.

"I did *The Artful Dodger* when nobody was particularly interested in my work apart from Bjørn, but these things have a way of sticking around for a second wind. Record companies are just big warehouses with a lot of records inside. They don't put anything in the window unless you scream at them morning, noon and night. The road back after Ronson was also very long. It was like starting all over again. We were playing little clubs in England, almost like cover band gigs, and it was pretty dispiriting, but I just wanted to play again. Over the years we wound up in town halls and theatres, but that was also part of the fun – to be climbing a ladder again – at my age."

Ian Hunter's Dirty Laundry was re-released by Cherry Red Records in 2007 and an 8/10 *Classic Rock* review reflected: "Although not strictly a solo album, every track is full of Hunter's influence and distinctive trademark swagger. It can hardly be described as perfection, but as a portrait of one of Britain's, nay the world's, greatest songsmiths in action, *Dirty Laundry* is unbeatable."

The Artful Dodger was reissued in 2014, MIG Music adding 'Fuck It Up' as a bonus track, but listing Hunter's song as 'All F%&k Up'. It would be a shock if the "ass end" of the music business ever changed.

CHAPTER ELEVEN

Worm's Eye View

Rant *remains fresh because it was fresh at the time.*

The *Artful Dodger* had demonstrated that a new musical heat was smouldering within Ian Hunter and in 2001 he ignited with his tenth studio album – the dramatic and distinctive *Rant*.

Rant was Hunter's uncompromising state-of-the-world thesis: a no-holds-barred, multi-faceted record that examined Ian's emotions surrounding his beloved but troubled homeland and a worrying political landscape. It was an exciting and challenging collection containing twelve tracks of truthful and sometimes provocative observation. *Rant* has also worn extremely well with the passage of time, remaining a vibrant suite of eclectic, perceptive and finely produced songs.

Importantly, in the late Nineties, Hunter reconnected with drummer Steve Holley, and it led to encounters with two great guitar players. Ian has always claimed that the right guitarist was a vital balancing factor in his output but that finding someone to take Ronson's place was virtually impossible; now he hit the bullseye twice, with Andy York and James Mastro. Hunter's music was about to shine and it would be the most amazing Indian summer.

IH: "Record companies were eating music alive and by the mid-Nineties I had to learn how to approach things properly again. I got back on track with *The Artful Dodger* and I'm still proud of most of that album, but I was looking for that 'other guy' – a Ralphs, a Ronson – and when I met Andy York, I knew I'd found him. *Rant*, and I guess The Rant Band, started when Steve Holley, who had played with Hunter Ronson, introduced me to Andy York at The Bowery Ballroom. Just like Mick in 1974, Steve said to me, 'You've got to get going here. You've got to do something.' Holley likes what I do and was great at getting me moving again. He had some involvement at a Bruce Henderson benefit gig in New York and called me, saying I should get out of the house and come down. So, in the end I went along, and this guy came out of the shadows and played tortured guitar. I'd said to Steve if I was going to get going again, I needed to work with a guitar player, as I used to do with Ralphs and Ronson. Steve told me at The Bowery Ballroom who this guitar player was. He was great. The sensibility was there, he knew his stuff and he struck me immediately. It was Andy York.

"I had quite a bit written and after that Bowery encounter I gave Andy five songs to consider. He was doing various things but came back with them all fully demoed about two months later, and then I learned that Andy York never does things in half measures. It took us a year to get together as he was touring with John Mellencamp, but it was worth the wait. Andy is one of those people who understands your songs when he hears them raw. York was like Ronson and Ralphs in the way he took my writing and moved it to the next level. He will get into the lyrics, but he is a music man and will suggest where I might develop things. Andy's finicky and I'm not, so we suit each other."

Andy York possesses huge talent as an amazing guitarist, an astute arranger and a great ideas man. He was a member of Jason and

The Scorchers, then Hearts and Minds, before collaborating with legendary Indiana rocker John Mellencamp of 'Jack and Diane' and 'R.O.C.K. in the U.S.A.' fame, where the fusion of country rock and raw guitar riffs suited York perfectly. Andy was influenced by delta blues, folk and avant-garde jazz, and he enjoyed Frank Zappa and listening to "masters of their craft". Working with Hunter in the studio, York's skills and focus were crucial to achieving the overall sound that suited Ian's songs. The production on *Rant* would be truly remarkable.

> **IH:** "Andy York knows exactly who he is, and his strengths lie in different areas. He's committed to the point of being committed and he's like Ronson in that he's a fine arranger. I also want to get in and get out of the studio as quickly as possible, but Andy will hang about and mop up and he played a big part for me on *Rant*. My confidence grew and he introduced me to New York's finest. Before that I didn't really know anybody in the area. I wouldn't swap Andy York for the world; he's a truly amazing chap on stage and off. Steve Holley played a big part as well – my favourite drummer – Mr Comfort, as he is known in New York, or Rhino as I know him."

As Hunter prepared to rant, he played a comeback gig at New York's Bowery Ballroom on 2nd June 2000; it was the night before his sixty-first birthday and his first US show in ten years. The concert rehearsals led to the introduction of another excellent guitarist, James Mastro, who would provide prolonged and stalwart support for Ian. Ironically, the Holley–York–Mastro era would eventually surpass Hunter Ronson in terms of longevity.

"James got in touch with me about possibly playing mandolin on 'I Wish I Was Your Mother', when he heard we were gearing up for Ian Hunter's big return gig at The Bowery Ballroom," says Andy York. "So, I had James come along to rehearsal to meet Ian and play the song and, of course, he was perfect. Ian was fascinated.

'Who is that bloke? He's great!' Ian Hunter came on stage for his first New York show in years and kicked ass. It was his birthday to boot and I remember Jesse, his son, bringing a cake on at the end."

James Mastro now became another important figure for Ian Hunter. As a New Jersey youngster, one of James's earliest bands, Fast Car, were regulars at CBGB and Max's Kansas City, and at seventeen he joined Richard Lloyd, the famed Television guitarist. Living in the middle of Hoboken's burgeoning music scene, Mastro played in The Bongos, Strange Cave and the Health and Happiness Show. Inspired by Lloyd, Ronson, Tom Verlaine and Ricky Wilson, and listing Television's *Marquee Moon*, Dylan's *Blood on the Tracks* and Bryan Ferry's *In Your Mind* among his favourite albums, James brought a wonderful range of great instrumental skill to Hunter's band.

Mott had also been an influential record for James Mastro and he would encapsulate his passion for the band in his 2013 liner notes for Sony Music's *The Essential Mott the Hoople* collection: "*Mott* is a concept album in many ways, dealing with the trappings of the rock life, and, sonically, it's their best. With the Mott the Hoople 'wall of sound' gone after Verden Allen's departure, some light shone through the windows. With Ian as writer there's a cohesive theme and sound that were previously lacking. This is the album that made me put down my air guitar and plug in a real one."

James appeared on three *Rant* tracks at first, but as a long-standing Rant Band member he now delights that Hunter's world ultimately became his world too: "My time with Ian has been great. His band, Mott the Hoople, was really the reason I started playing in the first place. I discovered Mott in 1973, when I heard 'All the Way from Memphis', a DJ favourite on New York City radio. It was five minutes of pure rock 'n' roll and I was hooked. I remember driving by The Uris Theatre as a kid, when Mott played their week on Broadway in 1974, begging my parents to let me out of the station wagon. 'I Wish I Was Your Mother' was probably the song that got me to play guitar as a youngster, then I discovered it was a mandolin and that really screwed me up. I always hold it as a goal to try and write a song. It's been my touchstone. It's also fantastic when you get to play with people that you so admire. Hunter remains an amazing writer and I think he's better now than when I first marvelled at him. He has a hard work ethic and is a brilliant songwriter and a great showman. The people who come to see Ian are just devoted."

> **IH:** "James is very much a team man. He turned up at the *Rant* sessions; we've worked together since 2000 and I don't think we've ever had an argument. Mastro's organisational ability is first class, as are his sweet touches of colour on whatever of the many instruments he happens to be playing. We often do a live version of 'Sweet Jane' and it was James who suggested an arrangement that took the song to another level."

Hunter had spent considerable time writing his new record, ditching almost an album's worth of material during the process, as he kept his sights set on "quality control". In July 2000, Ian moved into New York City to become more involved with his songs before the recording of *Rant* commenced at drummer Rich Pagano's New Calcutta Recording studio on Eighth Avenue in Manhattan. "I had some downtime in my studio and Ian and Andy knocked on my door and came in for the night," recalls Rich. "They stayed for three months. Recording *Rant* was a great experience and a lot of fun, and working with Ian Hunter was, in my opinion, possibly the closest thing to working with John Lennon. Ian's brilliance towers with his incredibly sensitive and poetic lyrics and biting wordplay. To watch Ian's lyrical editing process was a lesson in songwriting."

> **IH:** "I was scared starting all over again with *Rant*. In the lead-up to recording the album I couldn't get a record deal, so it was done on a very small budget. In the end it came in under 70,000 dollars, largely due to people helping me out. A Pro

Tools guy who worked on the record figured out that I was paying him only seven cents on the dollar. That's what was confronting us. *Rant* took three years to do because I kept writing and discarding songs, then, after a couple of years, I started to get things that I didn't want to get rid of. The first song that I felt was too good not to go on the record was 'Morons'. For *The Artful Dodger* I'd written largely on guitar, but for *Rant* I'd started playing piano, which makes it more involved. I hadn't touched a piano for about eight years, but 'Morons' arrived and it was great."

Hunter's original working title for the *Rant* album was *Worm's Eye View*, a phrase that appeared from nowhere and a line that Ian forgot was contained in his lyrics for Mott the Hoople's hit single 'Honaloochie Boogie'. Hunter and York produced *Rant*, Rich Pagano mixed the songs, which were all written by Ian, and Andy contributed considerably in terms of the arrangements, musical creativity and precision. The recording sessions for *Worm's Eye View/Rant* commenced in December 2000 and featured guitarists Andy York, Robbie Alter and James Mastro, drummers Steve Holley, Mickey Curry and Dane Clark, keyboard players Tommy Mandel and Doug Petty, plus bassist John Conte, brother of New York Doll Steve Conte. Ian's backing vocalists included Rich Pagano, Willie Nile, Jesse Patterson and Lisa Ronson, and Hunter stressed that he never worked on sentiment so Lisa and Jess were included on merit. As the sessions neared an end, Ian's album title changed.

IH: "The switch from *Worm's Eye View* to *Rant* came naturally. I'd forgotten that 'worm's eye view' was a line in 'Honaloochie Boogie'. For US release, one label wanted to call the album *Death of a Nation* and it was going to be *From the Knees of My Heart* for a while. Then I was putting down vocals one day in the studio and I said to Andy York that the record was a rant from one end to the other. The word 'rant' came into my mind again and again. I mentioned

347

it to Andy and he came back the following day and said, 'That's it. That's the title.' I guess the record named itself. The lyrics were kind of 'rantish', so we ended up calling the album *Rant* and then the band became The Rant Band. It's nice and short, like The Grease Band.

"*Rant* actually began in 1998 with the song 'Morons' and finished at the end of 2000 with 'No One' when everything stopped – twelve songs written, twelve songs recorded – that was it. The album was a great example of great people pooling their resources. We went for a performance mainly and wanted the record to be intimate rather than large. I think the performance is the key. There wasn't much room in the studio, so 'Paggy' had me jammed inside a vocal booth the size of a matchbox, Curry was thrashing away in the room and Andy was playing in the booth. That's how we did 'Wash Us Away', with everything else added later."

Rant would feature twelve thought-provoking songs, all written by Hunter: 'Rip Off', 'Good Samaritan', 'Death of a Nation', 'Purgatory', 'American Spy', 'Dead Man Walkin' (EastEnders)', 'Wash Us Away', 'Morons', 'Soap 'n' Water', 'Knees of My Heart', 'No One' and 'Still Love Rock and Roll'. In 2000, Ian signed with Papillon Records, a British label that had been newly established by the Chrysalis Group with long-time Chrysalis act Jethro Tull; one of Papillon's directors was Roy Eldridge, who had signed Hunter to Chrysalis Records in 1978. Papillon released *Rant* in May 2001, while independent record label Fuel 2000 issued the American version in April, with an alternative running order.

IH: "*Rant* UK had a different track order to *Rant* USA and the covers are different. The English version sounds better because that's the way it was conceived by Andy, Rich and me. The American CD was 'front-loaded' with the song 'Still Love Rock and Roll' to attract radio because I had a lot of ground to make up in the States. English and American

348

tastes are different; the US likes familiarity, but the UK looks for something new all the time. I chose a monochrome cover for England but Fuel Records wanted a colour shot for the US version. They said they had just done a survey which concluded that colour CD covers sell twenty per cent more than black and white – hard to believe, but we agreed to the American edition."

"It was a real shame about the US running order for *Rant*," says Andy York. "The powers that be decided that we had to have an 'obvious' choice for the beginning of the album because the Americans were too thick to appreciate the conflicted expat sentiment of 'Rip Off'."

Rant transcended much of the music that lay around it at the time – a powerful album, brilliantly arranged and produced, allowing Hunter to deliver a flurry of dramatic, emotional songs on a perfect musical canvas. Ian was frustrated by the British political situation under Tony Blair's "New Labour", but his angst was nothing new. He had been disillusioned before, but now Hunter brought age and greater experience to bear. Commenting on the world as an older guy, he still exhibited youth-like rage, but his world-gone-to-hell perspective was streaked with flashes of wit that helped dampen some of the fury. In 2001, Ian was just being truthful on *Rant*. In hindsight, his perspicacity was unerring.

IH: "*Rant* was me still raging against the English machine and was triggered by the same things that triggered 'Letter to Britannia from the Union Jack' twenty-five years earlier. British sovereignty had slowly been eroded since Ted Heath took Britain into the Common Market in 1972. Maggie Thatcher gave little bits away like weights and measures, but Tony Blair was not a traditionalist and it seemed to me that he wanted to make a good living, probably with designs on being president of the United States of Europe. Maybe a Federal Europe was evolution, but I didn't go along with it. I know that rock 'n' roll shouldn't get political, but if it's honest, that's okay."

While Hunter had given people co-credit in the past on certain songs, the expressions, words and music on his album were largely written by Ian before the other musicians became involved. *Rant* was a personal project.

> **IH:** "For some reason *Rant* had to be totally mine, songwriting-wise, but all the musicians loved the songs, we were all pretty new to each other and we all believed in the same goal. There was an us-against-the-world vibe and I really can't speak highly enough of all the people involved in the making of the record. I've been really lucky with the company I keep and that matters a lot. On *Rant* there's nostalgia, anger and love. I also think that *Rant* remains fresh because it was fresh at the time."

Hunter was swift to point out that his songs on *Rant* were not anti-England or pro-England, rather anti-British politics, penned with a sense of history but with a sharp eye on current events. Written in Open-G tuning, the album opener 'Rip Off' was a punchy rocker, possessing a riff finer than anything The Rolling Stones had penned in years. The song oozed frustration and was a no-holds-barred assault on England's green and pleasant land, and its economy. Ian may have become an all-American alien boy, but that was a good situation as he felt qualified to talk about poor British government, relaying opinions from his outside vantage point, looking in.

> **IH:** "That song was a little hard to digest, but it happened to be true. At the end of the day, the British press were fine with 'Rip Off' because it wasn't as if I was saying something they didn't already know. I had to comment, however fifth form it might seem. I was never a big fan of the ruling classes or high taxation as they never did anything with

the money they took back. I didn't rate Thatcher or Heath, while Wilson was socialism going through the roof. In the Seventies we got slaughtered tax-wise. I still thought music was a quickie, so I wanted to make sure I put some away before I went back to the factory, but, with ninety per cent tax, that wasn't on. I still get annoyed with things like *The Sunday Times'* '200 Richest People in Britain' list. How does that make the other fifty-eight million British people feel? It's just pure greed. You can understand it in America because it was built that way, but my country was built on care, vocation, fair play and tradition. The last thing Tony Blair wanted was tradition. England has been a rip-off for years. It made me angry and being angry is a good way to make a rock 'n' roll record."

Rant's second cut, 'Good Samaritan', was an unrelenting musical outing with sexual undertones, while the haunting 'Death of a Nation' saw Hunter expressing more concern about social decline in the *"cradle of civilisation"*, Great Britain. 'Death of a Nation' is a *"letter home"* and a powerful political song – but it is a protest song and a love song too, with Ian dreaming of a heavy-hearted Winston Churchill sadly observing England as a shadow of its former self.

IH: "'Good Samaritan' came from some old memory somewhere. I've had some alarming lapses of taste here and there, but I see no point in writing just for the sake of it. There has got to be reason. I do write some man–woman songs but my take on it is 'Good Samaritan' or 'Bastard'. That's my way of looking at it, truthfully. 'Death of a Nation' was really an end-of-an-era song and it was a drag to write. Nobody wants to say what I've said about England, but when you don't live somewhere you can comment. When I lived in Britain it felt like we were the best, maybe because we were an island – but when I went elsewhere, I found out we were used, and we weren't as free as we thought we were. Some people still feel the UK is the best place in the world, but they don't get the opportunity to get outside and have a look in. It was a pivotal time in England's history because the European idea was not a good idea in my opinion. It was a scary time because Blair was extremely good at rhetoric, like Clinton was, and, all the while, education and the health service remained appalling."

Rant's fourth track, the syncopated and slightly funky 'Purgatory', took Ian down a new avenue of sound, but the lyrics maintained the theme of frustration and disillusionment with cynical observations about the rich and beautiful people who are *"sent to destroy us"*.

IH: "We wanted to put 'Purgatory' out as a second single but were told by the Fuel label in America that it wasn't a good idea. 'Purgatory' and 'Good Samaritan' were different for me and were leaning in a more modern direction."

After a dark entrée to *Rant*, 'American Spy' proved that fun still flourished in some of Hunter's writing. The song's humorous lyrics had been inspired by an anecdote and a phrase uttered some years before by Ian's Sixties musical partner, Miller Anderson, and *Rant*'s CD booklet included the credit: *"Praise be to Miller Anderson for saying, 'Wanna buy a drink for an American Spy.'"*

IH: "Miller told me a story once about this guy who was a spiv. In Britain, spivs are guys who wear black suits and white socks and black shoes. They're usually pimply and usually the local loser, but they have these grandiose plans and make up stories. So, this guy that Miller mentioned joined the army and wound up in Cuba and went into a bar and said, 'Do you wanna buy a drink for an American spy?' – and they took him away – and he never came back. Miller told me this line and the thing stuck in my head for years. I thought it would be a great title for a song, but I could never quite write that story because I've never been to Cuba. It wasn't working. Then I got into me having left England in 1975 and I twisted it round that I go back there and use the loser's line. 'American Spy' was just good fun."

'Dead Man Walkin' (EastEnders)' remains one of Ian's favourite compositions. Constructed on a mesmeric blend of piano, groove box and drums, Hunter's lyrics described a figure in decline, painting a bleak picture of mid-life monotony – a man now conscious of mortality, past achievements and a lack of "newness".

IH: "I like the sound of 'Dead Man Walkin'", especially the piano. There is no process when I'm writing a song. Sometimes it's inspiration and a lot of the time it's accidents. 'Dead Man Walkin'" was the result of a wrong note being hit on the piano. I wrote it in F and the intention was F to G minor, to E flat, and back to F – but my finger on the left hand hit an E by mistake and 'Dead Man Walkin'" started to come. An accidental slip can alter an entire song. I had been writing 'No One' when the error occurred, but I dropped that immediately as I knew 'Dead Man Walkin'" was a better feeling. It wouldn't have happened on guitar so thankfully Robbie Alter had got me back on piano for *Rant*.

"'Dead Man Walkin'" is a truthful song about brutal self-assessment. In your late forties and early fifties, you are often a dead man. Life gets boring and every person goes past their peak. People know what they're doing with their job and their life, and nothing's new. At fifty, the idea of mortality also starts sneaking in. The line about EastEnders is a reference to life – real life. A lot of people live inside the British *EastEnders* TV show and when someone dies on that programme there's national mourning. The guy in the song is saying this isn't television, it's the real thing. When I took Mick Ralphs on one of my tours after *Rant*, he said he wouldn't play 'Dead Man Walkin" because it had too many chords, but, in fact, there are only four or five chords in it. The phrase 'dead man walking' had been used before, so that kind of pissed me off, but there's nothing you can do about that. I think lyrically the song is probably retarded imagination. Instead of people living their lives by *Coronation Street* and Manchester United, I was just saying: Is there room to think? We're so inundated with TV, computers and video games that nobody wants to think. It's too depressing to think."

'Wash Us Away' was a piece about the succession of liaisons that take place throughout life and how they become more adult. Referencing youthful ambition, Hunter's wordplay, such as *"the heart and the arrow, the rattle and the snake"*, was carefully honed, but the lyrics were completed only two days before the *Rant* sessions commenced.

IH: "We did 'Wash Us Away' as a live vocal, and Andy York and Mickey Curry were recorded live on guitar and drums too. We added bass later and complemented it all with James Mastro on mandolin. Originally, it was written to a totally different groove. It was Mickey's idea to change it and I'm glad he did. It is a tad abstract. I used the *'wash us away'* line as a vocal tool for melody over the chords, and slowly the song said it was called 'Wash Us Away'. It's nice when it comes looking for you."

On Mott's 1974 album *The Hoople*, Hunter devised the concept of a mini-opera and wrote the pioneering 'Marionette'. On *Rant*, 'Morons' adopted a similar slant. Ian's dramatic piano and the band's light-and-shade dynamics captured instant attention, but whilst the subject matter covered tough, acidic class warfare, the song also contained some slices of comedic theatre that equalled seasoned practitioners such as Randy Newman.

IH: "'Morons' is hysterical as well as historical. Robbie Alter asked me one day in 1998 to write a song like 'Marionette' and I asked why. He said because I was the only one who could do that, so I did 'Morons' just for fun. After he left that day I sat at the piano. I hadn't touched a piano in ten years and that song arrived, although the opening line had been rattling around in my head for a long time. I knew 'Morons' had got to go on a record, so that was a great start. I used to like that quasi-opera style a lot at one time. I'd been trying to write the lyric for ages and, once it was done, it opened the floodgates for *Rant*. 'Morons' is a good song. The title may be a little off colour in this precious little world that we live in, but songs should be judged by their content, not their title. 'Morons' could have been bigger but we couldn't afford it. It was like a *Hoople* track and the content was what *Rant* was about. I got it all out on 'Morons'. Then 'Rip Off' and 'Purgatory' came, and they gave the album form, which was nice."

Rant contained some dark matter and several frank political observations, but the personal 'Soap 'n' Water' pulled no punches either. It was directed at Mott's former drummer. Over the years, Ian had tired of jibes from Dale, in several of Griffin's interviews and reissue liner notes. The Hunter–Buffin alliance had seldom been a happy one, but aside from the *"slings and arrows"* aimed at him, Ian was particularly perplexed at a claim that Ronson had supposedly told the drummer he was "no good".

IH: "Oh dear! Sometimes people have it in for you and distort *so* much. One person distorted to the point that I had to write this song. I think stuff floats around your subconscious over time and then one day you manage to spit it out. The song was about Buffin, who was upset about Ronson for years. Apparently, there was a silly story that Buff felt insulted over a drumming rebuke, made by

355

Mick. There were times when Ronson had not liked some people's playing, but he always came to me first to discuss it. So, if Ronson had spoken to Buffin about his playing, why wouldn't he have said it to me? Mick never slagged off Buff's drumming. He did call Buff a miserable bastard after we did 'Saturday Gigs' on *Top of the Pops* and he may have had words then, but not about drumming. Things were not good on a personal level between Dale and me by the end of Mott. I just had to leave.

"Buff was a strange one. We were at an award event in London in 2009 when he rhapsodised about me at great length to my daughter, Tracie. I think Dale admired what I did, but he hated being stuck with me; he always worried about losing 'his band' and was a little paranoid about his timing. Buff's 'Moonie'-type rolls were huge, but we were never quite sure when he was coming out of one. He could be a pain, but I never doubted his commitment to Mott the Hoople for one second."

Parking politics, Ian recorded two touching and contrasting love songs for *Rant*. The wonderfully titled 'Knees of My Heart' paid homage to Trudi and recalled the newly wedded couple back in the early Seventies when they lived in Wembley, while 'No One' was a song of loneliness and, by default, a precursor to 'Dead Man Walkin''.

IH: "'Knees of My Heart' is a slice of Hunter married life, early on. I got some flak for the lyric and misspelling in the last verse – *'I bought you a house, with a burgular alarm system'* – but I fucking love that line. When I was writing 'No One' – a four-chord song in B flat – my left hand missed and hit a wrong note, but it was a great wrong note. You get a lot of stuff from mistakes. That's why band rehearsals are sometimes great, because somebody cocks up and you're off in another direction. Anyway, Andy York had heard 'No One' on a cassette, liked it and wanted us to do it."

Rant's final cut, 'Still Love Rock and Roll', was inspired by Hunter's early days absorbing Fifties music and it offered a light-hearted conclusion to the record. With references to Tommy Steele and Guy Mitchell, Ian tips his hat to his musical roots one more time but the song was originally earmarked as a bonus track. Hunter acknowledges that most of his albums carry on a tradition, usually featuring some form of homage to Jerry Lee Lewis.

> **IH:** "I write ballads, rockers and occasional 'groovers', but I've always had a penchant for Fifties music and that basic framework. 'Still Love Rock and Roll' is all about that music and a night I spent watching Little Richard and Sam Cooke at the Kettering Granada. It was written because I like writing songs with built-in power and because I remember that feeling. I don't think 'Still Love Rock and Roll' is as good a song as 'All the Way from Memphis' – I just like to acknowledge the individuals who gave my life meaning, but if I had my time again, I would take 'Still Love Rock and Roll' off *Rant*. That was a mistake, especially on the front-loaded US version. The *Rant* album is still one of my favourites, though, along with *Ian Hunter* and *You're Never Alone with a Schizophrenic*. With *Rant* you can walk in and out – it's a complete entity. I really liked it because it was something I would want to listen to, so at least I was happy."

With the cohesive but ferocious *Rant* completed, Ian mailed five carefully selected songs to his new label in Britain, as he felt there may be a timely single in the can. No Papillon single appeared but, seven years later, an unprecedented economic recession suggested that Hunter had been prophetic.

> **IH:** "I sent a CDR to my UK label and included 'Rip Off' and 'Death of a Nation', suggesting that they might make a single, in view of the impending political climate. It was just a thought. No takers! What do I know?"

357

Rant was acclaimed as *Mojo*'s 'Album of the Month', and under the headline 'Born to Bitch', *Footloose* enthused: "*Rant* sees Hunter back at his vitriolic, no-holds-barred best. As hard-hitting and emotionally direct as you would expect, the album highlights his increasing disillusionment with his homeland." *Q* wrote: "Geezer par excellence, Ian Hunter has done rather well here. Hunter can still craft a chorus and 'Dead Man Walkin'' is probably the album's standout" – while *Uncut* described *Rant* as: "Part memoir, part sobering visions of a world gone mad… its exalted anger awash in grief." In America, *Indianapolis Star* termed *Rant* an extraordinary collection of rock 'n' roll, while *Rolling Stone* ranked it with Hunter's best Mott the Hoople material. Topically relevant, politically aware and uncompromising, Ian opined that if people listened, they'd discover an optimistic and honest record.

> **IH:** "*Rant* comprised some personal views and I thought I'd get flak for it. I expected people to say, 'You don't live here anymore. What are you talking about?', but the reaction to it was great and it got great reviews. I think life's about where your heart is, not your feet, and my heart remains in Britain. I don't feel like an American even after forty-five years there. I'm British through and through – British passport; Green Card holder; I still live like a Brit, reading English papers and watching English soccer on television. I just prefer to live in the USA. I'm married to an American and I'm used to the laid-back US way. In Britain I think it's tighter, with people arguing over hedgerows and things like that. It's less frustrating in America and it's bigger. I live in Connecticut and love it because it's like Surrey, only cheaper. Connecticut is wonderful horse country. Why would I want to go back to the city?"

As *Rant* surfaced, Papillon Records elected that it would not sign any new rock acts. The label suffered and was closed by Chrysalis in 2002 while a subsidiary, The Hit Label, was left to trade in and deal

358

with back catalogue. *Rant* passed to the Echo imprint and was later issued in Europe by Repertoire Records.

> **IH:** "The problem with *Rant* was getting airplay because radio always wants to play 'classics'. If I write a crap new album, don't play it – but if I write a good one, play it. Stevie Nicks once said that she wasn't going to whinge about radio. Well, I think she should have because she'd got more power than me. The airplay puzzle was frustrating because, at first, the two record labels did get the CD into the shops for once. *Rant* was soon passed on to the Echo label when Papillon disintegrated. When we arrived in England to tour, Echo let us sell the CD at gigs but refused to service it to shops. It took me two years to write the album and then I had to fucking sell it for them as well."

Hunter had recorded and ditched almost an album's worth of songs before re-working *Rant*. The unused tracks included 'Rise and Shine', 'Famous Last Words', 'Requiem for the Dudes', '(It Never Rains On) Worthing', 'Abnormal', 'I'm in Awe', 'Avalanche', 'Salvation' and 'Just Want It Real', but Papillon Records only used album tracks when they issued the *Rant EP*, featuring 'Still Love Rock and Roll', 'Dead Man Walkin' (EastEnders)' and 'Death of a Nation'. A prospective Fuel 2000 single release, 'Death of a Nation', failed to pass the promotional stage after the terrorist attacks on New York's World Trade Center. A promo single appeared, the cover featuring a caricature of President George W. Bush as Alfred E. Neuman of *MAD* comics fame, taken from *The Nation* magazine. The promo CD was notable for two rare acoustic recordings from Ian's US TV appearance on *The Late Late Show with Craig Kilborn*; accompanied by James Mastro and Gary Louris of The Jayhawks, Hunter played 'Wash Us Away' and 'All the Young Dudes', although the latter was not broadcast.

During May, Ian embarked on a *Rant* promotional campaign visiting American radio stations talking about his new album and playing tracks acoustically with James Mastro. Andy York also started putting a band together for live work and, in June 2001, Hunter played eleven British gigs, including a show at Liverpool's reconstituted Cavern Club. "The Rant Band" line-up now comprised York, Holley, Ian Gibbons, guitarist Paul Cuddeford and bassist Gus Goad.

Gus Goad: "Paul Cuddeford got me involved with the 'UK Rant Band' in 2001, without an audition. I quickly realised how formidable Ian Hunter was and remember him yelling at me to 'Stay low!' when I got a bit adventurous at our first rehearsal. It wasn't until the first gig that I realised how great Ian is. He'd been massively underplaying during rehearsal and the sheer power of his performance on stage blew me away. And so it went on for three tours. I had the best seat in the house each night and was lucky to stand near Ian during his piano-based songs and watch him – sweat dripping from his nose, veins standing out on his neck – while he belted out 'All the Way from Memphis' or moved the whole room with 'Dead Man Walkin''. And what a band – Steve Holley, the greatest drummer I ever played with – Paul Cuddeford, Andy York and Mick Ralphs, three of the finest guitarists on the planet – Ian Gibbons, the most rock 'n' roll piano player I ever encountered – and some git on bass. I have enormous respect for Ian as an artist. It was obvious that he hated standing still, just relying on his old back catalogue, when he could be writing and performing new songs."

Paul Cuddeford: "When I first moved to London and joined a band, Mott the Hoople and Mick Ronson became my primary musical references. Within a couple of years, I answered an ad in *Melody Maker* and stood with Ian Hunter in a damp rehearsal room on the Holloway Road playing 'All the Young Dudes'. A few weeks before every tour, we'd receive a cassette with even more great songs from his incredible catalogue to learn. Then he sent us *Rant*, a fantastic album with an absolute stunner on it, 'Dead Man Walkin''. It still really gets me!"

> IH: "It started happening again for me with *Rant* because we started looking at it as a band, and got a band moving again. We did little gigs in England and the gigs started to grow.

It was gradual, though, because I was older, the business had changed and we were now faced with independents instead of major labels. It was tough. When Roy Eldridge and Papillon Records signed me, they hooked me up with a leading agent, Emma Banks, who was great. I subsequently met a hands-on guy, Mick Brown, who has looked after me on the road for years."

In 2001, Ian was invited to tour America with Ringo Starr and His All-Starr Band – the former Beatles' live "supergroup" of shifting musicians. Previous participants included Joe Walsh and Peter Frampton, and the players joining Ringo and Ian in 2001 were Howard Jones, Supertramp's Roger Hodgson and former King Crimson and ELP bassist Greg Lake.

IH: "I didn't know Ringo. David Fishof, who puts the whole thing together, rang me up and asked me to do the tour, which fitted between my American dates and an English tour. I thought it would be fun and interesting. I got back from England and Ringo was on the answering machine, then he rang me and welcomed me aboard. I'd never met any other Beatles, although I took a piss next to George Harrison one night in the Speakeasy, but I was a bit out of it so I never talked to him. Greg Lake was great to work with and I enjoyed his company a lot on that tour. We even discussed forming a band together, but it wouldn't have worked. Greg was a frustrated rocker.

"My 'spot' with Ringo included 'All the Young Dudes' and 'Still Love Rock and Roll', but we soon changed the latter for 'Irene Wilde' as Ringo liked the song and it was easy to learn. At a soundcheck one day Ringo said, 'What's that "Gonna Be Somebody Someday?" Do that.' He called it by a totally different title, but he enjoyed it and it worked fine. Ringo was a great guy and good fun to be with. The rehearsals were pretty hairy, but it was like a holiday. Ringo doesn't have to do it; he just plays, he's very proud of all the bands he's had and he's so normal it's frightening. I did Ringo's tour because it was just off the wall and I've always liked things that are odd. It's boring doing the same thing all the time. It was interesting working for somebody else because I got to know what a sideman is. Anyway, not many people get the opportunity to work with a Beatle."

In 2001, Ian co-wrote four songs with BDS, a band formed by Joe Bouchard of Blue Öyster Cult and former Alice Cooper members Dennis Dunaway and Neal Smith. 'Having the Time of My Life', 'Love You Too Much', 'There Was a Girl' and 'The Real Thing' appeared on *Back from Hell*, and Ian later guested on *Bones from the Yard* by the Dennis Dunaway Project in 2005.

IH: "I bumped into Joe Bouchard in my local paper shop one day and he asked me to go down and sit in with him and the original Alice Cooper rhythm section. They were geographical friends of mine who all lived locally in Connecticut, but I didn't really play with Bouchard Dunaway Smith and I'm not really on the BDS record. We used to get together on Mondays, just like lads again. I hung out with them, having a few beers, and I found myself helping with some songs, suggesting additions, and it worked. Joe's a good guitar player and I love Dennis and Neal. They're a great pair and the humour was like me and Ronson."

In December 2001, the matter of Mott the Hoople reared its persistent head once more and Ian was disinclined to consider any re-formation as he felt it could never meet expectations.

IH: "Mott will never re-form. We could make money, but a day is an eternity when you're doing something you really don't see the point in doing. It's not a question of personality differences – I've never met a band yet that got along – it's just a pointless exercise and I don't need it that badly. It's not all bloody show business. I just do what I want because that was the original idea of rock 'n' roll."

Having toured with Ringo Starr, Hunter turned his attention to a project that would take his music in a sparkling new direction, when Universal Records in Norway proposed that Ian perform live with an orchestra. The company had one eye on filming and recording, and the shows would feature Trondheimsolistene (The Trondheim Soloists), a musical chamber ensemble of string players. Hunter had not been convinced when the orchestral prospect was first raised by Universal, but his attitude had changed by 2001. The new release would be titled *Strings Attached*, comprising live recordings of Hunter's repertoire re-imagined, re-arranged and re-created.

IH: "The orchestral recordings came about because of Bjørn Nessjø and Petter Singsaas, the head of Universal in Norway, who was a fan. When they came and discussed it with me first time around, I didn't feel ready for it, nor did I see the point. Then, it was suggested again. They were saying to me, 'We think we can do it with beautiful lights, a sixteen-piece orchestra and a six-piece band' – and as they were reeling this idea off to me, I was mentally adding it all up and thinking, 'Yeah, but who's going to pay for all this?' It came to an alarming amount of money, but they said they would pay, so the big one was out of the way. It was truly wonderful. The Norwegians are very nice people and they actually do what they say they're going to do. Bjørn and Petter came to a London Astoria gig and took me out the following day and I was ready for it. That's how the Oslo project happened and I'm so happy that it did. Again, it was left field and that interested me greatly.

"Bjørn and Kjetil Bjerkestrand, a great keyboard player, came to my house in the States and recorded me on guitar and piano; then Kjetil made the tapes a cappella, removing the instrumentation once he was back in Oslo. He wanted a clean canvas – vocal only – so the grooves could be anything he wanted them to be. So 'Memphis' became almost half-time reggae, some songs were virtually re-hashed and with new arrangements behind the tracks – everything was so different and sometimes odd. Kjetil had worked with Miles Davis and Ray Charles and was not familiar with my songs, but he did his unique thing and instead of the orchestra playing round the chords, the whole delivery changed. Then, when we arrived in Oslo, Bjørn was making changes and Andy and I were still altering stuff on the day of the first gig. It was a project that was in preparation for a year, but with only four rehearsals. *Strings Attached* was fast and chaotic.

"The Oslo shows were performed with a six-piece rock band and a seventeen-piece orchestra. It was supposed to be eighteen string players, but we couldn't get the eighteenth bloke on the stage! The string players were only twenty to thirty-one years old; I called them Sigmund and The Little Freuds. The rehearsals for the two concerts were few but highly productive, and that accounts for the freshness. I was dealing with wonderful people: people with great musical memory and intuition. They were all well-versed in reading music and I was the only one there who didn't read, so I told Andy York what I wanted and he translated it musically to them. Everything centred around and went through Kjetil. He'd rehearse us one day, then rehearse the orchestra in Trondheim with the changing arrangements the next. That's how it went. I never met the orchestra until the night before the actual shows, but when you work with great people it becomes much easier. You just imagine the orchestra as a keyboard and then it's fine. They were wonderful and really into it, and that made it so much more special."

The two *Strings Attached* concerts, recorded on 29th and 30th January 2002 at Oslo's Sentrum Scene, were unique experiences for Hunter's hushed and attentive international audience, who had travelled from Britain and beyond. Playing alongside the orchestra, Ian's "rock band" comprised Andy York and some of *The Artful Dodger* session team, including guitarist Torstein Flakne, founder of Norwegian band Stage Dolls, and drummer Per Lindvall, who described Ian's music as "unique and timeless".

> IH: "Torstein may not be a recognisable name to people in the US or the UK, but he's an icon in Norway and one of the most tasteful players I've ever had the privilege of working with. During the first rehearsals for the Oslo shows we were running through 'Waterlow', and the solo, which had never been there before, happened quite by chance. The first time he did it I was over the moon. I don't know if he meant to do it, but I got the chills. Like all great players, Torstein's a thinker."

Kjetil Bjerkestrand's song arrangements injected new life, naked emotion and refreshing heart into the Hunter–Hoople back catalogue. 'Rest in Peace', 'All of the Good Ones Are Taken' and 'Seeing Double' were transformed and, for the first time, Ian delivered the stunning song that he had gifted to Ellen Foley in 1979, 'Don't Let Go'. There were also three new Hunter compositions in the set – 'Twisted Steel', 'Rollerball' and 'Your Way' – and one cover, not from the Bob Dylan songbook, as everyone anticipated, but Maschwitz and Sherwin's popular 1939 romantic song 'A Nightingale Sang in Berkeley Square', which Ian dedicated to his mum.

> IH: "When *Strings* came up, Universal asked if I could try to come up with something different for the set list, including one cover. I avoided Dylan because of the early comparisons that people had made in Mott the Hoople – it was too obvious anyway. I considered 'Somewhere' – that single that P.J. Proby had recorded in the Sixties. I loved P.J.'s version

so much, but I decided not to do it. Then I started thinking about 'A Nightingale Sang in Berkeley Square', because my mother always played the radio and it was often on the air in the Forties and Fifties. It's a really beautiful song and I love doing it. I've had a bit of stick for singing it and I can't see why. I think I do it great, in my own way. Anyway, if Elvis Costello can cover it, why can't I?"

Ian's new songs were warmly received and his live renditions became doubly important as Hunter would never complete or issue any studio versions. 'Twisted Steel' was inspired by the terrorist events of 9/11, while 'Rollerball' had been triggered by the 1975 movie of the same name; set in a corporate-controlled future where the ultra-violent sport of rollerball represents the world, the film and Ian's song addressed corporate greed and continued the thrust that Hunter had started on *Rant*. Ian considered that the individualistic lyric of 'Your Way' seemed slightly reminiscent of 'My Way', so Hunter and Andy dropped the song from the *Strings Attached* release, but regretted doing so.

> IH: "When the planes hit the World Trade Center in New York, I was in bed in Connecticut. Trudi woke me, and I saw the second one fly in and watched the buildings fall. My son Jesse sat on a roof a quarter of a mile away and watched the second plane from his job on 23rd Street. I had not intended to write about 9/11 at all. 'Twisted Steel' just came to me and I thought it was a simple and honest sentiment. It was written about Trudi's second cousin, Cookie, who was an exceptional young woman. She was on the phone to her mum as 9/11 happened and then she was gone. I was ringing somebody a few days later and phoned Cookie's mum in error and she could hardly speak. The song wasn't written about the event; I wrote it as a letter to Cookie's mother. America was pretty much oblivious until 9/11, then they realised they were in the middle of this, as Putin soon

366

realised. Nobody is safe anymore. Sadly, 'Twisted Steel' was written between albums; too late for *Rant* and a non-fit on the next record. To issue a studio version of the song on another album after *Strings* also seemed like cheating.

"'Rollerball' was about the corporate cults. James Caan had a line in that film, 'before the corporate wars', and it rang a bell with me. The world's situation is about greed and greed is in every business, including the music business, which is in a total mess. It's getting hard to have a good time."

Strings Attached: A Very Special Night with Ian Hunter was released in March 2005 as a double CD and DVD by Universal Europe and Sanctuary USA. *Classic Rock* described *Strings Attached* as a touching, special performance, noting: "'I Wish I Was Your Mother' and 'Waterlow' are given an extra dimension; they were beautiful and poignant to begin with and the addition of strings has made them mind-blowingly so. One of the most underrated songwriters these islands have ever produced, Hunter has never been happy to stagnate and this DVD is further proof of his desire to keep moving. May he never be still." *The New York Times* wrote: "Hunter has continued to make fine records and write songs that reveal a heart, soul and humanity that set him apart from nearly anyone else in music." Ian remains grateful to Universal Norway for making *Strings Attached* possible and retains fond memories of the experience.

IH: "The orchestral recordings were totally different to *Rant*, and I liked that idea. It also bought me some time to start another studio album. *Strings Attached* was an attempt to modernise my music; to go back and re-vamp some of the older stuff with a few surprises thrown in. The transformation of 'All the Way from Memphis' was one of Kjetil's more bizarre inventions and the Grieg inclusion at the end of '23a Swan Hill' came up during the rehearsals in Oslo; Kjetil did it by accident and I pounced! It was funny watching the orchestra's response to my songs and we had a great time. They put me in the Nobel Peace Prize Suite at The Grand Hotel in Oslo; it has the most famous balcony in Norway where all the recipients stand after they receive their prize, but my kids were throwing snowballs off it at people down below, to my undying shame. The logistics were arranged extremely well, and the record company was cooperative and worked like a record company should. I don't often get the opportunity to do things properly and here, for once, was a 'no-budget' situation. It was bloody hard work over a short period of time, but hopefully we got something special out of it. It certainly rang my bells and was one of the highlights of my life."

The new millennium had arrived with a flourish for Ian Hunter. *Rant* was an intelligent, dazzling album and, almost twenty years later, it retains a freshness and lyrical relevance. *Strings Attached* proved special too: an extraordinary live recording with orchestral treatments that re-sited several of Ian's classic songs in new musical landscapes. Hunter's renaissance would soon continue with another startling album.

CHAPTER TWELVE

Recreational Skull Diving

Shrunken Heads *was the American* Rant.

In 2002 Ian Hunter continued to play British live dates, but the shows would prove more significant than anybody realised at the time, when Mick Ralphs guested on second guitar. Including an appearance at London's Astoria Theatre, the 'Takin' the Mick Tour' were the first gigs Hunter and Ralphs had played together in twenty-nine years. Ian had tired of periodic questions about Mott the Hoople reunions, but the concerts with Mick turned out to be an important bridge.

> **IH:** "When Ralpher and I got together in 2002, he said he'd like to have a go again with me, as he liked some of my stuff – well not all of it! Neither of us really wanted to play Mott the Hoople songs. Mick much preferred playing *Rant*, so when it came to the Mott material at rehearsals, he and I would sit outside and have a cup of tea while the band played them. Fortunately, I had a great band and they made the Mott songs come alive. Then, and only then, did Ralpher and I get interested. There was no animosity when Mick left

Mott and when we met up again it was just like old times. Mott the Hoople was a long time ago and it was hard to go back. For years I said 'No' whenever a Mott reunion was suggested because I couldn't honestly see it coming off."

Following Sony Music's *All the Young Dudes* anthology in 1998, Angel Air issued *All the Way from Stockholm to Philadelphia: Live 71/72*, featuring two sought-after Mott the Hoople radio broadcasts. A review of the 2CD set by Dave Ling praised Mott's Swedish performance and their thunderous version of Mountain's 'Long Red'. Having celebrated the group's history in style with Sony's *Anthology*, the Stockholm/Philadelphia concert release was anticipated as the final excavation, but more albums appeared, including a 1970 Fillmore West set and a 1972 'Rock and Roll Circus' recording. Whilst these provided historical snapshots, many fans already possessed the material via bootlegs. Re-packaged Mott live discs flowed with some previously unreleased outtakes added as bonus cuts, including 'The Wreck of the Liberty Belle', 'The Ballad of Billy Joe' and 'If Your Heart Lay with the Rebel (Would You Cheer the Underdog?)', tracks that had been rejected by Sony. The quality of some discs was deemed disappointing, the nadir being *Rock 'N' Roll Circus: Live Wolverhampton 1972*, taken from an audience cassette. Arriving from various label imprints, CDs repeated material, re-moulded into "new" albums, with branding that became increasingly bizarre, including *Two Miles from Live Heaven*, *Live Dudes*, *Hoopling: Best of* and *Walkin' with the Hoople*. The tomb-raiding finally extended to an LP, *Live in Sweden 1971*.

After Sony's stalwart and attentive *Anthology* treatment it was sad to read a review of *Walkin' with the Hoople*: "The title, of course, puns on one of Mott's best-loved early classics and is just about lazy enough to warn you that *Walkin' with the Hoople* follows the customary path of licensing a grab-bag of previously released material and fashioning it into a whole 'new' album. It's an eccentric package. Arguably, Mott were at their purest during 1971–1972, but at their peak in 1974. Mixing the two eras together, however, with no regard for chronology or mood, really doesn't do anybody any favours, all the more so since the varying sound quality ensures that you spend more time fooling with the graphic equaliser, than you do actually listening to the album." *Pop Matters* wrote of *Live Dudes*: "If you're not an incorrigible Mott the Hoople archivist the CD is superfluous, and you'd be better off saving your money for the forthcoming Ian Hunter solo album."

Mott the Hoople's four original Island albums were reissued in 2003 along with *Two Miles from Heaven* as a first-time CD release. The re-mastered discs were welcome but there were oddities in the placement of scant bonus tracks. *Mott the Hoople* included 'Find Your Way' and the live version of 'Ohio', but Neil Young's song had not been written in 1969; 'Road to Birmingham' and Watts' favourite cut, 'Moonbus', would have been appropriate additions. Similarly, 'Midnight Lady' and 'The Debt' had been added to *Brain Capers*, but the songs were really relevant to *Wildlife*. *Classic Rock* would soon heap honour on Ian for the quality of his songwriting and solo work, but their reviewer, who had lauded Hunter Ronson in 1990, slaughtered Mott the Hoople's original Island albums. Opining that the fledgling band lacked clear focus and labelling one album "a stinker", five-star ratings were a relic of the past as a strange verdict was declared: *Mott the Hoople* (3/5), *Mad Shadows* (2), *Wildlife* (1), *Brain Capers* (3) and *Two Miles from Heaven* (2). Ian Hunter smiled. Joe Elliott screamed.

Ian contributed to a cover version of 'I Wish I Was Your Mother' on the 2003 album *From Hope* by Martin's Folly and cut a brilliant track for *Por Vida: A Tribute to the Songs of Alejandro Escovedo*, a 2004 CD release. Texan singer-songwriter Alejandro had collapsed from hepatitis C, and Hunter, John Cale, Billy Corgan and others recorded tracks for the project in response to Escovedo's health crisis. Escovedo was a Hunter fan who had covered 'Walkin' With a Mountain', 'Irene Wilde' and 'I Wish I Was Your Mother'. On the *Por Vida* (For Life) collection, Ian recorded 'One More Time' from Alejandro's 1992 album *Gravity*. Uplifted to a sunny, mid-paced rocker, Hunter's take ended with a repeat *"Austin"* refrain, echoing

371

"*Ohio*" on 'Cleveland Rocks'. Alejandro was moved by Ian's take of 'One More Time', which he had originally tried to write as a Mott the Hoople-styled song.

Alejandro Escovedo: "I remember listening to Ian's version of 'One More Time' and just breaking down. I thought about how many Mott the Hoople records I had listened to and then to have Ian make it sound like it was supposed to sound – it was an incredible moment. Most of the band's I've been in were modelled after Mott the Hoople. Ian combined a very literary kind of storytelling with a real rock 'n' roll band. He wasn't a songwriter trying to be a rocker – he was a rocker who was really a great songwriter. Ian has inspired me in music and life, or whichever comes first. I feel honoured to know him."

> **IH:** "I heard that Alejandro Escovedo was a fan and that he'd covered a couple of my songs. We met at a benefit in Chicago and I was struck by the genuineness of the man. Then someone in Austin got hold of me and said Alejandro was really ill and suggested that I do a song for a benefit CD. Andy York got a bunch of songs and we said we'd do 'One More Time'. I recorded it at Rick Tedesco's studio with York, Holley and Mastro. Alejandro is a good lad and a very, very nice guy. He's dedicated and is one of the true believers."

In 2004 Columbia released *Mojo presents... An Introduction to Mott the Hoople*, a seventeen-track compilation of CBS material that remains notable for being the only CD offering of Mott's edited 'Live Medley', employed as the B-side of their final single, 'Saturday Gigs'. *Mojo* wrote of the band: "It's all in the attitude – and Mott the Hoople had more than most. Hardened road-pros by the time they became bona fide rock stars, Mott boasted an unshakeable and infectious belief in rock 'n' roll. You want proof? Just ask the likes of Queen, The Clash, Morrissey or Def Leppard. The ballad of Mott the Hoople is a tale of thigh-high platform boots, enormous mood swings, big shades and black leather, and plans so ill-laid that arguably the best move they ever made was to break up – the first time at least."

A deluxe thirtieth anniversary *Mott the Hoople Live* collection was also issued by Sony Music in 2004. Swollen from its original eight cuts to twenty-one tracks, the twin CD set remedied the shortfalls of the 1974 LP and presented the original shows as far as possible from surviving tapes. 'All the Way from Memphis' and 'Hymn for the Dudes' at Hammersmith had been rendered unusable because of a mid-song tape switch and an out-of-tune organ, but DJ and founding member of Dramarama, Chris Carter, reviewed the reissue, saying: "The *Mott Live* long player was a half-assed chop job. Well, all that has now changed with the 30th Anniversary release of *Mott the Hoople Live*. Mott the Hoople in concert had basically two settings: loud and soft. When they turned it up Mott created a wall of sound that made Phil Spector's seem like a picket fence. When they turned it down, they were as mesmerising as anything Broadway ever had seen or heard. A+. The low spark of high-heeled boys lives on."

> **IH:** "The *Mott the Hoople Live* double CD made total sense. Fans got a load of previously unreleased music and the booklet was great too."

As 2004 reached an end, Hunter appeared on Jools Holland's twelfth New Year's Eve *Hootenanny* BBC TV show, along with Eric Clapton, Paul Carrack and Amy Winehouse. In 2005, Ian played harmonica for Ricky Warwick on The Almighty frontman's *Love Many Trust Few* album and toured America, Europe and Britain for three months. Miller Anderson deputised on lead guitar at Bergenfest in Norway and some fans still wondered if Ian might record with his longest-standing musical acquaintance.

> **IH:** "I haven't recorded with Miller Anderson again because he's my best and oldest mate, because he's absolutely brilliant on guitar and probably because he's a better singer

than me too. Miller can sing his ass off – why would he need my holler? I'm a great believer in fate. If it's meant to be it will happen, but, like Ralphs, Miller's a 'blueser' and I'm not. Miller's great at what he does and is big in parts of Europe. We have thought about it, but I just don't ever want to fall out with Miller and, it must be said, I am bossy."

Fine-tuning of The Rant Band continued with the addition of keyboard player Andy Burton and Mark 'M.C.' Bosch, an impressive guitarist who had worked with Elliot Easton, Benny Mardones and Carole King. Inspired by The Beatles, Townshend's "mind-blowing" guitar on The Who's *Live at Leeds,* Humble Pie and Paul Kossoff, Mark first started to learn music playing along to the American TV shows *Midnight Special* and *In Concert.*

Mark Bosch: "In 2002 a friend gave me a copy of *Rant* and the CD sat on my table for two months. One fine day I played it and I was amazed by what Ian Hunter was doing – and after all those years. I made a note to call James Mastro to say if they ever needed somebody, I'd love to help. Before I made that call, the same day, James called me and asked if I'd be interested in some Ian Hunter gigs. I couldn't believe it. My first show was in Santa Ana, California on 10th March 2005 and yes, I was a little nervous. Ian Hunter is a 'great' in all departments; travelling, playing, writing, lyrics and champagne! It's an amazing band with an amazing 'frontman', writer and rock God."

Andy Burton: "My first gig with Ian Hunter was a charity event at the Mercury Lounge in New York and it was also my 'try-out'. I'd studied the songs hard and was nervous at the rehearsal. The studio elevator wasn't working that day so I lugged my heavy Kawai keyboard up a few flights of stairs, but the case handle broke. We rehearsed and then I had to get that big Kawai back downstairs, but before I had gotten a grip on it, Ian had already grabbed one end to help me. I'd never seen a lead singer or frontman do that before. I thought, 'This guy's a gent. Rare indeed.' The set was only forty-five minutes that night, so

Ian stayed on guitar the whole time, rather than switch to piano for 'All the Way from Memphis'. I knew I was going to play that famous right-hand piano intro so there were more nerves as the song loomed. Finally, Ian said, 'Alright! Let's see what you're made of,' and I started playing that eighth-note pulse – and kept playing with Ian holding back – through an intro at least eight times the length of the original record. My wrist went numb – but I wasn't going to slow down or stop. At last Ian belted out 'One, two, three, four' with a grin and a nod. The band exploded and I was in. Ian Hunter. A gentleman indeed – and an expert at hazing."

In October 2005, as Ian worked on his next album, Snapper Music issued a Hunter live collection – a DVD titled *Just Another Night: Live at the Astoria* and a double CD, *The Truth, the Whole Truth and Nuthin' But the Truth* – recorded at London's Astoria in 2004 and featuring guest appearances by Joe Elliott and Brian May. *Stereophile* described Ian's release as fresh and vital, adding "This is as good as rock 'n' roll gets," while *Classic Rock* noted Hunter's glorious, ragged style and remarkable zeal – but as a live recording, *Welcome to the Club* it was not. Once again, more re-fashioned albums appeared when the Astoria recording was diced, sliced and released variously as *Behind the Shades*, *All the Young Dudes*, *Live in London* and *Ian Hunter and The Rant Band: Greatest Hits Live in London*.

At London's Café de Paris, on 4th October 2005, Ian Hunter was recognised with *Classic Rock*'s inaugural 'Classic Songwriter' award. There was special synchronicity when Ian's accolade was presented by guitarist Phil Manzanera, Roxy Music and Mott the Hoople having worked side by side at AIR Studios in 1973 on *For Your Pleasure* and *Mott*, two of British rock's landmark albums. Manzanera described Hunter as a fantastic songwriter and one of our national treasures, while *Classic Rock* wrote: "Ian Hunter's work revels in the romance of rock 'n' roll, so who better to be our Roll of Honour's first Classic Songwriter?" The acknowledgement of Hunter's talent was a richly deserved accolade.

IH: "The *Classic Rock* songwriter award was lovely. I've never been first in anything since the 100-yard dash for the under-twelves at Shrewsbury Police Sports Day, so it did engender a bit of a chill on the walk one morning. I saw Lemmy of Motörhead at the awards that night. I only ever saw two bass players louder than Pete Watts – Lemmy and John Entwistle. I used to play chords on the bass in my early days and Lemmy must have thought alike. At the *Classic Rock* event his band came over and had a chat with me, then a posh chap came over and asked me to meet Lemmy. He took me to the bar – where else – and I think Lemmy had written a book and I'd read it, so I said to Lemmy, 'I really enjoyed your book.' He snarled, 'You wrote two!' Who was I to argue?"

During 2006 Hunter was largely fine-tuning songs for his next album, but, on 23rd June, Ian played at New York's Beacon Theatre with Robert Plant, Garland Jeffreys and Nils Lofgren. Billed as 'We're Doing It for Love', the gig was a benefit for Arthur Lee, the ailing leader of pioneering Los Angeles band Love. *Rolling Stone* described Plant and Hunter's duet on 'When Will I Be Loved' as "heavy-glam Everly Brothers".

In November, at London's "posh" Langham Hotel, Ian Hunter and Mick Ralphs presented Brian May and Roger Taylor of Queen with *Classic Rock*'s 'Classic Songwriters' award in the same month that Sony Music issued *The Journey: A Retrospective of Mott the Hoople and Ian Hunter*. Presented in a deluxe die-cut box echoing the *Mott* album design, the triple CD set contained a career-spanning menu of fifty-three tracks. *The Journey* provided fresh focus on the depth of Ian's entire legacy, because, for the first time, a sampling of Mott's Island and CBS recordings and Hunter's solo work was harnessed in one collection. *Classic Rock* reflected that Bowie's 'All the Young Dudes' had been both a blessing and a curse as it had sometimes overshadowed the work of British rock's most gifted, insightful and underrated songwriter. "The proof is all here on this three-CD anthology," wrote reviewer Paul Elliott, as he admired the "brilliantly titled" 'Backsliding Fearlessly'. *Record Collector* described the collection as "the most complete picture yet of a man who's never been less than interesting". *The Journey* featured an early archive version of 'Morons' plus two shelved, unreleased tracks from the *Rant* era, 'I'm in Awe' and 'Avalanche'.

> **IH:** "I'd forgotten that I'd written those two tracks, so it was like listening to someone else's songs, or a new song I hadn't heard before, by me. I think 'Avalanche' and 'I'm in Awe' were shelved after I met Andy York and we started 'ranting'. 'Avalanche' was recorded in 1999 as I recall, and I met Andy in 2000 and we took a different tack with *Rant*. They're two of those songs that sometimes get caught up in that time warp, like 'Wings' on *YUI Orta*. It's just a matter of timing and what suits a specific record. I also had a song called 'It Never Rains on Worthing', but the lyrics are totally daft. It wouldn't have fitted on *Rant* at the time as it was basically skiffle music. 'Salvation' was another one of those songs that sometimes get shelved. It was written just before *Rant* and I have two versions: an early take and a second version with harmonicas on it, although I don't even recall who's playing on them."

Described as "the ultimate introduction to Hunter and Mott", grumbles over the omission of 'Rock and Roll Queen', 'Whisky Women' and 'Sweet Jane' missed the fundamental point that *The Journey* was conceived as a collage of Hunter's recorded work and *his* writing, both solo and within Mott the Hoople. In the US, Shout Factory would issue *Old Records Never Die*, a thirty-two-track Mott and Hunter collection that was essentially a watered-down version of *The Journey*, but with a cover that was bizarrely unattractive compared with Sony's artful packaging.

Hunter praised *The Journey*, but, always creative and in forward gear, he was ready to craft a new album – *Shrunken Heads* – his first new studio recordings in six years. It seemed ridiculous that *Rant* had failed to chart, but where that record politicised the UK, *Shrunken Heads* would exhibit frustration with the USA. Ian described the record as a mixture of politics and old-fashioned fun, and while *Shrunken Heads* dealt with American themes on tracks such as 'Soul of America' and 'How's Your House', Hunter was partly inspired by British imagery too. In a grave new world of narrowing attention spans, limitless texting and stunted conversation, Ian's field of vision and frank expressions seemed revelatory.

Shrunken Heads was recorded at A-Pawling Studio in Pawling, New York State, which was opened in 1987 by Peter Moshay and Daryl Hall to originate Hall and Oates recordings and productions for Sony Music. Here, Hunter had found an environment he liked and a great audio engineer in Peter Moshay. Ian also engaged with ex-Warner Brothers and Mercury Records CEO Danny Goldberg of Gold Village Entertainment, a newly formed artist management company.

Shrunken Heads remains one of Ian Hunter's finest albums and it presented eleven eclectic, thought-provoking songs: 'Words (Big Mouth)', 'Fuss About Nothin'', 'When the World Was Round', 'Brainwashed', 'Shrunken Heads', 'Soul of America', 'How's Your House', 'Guiding Light', 'Stretch', 'I Am What I Hated When I Was Young' and 'Reed 'em 'n' Weep'. The record was exceptional, Hunter reflecting on the foibles of modern life, consumerism, crass dressing, politics and personal situations. Ian proved capable of self-criticism on 'I Am What I Hated When I Was Young', while the youthful love song 'Reed 'em 'n' Weep' remains an under-appreciated diamond that easily sits alongside 'Waterlow', 'I Wish I Was Your Mother' and 'Irene Wilde' as one of Hunter's finest ever ballads.

> **IH:** "As a young guy you can write about love, but as you become older it becomes embarrassing, so I started searching for alternatives. President Bush arrived in 2001 and I thought there was a lot to write about there, so

Shrunken Heads was the American *Rant* I suppose, although it's a bit milder. *Shrunken Heads* is about small heads voting for small heads. Before you blame a politician, you can blame the people who voted for him. In the case of George W. Bush, they voted him in twice and to me that's a shrunken head. When Bush got re-elected, the average Republican said, 'Well, what else did we have?' They had a point. What was the alternative? If you've only got the choice of two parties and they're both crap, what do you do?

"I'm a Green Card and I love America, but it's run by about six huge oil and construction companies, and I think they are just another enemy. It's hard to be an American, but it's got nothing to do with your average American who's not allowed to see what's really going on. Most couples have a mortgage and kids and don't have time to analyse politics, and they play on this. Corporations want your loyalty as an employee, so your wife's working and you're working, and nobody's got any time, and nobody seems to be any better off, except the nanny, who is probably getting more than your wife's getting in wages. I can't do anything about the way the world's turning but you can increase awareness. People have to be smarter."

The musicians on *Shrunken Heads* included James Mastro, Steve Holley, Andy York, Andy Burton, bassist Graham Maby from the Joe Jackson Band, and guitarist Jack Petruzzelli. The album also featured guest appearances from E Street Band violinist Soozie Tyrell, Mark Bosch, Dennis Dunaway, Rick Tedesco, Jesse Patterson and Christine Ohlman; Ian would soon sing on 'There Ain't No Cure' on Christine's album, *The Deep End*. Jeff Tweedy of Wilco also contributed vocals to three *Shrunken Heads* tracks at Mastro's suggestion.

IH: "James knew Jeff Tweedy and I love his voice as there is a vulnerability in it that I would die for. Jeff joined me on stage

379

one night so we asked him to join us on *Shrunken Heads* and we went down to Chicago and he did three tracks. Jeff liked a song called 'Henry and the H-Bomb' that I did with Mott, but it was only ever an unfinished demo. I remember Jeff turned up at our Chicago gig and said, 'Let's do this' – 'Henry and the H-Bomb'.' I said, 'Well, there is no lyric to it.' And he said, 'Oh yes there is.' I said, 'There isn't. I wrote the song.' 'No, no, no, there's a lyric.' So, I said, 'What's the fucking lyric?' Jeff showed me a lyric and it was a great lyric, but I know I didn't write it. I think he'd listened to the junk on the Mott demo, wrote down what he thought I sang, and it was good. He kept insisting it was my lyric so I said, 'Fine.'

"James Mastro also introduced Mark Bosch to me and he became my guitarist and has filled in admirably over many years. York, Mastro and Bosch, after Ralphs and Ronson – I've been gifted with great guitar players. Andy and James had brought in bassist Tony Shanahan, who split his time with me and Patti Smith, and then Tony recommended Graham Maby, who was available when Joe Jackson wasn't touring."

Graham Maby: "I listened to Mott the Hoople in grammar school and used to play 'Once Bitten Twice Shy' in one of my first bands, but I didn't fully appreciate Ian until I saw him with Mick Ronson in Los Angeles. My lasting impressions of Ian are dedication and commitment to his art, his cynicism with humour, not bitterness, and having more fun in a recording studio with him than anyone else I can think of. My British tour with Ian Hunter was a career highlight. He's an example of hard work and humility."

Produced by Hunter and York, *Shrunken Heads* was recorded quickly as a band effort and all the songs were composed by Ian, apart from the opening track, co-written with Andy York: "In January 2006, I walked down the stairs to Ian's roomy basement studio to begin work. On the massive snooker table, the entire felt was covered in a myriad of yellow legal pad sheets, neatly stacked and organised in horizontal rows. Each stack represented a song lyric, rendered in Ian's calligraphic hand, and each lyric stack had an accompanying micro-cassette containing melodic and rhythmic ideas. There were probably twenty stacks in all. That's dedication to your craft. Clearly this man was, once again, on a mission. Thus began the adventure that resulted in *Shrunken Heads*. Ian had plenty to say. There was the loquacious scoundrel in 'Words', the visceral anger in 'Stretch', the self-deprecating humour of 'I Am What I Hated When I Was Young', a profound sense of loss in 'Read 'em 'n' Weep' and the uplifting hope of 'Guiding Light' – all just pieces of yellow legal paper, on a pool table, on that January day."

Shrunken Heads kicked off with 'Words (Big Mouth)', a humorous tale of regret that lamented the limitations of the English language. As the lyrics unfold, Ian falls over himself, apologising for careless comments, *"cruel little clusters"* and *"grammatical bacteria"*, blaming himself, alcohol and high spirits for the verbal damage and fall-out.

> **IH:** "'Words' was a song for Trudi and another true story. It's not the most startling ball-buster, but I like the song. We usually go to my friend Rick Tedesco's house once a week in Connecticut and get completely slaughtered, and the mood can turn ugly on the way home and has done on a few occasions over the years. The song is an apology to my wife."

'Fuss about Nothin'' was Hunter's reflection on George W. Bush and his "five-minute war" while 'Brainwashed' was an acerbic dig at herd-style thinking and consumerism, with a suggestion that gullible people rewind their lives and cut up their credit credits.

> **IH:** "'Fuss about Nothin'' concerned a chap who runs a nation and cons them into doing something. If you hear a slogan coming out of people's mouths non-stop in the news, you know there's a gimmick on the way. The repeated use of the term 'weapons of mass destruction' was a con to

get us into Iraq. 'Brainwashed' was about the great zombie proletariat – the working masses – and reality television. All the superfluous crap in life makes no real difference to anybody – slimming pills, branded clothes, make-up – they've become billion-dollar industries. People should spend their money on other things."

Hunter described 'When the World Was Round' as the first pop song he'd written in twenty-five years, but it carried a socially aware message, touching on globalisation, with Ian yearning for the simplicity of the past. Some wondered if Hunter's writing might have been influenced by *The World Is Flat* – Thomas L. Friedman's book asserting that the planet, in the information age, has become a level playing field.

IH: "I've never read that book and, in fact, the song was originally called 'When the World Was Young', but it didn't sound right. 'When the World Was Round' sounded better to Andy York. The song is about the world being off-balance, in that there's too many people with nothing and too few with too much, and how we've managed to con ourselves and put ourselves in a situation where it can only be a two-party system – Republicans and Democrats. There's a line in the song that I liked, '*too much information but not enough to go on*'. I'm a rock 'n' roller, not a politician, but I don't like idiots running the country. We try to make it as palatable as possible by making the songs sound great and the lyric is there if you want it. 'When the World Was Round' is a simple song about the world, before you find out what the world really is!"

The spine of *Shrunken Heads* was Ian's stunning pairing of the album's title song and 'Soul of America'. One commentator believed that Hunter had arguably "out-Dylaned Dylan again" with his impressive lyrics, not least on 'Shrunken Heads', where Ian bemoans the lack of political accountability and the gap between rich and poor.

> **IH:** "'Shrunken Heads' was written after I went to Blackpool Pleasure Beach in England one day and nobody smiled. Drugs have taken a lot of dignity. Britain really disappeared under Tony Blair and there's a large underbelly of people who don't give two shits about anyone but themselves. I like 'Shrunken Heads' because the chord sequence and the phrasing are good, and it's conversational. I liked the line *'The rich get richer and the poor get sorer'*. We seem to be going back to the Middle Ages with these enclaves that they're building for the super-rich and people paying a million for their daughter's wedding, while some people have nothing. 'Shrunken Heads' is about the electorate and the elected not doing their jobs properly. We really must get better leaders in the West because they're not up to it. They're just not clever enough."

Hunter's adopted homeland was still supplying a writing stimulus and 'Soul of America' was quintessential. The vivid song references John Adams (the second president of the United States), Thomas Paine (the political activist) and Geronimo (the Apache leader) set amongst images of the Alamo, Pearl Harbor, Philadelphia's Liberty Bell and the Manhattan skyline. Ian pulls no punches, describing apathetic politicians eroding the soul of the country and sending civilians to war, while they pursue their own political agendas and gain. There are souls all over the globe in Hunter's tale, except where they ought to be and where we need them in a crazy world.

> **IH:** "'Soul of America' concerned the George Bush regime which thankfully came to an end. You feel bad for the kids who are over there fighting, you hate the people who are sending them over there to do it and then you have to deal with the patriotism and the phoney patriotism, and the

religion and the phoney religion by certain people in political parties. For 'Soul of America' my snooker table was covered in verses trying to capture the bewilderment. In the end, I got so frustrated I said to Andy York, 'You're American; you choose the verses, 'cos I'm sick of the whole thing.' Andy put it together out of about four hundred verses."

The US saga continues with 'How's Your House', a party-chant song about Hurricane Katrina and the devastation following the cyclone that struck New Orleans and Louisiana in 2005. The song title was a phrase used by some of the flood victims and Hunter's lyric carries a serious message amidst depressing scenes where residents have no food or fresh water, families are torn apart and children float down streets inside cars swept away by the deluge. Many victims of the ruination turn in desperation to the US government's Federal Emergency Management Agency – then religious faith.

IH: "'How's Your House' was based on two chords and the lyrics came in ten minutes. When I played it to the band, I thought it wasn't going to work. It was just a poem originally, but The Rant Band convinced me to develop it."

After a run of politically oriented pieces, 'Guiding Light' was a low-paced, melodic love song that offered gentle respite on *Shrunken Heads*. It was also a nice prelude to the riff-driven and infectious 'Stretch' – a tribute song, heralded by a jangling guitar chord that was scruffier, stronger and more arresting than the Beatles' entrée to 'A Hard Day's Night'. Stretch was the nickname for Barry Parkes, who had been referenced in 'Rain', a song about Ian's early days in Northampton. Sadly, Barry passed away in 2003 and Hunter wanted to acknowledge the mixed-up and sometimes dangerous Jekyll and Hyde figure who had led a colourful life. The pictures of *"the pirate with the silver tongue"* were tinged with sadness, Ian regretting the eventual distance between them. The pair had followed radically different paths and Hunter emphasised their separation by adopting the dual meaning of 'stretch' – Ian riding in a limousine, while Barry served time in a jail cell.

> **IH:** "'Guiding Light' was an invented song, but it's a nice song. It could be about Trudi again and probably is. Stretch was a really unique friend that I had in Northampton. I love one-offs, and he was certainly a one-off. He went one way and I went the other. He had a great brain and a great sense of humour, but he had a very dark side too. Something had messed him up, and now and again he had to smack people for some reason, so he wound up not having much of a life. We met again around 2000 and we had a great couple of years. Then he got cancer and died. I miss him."

Like 'Skeletons (In Your Closet)' on *The Artful Dodger* album, Hunter included a humorous song on *Shrunken Heads*, exhibiting more playfulness in the fun-filled, country romp of 'I Am What I Hated When I Was Young'. A self-mocking, banjo-inflected essay in evolution, Ian reflects on ageing but extends a warning that we turn into our parents in the end. Reeling off things that he loathes about modern youth culture, Hunter bemoans his situation as an older man, admitting that he now embodies aspects he used to despise when he was a kid. The lyrical, light-hearted track may have seemed out of place on the record but it was rare, perhaps unique, to hear the word *"nincompoop"* used in an angst-ridden complaint.

> **IH:** "This song also started as another poem. It's clear to me that all kids think that a guy over thirty-five is dead and we all think they're stupid, so the song is just a generalisation and family fun. The young slag off the old – the old slag off the young. That's how it always has been and how it always should be."

Ian sometimes concluded albums with deeply moving renderings, like 'Sea Diver', 'God' and 'The Outsider', and he brought the curtain down on *Shrunken Heads* with a stylish, heart-breaking lament – 'Reed 'em 'n' Weep'. One of Hunter's most poignant ballads, the song relates a truthful tale of affection for a girl named Cathy, from his Shropshire youth. Ian's words echo the pain of 'Irene Wilde' as he tells of more rejection and declares his absolute desolation alongside wandering piano lines. As Dylan once remarked, a great song can walk on its own and here it was, Hunter placing a golden exclamation mark, with a believable wounded vocal, at the end of a superb album.

> **IH:** "'Read 'em 'n' Weep' actually happened and all came from the four-mile walk that I mention in the song. I lived in Shrewsbury and she lived in Meole Brace, a suburb which is four miles outside Shrewsbury. In those early days I couldn't afford the bus fare. It's a long way to walk home after you've been dumped and the song sort of grew from there."

Shrunken Heads was issued by Yep Roc Records in America, Mercury in Norway and Jerkin' Crocus Records in Britain, on 15th May 2007. The UK CD was presented in a card gatefold sleeve, the accompanying booklet containing illustrations for each song drawn by Max Maxwell, lead singer with the re-constituted Sensational Alex Harvey Band. Early album pressings also included a second limited-edition disc featuring three Hunter compositions as bonus tracks – 'Wasted', 'Real or Imaginary' and 'Your Eyes'.

> **IH:** "*Shrunken Heads* was a good album and the record ran right with eleven tracks. I suggested including 'Wasted' but Andy York insisted on 'Read 'em 'n' Weep'. I was also quite keen on 'Real or Imaginary', another war song, but it stayed off too. The bonus tracks on the EP weren't a ploy. The eleven songs on the album just stuck together. With 'Your Eyes' I was thinking that everybody would like to see the world through somebody else's eyes – a different life experience would be interesting. 'Wasted' was me in

underdog mode. I always had this thing about the little bloke against the world. Mott's drummer used to say that I made a career out of being the underdog and there's an element of truth in that. I favoured the underdog because my early life was difficult, I had a lot of rejection and it was difficult trying to make it. That never left me. Your formative years are important. 'Twisted Steel' was also considered for inclusion on *Shrunken Heads* and there was a new version of 'Irene Wilde' that we recorded, Chet Atkins style, but I don't think they were fully completed."

To promote *Shrunken Heads*, Jerkin' Crocus issued 'When the World Was Round' as a single and it reached No.91 on the UK national chart. The CD and vinyl picture discs featured live recordings of 'Twisted Steel', 'Once Bitten Twice Shy' and 'Words' as extra tracks, and an unusual animated promotional video was produced by creative filmmaker Andy Doran; described as "the testicle with fuzz" video, Hunter admired the visual interpretation of his song.

The British press praised *Shrunken Heads*. *Uncut* described the record as: "A heady cruise down Highway 61 – measured and polished where *Rant* is brash and ragged. 10/10." *Classic Rock* wrote: "Warm, witty and wise – it's not just one of Hunter's best albums but the kind of album Dylan fans dream of." According it a four-star rating, *The Daily Mirror* enthused: "Mott the Hoople man Hunter was one of the most timely and timelessly influential voices in Seventies Brit Rock. Long resident in America, his thirty-two-year solo career is studded with gems – and *Shrunken Heads*, where he's aided and abetted by a truly incendiary band, is a bit special. Hunter's songs are both reflective and anthemic."

In America, *Alternative Press* considered Ian fearless and creative, adding: "Really, do you think that in 2007 The Rolling Stones would write a song like 'I Am What I Hated When I Was Young'?" *Rolling Stone*'s David Fricke described Ian as the smartest guy in British glam: "*Shrunken Heads* is one of the best albums Hunter has made since the end of Mott, with its vintage surge and articulate fury. All the glitter in the world couldn't hide those shades of grey." *The New Yorker* opined that Hunter's vocals combined world-weariness, wisdom and honesty in a way that few rock singers could, while *The Village Voice* reflected: "George Bush, FEMA, and the various other shrunken heads that populate these songs should be so contrite. Hunter's at his best when dealing in the absurd, and these days there's plenty to go around."

Nominated as a *Classic Rock* record of the year, the publication's 'Top Fifty Albums of 2007' would soon rank *Shrunken Heads* at No.5. The record remains a wonderful high point in Hunter's repertoire. Laced with bursts of fun, warmth, honesty and masterful music, Ian was also writing at an unusual pace: having furnished three extra songs as a bonus EP, he already had more compositions in the bank.

> **IH:** "On *Shrunken Heads* I just continued writing and was halfway through the next album very quickly. To carry on like that was a huge buzz to me. *Shrunken Heads* sold a lot more albums than the ones immediately prior to it, which made it difficult, because when an album's done a bit of damage, I'm expected to do another one, quickly."

To coincide with the release of *Shrunken Heads*, Ian played three acoustic shows in the UK and the performances were rapturously received, especially a surprise airing of 'Ballad of Mott the Hoople'. In a review of Hunter's London's performance, Scott Rowley described Ian's *Shrunken Heads* material as effortlessly articulate, angry, wise and wonderful, adding: "It makes you wonder what so-called masters like Dylan have been playing at all these years."

Having toured widely in 2007, on 5th November Ian attended the 'Classic Rock Roll of Honour' in London, where Mick Ronson received the first ever 'Tommy Vance Inspiration' award. Hunter and Joe Elliott made touching speeches and presented Mick's posthumous accolade to Suzi and Lisa Ronson, who expressed thanks on behalf of her father with a heartfelt response.

> **IH:** "I was probably a lot closer to Mick Ronson than anybody else. We were both working-class boys and we were both lazy and nature took its course. Mick got bored very easily and I was a slow writer, so it was better that we didn't work sometimes and then come back together. Even when we weren't playing, we were socialising, and we'd have barbecues and he'd come and stay. Mick was a very strict singer and had perfect pitch. He was a frightening guitar player and he was also frightening to look at. I remember when he first joined Mott I thought, 'What am I gonna do?' Working with Ronno, especially early on, was great as we bumped off each other. It was a major blow when we lost Michael. He was a lovely man. I look at my life as before and after Ronson, but I don't think about epitaphs. It's important to have something new to look forward to."

Like Ronson, Hunter's mantra dictated that he always aimed for the next adventure. *Rant* and *Shrunken Heads* had been stellar albums, but there was more to come.

CHAPTER THIRTEEN

The X Factor

Success is doing what you want to do.

In early 2008, Ian was the most prepared he had ever been for a follow-up album, having adopted a breakneck pace for recording and touring. The acoustic–electric contrast that had developed in Hunter's music was refreshing and Ian praised the players around him who coped seamlessly with the transition.

> **IH:** "I'm really fortunate with The Rant Band as they play with me instead of for me, and that's important. They will adjust from rock to acoustic, to live sets with string players. They have no problem and I like doing all styles as it's nice to mix it up. The strings performances were left field and made a change, rather than just a rock thing all the time. There are always people who get pissed off, of course, because I do several ballads, but the change is good."

During February, Hunter advanced the stripped-down theme and performed ten acoustic concerts across the UK with James Mastro and Steve Holley. Ian dubbed them "The Runt Band" and the startling set list included 'Where Do You All Come From', 'The Other Man', 'Scars', 'Rain', 'Following in Your Footsteps' and 'Sons 'n' Lovers', Ian responding to pleas for older rarities and never-performed songs.

> IH: "On the acoustic tour we did stuff that we don't normally do live because we always got people requesting songs live, via my website. I remember after 100 Q&A sessions on *The Horse's Mouth*, I thought we should stop. I felt that the same poor people on there must have been grasping at straws, as the questions had all been asked. For years I'd had pockets of people with no contact from us or from other fans, so the internet and *The Horse's Mouth* were great for them."

'All the Young Dudes' was aired on Hunter's acoustic tour following its inclusion in the acclaimed coming-of-age film *Juno*, and Ian turned to piano for 'Honaloochie Boogie', 'Irene Wilde' and 'Ships' during each performance. Verden Allen sat in on 'Dudes' with Hunter at his final gig in Dartford and a discussion between the pair that night would change the course of Hoople history. Classy acoustic guitarist and singer-songwriter Amy Speace joined Ian's tour as support.

Amy Speace: "I was thrilled to play shows with Ian Hunter and be a fly on the wall. It was a master class. He is a kind man, a curious artist and a rock star of the highest order without any bullshit. He is a working musician and a superstar – a journeyman gentleman with class and edge. Ian is as fine a lyricist as anyone out there. I put him high on my list of favourite songwriters, up there with Townes Van Zandt and Bob Dylan. He writes the poetry of the universal and the specifically personal in the same breath and he does it with the rage of a young man and the wisdom of an elder. I feel blessed to know him and to have learned from him."

In October 2008, Ian returned to A-Pawling Studio to record his twelfth studio album. The record would be titled *Man Overboard* and feature eleven songs co-produced by Hunter and York, all taped, overdubbed and mixed in two weeks. It had been nearly twenty years since Ian released successive new albums so swiftly.

> IH: "The eighteen months between *Shrunken Heads* and *Man Overboard* were great because The Rant Band played so well that I thought we had to get back in the studio and record again. *Man Overboard* was probably the fastest album I'd done since Mott's *Brain Capers*. There was a lot of great playing and it was a good-sounding record that drew you in. When I was doing *Shrunken Heads*, I started picking up a twelve-string guitar and three songs flowed that didn't seem to suit that record, so they carried over. I really had a good time on *Shrunken Heads* and thought if I could write and record another album quickly then the situation will not have changed. My only thought was that George Bush was coming to an end and I knew Barack Obama would get in as president, so there might not be as much to write about."

As Ian worked on *Man Overboard*, rumours started to circulate that Mott may appear to celebrate the band's fortieth anniversary. Finally, in January 2009, an announcement attracted worldwide interest: Mott the Hoople would reform for two shows on 2nd and 3rd October at London's HMV Apollo, the concerts marking the first time the original line-up of Hunter, Ralphs, Allen, Watts and Griffin had played together in thirty-five years. The two dates sold out swiftly and, to Ian's amazement, three more shows were added. Hunter said that he was intrigued to see what the band could do and that, short of war, death and famine, the gigs were on. It was ironic that Verden had been the reunion catalyst at one of Ian's acoustic concerts, as Allen had been the first member to leave Mott the Hoople in 1973.

> IH: "Verden sat in with me on that Dartford gig and suggested a Mott re-formation, saying, 'If we don't do this now, we're never gonna do it.' That was a bit of a shock

to me as I'd never really thought of it like that, but it was true. I said to Verden, 'If it's painless, if everybody wants to do it, if it can go nice and easy without the usual bullshit, I'll do it.' Verden persuaded me, and said that Pete and Buff wanted to do it, and when I rang Ralpher he said it felt right. The question was whether we could cut it. Mick and I had worked continually, but the others hadn't. When I toured with Ralphs in The Rant Band, looking back, that was a big breakthrough. Mick began to realise he could trust me. There was no ill-feeling with Pete, but Buff and I didn't get on for a while. Every time Mott had come up before, somebody hated somebody, but, in 2009, the antagonism seemed to have evaporated. From the off, it was agreed that it had to be the five originals and all the old arguments didn't seem to be around."

Hunter wanted Mott to play at London's Roundhouse or the Hammersmith Odeon, and, when the latter was suggested, another jigsaw piece fitted. But the turnaround was amazing when one considered Dale Griffin's comments in the Nineties: that he "could see no good reason for re-forming Mott the Hoople"; that "it would not truly be fun anymore"; and that "there would be no point to 'All the Old Dudes'". In 1976, Hunter had denied that he was re-joining Mott; in 1981 the band discussed a re-formation; in 1990 Griffin and Watts had suggested to Hunter that Mott might re-form with Ralphs or Ronson; in 1997, during Sony's anthology project, Dale claimed that Mott the Hoople would record 'Like a Rolling Stone'. The rumours had become tiresome, but 2009 would be "The Year of the Dudes" and tickets for the fantasy went on sale nine months before the event.

In March 2009, Ian Hunter signed to New West Records for the release of *Man Overboard*. New West focused on indie rock and alternative country bands and was linked with Danny Goldberg's Ammal Records, whose signings included Steve Earle and Ray Davies. Hunter also sang on two tracks for Amy Speace's third album, *The Killer in Me*, produced by James Mastro, and appeared on 'Whiskey, Pills, Pornography', included on *Rich Pagano and the Sugarcane Cups*.

Mott the Hoople convened during June, and whilst they had not rehearsed any material, Hunter was optimistic about the reunion gigs. It was a case of "old dudes but no feuds", Ian admitting he was intrigued about the upcoming shows. He described Mott as a unique band that once possessed a powerful presence but, considering their advanced years, Hunter cautioned that people shouldn't expect perfection.

> **IH:** "We were always slightly chaotic. If Mott fans can relate to that then we should all be okay. Trepidation is part of the fun and I'm well aware of the pitfalls involved, but I feel like doing it. I thought we'd do a couple of shows and we'd have been happy with that. We didn't anticipate this much of a stir."

On 11th June, Mott the Hoople was presented with a 'Hall of Fame Award' at a *Mojo* Honours List event in London, attended by Hunter, Ralphs, Allen and Griffin. Judy Collins declared her admiration for Ian and Stephen Morris of New Order confessed that he had witnessed Mott the Hoople at the Buxton Festival in 1974. Hunter apologised for his failure to recognise Johnny Marr of The Smiths, explaining that he'd left the UK in 1975 and was unfamiliar with a lot of recent British musicians. Other award-winners included Yoko Ono, Blur, ZZ Top's Billy Gibbons and former Island Records supremo Chris Blackwell, who Hunter teased in the photo suite before the event.

Joe Elliott presented Mott's award and recalled how the journey began back in 1969 when Mick Ralphs kicked down the office door in Island Records; how the band discovered how to produce great records, reaching a zenith with *Mott*; how Mott the Hoople influenced a multitude of artists, including Morrissey, Queen and The Clash; and how they held the wonderful distinction of getting rock 'n' roll banned from The Albert Hall in 1971. "Not bad for a funny little band from Hereford," quipped Joe, as Ian accepted the award on Mott's behalf and responded stylishly from the stage.

> **IH:** "I had a speech prepared but then I saw John Cale, who's amazing – and then I saw Joe Brown, who's fantastic – and I saw Chris Blackwell. We were never Island Records' favourite band, owing largely to the fact we set fire to one of Chris's studios – and I was the person who had to ring Chris and tell him the studio was on fire. I asked Blackwell tonight if he was still as unhappy as ever to see us. Anyway, forty years ago last Tuesday we got together, and we played around for about five years in America and Europe, and then you look back on it and it seems like five minutes. To get a 'Hall of Fame' award for five minutes' work, I think, is a great deal."

After the *Mojo* event, Hunter gave Mott's trophy to Dale Griffin, but people commented on the drummer's appearance and speculated about his health. A TV news item featured Mott's arrival on the red carpet with predictable ageist asides but, in fact, the news was leaking out that Dale was suffering with Alzheimer's disease.

On 21st July 2009, Ian Hunter's *Man Overboard* album was released, featuring eleven self-penned songs: 'The Great Escape', 'Arms and Legs', 'Up and Running', 'Man Overboard', 'Babylon Blues', 'Girl from the Office', 'Flowers', 'These Feelings', 'Win It All', 'Way with Words' and 'River of Tears'. The highly talented supporting cast from *Shrunken Heads* was still involved – Holley, Mastro, Petruzzelli, Burton and York – one change being the engagement of bassist Paul Page, who had worked with Dion and John Cale.

> **IH:** "Graham Maby, Tony Shanahan and Steve Holley all recommended Paul Page, who said he'd waited seventeen years to get the gig; that always helps. Paul is a consummate

team player who locks with Steve like nobody else, and I've played with some great ones. Paul's got great character on stage and is a total upper off stage."

Although some fans anticipated a continuance of political themes from Hunter, *Man Overboard* was a gentler, meditative record that reflected on young romance, long-standing love, myth, mortality and morality. There was more truth at work in each song than any rancid political debate, but *Rant* seemed particularly pertinent in 2009 given an international financial crisis, a faltering British government that Gordon Brown had inherited from Tony Blair and a shocking MPs' expenses scandal. Despite a pledge from Prime Minister Brown that transparency was the only way to restore faith in democracy, many British politicians were condemned over disbursements claims. As the public buckled under recession, job losses and debt, 'Death of a Nation' and 'Rip Off' appeared retrospectively relevant.

> IH: "There was no future with all those chaps being caught with their hands in the till. MPs called it 'making mistakes'. Forgetting your car keys is a mistake. Rip-off! Pity nobody gave *Rant* much thought at the time. *Man Overboard* was lighter, medium-paced and a far more personal album than *Rant* or *Shrunken Heads*, with few explicit political songs. I knew in 2003 that we'd get Barack Obama as US president – he was destined – but Obama replacing Bush curtailed the political aspect of the music. This was unfortunate for me, but fortunate for America. *Man Overboard* wasn't intended to be autobiographical, but when Bush went I had to find something else to write about. I felt like a comedian looking for material.
>
> "People have spoken about that run of albums since I released *Rant* and debated which is best. *Rant* doesn't have to be better than *Shrunken Heads*, and *Man Overboard* doesn't have to be better than *Rant*. They're different

albums – different times – and people should just take them as they are. We were in and out of the studio in a week with *Man Overboard* and the vibrancy in the music came from the speed of recording. It is pretty much stream of consciousness when you get in there, so we just go for it. Andy and I wrote various sequences for the album. I would have liked another fast track, but it wasn't forthcoming and there is a point where you stop because the record says, 'That's it!'"

Man Overboard deftly mixed songs of regret, broken men and youth, Ian's sentimental lyrics and textures displaying heart and humour underneath an occasionally prickly exterior. Light in tone, 'The Great Escape' was a tongue-in-cheek, country-rock jangle that underpinned the album perfectly. Based on another true tale from Hunter's Northampton days, Ian describes ducking a potential bar-room brawl with the best left hook in town.

IH: "I was pleased with 'The Great Escape'. It is based on a true event but with some poetic licence. It was about 'getting away with it', literally – escaping a bunch of guys who want to smack you after a gig. It relates to getting out of a club through a window after the usual teenage bullshit – girlfriends and stuff. I didn't stand a dog's chance. They were seriously heavy, violent people but I made my escape in a friend's Austin Metropolitan. He was a mad chef who gave the pursuing hordes the Vs while we roared off. It was very exhilarating, but I didn't go back and left town *sans* guitar."

'Arms and Legs' was a catchy, heartfelt love song, built on skilful phrasing and melodic chord changes. The track rocked deftly and possessed a killer chorus, Ian's lyrics describing a *"ghostly shadow of a man"*, unsteady on his feet each morning, pondering lost opportunity, all in reflective mode. 'Arms and Legs' was certainly one of Hunter's smartest and more upbeat songs.

'Up and Running' was the first of two tracks that expressed the difference between rich and poor – creditors banging on people's doors while the powers that be make money out of others' misery. 'Man Overboard', originally titled 'Drunk and Disorderly', an acoustic-based anecdote, visualises alcohol rather than seawater overwhelming a dejected individual in a sad situation. The derelict wasn't born into booze but sunk there, as he tried to wash away internalised anger. Painting a downbeat picture of repossessed homes and crime, Ian's final verse marvels at technological advances and solutions for diseases, humorously noting that whilst cameras can now display our *"insides on TV"*, they still haven't found a cure for the song's narrator. Introspective, semi-autobiographical and displaying empathy for the ordinary man, 'Man Overboard' remains one of bassist Paul Page's cherished Hunter tracks.

Paul Page: *"Man Overboard was the first album I played on for Ian and the title song really stood out for me. The 6/8 feel was easy with Steve Holley, while Ian's lyrics and emotion were so real and poignant. Andy York played acoustic guitar along with Steve and me, and I had Ian's vocal way up in my mix, playing to and off his phrasing and lyric. It was one of those magic moments that can happen in the studio and I've always remained so grateful that I had that on my first album with Ian. It was a very special moment and it's still one of my favourite Ian Hunter songs."*

> **IH:** "'Up and Running' was another of my 'it's easy when you're rich' underdog songs, while 'Man Overboard' was a working man's blues – the only problem is he isn't working, so it must be an English blues song, which makes a change. The man overboard could have been me. I was there, but fortunately it didn't pan out that way. The way the world is going, working people are getting squeezed out, and I knew people like that. Before I got in bands, I worked in factories. I had a bit of luck, but a lot of people didn't. 'Man Overboard' was based on a person who is no longer with

us. The guy has ambition but doesn't know what to do with himself, so he winds up a mess."

'Babylon Blues' was Hunter's put-down of a self-destructive figure and an unsympathetic critique of celebrity meltdowns – a fine slice of boogie-style pop and a track handpicked by *Classic Rock* for their monthly Top Twenty songs, as soon as Ian's album was released. 'Girl from the Office', meanwhile, was another archetypal "early years" story of lust and bravado. Delivered with acoustic and bouzouki instrumentation, the track was cleverly sited, marking a natural halfway point on the album. While Ian often claimed reluctance to look back, his narratives like 'Girl from the Office' and 'The Great Escape' were founded on real-life experiences and situations, with a splash of poetic licence.

> IH: "The world's against precious people and 'Babylon Blues' was a song about another blind beggar on the road to fame. 'Girl from the Office' dates from me as a sixteen-year-old engineering apprentice. A girl is walking across the factory floor. The old men are wolf-whistling and the young ones are fancying their chances. It's an everyday English tale. My girl from the office worked at Sentinel in Shrewsbury. She was particularly good-looking and was called Margaret Oliver, and it struck me, as a totally nondescript person, that if I got to go with her then I'd be somebody. You think like that at sixteen, so I got to go with her and my estimation on the factory floor went sky high. Suddenly I was a happening dude. The Sabrina Dancing Academy in the song really did exist. I find it difficult to fabricate and there is an element of truth in many of my songs. I feel so much better if there's something I can see in the memory. You draw on what you know. 'Girl from the Office' is a sweet song and it's different. I had the lyric for a while, then one day we had a song. We did it for fun."

Alarm, Gene Loves Jezebel and Cure guitarist James Stevenson homed in on Hunter's reflective cut as another classic: "Ian is unquestionably one of the greatest songwriters and lyricists of our time. Everyone knows the hits, yet some of his more recent work is among his best. Always heartfelt without a cliché, his tribute to the late great Mick Ronson, 'Michael Picasso', is one of his most moving songs – and who but Ian Hunter would think of rhyming *'office'* with *'stand-offish'* in 'Girl from the Office'? Genius!"

The poetic and poignant 'Flowers' was a plea to humanity against a political backdrop, Hunter pushing sentiment sideways with a touch of exasperation. The plaintive song considered the custom of giving flowers in sympathy, but viewed the impotent act as a hollow, belated offering. Ian also noted the failure to learn from events that ultimately instigate sympathetic gestures, but prodded at America's "War on Terror" with lyrics that consider killing an insult to any religion.

> IH: "I guess people don't know what to do after the various catastrophes that assail us in life. So, people lay flowers, but it doesn't change anything; it's a traditional gesture, and they wither and fade. Somehow, I feel that flowers are not enough. Lessons should be learned. Eighteen- and nineteen-year-old kids go out to Middle East wars and all we seem to be able to do is hand flowers around. We should have outgrown this by now. I always remember that old Vietnam poster, 'Wouldn't it be great if there was a war and nobody turned up.' War is too stupid for words."

Hunter's autobiographical songs seemed more detailed and reflective than ever on *Man Overboard*. 'These Feelings' and 'Way with Words' were two of Ian's most affecting and atmospheric pieces – celebrations of long-term affection and friendship, touched with the simplicity and truth that often underscore his writing. 'Win It All' was a gentle, hymn-like track featuring soft

"Who was I to argue?"
Lemmy and Ian at the Classic Rock Awards,
Café de Paris, London, 5 November 2005

Campbell Devine

"Tickets for the fantasy"
Mick Ralphs and Ian Hunter, Mott the Hoople reunion concert,
Hammersmith Odeon, London, 1 October 2009

Harry Scott/Redferns

"New York City's the best"
Ian Hunter and the Rant Band, City Winery, New York, 8 September 2011:
Mark Bosch, Ian Hunter, James Mastro and Paul Page

Justin Purington

"Do you remember the Saturday Gigs?"
Ian with "new Maltese Cross guitar", second Mott the Hoople reunion,
O2 Arena, London, 18 November 2013

Matt Kent/WireImage

The Hollywood Vampires
Hunter with Joe Perry, Johnny Depp and Alice Cooper,
Ford Amphitheatre, Coney Island Boardwalk, Brooklyn, 10 July 2016
Kevin Mazur/Getty Images

"Have we got Dudes for you"
Ian with Brian May and Joe Elliott closing The Rock and Roll Hall of Fame Induction Ceremony, Barclays
Center, New York, 29 March 2019
Kevin Mazur/Getty Images For The Rock and Roll Hall of Fame

"And you see the green fields as you travel on by"
Hunter on tour, somewhere in the UK, June 2017

Dennis DiBrizzi

"Fingers Crossed"
Hoboken Music Festival, New Jersey, June 2016

Dennis DiBrizzi

"Hereford United's best"
Hunter with 'The Legendary' Stan Tippins,
Birmingham, England, June 2017
Dennis DiBrizzi

"My brother says you're better than the Beatles and the Stones"
Bob and Ian Patterson, Birmingham, England, June 2017
Dennis DiBrizzi

"The A-Team"
Ian Hunter and the Rant Band, Montclair, New Jersey, November 2017:
Rear: Mark Bosch, Steve Holley, Ian, Paul Page and James Mastro
Front: Dennis DiBrizzi

Dennis DiBrizzi

"Loose is nice"
Hunter at Mott the Hoople '74 rehearsals,
Birmingham, England, June 2018
Dennis DiBrizzi

"Showtime!"
Ian Hunter, Ariel Bender and Morgan Fisher,
Bilbao, Spain, June 2018
Dennis DiBrizzi

"Lisa Likes Rock n' Roll"
Ian with Lisa Ronson, Ramblin' Man Fair,
Kent, England, June 2018
Dennis DiBrizzi

"When the world was round"
Ian Hunter Patterson,
Connecticut, USA, 4 March 2020
Trudi Hunter

piano and sensitive accordion, topped off with Hunter's restrained vocal.

> **IH:** "I liked the way the chorus sounded on 'These Feelings' and Andy York gave it a mystical aura. I'm not keen on giving too much away in songs because I think ambiguity is a good thing: let people put their own interpretations on a song; let them think it applies to them. I've written songs that are direct, but I prefer the mistier ones. I have manufactured songs, but I don't get half as much fun out of them. I liked the melody on 'Win It All' and I remember the words came late on in the process; it's really a lullaby. I'll write a song like this now and again, like 'Don't Let Go'. One of the bonuses in this selfish business is people who say a particular song got them through a hard time. Some people listen to music when they are ill, and it makes them feel better. It's a perk that makes you feel slightly more justifiable. I can't even remember how 'Way with Words' developed. I was thinking that some people are clever with words and others aren't. Some are quick off the draw in any given conversation. Lyrics give you time to think, so you get it the way you want rather than talking off the top of your head. I'm a slow thinker."

Man Overboard's final track, 'River of Tears', was a folk-rock tune that told a tale of American legend, in this case the native Agoura people of California, clashing with the settlers who overwhelmed them.

> **IH:** "I was in Los Angeles in 2007, as we were playing at the Canyon Club in the Agoura Hills. The hotel I stayed in had a plaque on the wall about the Agoura Indians and one particular tribe. I thought it was a great little story so I converted it into a song. 'River of Tears' was literally taken from a wall as I was waiting for a lift in the hotel. The plaque was rather small and I wouldn't have read it at all, but the elevator took some time to arrive."

Rich and resonant, *Man Overboard* revealed more and more beauty with every listen. Hunter was still a rebel who rocked, who could taunt with a smile and a grin but also a writer who was not shy of sentimentality. *Man Overboard* was a strong, smart album that chronicled human triumphs and troubles. Presented in a gatefold card sleeve with lyric booklet, the CD's colourful front image pictured Ian beside Veterans Memorial Bridge, a Fifties iron structure that carries Route 202 over the Housatonic River near his Connecticut home. The photograph on the rear of the sleeve was taken quickly on a parking lot at a nearby shopping plaza, before Hunter and the crew were moved on by the local police.

The press continued to praise Ian's work, even if radio and television seldom gave people the opportunity to notice. *Record Collector* featured *Man Overboard* as 'New Album of the Month', awarding five stars, while *Uncut* considered that Ian was on the hottest songwriting streak of his career. *The Sunday Times* wrote: "On *Man Overboard*, the singer who fronted a band more acclaimed than bought, and who continues to be name-checked by contemporary acts, still refuses to succumb to bitterness, instead turning in an eleven-song set that is astonishingly vital from a septuagenarian, and puts to shame many toilers half his age. With that sandpapered voice, Hunter is as sharp and cussed as ever." *Mojo* described Hunter's songwriting as natural and as efficacious as breathing, adding: "Though the singer's October reunion gigs with Mott will likely lord it over his solo career, it would be a shame if dudes young or old missed out on this testament to Hunter's on-going vim."

Classic Rock's chief editor, Scott Rowley, accorded *Man Overboard* 8/10 and described the record wonderfully, noting a timely peak in form: "Do you remember The Album? Not what passes for albums these days – a couple of good songs and a whole load of filler – but a collection of tracks bound together by theme, pace, sound and consistency – a set of songs that work individually but take the listener on a longer, more satisfying journey? Ian Hunter does. Hunter has always been an album artist. *Shrunken*

Heads wasn't just a return to form, it was one of his greatest albums – and *Man Overboard* is its companion piece."

With weathered vocal rasps, slower musical tempos and fresh acoustic arrangements, *Man Overboard* expanded Ian's status as a writer and a man with a profound performance style. *USA Today* placed 'Girl from the Office' on its Top Ten playlist and the glowing reviews continued with *Crawdaddy*, who remarked that *Man Overboard* was the subtlest and perhaps best album that Ian had ever made. *The Chicago Tribune* said of Hunter: "His muse is as vital as ever. Artists like Jeff Tweedy, Alejandro Escovedo and Joe Strummer have covered Hunter's songs and David Bowie worshipped him. *Man Overboard* explains why."

There was a growing realisation that Hunter's recorded work was now richer and more diverse than ever, in marked contrast, at the time, to the output of two of his inspirations. In 2009, The Rolling Stones continued a reissue programme of their 1971 to 2005 albums, but, without any bonus material and with limited new recording, it seemed the Jagger–Richards well might be running dry. In the same period, it was announced that Bob Dylan would release an album of Christmas songs including 'Here Comes Santa Claus'. Ian Hunter was outdriving his heroes with new material, the impressive philosophical songs on *Man Overboard* proving that he possessed a more creative engine. At the end of the year, *Record Collector* placed *Man Overboard* in its ten '2009 Picks', describing the album as Hunter's solid gold personal triumph of autobiographical outings, shot with a simple honesty.

With Mott the Hoople rehearsals planned for September and five Hammersmith gigs booked for early October, there was little scope for Ian to support his new record. Even promotional radio appearances for *Man Overboard* were peppered with questions about Mott the Hoople. The Mott timing was not good for his solo album, but Ian realised that, with Verden Allen's forty-year milestone, it really was "now or never". On 23rd July, Hunter launched *Man Overboard* with a performance at New York's City Winery, delivering a set that included seven songs from the new CD plus 'Roll Away the Stone', 'Central Park n' West' and 'Dead Man Walkin''. In tandem with his live appearance, *New Yorker* raved about *Man Overboard* as its 'Pop Notes Record of the Week': "Ian Hunter, who recently turned seventy, is on a protracted winning streak that belies his age and finds him making full use of his experience. Hunter and his Mott bandmates are reuniting for a set of shows in October at the Hammersmith Apollo in London. Most likely, they won't play any of his solo material; their loss."

When Mott the Hoople had decided to re-form, Ian knew that, aside from the egos, the other mountain to climb was ensuring that the ensemble re-discovered the band's ethos and rock 'n' roll edge. Some of the Mott members had not set eyes on each other for thirty years and so Hunter was curious, remarking that the shows could not be "a Butlin's job". Staggered that Mott the Hoople was the quickest-selling show in London for three days, Ian found the concept of five gigs almost inconceivable.

> **IH:** "Mott the Hoople was never a perfect band. They could be bad, they could be brilliant, so we were looking for that odd X factor at Hammersmith, rather than perfection. I wasn't thinking about new Mott material because I'd always thought that no way in hell would we ever get together again. The song selection for the gigs was pretty easy as we all decided on a similar set list and it was just a question of what order to put them it. All I was worried about was whether we'd have that invisible thing which you could never quite put your finger on. Going into the 2009 gigs I really was intrigued about the X factor – then I suddenly realised that the X factor in Mott the Hoople was Pete Watts."

The four British-based Motts met towards the end of July to discuss preparatory work for the gigs and in August they started rehearsals at Usk in Monmouthshire, South Wales. Ian joined them at Rockfield Studios near Monmouth in mid-September, Ralphs bringing in one of Paul McCartney's team, in lieu of Stan Tippins, to sort out the inevitable Hoople politics.

> **IH:** "Mott the Hoople in 2009 was still fucking insane and fucking illogical. After touring with Bad Company, Ralphs rehearsed them. Before I arrived in the UK, I asked him what it sounded like. Mick said, 'It sounds like a pub band,' and at that point we had only ten days until the first show. We went down to Rockfield and that's where it came together, rehearsing in a very small room where I don't think I stood up once. Somehow, it all came back. I guess you never forget how to ride a bike."

Mott the Hoople was scheduled to play two "warm-up gigs" in Monmouth before their Hammersmith run, but, on 18th September, Dale Griffin's manager announced that Buffin's recent health had not been good and the drummer would be unable to participate fully in the concerts. "Herefordshire lad" Martin Chambers was engaged as drum deputy and Ian noted that Martin grew up watching Buff and knew his style backwards, so, "short of the real chap", Chambers was the best. Mick Ralphs enjoyed the reunion build-up and rejoiced over *Brain Capers*, still reflecting that commercial success had stripped the original band of something precious: "After forty years, Mott 2009 was amazing. The great thing about the original Mott the Hoople was the struggle. It was a bit like looking for the pot of gold; we never actually found it and that kept us going. When we had the hit, it became manufactured for me. We'd found something that worked, whereas before, we were trying everything. Early on, it was more 'don't-give-a-shit' experimental. *Brain Capers* really captured our essence."

Hunter valued the loyal audience that Mott had in the Seventies and was confident their admirers would feel the same forty years on. Fans *really* wanted to see Mott the Hoople one more time and Ian knew that the band never played *to* them, as the live experiences were communal experiences and people felt part of Mott. Hunter talked about the special chemistry in advance of the shows.

> **IH:** "If we're playing shit at Hammersmith, they won't criticise us – they'll feel like they've played shit, which is a good position to be in. Mott came and went in five minutes, forty years ago. That band could have been the biggest band that ever was, but it was all ass-backwards. At Hammersmith, we'll just do what we do. We didn't know what the fuck we were doing the first time around, but I'm sure we can manage."

Mott the Hoople appeared at the Blake Theatre in Monmouth on 25th and 26th September, Hunter likening the power of Mott to The Who or The Stooges. Following further rehearsal in London three days later, and after three decades of aborted reunions and rumours, Mott the Hoople was finally back at the legendary Hammersmith Odeon on 1st October 2009. Following the traditional 'Jupiter' introduction and the wiping of eyes by many audience members, to ensure that they were truly witnessing the moment, Mott launched into a subtle salvo of 'Hymn for the Dudes', then went for the throat with 'Rock and Roll Queen'. Martin Chambers was energised and explosive on drums, Watts wielded a home-painted pink Gibson Thunderbird and patrolled and posed for the gallery, while Allen proved once more that the swirling sound of the Hammond C3 was something special. But Ian Hunter remained the star, singing and playing with relish and brandishing a new customised Maltese Cross guitar for 'Angeline' and 'Walkin' with a Mountain'. The set contained acoustic versions of 'Original Mixed-Up Kid' and 'I Wish I Was Your Mother' and emotional renditions of 'The Moon Upstairs' and 'The Journey' prefaced by a snatch of 'Like a Rolling Stone'. The only songs played from the post-Ralphs period were 'Born Late '58', 'The Golden Age of Rock 'n' Roll' and 'Saturday Gigs'.

For five nights Mott the Hoople delivered two hours of down-to-earth charisma and, with a combined band age of over 320 years, tore up the tenet that rock is the stomping ground of youth. Hunter was happy, telling audiences it was lovely to be back, but that it was small and scruffy backstage and yet another establishment where he'd recommend the management "did a bit of hoovering". Crowds remained on their feet throughout each performance and Ian claimed it was the first time that Mott had received a standing ovation for an entire show. Hunter and Ralphs shook hands with fans in the front row while Watts remained eccentric, sporting an assortment of coloured shirts and neck ropes, and a pair of white moccasins with a large red hand-written 'O' and 'W' on each foot, and smaller scrawls alongside spelling out the words 'Old Wanker'. Pete once remarked that he used to watch support bands and think, "They're wearing the clothes Mott wore two years ago. They'll never make it." Now, in 2009, gone were the suits and the platform boots, but otherwise it was business as usual.

Two large video screens displayed images of the band and the iconic *Hoople* album cover served as a backdrop. With Hunter breaking into Dylan, Jerry Lee and Hank Williams fragments on piano towards the finale, and with Joe Elliott "leaping on" again for 'All the Young Dudes', the backing choir grew as the nights went on and included Jesse Patterson, Tracie Hunter, Jim Ralphs, Lisa Ronson and, of course, Stanley Tippins. Attendees at Mott's five shows included Morgan Fisher, Blue Weaver, Mick Bolton, John Fiddler, Ray Major, John Taylor, Jimmy Page, Mick Jones, Paul Simonon, David Gilmour, Bobby Gillespie, Brian May, Roger Taylor, Darrell Bath, Glen Matlock, Steve New, Noel Gallagher, Leee Black Childers, Clive Davis, Steve Popovich, Paul Hyde, Bob Rock, Mick Box, Suggs and Jay Jay French. Rock re-formations had sometimes shown that seductive liaisons with nostalgia can flatten the legend, but Mott blew fans, fellow stars and the media away. Victorious, happy and glorious, Guy Stevens would have been proud.

IH: "The first Hammersmith show on Thursday was very emotional and there was a hell of a crowd each night. The

band were still eccentric, Pete threatening to don hiking gear for the stage before sanity prevailed. Gentlemen of a certain age need to display a modicum of dignity, so we did. Watts played bass with an umbrella on one song, but Pete had a lot to do with the erratic nature of the band. Mott was always a totally diplomatic unit and Buffin was still involved, so that made it more complicated. That's what ruined the band the first time round and we were still doing it thirty-five years later. Mott 2009 was fun for a week, but I was very glad I wasn't joining again."

Support act for the final evening at Hammersmith was Down 'n' Outz – the band was a "one-off project" conceived by Joe Elliott and members of The Quireboys but their performance and the audience reaction would lead to a series of albums. "We obviously couldn't play Mott the Hoople songs at Hammersmith so we dug out some Ian Hunter, Mott and British Lions classics," recalls Joe. "After our set we went to the foyer bar and were nailed to the wall by tearful and enthusiastic fans. Somebody said, 'You have to go and record those songs' – so, we did."

Morgan Fisher, Mick Bolton and Blue Weaver held a "The Three Keys" event in Hammersmith around the gigs, including a screening of Morgan's forty-minute movie *Mott in America* with added Fisher soundtrack. Compiled from 8mm film shot during 1973 and 1974 in streets, hotels and airports, with humorous sequences and glimpses of Mott, Queen, Stan Tippins, Richie Anderson and Leee Black Childers, *Mott in America* was raw and ragged, Morgan admitting that much had been captured in semi-intoxicated and chaotic circumstances.

Mojo described Mott's 2009 Hammersmith shows as the most rapturously received reunion gigs in recent memory: "Grown men wept in the aisles of the Apollo as the grizzled team of originals and auxiliary drummer Martin Chambers delivered the signature Mott cocktail of wide-eyed rocking, phlegmatic cool and sartorial eccentricity. The boogaloo dudes carried the news."

IH: "Looking back, the *Rant* album and my 2003 and 2008 tours made it possible for Mott the Hoople to re-form in 2009. Mick Ralphs joining me on the road was a big thing because the original arguments about why we'd split, with me writing 'the hits', was cleared up. Mick knew fine well he'd written hits back in 1973, but they weren't working with my vocals so he went off with Paul Rodgers. In retrospect Ralphs and I realised what had happened and, when we toured in 2003, we got on great. That was the Mott the Hoople 2009 reunion breakthrough right there! Then, in 2008, Phally sat in with me and that was interesting too, because he had been the first to leave Mott the Hoople. He'd really hated me in the past but he turned up at my Dartford gig and after decades of fucking arguing, suddenly it clicked. Then the offer came in, which was substantial and it made even more sense."

Mott's 1st October performance was issued as a three CD set by Concert Live, and, to coincide with the Hammersmith shows, Sony released *The Very Best of Mott the Hoople*. *Uncut* wrote of the twenty-track collection: "Prior to the intervention of David Bowie with 'All the Young Dudes', Mott the Hoople were kick-ass rockers with mud on their boots and fire in the engine room. Pre-'Dudes' ballad 'Waterlow' shows Ian Hunter was already a writer of rare tenderness and in barely eighteen months they delivered gloriously self-referential, comedic, strangely moving and far-seeing rock 'n' roll soap operas. Every generation deserves the opportunity to discover them anew."

Mott the Hoople was recognised by *Classic Rock* with their 2009 'Comeback of the Year' award and *Man Overboard* was placed at No.20 in *Classic Rock*'s 'Fifty Best Albums of 2009' chart. Then, as Hoople excitement subsided, from April to June 2010, Ian and The Rant Band played in Britain, Europe and America. The shows finally afforded Hunter the opportunity to present music from *Man Overboard* as he featured on the UK TV show *Later... with Jools Holland,* performing 'Flowers' and 'Once Bitten Twice Shy'.

> IH: "I couldn't take my band on the road with the Mott gigs and *Man Overboard* did get a bit lost in the whole reunion. The album was overlooked but it could have been better promoted. It was kind of weird. I never met anyone from the label, either in the US or in the UK. I did my bit. I was kind of hoping they would do their bit."

In the summer of 2010, Mott the Hoople was lined up to play at the High Voltage Festival in London. Ian and the band were to be special guests supporting headliners Emerson Lake and Palmer on Sunday 25th July, until Watts declined.

> IH: "All I got out of the Mott reunion was being pissed off, as they probably were too. Pete was like an old horse trader who always wanted more than we could ever get, so Mott didn't play at Victoria. I don't think the band understood the business."

Instead of Mott the Hoople, Joe Elliott's Down 'n' Outz played at Victoria Park with Hunter appearing as their "special guest". Attendees included Jimmy Page, John Fiddler, Andy York and Maggi Ronson, and after a lengthy Down 'n' Outz set that commenced with a mammoth version of Elton John's 'Funeral for a Friend/Love Lies Bleeding', Ian was due to deliver seven songs. In the end, promoters pulled the power after two of Hunter's numbers to prepare the stage for ELP. At the cut-off point, Joe and Ian flew into an altercation with the stagehands and the battle continued backstage. The "Victoria violence" recalled the dramatic days of Mott the Hoople and national newspaper *The Sun* carried the headline 'Rock legends in gig brawl' and wrote: "AGEING rockers started a mass brawl when they were told to stop playing early. Def Leppard singer Joe Elliott, 50, and rock legend Ian Hunter, 71, charged roadies, wielding their guitars 'like axes' after power to their amps was cut off. The pair then kicked off a thirty-man punch-up. A roadie said: 'It was all in the spirit of rock 'n' roll.'"

> **IH:** "That was a mad afternoon. To add to the mix that article about the fight was on page 3 of *The Sun*, the UK's controversial daily tabloid which carried shots of topless models for years. We were next to the voluptuous Roxanne. Fame at last, accompanied by acute embarrassment."

Down 'n' Outz guitarist Guy Griffin and drummer Phil Martini had been proud of their involvement in Mott's final Hammersmith concert, but the duo said it was trumped by the enviable experience of rehearsing "classic Hunter classics" for their High Voltage appearance. "I remember being struck by Ian's rock 'n' roll piano hands," says Phil. "You could feel the effortless rhythm flowing from him and his vocals are rousing. Those who have seen Ian Hunter perform, with or without Mott, would agree that he's peerless."

In October, Hunter and The Rant Band played ten UK gigs, introducing four string players at three of the concerts to provide the live set with a different perspective. During his Birmingham Town Hall show, Ian was interrupted by chants of "C'mon Shrewsbury".

> **IH:** "I think my fortunes have been tied, with alarming consistency, to Shrewsbury Town FC, who have occupied the lower leagues of English football for some years. Those British gigs were good. I'd been in a London train station one day and I saw these guys in a quartet named Oopsie Mamushka and they sounded great. I figured I'd get an arrangement from the orchestra that I had worked with in Oslo and trim it down for a four-piece and take them on tour. So, we did. Initially they were wary and wanted half the money up front, but they discovered we were human."

On the first anniversary of Mott the Hoople's reunion, Ian admitted that he had been irked by the mammoth politics of the band's comeback and was still frustrated as Mott's personnel remained hilarious but utterly unmanageable. Hunter praised Martin

Chambers' magnificent playing as Dale's replacement, and the drummer retained admiration for Ian.

> **IH:** "In 2009, Mott was a lot more powerful than I imagined it was going to be. You tend to have rose-coloured spectacles, so you remember the better bits, but it lived up to expectations and that's why the reviews were so good. Walking out on stage was an amazing feeling and quite tear-provoking. It was very emotional when the five of us were together again, but it's not easy business-wise. There were three managers involved with Mott in 2009 and two managers killed off Mott the Hoople and Hunter Ronson in the Seventies. There was also a load of bitching, as before, if not worse. It was a blur but my favourite moments were walking on and walking off. What happened at Hammersmith was great but it took a year of bullshit. My solo situation is so much easier; I've got a band I don't argue with, we go out, we work and everything is great."

Martin Chambers: "I've been lucky enough to have known Ian Hunter for over forty years. Apart from advice he gave me after a gig at the Marquee Club in 1970, his writing has always grabbed my attention, as does his stage persona. There is undoubtedly a quality that chronicles the time we live in, not unlike that of Ray Davies and Bob Dylan. From my perspective as a drummer, Ian is a classic leader of the pack, in as much as, on stage, he is easy to read because he inhabits each song and conducts with every movement and expression. The 'feel' of his music is such an easy pleasure to roll out. In this situation the joy of the moment is equal to the amount of sweat produced. After all, that is rock 'n' roll… and so is Ian!"

Driven by Mott the Hoople's reunion, Start Productions embarked on a documentary production, *The Ballad of Mott the Hoople*. On 16th October 2010, the movie was premiered at the London Film Festival, an event attended by Ian Hunter,

Mick Ralphs, Verden Allen, Luther Grosvenor, Blue Weaver, Stan Tippins, Richie Anderson, Phil John, Jimmy Page, Andy Dunkley, Diane Stevens and Jeff Dexter. Issued on DVD a year later, extra footage included songs from the band's Hammersmith reunion and various interviews, while the accompanying booklet featured a note penned by Morrissey, who wrote: "Savage history always passes judgement in due course and here we are, in 2011, still studying Mott the Hoople."

In a 10/10 *Classic Rock* DVD review, David Quantick described Mott the Hoople as one of the greatest groups that we could ever hope for: "Everyone has their own definition of a 'rock band'. The simplest is three words: Mott the Hoople. If by some chance you've not been exposed to the brilliance of this band, there is a simple way out of your predicament. Three words again: Buy this DVD."

An American review by *The Nervous Breakdown* noted: "If you're interested in tales of dope, riots and groupies there is an impressive number of documentaries featuring Led Zeppelin, The Sex Pistols, The Rolling Stones and The Who. Yet eclipsed by the mega-stardom and misdeeds of those bands, England's Mott the Hoople quietly lived out a rich and compelling story. *The Ballad of Mott the Hoople* adheres to rock doc conventions; there is the break-up, the bitterness and the requisite reunion show."

The Ballad of Mott the Hoople drew together as much rare archive footage as possible but the documentary was not without omissions, with no reference to 'Honaloochie Boogie', 'Marionette' or 'Crash Street Kidds'. Interviewees included Hunter, Ralphs, Allen, Grosvenor, Griffin, Mick Jones and Roger Taylor. Dale commented in the documentary that he only ever wanted to be in one group – the strange, weird and wonderful Mott the Hoople – a band that came out of nowhere, except Guy Stevens' head. Former Sea Divers secretary Kris Needs rightly remarked: "Mott's story took place all in the space of five years. That's how long the Kaiser Chiefs have been around, but I don't believe we'll be talking about the Kaiser Chiefs in thirty years' time."

The Ballad of Mott the Hoople was described as a story of fun, fame, disagreements and, in the end, disillusionment, but the backwards glance allowed Ian to encapsulate the myths of the music industry once more. "The fun is the ride," said Hunter. "There ain't no station!"

CHAPTER FOURTEEN

Presidential Victory

The hardest part is getting the ideas.

As Ian Hunter prepared for another new studio album in 2011, concert appearances continued. His live set was revived with renditions of 'All-American Alien Boy', 'Sweet Jane' and 'Alice', played for the first time since Mott promoted *The Hoople* album in 1974, while Ian incorporated two "new" songs – 'Stand by Me' and 'Isolation' – from the Lennon albums *Rock 'n' Roll* and *John Lennon/Plastic Ono Band*.

> **IH:** "I was asked to participate in a John Lennon show in New York, so I learned a couple of Lennon tunes – well one Lennon and a Ben E. King song, which John recorded. Andy York suggested 'Isolation', because he knows my voice. When the Lennon tribute concert got shelved, I decided to play them anyway, just to make a change."

The inclusion of 'All-American Alien Boy' in Hunter's live set was a genuine highlight, as Paul Page faithfully nurtured the legendary bass interlude, originated by Jaco Pastorius, but applied his own interpretation and individuality. "It really has been an honour and a dream come true to be in The Rant Band," says Paul. "When I grew up in New York in the Seventies, Ian was my favourite singer-songwriter and Mott was THE coolest band. The Rant Band is a vehicle for Ian's music and legacy, but I've never been involved in as much of a real 'band' dynamic. I came on board in 2007 to tour *Shrunken Heads* and worked on *Man Overboard*. Ian and Andy York let me flesh out my own parts in my comfort zone, but, when they ask for something specific, I bend over backwards trying to please them. Well, they're both really good fuckin' bass players too, so you can't just shine them on."

In January 2012, Hunter re-entered A-Pawling Studios to record *When I'm President*. The album would be credited to "Ian Hunter and The Rant Band" and the group was more settled than ever. Ian stressed that his touring in 2011 had helped inflect his new songs, not Mott's reunion, as some commentators imagined.

> **IH:** "There was never going to be an album coming out of the Mott the Hoople reunion. It was simply a question of could we do it live – and we could – and we did. In terms of the next Ian Hunter record, The Rant Band toured the East Coast of America and the music got tight and my writing flowed. It sounded so good I thought we had to get it down and capture the sparkle and freshness. So, we had a nice Christmas and went into the studio and recorded *When I'm President*. We got the power and the passion, and it didn't turn into turgidity. The quicker it is the better, because all you're doing is killing the songs otherwise. We get in this space where I know the engineer and the studio is good, and four days later you've got yourself a record. Me and Andy York went back and mixed it in another nine days and most of the vocals were completed in four days too. *President* took about a year of writing and getting the songs together, but the recording took around twelve days, so it was pretty

painless. It was strange, because after all those years of being a sort of singer-songwriter, *When I'm President* was very much a group affair. The Rant Band was a pool of guys at first and then became a real group. There have been nine or ten 'Ranters' over ten years, so it was time for a band album."

With his record completed, on 13th March, Ian joined Jackson Browne, Art Garfunkel and other artists at New York's Carnegie Hall to perform in "The Rolling Stones' Hot Rocks Tribute", Hunter and The Rant Band playing '19th Nervous Breakdown'. During June, UK label 7T's issued a two CD set, *Ian Hunter: The Singles Collection 1975–83*, and The Rant Band flew into England for a 1st July performance at the Hop Farm Festival in Kent, Hunter appearing alongside Ray Davies, Peter Gabriel and Bob Dylan. *The Independent*'s review of the festival homed in on Ian's sand-blasted voice delivering a rejuvenating 'All the Young Dudes', with Mick Ralphs spirited in to solo, while Dylan's faltering set reportedly did little to win a generation of new fans.

> **IH:** "Bob Dylan played the Hop Farm Festival on the Saturday and we did the Sunday, so we didn't meet. Dylan's live shows can vary, but you're looking at a genius so he can do what he wants. For me, The Rant Band are great; they're loud, they keep me young and they're loyal. Before touring we rehearse for two or three days. It's all about homework and they are great at doing their homework, so rehearsals are just for tidying up and maybe some sequencing. The less rehearsal the better because you want it as fresh as possible."

In September, Ian helped launch "Cleveland Rocks: Past, Present and Future", playing a concert to support a venture aimed at assisting veterans of the Cleveland music scene and the Popovich Legacy Project. Then, as Ian's brand-new album surfaced, *Uncut* reflected on Hunter's previous decade, re-rating his recent studio trilogy highly: *Rant* (9/10), *Shrunken Heads* (10/10) and *Man Overboard* (9/10).

When *I'm President* was released on 4th September 2012, eight weeks before the US election, but it was not a protest record. Ian no longer exhibited the levels of angst witnessed on *Rant* and *Shrunken Heads*, and he was not as personally reflective as he had seemed on *Man Overboard*. Produced by Hunter and York, as "The Prongs" – Ian's new pseudonym for the new "twins" – there was a bounce, abandon and kick to *When I'm President*, but Hunter expanded his insightful interest in US culture with historical vignettes about Native American leader Crazy Horse, the outlaw Jesse James and the Civil War. Political topics had vaporised and were less inspirational now; for a decade many things had seemed unjust and that was an important instigator for new material, but while Bush and Blair were history, *When I'm President* still served up prickly, energetic music and an eclectic range of themes and songs.

> **IH:** "Politics was always good fun for writing, but on the *President* album the songs seemed to be more upbeat. The Bush years had passed so I wasn't 'ranting' as much. Songs came to me in the summer of 2011 and that grew into *When I'm President*. I'd get up every day with something ringing in my head. Songwriting is like a cat with a mouse; you're always playing with words, like a mathematician plays with numbers. A lot of it is thinking, not playing. The hardest part is getting the ideas, but once you know what the idea is you have the kernel to expand upon."

When *I'm President* featured eleven incredible tracks: 'Comfortable (Flyin' Scotsman)', 'Fatally Flawed', 'When I'm President', 'What For', 'Black Tears', 'Saint', 'Just the Way You Look Tonight', 'Wild Bunch', 'Ta Shunka Witco (Crazy Horse)', 'I Don't Know What You Want' and 'Life'. The CD was issued by Slimstyle Records in

America, Universal in Scandinavia and the Proper label in Britain, Ian describing the musicians as a group and summarising the album as "a rock 'n' roll record".

'Comfortable (Flyin' Scotsman)' was an unbridled, good-humoured presidential preamble, providing a Hoople-flavoured flashback. Most Hunter albums featured an appreciative nod to early rock 'n' roll and 'Comfortable' was stamped with strident Jerry Lee Lewis piano and Little Richard and The Upsetters saxophone.

> **IH:** "'Comfortable' is not in strict time and that was the fun with the song. I liked the line, *slip into something more comfortable*. Once I had the word 'imagination', that made all the verses easy. It's just a bluesy fun song."

After a buoyant opening cut, Hunter played his first lyrical ace with 'Fatally Flawed'. Musically the track was restrained, then explosive, driven by distorted and soulful guitar, while acidic lyrics related observations of addictive personalities and two deceased music stars. The inspiration was partly the decline of Whitney Houston and more openly Amy Winehouse, 'Fatally Flawed' referencing an incident that Ian had witnessed when he appeared alongside Amy in 2004, on Jools Holland's BBC TV show.

> **IH:** "The scales of life. Lyrically I was reflecting that some people have addictive personalities. They can't help it, but it can do them in. Some people need support systems while others seem to get along fine without them. Amy seemed particularly needy, like Marilyn Monroe, and it's difficult to deal with 24/7. I was playing something in Open-G one day and went to the C, fifth fret up, and that's how 'Fatally Flawed' started. The song is really all about dynamics as there are only two chords and it's like an old blues thing where you go from '0' in the verses to '10' in the hook, which always records well."

419

Via the album's tongue-in-cheek title track, Ian reiterated that the political left and right continue to fail and that new figureheads ultimately adopt a *"business-as-usual"* approach in spite of the passing years. Presidents may enter the White House with declared intent, but something happens to them *"up on the hill"* and real change is a rarity. With an over-the-shoulder glance to 'All-American Alien Boy', Hunter still sang of being an alien, but recited the names of former US presidents in lieu of Native Americans. The opinions in 'When I'm President' are expressed by the persona of a jaded know-it-all, bloke in the bar, criticising government and the money men and corporations who run America. As a Brit, Hunter could never be president, but his character can yearn for a 28th Amendment to the United States Constitution. He can envisage hitting the "haves" on behalf of the "have-nots". He can even dream of his face carved into South Dakota's sculpted rocky memorial alongside Washington, Jefferson, Roosevelt and Lincoln. The lyrical stretch offered by Ian was wonderful.

> **IH:** "'When I'm President' started off as a song called 'But I Will If I Have To' and I couldn't think of anything lyrically to go with that. I was in danger of running the melody into the ground then suddenly it became 'When I'm Superman', so that was good – and then it was electoral year, and it became 'When I'm President' – so it was a first-time round melody, third-time round lyric. I just took a chance. The song is about the misinformation that surrounds presidential politics and a guy in a bar, expounding what he's going to do if he's elected. In the final analysis, it's 'when pigs fly' – it's never going to happen! The president is never going to do anything positive, and the guy in the bar is never going to be president."

Ian had devised alternative working titles for *When I'm President* but often favoured using one of his songs as a focal point, from as far back as *All-American Alien Boy* and *Overnight Angels*.

IH: "Usually the title of an album will be one of my songs on the record, hence *Man Overboard* and *Shrunken Heads*. Sometimes titles emerge during recording and I opted for *When I'm President* for that reason. I thought of calling the album *Recreational Skull Diving* and I liked that, but it was too long. *Ancient Babies* was another one that got passed over and voted out."

The confrontational 'What For' was a rollicking Stones-style rocker, damning of modern society's trash television, magazines, mobile phones and unimaginative youth. Hunter's call and response chorus with The Rant Band was clever and catchy, and the track even concluded with a Jerry Lee Lewis 'Great Balls of Fire' refrain.

IH: "I find today's youth believing they are incredibly entitled. They've got all this stuff and they're as miserable as sin. They egg on their parents who try talking to them and all they get back is 'What for?' And we're paying for it. It's not actually my kids I'm talking about, but with some of these precocious, entitled little twats, it's time somebody gets back at them."

Hunter served up more spirit on 'Black Tears', another stunning song that was first sparked when Ian observed Chrissie Hynde at a Pretenders gig. Big and bluesy, heavy and melodic, Hunter's pen was pointed and his vocal stronger than ever. The track has stormy piano and wonderful chord changes and is movingly enhanced by Mark Bosch's brilliant, heart-wrenching solo. The tormented chorus is alluring, Ian describing blue eyes turning green – sad – red – then black, in an image-laden lyric that paints a pronounced picture.

IH: "I saw Chrissie Hynde at a gig once after Martin Chambers invited me to a Pretenders show. I immediately noticed that Chrissie was wearing very heavy eye make-up and soon it all

421

started to run under the stage lights. I thought 'black tears' was a good phrase. The guitar solo by M.C. is very special. I didn't know he was going to do it, but Boschy was quite insistent and really wanted to try it. Two takes later and we were all astounded. It's an unbelievable solo."

The Civil War and the Wild West influenced three songs on *When I'm President*. 'Saint', co-written by Hunter and Mastro, was the tale of an American Civil War hero who wanted to throw in his lot with Frank and Jesse James, but a one-legged casualty couldn't do that. The American theme continued with 'Wild Bunch'; revisiting the cowboy gangs of the Texas–Mexican border, Hunter took some inspiration from the classic Sixties film and the team of outlaws who had looked for one last score; the movie theme was fun, the track ending with a singalong chorus and group applause.

IH: "I read a lot and I love books that focus on certain historical eras, whether it's the Thirties, the Forties or the Fifties – anything just prior to the modern age. I'm fascinated by American events that transpired between 1840 and 1915. In England the history is thousands of years old, but in America you can almost reach out and touch it. Wyatt Earp, who took part in the gunfight at the OK Corral, died in 1929. I was born in 1939 so it feels close and it fires my imagination. For 'Saint' I had a vision of the Battle of Pig Point and a Union Man. I pictured a young guy with one leg and a tin, reflecting and begging on a street corner just after the American Civil War. That war was disgusting, a bloodbath. People go out and fight and come home maimed, and then they give them medals and parades, and fuck all else. Appalling. I liked the line *'it ain't the same without the music'*. There's no music on battlefields. 'Wild Bunch' was a situation when you first play what might become a song, and a phrase or saying comes with it. It was loosely based on the movie, but I had a problem. I had the music first and the words 'wild bunch' kept coming. I wondered how I could precis a film into four minutes. It took a while."

'Ta Shunka Witco (Crazy Horse)' was Ian's haunting lament to the legendary nineteenth-century leader of the Oglala Sioux tribe. After fighting against territorial encroachment, Crazy Horse surrendered to US troops, but died at the hands of a military guard while allegedly resisting imprisonment. Hunter found 'Crazy Horse' easy to deliver as it was more like a painting than a song. Complete with heartbeat tom-toms, occasional guitar stabs and flute, Ian had tried to channel the character of Crazy Horse during recording. 'Ta Shunka Witco' would become an atmospheric gem at Hunter's live shows, recreating the type of shimmering tension created by 'Standin' in My Light'.

IH: "There's always room for a little drama on record and on stage. Now and again it's a good thing. I read a lot about Crazy Horse. I've always been a fan of the underdog and to me he was the greatest underdog ever. Crazy Horse was a decent guy who went through hell. Nobody ever managed to take a photograph of him because he believed if you took his photo his shadow would disappear. With 'Crazy Horse' it felt like I was getting into this other person's body; that's how clear it felt. The history of his life affected me. He was petrified of white people and there was this horrifying inevitability. He was a young man when he died and he knew what was coming."

When I'm President featured three personal "family outings" that exemplified contrast and stylishness in Ian's writing – 'Just the Way You Look Tonight', 'I Don't Know What You Want' and an optimistic album-closer 'Life' – where Hunter quietly urges everyone to lighten up and relax. Father and son split the lead vocal delivery on 'I Don't Know What You Want', Jess singing the verses while dad scratches his head over the generational divide on the choruses.

423

IH: "'I Don't Know What You Want' started as a jam in my basement. Jess is a good singer so he walked in and did it in one take. He's a great guitarist and bass player too, and he sounds like a younger version of me, with a bit of grit in his voice. I was always shy as a youngster, but Jess is pushy, like Tracie. 'Just the Way You Look Tonight' was Trudi, again. 'Life' started out as a strong piano melody, but I didn't realise that it would be good at the end of a live show. I'd done 'Dudes' for forty years and thought it would be refreshing to put something new alongside it. I started writing the verses to 'Life' and it was a bit on the corny side, but that's what it was going to be. The essence is: don't take things too seriously. There are a lot of things that you can't do anything about so why worry about them? My dad died of a stroke because he took his job home; I'm very obsessed too and it's not a good thing to be. So, 'Life' is as much to me as anybody else, but it was also written partly for my kids. I tended to be very stubborn as a child, so I hoped that when my children heard 'Life' they'd relax a little bit more than me and my father."

Containing eclectic, sincere songs, Hunter was pleased that *When I'm President* was a band album, and was satisfied with the strength of his writing.

IH: "I like songwriting but if the tap's not running, it can be miserable. I was lucky with *President* because several songs came into my head and all I had to do was get them down. Most of them were faster songs too, and that was great because for three or four albums I'd written mainly slow stuff, so I was grabbing the fast songs with both hands."

When I'm President was released by Proper Records in a gatefold card sleeve with lyric booklet and the package echoed *Mott* and *The Hoople* with a literary quotation: "And music meets not always now the ear… those days are gone" – Byron. Proper also issued the album as a limited vinyl pressing and 'When I'm President' as a single to promote the record; a band performance video of the title track was also filmed in the basement of Hunter's home.

Describing *When I'm President* as wry, gritty and bittersweet, and possibly Hunter's best ever album, *Q* considered the record: "A rollicking stomp from start to finish" – while *Mojo* wrote: "It may be forty years since he first started out with Mott, but Hunter comes across as a young man here with energetic bones. A fiery spirited album." *Record Collector* loved *President*'s gleeful savagery and scorching swagger while *Uncut* opined: "Edging away from the weighty politics of his superb 2001–2009 trilogy, ageless Hunter turns in a rollicking set of no-frills rockers and ballads." *Classic Rock* praised 'Black Tears' as a stand-out track, Charles Shaar Murray adding: "With one foot firmly planted in rock and the other in singer-songwriter-ismo, the Old Bastard is still nobody's pushover."

When I'm President was an artistic album with a life force of its own and it hit various charts, including *Billboard* (Tastemaker Albums No.4), Amazon's American Best Sellers (Adult Alternative No.15) and No.97 on Britain's Official Album Chart. The positive response to *President* led to an Ian Hunter feature in the *Culture* supplement of *The Sunday Times*.

> **IH:** "I never thought I'd have my music set to strings and if anybody had told me when I was bumming around the streets of Northampton that they'd be interviewing me for the cultural section of *The Sunday Times*, I'd have fallen over."

October found The Rant Band playing Scandinavian and UK concerts and Hunter's walk-on intro music, proposed by Mastro, comprised an Alan Lomax chain gang tape of the 1947 prison song 'Early in the Morning'. Ian had turned seventy-three in June 2012, but he played with the commitment and panache of a man half his age. He joked that he was just hoping to survive the tour, but he was eager to go out and play songs from a great rock album with a great band. With Andy Burton committed elsewhere, Paul Page recommended keyboard player Dennis DiBrizzi to The Rant Band. DiBrizzi, a lover of *Abbey Road, Exile on Main Street* and Stevie Ray Vaughan's *Soul to Soul*, had worked with Genya Ravan, Dion and Gary US Bonds. In 2012, Dennis exhibited great character and played his way into The Rant Band with personality and style.

Dennis DiBrizzi: "*President* was already finished when I joined The Rant Band and Ian put eight songs from it in the set list for the 2012 tour. In concert the new material stood tall next to the classics, with 'Crazy Horse' quickly becoming a live favourite. Ian's integrity is second to no one. He leads by example and treats his fans and The Rant Band with respect. Rock 'n' roll is lucky to have him!"

Classic Rock described Hunter's live set as a schizophrenic three-act play: the first and third with Ian centre stage singing and knocking seven bells out of an acoustic; the second with Hunter at piano stage-right. The climax of Hunter's performances had been re-moulded to accommodate 'Life' in tandem with 'All the Young Dudes', but one UK review was less enthusiastic – and Ian noticed.

> **IH:** "I get a bum 2012 live review in *Record Collector* because I don't play more of the old stuff; but if I play more of the old stuff, I'm a parody. 'Life' suddenly cut into 'Saturday Gigs' live and it went down well because audiences didn't expect it. Then we went into 'All the Young Dudes', which I must play each night. If I went to see Procol Harum and they didn't do 'A Whiter Shade of Pale', I'd be pissed off, especially if they replaced it with some new song that wasn't as good. That's the dilemma. I try to give some of my songs a rest, but this pleases the regulars and annoys the casuals. I guess my set is one-third old Mott, one-third older me and one-third new me. I think that's a good balance."

426

In October 2012, EMI released *From the Knees of My Heart: The Chrysalis Years (1979–1981)*, a four-disc collection of former albums but with added alternative song versions and a CD of Hunter's 1981 New York concert, previously issued as the video *Ian Hunter Rocks*. In a 9/10 review, *Classic Rock* described 'Irene Wilde' as a confessional beaut, 'Sons and Daughters' as one of Hunter's most brutally moving autobiographical outings and the entire collection as vindication for the man who, for years, saw his music biz status as that of "The Outsider".

Rock 'n' roll now had one of its most astute and erudite song laureates in its ranks and, for many observers, Ian Hunter pooled the votes. The Rant Band was his exceptional Cabinet: one of the finest ensembles on the road and Ian's best group since the *Schizophrenic* days with Ronson. *When I'm President* really did represent a landslide victory and, by way of confirmation, *Classic Rock* included 'When I'm President' in their 'Top Fifty Songs of the Year' and wrote: "You're gonna see my ugly mug up on Mount Rushmore, rasps Ian Hunter as The Rant Band's country-rock guitars and mandolins dance winningly around him. You have to admit he'd probably do a better job than Mitt Romney. A very apt song in a US Presidential election year proved that one of the UK's finest songwriters has lost none of his skill."

In March 2013, Ian played European and UK live dates as The Ian Hunter Acoustic Trio, with guitarist Andy York and Nashville bassist Dave Roe, who had held a long tenure in Johnny Cash's band. The format was refreshing, Ian re-tooling a varied repertoire with renditions of 'Ships', 'Irene Wilde' and 'Now Is the Time'. Occasionally Hunter's set included 'Letter to Britannia from the Union Jack' and 'When My Mind's Gone', performed for the first time since Mott's *Mad Shadows* era. 'Michael Picasso' also sounded more poignant than ever, twenty years after Mick Ronson's passing, while 'Sweet Jane' took on a new lease of life with Roe's inspired musical embroidery.

Dave Roe: "The acoustic tour of the UK that I played with Ian was a very stripped-down affair, which showcased so many of his great songs. Ian Hunter is not only one of the best songwriters in rock 'n' roll history – he is one of the best songwriters in history – period."

During his engaging acoustic sets, Ian adjusted his lyrics on 'Now Is the Time', pointing a finger at the National Rifle Association once more and referencing the Sandy Hook school shootings that had occurred near his Connecticut home. The performances were an eclectic experience, Hunter adopting a different mindset, having fun and closing each acoustic show with the message: "I don't know if this is what you were expecting – but this is what you got."

On 2nd April, Ian entered Dean Street Studios in London's Soho to record with Island Records artists Tribes. The session, in Tony Visconti's former Good Earth Studio, had been suggested by Roy Eldridge, whose company managed Tribes and Plan B. In a fun, three-hour session, Hunter and Tribes taped a version of 'The Man in Me' from Bob Dylan's *New Morning* album plus a slowed-down take of 'Sweet Jane'. The two tracks were originally earmarked for possible release on Britain's 2014 Record Store Day, but Tribes disbanded.

Maggi Ronson hosted MickRonsonfest at the ICA in London on 27th April 2013, marking the twentieth anniversary of her brother's passing. She also released *Sweet Dreamer*, an album containing new interpretations of 'This Is for You', 'Michael Picasso' and 'Satellite of Love', the latter featuring backing vocals from Maggi, Lisa Ronson, Tracie Hunter and Hannah and Amelia Berridge, Mick's nieces. The anniversary date had given Maggi motivation to make an album as she entered the musical spotlight at last: "It's probably been a lack of self-confidence that held me back over the years. I remember when Mick worked with Van Morrison, Van asked if I wanted to sing, but I was so nervous. I didn't have the confidence to. I wish I had done."

In April, Sony Columbia released a two CD set, *The Essential Mott the Hoople*, as part of its Legacy series. Notable for a superb essay penned by James Mastro, Sony inexplicably omitted 'Ballad of Mott the Hoople' from the track listing and included a live recording of 'Marionette' rather than the studio version. Then, against all odds, it was announced in the same month that Mott the Hoople would reunite again, the line-up comprising Hunter, Ralphs, Allen, Watts and Martin Chambers. Dale Griffin's health was in continual decline and Ian felt sadness over the drummer's illness.

> **IH:** "In the old days Buff and I used to argue every day, but he was a gentleman in 2009. We didn't think we'd be back, but every once in a while someone comes up with an offer and this time around it got silly. It's one of the best bands in the world and the lure to get back together was strong again. Mott the Hoople live was blood and thunder and one hundred per cent in the old days. In 2009, the whole thing surprised us: how good the band was and how great the fans were too. When it was that good you think you might want another stab at it, but business got in the way and it took four years to sort that out."

On 5th May 2013, Steve Hyams passed away, aged sixty-two, having coped with heart problems for several years. A friendly spirit and a purveyor of vinyl and good taste in Mott's early days, Hunter felt that Hyams should have joined the band in 1975 and he admired Steve's second solo album, *Feather and a Tomahawk*. Luke Hyams recalled his father's humour and kind nature: "Dad partied with The Beatles, the Stones and many others, in stories that shouldn't be published until after everyone is dead. I remember him bursting into my kindergarten one day to announce, ever so politely, that I would be leaving early because our house was on fire. My father was on a rollercoaster ride of creative pursuit, misadventure and tragedy. He was a rock 'n' roll original."

> **IH:** "Steve was a great pal of Mott the Hoople when we started in 1969. He worked in a record shop on the Kings Road, just around the corner from the band flat, at the Chelsea Drug Store. Steve would bring stuff for us to listen

to and it was always good. He had impeccable taste. I don't think he was actually playing at that point. He played me some of his stuff later on and it was quite original and different. He was one of us. He had a couple of shots, but he wasn't too healthy some of the time and that held him back. I thought a fit Steve would have been great in Mott after I left, but it wasn't to be. He was unique. Steve's one that got away."

Unlike Mott the Hoople's reunion shows where audiences wallowed in nostalgia, Hunter's tours and albums continued to be "of the moment" and fans loved the experience. With Ian's refusal to rot or rust, June 2013 saw a brief return to the UK with two gigs preceding an appearance at the Isle of Wight Festival. The live set kicked off with 'What For' – a strident way to open any rock show – and included the best cuts from *When I'm President*. The band's Isle of Wight set was filmed for TV, but Ian remained hesitant about festival settings.

IH: "I don't like festivals because you get on and you don't know what's going to happen. It's not the crowd, it's more – 'Is it going to rain?' – 'Will the wind blow the sound away?' – 'Is the monitor guy good?' Sometimes it's fine and sometimes it's wrong, but if it is wrong, there's no time to get it re-organised."

The Rant Band played more US gigs in September and October before attention turned to Mott's November shows. Ian had concerns about the group's ability to fill the 20,000-seat O2 Arena in Greenwich, which seemed to be a booking choice oozing optimism. Hunter rightly considered The Roundhouse a more appropriate venue.

IH: "We played five nights at Hammersmith Odeon in 2009 and everybody thought we'd sold 20,000 tickets but we didn't really, because every night it was largely the same 3,000 die-hard people. So, in 2013, all the big guys got involved. There was an offer we accepted, then a bigger offer came from AEG Live, who must have thought we were Beyoncé, so then we're playing the O2 Arena, supposedly to 20,000 people and getting an absurd amount of money. I wanted to do The Roundhouse because it's mentioned in 'Saturday Gigs', but it was hard to turn AEG down. The first reunion was the magic one and was what people had wanted for years. Of course, 'The Law of Mott' was still there with different managers; the twain never meets. People asked about a new Mott the Hoople album, but it took four years to put together five gigs, so organising an album was beyond my lifespan. If they wanted a Mott record, they should have struck in 2009 when the band was hot."

Hunter joined Mott at Rockfield Studios again to begin tour preparations on 2nd November. During the second day, he picked up Watts' baritone guitar and wrote a new song titled 'Ain't That So', Ian expounding that every new guitar had a song in it. Ralphs noted that, whilst the other Motts had done some preparation in advance, the rehearsals really clicked after Hunter's arrival. An excited Verden Allen looked forward to the Newcastle City Hall gig and recalled a 1971 concert there, when Mott let fireworks off inside the venue. After a week of preparations, Mott the Hoople's mini-tour kicked off at Birmingham Symphony Hall on 11th November followed by shows at Glasgow Clyde Auditorium, Newcastle City Hall, Manchester O2 (filmed for DVD) and London's O2 Arena (recorded for CD).

Mott's set list was identical at every gig, the band kicking off powerfully with 'Rock and Roll Queen', 'One of the Boys' and 'The Moon Upstairs'. There was the surprise inclusion of 'Violence', and Watts and Allen procured some songwriting royalties from forthcoming discs via 'Born Late '58' and 'Soft Ground'; Ian did not want to play either song or the "shameful" 'Sucker', but the band grafted a fantastic section of 'Jailhouse Rock' onto the latter's introduction. 'Walkin' with a Mountain' included a nod to The Rolling Stones with a teasing *"the last time"* refrain, which left fans wondering if the final ballad really *was* being played. The set highlights for many followers, however, were the softer songs – 'Ballad of Mott the Hoople', 'Hymn for the Dudes', a medley of 'When My Mind's Gone', 'No Wheels to Ride' and 'The Journey', plus a wonderful rendition of 'Waterlow'. The obligatory hit singles closed the shows and 'The Right Honourable' Stanley Tippins returned to the stage.

> **IH:** "I'd taken Stan back on the road on some of my solo treks, including the tour with Ralphs and with Mott in 2009. He joined us again but now had a yellow card and a red card for behaviour. He also weighed the band every Thursday and handed out fines at £5 a pound, if you put any weight on. Martin Chambers played his ass off for us in 2013 and was great."

Unlikely to be banned from a concert hall again, reviews for Mott's gigs were mixed. A mean-spirited *Evening Times* feature described the Glasgow show as "lame" but the auditorium with its "sit down" bouncers did not help. The universally lavish praise in 2009 had included a five-star *Daily Telegraph* review that declared Mott the Hoople had stormed back to London for "a dazzling night" at the Hammersmith Apollo; now, *The Telegraph* hit a low blow, labelling the 2013 show grindingly consistent but acknowledging that Hunter's voice, phrasing, control and poise were the band's redeeming assets and wonderful throughout. *Classic Rock* wrote scathingly of the tour's best gig at a packed Newcastle City Hall, but Neal Keeling of *The Manchester Evening News* brightened the landscape when he enthused: "Right down to Ian Hunter's legendary Maltese Cross guitar, Mott the Hoople were everything I had hoped for when they kicked off their first concert in Manchester for forty years."

432

Between their Glasgow and Newcastle shows, *Classic Rock* presented Mott the Hoople with an 'Outstanding Contribution' award at The Roundhouse in London. Hunter gave thanks on the night and said, "The awards we used to get were ugly bits of wood and no one really argued if you took it home. There's going to be a punch-up over this one." Four days later, Ian Gittins of *The Guardian* felt that four years on from Hammersmith, the London spotlight was shining on Mott rather more harshly this time: "Empty seats are scattered around the O2 and while there is a palpable tidal wave of goodwill from their resolutely old-school fans, the main set is largely composed of stodgy, lumpen fare. Amid this muddy morass, the classic singles shine like diamonds."

Tacked alongside the tour, Phil John and Richie Anderson held events in Hereford, Birmingham and London, talking about life with the band and Phil's new publication – *You Rocked, We Rolled: Mott Road Crew Life* – based on his 1974 European tour diaries. A *Classic Rock* review noted the book's regular "getting lost – searching for porn musings", but the original road notes were never intended for public consumption. "It was just a scribbled diary," says Phil. "It was first publicised on an internet mag, then a private publisher asked if they could release it and added the footnotes and pics to bulk it out." Ian reflected on the grim rock 'n' roll circus of the Seventies and Mott the Hoople's 2013 gigs.

> **IH:** "When we were on the road in the early Seventies, England had amazing audiences, but it was a shithole in the grip of the unions. The US was like heaven, Germany made those of us who grew up after World War II wonder who came off best, and the rest of Europe made us wonder why we bothered getting off the ferry. Originally Mott the Hoople was quite anarchic, but some of the 2013 shows were too polite for me. The O2 was too big for us, but whilst I'd feared it would be a disaster, it turned out well. I thought the first three shows were great, before the lighting guy messed my throat up at Manchester with

dry ice. Newcastle City Hall was, by far, the best gig for me and was almost how we were in the old days. I didn't favour Watts' suggestion that we place 'Soft Ground' and 'Waterlow' together in the shows; that killed the set for us each night. The Mott dates were strictly for those who wanted to re-live days long ago, but the business end remained a gigantic pain in the arse. Ralpher and I ended up disagreeing with the other two and it was frustrating. Reunions are a dangerous manoeuvre and I wouldn't want to do them too much because Mott's an old band and we'd have to play the same songs every night. I enjoyed the first reunion more than the second, but the Mott audiences are big and that helps me and The Rant Band, who I regard as the group that I tour and record with."

It had taken thirty-five years for Mott the Hoople to reunite at Hammersmith after a tiresome trail of rumours. The 2009 reunion gigs had their internal politics and problems, but the 2013 shows created a bittersweet taste for some fans, with no Morgan Fisher or Ariel Bender involvement and expensive VIP tickets that were put on sale after dedicated followers had already snapped up standard seats. A commemorative concert photo book, *We've Got a Great Future Behind Us*, then tested loyalty and credit cards to breaking point at a punishing £200. The "limited edition" publication seemingly required a coffee table too, so some fans were forgiven for reflecting on Ian's prophetic *Alien Boy* couplet: "*There ain't no rock 'n' roll no more, just the music of the rich.*"

Before his return to the US, Hunter joined Mick Jones on 20th November in an Acton studio called The Bunker, to record and film for the *Rotten Hill* TV project. In front of a small invited audience, the duo played 'Laugh at Me' and 'Keep A-Knockin''.

IH: "We have had some obsessive fans like Joe Elliott and Mick Jones, and I think their interest has helped keep us going. It's interesting that a lot of these people who went on

434

to be punks and glam rockers were fans of Mott. We were a rock 'n' roll band before all that fragmentation took place and we had traces of metal, traces of punk and traces of glam. Now it's so compartmentalised."

On 13th January 2014, Consett's own Jerry Lee Lewis, Freddie 'Fingers' Lee, passed away in Newcastle. Aged seventy-six, he had previously suffered two strokes which halted his stage career and, on the day of his death, Ian released a message for Fred's family expressing his sorrow.

> **IH:** "Fred, Miller Anderson, Pete Phillips and I had some great times back in the day. Fred was a character. He told me he started with Sutch on ten bob a week AND he had to drive the van. We starved together in Germany – van broken down – club owner not paying us – but we got to play for hours every night and that was the buzz. Somehow disasters were averted, and we'd make it back. I always felt bad for Fred. He was – quite naturally – Jerry Lee Lewis's twin. Same range, same power on the keyboards, same arrogance and he could be really funny – same love of American country music – he would often sail into a song the band had never heard of. Fred loved the raw original beginnings of rock 'n' roll and remained staunchly loyal to it during a long, successful career. He had a lot of fans in Europe and never seemed to stop working – music was his life. We all went off and did different things, but I'll always be grateful to Fred for giving me a little hope at a time when I thought the factory was my only future. I'll always remember him saying to me, 'You're a good songwriter – but don't ever try to sing.' He was probably right!"

In March, Concert Live released *Mott the Hoople Live 2013*. With bare-bones packaging, the three-disc set comprised audio and film from Mott's Manchester Academy gig, the producers dropping the planned alternative London audio recording. *Classic Rock*'s review noted that the ballads provided the most moving moments and questioned if the *"Goodbye"* outro on 'Saturday Gigs' could be for real this time. Following their *My ReGeneration* CD, the Down 'n' Outz also issued *The Further Adventures of the Down 'n' Outz*, the band digging deep into Mott the Hoople's history for their second tribute disc, courageously re-igniting 'Marionette', 'Whizz Kid' and 'Crash Street Kidds'.

> **IH:** "The Down 'n' Outz get my approval. The solo by Paul Guerin on 'The Journey' is one of the best I've heard and Mott's songs really suit Joe's voice. It's a whole different side to him. Joe has the energy of ten men and the enthusiasm of twenty. It's great he's so keen on keeping the old stuff alive. More power to him, not that he needs any."

On 3rd June 2014, Ian and The Rant Band played the City Winery in New York. Billed as "Ian Hunter's Diamond Jubilee Birthday Bash", its guests included Ellen Foley, Alejandro Escovedo, Tommy Mandel, Jesse Malin, Wreckless Eric and Amy Rigby. Another attendee was Mick Rock, who remarked, "The gig was terrific. If I didn't know better, I would think Ian was lying. Seventy-five? He looks much younger."

In July, *Classic Rock* published its landmark 200th edition featuring 'The Soundtrack of Our Life; The 200 Greatest Songs of Classic Rock's Lifetime'. Ian's 'When the World Was Round' from *Shrunken Heads* was placed at No.60 – with Bob Dylan's 'Mississippi' from *Love and Theft* appearing at No.70, Hunter had out-Dylaned Dylan one more time.

During the same month MIG reissued Hunter's *Strings Attached*, the film and recordings receiving renewed praise when *Classic Rock* wrote: "There are very few artists who actually get better in the second half of their career and even fewer who improve in the third. Ian Hunter is one of those artists. His return to solo work in the twenty-first century has always been good, and sometimes

436

brilliant. Without exaggeration, this is one of the best live albums of all time."

Ian Hunter and the Rant Band: Live in the UK 2010 was released in September 2014, featuring 'Sea Diver', 'Waterlow', 'Irene Wilde' and a selection of tracks from *Man Overboard*. Ian admitted that he had no idea they were being recorded at the time, adding that fans should thank Trudi in that respect. Rejecting faded industry protocols, Hunter decided to release the album on his own label, JJM Records. The recording was more laid-back than the 2013 Rant Band tour, sitting midway between the subtlety of *Strings Attached* and the fire of *When I'm President,* and featuring string arrangements on 'Ships' and 'All the Young Dudes'.

Commencing in September, Hunter played a series of British, Scandinavian and American gigs. With no new material to showcase, the performances revolved around a selection of favourites and lesser-known songs from an extensive solo career. At London's Shepherd's Bush Empire, Mick Ralphs guested on 'Roll Away the Stone'. Former Overnight Angels member Rob Rawlinson also re-connected with Ian, the first time the pair had met in over thirty-five years, and the bassist was impressed: "Ian Hunter is a cornerstone of an era that may never come back. He gets up on stage and kills the audience every night. It's exactly how rock should be. At his age he should know better, but I'm glad he doesn't!"

Hunter's revival had begun with the landmark *Rant* and was followed by vibrant albums that were enhanced by the musical nucleus that became The Rant Band. Ian was full of praise for the participants.

IH: "The Rant Band has been together for some fifteen years and we've never had a problem. Mott the Hoople was together for five years and we always had a problem, every five minutes. In The Rant Band there is real camaraderie. I'm still doing this because I've got the motivation, which you have to have. People say I'm an old guy and I shouldn't be doing it, but that's the motivation. Mick Ronson's death

437

was very positive musically. Maybe Mick's still helping me because I've written great stuff since. After Ronson died it was a *long* way back. By then I didn't know anybody – musicians, managers, agents – nobody. Effectively, I was done. Then I met Steve Holley and Andy York and James Mastro, and I found the motivation.

"I encourage The Rant Band personality-wise; anybody can do what they want and there is a togetherness that's extremely appealing. Mott was five complete individuals and every one of them was a star. In The Rant Band I get the final say, but it seldom comes to that. James Mastro is more of a leader than I am most of the time. The big difference with Mott is that I'm only a fifth member. In The Rant Band, in essence, what I say goes, not that I have to say much because they've got it. They are incredible. We did forty gigs in 2014 and I remember looking at them before we started and thinking I'd never get through it. Not only did we get through it, we really did some damage!"

In January 2015, Hunter played at The Fillmore West in San Francisco and a sold-out "Welcome Back to the Club" gig at The Roxy in Los Angeles, then his first ever Japanese concerts followed with three shows at Tokyo's Garden Shimokitazawa. *Mojo* published 'Diary of a Rock 'n' Roll Star: Part Two', a Japanese "tour" follow-up to Ian's groundbreaking, early Seventies, warts-and-all memoir.

During June, Ian appeared at four gigs in New York, Brooklyn and Sellersville. The Rant Band had become one of the finest groups on the planet and their electrifying set at Brooklyn's Bell House on 15th June possessed a panache and power that blew Mott the Hoople 2013 sideways. Through August and September, Hunter played nine further shows as support to The J. Geils Band. Ian agreed to the tour after lead singer Peter Wolf extended a personal invitation and, along with a headlining festival commitment booked for January 2016, the shows helped fund Hunter's next studio album. *When I'm President* was a classy record that outshone the second

Mott reunion, and it became a firm fan favourite and an album close to keyboard player Dennis DiBrizzi's heart.

Peter Wolf: "I first met Ian when he was touring with Mick Ronson and I always found him to be an artist who defied any kind of category. He's one of a few, I would say, that is the 'Real Deal'."

Dennis DiBrizzi: "There are just too many great songs in Ian Hunter's catalogue to narrow the essence down to one song. *When I'm President* will always be a cherished album for me because it is songwriting at its finest. Emotion, sarcasm, innuendo and self-reflection – great rockers and soulful, eloquent ballads – it's all there, and more. There are songs that can make you move, and songs that make you think. 'Comfortable' says it best. *'All hail rock 'n' roll!'*"

2015 saw Ian Hunter crafting material for yet another album, but he also contributed to a planned retrospective of his solo career – an anthology that would be like no other. 2016 would be another victorious year.

CHAPTER FIFTEEN

Stranded in Reality

I was famous for a fortnight and that was enough.

The yellow legal pads were spread across Ian Hunter's basement floor again in 2015 as he assembled songs for his fourteenth studio album, *Fingers Crossed*. The working titles for the record included *White House*, *The Last Bus Home* and *Seein' Red*, and early song contenders were 'Everything's a Racket', 'Whatever It Takes', 'Sing for My Supper', 'Yellow Press', 'Room Full of Ghosts', 'Pain in the Ass' and 'Amen'. Hunter's subjects and writing scope remained wide-ranging and the process leading up to recording re-utilised The Rant Band's incredible skills and commitment.

> **IH:** "For a new album I write the music and lyrics. I really strive to keep it fresh and it is hard to do. It's random – like a joke comes into a comedian's head – it just appears. Then I run the songs past Andy York and The Rant Band. Once Andy's given the go-ahead for the songs that are up to par, we set a window to record them and everybody gets down to making them better. This is not easy because people have lives, so Rant Band members, one or two at a time, will start

visiting my home at odd intervals and arrangements develop. During this process songs can change, disappear or go in a different direction, and mistakes can be magical. The great thing about The Rant Band is they do a lot of homework so we're three-quarters done by the time we get together as a team. We bring our talents towards the finished article and record. Then, out the door to the masses, who mostly miss the point. Fun!"

As Hunter prepared to record in early 2016, the rock world gasped on 10th January when it was announced that David Bowie had passed away following a private eighteen-month struggle with cancer. Bowie had re-married in 1992 and became an almost invisible New Yorker, basing his family in Manhattan, but he could still surprise and generate attention, as with 2013's stage-managed release of *The Next Day.* However, on 8th January 2016 – his birthday – David unveiled his twenty-fifth album, *Blackstar,* with brand "Bowie" on the cover in fragmented glyphs and songs listed in Terminal font, from a design suite called Lazarus. Conspiracy theorists believed *Blackstar* was a coded warning of an apocalyptic collision between Earth and a giant hidden super-planet, but there was a different message behind the record.

The death of the rock star rebel, enthusiastic art collector and cultural icon shocked the globe, two days after his sixty-ninth birthday. Cryptic, jazz-infused and mournful, *Blackstar* carried the heavy aura of an epitaph and suddenly the world appreciated that Bowie's album was a parting gift. Keyboards clattered as journos realised that blackstar is a type of cancer lesion and an astrological term for a collapsed star. David had been given a three-month warning that his treatment was to be stopped as the cancer spread and his condition became terminal. Hearing of his unexpected passing, Ian Hunter immediately noted on his website: "David wrote some wonderful songs. I was lucky enough to sing one of them and it changed my life. My heart goes out to his wife, son and daughter. RIP David."

IH: "I only played two 'gigs' with David, when he got up with Mott the Hoople in Philly in 1972 and then at the Freddie Mercury show. He wanted Mott to play the 'Save the Whales' concert in London in 1972, but we wouldn't do it. If you opened for David, you only got part of the lights and PA and we weren't falling for that. We spent a few months with David over forty years ago and he was pivotal at that time for Mott, as Guy Stevens had been before. It was a great time and it changed our lives, but that was then. I was asked to appear at memorial concerts for Bowie in March 2016 but, for personal reasons, I decided against it. I regretted David's passing. It was a shock, but life goes on."

Following David's obituaries and the shelving of *Gods and Gangsters*, a book by former Bowie and Mott the Hoople manager Tony Defries, financial adviser Dan Atkinson noted that Tony had featured rather less frequently in David's tributes than he would have expected, because Defries had intersected the economic history of the Sixties and Seventies in three important ways. Atkinson wrote: "One, he [Tony] was a trade union official, serving on the ruling committee of the Association of Fashion and Advertising Photographers. After leaving AFAP, he tried unsuccessfully to unionise the fashion models themselves. Two, he spotted early the effect that the great wave of inflation would have on the gold price, which soared from about forty-five dollars a Troy ounce at the start of the Seventies to more than eight hundred dollars by January 1980. Three, he was one of those agents and managers who engineered a huge shift in power and money away from record companies, film studios and sports clubs towards artists, actors and directors, and players, a shift that has yet to be properly explored in a thorough-going book on the subject."

A week after Bowie's passing, on 17th January 2016, Dale Griffin died aged sixty-seven, at the Mountains Nursing Home at Libanus in Brecon, Wales. During his illness with Alzheimer's disease, Dale had given interviews to *The Express* and *The Telegraph*, promoting the fundraising event Memory Walk and talking about his dementia in the third person, calling it "My dreadful little bug, Mr Alzheimer". Buffin's funeral at Usk on 15th February was attended by Mick Ralphs, Verden Allen, Stan Tippins, Luther Grosvenor, Richie Anderson, Phil John, Mick Hince, Chris Whitehouse, Martin Chambers and Kingsley Ward.

Mick Ralphs thanked Buffin for the years of friendship and keeping the beat as the engine room of Mott; the guitarist was very affected by Dale's death and would opt out of Bad Company's 2016 US tour. Verden Allen said of the drummer's passing, "Dale was like family. We were very close. We went through a lot together. Dale was a nice, well-spoken man and a brilliant drummer. It's unbelievable that he's gone. I suppose in some ways it's a release for him now; he had suffered for many years."

At the end of January, Hunter and The Rant Band played three British gigs, including a headlining slot at a three-day indoor festival. The sets were a mirror of the previous year's live dates but, during each performance, Hunter included a home-run section comprising 'Sweet Jane', 'Rest in Peace' and 'All the Young Dudes' – a fine testimonial, without announcement or fanfare, to the departed Reed, Griffin and Bowie.

> IH: "We did three UK gigs in January 2016 and playing 'Rest in Peace' was special, and my way of honouring Dale and David. The last time I saw Buff was at the first Mott reunion. He was a very well-spoken guy and had it nailed. His illness was a terrible thing and there was nothing you could do. Buffin had a great time doing the encores at Hammersmith and I'm so glad he was able to do that. He would always talk to fans endlessly and was very into Mott the Hoople. Buff only played with the one band and when Mott folded, he stopped playing. I've seen so many people pass in my lifetime that I'm a bit of a stoic. Life is random and there's no logic. Genes play a huge part and sometimes how you live, but Buff wasn't much of a drinking man and never touched

drugs. He was the youngest Mott by far. Who would have thought it would turn out the way it did? It's all a bit back to front."

Before his return to the States, Ian played acoustic guitar and sang backing vocals for his daughter Tracie and her group The Rebelles on 'All the Young Dudes'. Released as a single in homage to Bowie, the London session included Glen Matlock and James Stevenson.

Hunter, The Rant Band and Andy York commenced the recording of Ian's new album on 5th March at Tony Shanahan's Hobo Sound Studios in Weehawken, New Jersey, the location employed by HBO for the soundtrack to the Mick Jagger–Martin Scorsese-produced TV series *Vinyl*. Hunter had thirteen songs prepared including a newly written tribute to Bowie entitled 'Dandy'. With enforced breaks during the process, courtesy of *Vinyl* sessions and a bout of laryngitis for Ian, by May the album was recorded, overdubbed, mixed and mastered.

> IH: "We recorded thirteen tracks with the band in four days: ten for the record and some bonus cuts for a Japanese release. I was glad that Andy York got hung up on some John Mellencamp stuff at one point, because three more songs came to me and they're the best three on the record. We had a great studio and engineer and the sound was there from the off. I'm blood and thunder and like the drama side of things, but Andy and the band are more sensible and rein me in. I feel very lucky to be in the gang. *Fingers Crossed* was kind of like *Schizophrenic*: good fun, new studio, new engineer and things just worked out fine."

During June, Hunter played three gigs in New York and in July guested on 'Sweet Jane' and 'All the Young Dudes', performed alongside Alice Cooper, Johnny Depp and the Hollywood Vampires in Brooklyn. Ian also featured on the TV show *Speakeasy*, filmed at Manhattan's Lincoln Center, where he was interviewed by Joe Elliott.

> **IH:** "I didn't know Johnny Depp had ever heard of me, but he asked if I wanted to get up with the Vampires when they came to New York. We were trying to get *Diary of a Rock 'n' Roll Star* out again at the time, assuming we could get a proper deal, and Johnny said he'd written two forewords for it. He's a real gentleman."

Fingers Crossed was released on 16th September 2016 and featured: 'That's When the Trouble Starts', 'Dandy', 'Ghosts', 'Fingers Crossed', 'White House', 'Bow Street Runners', 'Morpheus', 'Stranded in Reality', 'You Can't Live in the Past' and 'Long Time'. Session support for Hunter and The Rant Band included keyboard player Andy Burton, Andy York on acoustic guitars and recording engineer James Frazee, a thirty-four-year-old drummer who had worked with Blondie, The Whipsaws and Willie Nile. As ever, Hunter's fastidiousness was clear for all to see via the quality of his inimitable songwriting, and The Rant Band was enthused with *Fingers Crossed*. "The album was pretty much all recorded live and much faster than normal," said Steve Holley. "We played all the tracks in four days and, because it was done like that, it holds together really well."

Issued as a gatefold CD and limited-edition LP by Proper Records, Hunter's album offered music salutes, historic tales and personal commentaries spread across ten eclectic tracks. *The Last Bus Home* and *Seein' Red* had been dropped as possible album titles, the latter when the song of that name was removed from the draft track listing. Saddened by the American music business, Ian opted to release *Fingers Crossed* in the States on the JJM label; Respect Records of Japan issued the album in a mini-LP sleeve format.

> **IH:** "*Fingers Crossed* had nothing to do with the upcoming US election in 2016. The best two ideas that I had as album

titles were both titles to songs. 'Seein' Red' lost out to 'You Can't Live in the Past' as we tried to hinge a ten-track album together, so 'Seein' Red' became a bonus track. There was another ballad, 'Fingers Crossed', which came on really strong in the finishing stages of the record. That, and the fact that we always have our fingers crossed when any album is released, influenced the eventual title. Offers from US labels were ridiculous as indies are no different to the majors; they want to give you a pittance, way under what the album cost to make, then sit on the record until they amass a catalogue which they sell at a profit. No more! *Fingers Crossed* was special and I only wanted it with people who appreciate music. The offers I got did not involve listening to the record. They didn't care if it was good, bad or indifferent. The US music biz is composed of people who sit in offices with no real knowledge of music. If I could find an American label half as good as Proper UK, I'd do it, but they're not out there."

Fingers Crossed kicked off with the battle cry *"Yeah, yeah, yeah, yeah"* on 'That's When the Trouble Starts' – a ramshackle rocker that would have sat happily on any Keith Richards solo album and, at three and a half minutes, an attention-grabbing curtain-raiser. The song posted a warning for today's young fame-seekers, offering sage reflections for callow candidates who think "the biz" is easy, but highlighting that their arrogance leads them to believe they are cool when they are really *"fifty shades of stupid"*. One reviewer, Peter Gerstenzang, noted knowingly: "The minute Hunter's outraged rasp crashes in, growling about showbiz, getting old and all the other unbearable inequities of life, you know we have a live one here. Young punks would pull out their nose rings for such authentic anger."

IH: "Reality shows can rot your brain. 'That's When the Trouble Starts' is a shot at the Simon Cowell syndrome and

446

zombie audiences – flashing lights, crap music, and it's all over for them in fifteen minutes. I can't watch it – it drives me nuts – so I had a little dig."

Hunter played an early ace on *Fingers Crossed* with 'Dandy', a soaring and spiritual celebration of David Bowie with lyrics that painted a bright canvas of Ziggy Stardust's earth-shaking Seventies storm. The last song written for the album, it was a magnificent accolade featuring full-on, Mott-style swagger and a majestic chorus dusted with musical flakes of 'All the Young Dudes' and 'Saturday Gigs'. There was also a lyrical nod to Dylan's 'Ballad of a Thin Man', references to the classic Bowie songs 'The Prettiest Star', 'Life on Mars', 'Heroes' and 'The Jean Genie', plus a bridge that echoed 'Starman'. Ian's prose encapsulated the "Brixton boy" brilliantly – the ambitious guy who had it all: the voice and songwriting ability, the looks and style, a way with words and the necessary self-assurance – the *"keeper of the flame"* who turned our social-realist *Saturday Night and Sunday Morning* world from Sixties black and white into a startling Seventies rainbow. Hunter even name-checked Trevor Bolder and Woody Woodmansey of the Spiders directly, and paraphrased 'Dudes'. Interestingly, 'Dandy' mirrored 'Michael Picasso' in that neither piece mentions the central subject of the song directly by name. Later described as "the final glam rock anthem", Hunter's work felt like an instant classic. Proper Records released the song as their promo single from the album and *Classic Rock* immediately placed it on their 'Heavy Rotation' chart at No.2, describing it as a touching tribute.

> **IH:** "I was at home in January 2016 when David died, and I was working on a song called 'Lady'. The chord sequence and melody were written but the words weren't working. I liked the melody and was trying to write lyrics for 'Lady' and then David went, so I changed it easily to 'Dandy', as they have the same intonation. I thought it was all somewhat

affecting. David's death was a tremendous shock, so why not acknowledge it. The change only took forty-eight hours to write and was natural – it had to be, otherwise you might sound a bit Mickey Rooney. I knew Bowie for about a year when he was beginning his meteoric rise. He had a very powerful personality, was very generous with Mott and was a genuine fan of the band. David gave a lot and he took a lot too. He could be a bitch and a bit cruel, but I found him to be great when I knew him. I hadn't seen David in years. I spoke to him on his *Station to Station* tour when he tried to bum some cigarettes off me in the dressing room that night. He was a totally different type to me, so he went his way and I went mine. I knew he wasn't well but I didn't know it was that bad. The lyric for 'Dandy' was fluky and I was worried how Bowie fans might feel. I wondered if people might think I was trying to cash in, but I like how 'Dandy' turned out. I think the song is quite instant.

"Dandies were witty and confident. They were great dressers who were fastidious in their look, so it just seemed a natural thing to write 'Dandy' because David was so Technicolor. It's also a flashback to Mott's *All the Young Dudes* album cover. 'Dandy' has some nice guitar touches. I like the hook in the song – *'and then we took the last bus home'*. England was pretty drab in the early Seventies. When I was a kid you used to go to the Empire or the Granada and you'd see escapism via a Western movie, then come out and look up the street – and it was drab with bland shops, and you wanted to kick the windows in because the environment was so black and white. The early Seventies were boring, but you had that magic two hours at rock gigs; they were escapes too. Then Bowie arrived and his concerts were CinemaScope. He was probably the first Technicolor artist. I recall seeing him with make-up and shaved eyebrows, and it was quite shocking at the time, especially for the Americans. David took you to Magic Land, then you took the last bus

448

home and you were flying. I put myself in a fan's position for the song and was trying to illustrate the view of a kid going to see Ziggy Stardust. I remember watching Ziggy taking off from the wings. David was a mover, no question. The visual was so strong and a massive injection to music. We thought we were flash rockers in Mott, but Bowie was glam and Ronson looked spectacular. It was very classy the way Bowie died – it was typical David."

It was almost impossible to follow a song as strong as 'Dandy' but Hunter did it in style with 'Ghosts', Proper Records favoured choice for single release. 'Ghosts' was inspired by Ian's November 2014 visit to Sun Studios on Union Avenue in Memphis, rock 'n' roll pioneer Sam Phillips' legendary establishment and the hallowed ground where the presence of "The Gang of Four" – Elvis Presley, Jerry Lee Lewis, Johnny Cash and Carl Perkins – can still be felt. Framed around attractive acoustic guitar, bubbly bass and an enticing tempo, Hunter likened himself to a kid in a candy store, his lyrics hinting at *Alice in Wonderland* and Elvis, and recalling the life-saving moment in the late Fifties when music scratched the surface of his soul and told him who he was.

IH: "A guy called Rick Steph rang me up and said he'd seen that we were due to play in Memphis. Rick's father performed with Elvis Presley and he asked if we'd like to go to Sun Studios. So, we had this private studio tour, saw the bits that the usual tourists don't see and went in the booth too. There were guitars all over the walls, a double bass on a stand, a drum kit and Jerry Lee Lewis's piano, with the burn mark on it where he'd been told not to smoke. There were also three crosses on the floor marking the spots for Bill Black, Scotty Moore and Elvis. Suddenly Dennis DiBrizzi started barrelhousing the piano, Paul Page took the stand-up bass and Holley was on the drums using his fingers; you don't need sticks as the room is so live. Then Mastro and

Bosch take guitars down, so we get going and suddenly this room is swirling around. It sounded great in there and it really got me going. The piano was kind of 'ringy', but it was Jerry Lee's piano. Everybody was feeling something and by the end I just had to get back to the hotel room and write some words. Sun Studios was quite magic in a way. That room was eerie and there are ghosts. Nobody can tell me any different – you *can* feel it."

The last song that Ian captured for his album was the masterstroke within the masterpiece – the attractive and colourful 'Fingers Crossed' – another Hunter historical narrative, being an eighteenth-century tale of men being press-ganged into joining the navy, forced into service by *"nefarious rogues"*. With a tear-jerking chorus, the studio ensemble was in full flight, soaring behind a dramatic *"Hang me high"* climactic refrain, delivered sensitively and passionately by Ian throughout. 'Fingers Crossed' is one the finest and most emotional songs that Ian Hunter has ever written, and it was instantly picked out by DJ Johnnie Walker as the album's highlight on BBC radio.

IH: "It's difficult to write 'you left me for somebody else baby', when you're seventy-seven years of age, so on *Fingers Crossed* and *President* I seemed to zero in on history. 'Fingers Crossed' was not inspired by a book though; I've no idea where it came from. Again, I simply woke up one day with the opening line and from there the song took its own course. It was just C and F, and a little magic twirl on the piano. After the opening line, it was like 'Wild Bunch' on *President*: it could only go one way. Sometimes you get a run of words and you've got to stay with it. *'Pressed into service'* takes you back to the 1750s where you could have been a privateer or a pirate, and you weren't sure what you were until they brought you back to England, where they'd either knight you or hang you."

The mildly romantic and melodic foot-tapper 'White House' offered joyful release after the seriousness of the previous three tracks – a brilliantly placed fun song, based on real rural life and real living – while 'Bow Street Runners' related another eighteenth-century tale of the Fielding Brothers, who formed London's first professional police force to drive rogues and scallywags out of the city's gas-lit alleys and gin-soaked bars.

> IH: "I love The Traveling Wilburys and The Band, and 'White House' has that kind of feel. Wally, the beaver in the song, is real. We had recently found a new house, but it was empty for months before we moved in and he took over and was very upset when we arrived; he moved downstream. The 'Bow Street Runners' title came into my head first, so I had to write a song about that, and I started to check things out. In the 1700s half a million people lived in London and there were no cops, so crime was rampant. One of the Fielding Brothers was known as 'Blind Beak'; he couldn't see but he could smell crime and apparently recognised thousands of criminals by the sound of their voices, so the story goes. The brothers, Henry and John Fielding, were judges or part of the court system. They had night watchmen then but no police to control people, so the Brothers started a force – the Bow Street Runners – Britain's first Bobbies."

'Morpheus' was a stand-out track with a colossal lyric framed around the ancient Greek god who had the ability to mimic human form and shape, and morph into people's dreams. The opiate drug morphine derived from the name Morpheus and The Rant Band entangled the listener in a dreamy, spacey soundscape, Hunter grasping at lyrical lines in a night-time netherworld, floating between sleep and waking.

> IH: "Bosch plays some excellent guitar on 'Morpheus'. He is a great player and will show off a bit at times, but he is

451

fabulous. I didn't know that Morpheus was the god of sleep and dreams. Mick Ralphs told me he'd been deep in the arms of Morpheus one night after one of the Mott reunion shows and that it referred to the god of sleep. I loved the way Ralpher said it and something clicked with me, so I made a note of it."

The home run on *Fingers Crossed* comprised three songs that referenced Hunter's past and some of his milestones. The echoey, psychedelic sound collage of 'Stranded in Reality' carried one of Ian's cleverly unique and wildly offbeat lyrics, reflecting on the *"age of the deluded"* and opining that people have brains but no batteries to use them. The nostalgic 'You Can't Live in the Past', referencing Vera Lynn and yellow envelope telegrams that brought news of men missing in action, was a reflective and beautifully simple song. Applying colourful piano and mandolin, 'Long Time' offered a potted history of Hunter's musical path and life, including his early days in factories, Lynn's Café in Fifties Northampton, and meeting the "lunatic" Guy Stevens, who changed his musical course and showed him the way, as well as descriptions of Mott the Hoople, who made it, *"tripped the light fandango"*, ran out of steam and, one by one, *"fell off the edge of a dream"*.

IH: "Lynn's Café was around the corner from the ABC cinema in Northampton. It had a great jukebox, not as good as The Mitre's, but very good. 'Long Time' was another unchangeable line that arrived in the night. Three songs on *Fingers Crossed* started with words in my head as I woke up. A bit of a line will come and it's what you do with the 'bit' that counts. Songs are like houses – you've got to go into the kitchen, and the basement and the attic – you have to search every area. For 'Long Time' I sat at the piano one day and the hook just came out of my mouth. It was a straightforward, obvious chord sequence but sometimes simple is good. It's a bit reminiscent of *The Band*, an album that I loved."

Ian had recorded three extra songs at Hobo Sound: 'Racket' was not released but the "jazzy" 'Have a Nice Day' and 'Seein' Red' were added as bonus tracks to the Japanese edition of *Fingers Crossed*. 'Seein' Red' reflected on the American investigative reporter Gary Webb and his Nineties story concerning the Los Angeles cocaine trade. The episode was a bombshell at the time and, following an orchestrated campaign to discredit him, Gary lost his career, his family and then his life, when he was found dead in his apartment in 2004. In the hours before, he had enjoyed his favourite album and Spaghetti Western movie; when his body was discovered, *The Good, the Bad and the Ugly* was on the DVD machine – and Ian Hunter's *Welcome to the Club* nestled in the CD player.

> **IH:** "'Seein' Red' was good, but to me it didn't fit the mood of the album. The song was about Gary Webb, a Pulitzer Prize-winning journalist who was working on the West Coast and investigating the cocaine epidemic in LA. People were turning a blind eye so that the Nicaraguan contras could be funded but Gary was blanked by the media and his despair at their cowardice led directly to his death. He shot himself, then, many years later, the media owned up to how Gary was wronged. Apparently, he died listening to the live album that Mick Ronson and I recorded at The Roxy."

Press reviews reflected the breadth and excellence of *Fingers Crossed*, with four-star reviews awarded by *Q*, *Record Collector*, *Classic Rock*, *American Songwriter*, *The Sunday Express* and *Mojo*. *Q* wrote: "'Dandy' is as heartfelt as it's clear-eyed. It's not even the best thing here. Songs like 'Stranded in Reality' and the beautiful title track illustrate a talent for writing songs that are both stirring and melancholy. Hunter ends the LP on the aptly named 'You Can't Live in the Past' and his determination to address the future more than the present is admirable." *Classic Rock* praised Hunter's defiant "rocking and railing", according blockbuster status to the title track, while *Record Collector* noted that 'You Can't Live in the Past' beautifully summed up Ian's attitude and ethos.

American Songwriter considered that, track by track, hook by hook, growl by growl, Ian had never been better: "Ian Hunter's run of 21st Century records has been so consistently excellent that he doesn't have a contemporary in rock and roll even close in comparison. Starting with 2001's *Rant*, you'd have to look to literature's Philip Roth or film's John Huston to see such superb work coming from an artist in his seventies. Ian Hunter, 77, is now simply the finest practising songwriter from the classic rock era."

The Sunday Times included *Fingers Crossed* in their 'On Record: The Week's Essential New Releases' feature and *Soundchecks* noted: "Many rock stars grow old disgracefully, others never grow up or mature at all, and then there's a rare few that simply become immortal. Ian Hunter's follow-up to *When I'm President* offers ten tracks of excellent sounds with a timeless appeal from an enduring British luminary. Some old rockers don't die or fade away. The very best of them, like Ian Hunter, live forever."

Hunter issued *Fingers Crossed* in the week that Billy Joel played Wembley Stadium, London's *Evening Standard* noting: "The Piano Man hasn't released a collection of songs since 1993. Why bother when last year he pulled in almost 32 million dollars playing 30 concerts?" Drummer Nick Mason, meanwhile, was claiming on *Vintage TV* that Pink Floyd could sell concert tickets for £200 a throw, so why make the effort to record another new album that effectively becomes a giveaway? Stevie Nicks also suggested that there was no reason to spend a year and an amazing amount of money on a record that, even if it has great things on it, isn't going to sell. The industry was proving it had reached a new nadir. Rock may have sunk into something that many heritage bands neither liked nor recognised – and downloaded and streamed music might have left the Floyds and Fleetwoods seeking money from top-dollar touring instead – but Ian soared high, crafting stunning songs and playing wonderful gigs to an appreciative, knowing and dedicated following.

On 23rd September 2016, one week after its release, *Fingers Crossed* entered 'The Official UK Top Forty Albums Chart' at No.36 – Ian's highest charting solo record since *All-American Alien Boy* forty years before. The zenith of commercial recognition for Hunter may have been *Mott* and *You're Never Alone with a Schizophrenic* but, like *Rant* and *Shrunken Heads*, *Fingers Crossed* carried a stylishness and spirit that were justifiably rewarded. Ian had proved he remained a creative powerhouse who was still flourishing with flair, delivering some of his most meaningful and vital writing. Recording and gigging in his seventies, he was positive about his status and his life.

> **IH:** "There's two ways of approaching ageing: one way is to say, 'My God, I'm getting fat and stupid'; and the other way of looking at it is, 'I've been given this gift, why knock it on the head?' The only thing that keeps me happy is the constant creative process. Without that I'm an extremely miserable person. I enjoy writing. I have to do it. I can't see me recording Sinatra covers somehow and songs are still cropping up for me, so I'll probably stick to what I do best. It gave me life. It would seem chary to desert it now."

Individual reissues of Hunter's back catalogue had continued in recent times with *Ian Hunter* and *Live at Rockpalast* on vinyl, an *Original Album Classics* three CD box from Sony containing *Ian Hunter*, *All-American Alien Boy* and *Overnight Angels*, plus Japanese mini-LP CD editions of the same albums. However, after more than three years of work and planning, on 23rd October 2016 Proper Records issued the "gargantuan" *Stranded in Reality*, an unprecedented thirty-disc box set offering a swathe of rare tracks, previously unreleased recordings and film. Described as the ultimate assembly of Ian's influential and sparkling solo work, the collection contained a jackpot of over 400 tracks on twenty-eight CDs, including seventeen original albums on nineteen discs, nine CDs of hard-to-find recordings, intriguing unissued demos and live cuts, plus two DVDs of promotional, live, television and archive footage. The box was limited to 2,500 copies and included an eighty-eight-page book, signed *Alien Boy* lithograph and a twenty-page replica *Shades* music paper of historic 1975–2015 press features, dated 1st April 2016.

Fascinating titles were attributed to the nine 'new' albums, taken from Ian's personal notebook of song ideas and phrases – *Tilting the Mirror, If You Wait Long Enough for Anything, You Can Get It on Sale, Bag of Tricks, Acoustic Shadows, Experiments* and *It Never Happened.* The treasure trove also contained the expanded thirtieth anniversary editions of *Ian Hunter, All-American Alien Boy* and *You're Never Alone with a Schizophrenic,* plus special bonus track versions of *Overnight Angels, Welcome to the Club, Short Back n' Sides, All of the Good Ones Are Taken, The Artful Dodger, Shrunken Heads, When I'm President* and *Strings Attached,* the latter featuring two unreleased cuts, 'Your Way' and 'Dead Man Walkin' (EastEnders)'. All of the discs were presented in replica LP card sleeves, many with extra custom artwork. Proper Music also prefaced the box set with *Sampling in Reality,* a seven-track CD containing two unique tracks – a demo of 'American Music' and 'Sweet Jane' by Ian Hunter and Tribes.

> **IH:** "*Stranded in Reality* was a mind-boggling box set. I thought I'd only ever done twenty albums in my life, but they found twenty-eight CDs from somewhere. I wanted *Stranded* and *Fingers Crossed* out at the same time, because when you do an anthology it might sound like you're done, and I'm certainly not done. I agreed in 2012 that the box set could go ahead, but I viewed it with some suspicion at first. I wondered if it might sound like 'career over', but I went along with it because people took a lot of trouble over it. Proper spent a fortune licensing from various record companies, and Campbell Devine, Ian Crockett and Alan Price did piles of work assembling the set for over three years. It's nice that people would do that for me, because

going back is always a tad perplexing. I really appreciated their efforts as otherwise some of the unreleased stuff would have never seen the light of day. I've often said that the past doesn't interest me. I can only deal with what's in front of me, in any given circumstance at any given time. So, I came in halfway through the box set, but when I heard where *Stranded in Reality* was headed, I happily got involved. Going through the 'lost' material on Fostex and half-inch tapes was interesting. In the late Eighties and early Nineties, I was off the rails, messing about on my own and I did a lot of stuff then; it came in handy, eventually!

"Like Mick Ronson, over many years I've looked to the future, and still do. I don't know why that is. Once an album is done, I'm always on to the next one in my mind. I only look back when I have to, perhaps to prepare an old song for introduction to a live set. I guess it's like life – where there's hope there's life – so I seldom get involved in compilations. Sometimes they ask me, but sometimes I can't be bothered. Once they're gone, they're gone. I believe we reached the stage where there were over forty Mott the Hoople compilation albums and CDs by different labels, and we only recorded seven original studio albums and one official live LP. That's unreal!

"After decades of never looking back at my music, *Stranded in Reality* was different and a mammoth effort. I've had so many record labels over the years and every label I was ever on wanted paying per track, so it all adds up. The licensing was complex and created problems. It took a great deal of work so anybody who thought anybody was doing it for money is sorely mistaken. The compilation of the discs, the book and *Shades* music paper took up loads of time. I started to check what I had on various tapes and discs. My memory's not great so what was interesting to me was when we played it back and I had no knowledge of who was playing on it, or who wrote it, or who sang on it. It was just like listening to somebody else's records. Over the years, songs fell into gaps between albums. Some that I dropped were simple and not up to par; some were great but they just did not suit at the time; some were on old half-inch tapes from the late Eighties; some were tracks that nobody had ever heard, many of them home demos.

"I listened to 'If the Slipper Don't Fit', a backing track, for the first time since the *Alien Boy* sessions in 1976. It was great to hear Jaco again. There was talk of me writing a lyric and adding a vocal to 'Slipper' in 2015, as I did with 'One Fine Day' and 'Colwater High' in 2000, but it never happened because I was into my next studio album. I remember the original lyrical idea for the song though – *'If the slipper don't fit, then don't put it on.'* It's an interesting track that was too fast for *Alien Boy* at the time. 'Alibi' was a *Schizophrenic* jam and another stream of consciousness thing; I don't even remember recording or singing it!"

Stranded in Reality also included five live discs – *If You Wait Long Enough for Anything, You Can Get It on Sale*, a double set that included Hunter Ronson's stunning 1979 show from the Hammersmith Odeon – plus three individual volumes of live cuts, *Bag of Tricks*. These CDs brought together many songs that Ian seldom performed in concert, including 'Violence', 'Broadway', 'The Outsider', 'Theatre of the Absurd', 'Ill Wind', 'Purgatory', 'Good Samaritan' and 'Morons'.

IH: "The Hammersmith show with Ronson sounded better than *Welcome to the Club* when I heard it. Amongst the live stuff, we also found my version of Dylan's 'Is Your Love in Vain?' In retrospect this is overdone, but I liked it at the time. Mark Clarke, the bass player, was a great harmony singer and could arrange anything, but our version is maybe a bit too polished. 'Your Way' was a track that I wrote especially for the Oslo shows in 2002 but it wasn't included on the

Strings Attached album because Andy York and I weren't too keen on the performance at the time. A year or two later it sounded really good to us."

For many fans, the zenith of the *Stranded in Reality* box was *Experiments*, a disc of eighteen unreleased Hunter demos and outtakes recorded during the early Eighties onwards. Known but unissued tracks included 'You're Messin' with the King of Rock 'n' Roll', 'Money Can't Buy Love', 'More to Love', 'Look Before You Leap' and 'My Love (The Jar)'. Hunter also unearthed some songs that he'd forgotten about and that followers had never heard of.

IH: "There were several tracks that I gave for the box set where I had little recollection. In 2015, I could judge them as a punter rather than a writer. I could simply decide whether I liked the songs or not. My early Eighties writing had been eclectic because I was in the country, so we'd ended up back in Manhattan and I put my small 'studio' in an apartment bedroom. I'd read an interview with Phil Collins and it turned out I had the same studio set-up as him. I thought it would make me sound like Phil. It didn't. The difference was he knew how to use it. Everything I did using that studio sounded rubbish to me, mainly because I had no drums as we didn't have room in the apartment. I remember that Keith Reid, Procol Harum's lyricist, came by once and tried to write with me. I was told my songs were so good that it didn't matter about the home studio. Fatal. Being home demos, some of the songs sound mechanical now, but they're interesting.

"I found unissued songs on old half-inch tapes. There were tracks like 'Demolition Derby' – a demo that Trudi always liked – and 'Just Want It Real', a cute one with a great groove that I'd forgotten about completely. 'Coincidence' was a song about Keleel, a guy from New Orleans. He was our bus driver on a late Seventies Hunter Ronson tour, but he had an alarming fault: he had no sense of direction whatsoever. He was a great person, but fucking unbelievable. We'd drive and drive to a venue, and we'd say, 'It's not here!' – and he'd protest – 'I swear it was here before.' We'd driven eight hours when it was really only a two-hour journey – no GPS in those days. 'San Diego Freeway' was a fun track and 'Big Black Cadillac' was all me, playing everything. 'Nobody's Perfect' was the best love song to Trudi that I ever wrote. I'm not a very demonstrative person, so I guess I get the emotional side out in a few love songs.

"There were also two tracks from 'The Dodger' sessions, 'A Little Rock 'n' Roll' and 'Testosterone'. I've always had trouble with rockers. A line comes into your head sometimes and you write a song, and 'A Little Rock 'n' Roll' was one of them. It didn't make *The Artful Dodger* album, but it helped get me my *Rant* record deal – then I dropped it from *Rant*, much to the Papillon label's disappointment. 'Testosterone' was me and Bjørn Nessjø really going at it. I liked this track a lot, but it didn't fit *The Artful Dodger* record at the time. I'd done a demo of the song and then Bjørn did a great job on the version that missed *Dodger*, so it finally came out on *Stranded in Reality*.

"In 2013 I was asked if I would record a song with a young British band called Tribes, who were signed to Island Records and managed by Roy Eldridge's son. I was invited to sing Bob Dylan's 'The Man in Me' and went into a London West End studio but, on the day, Tribes asked me to do 'Sweet Jane' too. I did both and that was that. Our recording of 'The Man in Me' is a bit too Dylan-ish, but you can't do it any other way. People have foolishly asked me why I never did a Dylan covers album, but the trouble is, when I do a Bob song, I sound too much like Bob, so what's the point?"

The highpoint of *Experiments* was the mesmeric 'Salvation'. Ian had first played the song live in 1997 and remarked at that time:

"As you get older you worry a little bit more about those things that you did when you were young and foolish. Later, you start wondering where you're going when you leave here!" More recently, he expanded on the song's relevance.

> IH: "'Salvation' was one of the best things I've ever written. There are some songs that I ditch and there's a reason why I didn't record them. There were, however, a couple of exceptions, and one of them was 'Salvation'. I always vowed that I would save that as the last track for the very last record I ever put out, but I gave 'Salvation' as the last track for the last disc in the box set. It's hard to describe songs when you've spent weeks writing them, but this song is simply what it is. It's the wind-up. Everybody hopes they haven't been too naughty in the world. 'Salvation' is very important to me."

Stranded in Reality also included *It Never Happened*, a double DVD including the promo videos of 'Once Bitten Twice Shy', 'Irene Wilde', 'We Gotta Get Out of Here', 'All of the Good Ones Are Taken', 'American Music' and 'When I'm President' – plus rare live film of Hunter Ronson tearing through their acclaimed 1979 set in Toronto for a *New Music* TV special, along with the *Ian Hunter Rocks* and *Strings Attached* concerts. The box set also contained a signed photograph of Ian taken at the *All-American Alien Boy* sessions, used by the graphic artist Philip Hays as the basis for his painting on the reverse of the album sleeve.

> IH: "As they prepared the box set, they asked me to sign 2,500 lithographs of that photo. These turned up in boxes that weighed about half a ton, so I thought I would sign each one differently so that each person got a special one. After I'd signed 100 lithographs, I realised I was being an idiot, so I signed the other 2,400 and gave each a different mark. I thought the box set was great because it wasn't a

record company's stab at assembling something – it was a real fan putting something significant together – there's a big difference."

Classic Rock described *Stranded in Reality* as an astonishingly definitive archive-rummaging monolith and the most exhaustive career retrospective of any rock-related artist. *Record Collector's* five-star review, 'Hunter Gathered', considered the box set a spectacular package, *Experiments* the absolute jewel and the three-volume *Bag of Tricks* live CDs as endlessly fascinating discs.

Through September to November, Ian played almost thirty gigs in America, Britain and Scandinavia and his new songs translated to a live setting beautifully, especially 'Fingers Crossed'. Some of the juxtapositions in the set were smart too, with 'Honaloochie Boogie' prefacing 'Dandy' and Ian remarking between the tracks, "We wouldn't have done that song, unless we'd met this man" – plus a chilling rendition of 'Michael Picasso' prefaced by 'Ghosts'. The Rant Band kicked 'Cleveland Rocks' to a new level, 'The Truth, the Whole Truth, Nuthin' But the Truth' and 'American Spy' were sublime, and show-opener 'That's When the Trouble Starts' out-trumped the album cut with an extended intro allowing the group members to walk on stage in sequence – effectively a Roxy Music 'For Your Pleasure' set closer, in reverse!

At London's Shepherd's Bush Empire, Hunter was joined by guitarist Paul Cuddeford for 'All the Way from Memphis' and Graham Parker on 'All the Young Dudes'. The Rant Band shone throughout as astonishing, in-sync musicians, while Hunter just played it cool, with acoustic guitar centre stage, or poised at piano stage right, delivering a high-class set with real rock 'n' roll presence.

During Ian's British tour, Mick Ralphs suffered a stroke and was hospitalised in Oxfordshire, while Hunter was also aware that Pete Watts was in poor health and he referred to both "Motts" from the stage during his London performance. Ralphs had not been in a good space in early 2016 and was not feeling well, so he chose to miss Bad Company's swansong US tour, but played their British dates in October. Mick's health problems and stroke became public knowledge but, hidden from view, Pete was confined to a hospice in Hereford.

After his final European concert in Stockholm, during late November Ian returned to London and promoted *Stranded in Reality*, appearing on BBC's *The Art of Artists*, Vintage TV and Johnnie Walker's *Sounds of the Seventies*. In December *Classic Rock* published their Top Fifty albums of the year – 'The Best of 2016: The Year in Rock'. *Fingers Crossed* featured at No.23, ahead of Jeff Beck, Eric Clapton and The Pretenders, the publication noting: "Ian Hunter is 77. This is worth remarking on because musicians of this vintage aren't meant to be making music as remarkable as on Hunter's latest album. The centrepiece of *Fingers Crossed* is 'Dandy', a swaying boozy elegy to David Bowie that sounds like part two of 'All the Young Dudes'. Elsewhere the quality never really drops. And don't be wary. This album is fierce, cocky, defiant and very, very good."

Stranded in Reality was placed at No.9 in *Rolling Stone*'s 2016 'Reissue of the Year' chart, editor David Fricke describing Hunter as a working legend, a British Dylan who has steadily cut solo albums of visceral, probing rock since 1975 and a figure who is still touring harder than much younger men. 'Dandy' was also voted third 'Coolest Song in the World 2016' on Little Steven's *Underground Garage* US radio show.

Ian's live dates, new album and box set concluded an astonishingly buoyant year, but it was difficult to imagine explaining 2016 to an outsider – David Bowie, Dale Griffin, Glenn Frey, Keith Emerson, Prince, Sir George Martin, Leonard Cohen, Leon Russell, Greg Lake and George Michael all passed away, 'Brexit' began, and Donald Trump was elected US president.

On 22nd December 2016, renowned recording engineer Bill Price died from cancer, aged seventy-two. The unassuming studio maestro who possessed infinite technical knowledge and could handle even the most awkward characters was praised by producer Chris Thomas, the duo having worked on recordings by Roxy Music, The Clash and The Sex Pistols. Ian Hunter expressed sadness, saying: "Bill Price was one of the greatest engineers ever – he saved me a few times."

Dan Loggins, former CBS A&R man, paid tribute to a great music figure who had worked with Ian on *Mott*, *The Hoople*, *Mott the Hoople Live*, 'Foxy, Foxy', 'Saturday Gigs', *Ian Hunter*, 'England Rocks' and *Short Back n' Sides*. "I was very sad to learn of Bill Price's passing," said Dan. "He was so instrumental in making the *Mott* LP work on so many levels. He was really a brilliant sound man but with special people skills. Bill had the ability to communicate in tight pressure situations, dealing with artists and their egos, and record companies, producers, artist managers, 'deadlines' and 'budgets'. He was a gem of a man and we were lucky the fates allowed for our convergence at that moment in time. Bill was up there with the best of that generation, in an extraordinary era of British recording engineers."

Within Ian's circle, during 2016 Dale Griffin and Bill Price were gone, Mick Ralphs suffered a stroke and Richie Anderson and Pete Watts battled health problems. At seventy-seven years young, Hunter was one of music's greatest living inspirations.

Ian had crafted a British "Top Forty" LP in 2016 – his first in forty years – and, as one reviewer noted, the ongoing wonder of Hunter's career and the dedication of his fans had entered a new era. But, in December 2016, Ian recognised the great importance of his band and he was still looking forward.

> IH: "There was an upsurge for me in 2016, especially in Europe, so we'll go back there in 2017 on the back of *Fingers Crossed* and *Stranded in Reality*. Beyond that, I don't know. One thing at a time; well, two things at a time. In my career Guy Stevens, David Bowie and Mott the Hoople were pivotal, and now The Rant Band is pivotal. Music hit me when I was fifteen. I started out as a fan and then caught the

bug. I felt like I was running towards something: blind faith, I guess. It wasn't a popular choice, but I loved music then and I still love it."

Remarking that it was great to possess passion, Hunter's style and enthusiasm seemed endless. The pilgrim favoured progress.

CHAPTER SIXTEEN

Long Time

Rock 'n' roll is a young man's game – and I'm fifteen.

In 2016, *Stranded in Reality* afforded Ian Hunter a moment of rare reflection, but he retained absolute commitment to new material and the future.

> **IH:** "With *President* and *Fingers Crossed*, I was on the rise but I never expected to be. Playing live and recording are still fun. When your antenna is up, you're pretty fixated about writing and there isn't much room in your life for anything else. It's either that or sitting in the kitchen waiting for the inevitable. I have a great band and I enjoy their company, so I see no reason to stop. I'm not supposed to be doing it, so that's motivation in itself."

As Ian set about composing songs for another new album, it was announced that Pete Watts died on 22nd January 2017, having concealed his illness with throat cancer. Just over a year after Dale's passing, Ian noted on his website: "Oh dear. My extremely eccentric, lovely mate Peter Overend Watts has left the building – devastated." Verden Allen reflected that Pete was a funny, intelligent, talented and hugely charismatic person who was unique in all ways. Joe Elliott paid homage to Watts on his *Planet Rock* radio show and John Fiddler released a tribute song, 'Thunderbird'. Morgan Fisher said he was numb at the loss of his "dear, darling, crazy friend", noting that Pete's still devastatingly witty humour during his last days blew him away.

> **IH:** "The minute Pete died, I missed him badly. Watts and I got on like a house on fire in Mott the Hoople – then the house burnt down. I never realised how much he played a part in the oddness of Mott. I remember he invited Trudi and I round one evening for dinner. Pete produced this monster silver platter full of Indian food, proceeded to plonk a small dollop on each of our plates and then immediately demolished the rest himself. He could be madly intelligent and I just liked listening to him. He never stopped and I'd often be aching with laughter. I went to Pete's 'shop full of stuff' in Hereford once. There was a record section there and under one of the dividers – 'Horrible Blokes with Glasses' – I found an LP with a £5,000 sticker on it. The album was my 1981 record, *Short Back n' Sides*."

Peter Overend Watts was cremated on 12th February 2017 in Herefordshire with a thanksgiving service held immediately afterwards at All Saints Church in Brockhampton attended by Verden Allen, Stan Tippins, Martin Chambers, Kingsley Ward, Mick Hince, Jim Ralphs and Dicken and Pete Crowther from Mr Big. Watts' flamboyant nature was reflected in the music played, including Ralph Vaughan Williams, White Buffalo and Eels, while, under orders, Pete's hospice nurse brought a box of his walking book to sell copies. The solo album that Pete had threatened for years was released retrospectively in 2017 and, as eccentric as ever, Overend Watts' *He's Real Gone* featured 'Caribbean Hate Song', 'Belle of the Boot' and 'Prawn Fire on Uncle Sheep Funnel'.

With the passing of Griffin and Watts, and Ralphs' illness, Verden Allen considered in February 2017 that Mott the Hoople was "finished for good". Award-winning American journalist Ben Edmonds, who wrote beautifully about Mott's Broadway glory in 1974, had died from pancreatic cancer in March 2016 but not before he eulogised the band, reflecting that Ian gave brutally insightful commentaries on the rock madness that the group had found themselves in: "The music of Mott the Hoople, unclassifiable and always a little out of step with its time, has become timeless, an inspiration to each succeeding generation of rock 'n' roll outsiders."

> **IH:** "There was a lot of aggravation in Mott the Hoople but I'm proud of what we did. It was good that Buff got up to play a bit at Hammersmith in 2009 and I had great conversations with him at the reunion. I found him eloquent and a tad less angry than he was in the old days, and we buried the hatchet, so to speak. Tracie was present at one of our chats. We felt so bad for him; he was philosophical about his illness and any friction between us quickly melted. Buff and Pete – gone but not forgotten."

Hunter played two "pop-up" gigs at short notice in February at The Winery in New York City, delivering 'Ballad of Mott the Hoople' in his set, but soon there was further sadness. Stalwart rocker and cool country gent Richie Anderson had been fighting myeloma but his cancer spread. After failed treatments, Richie was given a new drug that had been successful in similar cases, but he passed away on 7th March 2017 at Dunedin Hospital in Reading, aged sixty-nine. Richie's funeral at Woolhampton on 24th March was attended by Stan Tippins, Mick 'Booster' Hince, Chris 'Crystal' Taylor from Queen's crew and Phil John, who delivered a wonderful eulogy praising the dependable, engaging and loyal figure that was Richard Anderson. Ian and Trudi issued a touching tribute to their friend: "RIP Richie Anderson, Mott the Hoople's original one and only road tech (back in the day they were called roadies). At the beginning, all we had was Richie; he kept turning help down, until, eventually, Phil John appeared and Richie grudgingly relented. Richie was a rock; up with the best; nobody better."

On 22nd April, Britain's tenth Record Store Day, 'Dandy' was released by Proper Records as an exclusive gold vinyl single. Limited to 1,000 copies, the hand-numbered disc featured the non-album track 'Seein' Red' as the B-side and was presented in a red and gold picture sleeve.

In the same month Sky Arts broadcast a sixty-minute documentary *Passions: Gary Kemp on Mick Ronson*. Concentrating on David Bowie's early Seventies albums with contributions from Mike Garson, Lulu, Roger Taylor and Bernard Butler, the film referenced Hunter Ronson briefly but made no major mention of Mick's solo achievements or collaborations. Then, in May, the Jon Brewer-produced movie that Suzi Ronson had started some years before was premiered in London. *Beside Bowie: The Mick Ronson Story* was a 100-minute production featuring recent voice-over sections recorded by David. Also lacking details of Ronson's solo work and weighted towards Bowie, the guitarist's eclectic and stunning history seemed smothered under commercial considerations. The essence of the film was that the humble boy from Hull provided the vital sonic muscle behind Bowie's songs and that Ziggy Stardust might not have arrived the way he did without Ronson and the Spiders, but as *Classic Rock* noted, it didn't really tell *the* Ronson story.

Mick's home town of Hull was nominated as the UK's City of Culture in 2017. The lacklustre Mick Ronson Memorial Stage and Café in Queen's Gardens were now vandalised, with the low-slung, grubby concrete and brick plinth standing as an unused tribute that was modest and unassuming, just like the man that it was meant to commemorate. The adjoining eatery was refurbished as the Ronson Rock Café and an eight-foot guitar sculpture designed by Hull college student Janis Skodins was unveiled by Maggi Ronson in a celebration garden in East Park, where Mick once worked.

Hunter played further concerts in 2017, including two "Seventy-eighth Birthday" shows in New York, the Sweden Rock festival and fourteen UK gigs. The latest live set, prefaced with more Mastro-inspired walk-on music – 'Prayer' from Huun-Huur-Tu's *The Orphan's Lament* – now contained 'Morpheus', '(Give Me Back My) Wings', 'Fatally Flawed' and a beautiful rendition of the underrated 'Guiding Light'. Proper Records released 'Ghosts' as a digital single on 9th June and Ian remarked that he wanted to tour widely in 2017 as the band retained absolute faith in their latest album.

> **IH:** "We believed in *Fingers Crossed* and wanted as many people as possible to hear it, so we kept playing. It's a special album to me. I could go out on my own or as a trio, but I like a band and The Rant Band is fantastic. Bosch plays lead and James is the colourist – the painter – so there's no room for another electric guitar. It would cloud things up. I think me on acoustic adds a little class to the sound. Mott the Hoople had only one guitarist, so I played electric. With The Rant Band it's different. The audiences are wonderful to me too and it's great to see young people at my gigs, at my age."

Hunter's concerts continued to be an increasingly refreshing experience. As "big guns" like U2 turned backwards in 2017 and exhumed *The Joshua Tree* album for a thirtieth anniversary £200-a-ticket tour, Ian parked populist tendencies and still elected to grandstand new fare in his live sets with admirable determination and doggedness. The Rant Band also deserved praise aplenty having developed an intuitive interplay, song-sensitive discipline and attention to detail. Reviewers of Ian's concerts noted the power of the hugely impressive Rant Band and that Hunter possessed energy, enthusiasm and the voice of a man half his age.

The rock scene had become a faded canvas of predictable milestones including "Best Of" collections, "Greatest Hits" tours and Christmas albums. For Ian, there were no cranky rock star moods and no bemoaning the state of rock 'n' roll. Hunter wasn't grumbling that music wasn't like the good old days; he was getting on with it, offering energetic and emotional songs with clever lyrics

470

centred on politics, people, events and history. Ian was reflecting his years, while one US journo wrote of The Killers' 2017 comeback: "If Brandon Flowers and his band started acting their age, The Killers could capture that magic that they seem to have decided has escaped them."

From September to October Hunter played further European and American concerts, Johnny Depp joining in on guitar at San Juan Capistrano and San Francisco's Fillmore West for five songs, which exceeded even Joe Elliott's enthusiasm. After warmly received gigs in Germany and Spain, Ian returned to America with more new songs evolving, but he also had a private wish to reignite Mott the Hoople for Morgan Fisher and Luther Grosvenor, who had missed out on the band's recent reunions. True to his word, in February 2018 it was confirmed that Mott would play at three summer festivals in Spain, England and Sweden.

Anchored by The Rant Band and starring Bender and Fisher alongside Hunter, Mott the Hoople's 2018 set reflected *The Hoople* and *Mott the Hoople Live* albums from their commercial zenith, with the band delivering the bizarre and angular 'Marionette', 'Rest in Peace', 'Rose' and the classic "Deadly Medley" that had sparkled on their 1973 tour. Hunter's Hoople had successfully re-heated the soufflé, something that Paul McCartney had said was impossible for The Beatles. Watts would probably have bristled that Mott was now Anglo-American, but Ian was eager that Morgan and Luther were acknowledged after their exclusion by some of the original Motts in 2009 and 2013. Fisher and Grosvenor had understood the reasoning behind earlier events and hadn't complained, Morgan attending all five nights at Hammersmith Odeon under his own steam. Mott the Hoople 2018 shone like a diamond, The Rant Band personnel giving "The Great Lord Ariel Bender" and "The Sartorial Morgan" much respect, while Grosvenor and Fisher retained absolute admiration for Hunter.

Luther Grosvenor: "When Ian called me to propose the 2018 Mott reunion, he explained that it had to be him, me and Morgan this time and that he felt bad we weren't involved in the 2013 gigs.

He said we'd played on *The Hoople* and *Mott the Hoople Live* and had been part of the band's most commercially successful period. I was worried by the prospect of so many Rant Band guitars on stage, but Ian said they were great people and wouldn't get in the way of the music – and he was right. It could have gone any way, but it was fantastic, and the camaraderie was amazing. It was a laugh a minute, we just got better and better over the three gigs, and by the end we were over the moon, because we *did it*! On 'Walkin' with a Mountain', the power of 1973 Mott came back. Ian was a ray of light and I think the 2018 comeback was the best. At the end of the day, Hunter is just extraordinary – for his talent, his age and rock 'n' roll look – Ian is amazing."

Morgan Fisher: "Bender and I understood why we were not included on the earlier reunion gigs, and there was no rancour once we heard of the complications. Ian is a decent bloke and made it up to us. There were only three gigs in 2018 and the idea of a warm-up show disappeared, or rather became a gig in Spain, in front of 30,000 people! Mott were the highest-energy live shows I ever did, but my hands had retained what I call muscle memory, and our rehearsals were a dream. Sadly, Pete and Buff, the best rhythm section I ever played with in my life, were missing, but Holley and Page are fantastic, and the power and passion were there. On the last day of rehearsals in Birmingham, we did the whole set quickly one morning and, at a lunch break, I asked Ian if we should run through it again. He said, 'Nah, I like it loose' – and those four words summed up Mott the Hoople perfectly."

> **IH: "The second part of the band never got a shot to play on the two previous reunions and I always felt it was a shame, as they kept Mott up for a year – so, Luther and Morgan eventually got their moment in the sun."**

Classic Rock reviewed Mott's 'Ramblin' Man' headlining performance and described 'Sweet Jane', 'Honaloochie Boogie' and the epic encore of 'Saturday Gigs' as monumental moments, adding: "Mott the Hoople are simply brilliant. Their energy, passion and obvious skills are a joy to behold – a band at the top of their game." More Hoople gigs were soon being planned, then, in November 2018, Universal Music, owners of Mott's Island Records back catalogue, released *Mental Train: The Island Years 1969–71*. Amid rare cuts that had surfaced previously, unheard studio outtakes included a vocal rehearsal of 'I'm a River', the instrumental backing track for 'Where Do You All Come From', unreleased rough diamonds and sprawling studio try-outs – the full eleven-minute version of 'You Really Got Me' and the sixteen-minute take of 'Can You Sing the Song That I Sing' – and alternative song versions, such as 'Blue Broken Tears' ('Waterlow').

Granting another *Classic Rock* 10/10 review, Emmy award-winning journalist David Quantick wrote of *Mental Train*: "Mott the Hoople were an extraordinary chaos of a group who became rock 'n' roll chart stars, and the rope that held them together was Ian Hunter. As a lead singer and solo artist, Ian's brilliance lies in his ability to connect heart and brain, and to see that rock is both ridiculous and incredibly important. From 'Waterlow' to 'Saturday Gigs', from 'When I'm President' to '23a Swan Hill', Ian Hunter's songs and records have been consistently great. He's one of the few artists who's as good now as he was forty years ago and in the first quarter of the 21st century, I still look forward to his next album."

On 29th March 2019, Roxy Music and Def Leppard were inducted into the Rock and Roll Hall of Fame at a ceremony in Brooklyn, New York. Even though Hunter Ronson had played the first fundraiser for the institution's museum in November 1989, shamefully there was still no place for Mott the Hoople or Ian. Magnanimously, Hunter agreed to play with Leppard and appear for the evening's closing showpiece, Elliott enthusing: "What a night – but to end with a version of 'All the Young Dudes' featuring Ian Hunter, Brian May, Stevie Van Zandt, Susanna Hoffs, Phil Manzanera, Rod Argent and Colin Blunstone – how mad and brilliant is that?"

In April Mott the Hoople played fifteen US and UK concerts, including a sold-out Beacon Theatre show in New York and two nights in London. American fans were excused for thinking the Milwaukee gig was an April Fool's joke as the band delivered their first gigs in the States for forty-five years. Mastro on sax was acclaimed, while Grosvenor and Fisher were credited with adding "punked-out, Marx Brothers-esque fun", Mott capturing all the mayhem, exhilaration and energy that the band had been famed for. At their London shows, on-stage participants included Brian May, Joe Elliott, Stan Tippins and the brilliant violinist Graham Preskett on 'Violence', while Bobby Gillespie of Primal Scream and Mick Jones of The Clash watched on in admiration from the balcony.

Graham Preskett: "I often worked at George Martin's AIR Studios and that's how I came to be part of the Hoople story. When we recorded 'Violence' there, Mott made me feel completely at home, offering me, I think, red wine and salad. It was very easy to come up with stuff and they knew what they liked when they heard it. After a bit of semi-Grappelli nonsense, I started to wail along with the violin and was really pleased, as were Ian and the band. I later went back to do a mock-sad brass band meets Wagner arrangement for 'Through the Looking Glass', of which I am also very proud. They were lovely people to work with and I am delighted to have been described by Mott as 'dishevelled'. The 2019 concerts with Ian and Mott the Hoople were an utter pleasure. Who would have thought that I would see them after so many years, and that it would be so much fun and the band so honest! Ian Hunter is the governor."

Bobby Gillespie: "Mott and Ian mean a lot to me. The ecstatic spirit of rock 'n' roll burns through every song they ever recorded – rocker or ballad. Countless times over the years, I lay there alone in the dark listening to 'Trudi's Song', feeling safe and warm in its womb-like spell – killing the sadness – a true soul-saver of a song. That classic run of Mott singles, on the radio all the time when I was a kid, still hits me deep and hard today. 'Roll Away the Stone' is my favourite; you carry that stuff with you. Mott the Hoople are an important band for us in Primal Scream – their story is mythic and legendary, and Ian Hunter is still an inspiration – a true rock 'n' roll romantic, a great songwriter and one of my favourite ever singers."

From 31st May to 3rd June, Ian Hunter and The Rant Band played four sold-out shows at the City Winery in New York to celebrate the singer's eightieth birthday. Delivering two Mott the Hoople-centred concerts and two solo sets, Ian continued to "own the stage", playing some fifty different songs across successive nights, including live airings of 'Too Much' and 'Restless Youth'. Lacking space across four lengthy sets for so many 'classics', suddenly observers appreciated the deep and spectacularly rich CV of a rock legend whose eclectic and peerless compositions still sparkled like polished jewels, having grown even greater through the years.

Fans were also reminded that where others had struggled in recent times, Ian retained an ability and sensibility to create diverse and mature excursions across entire albums – and the journey has not reached an end. In 2019, Madfish Music released two double vinyl gatefold sets – *Mott the Hoople Live at Hammersmith 1973* and *The Golden Age of Rock 'n' Roll* – the twenty tracks on the latter collection reminding us of Mott's heady essence: the balladry, power, craft, invention and realism, as well as the sheer joy of the songs and the band's exciting "flash rock" image. Looking forward, there is also much anticipation surrounding Hunter's remarkable voyage as he prepares to record another solo album; scheduled for 2020 release and tentatively titled *Overview*, the track list is set to include 'The Third Rail', 'One Trick Pony', 'People' and 'When the Dust Dies Down.'

In early August 2019, former Mott singer Nigel Benjamin and keyboard player Ian Gibbons passed away. Benjamin died at his home near Los Angeles, Morgan Fisher remarking: "Nigel could be particularly good on ballad-style songs. 'Career (No Such Thing as Rock 'n' Roll)' – my music, his lyrics – on *Shouting and Pointing* turned out spectacularly well. Joe Elliott agreed and recorded it later with the Down 'n' Outz. That was a very fine cover version, but I have to say Nigel really nailed his vocal. It was the peak of our work together in Mott. We succeeded in creating some powerful songs."

Joe Elliott: "Nigel Benjamin and Mott filled a void when I was a young, aspiring rocker and at the right age to be open-minded. I remember with great affection when I saw Nigel in Mott and with his next band, English Assassin. He was a big influence on me as a kid and when Def Leppard first started working with Mutt Lange and we were looking for a higher register for me to sing in, I would play him some of the stuff by Nigel and Mott. I still love the *Drive On* and *Shouting and Pointing* albums to death – always will."

> **IH: "I didn't know Nigel but his and Gibbo's passing was very sad. Ian Gibbons was not only a great musician and a lovely person, but great fun on the road. I'll never forget him and Paul Cuddeford doing their 'ventriloquist act' – after hours."**

It is amazing to witness Mott the Hoople five decades after their conception and to watch Hunter's continued creativity amongst a cache of classy guitarists that has included Ralphs, Ronson, York, Mastro and Bosch. But other associates of Hunter continue to admire his recordings and performances and, recently, several have had their say.

Stan Tippins: "Ian continues to amaze me with his songwriting and stage shows. He approaches everything with the hunger, keenness and freshness of someone just starting out in the business. While most songwriters from his generation, and much younger generations, have dried up and are 'finished', Ian continues to come up with absolute classics like *When I'm President*. Hunter has mellowed over the years and is a much better person for it."

Mick Ralphs: "I first met Ian in 1969, when Guy Stevens said, 'This is the guy you need!' I have a lot of love and respect for Ian as a great frontman, singer and fabulous songwriter. His lyrics are brilliant, and he always gets the point across in a way that is unique. Not only that; he is a wonderful human being."

Verden Allen: "When Ian Patterson auditioned for Silence in May 1969, he sat behind a piano at Regent Sound to play 'Like a Rolling Stone'. I was to join in on organ and I said to him before we started, 'If I drop any notes, don't worry, just carry on.' I wanted to help put him at ease, and Ian smiled. I remember the early days of Mott with affection. Ian Hunter is a fantastic songwriter. 'Original Mixed-Up Kid' was always a great song and so was 'Half Moon Bay' on our first album. I liked 'Once Bitten Twice Shy' a lot too – a fabulous single."

Richie Anderson: "Mott the Hoople 7th February 1970 – Chelsea College. Who's the red-haired maniac in the big shades beating an electric piano to death? Surely not the man I last saw as a calm bass player in the ill-fated New Yardbirds. And who's the man who could so easily have peaked around 1973 but forty years later, and still defying gravity, comes up with masterpieces like 'Ta Shunka Witco'? Ian Hunter! What a career. What an inspiration."

Richard Weaver: "I knew the rest of Mott the Hoople before Ian joined, but over the years I got to know him well and he became a good friend. I remember one time, when my life was at a particularly low ebb, he called in the middle of the night, just after returning from a tour. I asked why he was calling and he said he thought I might like to hear from a mate – a good mate, indeed. I have never forgotten that. It was indicative of his sensitivity, his amazing radar and, mostly, it says a great deal about the man. It was a privilege to witness Hunter's progress over time as he found his voice, both as a singer and as a writer of great songs – songs with a storyteller's magic – a cut above the usual pop and rock fare. His *Diary* was an amazing insight into the business from the inside. He's a great wordsmith and lyricist – a true artist."

Steve Holley: "It has been a pleasure and a privilege to spend so many years on and off stage with Ian Hunter. He has been a constant source of inspiration. Lyrically and musically, he is among the best in the world and I consider myself fortunate to have been a part of Ian's band for so long. I love the man."

Howard Helm: "My experiences with the Hunter Ronson Band were tremendous – on and off stage. I had always known of Ian and his amazing body of work since the earliest days of Mott the Hoople, but, until I worked daily with him, I hadn't realised the depth of his writing. He is truly an amazing songwriter. Ian's ability to take his experiences and turn them into a song lyric is very profound."

Bjørn Nessjø: "I'm impressed with Ian's stamina – his everyday chase for the 'perfect song' – the perfect match of exquisite lyric and melody. He is one of few remaining songwriters still focusing on quality over quantity and popularity: in other words, a rare breed in today's industry. I would like to hear him on an album – stripped down, bare-naked, with his voice in a low register as the focal point – taking advantage of a fully lived life, doing songs that will have the same profound impact on the very same people who related so closely to 'Irene Wilde' some forty years later."

Mick Brown: "Ian Hunter is the world's greatest ever songwriter. To steal Steve Earle's quote about Townes Van Zandt, 'And I'll stand on Bob Dylan's coffee table in my cowboy boots and tell him so.' Ian has always argued the case for Bob Dylan, but Dylan doesn't connect to my soul in the way that Hunter does. I've never seen a 'Pill Box Leopard Skin Hat', but I have experienced the sentiments expressed in 'Irene Wilde', a song that would be top three in my *Desert Island Discs*. Ian Hunter has a gift for heartfelt live performances and is one of the greatest set constructors that there is. Any of the musicians or crew who work for Ian will tell you the same thing; we all work with other artists, but there is something special about Hunter. No reflection would be complete without acknowledging his wife, Trudi. A true enabler: without her, I doubt Ian would be achieving the heights and setting the benchmarks that he is. She deals with all the 'crap' on a day-to-day basis and allows him to concentrate on his art. I love them both and am very humbled to be a small cog in the machine."

As Ian's music continues to thrive, so does *Diary of a Rock 'n' Roll Star*, a heart-warming echo from an era when the world really was round. In September 2018, Omnibus Press issued an updated version of Hunter's book: a glimpse behind the curtain from a moment in time that is more out of step than ever, and a tale that is all the more interesting for it. The new edition contained a foreword by actor Johnny Depp, who wrote of the diary, "It will sear your brain with a most staggering residue and may even have a profound effect on your life." Ian also contributed an epilogue which included the 2015 Japanese 'Diary of a Rock 'n' Roll Star: Part Two' feature, penned for *Mojo*. Hunter generously and humorously summed up The Rant Band at that time.

> **IH:** "Basically, we're all in James Mastro's band. He's a great organiser and takes care of the As to Bs. Steve Holley plays behind, and that suits me good – better than ever these days. Mark Bosch is the guitar player and a fine one at that; he can surprise and be exciting. Paul Page said he waited seventeen years to get this gig, poor devil! I'm a Paul fan – solid as a rock. Dennis DiBrizzi? What a strange kettle of fish this guy is: hilarious impressions of everybody and zero tolerance for anybody. Knows how to rock on a keyboard. Apparently, when James talked to him about working for me, Dennis said, 'Does he know what I'm like?' I do now – great fit! It's a nice balance, very responsible people."

The diary reissue was another milestone as Hunter hit fifty years in a music career, filled with eclectic experiences and encounters, and inevitable ups and downs. Mott the Hoople had been the launch pad, but Ian admits that when he looks back at the band, he doesn't feel much as he has always been a progressive figure.

> **IH:** "Mott the Hoople was genuine: a rock 'n' roll band that encompassed everything. Mott was great with Mick Ralphs, because he was a very tasty guitar player at a time when there weren't too many tasty guitar players around. Ralpher loved West Coast bands, but I was Jerry Lee Lewis and Little Richard forever: blood and thunder. I admire the blues and

I love gospel, but it's always been rock 'n' roll for me. That's what I grew up on, that's what I love to this day and that's what Mott was: a combination of assets, slamming into each other. I don't think as a band it was that great musically; it just seemed to have a lot of things going for it. The sound came because we really didn't know that much. Eventually we all got pretty tight in the original band, but there was always that invisible 'Hereford Ring' and I became 'the front-man' apparently, which didn't really help. We had great times though. The humour was intelligent but insane; when one stopped, another started, and it wasn't dumb humour. I was slightly older than the others, so when I wrote lyrics, I had a lot to say. I was a lucky guy too. They gave me the shot.

"As a solo artist, Mott was always annoying for me, but I loved them and to see them in recent years on a short-term basis was fine. I tend to recall the bad things about Mott the Hoople, but I do remember fondly the morning when they first rang me up and said, 'You've got the gig.' All my life I had dreamed about that. I think the first album was the best time because there was no stupidity at the start; there was just the joy of having a deal with Island Records and a label that was interested in us. CBS and 'All the Young Dudes' was fabulous for a while; we gave David's great song vital new blood and even after Mick and Verden left I was still gung-ho, although the chemistry worked best with the original line-up. Mott on Broadway was interesting, Heller was happening, and all the while we stayed genuine because I knew what I was talking about. Sadly, another good time was when I left the band.

"The end of Mott the Hoople was a slow burn following Ralphs' departure. After Ronson joined it went downhill fast and to my mind it was absolutely stupid. Together we could have risen above anything, but it went the other way. The band had become tedious, but I felt great when I left and I have never regretted leaving. Mott was school for us all; we

480

learned, we had fun learning and we got back together a couple of times. We were desperate and we wanted to make it. Every bit of Mott was scary, great, annoying, hilarious, triumphant and despondent – everything a band should be. The album covers were probably the only thing we never argued about!

"Mott was a very passionate band but they meant it and people relate to that. Sadly, it always seemed we were dogged by one thing or another. Roxy Music had EG Management and Bowie had Defries, while we flopped around like also-rans. It was a crazy band with no real leader actually, because they all thought they were stars in their own way. Mott the Hoople took a lot out of me and by 1974 my patience had evaporated; enough was enough. Throughout Mott I considered myself a songwriter and was totally into what I did, and, when I left, I was writing just the same as I always wrote. In a way, Ian Hunter was Mott the Hoople – in a way. But that was a fucking great band and they were all there 100 per cent at the point when we were great. We were a vaguely mysterious type of group, who disappeared at the right time."

Hunter had found the fame he craved via Mott the Hoople, but as journalist Charles Shaar Murray once observed of Ian, "I don't know anyone in rock who has as clear an understanding of just how much bullshit the star trip is, while simultaneously retaining such an obsessive love of its glamour." Having courted fame, however, Hunter would retreat from it.

IH: "Sadly, by the end of Mott, I discovered that the whole rock business is a bit disenchanting. You want something all your life and then you're doing 20,000-seaters, but, suddenly, fame seems boring. You struggled to get there and it's not what it seemed. I found that with fame there's absolutely nothing there. The ride was fun, but rock 'n' roll represented freedom at the outset, then when it happened it was great at first until I found that the freedom had disappeared. The 'superstar' bit used to make me laugh, but there is a really sad side to it. I've had a few friends who were superstars, but they got into a terrible mess. To me, going off the rails didn't make any sense. I didn't socialise much and play the game, and I didn't get invited to certain parties, but that's okay. I'm just a perfectly normal person who just happened to get into rock 'n' roll. This business can take too much out of you, and I'm not prepared to give that much and I won't surrender my privacy. I was famous for a fortnight and that was long enough for me.

"I'd never thought of music in terms of a career. I'd thought of it in terms of a life. I always felt that I'd hate to look back and have had no freedom, because that's the very thing that you joined bands for. The couple of years that I was really big with Mott the Hoople, I didn't enjoy it. Money doesn't mean anything and neither does being known. I always wanted to be famous but, when I was, I loved it for a fortnight and then it became a pain in the arse – girls outside the door morning, noon and night; you have to have a bath before you go and get the paper in the morning. Ronson had it bad because he looked like God. I prefer to come and go as I please.

"I have also preferred life as a solo artist because you live and die on your own. If I like what I do and it sells, that's fine, as it's my problem; in a band, everybody's blaming everybody else. My solo years have been great and thankfully my wife and my kids kept me grounded. I first met Trudi in England through Richard Weaver, who ended up doing some of Mott's promo videos, then I met her again in the USA on a Mott tour. She said she'd never marry a musician. I told her, 'I'm not a musician.' The last long-term job that Trudi had was as assistant to the principal of the United Nations School in New York, then we moved out of the city and she's had my back covered for years and is the bridge between me and the other side of a business that I cannot stand. She does what she does, and I do what I do. Trudi also keeps me healthy and I can honestly say that I don't think I'd be here without her. Nearly fifty years of rock 'n' roll marriage is a rarity and I don't know how Trudi has managed to do it because it's not easy when you're writing. It is daily frustration and failure, and you can get into some miserable moods between albums. It's not what it seems.

"I'm proud of my three kids and they're all great to me. Jess dabbled in music and had bands called American Degenerate and Audio Cartel with Tyson Schenker. Jess and Tyson worked well together; they're both intelligent kids. Tracie chose music for a while, had some great songs like 'Religion' and released a few albums, but I didn't want either of them to be in the business. It's not the nicest profession in the world and it is pretty dehumanising; in fact, it's a miserable business and the exact opposite of what most people think. If you get lucky enough to happen, the pressure is tremendous and it's coming from all angles and all levels. I told my kids I didn't want this to happen to them, but as long as they were happy that was fine for me, because life is doing what you want to do. I think I probably influenced Tracie in the beginning, and I taught Jess all I knew on guitar, which only took one afternoon. My eldest, Steve, is just as talented, but in another way. All three of my kids are great. I'm lucky."

Referenced as an inspiration by Queen, The Clash and Mötley Crüe, some sources termed Mott the Hoople the antecedents of punk and the "barons of Britpop", Blur's 'Charmless Man' single being evidence, with its Hunter-style vocal, Hoople piano and Ronsonesque guitar. Name-checks have abounded for Ian from the likes of John Taylor of Duran Duran, The Cult's Billy Duffy, Jim Kerr of Simple Minds and actor Johnny Depp, who all adored *Diary of a*

Rock 'n' Roll Star. Gene Simmons of Kiss, Mountain's Corky Laing, Mickey Bradley from The Undertones, The Georgia Satellites' Dan Baird, Ricky Warwick of Thin Lizzy and Robin Zander from the colossal Cheap Trick are further Hunter admirers. As vocalist Colin Blunstone once opined, you can best judge a great artist by the views and opinions of his peer group.

Gene Simmons: "Ian Hunter... even his name reeks of rock royalty. The swagger! The shades! The balls to push aside Ariel Bender when the guitarist dared get too close to Hunter singing mid-song! Ian could sing, but he never let melody get in the way of emphasising a lyric, by simply talking the words or spitting them out. Hunter has something in his vocal delivery few singers have. It's called gravitas. Weight! So, to all you aspiring rock groups, put aside the latest crop of emo bands. You will learn nothing from them. Put your headphones on and listen to 'All the Way from Memphis'... and learn from a master."

Corky Laing: "I first met Ian on a Texas tour in the early Seventies. Then we got together and collaborated in the mid-Seventies. Then Ian was touring in his late seventies. Go figure! I look up to Ian because he's older, he's taller and he's got great fuckin' hair. He's also a consistently brilliant artist, performer, writer – and a good mate."

Mickey Bradley: "When great singles weren't that common on Seventies TV shows, Mott the Hoople on *Top of the Pops* gave us hope. From the first *'Allo'* on 'Once Bitten Twice Shy', to the Liverpool docks and The Hollywood Bowl, Ian Hunter is the only shades-wearing rock star that we need – and he wrote the manual!"

Dan Baird: "There are those rock 'n' roll artists that we all know that have stayed true to their guiding star, but there is a place where it is vital to stay true to yourself, in spite of not achieving mass notoriety. It's a place just short of Mount Olympus, but a steady human greatness can be found there – a place that's not for the faint of heart. You have to work to not lose your foothold – a place where most will give in and agree to something idiotic, crash

484

and burn, or just flat give up the dream. Not Mr Hunter. You can look at a true career in his body of work – something to be truly proud of shaping – and he wants you to think his latest release is the best thing he's ever done. That is living it."

Ricky Warwick: "Ian Hunter has a way with words that speaks a universal magic. When he sings, he connects on every level. Always musically diverse and driven by pure intent, Ian is a poet, a rebel and a true rock 'n' roller – always has been and always will be."

Robin Zander: "My Mott the Hoople era was in the early Seventies when I was staying in Edinburgh, Scotland. Mott were so cool; no one could resist that glam 8th note piano and Mick Ralphs' guitar, songs that reflected a generation's angst. Mott the Hoople belongs in the 'Rock and Roll Hall of Fame' if any band does – and Ian Hunter's presence in rock 'n' roll is everlasting!"

> **IH:** "I've heard many people say that Mott the Hoople was influential and that puzzles me. I don't think we were the prettiest flowers in the garden, but it turned out we were perennials. It was the sum of the five people in Mott that counted. We weren't that good a band musically and that was fine because rock 'n' roll is best when it's halfway there; all the way there is twee. Mott were rambunctious and there's something nice about that. The influence we're supposed to have had was quite by fluke because we never seemed to be in our own time; we were either a bit behind or a bit ahead. People like Slade and Def Leppard say they admired Mott the Hoople and Ian Hunter; several joined us on stage, like Joe Elliott, Brian May, Axl Rose and Slash, and I met some great artists. I remember sitting backstage with Bryan Adams after a gig. He told me that night that he once lived with his grandma, in Shrewsbury. When I mentioned my early days in the town, Bryan said, 'Oh yeah, I lived there too.' I was gobsmacked – I thought he was a Canadian. His father was posted as a military diplomat round the world and had been at Sandhurst – my dad did a course at Sandhurst too.

We chatted about getting together and him producing me – this was in the late Eighties, because Trudi and I were still living in the New York apartment – but we never followed up. It would have been interesting, although I think Bryan's sound was in a different neck of the woods from me. A lot of people and bands say that we were an influence, but then I hear them and I don't see it."

The most avid Ian Hunter fan within the rock fraternity is undoubtedly Joe Elliott of Def Leppard. In recent *Classic Rock* features, Elliott cited *Mott* as 'The Greatest Album of All Time', Mick Ronson as 'The Guitar Hero', 'All the Young Dudes' as 'The Anthem', the "brilliant and underrated" *Wildlife* as his 'Desert Island Disc' and Ian Hunter as 'The Songwriter'. Joe praises Ian as a personal inspiration, but also a significant influence on other stars.

Joe Elliott: "I heard that when Queen supported Mott the Hoople at The Uris Theatre, Freddie Mercury was standing at the side of the stage watching them play 'Marionette'. That was Ian's 'mini-opera' and apparently Fred said that it was partly an inspiration for him writing 'Bohemian Rhapsody'. Hunter's 'The Golden Age of Rock 'n' Roll' was a call to arms for Def Leppard too. Things like 'Rock, Rock (Til You Drop)' and the *whoa, whoa* on 'Golden Age' came to mind when we were writing 'Photograph'. When I was growing up watching *Top of the Pops*, Ian Hunter had long curly hair and sunglasses. It was almost like you could never get to see him. It was like a mask, but not really. Ian is such a great writer, but he has put his stamp on other great songs too. When David Bowie gifted Mott the Hoople 'All the Young Dudes', it was like giving away the crown jewels. Mott's version is a million times better than any version that Bowie did though, right up until the *Reality* tour. David's version recorded in 2003 is good, but with every other take, Bowie never quite nailed it. Ian's original vocal treatment was brilliant. I can honestly say if it hadn't been for Hunter, I probably wouldn't have been in a band. He is a constant reference to me. He has the ability to write words that aren't as banal as your average rock lyric. Ian never pandered to that mundane approach and wrote more from the Dylan side of things, but, in my opinion, Ian Hunter is better than Bob Dylan."

The list of artists who have played and recorded Mott and Hunter songs includes Bad Company, Blue Öyster Cult, Shaun Cassidy, Contraband, Billy Cross, Def Leppard, Karla DeVito, Bruce Dickinson, The Dictators, Dramarama, Down 'n' Outz, Alejandro Escovedo, Ellen Foley, Scott Folsom, Great White, Hanoi Rocks, Juliana Hatfield, Jigsaw, Little Angels, Ian Lloyd, Barry Manilow, Brian May, Maria McKee, Martin's Folly, The Monkees, Mountain, Mr Big, Willie Nelson, The Pointer Sisters, The Presidents of the United States of America, Status Quo, Andy Taylor, Thunder, Bonnie Tyler, Urgent and The Yellow Monkey.

Cover versions of Ian's compositions extend to 'Walkin' with a Mountain', 'Angel of Eighth Avenue', 'Waterlow', 'Original Mixed-Up Kid', 'Ill Wind Blowing', 'Death May Be Your Santa Claus', 'The Journey', 'Sweet Angeline', 'The Moon Upstairs', 'Momma's Little Jewel', 'Jerkin' Crocus', 'One of the Boys', 'Sea Diver', 'All the Way from Memphis', 'Whizz Kid', 'Honaloochie Boogie', 'Violence', 'Drivin' Sister', 'Ballad of Mott the Hoople', 'I Wish I Was Your Mother', 'The Golden Age of Rock 'n' Roll', 'Marionette', 'Crash Street Kidds', 'Trudi's Song', 'Roll Away the Stone', 'Rest in Peace', 'Foxy, Foxy', 'Saturday Gigs', 'Once Bitten Twice Shy', 'Who Do You Love', '3,000 Miles from Here', 'Irene Wilde', 'Golden Opportunity', 'Overnight Angels', '(Miss) Silver Dime', 'England Rocks', 'Cleveland Rocks', 'Ships', 'Standin' in My Light', 'Bastard', 'The Outsider', 'Don't Let Go', 'Sons and Daughters', 'Central Park n' West', 'All of the Good Ones Are Taken', 'Every Step of the Way', 'Speechless', 'Big Time', 'Pain', 'Dancing on the Moon', 'Scars', 'Red Letter Day', 'The Other Man', 'Too Much', 'All is Forgiven' and 'Win It All'.

Collections of reinterpreted Hunter and Mott songs include the Down 'n' Outz' *My ReGeneration*, *The Further Adventures of the Down 'n' Outz* and *The Further Live Adventures of the Down 'n' Outz*. Scott McCaughey, of Young Fresh Fellows and The Minus 5, issued *Spain Capers* in 2015 as 'Scott the Hoople', with four covers and album artwork paying homage to *Brain Capers*. Swedish musician Wille Ahnberg released a 2016 tribute, *The Slow Hunters*, featuring ten of Ian's compositions recorded with Per and Sven Lindvall.

Mott the Hoople was also referenced directly in other artists' songs: Reunion's 'Life is a Rock (But the Radio Rolled Me)', REM's 'Man on the Moon', Mötley Crüe's 'Poison Apples' and Queen's 'Now I'm Here'. The Leighton Buzzard's single 'Saturday Night (Beneath the Plastic Palm Trees)' invoked the spirit of Mott and 'Saturday Gigs'. American bands The Phantoms and Mambo Sun recorded 'The Ballad of Overend Watts' and 'Overend Watts', and Scottish group Baby's Got a Gun cut 'Born Late '68' with *"golden age"* and *"crash street"* references. Ian retains mixed views on most covers, including re-interpretations of 'Ships', 'Who Do You Love' and 'Once Bitten Twice Shy', but he favours Maria McKee's version of 'I Wish I Was Your Mother'. He has also made it clear that he will never record a covers album as his favourite songs are perfect and don't require Hunter-ference.

> **IH:** "It is very flattering when people say my music is an influence and equally flattering when they cover my songs. I've never sold a song in my life, written for others or 'pitched' any songs. I can't write to order, apart from a few Eighties' movie tracks that I did when I was at a loose end. I worked with a couple of writers over the years, but I really want things all my own way. The covers of my stuff have been very eclectic, like The Monkees. I'm told there are about seventy covers and they're all over the place, but I'm no good at judging them. It doesn't bother me, as long as my name is on them and I get paid.
>
> "I remember once that my royalties from 'The Golden Age of Rock 'n' Roll' suddenly shot up and I couldn't figure out why. It wasn't in the charts anywhere, so I thought some DJ must have been using it in his programme, seven days a

week, because it was a lot of money. Then I was on tour in Sweden and this guy came into my dressing room who had covered four songs, translated them into Swedish and sold a quarter of a million. Of course, one of them was 'The Golden Age of Rock 'n' Roll', but he got a co-writing credit because he'd translated the lyrics. I never knew you could do that. Sometimes I think people should stop fucking with my art, but then I'm grateful they take the trouble now and again, because there were times when I was skint."

Countless Ian Hunter songs have become emblematic treasures to his fans in many ways. Having crafted some of rock's most inspired and intelligent lyrics, Hunter is a priceless figure on a withering musical landscape; an icon who has opened our eyes; a friend who has given us the most truthful of insights. But, whilst songwriting remains a frustrating battle of ideas, music and lyrics in Ian's world, he modestly maintains that he has simply been fortunate.

IH: "You get very frustrated writing songs because basically you're pulling things out of the air. I think it's as near to magic or conjuring as it comes. Where songs come from, I don't know. If there's any talent, it's messing about with the idea. Usually the music comes first for me and then there's the matter of finding lyrics, which is torture. I'm a big fan of humour, feel and groove. You really try to catch words, but just because they don't arrive doesn't mean the song is not good. 'Once Bitten Twice Shy' was written in ten hours and became a hit. 'Ships' took six years and became a hit. It's just more fun if you happen to get the lot in one go, because it's more organic.

"As you get older, it is also harder to break new ground, but music is a bottomless sea and I keep diving in. I just put my aerial up and hope for the best. Most of my lyrics are written around 4am – pad-by-the-bed stuff. You put a question into your head before you sleep and sometimes the computer gives the answer when you wake up. I use old cassette players all over the house, as I've lost at least half a dozen songs by not putting things down immediately. I write mainly on keyboard, because the left hand can take you different places. I ended up ruining all the white notes in Mott days, and I had to use the black notes, which I wasn't familiar with; that was great. Writing on bass is good because you hear one note and can wander round the universe; guitar chords will hem you in.

"In the Eighties my writing had not been good, then, when Mick Ronson died cruelly young, I realised that I couldn't fuck around anymore. I was writing songs at the time, but I was *only* writing them, as opposed to *being* them, *thinking* them. I was writing songs like Tin Pan Alley would write songs: *inventing* songs. I made my way back but it was tough.

"When I'm writing, I wish I was recording. When I'm recording, I wish I was performing. When I'm performing, I wish I was home in bed. When I tour, I can't write as it's a totally different head. On the road, you're basically a salesman, but touring must be done and that's another reason why you don't want to do it. It's not the stage part, which is fantastically gratifying; it's the rest of the day that gets to you. It's been a long road and I've lost count of the songs I've written, but I'm glad I made so many records for all those years."

Fifty years is a rare innings as a recording artist, live performer and songwriter, especially when a reputation is not founded on commerciality. How Ian Hunter has remained beneath the radar of wider recognition with his panoply of totemic songs and acclaimed albums remains a mystery. Hunter's record sales cannot compete with those of The Rolling Stones or Bob Dylan, but what sells en masse is bizarre and what is dismissed continues to be baffling.

IH: "I've got some gold and silver records on the wall and that's about it really. I guess you aspire to some hits when you start out, so I changed course for a while. After the success, I sat on the periphery and never did anything like you're supposed to do, or so I'm told. Sometimes it might not be fashionable and it might not be what other people think you ought to do, and sometimes you suffer for it, but life is doing what you want to do. If you choose to have a career and be monstrous, more power to you, but money's bullshit. Americans have a difficult time with people like me; they learn that to be successful you must have a lot of money, a nice house and all the appliances, but a lot of them find out that when they wind up in the big house full of things, there's really nothing there. That may not gel with what everybody thinks you should do, but I don't have to live with them. I'm not in it for *Billboard*. I'm in it for something much bigger than that, like having a complete life and looking back knowing that I did it according to me. According to me, my life has been a total success.

"In hindsight, *All-American Alien Boy* was great, because I'd wanted fame and fell for it. We'd become very precious in Mott for a while, but I didn't like my time in the sun. I prefer hovering in the dusk. I didn't handle pressure well, so, when *Alien Boy* died in 1976 and killed my career, I think it did me a favour in the long run. The kick in the teeth wasn't too bad as life has been no-hassle and no-hustle ever since. At the end of the day, when I was a teenager, my dad thought I was useless, my teachers thought I was no use and I had no personality, but music saved me and has given me everything."

Experts have tried to write Hunter off for years: when Mott flailed at Island Records; after the Bowie experience and 'All the Young Dudes'; when Ralphs quit Mott the Hoople; as Ian embarked on a solo career; in the aftermath of *All-American Alien Boy*; when he followed *Schizophrenic* with a "non-matching album" that was totally left field; to say nothing of the fallow Eighties and the recovery period after Ronson's passing. But *Rant*, *Shrunken Heads*, *Man Overboard*, *When I'm President* and *Fingers Crossed* are considered by many critics to be Hunter's best work, each song coated with a lived-in voice that gives appropriate attention to phrasing and texture, alongside heartfelt music that embellishes each track. Ian writes to a special standard, with command and comprehension – sharing personal subjects, situations and experiences – vocalising political opinion, historical stories and frustrations – the eclectic blend creating a special cocktail.

Reality has been woven through much of Hunter's rich repertoire – from the early psychological fences revealed in '23a Swan Hill' and 'The Loner', through the teenage career-igniting rejection of 'Irene Wilde' and 'Read 'em 'n' Weep', to marital breakdown in 'Waterlow' and 'Sons and Daughters'; from the mid-life emotions expressed in 'Beg a Little Love' and 'Dead Man Walkin'', through eulogies like 'Michael Picasso' and 'Dandy', to the question of mortality captured in 'Fingers Crossed' and 'Salvation'; from the political angst mapped out in 'Letter to Britannia from the Union Jack' and 'Shrunken Heads', to the historical fascinations depicted in 'Ta Shunka Witco' and 'Saint'; from sincere personal songs such as 'Nobody's Perfect', 'Irene Wilde' and 'Read 'em 'n' Weep', to the factual confessions laid bare in 'Ballad of Mott the Hoople', 'Boy' and 'Standin' in My Light' – and not least to the homages to the locations and musical nerve centres that gave Ian important inspiration, including Memphis, Cleveland and New York.

Yes, there are Ian Hunter songs that are "known", including 'Roll Away the Stone', 'All the Way from Memphis' and 'Once Bitten Twice Shy', but there are genuine gems that didn't receive the recognition they deserve – perceptive tracks such as 'Marionette', 'Rip Off' and 'Soul of America' – to say nothing of emotionally tender pieces like 'Too Much', 'Open My Eyes' and 'Black Tears'. In the final analysis perhaps only Ian Hunter had the skill to practise what he preached in the poetry of 'You Nearly Did Me In', adopting *"honesty"*, *"integrity"* and *"dignity"* in the challenging lyrics of 'Bastard', 'Rape', 'God' and 'Morons', without any hint of insensitivity or banality. Over a fifty-year period, Ian has built up an astonishing body of work and he holds fond memories of many musical milestones and episodes along the way.

IH: "Most guys my age got their shot in the Sixties but I didn't get my shot until the Seventies. I'd had forty jobs and eight years in factories at intervals before Mott, and all of that went into my lyrics. If you left school and went straight into a band, then you had no real experiences to relate. Then ideas behind songs get more difficult with time, so rather than keep covering standard boy–girl situations, I have always looked for something else. I'm not keen on giving too much away in songs because I think ambiguity is a good thing, so my writing has often been stimulated by issues that annoy me and I also read a lot. I'm old enough not to need musical influences and I don't pay attention to other artists' music because, when I did, I was accused of copying them.

"I never welcomed the Dylan comparisons and, in the early days of Mott the Hoople, I stopped listening to Bob Dylan. Jerry Lee Lewis and Little Richard is a thread running right through my musical life, but I still think Dylan's amazing; it is hard to get anywhere near the same league as 'Jokerman' or 'Every Grain of Sand'. When I met Bob, he was a very nice guy. When he contracted a lung illness in 1997, I was on tour and the early news was that it was worse than it actually was; that affected me greatly.

"I have had some amazing gigs; Mott the Hoople at Hammersmith in 1973 and 2009 were tremendous but the most memorable shows were the Freddie Mercury Tribute, Ronson's memorial at Hammersmith and Hunter Ronson at the Dominion Theatre. Cleveland, The Roxy run, Canada with Roy Young and The Star-Club in Hamburg were great too. It was fun all the way through. Most of all, I've loved the characters I've played with: people who were truly great like Jaco Pastorius, Steve Holley, Chris Stainton, David Sanborn and John Cale; and it was quite an event watching Queen on the recording of 'You Nearly Did Me In'. Ralpher was one of the funniest people I knew and a fine, unique guitarist. Ronson was fantastic, obviously. Andy York is more like Ronson than Ralphs: a great arranger and a brilliant player. Guitarists have always been important to me and I've never worked with horrible guitar players. I've always been lucky in that respect, but they're such bitches about each other I wouldn't dream of venturing an opinion.

"Ronson was something else. A lot of people didn't get Mick, and if you met him casually you'd think he was daft, but he was an incredibly sharp guy. I *did* see him score strings and horn sections on the back of a fucking fag packet, and the episode with 'Jack and Diane' for Mellencamp was amazing, when Ronson *did* suggest various changes to the song after picking a cassette out of a rubbish bin. That was one of Mick's arts. He was such a character too. Ronson had virtually no ego and he made people feel at ease almost instantly. He was naturally gifted, but he'd also worked hard in his apprenticeship years. He played piano so well and could talk orchestral parlance if need be. Mad as a brush, he could be a little crazy but he was thoughtful and kind. I guess we didn't help each other in some ways; sometimes when we were 'working', we'd smoke and drink and congratulate each other on how we weren't smoking and drinking.

"Mick was amazing in so many respects. People used to say Hunter Ronson was great, which was nice, and sometimes they'd ask us how we did it. Mick said it best at a radio station one day, when this DJ asked him, 'How do you and Ian work?' And Ronson said, 'Well, I play a bit of guitar – and he comes in singing – and when he stops singing – I play a bit more guitar – then I stop when he starts singing again

494

– and when he finishes singing – we stop again.' That was *so* Mick. He was a very modest guy and extremely funny. Mick would tell the same joke in the dressing room for a year, to everyone who came in to see us – and he laughed the loudest – but they were laughing at him, not at the joke."

The hardest attribute to find in the rock business is sincerity, but the star with the shades has it in spades. Ian Hunter – frank, down to earth, thought-provoking – the literate legend who observes astutely and writes with humanity and heart as an everyman – the fascinating spokesman and the figure who kept the spirit of Mott the Hoople alive, performing and preserving their great songs through the decades. Hunter fought for fame but didn't want to be a superstar; he just wanted to be a songwriter and musician. Now, he is probably the most qualified figure in contemporary music to comment on the rock world, but he has reservations.

IH: "People think rock music is glamorous, but it's not good, so I just try and keep on the edge. I've never liked any institutions and I don't give a fuck about rock 'n' roll as some institution. What I do isn't a religion – it's a hobby – one that just happened to give me a life when I was fifteen. It would take a genius to avoid being screwed in this business and I've had good people working with me so fortunately I came through fifty per cent unscathed. I loved music so much when I started, I didn't care. This game is not for the faint of heart but losers can get lucky. Blind optimism is a plus and talent plays its part. I think the music biz stinks in general, so the web seemed a breath of fresh air. Unfortunately, the same sort of people who stunk the biz up stunk up the web. Rock has never been the most innocent of businesses anyway and it is in such a mess that I won't have anything to do with it. You have to be yourself. I just do what I do and for me it's the quality of my work that matters most. Fear of irrelevance is the philosophy.

"As for fame, I do admit that I once wanted fame so badly, but when I became famous it was a pain. If you become big, you have to do stuff seven days a week and you become something you don't like. Money doesn't mean anything and neither does being known. I don't want to be in the middle of that storm. I tried it and I didn't even like myself. I never enjoyed when things were lined up for me; recording, gigs, singles, albums, press, British tours and American tours. I like *not* knowing what's coming next, not planning. That's the fun of it. You're only as good as what you do next anyway and the rest doesn't matter much to me. I've slipped a lot as a result, but I like it. It's hanging in that's important, no matter how many people tell you that they think you are crap."

Hunter's central target as a solo artist has been a quest for quality. With a different pedigree and nature to the standard 'singer-songwriter' breed, he applies fresh twists to so many topics, in so many ways. He never tried to camouflage his musical sources or inspirations and not too many songs were taken from his imagination or based on falsehood. His three-dimensional, poetic lyrics were often direct but sometimes open to interpretation, and fans frequently felt that Ian was singing for them, or to them. Refusing to worship at the temple of commercialism, Ian carved out a widescreen career, sometimes taking abrupt changes in direction.

IH: "From *Alien Boy* onwards I've concentrated more on the body of work and not really thought about hits. My idea of a successful record is when you write a complete album that hangs together as one piece. My business is to make albums whether they're in date or out of date. I don't care what anyone else is doing. I love making music and as long as I'm doing what I like and what I respect, I'm fine. I still showcase Mott songs in my live sets because I wrote them, they work

496

all the way through and they're part of me. All the songs sound like Ian Hunter anyway.

"Music was never really a career – it's a life – and my life has been interesting. It's been up and down. I've never been huge but I've never gone down the tubes either. Interesting is much better than if I'd been successful all the way through because I wouldn't have learned much at all, and I'd have hated to fail all the way through. I think I never got recognition because of management, labels and me, but I've done some good things. Sometimes you lose the truth and it just sneaks off. Fortunately, it snuck back again with *Rant* and *Strings Attached*, and the albums following them were good too. Ever since Mick died, I vowed I'd do great work and that's what I'm doing. I don't think the same way as most people do so my stuff doesn't appeal to the hordes. I'm only a marginal artist, but I won't stop playing music. Anyway, rock 'n' roll is a young man's game – and I'm fifteen!"

History is invariably written by the winners and Ian Hunter is a victor. An articulate writer, he penned angst-ridden rockers that made Mott the Hoople the "lads" of their day, elevating anger to an art form and crafting lyrics that conveyed rejection and disconnection, but also sentimentality. Debunking superstardom and demythologising the rock business, he earned his place as a great British artist with countless classic songs, lasting influence and a fascinating myth. He has given us inspiration at times of personal tragedy. He has displayed interesting insights and important ideas in his writing. But he never brandished his intelligence as a weapon; he shared it. Hunter kept one hand on the tiller of real rock 'n' roll and, while Bowie and Ferry delivered periodically in recent times, Ian's records and critical reviews were more consistent. The thirty years of music that flowed from *Stranded in Reality*, and five successive five-star albums between 2001 and 2016, proved that Ian's output is still based on "new" songs and a "now" band, rather than the nostalgic shadows of Mott the Hoople. As the years have passed, Hunter's writing has developed at an unremitting pace, outstripping most rock stars.

Respected by numerous peers, Ian Hunter has stayed discerning, astute and perceptive, establishing an unfeigned heritage for those who are smart enough to appreciate it. Perhaps the journey, his work and his persona could be summarised in four lines, using observations offered by countless rock luminaries for *Stranded in Reality* and this biography: "Solid, inspirational, masterful, gravity-defying, honest, frank, charismatic, gifted, professional, legendary, mysterious, compassionate, truthful, intelligent, formidable, sensitive, poetic, rousing and peerless – a commanding genius – a stand-up guy."

Having witnessed many musical highs and lows, Hunter can be proud that he ploughed an individualistic furrow as someone who understands rock 'n' roll. He confesses that the ideas for songs are more difficult than composition. He acknowledges that he has strived to write about real-life situations, avoiding love songs and adolescent anger, topics that are no longer appropriate at his age. He has maintained a credible place in the shifting sands between sales success and critical acclaim, retaining stature in the process; a survivor in a cruel business; a visually captivating figure; a special writer of veracity and individuality. Hunter's expression, music and words have challenged us, thrilled us, comforted us and made life so much better.

Unquestionably, Ian Hunter should be discussed, understood and appreciated more than he is, but, as awareness of his longevity continues to grow, the delivery and dexterity of his material have been noted as important differentiating factors. He is increasingly regarded as one of Britain's most influential songwriters, an American review of *Fingers Crossed* opining that his recent run of golden records has been so consistent and excellent that he no longer has a rock 'n' roll contemporary who comes close. With David Bowie and Leonard Cohen gone and with the glory of Bob Dylan and Neil Young seemingly in the past, Ian Hunter, at the age of seventy-seven, was recently termed "the finest practising songwriter from the classic rock era".

Hunter harbours an addictive and persistent need to create music, hoping that it will connect with as wide an audience as possible. Refusing to sleepwalk through past hits or nostalgia, he has remained centred throughout a roller-coaster trip, never betraying his talent. Ian's songs can be controversial, confessional or tongue-in-cheek, but they are always perceptive, offering windows on interesting landscapes and revealing fascinating trains of thought. Yes, he re-plotted his journey and exited the fast lane. Indeed, the intense dynamic of being in the light and attracting attention always sits alongside life-changing restrictions. Inevitably, there is a dark side to a shady industry. Ian Hunter simply found that navigating the extremes and achieving balance was the key.

Gifted at marking a moment or opinion, Ian found a special way of conveying views or situations via his words and his music. With multi-dimensional lyrics sometimes suggesting more than they say, fans can listen with their own doors of perception. Retaining fifty years of ragged rock 'n' roll yearning and focus, Hunter also appreciated that if you can play live, hits don't really matter because you will be successful, at least by his definition. As Ian once remarked: reviews mean nothing, queues mean everything.

> IH: "Things around me go into me and songs come, eventually. I am not a part of the music industry. I've hovered on the periphery since the Eighties when I became disenchanted with record labels who thought they could take over music. I combined that general apathy with some laziness and let things fall away for a while, but I headed back after we lost Mick Ronson. I have no ambitions now, but I like surprises. The desire has got to be there, and, for me, it still is. The key? The key is to stay off the hard stuff – and stay out of the Premiership!"

The corporate expectations and commercial accommodations of rock 'n' roll never appealed to Ian Hunter – the individualistic writer who makes genius seem effortless, the man who seems to have endlesss talent to burn. King Crimson's fascinating guitar master Robert Fripp expounded in 2002 that, professionally, "The aim is always to be true"; Ian Hunter has the same target. During a 2013 *Talks Music* interview, Kinks songwriter Ray Davies also proclaimed, "In this industry, you don't come back" – but Ian Hunter has.

With a dash of irony, two other figures who became intertwined with Ian's image and music had a similar approach in terms of artistic ethic: Maurits Cornelis Escher, who once remarked that his work was a game, a very serious game; and Bob Dylan, who opined that a man is successful if he gets up in the morning and goes to bed at night, and in between he does what he wants to do.

Hunter's dedication, independence and expression have created a legacy that sets his name apart. For those who appreciate authentic music with an intriguing dimension, Ian has burned moving musical shadows into our souls and has left an indelible mark. He has captivated his fans, and two of the amazing players who shared "just a little bit of the journey" are qualified to reflect on Ian Hunter the man – past, present and future.

Morgan Fisher: "When Ian left Mott the Hoople in 1974, it was reminiscent of my father leaving when I was sixteen. There was a sense of great loss – not upset, but almost a depression. Glam rock was disposable really, whereas Mott the Hoople's music was serious via Ian Hunter's writing. The band should have given his lyrics more attention, but we didn't care – we just got on and gave the best musical support that we could. Ian left Mott, as far as I know because of all the pressures and demands to write hits, but it was funny he went straight back into it, with a big label and a hit solo album. I didn't have time to follow Ian's career consistently over the decades, but I got a copy of *Fingers Crossed* and it is obvious to me that he is Britain's Bob Dylan.

"Ian has a great depth of lyric and writes with balance, humanity and sensitivity, and good on him for trying out different things across his career, like working with Jaco Pastorius and Mick Jones. Hunter is a very smart man. He wrote about gun control in the Eighties and now it's terribly relative in this nightmarish world we find ourselves in. He is good at writing songs about friends too – he eulogised Ronson and Bowie, and there's two classics right there that are not maudlin – they're celebrations. I think 'Michael Picasso' is one of Ian's greatest songs, and there have been many great Ian Hunter songs. There was a film director once who was asked what his favourite movie was, and he said 'the next one' – and that's the way Ian looks at music and what he says. It is a very intelligent response. Why Ian Hunter has not been more feted and awarded as possibly our best songwriter, I do not know. There are other candidates, but Ian has more depth and directness. I just totally admire what he did – and what he does."

James Mastro: "If I were Ian Hunter right now, I'd be sitting back on the laurels I'd gathered through the years, enjoying the money I'd made and thinking about the good old days. I'd be awestruck by some of the musicians, artists and people I'd inspired over the decades. I'd look at it all and say to myself, 'Not bad work at all. Now I can rest.' But fortunately for all concerned, I am not Ian Hunter and he still is. For when it comes to said Hunter, the 'good old days' are still in the making. And that gives us all something to look forward to – doesn't it?"

Hunter's journey has been remarkable and, as the great trip continues, followers, converts and casual listeners increasingly ask, "How does Ian do it?"

Well, as Ian Hunter Patterson once declared, "I was just being myself – because that was all I'd got."

Salvation

There are ways to escape
There are so many roads you can take
Burning shadows on your soul
When you're naive and young

But the older you get
You tend to look back on those things you regret
Will you ever find
Your own salvation

Everyone lies
We've all got those secrets we've all got to hide
Everyone fails
You're not the only one

There are knots in my heart
That I try to untie but they won't come apart
Will I ever find
My salvation

So, if it ain't too much, help me get in touch, with my salvation
When it's cold outside, won't you help me find, my salvation
Take these shades off me, help me find the key, to my salvation
So, if it ain't too much, help me get in touch, with my salvation

When there's nothing to cling to, when there's no one to turn to
I know you will come – I know you will come
When there's nothing to say, and there's nothing to hold on to
but life
I know you will come – me and my shadows, you and your
salvation

At the end of the day
You've got to live with yourself
It's just a question of how
You learned your lessons

Whatever you do
It's going to come back on you
Never be too proud to beg
For your salvation

So, if it ain't too much, help me get in touch, with my salvation
When it's cold outside, won't you help me find, my salvation
Take these shades off me, help me find the key, to my salvation
Oh, I just can't wait, to come face to face, with my salvation

Ian Hunter (2016)

Afterword

CAN'T KEEP A GOOD MAN DOWN

As a fifteen-year-old kid, in 1975, I had four paper rounds to sustain my increasing hunger for buying records: two rounds before school and two after. One evening in March, I was waiting for the papers to arrive and glanced through a weekly music "red top". I saw an ad for Mick Ronson's *Play Don't Worry* album, but at the foot it read, "On Tour with Ian Hunter", and the dates included Sheffield City Hall, that night. Once the papers arrived, I ran the whole round, begged my wages up-front and headed off to my first gig since T. Rex in 1971.

I'd become a fan of Mott the Hoople after hearing 'Original Mixed-Up Kid' on Island's *El Pea* compilation in 1971, and I'd followed Mott until they split in 1974, but that night in 1975 reignited my love for all things Ian Hunter. The dude with the curly hair and ever-present shades was out on his own (sort of) for the first time. He had an amazing start as a solo artist, releasing the hit single 'Once Bitten Twice Shy' and one of THE best debut albums of all time: *Ian Hunter* is laced with class – it's timeless, poignant, happy, sad – everything a record should be. Hard to follow? Maybe. I had difficulty with *All-American Alien Boy*, but I've since learned that Ian doesn't do "same" and the album has become a firm favourite.

Overnight Angels followed and I went to see Hunter live again, sneaking backstage and meeting Ian for the first time. After the *Schizophrenic* album I began my music career and it presented opportunities to see Ian further afield, at The Ritz in New York and Toronto's Rock 'n' Roll Heaven in 1988, after a Def Leppard gig, when I joined Ian on stage for the first time.

In the Eighties new Ian Hunter music was restricted to a few movie soundtracks – more of a reflection of the times than the man – before a momentous return to form with Hunter Ronson's *YUI Orta*. Tragically, Mick passed away in 1993 but Ian said it "kicked his arse", musically. Following *The Artful Dodger* there was a kind of renaissance. The crowds came back, they embraced the new and invited it in with the old – and the new kept coming. 2001's *Rant*, with the brilliant 'Morons', was his best work in decades; *Shrunken Heads* featured the beautiful 'When the World Was Round'; *Man Overboard* had the tongue-in-cheek 'Girl from the Office'; *When I'm President* included one of Ian's best-ever songs, 'Black Tears' – no mean feat for a man who's been doing this as long as The Rolling Stones. But it didn't end there. 2016's *Fingers Crossed* was bursting with supreme songs, like his hymn to Bowie, 'Dandy', as well as 'Ghosts' and the stunning 'Morpheus'. There was also the very nice tidy-up of Ian's affairs with the awesome thirty-disc box set *Stranded In Reality*, and continued Hunter and Mott gigs have stoked even more coke on the fire since then.

Ian has written and performed special music for fifty years; there is no stopping the man; and there is no question, there will NEVER be another like Ian Hunter, EVER!

Joe Elliott
Def Leppard

505

Ian Hunter Discography

Albums

Ian Hunter

Once Bitten Twice Shy (Hunter) 4.44
Who Do You Love (Hunter) 3.51
Lounge Lizard (Hunter) 4.32
Boy (Hunter/Ronson) 8.52
3,000 Miles from Here (Hunter) 2.48
The Truth, the Whole Truth, Nuthin' But the Truth (Hunter) 6.13
It Ain't Easy When You Fall/Shades Off (Hunter) 5.46
I Get So Excited (Hunter) 3.48

Recorded: AIR No.2 Studio, London – January and February 1975
Released: CBS Records 80710 – March 1975
Personnel: Ian Hunter (Lead and Backing Vocals, Guitar, Piano, Percussion); Mick Ronson (Lead Guitar, Organ, Mellotron, Harmonica, Bass); Geoff Appleby (Bass Guitar, Backing Vocals); Peter Arnesen (Piano); Dennis Elliott (Drums, Percussion); John Gustafson (Bass Guitar on 'Lounge Lizard')
Producers: Ian Hunter and Mick Ronson, Arranger: Ian Hunter, Engineer: Bill Price

Hunter's debut album provided confirmation that the combination of Mott the Hoople and Mick Ronson could have been sensational. *Ian Hunter* remains a Seventies classic that far exceeded post-Hoople expectations. Stripped of saxes, cellos and high drama, Mick's sparkling and inventive guitar playing added energy to some of Ian's finest compositions, including the hit single 'Once Bitten Twice Shy', 'Lounge Lizard', 'The Truth, the Whole Truth, Nuthin' But the Truth' and 'It Ain't Easy When You Fall'. *Sounds* termed the three opening cuts a rock 'n' roll masterpiece. An adapted Escher cover echoed Mott's first LP. Hunter turns killer!

All-American Alien Boy

Letter to Britannia from the Union Jack (Hunter) 3.48
All-American Alien Boy (Hunter) 7.07
Irene Wilde (Hunter) 3.43
Restless Youth (Hunter) 6.17
Rape (Hunter) 4.20
You Nearly Did Me In (Hunter) 5.46
Apathy 83 (Hunter) 4.43
God (Take One) (Hunter) 5.45

Recorded: Electric Lady Studios, New York – January 1976
Released: CBS Records 81310 – May 1976
Personnel: Ian Hunter (Lead and Backing Vocals, Rhythm Guitar, Piano); Chris Stainton (Piano, Organ, Mellotron, Bass on 'Restless Youth'); Jaco Pastorius (Bass, Guitar on 'God'); Jerry Weems (Lead Guitar); Aynsley Dunbar (Drums); David Sanborn (Alto Saxophone); Don Alias (Congas); Dave Bargeron (Trombone); Dominic Cortese (Accordion); Cornell Dupree (Guitar on 'Britannia'); Arnie Lawrence (Clarinet); Lew Soloff (Trumpet)
Backing Singers: Erin Dickens, Gail Kantor, Ann E. Sutton, Bob Segarini
Backing Vocals on 'You Nearly Did Me In': Freddie Mercury, Brian May, Roger Taylor
Producer: Ian Hunter, Engineer: David Palmer

507

Hunter recorded this insightful, thematic record in three weeks at New York's Electric Lady Studios, revealing his impressions on being "hit" by America, where he was now resident. 'Irene Wilde' and 'You Nearly Did Me In' were stellar and Ian's lyrical skill was further exemplified in 'Letter to Britannia from the Union Jack', 'Rape' and 'God (Take One)'. With astonishing musicianship in abundance and featuring the late great Jaco Pastorius, this was Mick Ronson's favourite Hunter solo album even though he had headed off to tour with Bob Dylan. Ian labelled the record commercial suicide; the critics loved it. Hunter turns up trumps.

Overnight Angels

Golden Opportunity (Hunter) 4.31
Shallow Crystals (Hunter) 3.58
Overnight Angels (Hunter) 5.12
Broadway (Hunter) 3.46
Justice of the Peace (Hunter) 3.01
(Miss) Silver Dime (Hunter/Slick) 4.34
Wild n' Free (Hunter) 3.08
The Ballad of Little Star (Hunter) 2.32
To Love a Woman (Hunter) 3.54

Recorded: Le Studio, Morin-Heights, Canada – January and February 1977
Released: CBS Records 81993 – May 1977
Personnel: Ian Hunter (Lead and Backing Vocals, Rhythm Guitar, Piano); Earl Slick (Lead, Slide and Rhythm Guitars); Peter Oxendale (Keyboards); Rob Rawlinson (Bass, Harmony Vocals); Dennis Elliott (Drums, Percussion on 'Justice of the Peace'); Roy Thomas Baker (Percussion); Miller Anderson and Lem Lubin (Harmony Vocals on 'Broadway'); Bud Prager (Percussion on '(Miss) Silver Dime')
Producer: Roy Thomas Baker, Engineer: Gary Lyons

Overnight Angels may be one of Ian's least favourite records, but it contained several great songs, including 'Shallow Crystals', 'Wild n' Free', '(Miss) Silver Dime' and 'Broadway'. 'Justice of the Peace' was a sure-fire hit single that missed the charts when it was shamefully ignored by UK record-buyers. Recorded at Le Studio in Morin-Heights, Canada, with Earl Slick on guitar, Queen's former producer Roy Thomas Baker applied his supersonic treatment and Rob Rawlinson added brilliant bass flourishes. *Sounds* termed the album "Overnight Sensation."

You're Never Alone with a Schizophrenic

Just Another Night (Hunter/Ronson) 4.36
Wild East (Hunter) 3.58
Cleveland Rocks (Hunter) 3.48
Ships (Hunter) 4.11
When the Daylight Comes (Hunter) 4.27
Life After Death (Hunter) 3.49
Standin' in My Light (Hunter) 4.35
Bastard (Hunter) 6.37
The Outsider (Hunter) 5.57

Recorded: The Power Station, New York – January 1979
Released: Chrysalis Records CHR 1214 – April 1979
Personnel: Ian Hunter (Lead and Harmony Vocals, Piano, Moog, ARP, Organ, Guitar, Percussion, Backing Vocals); Mick Ronson (Guitar, Percussion, Vocals); Roy Bittan (ARP, Organ, Moog, Piano, Backing Vocals); Garry Tallent (Bass); Max Weinberg (Drums): John Cale (Piano and ARP on 'Bastard'); George Young (Tenor Saxophone); Lew Delgatto (Baritone Saxophone)
Backing Vocals: Ellen Foley, Rory Dodd, Eric Bloom
Producers: Mick Ronson and Ian Hunter, Arrangers: Mick Ronson, Ian Hunter and Roy Bittan, Engineer: Bob Clearmountain

In 1978 Ian signed with Chrysalis and released *You're Never Alone with a Schizophrenic*, one of his finest albums, recorded with Ronson and members of Bruce Springsteen's E Street Band. 'Cleveland Rocks', 'Standin' in My Light', 'Bastard' and 'The Outsider' were exceptional and the record was one of the Chrysalis label's biggest sellers. It later furnished a Top Ten hit for Barry Manilow, who covered 'Ships', but it didn't yield a chart single for Hunter. Ronson found the title for the album scrawled on a toilet wall. A stunning record that ticked all the boxes.

Welcome to the Club

Disc One
FBI (Gormley) 3.51
Once Bitten Twice Shy (Hunter) 5.25
Angeline (Hunter) 4.56
Laugh at Me (Bono) 3.40
All the Way from Memphis (Hunter) 3.33
I Wish I Was Your Mother (Hunter) 6.47
Irene Wilde (Hunter) 4.56
Just Another Night (Hunter/Ronson) 6.03
Cleveland Rocks (Hunter) 6.01

Disc Two
Standin' in My Light (Hunter) 5.49
Bastard (Hunter) 8.12
Walkin' with a Mountain (Hunter)/Rock and Roll Queen (Ralphs) 4.19
All the Young Dudes (Bowie) 3.30
Slaughter on 10th Avenue (Rodgers) 2.25
We Gotta Get Out of Here* (Hunter) 3.14
Silver Needles* (Hunter) 5.56
Man O'War* (Hunter/Ronson) 4.19
Sons and Daughters (Hunter) 5.04

Recorded: The Roxy, West Hollywood, CA – 5 to 11 November 1979; *Media Sound, New York – 10 and 11 January 1980
Released: Chrysalis Records CJT 6 – April 1980
Personnel: Ian Hunter (Lead Vocals, Guitar); Mick Ronson (Guitar); Tommy Morrongiello (Guitar); Tommy Mandel (Keyboards); Martin Briley (Bass); Georgie Meyer (Keyboards, Saxophone, Vocals); Eric Parker (Drums); Ellen Foley (Vocals)
Producers: Ian Hunter and Mick Ronson, Engineer: Harvey Goldberg

A full-blooded live album recorded at the infamous Roxy Theatre on Sunset Boulevard. Mixing Mott and solo classics with aplomb, Ian applied interesting twists to some older songs, including 'Laugh at Me' and 'The Golden Age of Rock 'n' Roll'. The 2LP set featured Ronson's version of 'FBI' and some 'live-in-the-studio' tracks, notably 'Silver Needles'. *Welcome to the Club* successfully captured the explosive energy of Hunter Ronson; the songs and playing are stunning, and the connection between Ian, band and audience is quite brilliant. If only they'd stuck to the original nifty album title, *From the Knees of My Heart*!

Short Back n' Sides

Central Park n' West (Hunter) 4.00
Lisa Likes Rock n' Roll (Hunter) 3.56
I Need Your Love (Hunter) 3.34
Old Records Never Die (Hunter) 4.18
Noises (Hunter/Morrongiello) 5.51
Rain (Hunter) 5.54
Gun Control (Hunter) 3.12
Theatre of the Absurd (Hunter) 5.49
Leave Me Alone (Hunter) 3.29
Keep on Burning (Hunter) 4.46

Recorded: The Power Station, Wizard Sound and Electric Lady Studios New York; Wessex Studios London – 1980–81

Released: Chrysalis Records CHR 1326 – August 1981
Personnel: Ian Hunter (Vocals, Guitars, Piano); Mick Ronson (Guitar, Keyboards, Vocals); Tommy Morrongiello (Guitar, Bass); Tommy Mandel (Keyboards); Georgie Meyer (Keyboards, Vocals); Martin Briley (Bass); Eric Parker (Drums); Mick Jones (Guitar, Vocals); Topper Headon (Drums, Percussion); Tymon Dogg (Violin); Miller Anderson and Ellen Foley (Backing Vocals)
'I Need Your Love': Todd Rundgren (Bass, Vocals); Gary Windo (Alto); Roger Powell (Vocals)
'Gun Control': Mick Barakan (Guitar); John Holbrook (Bass); Wells Kelly (Drums)
Producers: Mick Ronson and Mick Jones, Mixed by: Bob Clearmountain and Dave Tickle
'Gun Control': Mixed and engineered by John Holbrook at Bearsville Studios, Woodstock, NY
'I Need Your Love': Mixed and engineered by Todd Rundgren at Utopia Sound, London

Hunter and Ronson commenced recording sessions for *Theatre of the Absurd* and decided to invite Mick Jones of The Clash to produce the reggae-flavoured title track; in the end, he stayed for "the works". No one can accuse Ian of repetition. Like *All-American Alien Boy*, *Short Back n' Sides* was an unexpected bolt from the blue. 'Central Park n' West', 'Rain' and 'Gun Control' were particularly strong but Guy Stevens heard the introduction to 'Noises' and considered it pretentious. Bold and brave, Hunter called the record his garage album. Chrysalis Records hated it!

All of the Good Ones Are Taken

All of the Good Ones Are Taken (Hunter) 3.42
Every Step of the Way (Hunter/Clarke) 3.55
Fun (Hunter/Clarke/Michaels) 4.21
Speechless (Hunter) 3.49
Death 'n' Glory Boys (Hunter) 5.57

That Girl Is Rock 'n' Roll (Hunter) 3.18
Somethin's Goin' On (Hunter) 4.33
Captain Void 'n' the Video Jets (Hunter) 4.12
Seeing Double (Hunter) 4.24
All of the Good Ones Are Taken (Hunter) 3.48

Recorded: Wizard Sound Studios, New York State – 1982–83
Released: CBS Records 25379 – September 1983
Personnel: Ian Hunter (Vocals, Guitar, Piano); Robbie Alter (Guitar, Vocals); Mark Clarke (Bass, Vocals); Hilly Michaels (Drums); Tommy Mandel (Keyboards, Vocals); Bob Mayo (Keyboards); Lou Cortlezzi (Alto Saxophone); Clarence Clemmons (Sax on 'All of the Good Ones Are Taken' and 'Seeing Double'); Dan Hartman (Bass on 'Speechless'); Jeff Bova (Keyboards on 'Speechless'); Mick Ronson (Lead Guitar on 'Death 'n' Glory Boys'); Jimmy Ripp (Guitar on 'All of the Good Ones Are Taken' and 'That Girl Is Rock 'n' Roll'); Rory Dodd and Eric Troyer (Backing Vocals on 'All of the Good Ones Are Taken')
Producers: Max Norman in association with Ian Hunter, Engineer: Mike Scott

A record that attracted interest because of the sparkling title track and Hunter's accompanying promotional video that parodied the Dudley Moore comedy *Arthur* and received an MTV Awards nomination. Ronson featured on 'Death 'n' Glory Boys', 'Seeing Double' was superb, Status Quo covered 'Speechless', and The Monkees recorded 'Every Step of the Way'. Lighter, thinner-sounding and mildly political, the album was not typical of Ian's work, but interesting nonetheless. Hunter was about to enter the wilderness years.

YUI Orta

American Music (Hunter) 4.12
The Loner (Hunter) 4.47

Women's Intuition (Hunter/Ronson) 6.31
Tell It Like It Is (Hunter/Ronson) 4.23
Livin' in a Heart (Hunter) 4.34
Big Time (Hunter) 4.03
Cool (Hunter/Ronson) 4.30
Beg a Little Love (Hunter/McNasty) 6.26
Following in Your Footsteps (Hunter/Ronson) 5.02
Sons 'n' Lovers (Hunter) 4.55
Pain (Hunter/Kehr) 4.43
How Much More Can I Take (Hunter) 3.48
Sweet Dreamer (Gibson/Ronson) 6.28

Recorded: The Power Station, New York – June and July 1989
Released: Mercury Records 838-973-1 – January 1990
Personnel: Ian Hunter (Vocals, Guitar, Piano on 'Sweet Dreamer'); Mick Ronson (Guitar, Backing Vocals); Pat Kilbride (Bass); Tommy Mandel (Keyboards); Mickey Curry (Drums); Bernard Edwards (Bass on 'Women's Intuition')
Backing Vocals: Carmela Long, Joey Cirecano, Donnie Kehr, Robbie Alter, Carola Westerlund
Producer: Bernard Edwards

At last, a Hunter Ronson album, and it was a great one, featuring a tremendous band. Super songs abound, including 'The Loner', 'Women's Intuition', 'Beg a Little Love', 'How Much More Can I Take' and 'Pain'. Ronson's instrumental 'Sweet Dreamer' remains a heart-breaking tour de force. An exciting record with a classic album title based on a Three Stooges catchphrase, but most DJs couldn't pronounce it. U Orta Buy It!

Ian Hunter's Dirty Laundry

Dancing on the Moon (Hunter/Bath/Plain) 5.24
Another Fine Mess (Hunter/Bath/Plain) 3.28
Scars (Hunter/Bath/Plain) 5.04

Never Trust a Blonde (Bath) 5.19
Psycho Girl (Plain) 2.48
My Revolution (Steel/Hunter/Dangerfield) 4.08
Good Girls (Plain) 4.01
Red Letter Day (Hunter) 5.11
Invisible Strings (Hunter) 3.53
Everyone's a Fool (Bath/Roig) 2.41
Junkee Love (Matheson/Steel) 2.46
The Other Man (Hunter) 5.23

Recorded: Abbey Road Studios, London – July to August 1994
Released: Norsk Plateproduksjon IDCD 44 – March 1995
Personnel: Ian Hunter (Vocals, Guitar); Darrell Bath (Guitar, Vocals); Honest John Plain (Guitar, Vocals); Casino Steel (Keyboards, Percussion, Vocals); Glen Matlock (Bass); Vom (Drums)
Producer: Bjørn Nessjø

After Ronson's passing in 1993, Hunter agreed to record at Abbey Road Studios with Glen Matlock, Casino Steel and guitarists Honest John Plain and Darrell Bath for a project called *The Gringo Starrs*. Swept up by the band of punk pseudo-legends, it became *Ian Hunter's Dirty Laundry*. Largely written in the studio and cut at speed, this sparkling set of songs includes the beautiful 'Scars', a brilliant ode to life on the road with Ronson entitled 'Another Fine Mess' and the humorously anthemic 'My Revolution'. Fun and "Stonesy", it wasn't really an Ian Hunter solo album, but it was far too good to miss.

The Hunter Ronson Band: BBC Live in Concert

Once Bitten Twice Shy (Hunter) 4.59
How Much More Can I Take (Hunter) 4.06
Beg a Little Love (Hunter/McNasty) 7.18
Following in Your Footsteps (Hunter/Ronson) 5.41
Just Another Night (Hunter/Ronson) 5.41

Sweet Dreamer (Gibson) 7.42
(Give Me Back My) Wings (Hunter) 6.56
Standin' in My Light (Hunter) 5.33
Bastard (Hunter) 8.38
The Loner (Hunter) 5.22
You're Never Too Small to Hit the Big Time (Hunter) 6.47
All the Way from Memphis (Hunter) 4.55
Irene Wilde (Hunter) 5.51

Recorded: The Dominion Theatre, London – 15 February 1989
Released: Windsong Records WINCD 078 – November 1995
Personnel: Ian Hunter (Vocals, Guitar); Mick Ronson (Guitar, Backing Vocals); Howard Helm (Keyboards); Pat Kilbride (Bass); Steve Holley (Drums)
Producer: Pete Ritzema

Another great live testament that showcased seven new songs from the soon-to-be-recorded *YUI Orta*. Includes '(Give Me Back My) Wings' – featuring the amazing Pat Kilbride and "The Great Steve Holley" – and stalwart versions of 'Standin' in My Light', 'Bastard' and 'Irene Wilde'. One reviewer wrote that Hunter Ronson rocked London's Dominion to its very foundations and there truly was tremendous power from Ian and a stunning, stripped down, four-piece band. Mick Ronson: "Less is more!"

The Artful Dodger

Too Much (Hunter) 4.44
Now Is the Time (Hunter) 4.54
Something to Believe In (Hunter) 5.46
Resurrection Mary (Hunter) 6.11
Walk on Water (Hunter/McNasty) 3.48
23a Swan Hill (Hunter) 4.47
Michael Picasso (Hunter) 5.45
Open My Eyes (Hunter/Bath) 5.42

516

The Artful Dodger (Hunter) 4.21
Skeletons (In Your Closet) (Hunter/Bath/Plain) 4.00
Still the Same (Hunter) 5.06

Recorded and mixed: Nidaros Studios, Trondheim, Norway
Additional recording: The Time Machine, Vermont, USA
Released: Polydor Records 531 794-2 – September 1996
Personnel: Ian Hunter (Lead Vocals, Electric and Acoustic Guitars, Harp);
Darrell Bath (Acoustic, Electric and Baryton Guitars, Vocals);
Torstein Flakne (Guitar, Vocals); Frode Alnaes (Guitar); Robbie Alter
(Acoustic, Electric and Slide Guitars); Kjetil Bjerkestrand (Keyboards
and String Arrangements); Sven Lindvall (Bass); Pat Kilbride (Bass,
Acoustic Bass); Per Lindvall (Drums, Percussion); Dennis Elliott
(Drums); Honest John Plain (Backing Vocals, Lead Vocal); Mariann
Lisland (Vocals); Per Oisten Sorenson (Vocals); Valvano String
Quartet
Producer: Bjørn Nessjø, Assistant engineers: Rune Nordal and
Steve Moseley

Mick Ronson's passing brought about a self-awakening in Ian
Hunter; he became determined that his future work would be
top-drawer and he has consistently achieved that aim. *The Artful
Dodger* featured '23a Swan Hill' (the family home that Ian left when
he was sixteen), 'Now Is the Time' (inspired by Freddie Mercury) and
'Michael Picasso' (Hunter's eulogy to Ronson). Other compelling
highlights include 'Resurrection Mary', 'Too Much' and 'Open My
Eyes'. Darrell Bath justifiably termed the record a classic album. It
took four guitar players to replace Ronson.

Rant

Rip Off (Hunter) 4.50
Good Samaritan (Hunter) 4.07
Death of a Nation (Hunter) 5.35
Purgatory (Hunter) 4.46

American Spy (Hunter) 4.30
Dead Man Walkin' (EastEnders) (Hunter) 6.20
Wash Us Away (Hunter) 3.57
Morons (Hunter) 5.32
Soap 'n' Water (Hunter) 5.18
Knees of My Heart (Hunter) 3.35
No One (Hunter) 3.37
Still Love Rock and Roll (Hunter) 4.34

Recorded: New Calcutta Recording Studio, New York City – December 2000 to January 2001
Released: Papillon Records BTFLYCD 0016 – May 2001
Personnel: Ian Hunter (Vocals, Keyboards Piano, Guitar, Harmonica, Backing Vocals); Andy York (Guitar, Bass, Mandoguitar, Mandolin, Groovebox, Autoharp, Zither, Organ, Keyboards, Backing Vocals); James Mastro (Electric Slide Guitar, Twelve-String Acoustic and Electric Guitars, Mandolin, Six-String Fuzz Bass); Robbie Alter (Guitar, Bass, Piano); Rick Tedesco (Guitar); John Conte (Bass); Mickey Curry (Drums); Dane Clark (Drums); Steve Holley (Drums, Percussion); Rick Pagano (Drums, Bongos, Backing Vocals); Doug Petty (Organ, Keyboards); Tommy Mandel (Keyboards, Organ, Loops)
Gang Vocals: Willie Nile, Jesse Patterson, Lisa Ronson, Rick Tedesco
Producers: Andy York and Ian Hunter, Co-produced, recorded and mixed by: Rich Pagano

Angered by British politics, this powerful contemporary collection found Hunter raging at his homeland with 'Death of a Nation', 'Morons' and 'Rip Off'. *Rant* contains several of Ian's most popular tracks, including 'Wash Us Away' and the mid-life reflections of 'Dead Man Walkin'', one of his finest songs. Nearly twenty years on, the album still sparkles with hard-hitting relevance and brilliant production from Andy York. Part memoir, part sobering vision of a world gone mad, *Rant* was outstanding. Hunter had dealt with Blair. Bring on Bush.

Strings Attached

Disc One
Rest in Peace (Hunter/Watts/Griffin) 6.31
All of the Good Ones Are Taken (Hunter) 3.32
I Wish I Was Your Mother (Hunter) 5.48
Twisted Steel (Hunter) 3.10
Boy (Hunter/Ronson) 9.10
23a Swan Hill (Hunter) 5.23
Waterlow (Hunter) 3.49
All the Young Dudes (Bowie) 5.43
Irene Wilde (Hunter) 4.06
Once Bitten Twice Shy (Hunter) 5.28

Disc Two
Rollerball (Hunter) 5.27
Ships (Hunter) 6.10
A Nightingale Sang in Berkeley Square (Maschwitz/Sherwin) 3.59
Michael Picasso (Hunter) 8.21
Wash Us Away (Hunter) 4.28
Don't Let Go (Hunter) 3.56
All the Way from Memphis (Hunter) 5.29
Roll Away the Stone (Hunter) 5.03
Saturday Gigs (Hunter) 6.31

Recorded: Sentrum Scene, Oslo – 29 and 30 January 2002
Released: Universal Records 067 711-2 – October 2003
Personnel: Ian Hunter (Vocals, Guitar); Andy York (Guitar); Torstein Flakne (Guitar); Kjetil Bjerkestrand (Keyboards); Sven Lindvall (Bass); Per Lindvall (Drums)
Orchestra: Trondheimsolistene Strings, Arranger: Kjetil Bjerkestrand
Producer: Bjørn Nessjø, Engineer: Jan Erik Kongshaug
Mixed: Nidaros Studios, Trondheim by Bjørn Nessjø and Rune Nordal

Recorded and filmed in Oslo with a string orchestra, guitarist Andy York and Ian's Scandinavian band. Features refreshing re-workings of solo and Mott material plus some new songs and surprises – 'Don't Let Go', 'Rollerball', 'Twisted Steel' and one cover – not Bob Dylan, not P.J. Proby, but 'A Nightingale Sang in Berkeley Square'. *Classic Rock* described *Strings Attached* as one of the best live albums of all time. Hunter considers the project one of the highlights of his life. Little wonder!

Shrunken Heads

Words (Big Mouth) (Hunter/York) 5.03
Fuss About Nothin' (Hunter) 3.44
When the World Was Round (Hunter) 4.50
Brainwashed (Hunter) 3.40
Shrunken Heads (Hunter) 7.45
Soul of America (Hunter) 4.43
How's Your House (Hunter) 4.18
Guiding Light (Hunter) 4.09
Stretch (Hunter) 4.12
I Am What I Hated When I Was Young (Hunter) 3.05
Reed 'em 'n' Weep (Hunter) 5.02

Limited Edition Bonus EP
Your Eyes (Hunter) 3.51
Wasted (Hunter) 5.07
Real or Imaginary (Hunter) 3.39

Recorded and mixed: A-Pawling Studios, Pawling, New York and Hangar Studio, Brookfield, Connecticut – January 2007
Released: Jerkin' Crocus Records JERK 9 – May 2007
Personnel: Ian Hunter (Vocals, Acoustic Guitar, Piano, Harmonica, Backing Vocals); Andy York (Acoustic, Electric and Twelve-String Guitars, Banjo, Ukelele, Piano, Wurlitzer, Backing and Gang Vocals); James Mastro (Slide, Electric, Buzzsaw and Baritone Guitars, E Bow,

Backing Vocals); Mark Bosch (Solo Guitar); Graham Maby (Bass, Gang Vocals); Steve Holley (Drums, Percussion, Gang Vocals); Andy Burton (Keyboards, Wurlitzer, Organ, Accordion, Piano); Pete Moshay (Keyboards); Rick Tedesco (Staccato Piano); Jack Petruzzelli (Mando, Electric, Leslie and Phaser Guitars, Omnichord, Wah Wah); Tony Shanahan (Upright Bass); Soozie Tyrell (Strings); Jeff Tweedy (Vocals on Tracks 1, 2 and 8)
Backing and Gang Vocals: Jesse Hunter, Dennis Dunaway, Mary Lee Kortes, Christine Ohlman
Producers: Andy York and Ian Hunter, Recorded and mixed: Peter Moshay
Booklet illustrations: Max Maxwell

Rant had dealt with Britain so *Shrunken Heads* had to politicise America, to some degree. Although this album addressed US life on tracks like 'Soul of America' and 'How's Your House', it also contained some English topics and imagery. Another tale of lost love from Ian's youth, 'Reed 'em 'n' Weep', easily sits alongside 'I Wish I Was Your Mother' and 'Irene Wilde' as one of Hunter's finest ballads. Brimming with single-minded spirit and originality, the record was nominated as a *Classic Rock* 'Album of the Year 2007'. *Shrunken Heads* sparkled and confirmed that rock's most astute dude still carried the news.

Man Overboard

The Great Escape (Hunter) 4.29
Arms and Legs (Hunter) 4.34
Up and Running (Hunter) 3.47
Man Overboard (Hunter) 5.16
Babylon Blues (Hunter) 4.54
Girl from the Office (Hunter) 4.35
Flowers (Hunter) 3.23
These Feelings (Hunter) 4.01
Win It All (Hunter) 2.24

Way with Words (Hunter) 4.15
River of Tears (Hunter) 5.35

Recorded and mixed: A-Pawling Studios, Pawling, NY – September and October 2008
Additional overdubs at: Stilson Hill, Indianapolis and Tannery Row, Hoboken, NJ
Released: New West Records NW 6167-2 – July 2009
Personnel: Ian Hunter (Vocals, Acoustic Guitar); Andy York (Acoustic Guitar, Backing Vocals);
James Mastro (Electric Guitar); Paul Page (Bass, Gang Vocals); Steve Holley (Drums, Percussion); Andy Burton (Grand Piano, Hammond Organ); Jack Petruzzelli (Electric Guitar)
Producers: Andy York and Ian Hunter, Recorded and mixed: Peter Moshay

A relaxed and meditative Hunter exhibited a greater emphasis on restraint and acoustic-based songs on *Man Overboard*. 'Arms and Legs' had a melody to die for and there was touching humour in 'The Great Escape' and 'Girl from the Office', based on more early, real-life Ian Patterson experiences. A mature and introspective record that flowed beautifully, it garnered further five-star reviews. Ian might have carried an unashamed Dylan admiration, but, at seventy, Hunter had surpassed his hero.

When I'm President

Comfortable (Flyin' Scotsman) (Hunter) 3.02
Fatally Flawed (Hunter) 5.03
When I'm President (Hunter) 4.21
What For (Hunter) 4.22
Black Tears (Hunter) 3.37
Saint (Hunter/Mastro) 3.35
Just the Way You Look Tonight (Hunter) 3.34
Wild Bunch (Hunter) 3.54

522

Ta Shunka Witco (Crazy Horse) (Hunter) 5.47
I Don't Know What You Want (Hunter/Patterson) 3.47
Life (Hunter) 4.58

Recorded: A-Pawling Studios, Pawling, New York – January and February 2012
Released: Proper Records Proper 104 – September 2012
Personnel: Ian Hunter (Vocals); Andy York (Guitar, Backing Vocals); James Mastro (Guitar); Mark Bosch (Guitar); Paul Page (Bass, Gang Vocals); Steve Holley (Drums, Percussion); Andy Burton (Organ, Piano)
Producers: The Prongs (Ian Hunter and Andy York), Recorded and mixed: Peter Moshay

Generously co-credited by Ian to The Rant Band, *When I'm President* contained some of Hunter's best writing, including 'When I'm President', 'Fatally Flawed', 'What For' and 'Ta Shunka Witco'. 'Black Tears' was absolute genius, bolstered by pure emotion, subtle intensity and a blistering Bosch guitar solo. Exuding controlled energy, The Rant Band shone in style while Hunter kept raising the bar. A landslide victory!

Ian Hunter and The Rant Band: Live in the UK 2010

Sea Diver (Hunter) 2.51
Arms and Legs (Hunter) 4.37
Words (Big Mouth) (Hunter/York) 5.36
The Great Escape (Hunter) 4.41
Ships (Hunter) 5.05
Irene Wilde (Hunter) 4.18
Flowers (Hunter) 3.37
Soul of America (Hunter) 4.34
Man Overboard (Hunter) 6.00
Waterlow (Hunter) 3.54
Michael Picasso (Hunter) 8.00

Wash Us Away (Hunter) 4.25
23a Swan Hill (Hunter) 4.49
Sweet Jane (Reed) 4.23
All the Young Dudes (Bowie) 7.05

Recorded: UK concert venues – October 2010
Released: Rant Records JJM 001 – September 2014
Personnel: Ian Hunter (Vocals); James Mastro (Guitar); Mark Bosch (Guitar); Paul Page (Bass, Gang Vocals); Steve Holley (Drums, Percussion); Andy Burton (Organ, Piano)
Producers: Andy York and Ian Hunter

A gold-nugget set recorded on Ian's 2010 British tour, this album captured seven of Hunter's more recent songs for the first time in a live setting, and offered rare outings for the gorgeous Mott the Hoople classics 'Sea Diver' and 'Waterlow'.

Fingers Crossed

That's When the Trouble Starts (Hunter) 3.37
Dandy (Hunter) 4.42
Ghosts (Hunter) 4.08
Fingers Crossed (Hunter) 5.12
White House (Hunter) 3.36
Bow Street Runners (Hunter) 4.58
Morpheus (Hunter) 5.10
Stranded in Reality (Hunter) 4.49
You Can't Live in the Past (Hunter) 5.11
Long Time (Hunter) 4.29

Bonus tracks on Japanese CD
Seein' Red (Hunter) 3.16
Have a Nice Day (Hunter) 4.16

Recorded and mixed: Hobo Studios, Weehawken, New Jersey –
March to May 2016
Released: Proper Records PRPCD137 – September 2016
Personnel: Ian Hunter (Vocals, Acoustic Guitar, Piano); James
Mastro (Electric Guitars); Mark Bosch (Electric Guitars); Paul Page
(Bass, Vocals); Steve Holley (Drums, Percussion); Andy Burton
(Keyboards); Dennis DiBrizzi (Piano); Andy York (Acoustic Guitars)
Producers: Andy York and Ian Hunter, Recorded and mixed: James
Frazee

One of Hunter's finest and most dynamic albums: 'Dandy' was a
heartfelt homage to David Bowie, 'Fingers Crossed' illustrated a
unique talent for writing stirring lyrics and music, and the aptly
named 'You Can't Live in the Past' beautifully summed up Ian's
attitude and ethos. 'Ghosts' and 'Morpheus' were stunning high
points too. *American Songwriter* wrote: "Ian Hunter's run of 21st
Century records has been so consistently excellent that he doesn't
have a contemporary in rock and roll even close in comparison.
Ian Hunter is now simply the finest practising songwriter from the
classic rock era." Nuf said!

UK Singles

Once Bitten Twice Shy/3,000 Miles from Here
CBS 3194 – April 1975

Who Do You Love/Boy
CBS 3486 – July 1975

All-American Alien Boy/Rape
CBS 4268 – April 1976

You Nearly Did Me In/Letter to Britannia from the Union Jack
CBS 4479 – August 1976

Justice of the Peace/The Ballad of Little Star
CBS 5229 – May 1977

England Rocks/Wild n' Free
CBS 5497 – July 1977

When the Daylight Comes/Life After Death – picture sleeve, white
vinyl
Chrysalis CHS 2324 – April 1979

Ships/Wild East – picture sleeve
Chrysalis CHS 2346 – August 1979

Cleveland Rocks/Bastard – picture sleeve
Chrysalis CHS 2390 – November 1979

We Gotta Get Out of Here/One of the Boys/Sons and Daughters/
Live Medley – picture sleeve, gatefold double single
Chrysalis CHS 2434 – May 1980

Lisa Likes Rock n' Roll/Noises – picture sleeve, clear vinyl
Chrysalis CHS 2542 – August 1981

All of the Good Ones Are Taken/Death 'n' Glory Boys – picture
sleeve seven-inch
All of the Good Ones Are Taken/Death 'n' Glory Boys/Traitor –
picture sleeve twelve-inch
CBS A3541 – August 1983

Somethin's Goin' On/All of the Good Ones Are Taken (Slow Version)
CBS A3855 – October 1983

American Music/Tell It Like It Is – picture sleeve seven-inch
American Music/Tell It Like It Is/Sweet Dreamer – picture sleeve twelve-inch and card sleeve CD
Mercury MER 315 – February 1990

The Artful Dodger/Now Is the Time/Fuck It Up
Citadel CIT 101CDS – April 1997

Michael Picasso (Live)/Michael Picasso (Studio)/23a Swan Hill
Citadel CIT 102CDS – February 1998

Rant EP: Still Love Rock and Roll/Dead Man Walkin' (EastEnders)/Death of a Nation
Papillon BTFLYS0017 – April 2001

When the World Was Round (Edit)/Words (Big Mouth) (Live) – seven-inch picture disc
When the World Was Round (Edit)/Once Bitten Twice Shy (Live)/Twisted Steel (Live) – CD
When the World Was Round (Video)/Interview – DVD
Jerkin' Crocus LIL JERK2 – November 2007

Dandy/Seein' Red – numbered, limited edition, seven-inch gold vinyl with picture sleeve and sticker
Proper Records PRP7S137 – April 2017

Compilations, Rarities and Bonus Tracks

Several Ian Hunter live, compilation and expanded album releases encompass previously unheard material and rare tracks, including:

Welcome to the Club (Chrysalis 1994)

Bonus tracks on reissue CD: The Golden Age of Rock 'n' Roll (4.04)/When the Daylight Comes (9.00)/One of the Boys (7.21)/Live Medley: Once Bitten Twice Shy–Bastard–Cleveland Rocks (6.10)

Long Odds n' Outtakes (Chrysalis 1994)

Limited Edition *Short Back n' Sides* bonus disc: Detroit (Rough Mix Instrumental) (3.42)/Na Na Na (4.13)/I Need Your Love (Rough Mix) (3.46)/Rain (Alternative Mix) (5.50)/I Believe in You (4.15)/Listen to the Eight Track (6.08)/You Stepped into My Dreams (4.41)/Venus in the Bathtub (4.29)/Theatre of the Absurd (6.08)/Detroit (Outtake 5 Vocal) (4.00)/Na Na Na (Extended mix) (4.29)/China (Ronson Vocal) (4.36)/Old Records Never Die (Version 1) (4.18) (All Songs Written by Ian Hunter)

The Secret Sessions (Pet Rock Records 1999)

The 1978 Pompeii tapes – Laing, Pappalardi, Hunter, Ronson tracks – Easy Money (Laing/Hunter)/Silent Movie (Laing/Hunter)/I Ain't No Angel (Laing/Hunter)/The Outsider (Hunter)

Missing in Action (Burning Airlines 2000)

CD1: Missing in Action: Ian Hunter Live 1979–89 – Life After Death/ Ships/Letter to Britannia from the Union Jack/We Gotta Get Out of Here/While You Were Looking at Me/(I'm the) Teacher/Day Tripper/ Tell It Like It Is/Pain/Women's Intuition/Wild East/Na Na Na
CD2: Collateral Damage: The Ian Hunter Band featuring Mick Ronson Live 1979–80 (Limited Edition Bonus Disc) – FBI/Once Bitten Twice Shy/When the Daylight Comes/Laugh at Me/I Wish I Was Your Mother/Cleveland Rocks/Bastard/Standin' in My Light/ Angeline/All the Way from Memphis/Walkin' with a Mountain/Rock and Roll Queen/All the Young Dudes/Slaughter on 10th Avenue

Once Bitten Twice Shy (Columbia 2000)

CD1: Rockers – Once Bitten Twice Shy/Who Do You Love/Colwater High*/One Fine Day*/The Truth, the Whole Truth, Nuthin' But the Truth/Common Disease*/Justice of the Peace/When the Daylight Comes/Cleveland Rocks/Bastard/Gun Control/Speechless/Traitor/(I'm the) Teacher/Great Expectations (You Never Know What to Expect)/Good Man in a Bad Time/Women's Intuition/Ain't No Way to Treat a Lady*/All the Young Dudes* (Live Version with Def Leppard)
CD2: Ballads – Shades Off/Boy/Letter to Britannia from the Union Jack/You Nearly Did Me In/(God) Advice to a Friend*/Shallow Crystals/Ships/Standin' in My Light/The Outsider/Junkman*/Old Records Never Die/All of the Good Ones Are Taken/Seeing Double/Bluebirds*/Sunshine Eyes*/Ill Wind*/All is Forgiven*/Michael Picasso (Live)*

Two discs titled 'Rockers' and 'Ballads' by Ian and notable for the inclusion of several rare and previously unreleased tracks*.

Overnight Angels (Columbia 2002)

Bonus track on reissue CD: England Rocks (Hunter) (2.53)

The Truth, the Whole Truth and Nuthin' But the Truth (Snapper Records 2005)

CD1: Rest in Peace/Rock and Roll Queen/Once Bitten Twice Shy/Twisted Steel/I Wish I Was Your Mother/Knees of My Heart/23a Swan Hill/Irene Wilde/The Truth, the Whole Truth, Nuthin' But the Truth/Rollerball
CD2: A Nightingale Sang in Berkeley Square/Roll Away the Stone/Saturday Gigs/All the Young Dudes/The Journey/Dead Man Walking/Just Another Night/Cleveland Rocks/Michael Picasso/Standin' in My Light/All the Way from Memphis

A 2CD and DVD release recorded at the London Astoria in 2004. Subsequently repackaged as *Behind the Shades*, *All the Young Dudes* and *Live in London*, *Greatest Hits Live*

Ian Hunter (Sony Music 2005)

Bonus tracks on thirtieth anniversary CD: Colwater High (Hunter) (3.12)/One Fine Day (Hunter) (2.21)/Once Bitten Twice Shy (Single Version) (3.52)/Who Do You Love (Single Version) (3.17)/Shades Off (Poem) (1.37)/Boy (Single B-side) (3.42)

All-American Alien Boy (Sony Music 2006)

Bonus tracks on thirtieth anniversary CD: From Rule Britannia to Union Jack (4.08)/All-American Alien Boy (Early Single Version) (4.04)/Irene Wilde (Number One) (3.52)/Weary Anger (5.45)/Apathy (4.42)/(God) Advice to a Friend (5.31)

The Journey: A Retrospective – Mott the Hoople and Ian Hunter (Sony BMG 2006)

CD1: Road to Birmingham/Backsliding Fearlessly/Walkin' with a Mountain/Angel of Eighth Avenue/Waterlow/The Debt/One of The Boys/The Journey/The Moon Upstairs/All the Young Dudes/ Momma's Little Jewel/Jerkin' Crocus/Sea Diver/Honaloochie Boogie/The Ballad of Mott the Hoople/Hymn for the Dudes/Whizz Kid/I Wish I Was Your Mother
CD2: All the Way from Memphis/Violence/Roll Away the Stone/ The Golden Age of Rock 'n' Roll/Marionette/Crash Street Kidds/ Foxy, Foxy/Saturday Gigs/Once Bitten Twice Shy/Who Do You Love/Lounge Lizard/3,000 Miles from Here/The Truth, the Whole Truth, Nuthin' But the Truth/It Ain't Easy When You Fall–Shades Off/Letter to Britannia from the Union Jack/Irene Wilde/You Nearly Did Me In/Justice of the Peace

CD3: Cleveland Rocks/Standin' in My Light/Bastard/The Outsider/ Gun Control/All of the Good Ones Are Taken/Speechless/Ill Wind/ The Loner/23a Swan Hill/Michael Picasso/I'm In Awe/Avalanche/ Morons/Wash Us Away/Knees of My Heart/Dead Man Walkin' (EastEnders)

The first collection that entwined Hunter's Hoople and solo repertoire, featuring two shelved *Rant* tracks, 'I'm in Awe' and 'Avalanche', plus a demo version of 'Morons'. Generous artwork by Sony including a die-cut slipcase echoing the *Mott* LP. Described as the ultimate introduction to Ian and Mott, *Record Collector* wrote: "This is the most complete picture yet of a man who's never been less than interesting."

All of the Good Ones Are Taken (American Beat 2007)

Bonus track on reissue CD: Traitor (Hunter) (3.57)

You're Never Alone with a Schizophrenic (EMI Chrysalis 2009)

CD1: Just Another Night (4.36)/Wild East (3.58)/Cleveland Rocks (3.48)/Ships (4.11)/When the Daylight Comes (4.27)/Life After Death (3.49)/Standin' in My Light (4.35)/Bastard (6.37)/The Outsider (5.57)/Don't Let Go (Demo) (4.14)/Ships (Take 1) (5.24)/Daylight (Early version) (4.38)/Just Another Night (The Other Side of Life; Early version) (5.23)/Whole Lotta Shakin' Goin' On (2.27)
CD2: Ian Hunter Live 1979 – FBI*/Once Bitten Twice Shy*/ Life After Death*/Sons and Daughters**/Laugh at Me**/Just Another Night**/One of the Boys**/Letter to Britannia from the Union Jack***/Bastard***/All the Way from Memphis*/Cleveland Rocks*/All the Young Dudes**/When the Daylight Comes*/Sweet Angeline*
Recorded 1979 at the Agora Ballroom, Cleveland* (18 June), Hammersmith Odeon, London** (22 November) and Berkeley Community Theater, California*** (13 July).

A twenty-eight-track thirtieth anniversary collection adding five studio outtakes and a complete disc of 1979 live performances, all previously unreleased, alongside the original album.

Live at Rockpalast: The Ian Hunter Band featuring Mick Ronson (MIG 2011)

FBI/Once Bitten Twice Shy/Angeline/Laugh at Me/Irene Wilde/I Wish I Was Your Mother/Just Another Night/We Gotta Get Out of Here/Bastard/All the Way from Memphis/Cleveland Rocks/All the Young Dudes/Slaughter on 10th Avenue

CD and DVD release, recorded for German TV in 1980 and notable for the live version of 'We Gotta Get Out of Here'.

From the Knees of My Heart: The Chrysalis Years (1979–81) (EMI Chrysalis 2012)

A four-disc set with bonus and unreleased tracks comprising CD1: *You're Never Alone with a Schizophrenic*; CD2: *Welcome to the Club*; CD3: *Short Back n' Sides*; CD4: *Ian Hunter Rocks.*

Rare and first-time CD tracks:
CD1: Ships (Early Version) (5.24)/Just Another Night (Version #3) (4.29)/The Outsider (Early Version) (6.52)/Alibi (4.38)
CD3: China (Rough Mix with Ronson Vocal) 4.24
CD4: Live in New York 1981: Once Bitten Twice Shy (5.34)/ Gun Control (3.47)/Central Park n' West (4.33)/All the Way from Memphis (4.13)/I Need Your Love (6.48)/Noises (5.44)/Just Another Night (7.04)/Cleveland Rocks (7.51)/Irene Wilde (4.40)/All the Young Dudes–Roll Away the Stone–Ships (9.20)/We Gotta Get Out of Here (Alternate Version) (3.16)

Sampling in Reality (Proper Records 2016)

A Little Rock 'n' Roll (5.20)/Your Eyes (3.49)/Waterlow (Trio Version) (3.11)/Sons 'n' Lovers (Live Acoustic 2008) (5.01)/When I'm President (Live Acoustic 2013) (5.49)/American Music (Early Version) (3.50)/ Sweet Jane (Ian Hunter and Tribes) (4.40)

A sampler CD to promote the *Stranded in Reality* anthology. Tracks 1 to 5 are taken from the box set, while tracks 6 and 7 are totally unique to the sampler disc.

Stranded in Reality (Proper Records 2016)

Disc 1: Ian Hunter (Thirtieth Anniversary Edition)
Disc 2: All-American Alien Boy (Thirtieth Anniversary Edition)
Disc 3: Overnight Angels (Thirtieth Anniversary Edition)
Disc 4: You're Never Alone with a Schizophrenic (Thirtieth Anniversary Edition)
Disc 5: Welcome to the Club (Bonus Tracks Edition)
Disc 6: Welcome to the Club (Bonus Tracks Edition)
Disc 7: Short Back n' Sides (Bonus Tracks Edition)
Disc 8: All of the Good Ones Are Taken (Bonus Tracks Edition)
Disc 9: YUI Orta
Disc 10: Ian Hunter's Dirty Laundry
Disc 11: The Hunter Ronson Band: BBC Live in Concert
Disc 12: The Artful Dodger (Bonus Track Edition)
Disc 13: Rant
Disc 14: Strings Attached (Bonus Tracks Edition)
Disc 15: Strings Attached (Bonus Tracks Edition)
Disc 16: Shrunken Heads (Bonus Tracks Edition)
Disc 17: Man Overboard
Disc 18: Ian Hunter and the Rant Band: Live in the UK 2010
Disc 19: When I'm President (Bonus Track Edition)
Disc 20: Tilting the Mirror (Rare Tracks and B-sides)
Disc 21: Tilting the Mirror (Rare Tracks and B-sides)

Disc 22: If You Wait Long Enough for Anything, You Can Get It on Sale (Live 1979–1981)
Disc 23: If You Wait Long Enough for Anything, You Can Get It on Sale (Live 1979–1981)
Disc 24: Bag of Tricks: Volume 1 (Live and Rare)
Disc 25: Bag of Tricks: Volume 2 (Live and Rare)
Disc 26: Bag of Tricks: Volume 3 (Live and Rare)
Disc 27: Acoustic Shadows (Live Acoustic)
Disc 28: Experiments (Previously Unreleased Demos & Outtakes)
Disc 29: It Never Happened (DVD)
Disc 30: It Never Happened (DVD)

Tilting the Mirror

CD1: All-American Alien Boy (Hunter) (Single A-side) (3.50)/You Nearly Did Me In (Hunter) (Single A-side) (3.34)/Common Disease (Hunter) (Alien Boy Outtake) (3.53)/If the Slipper Don't Fit (Alien Boy Outtake) (3.04)/The Outsider (Hunter) (Early Version) (6.51)/ Alibi (Hunter) (Schizophrenic Jam) (4.38)/When the Daylight Comes (Hunter) (Single A-side) (3.45)/Just Another Night (Hunter/Ronson) (Electric Version #3) (4.29)/Detroit (Hunter) (Rough Mix Instrumental) (3.42)/Na Na Na (Hunter) (4.14)/I Believe in You (Hunter) (4.16)/ Listen to the Eight Track (Hunter) (6.08)/You Stepped into My Dreams (Hunter) (4.43)/Venus in the Bathtub (Hunter) (4.29)/China (Hunter) (Ronson Vocal) (4.36)/Detroit (Hunter) (Outtake 5 Vocal) (4.00)/Na Na Na (Hunter) (Extended Mix) (4.28)
CD2: Bluebirds (Hunter) (Demo) (4.18)/All is Forgiven (Hunter) (Demo) (3.14)/Sunshine Eyes (Hunter) (Demo) (4.21)/(I'm the) Teacher (Hunter/Ronson) (4.34)/Great Expectations (You Never Know What to Expect) (Hunter) (3.54)/Good Man in a Bad Time (Tanner/Reede) (3.41)/ Wake Up Call (Baker/Tina B/Mandel) (4.52)/ Ill Wind (Hunter) (Demo) (3.22)/Women's Intuition (Hunter/Ronson) (US Single Edit) (4.21)/Ain't No Way to Treat a Lady (Hunter) (Artful Dodger Outtake) (4.33)/Resurrection Mary (Hunter) (Trio version) (7.01)/Something to Believe In (Hunter) (Trio Version) (5.16)/

Waterlow (Hunter) (Trio Version) (3.10)/I'm In Awe (Hunter) (Early Rant Demo) (4.39)/Avalanche (Hunter) (Early Rant Demo) (5.00)/ Morons (Hunter) (Rant Demo) (5.33)/One More Time (Escovedo) (4.14)

If You Wait Long Enough for Anything, You Can Get It on Sale

CD1: FBI (Gormley) (5.12)/Once Bitten Twice Shy (Hunter) (5.31)/ One of the Boys (Hunter/Ralphs) (5.03)/Laugh at Me (Bono) (4.06)/I Wish I Was Your Mother (Hunter) (6.30)/ Sons and Daughters (Hunter) (5.23)/Irene Wilde (Hunter) (4.25)/Just Another Night (Hunter/Ronson) (7.51)/Life After Death (Hunter) (5.16)/Angeline (Hunter) (5.00)/Standin' in My Light (Hunter) (6.03)/Bastard (Hunter) (7.48)/The Golden Age of Rock 'n' Roll (Hunter) (4.34)/All the Way from Memphis (Hunter) (6.12)
CD2: All the Young Dudes (Bowie) (4.24)/Walkin' with a Mountain (Hunter)/Rock and Roll Queen (Ralphs) (5.45)/Cleveland Rocks (Hunter) (8.41)/When the Daylight Comes (Hunter) (16.47)/Letter to Britannia from the Union Jack (Hunter) (3.52)/Ships (Hunter) (6.49)/ Gun Control (Hunter) (3.36)/Violence (Hunter/Ralphs) (4.56)/Is Your Love in Vain? (Dylan) (5.58)/Lisa Likes Rock n' Roll (Hunter) (4.12)/ Theatre of the Absurd (Hunter) (4.36)/Walkin' with a Mountain (Hunter) (4.21)

CD1 and CD2 Tracks 1–4: Hammersmith Odeon, London – 22 November 1979
CD2 Track 5: Berkeley Community Theater, Berkeley, CA – 7 July 1979
CD2 Track 6: My Father's Place, Long Island, NY – 12–13 June 1979
CD2 Tracks 7–12: The Old Waldorf, San Francisco, CA – 26–28 October 1981

Bag of Tricks: Volume 1

Radio Flash #1/A Sane Revolution (Lawrence) (0.45)/Wild East (Hunter) (1987 Toronto) (4.29)/(I'm the) Teacher (Hunter/Ronson) (1987 Toronto) (3.52)/While You Were Looking at Me (Van Zandt) (1988 Toronto) (4.26)/Day Tripper (Lennon/McCartney) (1988 Toronto) (5.18)/Pain (Hunter/Kehr) (1989 San Jose) (5.56)/Resurrection Mary (Hunter) (1994 Mick Ronson Memorial London) (7.28)/Michael Picasso (Hunter) (1994 Mick Ronson Memorial London) (6.44)/ Shades Off/Boy (Hunter/Ronson) (2000 Bilston) (10.00)/Ill Wind (Hunter) (2000 Bilston) (4.52)/Good Samaritan (Hunter) (2002 Manchester) (5.45)/Purgatory (Hunter) (2002 Manchester) (4.55)/ American Spy (Hunter) (2002 Manchester) (5.06)/Death of a Nation (Hunter) (2002 Manchester) (7.15)

Bag of Tricks: Volume 2

Radio Flash #2/Rock and Roll Queen (Ralphs)/Death May Be Your Santa Claus (Hunter/Allen) (2002 Manchester) (9.14)/One of the Boys (Hunter/Ralphs) (2002 Manchester) (5.25)/The Original Mixed-Up Kid (2002 Manchester) (5.33)/Knockin' on Heaven's Door (Dylan) (2002 Manchester) (5.04)/Twisted Steel (Hunter) (2002 Manchester) (4.04)/23a Swan Hill (Hunter) (2002 Manchester) (6.24)/Dead Man Walkin' (EastEnders) (Hunter) (2002 Manchester) (7.00)/From the Knees of My Heart (Hunter) (2004 Barcelona) (4.15)/The Truth, the Whole Truth, Nuthin' but the Truth (Hunter) (2004 Barcelona) (8.30)/ Rollerball (Hunter) (2004 Barcelona) (5.20)/Irene Wilde (Hunter) (2004 Barcelona) (5.15)/Roll Away the Stone (Hunter) (2004 Barcelona) (3.15)/ Lounge Lizard (Hunter) (2005 Austin) (4.58)/The Outsider (Hunter) (2005 Trondheim) (5.00)

Bag of Tricks: Volume 3

Radio flash #3/Hymn for the Dudes (Hunter/Allen) (2005 Trondheim) (5.40)/All-American Alien Boy (Hunter) (2005 Trondheim) (5.47)/

536

Morons-Marionette-Broadway (Hunter) (2005 Trondheim) (6.27)/ Following in Your Footsteps (Hunter/Ronson) (Acoustic) (2008 Manchester) (5.15)/ Dancing on the Moon (Hunter/Bath/Plain) (2010 Newcastle) (5.42)/Shallow Crystals (Hunter) (2010 Newcastle) (3.55)/The Ballad of Little Star (Hunter) (2010 Newcastle) (2.49)/ Just the Way You Look Tonight (Hunter) (2012 Oslo) (3.55)/Black Tears (Hunter) (2012 Oslo) (3.36)/Isolation (Lennon) (2012 Oslo) (4.32)/Alice (Hunter) (2012 Oslo) (4.40)/The Moon Upstairs (Hunter/ Ralphs) (2012 Oslo) (5.20)/Ta Shunka Witco (Crazy Horse) (Hunter) (2012 Oslo) (6.39)/ When I'm President (Hunter) (Acoustic) (2013 Sheffield) (5.49)/Now is the Time (Hunter) (2015 Tokyo) (5.29)/ Shades Off (Hunter) (0.22)

Acoustic Shadows

Where Do You All Come From (Hunter/Ralphs/Watts/Griffin) (4.59)/ Wash Us Away (Hunter) (4.26)/The Other Man (Hunter) (2.42)/ Scars (Hunter/Bath/Plain) (4.37)/Soul of America – I Wish I Was Your Mother (Hunter) (6.42)/Shrunken Heads (Hunter) (6.38)/Rain (Hunter) (6.24)/Sons 'n' Lovers (Hunter) (5.01)/Sweet Jane (Reed) (5.22)/Irene Wilde – Ships – Letter to Britannia from the Union Jack (Hunter) (10.08)/Honaloochie Boogie – How's Your House (Hunter) (6.11)/Twisted Steel (Hunter) (3.19)/When the World Was Round (Hunter) (5.21)/Once Bitten Twice Shy (Hunter) (6.01)

Recorded: The Mick Jagger Theatre, Dartford, Kent – 2 March 2008 Personnel: Ian Hunter (Vocals, Guitar); James Mastro (Guitars); Steve Holley (Percussion)

Experiments

You're Messin' with the King of Rock 'n' Roll (Hunter) (4.57)/Money Can't Buy Love (Hunter) (3.09)/More to Love (Hunter) (4.27)/Look Before You Leap (Hunter) (5.24)/My Love (The Jar) (Hunter) (3.46)/ Demolition Derby (Hunter) (4.03)/Just Want It Real (Hunter) (3.27)/

Coincidence (Hunter) (4.37)/Big Black Cadillac (Hunter) (4.03)/ San Diego Freeway (Hunter) (4.05)/Nobody's Perfect (Hunter) (3.15)/Too Much (All I Ever Wanted) (Hunter) (Early Version) (4.27)/ Artful Dodger (Hunter) (Early Version) (4.07)/Michael Picasso (Hunter) (Early Version) (6.56)/A Little Rock 'n' Roll (Hunter) (5.20)/ Testosterone (Hunter) (4.59)/The Man in Me (Dylan) (Ian Hunter and Tribes) (3.02)/Salvation (Hunter) (4.47)

It Never Happened

DVD1: Once Bitten Twice Shy (CBS promo video 1975)/All-American Alien Boy (Studio film 1975)/Standin' in My Light [fragment] ('Top Pop' Holland TV 1979)/Irene Wilde (Chrysalis *Welcome to the Club* promo 1980)/Once Bitten Twice Shy (Chrysalis *Welcome to the Club* promo 1980)/We Gotta Get Out of Here (Chrysalis *Welcome to the Club* promo 1980)/Laugh at Me (*Rockpalast* 1980)/Irene Wilde (*Rockpalast* 1980)/I Wish I Was Your Mother (*Rockpalast* 1980)/All of the Good Ones Are Taken (CBS Promo Video 1983)/ While You Were Looking at Me (Rock 'n' Roll Heaven, Toronto 1988)/Day Tripper (Rock 'n' Roll Heaven, Toronto 1988)/Beg A Little Love (Dominion Theatre, London 1989)/Following in Your Footsteps (Dominion Theatre, London 1989)/(Give Me Back My) Wings (Dominion Theatre, London 1989)/The Loner (Dominion Theatre, London 1989)/American Music (PolyGram Promo Video 1990)/My Revolution (Scandinavian NRK TV Session 1995)/Michael Picasso (MTV VH1 *Take It to the Bridge* session 1997)/Irene Wilde (MTV VH1 *Take It to the Bridge* session 1997)/When the World Was Round (Jerkin' Crocus Promo Video 2007)/Flowers (Jools Holland BBC TV session 2009)/Once Bitten Twice Shy (Jools Holland BBC TV session 2009)/ When I'm President (Proper Promo Video 2012) DVD2: (*The New Music*: Ryerson Theatre, Toronto 1979) – Trailer/ Hunter Ronson interview/Life After Death/Just Another Night/ The Golden Age of Rock 'n' Roll/Standin' in My Light/Bastard/ Cleveland Rocks/All the Young Dudes/When the Daylight Comes/ Slaughter on 10th Avenue; (*Ian Hunter Rocks*: The Dr Pepper

538

Festival, New York 1981) – Once Bitten Twice Shy/Gun Control/ Central Park n' West/All the Way from Memphis/I Need Your Love/ Noises/Just Another Night/Cleveland Rocks/Irene Wilde/All the Young Dudes; (*Strings Attached*: The Sentrum, Oslo 2002) – Rest in Peace/All of the Good Ones Are Taken/I Wish I Was Your Mother/ Twisted Steel/Boy/23a Swan Hill/Waterlow/All the Young Dudes/ Irene Wilde/Once Bitten Twice Shy/Rollerball/Ships/A Nightingale Sang in Berkeley Square/ Michael Picasso/Wash Us Away/Don't Let Go/All the Way from Memphis/Roll Away the Stone/Saturday Gigs

Released: Proper Records (SHADES 1) – October 2016
Limited edition – 2,500 copies in LP-size Escher-style deluxe box

A rock 'n' roll jackpot of over 400 tracks on thirty discs in replica card sleeves plus eighty-eight-page hardback book with "track by track" narrative for every song, *Shades* replica music paper and signed *Alien Boy* lithograph. Discs 22 to 30 comprise nine new discs of buried treasures including previously unreleased tracks, demos, alternative takes, rare live cuts, videos, film footage and first-time CD/DVD material. *Classic Rock* termed Ian's anthology box set: "The most exhaustive career retrospective any rock-related artist has had assembled in one package." No coffee table required!

International Singles and Promo Discs

Who Do You Love/It Ain't Easy When You Fall – Australia – CBS 1976
When the Daylight Comes/When the Daylight Comes – twelve-inch promo – USA – 1979
Just Another Night/Ships – Spain – Chrysalis 1979
Just Another Night/Cleveland Rocks – USA – Chrysalis 1979
Ships/Cleveland Rocks – France – Chrysalis 1979
Standin' in My Light/Wild East – Holland – Chrysalis 1979
Bastard/Cleveland Rocks – Italy – Chrysalis 1979
We Gotta Get Out of Here/Sons and Daughters – Belgium, USA – Chrysalis 1979

We Gotta Get Out of Here/Standin' in My Light – France – Chrysalis 1979

We Gotta Get Out of Here/All the Young Dudes/All the Way from Memphis – Canada – Chrysalis 1979

We Gotta Get Out of Here/All the Young Dudes – Germany, Italy, Holland – Chrysalis 1979

We Gotta Get Out of Here/All the Way from Memphis – Australia – Chrysalis 1979

Central Park n' West/Rain/I Need Your Love – twelve-inch promo – USA – Chrysalis 1979

Irene Wilde/Ships – Brazil – Chrysalis 1980

I Need Your Love/Keep on Burning – USA – Chrysalis 1981

Central Park n' West/Rain – Spain, USA – Chrysalis 1981

Central Park n' West/Keep on Burnin' – Canada – Chrysalis 1981

Central Park n' West/Noises – Holland – Chrysalis 1981

All of the Good Ones Are Taken/All of the Good Ones Are Taken (Slow Version) – Holland – Columbia 1983

All of the Good Ones Are Taken – twelve-inch promo – USA – Columbia 1983

That Girl Is Rock 'n' Roll/Seeing Double – USA, Canada – Columbia 1983

That Girl Is Rock 'n' Roll/Every Step of the Way – twelve-inch promo – USA – Columbia 1983

Somethin's Goin' On (Radio Edit)/All of the Good Ones Are Taken (Slow Version) – seven-inch promo – UK – CBS 1983

(I'm the) Teacher (Long Edit) – twelve-inch promo – USA – Capitol 1984

American Music/Women's Intuition/Cool/Big Time – promo CD – UK – Mercury 1989

American Music/Women's Intuition/Pain/Beg a Little Love/Big Time – YUI Orta five-track sampler promo cassette – USA – Mercury 1989

American Music – promo picture disc CD – USA – Mercury 1989

American Music/American Music – twelve-inch promo – Canada – Mercury 1989

American Music/Tell it Like It Is – cassette – USA – Mercury 1989

Women's Intuition – promo picture disc CD – USA – Mercury 1990

Women's Intuition/Women's Intuition (Remix) – twelve-inch promo – Canada – Mercury 1990

Women's Intuition/Following in Your Footsteps – cassette – USA – Mercury 1990

Red Letter Day (Edit)/Red Letter Day – promo card sleeve CD – Norway – Norsk Plateproduksjon 1994

My Revolution/Dancing on the Moon – CD single – Norway – Norsk Plateproduksjon 1995

Too Much – promo picture disc CD – Norway – Mercury 1996

Too Much – promo CD – Germany – Polydor 1997

Death of a Nation/All the Young Dudes (Live)/Wash Us Away (Live) – promo CD – USA – Fuel 2000 Records 2001

When I'm President (Radio Edit) – promo CD card sleeve – UK – Proper 2012

When I'm President (Radio Edit) – jewel case USA – Slimstyle 2012

Dandy – promo CD card sleeve – UK – Proper 2016

Compilation albums

Shades of Ian Hunter and Mott the Hoople (2LP/2CD) – CBS 1980

Shades of Ian Hunter (CD) – Chrysalis 1988

The Very Best of Ian Hunter (LP/CD) – CBS 1990

The Collection (CD) – Castle 1991

Once Bitten Twice Shy (2CD) – Sony Columbia 2000

The Best of Ian Hunter (CD) – EMI Capitol 2001

Standing in the Light (Missing in Action reissue) (2CD) – Alchemy Pilot 2004

Behind the Shades (Live 2004) (CD) – Airline Records 2008

All the Young Dudes (Live 2004) (2CD) – Secret Records 2009

Live in London (2004) (CD) – Great American Music Company/ Secret Records 2009

The Singles Collection 1975–1983 (2CD) – 7T's 2012

Original Album Classics: Ian Hunter, All-American Alien Boy, Overnight Angels (3CD) – Columbia 2012
From the Knees of My Heart: The Chrysalis Years (1979–1981) (4CD) – EMI Chrysalis 2012
Live at Rockpalast: The Ian Hunter Band Featuring Mick Ronson (1980) (2LP) – Let Them Eat Vinyl 2016
Ian Hunter and the Rant Band Greatest Hits: Live in London (2004) (LP) – Secret Records 2017

Soundtrack LPs

Up the Academy – We Gotta Get Out of Here (Hunter) – Capitol 1980
Up the Creek – Great Expectations (You Never Know What to Expect) (Hunter) – Epic 1984
Teachers – (I'm the) Teacher (Hunter/Ronson) – Capitol 1984
Fright Night – Good Man in a Bad Time (Hunter/Ronson) – Epic 1985
The Wraith – Wake-up Call (Baker/Tina B/Mandel) – Scotti Bros Records 1986
Light of Day – Cleveland Rocks (Hunter) – Blackheart Records 1987

Video

Ian Hunter Rocks (1981) – Chrysalis VHS 1983
Strings Attached (2002) – Universal DVD 2003
Just Another Night: Live at the Astoria (2004) – Secret Films DVD 2005
All the Young Dudes: Live at the Astoria (2004) – Secret Films DVD 2009
Live at Rockpalast: The Ian Hunter Band Featuring Mick Ronson (1980) – MIG Music DVD 2011
The Ballad of Mott the Hoople – Start Productions DVD 2011
Strings Attached (2002) – MIG Music DVD 2014
It Never Happened – Proper Music 2DVD 2016

Permissions

All-American Alien Boy
Words & Music by Ian Hunter
© 1976
Reproduced by Permission of Ian Hunter Music Inc./EMI Music Publishing Ltd, London W1F 9LD.

Guy Stevens Poem
Words by Ian Hunter
© 1981
Used by permission of Jesse John Music.

If the Slipper Don't Fit
Words by Ian Hunter
© 2016
Used by permission of Jesse John Music.

Knees of My Heart
Words & Music by Ian Hunter
© 2001 Jesse John Music
All Rights Administered by BMG Rights Management (US) LLC.
All Rights Reserved. International Copyright Secured.
Used by permission of Hal Leonard Europe Limited.

Michael Picasso
Words & Music by Ian Hunter
© 1996 Jesse John Music
All Rights Administered by BMG Rights Management (US) LLC.
All Rights Reserved. International Copyright Secured.
Used by permission of Hal Leonard Europe Limited.

Salvation
Words by Ian Hunter
© 1997
Used by permission of Jesse John Music.